D1258170

Communications
Architecture
for
Distributed
Systems

Communications Architecture for Distributed Systems

R. J. CYPSER
IBM Corporation

ADDISON-WESLEY PUBLISHING COMPANY
Reading, Massachusetts • Menlo Park, California
London • Amsterdam • Don Mills, Ontario • Sydney

ISBN 0-201-14458-1
BCDEFGHIJK-HA-798

To Betty

THE SYSTEMS PROGRAMMING SERIES

*The Program Development Process Part I—The Individual Programmer	Joel D. Aron
The Program Development Process Part II—The Programming Team	Joel D. Aron
*The Design and Structure of Programming Languages	John E. Nicholls
Mathematical Background of Programming	Frank Beckman
Structured Programming: Theory and Practice	Richard C. Linger Harlan D. Mills
*The Environment for Systems Programs	Frederic G. Withington
Coded Character Sets; History and Development	Charles E. Mackenzie

*An Introduction To Database Systems, Second Edition	C. J. Date
Interactive Computer Graphics	Andries Van Dam James Foley
*Sorting and Sort Systems	Harold Lorin
*Compiler Design Theory	Philip M. Lewis II Daniel J. Rosenkrantz Richard E. Stearns
*Communications Architecture for Distributed Systems	R. J. Cypser
*Recursive Programming Techniques	William Burge
Conceptual Structures: Information Processing in Mind and Machines	John F. Sowa
Modeling and Analysis: An Introduction to System Performance Evaluation Methodology	Hisashi Kobayashi

*Published

IBM EDITORIAL BOARD

Foreword

The field of systems programming primarily grew out of the efforts of many programmers and managers whose creative energy went into producing practical, utilitarian systems programs needed by the rapidly growing computer industry. Programming was practiced as an art where each programmer invented his own solutions to problems with little guidance beyond that provided by his immediate associates. In 1968, the late Ascher Opler, then at IBM, recognized that it was necessary to bring programming knowledge together in a form that would be accessible to all systems programmers. Surveying the state of the art, he decided that enough useful material existed to justify a significant publication effort. On his recommendation, IBM decided to sponsor The Systems Programming Series as a long term project to collect, organize, and publish principles and techniques that would have lasting value throughout the industry.

The Series consists of an open-ended collection of text-reference books. The contents of each book represent the individual author's view of the subject area and do not necessarily reflect the views of the IBM Corporation. Each is organized for course use but is detailed enough for reference. Further, the Series is organized in three levels: broad introductory material in the foundation volumes, more specialized material in the software volumes, and very specialized theory in the computer science volumes. As such, the Series meets the needs of the novice, the experienced programmer, and the computer scientist.

The Editorial Board

Preface

First, it may be well to state what is meant by the title of this text. Architecture is the specification of the relationships between parts of a system. Communications architecture for distributed systems includes the description of the *formats, potocols, operational sequences, and logical structures* for functions needed to achieve *meaningful communication* among units that have diverse data-processing, data-input, or data-output capabilities. These units may be physically close or widely separated, and the data transmission may use a wide variety of transmission media (e.g., wires, satellites, optics), which are not part of the architecture.

Those associated with data processing have come to recognize clearly (and sometimes painfully) the need for a communications systems architecture that facilitates the distribution of information processing. Such an architecture must provide common protocols for communication among diverse products whose internal structures are different and whose user interfaces are different. The objective is to facilitate more general communicability in systems of great diversity and rapid change. The structure must permit future changes to take place in a way that preserves parts of the system investments and still facilitates rapid evolution of other parts of the system.

This text addresses distributed systems by using a specific architecture, the Systems Network Architecture (SNA), as the prime illustration and reference. Chapters 6 to 15 are devoted largely to this. Since SNA is a comprehensive well-documented approach, it helps to define the problems and establish principles, as well as provide an illustrative architecture. Some comparisons with parallel developments, outside SNA, are also included.

Only a basic understanding of data processing and communications is assumed. Part 1 of the text (Chapters 1-5) provides most of the background needed for the architectural discussions in subsequent chapters. The level of description is more than conceptual. It is primarily intended to provide an understanding of the concepts and rationale of the architecture for distributed systems, but beyond that it seeks to provide, by its specific illustrations, enough knowledge about protocols so that the reader will be equipped to undertake preliminary design of potential systems. This level is appropriate for some university studies in architectural concepts and facilities, and for the continuing education of professional engineers and programmers. It has been found, in a series of courses, that (1) an introductory course in teleprocessing and architecture needs to include only the first six chapters; (2) a course that emphasizes architectural concepts and network services can include Chapter 6, Sections 7.1-7.3, and Chapters 12 and 15; (3) those desiring more detail on SNA can then use Chapters 8, 9, 10, 11, and 14, in addition; and (4) Chapters 13, 16, and 17, covering finite-state machines, routing techniques, and new data networks, can be extensions of either (2) or (3). Although considerable specific information can thus be chosen, the level of description in the text is not intended to be sufficient for detailed system design, which would require reference to published architecture specifications for the particular architecture used. The text is organized in four parts, as follows.

Part 1 (Chapters 1-5) provides an overview of this evolving environment to generate a perspective of the relationship between data-processing and communication systems. The scope of today's teleprocessing systems, their diversity, their structural evolution, and their major cost components are reviewed. The technological trends in data processing and data transmission are described, to substantiate the trends to greater decentralization and distribution of function. The basic functions that can be distributed and the key design questions to be addressed by distributed systems are introduced. Part 1 thus describes the system components, provides the objectives of a distributed system, and introduces some of its architectural concepts. Part 1 is an introduction to the other parts. Those already sufficiently familiar with current TP systems and their trends may choose to begin the text at Part 2.

Part 2 (Chapters 6-11) describes the concepts and some of the facilities of a specific architecture, the Systems Network Architecture (SNA). The concepts of network addressable units, sessions, peer protocols for functional layers, function subsets, and control domains are explained. The major SNA components and their operations are described.

Part 3 (Chapters 12–14) then describes overall SNA systems in three ways. In Chapter 12, typical operational sequences are traced across all layers of the system. Chapter 13 illustrates how finite-state machines can be used to give a more precise definition of the architecture. Chapter 14 presents an overview of recovery, integrity, and security facilities.

Part 4 (Chapters 15–17) describes the areas of multiple control domains, routing techniques, and the interfaces (X.21 and X.25) to some new data networks that are offered by communications carriers.

This organization of the text reflects the facts that teleprocessing systems are moving toward a flexibility of interconnection of heterogeneous boxes, and system architectures are evolving to make this possible. An early feature of that evolution has been the extension of centralized data processing to tree-structured data processing and communications, with gradual distribution of DP functions to remote nodes of the network. Parts 2 and 3 are largely devoted to this. The next step has been the interconnection of tree structures. The goal is a more generalized ability to communicate among programs, operators, and storage media, which may be located in different control domains. This topic is treated in Part 4.

In reading the text, one should distinguish among requirements, architecture, and implementations:

1. *The required set.* This includes all those functions that are judged by the network owner to be requirements for total network operations. Many of these are discussed in Part 1.

2. *The architected set.* This is only a subset of the required set. Not all functions can or should be architected as part of a systems architecture. Some functions are best left unique to a given product; if they do not affect internode operations, they are best left unconstrained. The functions in the architected set are very carefully defined, and include a set of protocols for the relations among function components. The total architected set must be completely consistent and must offer options of functions as needed for different requirement subsets. Parts 2, 3, and 4 address candidates for this set.

3. *The implemented set.* In any product, the implemented set of functions is usually only a subset of the architected set. Different products may use different subsets of the architecture, depending on market needs and cost tradeoffs.

To illustrate, the currently implemented set of SNA functions is referred to as SNA-3. Subsets of SNA-3 are implemented in a variety of current products, such as operating systems, TP access methods, terminals, terminal controllers, and communications controllers. Different sets of products may implement different subsets of the architecture. The text attempts to illustrate the concept that such diversity must be orderly, and that it can be so if the structure of the architecture facilitates it.

Thus, though the text mentions products for illustrative purposes, it does not define any specific equipment or programs that implement SNA, nor does it presume to define any particular implementation subsets or deviations from the architectural description that appear within any product. These matters are described in the appropriate publications that pertain to the particular equipment or program to be used.

Poughkeepsie, New York   R.J.C.
January 1978

Acknowledgments

This text draws heavily on the experience and work of the IBM Communications Systems Architecture departments located in Research Triangle Park, North Carolina, Kingston, New York, and La Gaude, France, and on the complementary architecture support by people working on communications-oriented products. Though they represent only a partial list, the following people are acknowledged for their major contributions to this work.

E. H. Sussenguth, P. O. Lindfors, and V. L. Hoberecht provided the overall direction of the SNA development teams. Much of the initial architectural structure of SNA was provided by E. M. Thomas. Basic conceptual contributions across the entire range of SNA were made by W. A. Bernstein, J. C. Broughton, E. E. Cobb, J. P. Gray, and E. M. Thomas. Major contributions in specific areas were made by W. S. Arell, W. Bergman, L. W. Brown, A. Burke, R. A. Donnan, J. Knauth, M. A. Lerner, L. Loucks, J. Oseas, T. F. Piatkowski, D. R. Reed, and W. R. Wheeler. Specific credits are given in some chapters.

This text would not have been possible without the support and cooperation of Dr. E. Sussenguth, the director of communications systems architecture at IBM. I am also indebted to the many who reviewed sections of the text and generously provided me with their comments and corrections. I want to thank particularly J. Aron and B. D. Moldow who commented on many sections.

My wife, Betty, deserves special thanks for her encouragement and support of my work in preparing this text. She and the rest of the family cheerfully kept this going despite the frequent usurpation of the dining room and the regular siphoning of time from the family to the book.

Almost all of the manuscript typing, including a mountain of revisions, were done with skill and great patience by Miss Carol Stokrocki, using a computer-based text-editing system. Many thanks go to her for her fine cooperation. In addition, I want to thank Ms. Harriet Harrison for her assistance in editing and typing some of the tedious appendixes.

Contents

PART 1
THE COMMUNICATIONS-SERVED DATA-PROCESSING SYSTEM

CHAPTER 1
TODAY'S TELEPROCESSING SYSTEMS

1.1	Introduction	3
1.2	Scope of Teleprocessing Systems	3
1.3	Early Transmission Facilities	19
1.4	System Costs	30
1.5	References and Bibliography	32

CHAPTER 2
SYSTEM TRENDS

2.1	Introduction	35
2.2	Computer Technology Trends	35
2.3	Information Spectrum Trends	37
2.4	Transmission Trends	44
2.5	Trends in Programming	68
2.6	Trends in Distributed Function	72
2.7	References and Bibliography	78

CHAPTER 3
EVOLUTION OF CONFIGURATION AND FUNCTION DISTRIBUTION

3.1	Introduction	81
3.2	Divergence of Early Designs	81

3.3   The Early Host Structures 86
3.4   Application Subsystems 94
3.5   Communications Controllers (COMC) 98
3.6   Cluster Controllers and Subhosts 104
3.7   Growth of Regional Networks 109
3.8   Multidomain Networks 113
3.9   Configuration Prognosis 118
3.10 Exercises 121
3.11 References and Bibliography 121

CHAPTER 4
IMPROVING LINE UTILIZATION

4.1   Introduction 123
4.2   Multidrop Lines 123
4.3   Multiplexing versus Concentration 129
4.4   Synchronous TDM and FDM 130
4.5   Asynchronous TDM and Concentration 133
4.6   Positioning Multiplexors or Concentrators 136
4.7   Effects of Digital Transmission 138
4.8   References and Bibliography 139

CHAPTER 5
SYSTEM OBJECTIVES SUMMARY

5.1   Introduction 141
5.2   General Design Objectives 141
5.3   Key Design Questions 144
5.4   Migration Objectives 145
5.5   References and Bibliography 148

PART 2
THE ARCHITECTURAL LAYERS

CHAPTER 6
BASIC CONCEPTS OF SYSTEMS NETWORK ARCHITECTURE

6.1   Introduction 151
6.2   Network Addressable Units 153
6.3   End-Users 159
6.4   Nodes, Terminals, Devices, and Work Stations 162
6.5   Sessions 164
6.6   Distributed SNA Services 166
6.7   Functional Layers 167
6.8   Formats and Protocols 177
6.9   Apparent Peer Flows 188

6.10   Asymmetric Session Protocols 192
6.11   Networks at Various Levels 195
6.12   Function Subsets 196
6.13   Control Domains 198
6.14   Parallel Developments 201
6.15   Exercises... 207
6.16   References and Bibliography 208

CHAPTER 7
HIGHER-LEVEL SERVICES OF SNA NETWORK

7.1   Introduction 211
7.2   Use of NAU Services....................................... 213
7.3   Network Services 214
7.4   Presentation Services 235
7.5   Presentation Services for Data Transfer...................... 242
7.6   Presentation Services for Text Processing.................... 250
7.7   Presentation Services in an Interactive Environment 251
7.8   Parallel Developments 256
7.9   Exercises... 261
7.10   References and Bibliography 262

CHAPTER 8
DATA FLOW CONTROL

8.1   Introduction 265
8.2   Send/Receive Modes 267
8.3   Chains 269
8.4   Control Modes (Waiting for Responses) 273
8.5   Response Order 275
8.6   Response Synchronization................................... 275
8.7   Brackets 277
8.8   DFC-RUs 281
8.9   Interacting with Data Flow Control 284
8.10   Summary of DFC Functions................................. 286
8.11   Exercises... 288
8.12   References and Bibliography 289

CHAPTER 9
TRANSMISSION CONTROL

9.1   Introduction 291
9.2   Connection Point Manager 292
9.3   Session Control 303
9.4   Pre-session Routing.. 308
9.5   Transmission Control Boundary Functions 308
9.6   Network Control (NC) 310

9.7   Establishing an LU-LU Session 310
9.8   Parallel Developments 325
9.9   Exercises 328
9.10   References and Bibliography 332

CHAPTER 10
PATH CONTROL

10.1   Introduction 333
10.2   Addressing 335
10.3   Boundary-Function Address Transformation 339
10.4   Segmenting and Blocking 343
10.5   Transmission Header 348
10.6   Parallel Developments 354
10.7   Exercises 356
10.8   References and Bibliography 358

CHAPTER 11
DATA LINK CONTROL

11.1   Introduction 359
11.2   History of Data Link Control 360
11.3   Data Link Control Requirements 368
11.4   Positional Significance 369
11.5   DLC Structure 371
11.6   Error Detection 385
11.7   Illustrative SDLC Sequences 390
11.8   Classes of Procedure 399
11.9   Parallel Developments 403
11.10 Exercises 403
11.11 References and Bibliography 406

PART 3
OVERVIEW OF OPERATIONS

CHAPTER 12
PUTTING IT TOGETHER

12.1   Introduction 411
12.2   SNA Node Types 411
12.3   SNA Layer Capability in Each Node Type 413
12.4   Bringing the System Up 419
12.5   Dial Sequences 430
12.6   Other Physical Network-Service RUs 443
12.7   Log-on Sequence 446
12.8   Logging Off 452

12.9   Example of LU Services in Operation 453
12.10   Header Assembly and Disassembly 456
12.11   Exercises 463

CHAPTER 13
FINITE STATE ARCHITECTURE

13.1   Introduction 465
13.2   Graphical Representation of FSMs 467
13.3   Location of FSMs Within Each Layer 467
13.4   Basic FSM Pairs 470
13.5   FSM-Naming Conventions and Symbols 475
13.6   Illustrative FSMs 477
13.7   Exercises 494
13.8   References and Bibliography 495

CHAPTER 14
RELIABILITY AND SECURITY CONTROL

14.1   RAS Strategy 497
14.2   Error Recovery Hierarchy 498
14.3   SNA Request Recovery 503
14.4   Application-Program/Subsystem Failure 508
14.5   Network Operator Recovery Aids 509
14.6   Data Security 510
14.7   References and Bibliography 516

PART 4
ADVANCED FUNCTIONS

CHAPTER 15
MULTIDOMAIN NETWORKS

15.1   Introduction 519
15.2   Control Domains and Networks 520
15.3   Cross-domain Connections 525
15.4   Use of the SSCP 533
15.5   Bypassing a Host (for Data Flows) 540
15.6   Networking Facilities 540
15.7   SSCP-SSCP Sessions 541
15.8   Cross-domain LU-LU Sessions/Setup 548
15.9   Cross-domain Link Connection 558
15.10   Multidomain Network Recovery 560
15.11   Parallel Developments 570
15.12   Exercises 571
15.13   References and Bibliography 572

CHAPTER 16
ROUTING TECHNIQUES

16.1   Introduction 575
16.2   Alternate versus Parallel Routes 577
16.3   Types of Routing Techniques 579
16.4   Explicit Path Routing 585
16.5   Distributed Stochastic Routing 587
16.6   Multidomain Routing 590
16.7   References and Bibliography 591

CHAPTER 17
INTERFACING TO NEW DATA NETWORKS

17.1   Introduction 593
17.2   X.21 Interface 600
17.3   X.25 Interface 607
17.4   Conclusion 622
17.5   References and Bibliography 622

APPENDIXES

A   RH, TH, and Link Header Formats in SNA 627
B   Profiles and LU-Types in SNA 631
C   Request-Response Unit (RU) Formats in SNA 640
D   FM Headers and Character String Controls in SNA 662
E   Exception Codes 675
F   Answers to Exercises 682
G   Acronyms and Abbreviations 688

ABOUT THE AUTHOR 697

INDEX 699

Part 1
The Communications-Served Data-Processing System

An introduction to the subsequent chapters on architecture, Part 1 describes and defines the objectives of a distributed system.

- Chapter 1 examines today's teleprocessing systems, the scope of the data-processing system, and the characteristics of early transmission facilities.
- Chapter 2 looks at future trends in computer technology, the types of information to be transmitted, transmission systems, and programming. It also reviews the consequent trends toward the distribution of functions throughout a network.
- Chapter 3 traces the evolution of hardware and programming structures and of functional layers, along with the grouping of function into hosts, communications controllers, and cluster controllers. The growth to regional computer networks and multiregion networks is described.
- Chapter 4 provides a review of the principal techniques for improving communications-line utilization—namely, polling, multiplexing, and concentration. The roles of message switching and packet switching are introduced in this context.
- Chapter 5 summarizes a set of guidelines and key design questions for the evolution of an architecture for distributed systems.

1
Today's Teleprocessing Systems

1.1 INTRODUCTION

Chapter 1 introduces the reader to the basic facilities and the key parameters in data-processing/communication systems. The broad range of applications, configurations, and transaction rates are described. Earlier transmission facilities, and their attributes that are pertinent to a systems architecture, are reviewed, and the primary factors of total system cost are examined.

1.2 SCOPE OF TELEPROCESSING SYSTEMS

1.2.1 Application Breadth

As the saying goes, "We've come a long way." It was only in 1941 that telegraph paper tape information was first converted directly into punched cards to enter telegraph information into the computer. And it wasn't until 1954 that the Transceiver (a terminal attached to telephone lines) first transmitted punched-card data directly, without conversion to telegraph paper tape. But the late 1950s saw an explosion of techniques for remote computer usage. The SAGE Air Defense system, for example, drew digitized radar data from sites located over hundreds of miles, to feed dozens of computer centers that were tied into a semiautonomous national computer network, involving one and a half million miles of communication lines and thousands of interactive display consoles. In

1962, SABRE, the first large, real-time, on-line airline reservation system, went into operation, linking 1200 reservation terminals to a central processing center.

Since then, teleprocessing has grown steadily. We see processors increasingly serving many remote users by remote job entry, with remote output of the results. We have seen the accumulation of large data bases, which hundreds and even thousands of people can interrogate. We have witnessed the development of conversational techniques, whereby individuals can utilize remote processing power to develop, in a close interactive mode, new programs or procedures. We have seen, in general, an increasing sophistication in the tools made available to individuals for their use of data-processing resources in multiple locations.

Applications for teleprocessing systems are now extremely diverse. To illustrate:

1. On-line cash transaction applications, and branch-to-central accounting, in the banking industry
2. On-line freight loading, freight movement, and bill-checking information systems in the transportation industry
3. On-line order processing, and terminal-oriented bill of materials and inventory control, in the manufacturing industry
4. On-line reservations in the travel and airlines industries

These are from lists of many hundreds of important TP applications. The growth of such applications accelerates as costs come down and ease of use increases.

These applications can be classified as

- Conversational
- Inquiry/response
- Data entry
- Batch
- Application to application
- Sensor base

Each has different characteristics and different requirements on an architecture for distributed systems.

Conversational applications. These are characterized by a series of rather short messages that are related to one another. The amount of traffic is about the same in both directions. (It is said, therefore, to be "balanced.") A wait for a reply to each message is a normal mode.

Conversational program development, using a time-sharing subsystem, is one example of this class [1.14]. Some of the simple inquiry systems also can approach the conversational mode. Airline reservations are typically conversational within a reservation transaction. The size of messages is usually less than 100 characters (or 100 bytes of 8 bits each). Since the messages are small, and the processing to generate each reply is relatively small, the overhead in both the communications and data-processing systems must be kept relatively low; otherwise, the achievable transaction rates may be severely limited by this overhead. In conversational applications, overall system response time is a prime requirement; response times less than three to four seconds are usually needed to keep the level of human efficiency high. Because the operator is continuously involved in the conversation, he or she can also be depended on to handle some recovery situations.

Inquiry/response applications. These are typified by longer replies to short queries, and by *a greater independence of one request from another.* The reply is typically four or five times longer than the inquiry, and this ratio can be much higher. (This traffic, then, is said to be "unbalanced.") The inquiry can be fairly complex, as the following examples indicate: "Give me a list of all the subassemblies that use part number 5179," "Give me the projected reorder dates for the parts in assembly 224," or "Give me the names of all the PhDs in chemistry who work at our plants in New York and Philadelphia."

The number of accesses to data storage and the sophistication of data-management services are usually greater in inquiry applications. The communications overhead and the time spent in communications are, therefore, a smaller percentage of the total round-trip overhead and processing time. Response time in the range of two to twenty seconds is still very important, but response times that are longer than three seconds are more acceptable than in conversational applications. As in conversational applications, consistency of response time is important to user satisfaction.

Data entry. Data-entry and data-collection activities are often characterized by relatively long input messages and very short replies. The amount of host processing per message is minimal, but may include validity checks, editing, and formatting.

Batch applications. These are typified by remote job entry and the distribution of voluminous output to one or more remote locations. The input may be limited to parameters to be used by the program that was previously stored in the central site. Or, the program itself may be the input which then processes data that is kept at the central site. Or, both program and data may have to be the input. Both input and output may be voluminous. Turnaround time, in the order of minutes or even hours, is the response criterion for batch applications. In some cases, deadline-scheduling is used instead, stating that a particular job must be completed before, say, 8:00 A.M. tomorrow.

Batch applications enter the system in groups and are processed in a sequence that maximizes system throughput. They are expected to operate without direct operator involvement with a particular job. Therefore, a high degree of automatic recovery from communication error, without manual assistance, is required. Message lengths are, of course, likely to be very long and variable in both directions.

Application-to-application. These occur when there is considerable computational power at both ends of the communication line, and *the communications are directed by application programs or system service programs at both ends.* This is becoming the case more and more as the cost of data-processing technology decreases, and as it becomes more feasible to locate more function at each remote node.

The processor-to-processor traffic can be either balanced or unbalanced. It can have some of the characteristics of conversational, inquiry, or batch applications, depending on the division of function between the two processors. There is a high requirement for automatic error detection and automatic recovery from errors, with an absolute minimum of operator intervention.

Sensor base applications. The primary requirement in these applications is fast response time, measured from the instant that the sensing device requests the attention of the processor until the moment (after the processor has completed the processing of the transaction) when the total reply is delivered to the sensor. The message may be only a few bytes containing data from a single sensor, or hundreds of bytes containing data from many sensors. Because access to mechanical storage, such as tapes or disks, is time-consuming, all necessary data is kept in high-speed storage.

The time to interrupt the processor and begin processing the transaction must be very short and higher-speed transmission lines must be used so that the total response time is measured in milliseconds.

1.2.2 Configuration Breadth

Processing power may be either entirely in one location or distributed among many different locations. Most installations begin with one central processor and a few simple terminals, and expand to more distributed processing and more functional terminals. A manufacturing complex may, for example, grow to have twenty cluster controllers (that is, units for the control of a group of terminals), each with five to fifteen display units, keyboards, and/or printers. A single large reservation system spanning the nation may have several thousand terminals working through 50 or so concentrators (units that merge data from slow speed lines onto a higher speed line). The teleprocessing network may be restricted to a single building, or it may span a city, a state, or the nation. Groups of data-processing centers are also, in turn, linked by communications systems; these networks may cover any area, even extending from country to country.

Data-processing centers may be dedicated to only one application, while in other cases, economy of scale leads to DP centers that serve multiple applications. Teleprocessing has provided the means for remote users to access both types of center. When the center contains integrated data bases that are capable of serving a range of applications, the added value of the file makes it worthwhile for more users to access the center.

As applications multiply in number and size, data bases (both dedicated and integrated) tend to develop at multiple data-processing centers. Since data is the raw material of data processing, a need often develops for access (occasional or periodic) to more than one data base. This motivates users to demand interconnected networks of machines and applications. *Thus three factors, data-base development, remote access, and sometimes economy of scale, combine with lower cost technologies to advance the trend toward networking of data-processing facilities.*

Processors may be interconnected in a local network (for example, via computer channel to computer channel), or in a remote network via common-carrier or PTT facilities, or combinations of remote and local networks. Connecting networks may be tree structures (with a single path from the root to other elements) or they may be mesh structures (with alternate paths). The architecture for distributed systems must be able to accommodate a wide variety of such configurations and to facilitate changes in the configuration as the system matures.

1.2.3 Messages and Transactions

Messages. A message is a single transmission of a user's data between two points. Some illustrative message sizes in today's systems are shown in Fig. 1.1. If the input is an inquiry from a keyboard, it typically will be short, in the range of 20 to 50 characters. The response to the inquiry will often be in the form of a display, which can be quickly presented even though it amounts to anywhere from 100 to 1000 characters. The unit of

Industry:	Banking	Airline	Broadcasting	Public Utility
Application:	Data Collection	Reservation	Inquiries	Remote Job Entry
Characters/message				
Input	200	20	20	100–1000
Output	60	100	400 .	
Lines Printed/job				100–2000

Fig. 1.1 Illustrative message sizes and printed output.

work in batch applications may be tens of thousands of characters, but these are usually broken into smaller components (of perhaps 256 to 1000 characters) for transmission as a series of messages.

The message rates of different terminals range from one-tenth of a message per hour to hundreds of messages per hour. A message rate at the central processor may range from one-tenth of a message per second to hundreds of messages per second, depending on the type of messages. For example, the complexity of the message, in terms of the amount of computer processing involved, can vary from 100 to 1,000,000 instructions per message.

A typical airlines reservation message, for example, involves about 15,000 instruction executions and ten data-base accesses. The more complex messages may contain statements of a higher-level language (for example, COBOL or APL); they may contain macro instructions known only to the destination; or they may contain a request for a complex search of a data base. Cases are known that involve over a million instructions and up to thirty data-base accesses per message. The amount of input and output data that is transmitted per message can vary by factors of a thousand or more.

Message size and the amount of message processing tend to vary inversely with message rates. On the other hand, for a given message rate, message size and processing tend to increase with time, as the complexity and breadth of computer-aided operations increase. The growth in message rate and complexity results in a steady pressure for improved performance of both the data-communications and the data-processing systems.

Transactions. A transaction involves a series of messages, in one or both directions, which together achieve a unit of work. The transaction is a characteristic of the application. For example, in the airline industry, a transaction might span the series of messages involved in reserving a seat in a flight reservation system. The transaction duration in this case is affected by the time for interaction between the passenger and the agent, as well as the time to process the transaction at the computer site.

In the banking industry, a transaction may consist of the entry of a customer's deposit and the updating of the customer's balance. In the retail industry, a transaction might be the process of recording item sales, or processing refunds, or verifying checks before accepting them as tender. In remote batch entry, the transaction may be a job step or an entire job, while in application program development, it may be the entry of a long series of programming statements and their trial execution.

In each case, the transaction time includes data-processing time and, often, human-interaction time. The time for actual data transmission may be a small or large fraction of the transaction time, depending on transmission speeds and the amounts of data-processing and/or human-interaction time.

The frequency and duration of transactions can vary over wide ranges. A rough approximation of this range is given in Fig. 1.2 as a function of application class. A relative measure of the activity per terminal is given by the product of the two coordinates; in Fig. 1.2, this is loosely expressed in erlangs, which strictly speaking is the ratio of mean service time to mean time between customer arrivals.

One or more transactions could be the subject of a distinct call on the switched network, with a *physical* connection established between two parties only for the duration of the transactions. On the other hand, the physical connection may be made on a long-term basis (for example, with a nonswitched line); then a *logical* connection may be made for two parties for only the duration of one or more transactions. In still other cases, if the disconnect/connect time is short enough, it is possible to have a physical connection only *for each message* within a transaction, disconnecting for the pause between messages.

1.2.4 Illustrative Distributed Systems

The features of data-processing/communications systems thus span a wide spectrum that almost defies illustration. Nevertheless, we'll try to illustrate the fact that systems of today are distributed in two ways: first *in a hierarchical fashion* and then *in a peer fashion*. The degree of centralization and distribution will first be illustrated by examining typical systems in three industries:

1. Airline reservation systems using a centralized data base
2. A banking system, where the data base is centralized but some of the message processing is distributed
3. A retail system, where more of the processing is distributed

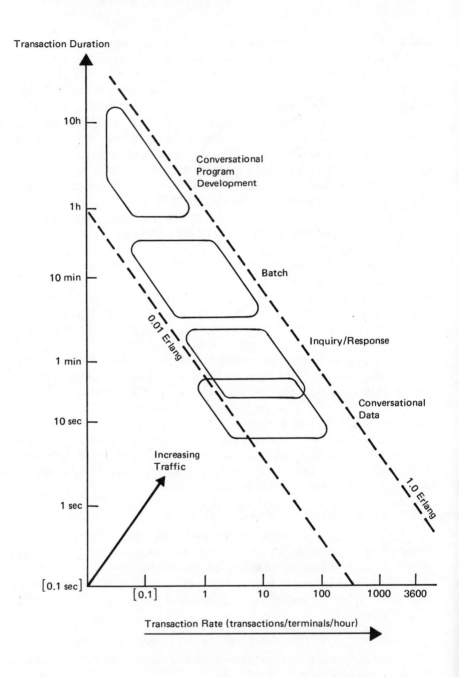

Fig. 1.2 Spectrum of transaction characteristics by application class.

Then we will consider how, in addition, each of these systems might involve the use of peer processors and peer data bases.

Centralized reservations.   One of the pioneering developments in on-line, interactive, data-base-oriented teleprocessing systems has been for airline systems [1.18, 1.19]. Out of the development of PARS (the Programmed Airline Reservation System) came a generalized Airlines Control Program (ACP) that was optimized for short standard messages, fixed formatted file records, and high transaction rates. Today, a typical ACP system might consist of 2000 to 5000 terminals. Some ACP systems also exist with a few hundred terminals and 10,000 terminal systems have been envisaged for the near future [1.19].

Often, these networks span a large area, typically nationwide, connecting agents in the major cities of a country to a *centralized data base*. Thus, any agent can sell, change, or cancel a reservation for any flight segment in the system, and know that all information is accurate and current to that instant.

In airline reservation systems, long-distance communication lines are shared among many agents through the use of concentrators (see Chapter 4) at key locations. Traffic to and from a number of agents is multiplexed by the concentrator onto a single long-distance line (see Fig. 1.3). A number of these concentrators may all share a single 2400-bit/sec (bps) communication line to the central site; polling manages this sharing (again, see Chapter 4) by allowing each concentrator, in turn, to use that line. The agent work stations may be locally attached to the concentrator or remotely attached via communication lines operating at 2400, 1200, or 148.8 bps. (A still higher level of sharing may be done by the telephone company, in which many such individual lines share a broadband transmission facility for the intercity and long-distance traffic. This sharing, however, is completely transparent to the subscriber.)

As an example [1.19], a system using an IBM S/360 Model 195 was designed to process 180 typical reservation messages each second, with the central processing unit operating at 85 percent utilization. The average response time was designed to be within two seconds, the response time at the 90th percentile to be within four seconds, and the average processing time per message to be less than 4.7 milliseconds.

Centralized data and distributed processing.   Many financial institutions are using distributed programmable units to handle transactions locally. We will describe a hypothetical but representative system in which large numbers of work stations, spread over large areas, operate on-line in this type of distributed-function network.

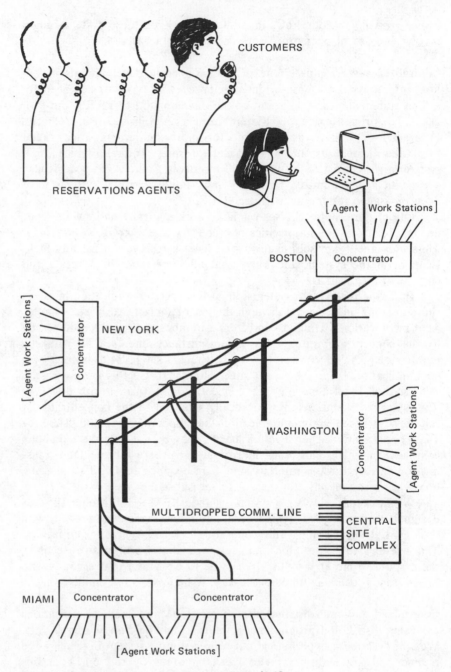

CUSTOMERS

RESERVATIONS AGENTS

[Agent Work Stations]

BOSTON Concentrator

[Agent Work Stations]

Concentrator NEW YORK

WASHINGTON Concentrator

[Agent Work Stations]

MULTIDROPPED COMM. LINE

CENTRAL SITE COMPLEX

MIAMI Concentrator Concentrator

[Agent Work Stations]

Fig. 1.3 Centralized airline reservation system [1.18].

Each work station typically is composed of a number of terminal facilities. This usually consists, for example, of

1. A programmable keyboard
2. A reader of prerecorded information in magnetic stripes
3. An alphanumeric character display (for example, a 240-character gas display panel)
4. A receipt and journal printer (for example, a 30-character/second, 80-column printer)

Alternatively, a work station might be a higher-speed administrative line printer. A group of such work stations is managed by a *programmable cluster controller*, as shown in Fig. 1.4. The work stations are connected to the programmable controller via private, on-premises loops at 1200, 2400, or 4800 bps, or via common carrier at—say, 1200 bps.

The programmed cluster controllers execute application-oriented programs and store data that are pertinent to local operations. They can be programmed to act as an "electronic journal," maintaining local totals, logging transactions performed on attached terminals, and providing a detailed audit trail. They can also be programmed to capture transactions during off-line operation for later transmission to a

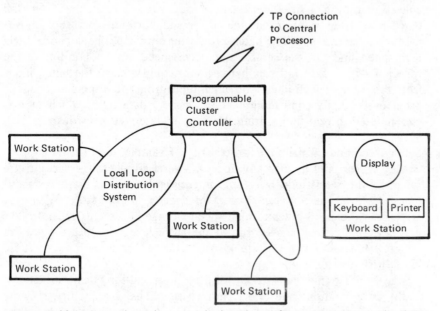

Fig. 1.4 Multiple work stations attached to loops from a programmable cluster controller.

central computer site. In one type of controller [1.22], a removable random-access diskette can store up to $560K$ bytes of data. In addition, certain members of that controller family have nonremovable disk storage of up to 9.3 million bytes. Many transactions, however, may also draw data in real time from the central data base to which each programmable controller is connected. The programmable controllers are, in effect, *local coordinators and preliminary processors* for the operations at the multiple work stations.

Each of the programmable cluster controllers in a typical installation will be connected to a central host site via lines of 1200–4800 bps. In some applications, the central site contains the central data base that is updated in real time by certain transactions entered at each work station. Every transaction across the entire network thus can draw on information that is accurate up to that instant, regardless of the number and/or location of the transactions. An illustrative duplexed configuration for a central site is given in Fig. 1.5, showing dual processors, shared disk storage, shared tape files, and shared communications controllers. Although an I/O device may be shared, only one processor, with the required amount of equipment dedicated to it, would be on-line at any given time.

Another part of the financial network may involve high-speed data collection during a brief period each day. Data is collected from the batch-processing centers at the dispersed locations to the above-mentioned central site. The batch-processing sites could be connected, via high-speed lines, to the central site. High-speed tapes, operating in the range of $470K$–$1250K$ bytes per second, would receive the batch input from these high-speed lines. The batch input from the dispersed locations provides the daily confirmation of the central data base, which then is incremented in real time during the day, as described previously.

Semiautonomous distributed processing. Examples of distributed processing, where still greater autonomy is exercised at each processor, are found in the retail industry. *Here programmable controllers operate autonomously, for the common types of transaction,* in each store. With over a hundred thousand bytes of high-speed storage in the cluster controller, multiple applications can be run at the store level. For other types, an interaction with a central site is used. Let us examine one of these "in-store" systems.

Sales personnel use a "point-of-sale" terminal for sales transactions, credit authorization, and some inquiry functions. Data entry may be through a magnetic or optical wand, whose passage over a label reads the identity of the item, or through a numeric and function-key keyboard.

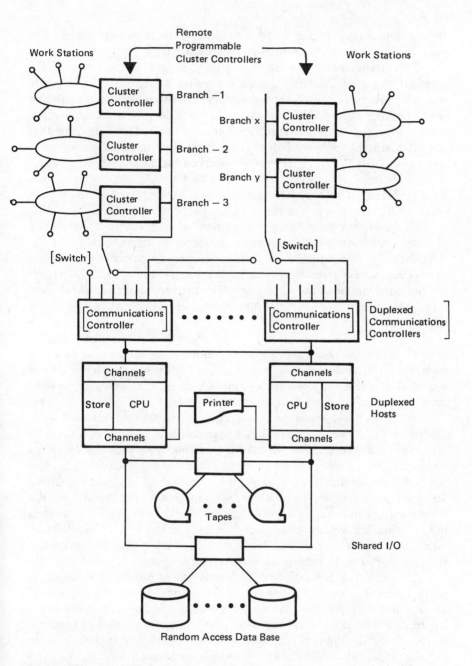

Fig. 1.5 Illustrative duplexed central processing site, and work stations on remote cluster controllers.

Instructions to the operator and data being entered are displayed; data provided in response to an inquiry may be printed.

Cash transactions are handled solely by the interactions of the terminal and a programmed cluster controller located in each store. In this role, the programmed controllers operate autonomously. Credit and check-cashing authorization, on the other hand, involve a check against a master file at a central computer location. Also, once a day, another central computer application draws data from all of its connected controllers so as to establish register balances and conduct an overall sales audit.

Another set of applications concerns the flow of inventory, and relies on a few separate display terminals per store. *Order entry* is the creation of purchase orders and the input to the purchase-order data base. The *receiving* application controls the movement of merchandise received and checked. *Accounts payable* includes the entry of invoice data into the data base, the calculation of cost and retail sales dollars, and information verification. These types of application are executed partly in the controller and partly in the central processor. The interaction is from the display terminal *via the same controller that handles the sales transactions* to the central computer.

Let us take as an example a chain of stores that is located throughout several states. In this installation, a group of 20 department stores is being brought on-line, with one programmed controller in each store and a central computer to coordinate them all. In at least one case, several stores can share a single programmed controller.

In our example, terminals are connected to the programmed store controller via a 2400- or 9600-bps transmission loop. The controllers, in turn, are each connected to the central computer by a separate 4800-bps telephone line. Each programmed controller manages from 60 to 120 point-of-sale terminals plus a display terminal and a printer. These terminals may handle from 20 to 30 transactions per hour, and the programmed controller in a store may handle 2000 to 3000 transactions per hour during a peak sales period. Response times at a point-of-sale terminal probably average less than a second, and less than ten percent of the responses should take more than, say, 1.5 seconds.

Each credit authorization requires only one or possibly two messages to the central computer. However, transactions of the inventory-flow applications may involve four or five messages to the central computer per transaction. The central computer, then, must be capable of handling in the order of eight to ten messages per second during peak sales periods, even though all cash transactions are handled locally, using the in-store programmed cluster controller.

When the day's transactions are batched from all the store controllers to the central computer, the transmission must take place in a short time, say, 0.5–1.5 hours. The records for tens of thousands of transactions must be transmitted in this mode, and the central computer must be capable of handling an equivalent of 10 to 20 messages per second during this time.

Multiple peers. The preceding examples illustrate a *hierarchical distribution of functions among three levels: the intelligent terminals, the programmed cluster controllers, and the central processing unit.* Both data bases and processing capabilities can be so distributed.

Given this hierarchy of distribution, one can, in addition, have multiple servers that operate as peers. To illustrate, any of the central processing units in the above examples might be replaced by multiple CPUs and multiple data bases. These might be at different locations. Different types of operation with such peers can be identified as follows.

1. *Transaction routing to peer data bases.* In some cases, the data base is partitioned by geography or function, and separate data bases are managed by different processors. These are peers of one another that can be coupled together. An illustrative configuration for systems with peer coupling is shown in Fig. 1.6. It may be desirable that terminals at any location be able to access any data base, and that the terminal user be unaware of the data-base partitioning.

In such systems, if a request arrives at any CPU it should be rerouted automatically to the site where the appropriate data base is located. With transaction routing, the routing to the correct data base is based on a transaction code in the user's request. Similarly, a request from the data base to any terminal can be routed to that terminal, via an intermediate host if necessary, using the terminal name in the request. In this example, *the routing is achieved in an application-like program by examining the contents of the request* that is provided by the user of the network.

2. *Job routing to peer processing units.* This is another form of transaction routing in which the work scope is a job (that is, an application program). As before, special fields within the user's request that accompanies the job can be used to achieve the routings. These fields can be interpreted by a so-called Job Entry Subsystem (JES) which functions as a pseudo-application program. JES performs the routing and coordinates the scheduling of jobs at multiple CPUs.

In one implementation [1.23], for example, the submitter of a job may specify the host upon which a job is to be executed and also the destination of the output resulting from job execution. A job may be entered into the network from any job entry station that is local to one of the hosts, or from a remote terminal. A job may also be entered into the network via any of the internal job queues within any of the hosts. Jobs

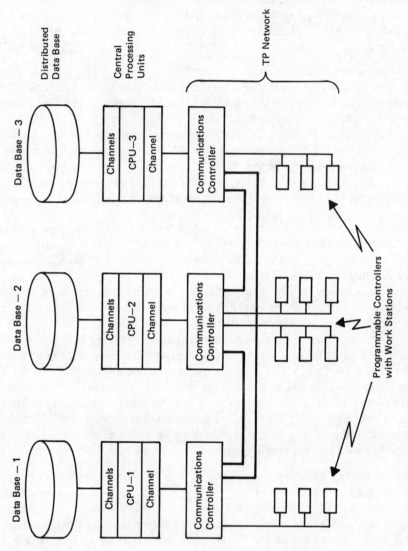

Fig. 1.6 Configuration with peer-coupled distributed data bases.

may be transmitted directly from an originating host to an execution host, without incurring store-and-forward overhead at intermediary hosts. When the job has been received at the execution host, it is queued to await execution. During execution of the job, output data sets are queued for transmission to the destination specified by the submitter of the job.

3. *Transaction-routing network service.* In the two cases cited above, the routing of the transaction (or job) is performed by a subsystem that operates as an application program external to the network. An alternative is to build the system so that the routing function is a part of the network services, even though examination of the content of the request is involved.

4. *Connection to alternate peers.* Quite a different approach is to build into the network architecture an ability to achieve logical connections to any program that may be located in any CPU *without examination of the content of each of the user's requests.* The connection (or session) usually pertains to the exchange of a series of bidirectional messages, which may proceed for a short or an extended length of time. Such a connection involves separate set-up messages to establish an initial connection. At that point, the user of the network specifies the name of the desired destination, for example, to which program subsequent messages will be sent. The subsequent dialogue employs addressing facilities that use headers supplied by transmission services of the network (rather than fields within the user's request).

More than one of these four types of operation may coexist in the same system.

1.3   EARLY TRANSMISSION FACILITIES

1.3.1 Introduction

Teleprocessing architecture is not greatly influenced by the types of transmission facilities to be employed. Nevertheless, there are some important localized influences, so it is appropriate to review transmission characteristics. We will first review the earlier transmission facilities, while new facilities and their trends will be discussed in Chapter 2.

1.3.2 Communications Common Carrier and PTT Facilities

The communications common carriers in the United States, which are independent but regulated companies, and the government agencies known as Postal Telephone and Telegraph Administrations (PTTs) both provide a public communication service. The responsibility of the common carriers and PTTs includes, in part, accepting a signal from a portion of a data-processing system (or business machine), transporting that signal to a distant point, and delivering the signal with exactly the same bit sequence it had when received. The method used to transport the signal varies according to the carrier's internal equipment, and should be of no concern to the data-processing equipment or to the end-user. Of course, the signals at the end points must conform to accepted standards, and the overall performance, in cost, reliability, delay, and throughput, must be satisfactory. In the United States, the primary common carriers have been the Western Union Telegraph Company and the many independent telephone companies. The largest, by far, of the American telephone companies is American Telephone and Telegraph Company, which with the Bell operating companies provides most of the nation's telephones. General Telephone and Electronics is the next largest, but there are about 1600 independent telephone companies. In addition, there are specialized carriers and domestic satellite carriers in the United States (see Chapter 2). In many other countries, the communications facilities are managed by national agencies referred to as PTTs or by private companies operating under the supervision of the government, which often has sole responsibility for all such facilities in that country.

Both common carriers and PTTs offer nonswitched (dedicated) and switched (public) facilities. Nonswitched facilities are dedicated to the use of only one subscriber. The entire capacity of a nonswitched facility is available to that subscriber exclusively, and payment is made on a monthly basis, irrespective of the traffic on the line. The nonswitched facility may be only a reserved capacity, such as a frequency band of a broadband link, rather than a physically separate line. If necessary, even a dedicated (nonswitched) line may be replaced, by the carrier, during periods of normal maintenance. Switched facilities are physically switched, usually on an individual call basis, from one subscriber to another. The familiar Direct Distance Dial (DDD) facilities of AT&T are a prime example of this; with this system multiple switching centers establish a physical connection between source and destination, but only for the duration of a call.

Bandwidth and bit rate.   The term bandwidth does not refer to transmission speed; that is, the rate at which bits are actually sent on a line. Rather, it refers to a characteristic of the line itself and the range of frequencies that the line can actually carry. This bandwidth is usually measured in kilohertz (one kilohertz is equal to 1000 cycles per second). The theoretical maximum transmission capacity of a line (in bits per second) is usually much larger than the bandwidth and depends on the signal-to-noise ratio. The practical transmission speed (or bit rate) is always some fraction of the theoretical maximum transmission capacity. Thus, a line with a *bandwidth* of 4 kHz may permit a *transmission speed* of 2.4, 4.8, or 9.6 kilobits per second (kbps), depending on the modulation technique and signal-processing technique used. Its theoretical maximum transmission capacity would be much larger than 9.6 kbps, but practical consideration limits the use of this larger capacity.

Communications facilities have been available in the following three ranges.

1. *Narrowband facilities.* Narrowband channels permit speeds in the range below 200 bits per second (bps). Both nonswitched and switched services are available.

2. *Voiceband facilities.* The voice-grade network provides a medium to facilitate data communication in virtually any location, with a bandwidth that is nominally 4 kilohertz (kHz). By the use of special modulation and demodulation units (modems), switched lines are operated with data transfer rates in the range of 600 to 4800 bps. Nonswitched lines, with special conditioning, operate at speeds of 4800, 7200, and 9600 bps.

Private vendors have offered equipments to combine several voiceband facilities so as to give an appearance, to the data-processing equipment, of a higher bandwidth line. For example, two 9.6-kbps lines can be combined by such special equipment to provide, in effect, a 19.2-kbps facility. In some cases, this is sufficient and also less expensive than the next higher available line, say, one of 50 kbps.

3. *Wideband facilities.* This refers to all communications facilities having a bandwidth considerably wider than those of voice channels. TELPAK, for example, is a nonswitched service offered by AT&T that is capable of handling data speeds of up to 230,400 bps. Each TELPAK channel can be used as a single wideband channel, or it can be subdivided into independent voice channels.

Wideband facilities can be obtained in the United States in a hierarchy of capacities, equivalent to 60 or 240 voice-grade channels (using Type 5700 and Type 5800 lines, respectively). Although not a TELPAK offering, Series 8000 is another wideband service in the United States that permits high-speed data transmission at rates of up to 50,000 bps. A 12-channel (48-kHz) facility is available in many other countries (for example, Japan, Norway, Germany, the United Kingdom, France, Italy). The 60-channel (240-kHz) and higher bandwidth facilities are less common.

Another nonswitched wideband AT&T service, the T1, provides 1.544 megabit/second (Mbps) capability in certain areas over limited distances (80–160 km). For voice transmission, the T1 carrier uses pulse-code modulation (PCM) to convert the analog signals into 64-kbps bit streams. Then by time-division multiplexing (see Chapter 4), it combines many such signals into a 1.544-Mbps bit stream. These same lines can be used for data transmission.

The T2 carrier system operates at 6.3 Mbps at distances of up to 800 kilometers. Multiples of T1 (at 1.5 Mbps) are multiplexed to form T2 (at 6.3 Mbps).

One used to be able to see a physical copper *line* and a unique physical *circuit* that were used to carry a single telephone conversation. Now we have the preceding spectrum of bandwidth offerings and operating speeds. There obviously is no physical copper line dedicated to each channel of these offerings. Many of these channels might be multiplexed on a coaxial cable, a microwave link, or a satellite system. Nevertheless, it is still customary to refer to lines or circuits, such as a "voice line" of 4 kHz or a "broadband circuit" operating at, say, 48 kbps. They usually function, so far as the end-user is concerned, as though they were a line and an isolated circuit, and so the terms have persisted.

Economy of bandwidth. It is typical of the recent tariff structures for cost-per-character-transmitted to be 10 to 20 times higher for narrow-band facilities than for voice-grade facilities, assuming the same percentage of utilization for both. Major savings (on a per-character basis) are also possible in going from voice-grade to wideband facilities, if the facilities are fully utilized.

Modems. Most transmission facilities have been designed to handle analog signals, rather than digital data. In voice-grade lines, for example, the use of transformer coupling results in severe attenuation at frequencies below 400 Hz, and attenuation is also high above 3 kHz. In order to transmit digital information over such facilities, the digital signal must be altered so that its energy is mainly between 500 and 3000 Hz. The digital signal, in effect, modulates a carrier in the proper frequency band. At the receiver, the signal is demodulated. The equipment at both ends of the line is called, accordingly, the modulator–demodulator, or modem.

Amplitude and phase distortion will still be present because of nonideal transmission-line characteristics. Filters may be included in modems to compensate for line distortions. These so-called "equalizers" reduce signal distortion, hence permitting higher transmission speeds or greater reliability. The drive for higher transmission speeds using relatively low bandwidth lines forced modem designers to use more complex modulation methods. This led to a higher degree of complexity in the modem, so that today a 9600-bps modem is really a small computer. Its program might, for example, work with a signal composed of eight distinct phases and two amplitude levels.

In some countries, modems must be supplied by the PTTs. In other countries, they may be supplied by either the user or the common carrier or the PTT.

Transmission sections.   There are three main transmission sections in the carrier's plant:

1. The local distribution
2. The short-haul transmission system
3. The long-haul transmission system

A single "line" may use all three, or only some, of these sections.

The local distribution is generally a twisted pair of wires linking users and the local central office. Large multipair cables converge all these loops into a minimum number of routes. The short-haul system spans distances from 80 to 160 km. Usually, frequency or time-division multiplexing is used to handle multiple voice-grade channels. In long-haul systems, thousands of voice channels can be multiplexed, using coaxial cable or microwave radio circuits. In the United States, voice channels are commonly assembled into groups (12 voice channels in a 48-kHz bandwidth), supergroups (5 groups in a 240-kHz bandwidth), and master groups (10 groups in approximately a 2.4-MHz bandwidth). These systems typically span distances of over 160 km, but such distances are widely variant.

1.3.3 Switched versus Nonswitched Lines

When using a *switched* network, a given line can be mechanically or electronically switched among end-users. A user, then, may employ a different line on successive calls. A *nonswitched* facility, on the other hand, is preselected and reserved for exclusive use by one subscriber.

In the case of a switched network, the use of the network is preceded by a *signaling phase.* In this initial time period, there is an exchange of information between the originating terminal device or user and the communications system that will provide the basic transportation service. This information is required by the communications system to establish a transmission path (real or virtual) between the originating user and the receiving user. (The dial sequences in this signaling phase are described in Chapter 12 for circuit switched networks and in Chapter 17 for packet-switched networks.)

The choice of nonswitched or switched lines depends on the amount of traffic, need for fast response time, cost of the particular line configuration, speeds obtainable, and required reliability. All are technology-dependent. The factors are briefly reviewed here, and will be reexamined in Section 2.4.

To connect or establish a call on the public switched telephone network (in the United States) requires a significant call-establishment time, as shown below [1.10].

Airline distance (kilometers)	Connect time (seconds)	
	Mean	Standard deviation
0–290	11.1	4.6
291–1166	15.6	5.0
1167–4666	17.6	6.6

This time is consumed in dialing, central-office switching and ringing, and (in data-communications applications) modem handshaking. Disconnect times for the public telephone network are about three seconds. Under these circumstances, response time on switched lines in the past has been unacceptable for many applications.

Costs of nonswitched lines may be lower than those of switched services when the usage exceeds a given amount. (A very rough rule of thumb for nonswitched lines in the United States in the 1970s has been a dollar per mile per month.) The crossover point depends on distance and tariffs, but can be considered generally to be between one and four hours of billable usage per day.

Comparisons by Lissandrello [1.5] showed widely varying breakeven points between nonswitched voice-grade and the public switched network in different parts of the world. The data from that study (circa 1971) showed that if one used the public switched network in the United States for 1–1.5 hours per day over a distance of 300 kilometers, it would be cheaper to lease a nonswitched line. On the other hand, Germany and Sweden would require four hours of operation per day, while France and Italy would require two hours of operation per day over a distance of 500 kilometers in order to break even.

The characteristics of a nonswitched line are relatively fixed; therefore, steps can be taken to optimize the line and its usage. A so-called "conditioned" line has been checked over to ensure its characteristics; this checkup may include some cleanup of undesirable characteristics.

Given a stable, nonswitched line, the modem may contain equalization circuits that can be tuned to compensate for line distortion. This compensation can result in either a lower error rate or a higher transmission speed. Methods for dynamic equalization have been developed, but these add to the cost of the modem.

In general, switching equipment can be of diverse types and vintages. The circuits obtained may vary from call to call. A result is that switched lines have generally had higher noise and hence more errors for a given transmission speed than have nonswitched lines. Also, because of this diversity, the probability of a line outage is greater with switched lines. Thus, in the past, nonswitched lines have been generally preferable to switched lines for the following reasons:

- Greater economy with heavy use
- Better performance definition and stability
- Better availability
- Faster response to short inquiries

1.3.4 Half-duplex and Duplex Lines

A transmission line connecting two or more users of the line can be used in several ways. Protocols, or agreements among the users of the line, can be established to determine who can transmit at what time. A half-duplex (HDX) protocol permits only one terminal to transmit in only one direction at any one time. A duplex protocol permits bidirectional flow on the "line," so that two terminals may be sending to each other simultaneously. These two protocols have implications about the physical capabilities of both the line and the terminals.

Half-duplex "lines" are physically capable of flow in only one direction at a time. They require a pause for "line turnaround" which includes turning off echo suppressors (that isolate the return path) and allows decaying oscillations on the line to settle down. Turnaround delay is usually 75–100 milliseconds. Only after the pause can transmission take place in the opposite direction. Duplex lines do not have this restriction. Half-duplex lines are physically incapable of supporting duplex flows. In local loops, for example, four-wire circuits (rather than two-wire) are usually needed for duplex operation. Many of the local circuits, from a telephone to a local exchange, have been only two-wire. Most intercity lines are four-wire, or equivalent to four-wire. When necessary, two half-duplex circuits can be used to provide a duplex capability.

A duplex terminal is equipped to send and receive at the same time, while a half-duplex terminal is not. The modem, also, must be tailored to provide either duplex or half-duplex operation. A duplex line can handle transmissions with greater efficiency than a half-duplex line of the same bandwidth can. Yet the duplex line often costs little more than the half-duplex line. In the United States (in 1976) the duplex line has been about 25 percent more expensive than the half-duplex, but that differential is often less in other countries.

In the past, the costs of terminals and modems for duplex operation has been high enough to encourage half-duplex operation. This cost increment for duplex is decreasing as technology permits. On the other hand, much of the benefit of duplex operations has been obtained by a combination of half-duplex terminals and a duplex line. In this mode, called duplex multipoint, one duplex terminal (or station) communicates with multiple half-duplex terminals (or stations) via a duplex line (see Section 4.2).

1.3.5 Response Time

Response time is the elapsed time between the end of a request to a data-processing system and the beginning of the reply (for example, the length of time between the entry at a terminal of the last character of an inquiry and the display of the first character of the reply at a user terminal). Usually, we think in terms of an average response time, but it may also be necessary to specify that, say, 95 percent of the time, no wait will exceed some maximum figure. The delay in traveling from source to destination is due to a number of factors, including some or all of the following (see Fig. 1.7).

1. Message-serializing time, or the time it takes to get the full message onto the line, one bit at a time, at the rate fixed by the transmission speed (for example, 1200 bps). This time is given by the length of the message (in bits) divided by the transmission speed (in bits per second). This delay occurs at the source and at each intermediate node where data is buffered.

2. The propagation time, or the time for a signal to physically travel along the lines from source to destination.

3. Line turnaround time, or the time required to reverse the direction of transmission when using a half-duplex communications channel.

4. Modem delay time.

5. The processing time required for routing within the origin node, at each intermediate node, and at the destination.

6. The queuing time involved in each node, waiting for a resource (such as a line or a processor) to be free.

The response time includes these factors for both directions of flow, and the time for message processing at the destination.

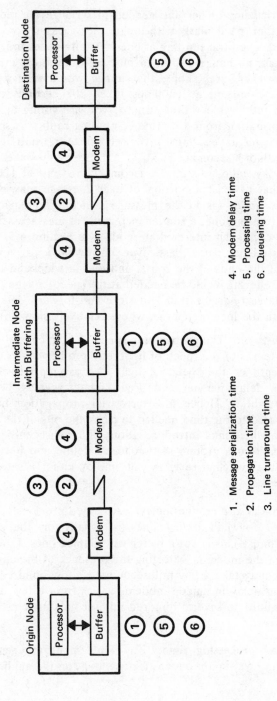

Fig. 1.7 Potential delays of a message traveling from source to destination.

1. Message serialization time
2. Propagation time
3. Line turnaround time
4. Modem delay time
5. Processing time
6. Queueing time

Message serializing. The time needed to serialize the message is often most important, particularly with longer messages or slower speed lines. For example, when transmitting at one megabit per second, a quarter of a million bits for an image display or plot are transmitted in a quarter of a second. However, at 50 kbps, that image would take five seconds to transmit. Transmitting at 1200 bps takes 208 seconds or almost 3.5 minutes, an intolerable waiting time if you are sitting at a display and seeking information from a remote computing center. A shorter inquiry, of say 1000 bytes, takes almost seven seconds to transmit at 1200 bps, but only one-sixth of a second at 50 kbps. A 100-byte message, which is quite common today, takes less than a second to transmit at 1200 bps.

Note that at least a portion of each message may be buffered at intermediate nodes (as in the message switching and packet switching systems). If this is done, a similar increment of message-serializing delay is added at each such intermediate node (see Section 4.5).

A transmission may pass over narrowband or voiceband local networks, at the ends of the route, and over a wideband facility for the long haul. Buffering would be needed at the speed-change points. In such cases, the largest serialization and store-and-forward delays will be associated with the local networks, where relatively slow links are used.

Propagation time. The propagation speed [1.6] in coaxial cables may be about nine-tenths of the speed of light, but in other cables, it may be less than one-tenth of the speed of light. An assumption of one or two milliseconds delay per one hundred kilometers may be average for terrestrial facilities. Hence, the terrestrial propagation time is usually small compared to the time needed to clock the bits of the message onto the line. Satellite links introduce about 300 milliseconds per hop (one transmission from a ground station to a satellite and back to a ground station). Some switched services can employ either a satellite link or a terrestrial link.

Line turnaround and modem delay. As stated previously, the line turnaround time for half-duplex lines is usually on the order of 75–100 milliseconds. This is not a factor with duplex lines. In addition, there are delays in the modem. Detecting the presence of the analog carrier at the receiver may take a few milliseconds to a few hundred milliseconds. Transmission delay in analog modems varies from a few milliseconds in the simpler units to several hundred milliseconds in some very complex units.

Queuing and processing time. The time spent at each node doing processing and waiting in queues is dependent on the application and the transmission system design. This time can range from milliseconds to seconds and longer. In the intermediate nodes, which use buffering or store-and-forward techniques, critical factors are the sizes of the messages, the amount of buffering available, and the speed of the processor. The waiting time for line availability obviously is dependent on the line load. With reasonable designs, the delays are often in the range of 20–100 msec per intermediate node, but this can be larger at times of heavy line congestion.

Improving response time. The accumulation of all of the above propagation and equipment delays can, in some cases, be significant; but at lower data rates, the local bit transmission speed and the block length are often the key factors in determining response time.

In other cases, queueing time may be the key factor. For a given block length, the problem is often stated to be one of inadequate capacity for the throughput desired, resulting in too great a utilization of the facility. Actually, improvements in response time can be obtained by either of two approaches [1.24]: (1) reducing the utilization of the facility by (a) increasing the system capacity or (b) reducing the throughput, and (2) maintaining a constant utilization rate but scaling up both the capacity and the throughput.

1.3.6 Transmission Error Performance

Average bit error rates for various communications services around the world are said to range from one in 50,000 for narrowband lines to one in 500,000 for voice-grade lines operated at 600 bps [1.3]. However, average failure rates can be misleading. One observes, from test data, that different lines in the same speed category may differ in their reliability by three orders of magnitude. This is illustrated in Fig. 1.8, which combines the results of four surveys, two in the United States on Bell System facilities and two in the United Kingdom [1.7]. The data span a range of error rate from 10^{-3} to 10^{-6}, which is wider than the averages cited above. Moreover, the best ten percent of a given type line are about 1000 times better than the worst ten percent. This extreme variability is partially a result of the widely varying ages of the equipment in a typical system and the widely varying environments of that equipment. The performance of switched network services can even vary by time of day, because of the effect of switching activity and the likelihood of longer (alternate) routes during peak periods.

A realistic approach to this problem of variable performance has been to concede that almost every major network is likely to encounter a wide variety of line qualities. An architecture that must apply to many of

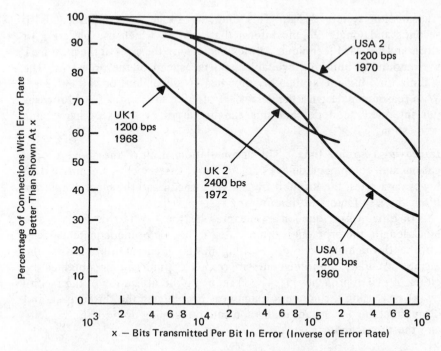

Fig. 1.8 Distribution of error rates on switched telephone connections [1.7].

the networks must aim to provide highly reliable transmissions in, say, all but the worst five percent of the lines expected to be found. This has led to the incorporation of highly effective error detection and automatic retransmission facilities in many of the data link controls. The criterion of goodness then shifts to block error rates (BER) and frequency of undetected block errors (rather than bit error rates). Block error detection is discussed in Chapter 11.

Catastrophic outages of long duration are, of course, a special hazard. Not all sections of a circuit are equally prone to such outages. Several studies [1.25] have indicated that the local distribution loops cause a high percentage of them. Unfortunately these often cannot be guarded against by having dual routes, and cannot be bypassed, because all available local circuits, dial and leased, may go through the same cable.

1.4 SYSTEM COSTS

1.4.1 Introduction

The teleprocessing system is often a key ingredient in making an application feasible. While minimizing the cost of each component in a system must be considered, the larger payoff is usually found in tackling the major cost factors of that system, even when this means higher costs in other areas. An architecture with the proper structure can have a major effect on the feasibility of the application and on total system cost, by affecting the larger (and increasing) cost factors.

1.4.2 System Cost Factors

The costs of systems and their components vary over a very wide range. It is interesting to observe, however, that the percentages of expenditures for the various classes of equipment and services often do not change greatly when comparing small systems to large systems or when comparing very different data-processing application areas.

The costs of personnel have usually been the largest single factor in data-processing/communications systems. These personnel include customer programmers, system operators, system analysts, keypunch operators, network operators, and so forth. It is not unusual to find personnel costs in the range of 35 to 50 percent of the total data-processing and communication expenses. The second largest expense item is often hardware costs, exclusive of teleprocessing costs. Communications costs, including the communications hardware and lines, very often trail third in this comparison, with frequent showings of between 5 and 25 percent of the total expense. It is possible today to provide a wide range of teleprocessing system designs with line costs small in comparison to the cost of computers, terminals, software, and operations.

On the other hand, the trend is toward ever-wider use of communication facilities. Communications costs can therefore be expected to grow; hence more emphasis is put on resource sharing to limit the cost growth. New (and more economical) transmission services also become more attractive as load builds up.

The rate of application development is an additional issue. The shortage of skilled systems personnel can easily extend the development of a new teleprocessing application for years, or it may prevent the development altogether. The potential cost savings of the application are thus deferred or lost completely. This is often the key consideration.

1.4.3 Design Priorities Regarding System Cost

With improvements in price/performance of hardware (see Chapter 2), hardware cost will be a decreasing percentage of the total cost. Communications costs promise to increase and become a somewhat higher percentage of the total, despite improved tariffs, as the number of terminals and geographic dispersion increase. Of primary importance, however, is the fact that with continuing inflation, the personnel costs can be expected to remain high or to increase further.

Clearly, the total system architecture and design should give priority to those factors that promote ease of system development, of application program development, of system use, of system change to meet new requirements, and of system expansion, and similar considerations where skilled personnel are involved and tend to be a limiting factor.

We must profit from experience with today's systems to discern the types of architecture that can lead to longer-term total cost savings. A structure which seeks to separate and keep physically independent those functions that are logically independent is a first step in that direction; such separation can permit change and evolution in a part of the system without requiring the consumption of skilled resources to constantly modify other parts.

1.5 REFERENCES AND BIBLIOGRAPHY

See also [3.1].

1.1 P. E. Jackson and C. D. Stubbs. "A Study of Multiaccess Computer Communications." *AFIPS Conf. Proc.* **34** (May 1969): 491.

1.2 J. Martin. *Systems Analysis for Data Transmission.* Englewood Cliffs, N.J.: Prentice-Hall (1972).

1.3 J. Martin. *Teleprocessing Network Organization.* Englewood Cliffs, N.J.: Prentice-Hall (1970).

1.4 B. Skoldborg. "Real Time Banking System As An Application." *Proc. ICCC, Stockholm* (12–14 August 1974).

1.5 G. J. Lissandrello. "World Data Communications As Seen By The Data Processing Systems Designers." *ACM/IEEE Second Symposium on Problems in the Optimization of Data Communications Systems,* Palo Alto, California (20–22 October 1971).

1.6 Electronic Industries Association. "Application Notes for EIA Standards 232-C." *Industrial Electronics Bulletin* **9**.

1.7 D. W. Davies and D. L. A. Barber. *Communication Networks for Computers.* New York: John Wiley (1973). (Figure 1.8 reprinted by permission of John Wiley.)

1.8 *Electronics* (8 January 1976): 94.

1.9 *Datamation* (November 1975): 47, 49.

1.10 Bell System Technical Reference. "Data Communication Using the Switched Telecommunications Network." PUB41005 (May 1971).

1.11 J. Martin. *Telecommunications and the Computer.* Englewood Cliffs, N.J.: Prentice-Hall (1969).

1.12 D. A. Dunn and A. J. Lipinsky. "Economic Considerations in Computer Communications Systems." In N. Abramson and F. Kuo (eds.), *Computer Communications Networks.* Englewood Cliffs, N.J.: Prentice-Hall (1973).

1.13 P. E. Muench. "Bell System Private Line Data Service." *Proc. 1971 IEEE Intern. Conv.* New York City: (22–25 March 1971).

1.14 *OS/VS2* IBM Form No. GC20-0001.

1.15 W. P. Davenport. *Modern Data Communication.* New York: Hayden (1971).

1.16 L. M. Branscomb. "Trends and Developments in Computer/Telecommunications Technologies." *OECD Conference on Computer/Telecommunications.* Paris (February 1975).

1.17 P. E. Green, Jr., and R. W. Lucky (eds.). *Computer Communications.* New York: IEEE Press (1975).

1.18 J. R. Knight. "A Case Study: Airlines Reservation Systems." *Proc. IEEE* **60** (November 1972): 1423–1431. (Figure 1.3 reprinted by permission of IEEE.)

1.19 J. E. Siwiec. "PARS/ACP-High Performance DB/DC System." *IBM Systems Journal* **16,** No. 2 (1977).

1.20 P. V. McEnroe, H. T. Huth, E. A. Moore, and W. W. Morris III. "Overview of the Supermarket System and the Retail Store System." *IBM Systems Journal* **15,** No. 1 (1975).

1.21 J. H. Winbrow. "A Large Scale Interactive Administrative System." *IBM Systems Journal* **10,** No. 4 (1971): 260–282.

1.22 *Advanced Function for Communications System Summary.* IBM Form No. GA27-3099-1.

1.23 *Network Job Entry Facility for JES-2, General Information.* IBM Form No. GC23-0010.

1.24 L. Kleinrock. *Queueing Systems,* Volume II. New York: John Wiley (1976).

1.25 J. Martin. *Telecommunications and the Computer,* 2nd ed. Englewood Cliffs, N.J.: Prentice-Hall (1976).

2
System
Trends

2.1 INTRODUCTION

Having reviewed the state of today's systems, we must next consider how
future trends are likely to affect the requirements of a future architecture
for distributed systems. The dramatic reductions in digital-technology
costs, the widening range of types of information to be transmitted, new
common-carrier data networks, and advances in programming techniques
all provide both new opportunities and new requirements. These contribute to a trend toward greater distribution of function through the
network, with associated architecture needs.

2.2 COMPUTER TECHNOLOGY TRENDS

There is no doubt that there has been a dramatic reduction in the cost of
digital technology, particularly for logic circuits and for storage. This is
illustrated by the cost reductions for integrated circuits as shown in Fig.
2.1 [2.1]. From 1965–1966 to 1970–1971, the number of electrical
circuits that could be placed on a single chip of silicon, with metal-oxide
semiconductor devices imbedded in it, increased by a factor of 100. The
switching delay of these circuits was improved by a factor of 10. During
this same period, the price per gate or circuit function fell by a factor of
between 15 and 25, while the price per bit of storage fell by a factor of
between 65 and 100. Another projection [2.34] shows the price per logic
gate, using bipolar LSI technology, dropping by a factor of 100 in the
eight years between 1972 and 1980. This has resulted from advances in
the semiconductor fabrication technology that have permitted higher and

Function	1965–66	1970–71	Factor Of Improvement
Switching Delay (nanoseconds)	12	1.2	10:1
Device Complexity Per Chip			
Gate Circuits			
Bipolar	12–16	150	1:10
MOS	100	5–10,000	1:100
Bit Density			
Bipolar	4	256	1:64
MOS	32	1,024	1:32
Price Per Device Package	$2.00	20¢	10:1
Per Gate Or *Circuit Function*			
Bipolar	$1.00	4¢	25:1 ←
MOS	$0.30	2¢	15:1
Per *Memory Bit* (RAM)			
Bipolar	$4.00	6¢	65:1 ←
MOS	$1.00	1¢	100:1

Fig. 2.1   Integrated circuit cost reduction [2.1].

higher densities of logic and storage to be achieved. The cost of fabrication of a silicon wafer remains relatively static while the number of logic elements or storage cells within that same wafer steadily increases. Hence, the cost per unit of logic or storage goes down. The average number of components (transistors, diodes, resistors) per integrated circuit has about doubled every year since 1960. Predictions [2.37] are that by 1980 the most advanced circuits will contain the equivalent of one million components.

How these reductions in circuit costs are reflected in the price of the final product (such as a central processing unit) depends, of course, on other factors, such as the costs of power supplies, frames, and connectors which do not decrease at nearly the same rate. One comparison of central-processing-unit prices from 1960 to 1967 indicates that the price per instruction executed dropped by a factor of seven every five years. A more recent indication is given in Fig. 2.2 [2.2], which shows the reductions in the computing cost when performing a single job, namely, the computing for the packet switching function. Shown there is the change in the computational cost associated with moving a million bits over an average distance of 1940 kilometers within a nationwide network. That cost was calculated from the purchase cost for several small computers of different manufacturers. This examination indicates a reduction by a factor of ten in five years. While such analyses vary greatly with the

Dollars/Million Bits Transmitted

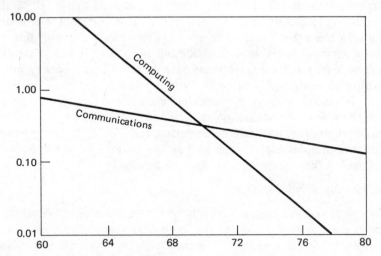

Fig. 2.2 Relative costs of communications and computing in a packet switching network (from a paper by L. G. Roberts [2.2]).

nature of the jobs to be performed by the equipment, it is clear that over, say, a fifteen-year period, we are witnessing price reductions per unit of work ranging from factors of several hundred to a thousand. One of the results of this trend is the widespread use of minicomputers with power comparable to machines of the 1960s and early 1970s. The prospects for continued improvement over the next decade are excellent.

As computing technology costs decrease, that technology can be used more widely to conserve communication bandwidth. This is accomplished by a wide variety of approaches, such as polling, multiplexing, concentration, fast-connect digital switching systems, packet switching systems, and satellite-borne switches (all of which are discussed later in this chapter or in Chapter 4).

2.3 INFORMATION SPECTRUM TRENDS

2.3.1 Introduction

System designs tend to be optimized about an assumed set of characteristics of the information being transmitted. The architecture often caters to these assumed characteristics and the expected use to be made of that information.

We find that analog voice channels characteristically handle data transmission at speeds of between 200 and 9600 bps, depending on terminal complexity and type of application. The digital telephone channel, on the other hand, is in the neighborhood of 56,000 bps and the video channel is higher than 6,000,000 bps. The message characteristics range from short conversational packets to endless one-way bit strings, with many varieties in between.

What will be the important characteristics of the information and the usage to be made of that information, as we continue to expand the new application programs, new characteristics of bulk digital storage, and new input/output devices? A look at these trends may influence the degree of versatility that we build into the architecture.

2.3.2 New Applications

We already have a great diversity of data-processing applications. However, there is an expectation that new classes of applications will involve substantially different kinds of input/output mechanisms and information transfer. Some possible examples follow.

1. *Image processing.* The entry in digitized form, via the network, of the results of electronic scanning of documents; the filing of documents in an image data base and the processing of these documents, with human interaction via high-resolution displays; and the distribution, via the network, of image-enhanced output.

2. *Document distribution.* The high-volume transfer of facsimile and/or digitized image among document-distribution centers and the subsequent distribution, partially electronic and partially manual, from these distribution centers to the recipients. A subset of this application class is electronic-mail, which attempts to use similar techniques in current mail systems.

3. *The automated office.* Electronic capture of keystrokes on electronic typewriters and the use of communications and data processing to support the logging, filing, retrieval, copying, and distribution functions of the office complex.

4. *Computer tutor.* From a library of self-help programs, computer programs coaching the pupil (typically adult) in an interactive mode [2.25].

5. *Cashless society transactions.* Recording of financial transactions, with an immediate printed output for buyer and seller, and updating of balance in computer storage [2.25].

Such new on-line applications will come into wider use as the cost of computing, communications, and terminals decreases, and as the cost of other existing methods increases. To illustrate [2.29], the cost of a single piece of medical literature to a library has been rising at a compound growth rate of seven to nine percent per year. At the same time, the amount of such literature has been increasing at four to seven percent per year. Hence, the rate at which library costs would rise, if a library attempted to cover a constant fraction of relevant literature, would be about fourteen percent per year. Thus, this cost has been doubling about every five years. At some point, as on-line computing services decrease in cost, the on-line storage and distribution of some of these documents become economically feasible. Such crossover points are expected to be reached, for some of the above applications, during the coming decade.

Noncoded information

Two of the above examples involve the transmission of *noncoded information* from a page or a form. By this we mean the transmission of a bit (or byte) stream, whose successive values correspond to successive points in a linear scan of an image. The image is digitally recorded and then reproduced without the use of coordinate data. No character coding is involved. Insurance company forms and engineering drawings are examples of documents containing information that does not always lend itself to character-string encoding. Instead, a scan of the entire image preserves all information. The retention of the image itself, with artwork, handwritten inscriptions, and explanatory notes or diagrams, is often necessary for the retention of essential information.

Digital images were once processed only by relatively complex systems having large amounts of special-purpose hardware and programming. The rapid development of raster-scan technology, however, promises to make the handling of images economically feasible in relatively simple input/output equipments.

The raster scan is the technique of generating or recording the elements of a display image by a line-by-line sweep across the entire display surface; an example is the generation of a picture on a television screen. In a raster scan, the image is scanned to detect all changes in light intensity (or color) in a series of very closely spaced scans, say, 120 per inch. The data can be digitized to give a binary value for light (or color) for each of, say, 120 sample points per inch of scan. The stored matrix of intensity values can be used in an output scan to reproduce the stored image.

Laser-beam technology facilitates the scanning of documents for input purposes and the rapid scanning of sensitized papers for output documents. Cathode-ray tubes also lend themselves to raster scanning. A storage technique inherent in the display tube or storage provided by low-cost semiconductors (or magnetics) can be used. Thus, a combination of digital, cathode-ray tube, and laser technologies now permits image input/output devices to be harmoniously linked with digital storage, digital computing, and digital transmission systems.

If we assume image devices operating at resolutions in the range of 120 to 240 sample points per linear inch, the potential amount of image information in a standard $8\frac{1}{2}$-by-11-inch document can be quite large. Allowing only one bit per sample point (that is, either black or white, with no shades of gray or color per sample point), the requirement is for $168K$ bytes at the lower resolution or $672K$ bytes at the higher resolution. Many coding techniques are available to take advantage of the strings of unchanging black or white, or strings of unchanging color. Coding of black and white images, for example, can result in a compression of the byte string by factors in the range of two to ten. If large areas of a page are unoccupied, simple techniques such as automatically skipping white zones can greatly reduce the number of bytes per page. Nevertheless, we are talking about tens of thousands of bytes per page.

2.3.4 Bulk Store

The transmission of very large amounts of information will depend in part on the availability of large, inexpensive storage. Very large on-line libraries of digital data are in use today. Examples include the Unicon store of Precision Instruments, the Masstape of Grumman, the Terabit file of Ampex, and the 3850 Mass Storage System of IBM. These are the forerunners.

Magnetic technology is more mature than that of semiconductors. Nevertheless, the cost of digital storage media, such as rotating magnetic disks, magnetic tape, and magnetic cartridges, has been dropping substantially. Improvements in the price per bit of on-line storage have been steady and dramatic over the past 15 years, as illustrated in Fig. 2.3 [2.16]. For example, the monthly cost on the IBM 3850 mass storage device is less than 25 cents per million bits. The steadily decreasing cost of this type of storage has enabled data-processing systems to increase their storage capacity from tens of thousands of bytes to millions of bytes and then to hundreds of billions of bytes.

The continuation of this trend of decreasing cost per unit of storage and the technical feasibility for very large capacities of storage complement the use of long byte strings for digitized images. As the storage of vast numbers of images becomes economically feasible, it then becomes feasible to provide for image retrieval, and also image processing via

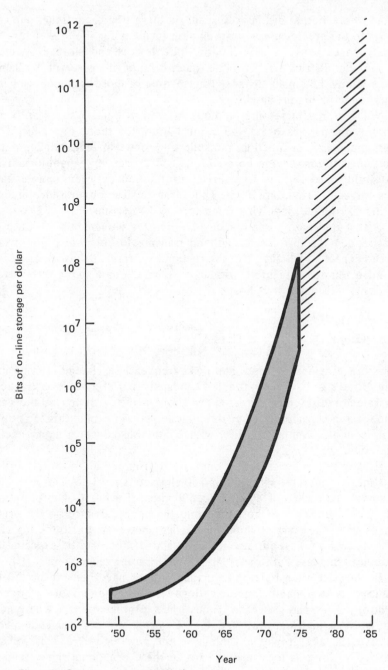

Fig. 2.3 Storage per dollar [2.16].

human interaction at display consoles. As these trends continue, one can anticipate the greater use of transmission facilities for the interchange of digital images between new input/output devices and storage systems. The on-site distribution of large quantities of images will be complemented by the longer-distance transmission of those documents having higher value or urgent need.

We also find increasing amounts of storage being located with the terminals themselves or in the control units for those terminals. The programmable, high-function controllers become, in fact, smaller data-processing centers, having both storage and processing capabilities. This creates the need for the transfer of information between remote data bases and centralized data bases. These transfers can be both incremental and batch-oriented, involving small to very large transfers.

Distributed data bases that involve massive movements of data will be dependent on low-cost broadband transmission facilities. Otherwise, one can expect a high degree of interaction by terminals that are clustered around a remote data base, with only summary data being transferred over longer distances to a host.

2.3.5 Other Device Data Rates

Such storage devices as tapes and disks frequently exchange information today at rates of between 4.0 and 12 megabits per second. The practical data rate for disks has increased by about a factor of ten in the past decade. From considerations of trend alone, we can expect this to double or triple in the coming decade, with continuing advances in magnetic technology.

High-speed printers today operate at from 2000 to over 15,000 print-lines per minute, with 150 or 250 characters per line. This amounts to average data rates of 40 kbps to 500 kbps. If a burst of information were needed during the short time that the paper advances, a data rate perhaps five times faster would be needed; however, full buffering can eliminate such burst requirements. Print speeds, too, can be expected to continue to increase with newer nonimpact printing technologies.

In the past, such high-performance devices have been restricted to local use. As broadband communications services become more economical, however, we can expect to witness the "turnpike effect," where new users (such as high data-rate feeding of storage devices and high-speed printers) will take greater advantage of the new highways. This will be restricted so long as local access lines to these broadband links remain expensive. However, optical fibers, on-site satellite ground stations, and CATV systems may break this restriction (see Section 2.4).

On the other hand, we see increasing logic and storage associated with devices and cluster controllers. This tends to reduce the frequency of interaction between devices and hosts. As G. B. Thompson observed [2.21], the instantaneous data rate at any given moment will have an increasing tendency toward higher and higher bit rates, but the rate from a given terminal becomes "lumpier and lumpier" when viewed along the time axis.

2.3.6 Effects of I/O on Architecture

The spectrum for transmitted information is already wide and can be expected to continue to grow as the technologies permit more and more forms of information to be economically captured, transferred, stored, and processed. The widening of the spectrum brings with it increasing intelligence at both ends of the communication line to capture, transform, and manipulate this information.

The message may contain alphameric data, graphs and curve-plots, an image of a handwritten insurance form, or combinations of these. In any case, the physical nature of the receiving device and/or the operational needs of the human user may call for a transformation or mapping of the message, so as to obtain the desired presentation format. This leads to a layer of function (called Presentation Services in Systems Network Architecture) which transforms the transmitted message so as to serve the changing needs of the particular I/O device, storage device, program, or person.

An architecture for distributed systems must be able to provide protocols for the management of these higher-level functions as they are introduced. Because they will change, these higher-level protocols must be independent of the transmission system. In other words, this layer, like all other layers of the architecture, should be independently changeable and be isolated from changes in other layers. The widening spectrum of information to be transmitted also emphasizes the need for a network architecture that will accommodate a wide range of information block sizes and data structures.

Finally, the trends in application, storage, and I/O devices promise increased use of broadband facilities, if they become available at a lower cost. However, this would have to be site-to-site broadband transmission, including the local loops as well as the longer-distance sections of the line.

2.4 TRANSMISSION TRENDS*

2.4.1 Introduction

Section 1.3 introduced the early transmission facilities, the factors that influence the selection of facilities, and the diversity of services that a teleprocessing system must accommodate today. This section examines future transmission trends.

The coming decade will be a period of rapid development in the techniques used by communications carriers. This will accelerate cost reductions and improve price-performance somewhat. The system architecture of the future must take advantage of at least four major developments:

1. Satellite transmission

2. Digital (as distinct from analog) transmission networks

3. Fast-connect networks

4. Value-added networks

These developments are introduced in the following discussion. Further architectural considerations for new data networks are given in Chapter 17.

2.4.2 Transmission Cost Improvements by Traditional Means

The primary motivation for new transmission facilities has been cost reduction. We have already noted the dramatic cost reductions in the data-processing portions of the network. We next look at cost trends in the transmission portion.

Terrestrial transmission will often involve a combination of ordinary cable and either microwave or coax. A given message will pass over some links that are relatively new and other links in which the capital investment was made many years ago. The average cost improvement, with such a broad mix of equipment, is bound to be much lower than the improvement in one segment. New sets of facilities will reduce, but in many cases not eliminate, this problem.

But what about advances in transmission technology? Figure 2.4 shows the improvements in cost per circuit mile for several technologies in terrestrial transmission as a function of the number of circuits in the particular link [2.14]. Where small numbers of circuits are involved, the improvements are not great. In all, the cost per mile of transmission lines

---

* I am indebted to A. Brezovac, of IBM Zurich, and J. E. Merkel, of IBM Raleigh, for information on the future trends in data transmission.

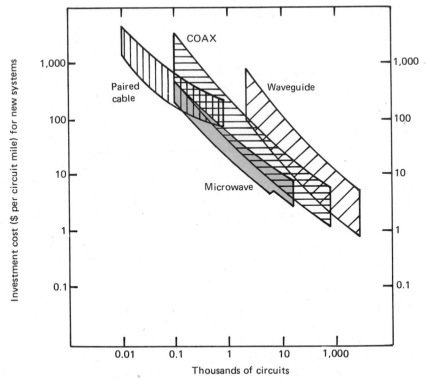

Fig. 2.4 Cost trends in terrestrial transmission.

changes radically only when the very high bandwidth capabilities of microwave, coax, and waveguide can be utilized efficiently. Efficient utilization of such a broad bandwidth depends heavily on the volume of voice traffic which today, and for the foreseeable future, will be many times greater than that of data. This leads to the desirability of sharing resources among voice and data traffic. However this may forego potential economies of specialization, and may lead to a more limited range of standardized services. Not shown, but very hopeful, are potential cost savings using optical-fiber transmission, all digital rather than analog modulation techniques, and satellite transmission, to be discussed in the following sections.

Figure 2.2 (see p. 37) shows the reduction of communication costs in recent years for the particular case of line costs for packet transmission. (This cost pertains to the movement of one million bits over a distance of 1940 kilometers.) As indicated in that analysis, the rate at which communications costs are improving is much less than the rate at which computer costs are improving [2.2].

2.4.3 Transmission by Optical Fiber

It has been predicted [2.20] that optical-fiber transmission systems will be incorporated into PTT networks by the early 1980s. These are likely to be in the heavily loaded parts of existing networks, where optical fibers can provide an increase in capacity for critical links.

Optical fibers are thin threads of dielectric inorganic glass surrounded by a layer of another material that generally has a lower refractive index. Light travels in this filament much as electromagnetic waves travel in a waveguide; both single-mode and multimode transmission can be supported. The very thin fibers (about 2 to 5 μm) that are needed for multimode transmission offer bandwidths of up to tens of gigahertz (that is, tens of billions of cycles per second). Larger fibers (for example, those of 10 to 30 μm) provide less bandwidth (for example, 10–100 megahertz).

Some existing and proposed metallic cable systems [2.20] are compared with proposed fiber-optic systems in Fig. 2.5. Note the projected advantage of fiber-optic systems in the distance between repeater stations. Systems with optical repeaters are not assumed, but may be feasible in later installations. In the interim, conversion from light to electronic signals and then back to light is assumed.

The two critical areas have been attenuation in the fiber and the life of light sources. Losses as low as 2 db/km have been reported in both monomode and multimode fibers [2.20, 2.31]. Light sources have had lifetimes of 10,000 hours, and lifetimes of 100,000 hours are projected [2.20].

The fiber-optic cable appears to be a technology with promise for low-cost, very high-capacity, long-haul transmission, and also flexible

System Capacity		Metallic Cable Systems	Fiber-Optic Systems	
Mbps	Voice Channels	Repeater Spacing (km)	Loss* (dB/km)	Repeater Spacing (km)
2.048	30	2	10-3	6-16
8.448	120	3-4	10-3	5-15
34.304	480	2	10-4	5-12
140	1920	2	10-4	4-10
560	7680	1.6-2	10-4	3-8
		1		

*Loss (dB/km) Includes An Allowance For Jointing

Fig. 2.5 Some existing or proposed metallic cable and possible fiber-optic digital systems for comparison [2.20].

transmissions in short-distance, local transmission. In the 1980s fiber-optics should be a significant factor in reducing bottlenecks in existing transmission facilities, and in providing some new broadband capability at a lower cost.

2.4.4 Transmission by Satellite

Satellite systems. Satellite communications offer a broad bandwidth at improved prices for medium and long distance, with inherent point-to-multipoint properties. Most suitable for relatively long distances (hundreds of miles or more), satellite communication reduces the complications of intermediate nodes and complex routing algorithms while promising a high degree of reliability of broadband transmission between ground stations. The INTELSAT IV satellite carried twelve transponders, each having a bandwidth of 36 MHz. Proposed satellites [2.34] can carry eight or more transponders, each with a data-transmission relay capacity of up to 54 million bits per second.

The satellite serves the function of a relatively simple repeater, which broadcasts each message to all ground stations within the range of a spot antenna. Each satellite may have a number of separate spot antennas that cover different terrestrial areas. Among the ground stations in a given "spot," no other physical switching is needed. With addressing per message, each ground station selects only those messages addressed to it.

One of the attractive features of the satellite is that channels can readily be combined to provide a wide range of bandwidths, serving few or many users concurrently. Also, as load patterns change in different geographic areas, the capacity is readily shifted to wherever it is needed. This can be done dynamically to accommodate the requirements of the time of day in each time zone as well.

Satellite costs. The projected INTELSAT costs [2.2] and circuit capacity are shown in Fig. 2.6. As shown in Fig. 2.7, the rate at which satellite transmission costs fall is comparable to that of the 10-fold reduction every five years that was experienced in the case of the computer costs for packet switching [2.2]. The rates of improvement shown for both a national land net and a regional land net (averaging 100 km) are much less than that for satellites.

By the early 1980s, the economic crossover for communication satellites has been projected to be only a few hundred miles for bandwidths of up to 9600 bps, and even less than that for broadband transmission. As with any service, the economy of satellites can also be aided by the integration of voice, data, and image in the same system. In those cases where the data transmission is a small fraction of the voice load, the data

INTELSAT	Usage Year	Number Of Circuits	Lifetime Years	Total Cost	Cost Per Circuit Per Year
I	1965–67	240	1.5	$ 8.2M	$22,800
II	1967–68	240	3	$ 8.1M	$11,300
III	1968–71	1,200	5	$10.5M	$ 1,800
IV	1971–78	6,000	7	$26.0M	$ 600
V	1978–85	100,000	10	$28.5M	$ 30
Estimated					

Fig. 2.6 Cost estimates for INTELSAT communication satellites [2.2].

transmission should be obtainable as a small incremental cost to the voice facility.

Smaller earth stations. Earlier satellite systems operate in the 4–6 gigahertz (GHz) frequency range, requiring large and very costly ground stations. Each of these ground stations necessarily serves a wide geographical area, with the result that considerable cost is involved in the local lines from the user to the ground station. This is aggravated by the fact that 4–6 GHz is also the frequency used by many microwave systems; therefore, to avoid interference, these ground stations must be located at some distance from microwave systems which serve many metropolitan

Dollars/Million
Bits Transmitted

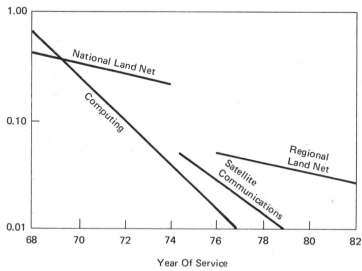

Fig. 2.7 Satellites' cost impact.

areas. Later satellite systems, operating at higher frequencies (for example, 12–14 GHz), will have this problem to a lesser degree. There is a greater susceptibility to rain at this higher frequency, however; this may be dealt with, perhaps, by placement of redundant earth stations and/or temporary off-load to terrestrial facilities. As technology improves and ground-station costs are reduced, the number of ground stations can dramatically increase, and the locations can be such as to minimize local transmission costs. Indeed, for the large user, location of the earth station with a 5–7 meter antenna on customer premises will be economically feasible, thus offering a possibility for major cost reductions. With source-to-destination transmission by satellite, the high costs involved in local carrier services can be eliminated.

Satellite delay. Satellite transmission has, however, suffered from a longer propagation delay, with a round-trip propagation time of about 600 milliseconds. Delays over the satellite link, delays in terrestrial "tail" circuits, and delays in modem equipments can conservatively amount to a round-trip delay of about 700 msec. This does not necessarily mean that response time is longer when using satellite transmission. As noted in Section 1.3.5, response time is due to many factors. Some of these are improved in satellite systems, and this compensates for the longer propagation delay. Usually, two of the key factors in response time are

1. The local message-serializing time (message length divided by line speed in bits per second)
2. The number of intermediate nodes at which additional message queuing, message processing, and message serializing take place

The message-serializing time, for example, is very different if 19.2 kbps or 50 kbps, rather than 1.2 kbps, are used. A 1000-bit message requires 1000 msec to be encoded on a 1000-bps line. On the other hand, the low cost of the higher bandwidth that is available in satellites permits the use of a high transmission speed there. If on-site antennas are used, the longer serializing delays of low-speed local lines are eliminated. Moreover, the single high-speed repeater station in the satellite eliminates any need for multiple intermediate nodes, when site-to-site transmission is involved. The addition of low-speed terrestrial "tails" to the satellite link for local connections can, of course, again increase the response time.

One other factor affecting many present-day systems is the turnaround time when using half-duplex circuits. The satellite links are expected to be duplex, and this capability eliminates the turnaround component of delay. Of course, newer terrestrial facilities will be duplex as well.

The net result is that the response time, when using site-to-site satellite transmission, can be very good. It can be equal to or better than that experienced in common terrestrial systems of today that use lower frequencies. Response-time requirements of some applications will, nevertheless, preclude the use of satellite transmission when fractional-second response is needed. This will further the distribution of function to remote centers, so that the very rapid responses are provided there and only the less demanding transactions are sent over the longer distances.

Retransmissions.   A high reliability of transmission is essential because retransmissions are time-consuming, and frequent retransmissions adversely affect the average response time. The expected high reliability of satellite transmission (under most atmospheric and sunspot conditions) should reduce the need for retransmission on the occasion of error. This should also permit the use of larger blocks of data (for example, 1000–10,000 bytes per block) in each transmission. This factor plus the reduced use of bandwidth for retransmission can improve the effective line utilization for useful data.

The long propagation delay does mean that if messages are to be retransmitted on the occasion of error, a longer sequence count must be maintained, because so many messages can be in transit at any one time. Also, when an error does occur, it is more efficient to selectively retransmit only the mesage in error, rather than retransmit all subsequent messages (as is frequently done in terrestrial transmission).

Waiting for an acknowledgment to each message would also be very time-consuming, resulting in major reductions in channel utilization. The HDLC technique (described in Chapter 11) of transmitting up to seven (or 128) messages before requiring acknowledgment greatly reduces this problem. The use of duplex transmission further improves the channel utilization because error indications can be sent as soon as the error is detected. Retransmissions may also be reduced, in some satellite systems, by the use of forward error-correcting codes.

2.4.5 Digital Transmission Networks

The previously mentioned trends toward lower costs in digital technology are also resulting in lower communication costs in those carrier networks that employ digital technologies. This stems from several factors.

Analog networks use linear amplifiers, which amplify the noise along with the signal. A digital network uses nonlinear repeaters, which do not pass noise that is below a given clip level. Therefore, digital transmission networks inherently offer the potential for improved reliability.

This property can also be used to improve performance. Higher-speed transmissions, on a given line, are accompanied by greater distortion. In the presence of noise, this can be disastrous on an analog line. With digital regeneration, however, a higher degree of distortion can be tolerated because each pulse is regenerated at each repeater. A given line, therefore, can be operated at higher frequencies when digital transmission is used. The key is to provide repeaters in order to regenerate the signal sufficiently often that the signal survives the distortion.

AT&T frequently places repeaters every 6000 feet, because that is the spacing of the loading coils on the analog lines, so access facilities are available there. The digital repeaters sometimes replace the loading coils on existing lines.

Switching systems designed for analog voice have had a complexity, in signaling, ringing, and switching, that is well beyond that occurring in systems for digital data alone. Digital switching systems are simpler, and the steady reductions in cost of digital circuits and memory make digital switching costs considerably lower. As channel capacities increase, the degree of multiplexing and switching increases and becomes a higher percentage of the total transmission costs, making the savings from the use of digital techniques more important. Costly modulators and demodulators (modems) have also been used at each end of the analog telephone lines to shift the baseband signal to a band near the middle of the voice channel. With all-digital transmission systems, the need for modems is eliminated, in favor of a simpler attachment unit.

Various carrier techniques, such as Data Under Voice (DUV) and Data Over Voice (DOV), have been used to frequency multiplex a digital data channel along with voice channels in a basically analog system. While such incremental investments often yield good payoffs, they do not offer all the benefits of a totally digital system design. Piecemeal insertion of digital techniques into existing systems may not fully utilize digital capabilities, and may have cost problems because of the high cost of equipment used to interface several generations of technology.

Installation plans for new data networks are changing continuously, so specific carriers must be contacted for up-to-date information. An idea of the scope of these plans can, however, be determined from Fig. 2.8, which shows some of the proposed data networks in the United States.

The movement to digital techniques in transmission is of great long-range significance, so a brief resume of several major offerings follows.

Dataphone Digital Service.   With the introduction of Dataphone Digital Service (DDS) for private-line service in early 1975, American Telephone and Telegraph (AT&T) initiated a program to make digital transmission available to a majority of its customers. The major metropolitan areas are being serviced, and the rate of development is high enough so that about 80 percent of the potential United States teleprocessing market should be covered by 1978 (see Fig. 2.8).

DDS can be transparent when using the standard interfaces to the service. There is no need for the transmission system to examine or interpret the information sent into the system, and there are no restrictions on the character of the data in the customer use of the transmission facility. A DDS objective was established [2.8] to provide transmission that is error-free 99.5 percent of all one-second intervals. Another objective is that a customer's service will be available for his or her use 99.96 percent of the time. (This would permit an average downtime no greater than 210 minutes per year.) DDS tariffs now are substantially lower than comparable-speed analog services [2.22].

AT&T has also expressed interest in offering switched digital service. As of this writing, its application, filed with the Federal Communications Commission, calls for a dataphone switched digital service (DSDS) operating at 56 kilobits per second on a station-to-station dial-up basis. Initial service to 18 cities will be followed by extensions to other major cities across the nation. Each station will be charged for an access line and for an attachment unit, called a switched-data-service unit. That unit encodes and decodes signals, recovers timing, samples synchronously, formats the data, and generates and recognizes signals. DSDS tariffs reportedly will be time- and distance-dependent, and billing will be for an initial ten-second period with one-second increments.

Microwave networks. Microwave transmission equipment lends itself well to digital as well as analog transmission. Special microwave networks, therefore, are participating in the movement toward digital techniques.

Microwave Communications Incorporated (MCI) is a special service common carrier (SSCC), now operating a nationwide network to major cities (see Fig. 2.8). MCI provides both analog and digital transmission [2.14], offering

- Point-to-point analog or digital service
- A wide variety of bandwidths: 200 to 960,000 Hz
- Channels available full- or part-time
- Customer sharing of channels

The proposed mode of usage of the MCI-affiliated companies is distinctly flexible. For example, a customer reportedly could lease channels of the

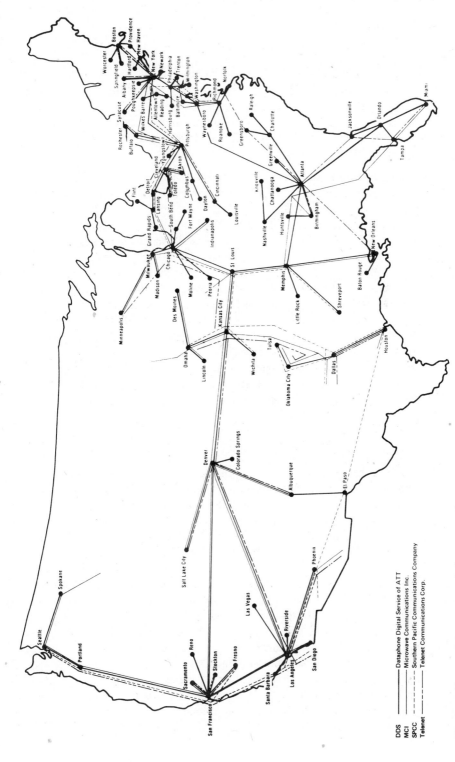

Fig. 2.8 Some of the proposed data networks.

DDS ——————— Dataphone Digital Service of ATT
MCI ——————— Microwave Communications Inc.
SPCC ————————— Southern Pacific Communications Company
Telenet ————————— Telenet Communications Corp.

exact bandwidth required, transmit any form of signal (voice, data, facsimile, etc.), arrange two-way channels with different bandwidths in each direction, use his or her own multiplexor and terminal equipment, and resell the unused portion of the channel to another organization.

Announced MCI plans [2.22] include switched data transmission at up to 4800 bps and high-speed, switched, digital facsimile.

DATRAN/Southern Pacific. DATRAN was another of the special service common carriers (SSCC) authorized in a 1971 ruling of the FCC to meet special communications needs not being met by the established common carriers. Though DATRAN encountered financial difficulties amid tariff disputes (resulting in a termination of operations), their initial installations demonstrated the technical feasibility and advantages of digital data transmission. The DATRAN offering was exclusively digital, and provided both switched and nonswitched lines. Time-Division Multiplexing (TDM) was widely used, with regeneration at each microwave repeater station, without demultiplexing the signal. DATRAN, like the AT&T DDS, was fully transparent so far as the user was concerned. The billing increment was lowered to make the short switched call more practical. The guaranteed performance of the DATRAN network was an average of 99.95 percent error-free seconds. The DATRAN facilities were purchased by the Southern Pacific Communications Company.

Digitized voice. It sometimes appears that digitized voice should share the same facilities as digitized data, so let us have a brief look at the nature of digitized voice. With pulse-code modulation, the bandwidth required for digitized voice is much greater than for analog voice. A sampling rate of about 8000 samples per second is needed to reproduce a voice signal of 4 kHz. With, say, seven bits per sample (for 128 amplitude levels) a data rate of 56 kbps would be needed. On the other hand, delta modulation and linear-predictive encoding have yielded good voice reproduction at 32 kbps and lower. In any case, however, the bandwidth needed is large indeed, when compared to analog voice circuits.

Despite this large bandwidth requirement, the overall costs of digitized voice are often favorable, when compared to analog voice circuits. This is the result of steadily improving digital technology and the falling costs of digital-amplification signal regeneration and switching. Hence, digitized voice is often, and increasingly, economically viable. As digitized voice spreads, so will the opportunities for sharing facilities with digitized data, but not without complications. One complication is that the voice sampling should be synchronous to avoid further distortion. To achieve this synchronous sampling, one approach is to reserve a portion of each time slot for voice, leaving the remainder of the time slot to be filled in by data transmission as data is available. To better utilize the line capacity, other techniques have been developed to use the whole time slot for data whenever there is a momentary pause in the voice transmission.

Because of the different requirements for voice and data, the current trend in some countries seems to be to plan separate data facilities. However, long-term plans often include at least a partial sharing of facilities between voice and data, as technical problems are overcome.

2.4.6 Fast-Connection Networks

As we noted in Section 1.3, switching facilities of the past have been inadequate for some applications because of relatively long delays in the connection and termination of a call. Another problem has been the long minimum billing period, when data transmissions can be very short. New fast-connect digital switching systems promise to reduce both problems.

Connection times. Digital switching, first of all, provides greatly improved connection and disconnection times. Connection times of less than one second are being experienced with present facilities. The digital switching service (called Datadial) of DATRAN had been advertised with a 0.8-second average call set-up time, and a 0.2-msec clear-to-send time. The DATRAN billing increment had been one second, with a minimum call period of six seconds and a minimum charge per call of about one cent. AT&T has also filed tariffs for switching of the Dataphone Digital Service (DSDS), as described above. Connect times for this service are expected to be under six seconds. The Electronic-Data Switching (EDS) system in Germany, as another example, is specified to provide call set-up and clear-down times on the order of 0.2 second. Current indications are that the charging interval will be about one second, and that full data transparency will be provided after call establishment. In the Nordic Public Data Network [2.36], the call set-up time is projected to be between a "normal" value of 100–200 msec and an upper value of 500–2000 msec in extreme cases (<1%) during the busy hour.

The fast-connect trend of digital switching networks is clear. Hence, switched systems of the future will be capable of meeting more of the response-time requirements that were formerly the sole province of nonswitched lines. In particular, some inquiry and conversationally interactive systems that can tolerate response times of, say, one to four seconds will find switched systems capable of satisfying a larger portion of their connection needs, but only when the entire path is served by fast-connect facilities. This latter condition, unfortunately, will often not be fulfilled in most countries, given the large capital investment in local facilities.

Transparency. Signaling between users and the digital network first establishes the transmission path. Once the communication system detects the end of the signaling phase, users of the digital switched network are no longer required to meet the disciplines, protocols, or languages required for signaling. The users may send any bit-code combination that may be required by the application, computer, or terminal equipment.

Switched digital costs. On switched digital systems, there is a minimum charge per call and a monthly equipment charge, in addition to a usage charge. The transmission time for one unit of data (that is, the call duration) in interactive and inquiry/response systems is often on the order of a fraction of one second. However, the minimum charged time per call must be based on a transmission time that compensates for the actual call set-up cost of the carrier. Extremely fast connect/disconnect cycles consume more switching capacity, whose costs would also have to be passed on to the subscriber. Minimum charge times on the order of seconds are, therefore, more reasonable than milliseconds. Thus, extremely short messages may carry a substantial "front-end load," and the switching systems may therefore be a better buy for longer messages and for calls that involve multiple messages.

Because the costs of a switched line ordinarily increase with usage, there is also some usage figure, in hours per day, beyond which a dedicated, nonswitched line will be more economical. (Recall the discussion of nonswitched versus switched lines in Chapter 1.) An AT&T market study [2.17] of many of its largest customers reportedly concluded that, on the average, each company transmitted the equivalent of about 1.1 hours of 56-kbps traffic per day—not enough (at that time) to justify a nonswitched high-speed line. However, studies of call rates, message size, and call duration, taking into account billing periods, minimum call charge, and maximum monthly charges, are necessary for any particular decision.

Cost calculations must be made for each particular network and tariff structure. However, trends do appear. If one considers only the distances involved and the hours of usage per day, one gets a first approximation, such as that shown in Fig. 2.9, of a cost-effective demarcation line between nonswitched and switched digital service [2.17]. This chart reflects only bulk transmission and the DDS and DSDS 56-kbps tariffs proposed by AT&T. Very roughly, it indicates a lower cost for 56-kbps switched lines with

- Less than 1 hour usage/day at 200 miles or less
- Less than 2 hours usage/day at 400 miles
- Less than 3 hours usage/day at 700 miles
- Less than 4 hours usage/day at 900 miles

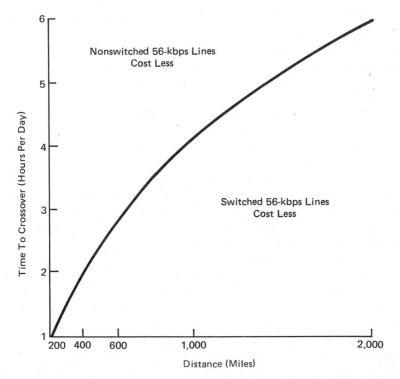

Fig. 2.9 Proposed crossover on nonswitched versus switched digital transmission lines (reprinted from *Data Communications*. Copyright 1976 by McGraw-Hill Inc. All rights reserved.).

Other message characteristics and data rates will, however, give different crossovers.

Peak load conditions. All switched systems (whether line-switched or packet-switched, which will be discussed in Chapter 4) share transmission facilities among multiple users whose peak demands can cause delays in each other's service. Response times and busy times can be specified only statistically, and the user must accept the fact that transmission delays may be greater in peak load periods, when the total system is most congested. To ease the problems of busy conditions, switched digital networks can offer an automatic call-back function, which will queue calls (up to a fixed maximum number) on a busy number, and then connect each call in order as the called number becomes free.

2.4.7 Interfacing to Communications Networks

The connection of data-processing systems to digital networks, whether nonswitched or switched, promises to cause minimum disruption to the existing data-processing complex. Physical interfaces between data-processing equipments and communication equipments are standardized in the United States through the efforts of the Electronic Industries Association (EIA), and worldwide through the International Telegraph and Telephone Consultative Committee (CCITT). The EIA and the CCITT standards are almost universally adhered to in order to promote general communicability. The standard interfaces, EIA RS-232-C for data and EIA RS-366 for Autocall, are used for both analog and digital switched networks. (The CCITT V.24 is the worldwide counterpart, but not the exact equivalent, of the EIA's RS-232-C.)

RS-232-C defines electrical signal characteristics, interface mechanical characteristics, and the functional description of interchange circuits. It is applicable to nonswitched service (two- or four-wire, point-to-point or multipoint), and switched network service (two- or four-wire). Applicability includes automatic answer and automatic call, but some of the necessary circuits for automatic call are in CCITT V.24 or RS-366.

AT&T's 2400-, 4800-, and 9600-bps DDS units have an interface that conforms with RS-232-C, whether type D or E. The 56-kbps unit conforms with the CCITT V.35 balanced dc interface and its control signals conform with RS-232-C.

The newer CCITT X.21 interface provides a cleaner interface for synchronous modes of transmission on public data networks (see Fig. 2.10). Again, this interface does not affect the higher levels of the architecture. As X.21 ultimately becomes the accepted standard for the interface to digital networks, there will be three sets of commonly used interfaces, as follows:

1. Digital networks
    -   Switched: full X.21
    -   Nonswitched: X.21 subset
2. Analog networks
    -   Switched: V.24 and V.25 (RS-232 and RS-366)
3. Packet networks: X.25 (which includes the X.21). The X.21 and X.25 interfaces are discussed in greater detail in Chapter 17.

2.4.8 Digital Carrier Architectural Requirements

The requirements on the remainder of the data-processing/ communications system, in order to utilize such digital transmission systems as DDS and EDS, are relatively small. Auto-call and auto-answer features, of the type already available, are required if the lines are switched without manual intervention. Automatic recalling on

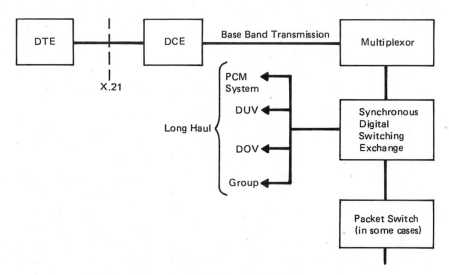

DTE = Data Terminal Equipment (represents the data source or data sink)
DCE = Data Circuit Terminating Equipment (includes any signal conversion
        equipment needed beyond the standard interfaces)
DUV = Data Under Voice
DOV = Data Over Voice

Fig. 2.10 Synchronous circuit-switched digital networks.

busy conditions should then also be accommodated. Another relatively
manageable change needed for fast-connect networks is that the logical
connections, or sessions, must be maintained even though the physical
connection is broken. This is a change in concept, for even with today's
dial connections, the logical and physical connections usually go together.

  The simplicity of satellite switching enables it to appear, potentially,
as either a nonswitched line or a fast-switched facility, benefiting therefore from these same architectural modifications.

  Thus, the technical and architectural match between digital transmission systems (both nonswitched and switched) and data-processing systems is very good, with little disruption in the data-processing complex.
The transparency and the standard interfaces for physical connection to
digital networks also facilitate the ability to use the new transmissions
facilities in combination with the old. The same can be said about the
match between satellite systems and DP systems.

  With modest architectural extensions, nonswitched digital networks,
switched digital networks, and satellite systems that link customer sites all
promise to be viable alternatives that will enable a user to choose one or

another at different times. Periodic switchover among these three appears to be readily achievable, when required, with minimum expense for this "switchover" capability.

2.4.9 Packet-Switching and Value-Added Networks

Packet switching uses asynchronous time-division multiplexing (ATDM) of messages (see Chapter 4) on each segment of each path. To understand how this differs from other facilities, consider first that a circuit connects two nodes of a subscriber's network. That circuit might be a nonswitched (dedicated) facility or a switched facility. If the latter, the circuit is set up by a special signaling message that threads its way through the network seizing channels in the path as it proceeds. After the path is established, a return signal informs the source that data transmission may proceed, and all channels in the path are used simultaneously. A given message, going from node to node, ties up an entire circuit between that pair of nodes. This is true for both switched and nonswitched lines.

The subscriber may multiplex messages (i.e., packets) from his or her own users onto that circuit. However, this sharing, using ATDM, would be limited to the users of that one subscriber, unless some private multiple-subscriber agreement existed (see Section 2.4.12). Assume that the utilization of that circuit is still low.

If, beyond the above use of ADTM, the services of a packet carrier are used, then the packet carrier would provide additional store-and-forward nodes between the two nodes of the subscriber. The packet carrier could then share that circuit (that was between packet-carrier nodes) with still other subscribers. There may be a series of store-and-forward nodes in the path, in which case each segment could be individually time-shared among subscribers. These intermediary store-and-forward nodes may be owned by the carrier that owns the lines or by a third party. Thus, sharing a line using multiplexed packets of different users can be done by a subscriber, by common carriers or PTTs, and by third parties who form value-added networks (VANs).

Various authorities, including D. W. Davies [2.35], have advocated that a packet-switched network should have two levels. The lower level would be the local area network; the higher level would be the long-distance packet transmission and switching network. In some configurations, this will naturally occur through the use of ATDM in private networks as well as in the network of the packet carrier. The circuits provided by packet carriers (exclusive of access lines) are called *virtual circuits* in that they appear to be available to a subscriber but may in fact be shared with other subscribers unknown to him. A virtual circuit may be *switched*, and so need a call-establishment and call-disconnection procedure. Or it may be *permanent*, in which case no call set-up or disconnection is needed.

The Value-Added Carriers (VACs) are a new type of common carrier, initiated in 1973. They plan to subscribe to conventional common-carrier nonswitched services, and then provide store-and-forward packet-switching services to the public. For example, United States VACs, such as TELENET, will probably use AT&T's leased DDS offering. Messages are handled in packets of standard size to facilitate data movement through the network. Similar packet switching systems are under development by common carriers and PTTs in different countries.

The VACs serve to share a given nonswitched line among many independent subscribers (for example, different corporations), and thus build up line utilization for broadband links. The value-added networks (VANs) provide the effect of a switched network (by accepting calls to any destination in the network) even though nonswitched lines of the carrier are used. The routing mechanism is supplied by the VAC rather than by the carrier that owns the lines. Net savings that accrue from providing this service potentially can be reflected in lower rates per packet transmitted. Whether the purchase of value-added services will prove to be as attractive as a combination of the three preceding offerings (of nonswitched digital, fast-switched digital, and satellite transmission) will depend on customer-traffic characteristics, as well as on the tariffs of the different offerings.

Charges for packet services have included a flat rate for each thousand packets transmitted, regardless of distance, plus monthly charges for each access port to the network. In addition, customers may dial up or lease a local line to the VAN and lease a special interface controller to the network. Both fixed monthly costs and usage costs must be considered, particularly when the hours of usage per day are lower. The usage costs tend to dominate, of course, as volume increases, particularly with bulk transmissions.

The packet-switching services offered by PTTs in Canada and France are similar to those offered by the TELENET VAN in the United States [2.27, 2.28]. Another packet-switching service, called the Transaction Network (TN), has been announced by AT&T.

On packet-switching and VAN packet-switching networks, there must be a separate and distinct signaling phase, in which the user exchanges control packets with the network, to advise the network of the address of the called party. This is illustrated by the procedure defined for switched virtual call service in the interface proposal for packet networks, the CCITT Recommendation X.25 (see Chapter 17). After access is granted and initial signaling is completed, each user information record not only must contain the normal data link controls (see Chapter 11), but in addition must contain a packet header field. Once the system determines that it has reached the end of the packet header field, the user should be (but is not always) free to use any code or bit sequences for either coded or noncoded information. Some packet carriers provide this transparency and others do not.

Some of the packet carriers and VANs include device control, code conversion, buffering, error control, polling, and addressing, all of which fall in the grey area between data processing and data communications. Some require no knowledge of the application or the end-use device; others do. As a result, some of the networks must make certain assumptions about the users.

2.4.10 CATV Networks

The costs of local (as distinct from long-distance) transmissions often are the major portion of system transmission costs. The capital costs for the local loops are high because there is no sharing, at a given instant, among subscribers; there usually is insufficient bandwidth in the local lines for sharing. The ratio of capital costs per mile for long-haul segments to that for intracity segments has been on the order of $1:10$. This ratio is not likely to increase for a long time because of the large investment in the present local telephone plant and the decreasing costs for long-haul transmission. However, one possible source of lower local transmission costs is the growing CATV network, which deserves some mention here.

Estimates of CATV penetration in the next ten years range from 40 to 60 percent of all the households in the United States. Industry sources predict that 90 percent of American households will be fronted (with a readily available cable) within the next ten years. (Substantial CATV activity also exists in Canada, the United Kingdom, and Japan.) Even such cities as New York and Los Angeles are being supplied with CATV, although the distance from TV transmitters is small in these cities. Usage will concentrate in population centers, but a portion of business offices similarly wired is a reasonable expectation, since some business areas tend to coincide with population areas. Extensions of the CATV net to pick up a business can be more easily justified than a similar extension to pick up a home. Thus, the CATV networks have the possibility of emerging as another carrier for digital, as well as for video, services. These transmission networks and computer systems can conceivably combine to produce an interactive display terminal capability featuring the use of broad bandwidth at relatively low prices.

Cable TV provides a multidrop facility. The trunk cable has a bandwidth of approximately 300 megahertz. Individual channels might be employed in the 6-MHz region. The present state of the art would permit 24 6-MHz channels in one direction within the 300-MHz cable, with potential expansion to 40 channels. Standard TV sets can receive 12 VHF channels plus UHF channels. Thus, extra capacity exists for other information services. Bandwidth on the same cable, or a second cable, can be used to provide bidirectional communication. CATV installations might involve very high data rates (for pictures and voice) in one direction and low data rates (from terminal keyboards) in the opposite direction.

Computer-to-computer links are also provided via leased CATV channels. In one installation [2.18] multiple lower-speed lines (2.4–19.2 kbps) from each computer are time-division multiplexed to a single 50-kbps or 230.4-kbps CATV channel. These channels can be backed up by telephone-company facilities operating at the same frequencies. Tandem CATV/satellite links are also in operation.

Most agree that the CATV industry is in its infancy. How rapidly it will develop is very speculative, but the potential for a broadband system in a majority of the high-density areas of the developed countries is very real. The 1980s will probably see significant developments in this area. To the extent that this industry does mature, we should find this broadband capability being gradually taken advantage of by computer-related data services.

2.4.11 Encryption Requirements

Higher levels of security are becoming a requirement as more and more vital business data are being continuously transported. Encryption of users' data at the origin and then reconstruction (deciphering) of the information at the destination is becoming increasingly popular as an approach to high-level data security. A new standard algorithm has been adopted by the National Bureau of Standards as the United States Federal Information Processing Data Encryption Standard [14.8]. Encryption is most effective if it is user-controlled and provided on an end-to-end basis, rather than for links or segments of the path.

If the data is encrypted, there is no way for the carrier to act on or "process" the user information because it is scrambled and unintelligible in its transmitted form. It follows that for the user to be free to implement (independent of the communication supplier) a system having encrypted records, the carrier system must be completely transparent.

2.4.12 Resale and Shared Use

Tariffs of the past have often included restrictions on the resale and shared use of communication facilities. This has often prevented, for example, the joint use of a broadband facility by special agreements among multiple subscribers. However, policies in this area are in the process of changing, and this too can have major effects on the costs, modes of use, and management of communication networks.

Resale is the subscription to communication services and facilities by one entity and the reoffering of these to the public (with or without "added value" for profit). *Sharing* is a nonprofit arrangement in which several users collectively use communications services and facilities provided by a carrier, with each user paying the communications-related costs according to its pro rata usage.

A key decision in this area was rendered by the (United States) Federal Communications Commission in July 1976. Pertaining to Docket No. 20097 the Commission issued a Report and Order finding that "existing restrictions on the sharing and resale of private line service are unjust and unreasonable and unlawfully discriminatory" [2.30]. Carriers have in the past decided themselves who may resell and share services and facilities. This FCC decision requires American carriers to treat all of its customers alike, unless valid reasons exist to the contrary. The Commission further found that: "Because sharing does not constitute the offering of a service by one entity to others for a profit, entities engaged in sharing arrangements are not subject to regulation under Title II of the Act." Thus, sharing (as distinct from resale) could be conducted free of regulatory complexity.

2.4.13 Worldwide Movements

As we noted in our discussion of terrestrial transmission in the United States, there are strong movements toward the use of digital transmission (for example, DDS) and faster circuit-switched networks (for example, DSDS). In addition, there are value-added carriers, such as TELENET, which make use of newer leased digital services for packet-switching services. There are also worldwide developments paralleling those cited here.

Nonswitched (dedicated) lines are being upgraded to digital transmission in many parts of the world. The addition of fast circuit-switching and packet-switching facilities is also progressing, as follows.

1. Germany, Japan, Italy, the Nordic countries (Norway, Sweden, and Finland), and CNCPT (Canadian National/Canadian Pacific Telecommunications) in Canada are committed to fast circuit-switched data transmission facilities.

2. France and the United Kingdom, while developing long-range plans for integrated-voice fast circuit-switched digital networks, are introducing packet-switched networks in the near term.

3. Australia, Bell Canada, and Spain are introducing packet switching while remaining relatively uncommitted to fast circuit switching.

An approximate mapping of four classes of new data networks against time is shown in Fig. 2.11 for various countries (this data was collected at the IBM Data Communication Center in Zurich). The name for each system is given in parentheses beneath the name of the country in which it is located. These four classes are the following.

1. *Nonswitched digital:* networks that employ digital transmission, are digitally multiplexed, and use dedicated, duplex, data circuits.

2. *Interim circuit-switched:* networks that employ conventional analog transmissions, but typically feature faster call set-up time than the normal public switched networks. They appear as dedicated end-to-end circuits after call establishment.

3. *Synchronous circuit-switched:* networks that employ digital transmission, where the synchronization and bit timing are provided by the networks.

4. *Packet-switched:* where the physical channel is occupied by any one message only for the duration of the packet.

2.4.14 Transmission Prognosis

As the foregoing indicates, this is a time of experiment and change in the data-communications field. A summing up of expectations is attempted in four steps as follows.

Primary facilities

1. Private-line (nonswitched) services will continue to be available at reasonable tariffs in almost all countries. In many countries, they are being upgraded to digital transmission to realize cost and performance advantages. The result is that private-line services will continue to satisfy the needs of a large part, probably the majority, of the data-processing applications in the foreseeable future.

2. The public switched networks (circuit switching) will also continue to be used for data in almost all countries. Long connect times and transmission capacity will continue to limit the applicability of older equipments. However, in many countries, fast circuit-switched services, with tariffs structured for data application, have been introduced. These services will find increasing use when economy via concentration of traffic of independent subscribers is the dominant consideration.

3. Satellite transmission services will compete effectively with short- and long-haul digital transmission services. They will provide a unique point-to-point service when ground stations can be on user premises.

	Nonswitched Digital	Interim Circuit-Sw. Improved Analog	Syn. Circuit-Switched Digital	Packet-Switched
		CANADA (Multicom)		
1972		FRANCE (Caducée)		SPAIN (CTNE)
	CANADA (Dataroute) FRANCE (Transplex) U.K. (Dataplex)			
	CANADA (Infodat) GERMANY (Digital Nonswitched)	GERMANY (EDS I)		AUSTRALIA (CUDN)
		ITALY (SIP-RFD)		U.K. (EPSS)
	BRAZIL (RNTD)		CANADA (CNCPT) (Info-Switch)	CANADA (Datapac) AUSTRALIA (APS Network)
	FRANCE (Transmic) SWITZERLAND (Digital Nonswitched)	SWITZERLAND (EDW)	JAPAN (DDX)	
	ITALY (Digital Nonswitched)	AUSTRIA (OPT Data Network)	NORDIC DATA NETWORK	FRANCE (Transpac)
	UK (Digital Nonswitched)		GERMANY (EDS II)	JAPAN (DDX)
1980 Or Later	BELGIUM (RTT Digital Service)		NORDIC DATA NET. (Phase II) FRANCE (Hermes) ITALY (SIP Integrated Digital Network) U.K. (DDS) SWITZERLAND (IFS I) BELGIUM (RTT Data Network)	

TIME (downward arrow at left)

Fig. 2.11 Probable new data networks outside the United States.

4. New regulations permitting sharing and resale will promote wider use of the above with savings for the participants.

5. Packet-switched networks, which may incorporate additional (value-added) functions while using the newer digital transmission facilities, will compete with the above, particularly for applications involving short messages, low volume, and wide geographic spread.

6. The preferred service in some countries will be determined by national objectives, which may be reflected in the tariffs established for each type of service.

Performance. Technology now makes possible major improvements in key parameters.

- Channel bandwidth can be improved by the use of digital time-division multiplexing, improving three to six fold (e.g., from 9600 bps to 56 kbps).

- Error rates can be improved by a factor of about 100, from approximately 10^{-5} to 10^{-7}.

- Connection time can be improved by a factor of about 10, from more than 10 seconds to less than one second.

Various services achieving this level of performance will be offered in the coming decade.

Net cost. What will be the net effect of this on communications costs? It appears that the major effects (at least initially) will be on the cost and reliability of long-distance transmission (for example, above 80 km) where steady improvements can be foreseen. This will favor geographically more extended teleprocessing systems, and result in a still higher percentage of the transmission costs being incurred by the local, shorter-distance portions of the network.

A second effect, already evident, is in improvements in the relative cost of broadband facilities. This will encourage higher volume transfers (for example, more traffic in larger blocks) and also more multiplexing or concentration of low-speed traffic to take further advantage of the higher-speed lines. Where this is feasible, the lower communications costs will encourage larger concentrations of data-processing capacity, and regional coordination of distributed operations. Distributed operations, in turn, will tend to have increasing function.

The consequence of these trends will probably be a reduction, but not a major one, in the transmission costs of most existing systems. Costs of local connections will remain high except for source-to-destination satellite transmissions (and the more remote possibility of local CATV data services). Installation, maintenance, and operations costs of transmission systems will remain labor-cost sensitive and will partially offset reduced costs from technical improvements.

Architectural requirements. The distributed-systems architecture must be able to accommodate diverse transmission media, including both analog and digital transmission. Narrowband and voiceband services will continue to be of prime concern, but broadband facilities, such as those of 50 kbps or more, will be of great value for both transmission economy and short response times. The architecture must accommodate a variety of broadband systems, including terrestrial, satellite, and CATV systems. The data-link-control protocols must be independent of the media used.

The distributed-systems architecture must make it possible to use these diverse transmission facilities in different customer networks, in different parts of the same network, and/or at different times in the same parts of the network. Products and user systems must be able to be moved to and from specific communications carrier facilities, with a minimum of product modifications in the transition.

2.5   TRENDS IN PROGRAMMING

As labor costs mount and hardware costs decrease, the programming costs assume an even higher percentage of the total system cost, and become the prime target for cost improvements.

2.5.1   System Services

Very simple control programs can exist in different data-processing nodes of the network. Some may use simple sequential processing, rather than overlapped multiprogramming. However, the more primitive systems may put a larger burden on the user. System services, such as improved data management, storage device management, network management, I/O processing, accounting, security, and recovery, all can reduce the burden on the application programmer. This is true, however, only if these services can function independently of the application, and can themselves evolve with minimum impact on the application.

The scope of such services is implied in the growing size of system control programs, or "operating systems." These provide many optional services from which a given customer can build a system suitable for his or her needs. The growth of the total number of modules (which vary in size, but are often about 1000 lines of code each), as a major operating system evolves, is illustrated in Fig. 2.12. The number of modules in a

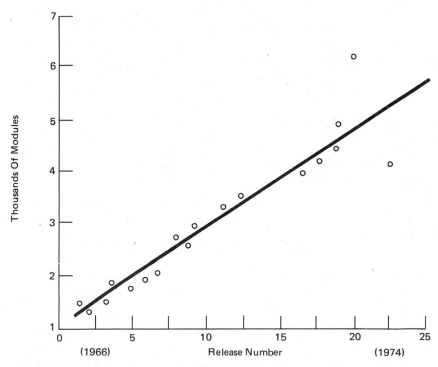

Fig. 2.12 Size of operating systems [2.1].

mature host operating system is on the order of thousands, and the diversity of services offered by an operating system grows steadily over a ten-year period.

The operating system, within a given node of the network, often provides basic services, such as task scheduling, data-base access methods, input/output supervision, and teleprocessing access methods. Supplementary services, more tailored to a class of applications, are frequently provided in application subsystems. Examples of these, taken from IBM OS/VS 370 and its associated program products, are

- Data-base/data-communications subsystems, such as the Customer Information Control System (CICS) and the Information Management System (IMS), for the coordination of transactions dealing with data-base inquiry or update [3.5, 3.11].

- Job entry subsystem (JES) for the coordination of remote job entry and remote job output distribution [2.32].

- Time-sharing option (TSO) for the coordination of program-development tasks on a time-sharing basis [1.14].

Therefore, it is either an application itself, or an application subsystem (which represents a group of applications), or an application service within the operating system, that often provides the user-interface to the network. It follows that these intermediary service programs must also be given the ability to appear to the network as the network addressable unit.

2.5.2 Modular Structures

The trend in programming is strongly toward modularity of structure, with well-defined functional interfaces. While the goal is elusive and never completely achievable, progress is being made so that:

1. The application program is becoming largely independent of the following.
   - The data-base structure (for example, types of storage devices and organization of data itself)
   - The physical structure of the data-processing complex (for example, single or multi-processor, integrated or stand-alone channels, single or multiple levels of store)
   - The structure of the communications system (for example, number and location of nodes, types of line control and path control)
   - Some physical characteristics of end-use devices (for example, carriage size, screen size, and similar common attributes)

2. Any one major operating-system service can be functionally altered with minimum effects on all other services to permit asynchronous evolution of services.

3. Failure within any one major service can be detected and localized more often to that service to reduce propagation of the effects of that failure to other parts of the system.

Operating counter to this trend is the fact that short-term gains can always be obtained by tuning an application to a particular data-base structure, processor design, system configuration, or I/O device. These application dependencies then inhibit changes in any of these parameters.

2.5.3 Distributed Programming

The complexity of a centralized data-processing system can increase to the point where the system overhead for the sharing of resources, protection of multiple users, and facilities for system recovery can consume a major part of the system capacity (for example, a major part of the available CPU cycles). At the same time, the cost of computer hardware has been dropping rapidly so that computer cycles are less expensive. The "economy-of-scale" argument is still valid, but the crossover points are clearly changing.

This, coupled with the modularity of structure referred to above, leads to the greater possibility of "off-loading" of function from the central complex. Services that can be physically removed from the central processor are appearing in "front-ends," or in remote programmable cluster controllers, or in subsystems that are associated with the central complex but are not necessarily physically close to it.

The way in which processes invoke one another and the way in which data is transferred among processes are quite different when a distribution of programs is anticipated [2.19]. In conventional DP systems, this is usually done by sharing a common address space in high-speed memory. In distributed systems, on the other hand, each process communicates with other processes by sending messages and arranging for the activation of the desired process. The operating system's job is to awaken a process for which a message has arrived. In addition to delivering a message to its destination process, the system may serve to activate a process, depending on some characteristic of the message or the receipt of a special control message.

Each separate node may have a unique hardware architecture. Nevertheless, communication between programs in the separate nodes is required. The communication among program modules then is recognized as a communications problem fundamentally; and the protocols for communication must be carefully defined. The architecture for such communication must obviously be independent of the node hardware architecture, and a total system architecture that generally serves distributed function is needed. A closer examination of these distributed functions is made in Section 2.6.

2.5.4 Program Maintenance

Currently a key factor in determining the cost of reconfiguring networks is the "maintenance" of application programs, I/O device-support programs, and data-base management programs. Maintenance is a popular misnomer that includes the process of correcting and/or converting programs and data to work under changing conditions. It is not unusual to find that one-half of an establishment's programmers are consumed in "maintenance" of old applications, system-program maintenance, and system conversions. It is in both the customer's and network vendor's interests to reduce maintenance that is incurred on the occasion of reconfiguration. The availability of such capability would release customer effort for new application development and shorten the reconfiguration time. This is helped if system design keeps applications relatively independent of the network configuration and if changes to the devices and/or the transmission system can be shielded from the applications.

Even when an application program is changed or split among locations, if the user interface to the terminal remains unchanged, the operator should be shielded from the application change so that the old services are still obtainable with the old terminal operating procedures. Such reconfiguration requirements lead directly to a need for a layered system structure, where layers can change independent of other layers, and system changes can be shielded from application programs and other end-users.

2.6   TRENDS IN DISTRIBUTED FUNCTION

2.6.1   Introduction

Technology will permit us to have computer-like capability in almost every node of typewriter size and larger. The rapid reductions in the cost of computer logic and computer storage provide increasing opportunities for associating a higher degree of function in physically separate nodes that span a very wide range in price. Therefore, the trend is for the distributed nodes, with increasing function, to be connected by a variety of transmission facilities. This section provides an overview of this trend, addressing these two questions.

1. In a data-processing/communications system, what are the basic functions that are potentially distributable?
2. What are the primary benefits that justify an architecture to facilitate distributed function?

2.6.2   Definition of Distributed Function

In general, a function is said to be distributed if either of the following holds:

1. The same function can be executed at more than one node in a network and/or
2. The function is not completely executable in a single node and parts of that function are executed cooperatively in separate nodes.

In either of these two cases of distributed function, one must have the following:

1. The information, stored within a node that is needed by the distributed function.
2. The decision logic within a node for that function,
3. The capability within a node to execute the logic of the distributed function (this capability may be active or it may be latent, requiring an activation or even a program load), and
4. The capability to invoke that function from another node, or to allocate work to that function from another node.

2.6.3 Six Distributable Functions

Six sets of functions are potentially located within any node of a distributed network, and are potentially related to like functions in other nodes by a set of internode protocols. These six, illustrated in Fig. 2.13, are as follows.

1. The management of application processing
2. The management of the data that may be stored on a hierarchy of storage devices
3. The management of communications and of the dependent source/sink devices
4. The customer application programs (which utilize all of these management functions to a greater or lesser extent)
5. An intermediary set of application subsystems (between the customer's application code and the main operating system) oriented toward a particular application class, and/or toward the management of a set of attached devices. (Application subsystems are functionally related to operating systems, but are often structured as a pseudoapplication—examples are IMS, CICS, and RJE. A somewhat analogous function is provided in some cluster controllers.)
6. Input/output mechanisms which (though not strictly "within" a node) are completely dependent on that node for their management (including the means for their being addressed by other nodes)

Increasingly, as the costs of processing and storage decrease, it is more feasible that nodes will contain at least the first three management functions, in varying degrees. However, a given node could be restricted to only one or two of these.

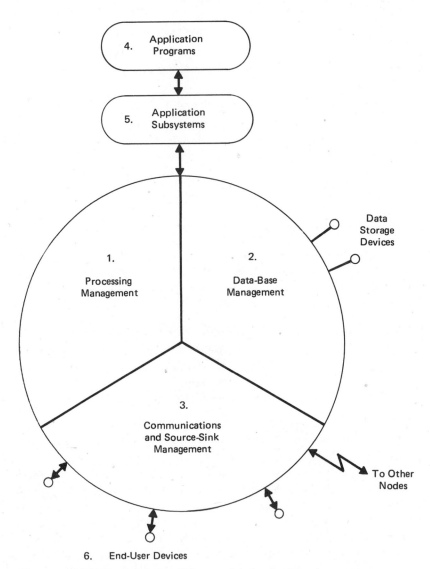

Fig. 2.13 Potential functions within a node of a distributed network.

The evolving data-processing/communications network can be visualized as an archipelago of islands of many sizes and shapes, each having some or all of the six functions shown in Fig. 2.13. These range from the spartan computer-like capability within a terminal keyboard, to the mass-storage systems and multiple-application processors of central data-processing systems. The industry-oriented subsystems, consisting of small data processors with specialized applications controlling terminal clusters, lie between these extremes. Technology permits almost every node to have a surprising (and steadily increasing) amount of function, and this can vary widely. An architecture for distributed systems should provide a common structure, and subsets of that structure should be readily available to meet the varying needs for communication among these nodes.

2.6.4 Why Centralize and/or Distribute Function?

Centralization. In a centralized system, all applications are executed in a single host. This may be a multiprocessor, which operates as a single host because it has a single operating system. The centralized system offers obvious advantages in the development and use of applications that share a large data base. All of the data can be managed centrally under the control of a single person (the data-base administrator) so that data-base structure, protocols, and security are all tightly managed. New applications can be created using different subsets of the total data base. Applications can be written independently, with assurance that the data needed for a particular application will be available at that central node. Sharing of all resources can be controlled directly.

The data-base management facilities and the communications management facilities at the single central node can be relatively rich in function. Ease of use, security, and recovery can be facilitated. Economy of scale makes these richer functions justifiable because they benefit a larger number of users. In general, only somewhat leaner functions can be afforded in the smaller nodes when the data base and other functions are distributed to smaller nodes.

Distribution. There are, however, many situations where more than one central site is desirable, and where one or more central sites can best be augmented by specialized or supporting subsystems that are operationally separate from and perhaps physically remote from these central sites. The advantages of distributed function are often one or more of the following.

1. It satisfies the needs for local autonomy, local physical accessibility, local security, or local application development in the subdivisions of the user's organization. Ease of management of the subdivisions and/or a desire to build the system "from the bottom up," dictated by local needs and under local control, may be a factor.

2. It provides greater availability to the users of the network, by reducing dependence on relatively unreliable transmission lines.

3. It provides better performance from the viewpoint of the local users. (For example, distributed function shortens the response time for processes that could be done locally, when line transmission delays are an important factor.)

4. It reduces the data bandwidth required between nodes to reduce lin
costs and hence system costs.

5. It provides for smooth growth, or for growth beyond the top of th
processor line, by off-loading the "central processor," augmentin
the host with controllers, adding hosts, etc.

6. It utilizes the more efficient properties of distinct nodes. (For exam
ple, the instruction set of one node may be more suitable fo
executing some function than another node.)

7. It localizes the effects of product change. (For example, one ca
locate device-dependent support closer to the devices so as t
localize the effects of additions of new devices to the system, an
thus make the development of new devices more manageable.)

8. It accommodates changes in local load patterns and application
(for example, with economic change, growth, or reorganization)
without major disruption or expense at the central site.

9. It improves the quality of input data leaving the source area wit
local aids such as edits, operator guidance, and validity checks.

10. It simplifies the programming support used for a given application b
tailoring the support to that limited application.

Obviously, these reasons do not apply in all cases. In some cases
distributing functions poorly could have the opposite effects. Fo
example:

1. In some cases, distribution of function could increase costs at the ne
nodes for I/O equipment, personnel, etc., or increase line traffic due to
new need to coordinate the access to and the maintenance of integrity o
distributed data sets.

2. Separate processors will have superior response times only if thei
work load is low enough, and they are not hamstrung by many inquirie
to a central data base. Poor response time could well result from a remot
processor that is slower than a central processor, depending on thei
capacities and work loads.

3. In practice, availability can be gained by distribution only if th
function and data can be efficiently partitioned so that the parts ca
operate independently for a time. As an example, availability of the IBM
3660 Supermarket subsystem was greatly improved by function distribu
tion, because that subsystem can operate efficiently with only occasiona
host interaction; those distributed functions could be clearly partitione
from the centralized functions. On the other hand, the early airline
system designers decided that their national data bases could not b
efficiently partitioned and distributed, even to regions.

These examples illustrate that (1) the optimum distribution of function can be very application- and configuration-dependent, and (2) the configuration and the distribution of function should be changeable to meet changing customer requirements. The diversity of trade-offs makes it clear that many shades of distributed function can be optimum for different situations. An architecture for distributed systems, therefore, must provide completely general communicability among network addressable units (NAUs) without any assumptions about the characteristics of the programs or the devices that the NAUs may represent.

Distributed data. The following different approaches to the management of the data base can be seen.

1. *Centralized data base.* All data are in one location, are accessible to all users, and are updated in real time.

2. *Distributed common data base.* This approach conceives of a single common data base that is kept up to date and is shared by all users, despite the fact that parts are physically separated and are separately managed. In this concept, all parts of the data base are managed as peers of one another. An inquiry will be automatically rerouted by peer coupling to the site where the pertinent data is kept and the request can be satisfied.

3. *Dual-version data base.* This approach conceives of two versions of the data base: multiple distributed parts of the data base (each of which represents a portion of the master file) and a centralized batch version of the data base. The distributed parts are used on-line for fast response applications, such as production control or customer service, but may disagree with the central batch version, as updates occur during the day. Once a day, the central batch version and the multiple parts of the distributed version are brought into synchronism. Another related approach occurs when the central data base is also on-line and is updated in real time during the day, but the legal data base is in the distributed parts. The central data base is then made to coincide with the distributed parts once each day.

4. *Independent data bases.* With this approach, the data is divided along geographic or functional lines so as to make the parts independent of each other; the parts are managed as separate data bases. This attempts to minimize the need for any one application or terminal user to have access to more than one part of the data base, or to more than one site. There are no facilities for automatically rerouting a request that does need access to another part. The selection of the site containing the desired data is up to the user.

Decentralization. The word decentralization implies not only the transfer of function to outlying locations, but also an independence of operation at each site. Such independence may be organizationally necessary. The different sites then operate as independent peers; one avoids splitting function between sites and any operation as dependent pairs. The operation is rather "at arms length."

Two points must be emphasized here. First, the avoidance of dynamic functional dependence among sites may not be the same as limiting communicability. It may still be necessary to provide a rather general ability for multiple units in one location to be able to communicate with one or more units in another location. Second, the development of a system, on the assumption of a completely decentralized mode with very restricted communicability among sites, is likely to need major architectural changes later on, in order to expand the generality of communications for newer applications.

2.7 REFERENCES AND BIBLIOGRAPHY

2.1 L. M. Branscomb. "Trends and Developments in Computer/Telecommunications Technologies." *OECD Conference on Computer/Telecommunications*, Paris (February 1975). (Figures 2.1 and 2.12 reprinted by permission of L. M. Branscomb.)

2.2 L. G. Roberts. "Data by the Packet." *IEEE Spectrum* (February 1974). (Figures 2.2 and 2.6 reprinted by permission of *IEEE Spectrum*.)

2.3 J. J. Mahoney, Jr., J. J. Mansell, and R. C. Matlack. "Digital Data System: User's View of the Network." *Bell System Technical Journal* **54,** No. 5 (May–June 1975): 833–844.

2.4 N. E. Snow and N. Knapp, Jr. "Digital Data System: System Overview." *BSTJ* **54,** No. 5 (May–June 1975): 811–832.

2.5 A. G. Fraser. "The Present Status and Future Trends in Computer/Communications Technology." Presented at a meeting of the Japanese Electronics Industries Development Association, Tokyo (October 1975).

2.6 A. Danet, R. Despres, B. Jamet, G. Pichor, and P. Y. Schwartz. "Packet Switching in a Public Data Transmission Service: The TRANSPAC Network." *European Computer Conference* **75,** London (September 1975).

2.7 N. Abramson. "The ALOHA System—Another Alternative for Computer Communications." *AFIPS Conf. Proc.* **37** (November 1970): 281.

2.8 L. W. Ellis. "The Law of Economics of Scale Applied to Communication System Design." *ICCC Proceedings, Stockholm* (August 1974): 299–306.

2.9 J. Martin. *Future Developments in Telecommunications.* Englewood Cliffs, N.J.: Prentice-Hall (1971).

2.10 K. Hirota, M. Kato, and Y. Yoshida. "A Design of Packet Switching Systems." *Proc. ICCC, Stockholm* (12–14 August 1974).

2.11 C. F. Stuehrk. "The Bell System's Dataphone Digital Service." *Proc. ICCC, Stockholm* (12–14 August 1974).

2.12 K. C. Knight. "Evolving Computer Performance." *Datamation* **14** (January 1968).

2.13 D. A. Dunn and A. J. Lipinski. "Economic Consideration in Computer Communication Systems." In N. Abramson and F. Kuo (eds.), *Computer Communication Networks.* Englewood Cliffs, N.J.: Prentice-Hall (1973).

2.14 P. M. Walker and S. L. Mathison. "Communications Carriers: Evolution or Revolution?" *Technology Review* (October/November 1970).

2.15 P. D. Moulton. "Datran's Datadial and Telenet's VAN Service: A Cost Comparison." *Modern Data* (March 1976).

2.16 L. M. Branscomb. "Technology Trends in Peripheral Devices." *IEEE Computer Society International Conference,* San Francisco (26–28 February 1974). (Figure 2.3 reprinted by permission of IEEE.)

2.17 "AT&T offers to provide switched 56 Kb/s lines." *Data Communication* (May–June 1976): 15–17.

2.18 A. C. Maltz. "Television Cables Save Money for Bankers Trust in Wideband Data Network." *Data Communication* (May–June 1976): 81–86.

2.19 D. F. Farber. "Distributed Machines Software Considerations." *IEEE 1974 Compcon Spring,* San Francisco (February 1974): 75–77.

2.20 K. C. Kao and M. E. Collier. "Fibre-Optic Systems In Future Telecommunication Networks." *1975 World Telecommunications Forum,* Geneva (October 1975). (Figure 2.5 reprinted by permission of International Telecommunications Union, Geneva, Switzerland.)

2.21 G. B. Thompson. "Network Implications of Intelligent Peripherals." *IEEE 1974 Compcon Spring,* San Francisco (February 1974).

2.22 *Data Channels* (December 1975).

2.23 *Computerworld* (30 January 1974): 4.

2.24 E. R. Cacciamani and K. S. Kim. "Circumventing the Problems of Propagation Delay on Satellite Data Channels." *Data Communications* (July/August 1975).

2.25 P. Baran and A. J. Lepinski. "The Future of the Telephone Industry 1970–1985." *Institute for the Future,* Report R-20. Middletown, Conn. (1971).

2.26 R. Bernstein. "Digital Image Processing of Earth Observation Sensor Data." *IBM J. of Research and Dev.* **20,** No. 1 (January 1976).

2.27 "Systems Planners Guide for Host Computer Systems." Telenet Communications Corp. (March 1975).

2.28 A. Danet. "Packet Switching in a Public Data Transmission Service: The TRANSPAC Network." *French PTT Research Center* (September 1975).

2.29 D. B. McCann. "Trends in Information." *Proc. ASIS Meeting,* Atlant (October 1974).

2.30 "Resale and Shared Use of Common Carrier Services and Facilities. *Federal Register* **41,** No. 144 (26 July 1976): 30657–30688.

2.31 C. J. Lucy. "Fiberguide Projections—Performance and Price." *Proc. IEE 1976 Communications Conf.,* Philadelphia (June 1976): 50-1-50-2.

2.32 *Job Entry Subsystem-JES2.* IBM Form No. SC 23-003.

2.33 *Management Report on Satellite Business Systems.* Washington, D.C.: Sate lite Business Systems (May 1976).

2.34 R. Allen. "Components: Microprocessors Galore." *IEEE Spectru* (January 1976): 50–52.

2.35 D. W. Davies. "The Principles of a Data Communications Network fc Computers and Remote Peripherals." Presented at IFIP Congress, Edinburg (1968).

2.36 B. Allonen, L. Haglund, G. Hellman, and O. Olofsson. "Technical Descri tion of the Nordic Public Data Network." *TELE* (January 1976): 13–23.

2.37 E. W. Pullen and R. G. Simko. "Our Changing Industry." *Datamation* (Janua 1977): 49–55.

3
Evolution of
Configuration and
Function
Distribution

3.1 INTRODUCTION

The physical and functional structures of the dataproc-essing/communication system have followed an evolution consistent with the gradual maturing of data-processing services, the rapid improvements in computer-hardware price/performance, and the improvements of techniques for effective transmission-line utilization. This chapter traces the evolution of physical configuration and relates it to the distribution of function in three primary types of nodes in the network: hosts, communication controllers, and cluster controllers or subhosts. This leads to the evolution of layered functions in these nodes and to the concept of general communicability among network addressable units.

3.2 DIVERGENCE OF EARLY DESIGNS

3.2.1 Introduction

During the 1960s, large on-line systems were created for applications having a high return on investment. A great deal of expert handcrafting was applied to each system, which was constructed of customized hardware, programming, and communications links. Each system was optimized for the application as it was understood at the time. We must evaluate this earlier experience and appreciate the problems encountered in order to understand the need for structure in the architecture for distributed systems.

3.2.2 Intermixed Protocols

We use the word *protocol* to refer to the agreements reached between two parties on the format and meaning of control messages and the sequence of control messages that are to be exchanged between the parties. Special control characters and message headers with specified formats have been used in such exchanges. Three distinct sets of protocols have tended to be intermixed, namely, device-control protocols, data-link-control protocols, and end-to-end data-format protocols. Let us first define these.

1. A *terminal* or *work station* may have one or more input/output mechanisms, such as a keyboard, a printer, a display, etc., that are often referred to as *devices*. Each device has attributes, such as carriage return, line feed, tabs, coordinate positioning, new page, scroll, etc. *Device control* refers to the sending of commands to activate or use these device attributes. Such commands are the formats for the *device-control protocol.*

2. Data link control concerns the operation of a data link between nodes. *Data-link-control protocols* are needed to manage the operation of the link, which may be shared by multiple stations. The protocols regulate the initiation, checking, and retransmission (if necessary) of each data transmission.

3. *End-to-end data-format controls* involve data-format indicators and headers to characterize the data being sent rather than its transportation. This category of controls includes, for example, the following:

   ▪ Delimiters of text, to indicate the end of text or the separation of text from a header that describes the text.

   ▪ Indicators for chaining together a group of data units

   ▪ Headers that identify the type of message being sent

   ▪ Indicators of whether or not a message obeys a prescribed format

One result of the early growth of on-line systems was a multiplicity of incompatible data-link-control protocols, device-control protocols, and end-to-end data-format protocols. These three were often considered to be a single problem, and were intermixed.

The same control character came to mean different things for device control and link control or data-format control. For example, a negative acknowledgment (NAK) might occur because of a line error or because of buffer unavailability. Since the end-user (usually an application) inserted these control characters, each application could assign its own conditions for the use of the control character. It thus became impossible to handle link controls at the link control level; all control characters had to be interpreted within the application.

Application programs were written to take advantage of the existing TP designs; thus they came to contain increasingly diverse control functions that were both link- and device-dependent. Formatting of the data within the application in a manner that was unique for each device was also commonplace, so the application became still more device-dependent. Any change in a device or a line protocol required an application rewrite.

Terminals and lines. At first, it was entirely satisfactory for terminals and lines to be dedicated, or rather restricted, to only one application. The sharing of lines and terminals among applications was not facilitated in the conventional access methods. The use of a given line for different types of terminal was often impossible, because different terminals had different device controls and hence different requirements on the protocols used to manage the line. In order to economize on terminal-product cost, the line controls had been simplified to the extent that the full two-way or duplex capability of many lines could not be utilized; and the designers settled for half-duplex or one-way-at-a-time capabilities.

Later, the number of terminals connected to a system increased rapidly, rising from very few to tens or hundreds, and in some cases even thousands, of terminals per system. Line costs thus became a major factor and a significant percentage of total system operational expenses. These costs were unnecessarily increased by the fact that different line control disciplines and different terminal types could not be mixed on the same line; and the lines themselves were used inefficiently, because of the limitation to half-duplex operation.

It was not uncommon to find, in a given remote location, a number of terminals all going to the same remote center but each dedicated to a different application and each connected to an independent line. The consequent line utilizations were much lower than necessary. Both terminals and lines were unnecessarily duplicated, and hence more costly.

Thus, as data-processing users grew toward multiple TP applications, it became increasingly important to support the sharing of network resources, such as lines and terminals, across multiple applications. Subsystems, concerned with remote job entry, data-base interaction, and conversational programming, likewise grew in importance, so that resource sharing among them became economically important.

Access methods. The Basic Telecommunications Access Method (BTAM) provides a set of relatively primitive macros that can be incorporated into application programs to achieve read, write, and recovery functions. (A macroinstruction is a source language that is to be replaced by a defined sequence of instructions.) With BTAM, line-scheduling logic is part of the application program. The application is also responsible for polling, which must be done separately for each link (see the discussion of polling in Section 4.2). The Remote Terminal Access Method (RTAM), developed for Remote Job Entry (RJE) support, was also based on BTAM, but provided message multiplexing capabilities that were of value with multiple I/O mechanisms at one RJE work station. This was followed by queued access methods (such as QTAM) which, by virtue of both disk and core queuing of messages, provided a fine service for those interested in store-and-forward message switching but unfortunately did not provide the more direct control needed for higher performance applications. Different access methods thus came to be used by different applications, which thwarted resource sharing among applications. Without the sharing of resources, such as lines, terminals, and software support, resource utilizations were low; hence costly resources were unnecessarily duplicated. The choice of the access method depended on a number of factors, particularly the types of terminal supported, the types of application program, and the performance requirements. Most access methods intermixed link-control, device-control, and data-format protocols. In view of all the above factors, it became increasingly evident that resource sharing required either a new approach to provide consolidation of access methods or a better means for the joint use of different access methods.

Network management.   Along with this diversity, of course, came multiple protocols for network management. The subdivision of a network into zones having different start-up, shut-down, and operational protocols came to be a major problem. Efficiency of facilities management required that a common set (or at least related sets) of procedures be provided for the configuring of the network, the activation of its various units, and the dynamic modification of the network to meet load requirements. It was realized that, even though such network management had been implemented as part of the TP access method, it is a function that is logically distinct from other access-method functions, and could be structured accordingly.

3.2.3 Code Sprinkling

Figure 3.1 illustrates the resulting situation in which a variety of terminals were supported on a computer of the System 360 generation [3.10]. Device-dependent code was sprinkled among applications, in management information sybsystems, in a variety of access methods, and in the input/output supervisor. A change in a device, its device-control protocols, the line-control protocols, or the data-format protocols could

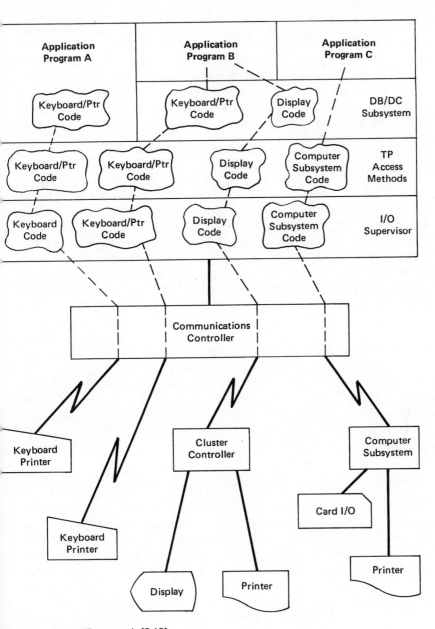

Fig. 3.1 Early TP network [3.10].

affect code at many levels. The amount of reprogramming that accompanied changes to the transmission system proved to be so great that expansion of applications became slower as the system grew. The replacement or enhancement of a given functional capability often affected other system components that were in the path (see Fig. 3.1), so that an increasing effort had to be devoted to the "maintenance" of the old applications and system components at the expense of true evolution of the customer's system.

3.2.4 The Architectural Requirements

Thus the growth of the teleprocessing technology from the mid-1950s to the early 1970s experienced the usual multiplicity of approaches. This was followed by a gradual consolidation of concepts. As technical knowledge and experience grew, it became apparent that a convergence of the best design practices was possible. It was sometimes painfully clear that an integration of facilities was needed to promote resource sharing. However, new structure was needed which formally separated those functions that are logically independent, in order to facilitate further change.

The essence of the desired architectural approach is to separate data-link-control protocols, end-to-end data-format protocols, and device-control protocols, all of which had been intermixed in earlier systems. In addition, however, it became apparent that the network architecture had to accommodate two trends made possible by advancing technologies. These are the trends toward the distribution of function among widely scattered network nodes and the growth of a wider variety of communication-carrier offerings.

3.3 THE EARLY HOST STRUCTURES

In the early teleprocessing systems (beginning in the 1950s and extending into the late 1960s) the primary goal was to make available, at remote locations, the power of a central data-processing system, as illustrated in Fig. 3.2. The remote keyboards and printers, quite naturally, were considered to be simple input/output units for the computer, even though the connecting cables were somewhat long (see Fig. 3.3). This was the background for the incorporation of TP controls into the central complex.

The treatment of device and network controls passed through a series of phases. At first these functions were completely embedded within applications and were the complete responsibility of the application programmer. Later, separate system services were established outside the application, which served multiple applications. These system services, for

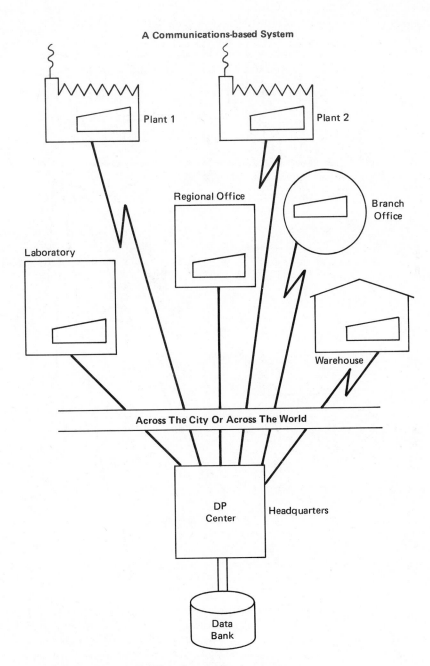

Fig. 3.2 Remote availability of centralized resources.

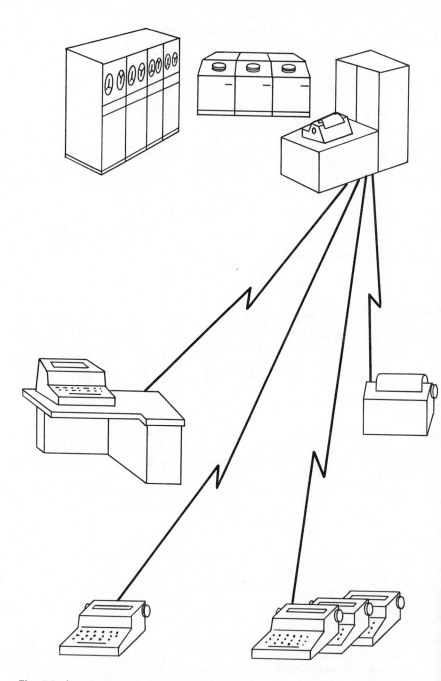

Fig. 3.3 Input/output devices via TP.

device and network controls, were located first in the host and then in adjacent or remote control units. To begin, let's recall the changes in the treatment of line controls, line scheduling, and path-finding functions. This evolution is illustrated in Fig. 3.4 [6.4].

3.3.1 I/O Scheduler (IOS)

Initially, of course, all the devices were local to the central processor and the control of these devices was completely within the application program, as shown in Fig. 3.4(a). A separate function was then created that was called the I/O scheduler (IOS), as shown in Fig. 3.4(b). A point of control was established there so that a connection was provided between a given application and a given I/O device for the duration of the job. A path-finding function was provided so that a request from a particular application would be routed to the correct device, and vice versa. Design differences and device control differences, among devices in a given class, tended to be masked from the application programmer by having common request formats for all devices within the given class. As TP lines came into initial use, it was natural to consider the remote TP device as simply a peculiar form of local attachment; and the same I/O scheduler was slightly adapted to route the data from the remote lines to the application program, as illustrated in Fig. 3.4(c).

The central processing units developed the means for handling I/O and TP interrupts in an efficient manner. Hardware and programming interrupt handlers recognized an interrupt from outside the CPU, and the interrupt handler was designed to transfer control to the desired application or to response routines that were tailored to the type of interrupt being fielded. These response routines could be vendor-supplied or user-written.

When the TP terminals were first accommodated by IOS, it was expedient to consider the line and the terminal as an entity because the TP line protocols of that time combined both line-control and device-control functions.

Up until this point, there was little, if any, sharing of TP resources among applications. The basic telecommunications access methods still required that each application program essentially own and manage its lines and terminals, and the application programs themselves still contained considerable awareness of the operation and characteristics of each line and terminal.

The application program at this point used the relatively "low-level" READ/WRITE interface. The READ command permitted the application to accept an input message coming from a device, via a predesignated

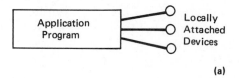

(a)

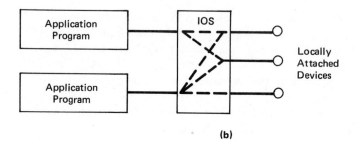

(b)

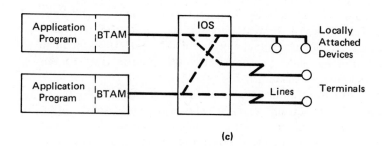

(c)

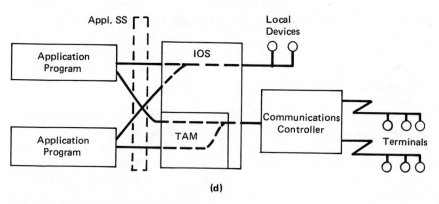

(d)

TAM   = Teleprocessing Access Method
Appl. SS = Application Subsystem

Fig. 3.4 Evolution of control structure.

buffer. The WRITE command made the output message, which had been placed in a predesignated buffer, available for output operations. What was put in the buffer by the application was exactly what was sent: no more, no less. All line-control and device-control information, if any, had to be part of that buffer content. In most cases, the application issuing the READ or WRITE waited until that operation was completed.

Devices and links were referred to by absolute physical addresses, which were designated at the time that the total physical configuration was defined (called systems generation or sys-gen). User-written exits were sometimes employed as part of the READ/WRITE command to convert from symbolic names to physical addresses.

3.3.2 Queued Access Methods

The Tele Communications Access Method (TCAM) [3.3] provided line sharing among applications and terminal access to any one of a set of message-processing programs. It did this by employing a set of message queues between the applications and the TP network. (Of course, all terminals on the same line had to be built for the same line control discipline, and had to operate at the same line data rate.) Terminals could be logically connected to a user-written message-control program, which could then pass the message to a user-written message-processing program. User macros were provided by TCAM to facilitate the writing and compiling of such message-control and message-processing programs. System code provided queuing which held the data for routing and for recovery purposes. This practice of dividing the application into two parts (the application proper and the message control) was also adopted in most later application subsystems. That way, a higher-level call could be used by the message-processing program. The message-control program would handle the queuing, routing, acknowledgment-generation, and correlation of received acknowledgments with sent requests. The message-control program could also control the establishment of connections and handle recovery.

A step toward device independence was taken in TCAM with user-specified message-handling code. As each message passed through the message-control program, both on its way from the origin to the message queue maintained for its destination and on its way from the message queue to the actual destination, the message-handling code could be used to analyze, validate, and/or edit the message data. Many device-dependent characteristics could thus be edited out before the message was passed to an application program, and messages could be formatted for necessary device peculiarities before they were passed to the TP line.

Applications could therefore be written largely independent of line disciplines and device peculiarities. The interface between the application (the message-processing program) and the message-control program could also be at a higher level that was oblivious to TP factors. That interface, in TCAM, was chosen to provide maximum compatibility with local device access methods; that is, with the basic sequential access method, BSAM (READ/WRITE level) and the queued sequential access method, QSAM (GET/PUT level). Macro instructions enabled the application program to request message transfer to or from a work area within each application program. The TP independence of this approach is indicated by the fact that it is possible to test and debug such applications in a non-TP environment, providing inputs from and outputs to a local sequential device (for example, magnetic tape, disk, punched card, etc.).

Thus, at this point, a more general communicability among applications and terminals was provided, so long as the particular queuing approach provided adequate performance and was compatible with the desired design. The application was also relieved of much of the path control and session management functions.

3.3.3   Generalized TP Sharing

Increasingly, a very wide range of applications needed to share lines, and a given terminal needed to have access to these different types. Some applications were transaction-oriented, some were conversationally interactive, and some were batch-oriented. Some types of application could achieve maximum performance by a direct, nonqueued type of connection, somewhat analogous to that provided by BTAM. Other applications (and application subsystems) were best served by unique types of queueing and special recovery facilities that were closely associated with that queueing. The need grew, therefore, for an access method that could provide line sharing and terminal sharing to applications whether or not they employed queueing of messages and regardless of the type of queueing facilities, if such were employed. The ability to share, without the necessity of queueing, was built into a facility referred to as VTAM (Virtual Telecommunication Access Methods) [3.4].

VTAM, like TCAM, relieved the user from the need to write line scheduling and polling code. VTAM supported multiple terminals on a single TP line; terminals on shared lines could be distributed among applications of all types. VTAM converted the I/O message to transmission format, adding the necessary TP headers to the information. A "path-control" function routed the messages to and from the multiple applications. The older IOS package was still utilized for managing the channel interface, and the VTAM function operated through the IOS.

The application program was, at the same time, provided with a somewhat higher-level interface than that used in BTAM, called SEND/RECEIVE. This had several major characteristics, as follows.

In the SEND/RECEIVE environment, the "session" established a logical connection between two network addressable units—say, between an application and a terminal. Control tables, with associated ground rules for data flow, could be established for each session. An application program could have many sessions with many devices, but only one session at any one time between a given application program and a given device. The system managed the flows by session and ensured the integrity of the session; that is, it kept extraneous messages from intruding into a session. Symbolic addresses used in application programs were converted by system-provided code to physical addresses. System code constructed and added the necessary headers to the data that were needed for path finding and flow control.

However, with VTAM, some of the actual I/O processing was executed outside VTAM. This might be in a message-control part of an application program or in an application subsystem, such as IMS or JES. For example, the indicators for data flow control, such as "My turn, your turn" or "Group this chain of messages together as a unit," came to VTAM. VTAM then issued the READ and WRITE command. At the same time, VTAM absorbed responsibility for detecting lost messages, and for helping the user to resynchronize data flows when necessary.

Even with VTAM, device-dependent programming still could be partially embedded in application programs, and an application could be written to support only specific device types. Of course, applications were more often subdivided, as TCAM was, into device-independent portions and device-dependent portions, so that the heart of each application was in reality device-independent. Nevertheless, there was a need for system-provided code to facilitate device independence. Such system facilities for handling device dependencies external to the application were provided not in VTAM itself, but in complementary "application subsystems" that were designed to serve multiple applications of a given class. These are discussed in Section 3.4.

The structure then looked roughly like that shown in Fig. 3.4(d). The BTAM code that had been embedded in the application was removed. The teleprocessing access-method (TAM, standing for either TCAM or VTAM) functions were separated from the application. IOS was still used by the TAM to manage the physical data link (called the channel) between the host and attached controllers. And, as we will discuss in a later section, more of the TP line management functions were moved to a separate communications controller.

3.4 APPLICATION SUBSYSTEMS

3.4.1 Multiapplication Structures

Multiple applications, or multiple message-processing programs for different types of message, required a family of related services. An interim structure and the distribution of function between the host and the communications controller (COMC) are shown in Fig. 3.5. A distinct transmission control function became identified whose function is to manage and keep track of each logical connection (or session) between a remote destination and one of the local applications. Each transmission control element also served as a mailbox to which were routed the incoming messages for a particular application program.

The path control in the host routes messages to the correct COMC, or to one of the locally attached device control units. The path control in the COMC then routes the message to the correct line attached to the COMC. So, each successive instance of path control finds the next link in the path to the destination. If a remote cluster controller or a remote COMC were attached to the local COMC, then still another stage of path finding would take place in the remote nodes.

The network management function relieved the multiple applications of many of the procedures for resource control throughout the network. The network services were made logically distinct from the applications and from the normal data flow functions of the teleprocessing access method. This included procedures for

1. The initiation and termination of logical connections between terminals and an application
2. Network start-up and network shut-down
3. Network reconfiguration as nodes or links need to be activated or deactivated
4. Coordination of traffic measurement and monitoring
5. Coordination of some network recovery situations that are not handled at lower levels

It thus became a common network-management control point for system services (known in SNA as the System Services Control Point, or the SSCP). This became logically distinct from those access-method functions that concerned flows once a connection was established.

3.4.2 DB/DC Subsystems

A concurrent and largely independent development was that of the database/data-communication subsystem, such as CICS [3.11] and IMS [3.5]. These subsystems performed the following three functions.

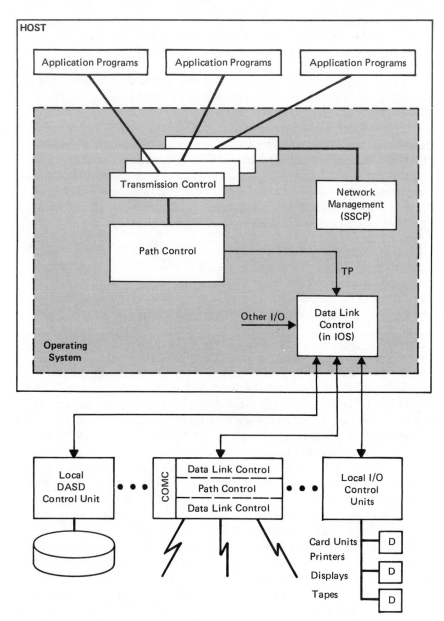

Fig. 3.5 Key TP functions in operating system and communications controller in middle time period.

1. They coordinated all the recovery dealing with a particular transaction, whether that recovery involved communications, message-processing in the host, or data-base processing in the host.

2. They developed a user interface for the message-processing programs which could shield the application program from the fact that there were design peculiarities in either the line protocols or in the attached devices. A considerable degree of device independence and line-protocol independence was thus achieved by the insertion of intermediary programs (called presentation services in SNA) for these purposes. The application programmer, therefore, did not have to be concerned with the nature of the line protocols or the details of the device-control codes. In general, moreover, the DB/DC subsystems tended to shield the user from the peculiarities of the teleprocessing access method being used.

3. In a similar way, their user interface shielded the message-processing programs from the peculiarities of the data base. This contributed a considerable degree of data independence. The application programmer did not have to be concerned with the physical characteristics of storage devices or the way in which data fields were physically grouped together. Instead, the application programmer worked with a logical structure of the data segments.

As shown in Fig. 3.6, the DB/DC subsystem itself usually runs as a specialized application program (perhaps with some privileges not given to all application programs) using the facilities of the operating system. Its presentation services to achieve device independence, line-protocol independence, and data independence are intermediaries between the transmission subsystem and the message-processing programs.

The DB/DC subsystem, as well as normal applications, uses the transmission control and path control services, which are part of the TP access methods, within the host operating system. However, message-control programs, within the DB/DC subsystem, also perform a routing function among the message-processing programs serviced by the subsystem. Requests are analyzed to determine, by the content of the request, what action to take on that request. Normally, requests are routed between application programs and terminals. In many DB/DC subsystems, however, it is also possible to route requests between application programs or between terminals.

In some subsystems, the messages are stacked in a message queue. In others, no queue is built in the host, and only one message per terminal entry is kept. In that case, if the host is busy, the queues develop either at the device itself (no further keying is possible) or in the cluster controller.

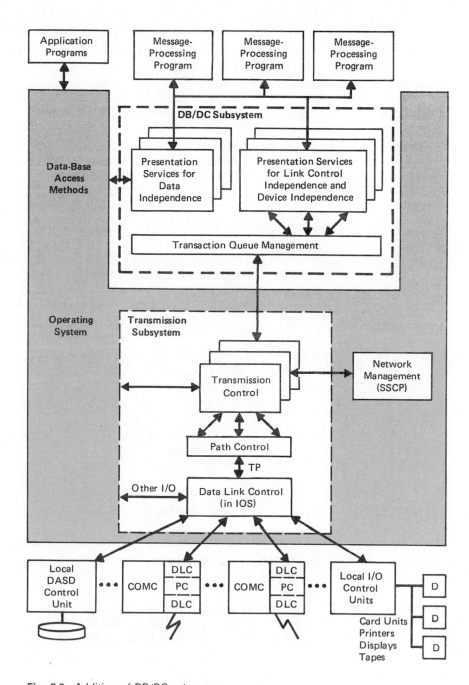

Fig. 3.6 Addition of DB/DC subsystems.

For example, CICS and IMS differ fundamentally in that IMS is queued and CICS is not. CICS is referred to as a "direct-control system."

The DB/DC subsystem usually also performs a scheduling function, calling on the operating systems for resources as necessary. CICS, for example, has a "task control program" to initiate a new task for each transaction, and to maintain a thread of control for each transaction. When one thread is delayed, as when waiting for a disk access to complete, another thread is given control of the processing resource.

3.5 COMMUNICATIONS CONTROLLERS (COMC)

3.5.1 Basic COMC Functions

In the above discussion, we traced the separation of functions so that logically distinct functions came to be designed in distinct layers of the system. Another aspect is the search for performance and reliability of transmission-related functions. This search led to a decrease in the sharing of hardware and programming resources between application-processing functions and some of the transmission-oriented functions (such as line control and some path control functions). Less sharing of resources does not necessarily imply physical unit separation. However, in many cases, the logical separation was achieved by creating a physically separate stand-alone unit that is referred to as a communications controller (COMC) in Fig. 3.4(d).

The nature of the line control functions required very frequent interruptions of the processor, when that processor was required to perform the relatively menial tasks of line controls such as message assembly and polling. Each interruption of the central processing unit (CPU), of course, had a certain amount of overhead involved, and the small amount of work to be done on the occasion of each interruption often did not justify the expense of the interruption overhead. Hence, in the search for better performance, it was natural to move the line control function to a separate unit outboard of the processor, which was specially designed for that mode of operation.

Early communications controllers, nevertheless, continued to interrupt the host whenever a byte had been assembled from bits received over a particular line. The frequency of host interruption was further reduced in later front-ends by the inclusion of sufficient buffering and controls in the front-end units, so that the host was interrupted only on the occasion of either a complete computer word (for example, 32 bits) or a complete message [3.7, 3.9, 3.12, 3.14]. This served also to increase the

data-handling capability of the communications controller. The capacity
of such units now ranges from 15,000 to 100,000 characters per second.

The details of line scheduling (for example, "Now get the next
message for line X from the message queue") and polling were first done
in the host. Later, with more capability in the front-ends (for example, in
the IBM 2701, 2702, and 2703), polling was partly delegated outward,
and much more of the line-scheduling function was likewise moved
outward. Then (with the IBM 3705), polling was completely moved to the
COMC, and the destination addresses within the TP network were
separated from the CPU's local I/O address structure. The front-end itself
could be a single address, so far as the host was concerned, and the
network addressing was handled by the front-end with no restrictions
because of CPU-addressing limitations.

The data link control (DLC) in the COMC became more self-
sufficient, so as to initiate, control, check, and terminate data transfer
over the data link. [Note that the term "line" strictly refers to the physical
medium; the term "data link" also includes the modem (or other attachment unit) and all stations connected to the line; and data link control
uses the data link and includes the protocols used to manage the link.]

Local devices remained directly attached to the CPU channels. A
path control function remained in the CPU for the routing of messages
among its directly attached devices, such as the local I/O control units,
controllers for local terminals, and communications controllers. Within the
communications controller, in turn, a second level of path control existed
for the routing of messages to the proper TP line. Both hosts and COMCs
developed the so-called intermediate function, which is the capability to
route received messages on to COMCs which finally attach the destination node. The host or COMC routing table shows which output link
should be used to send a message on its way, but the host or COMC need
have no knowledge of what happens to a message after the adjacent node
has accepted responsibility for it.

We also see, as we would expect, the existence of two or more data-
link-control disciplines, some pertaining to the remote network attached
to the communications controller and some pertaining to the local network (channel bus) attached directly to the host.

Initially, the data link controls in the COMC reported link errors (for
example, parity checks on data) to the application or its recovery exit
routine. Later DLCs incorporated automatic retransmission facilities into
the COMC itself. Copies of one or more messages were retained by the
sending node until the adjacent receiving node acknowledged a valid and
error-free reception of those messages. Retransmissions were scheduled
either after time-outs or on the occasion of some indicator or count from

the receiving node. Eventual failures to achieve a successful transmission were reported back to the application.

Another useful feature of COMCs offered by different companies may be speed recognition, that is, the automatic determination of the bit rate used by the attached node. When attaching nodes (or devices) dial in, the probability of obtaining a free port will be greater if all ports are accessible to any speed device than if certain ports can only handle certain speeds. The attaching node (or device) can also dial a single number regardless of the speed of that attachment. The ports themselves can be on a rotary so as to connect the next available port. The chosen port can then adapt to the speed of the attaching unit through automatic speed recognition.

3.5.2   COMC Physical Unit Services

The division of work between the functions in the communications controller and the corresponding functions in the host further evolved so as to give greater self-sufficiency to the COMC. One of these delegations of function pertains to the physical resources in, and the lines attached to, the communications controller. The knowledge of these resources, their general status, and the control tables for the activation, monitoring, testing, and deactivation of these resources needed to be physically located within the node itself. Hence, a part of the network services was built into the COMC under a function called the physical unit services. This provided a degree of local management of the physical resources of the COMC and of lines attached to the COMC. The physical unit services, in turn, were coupled to the system services control point (SSCP), so that all COMCs could be coordinated.

The physical configuration of the network is defined, for these network services in the COMC, by a *network-definition* procedure. This specifies the numbers, types, and configurations of terminal nodes and cluster controllers to be attached. A COMC may have more than one network definition generated for it; which definition it will use can be determined as the need arises. Each definition can have a symbolic name, so it can be called on to alter network configuration as demands on application programs change. Operator commands also can be used to make more minor changes in the configuration if that becomes necessary.

3.5.3   COMC Boundary Functions

Further functions of the COMC came to be the support of adjacent terminal controllers, particularly for *address translation*. In a sense, the communications controllers stand at the boundary of a world of common network addressability. However, each of the units attaching to the COMC may have an addressing world all its own, which is first of all different from that of the COMC network, sometimes more restricted in scope, and probably specialized to the manufacturer. Units that radiate from the communications controller may only be aware of their own subordinate devices and the COMC, and not of the total network's existence or of the addressing needs of other units.

There has developed, therefore, a set of boundary functions which exist in communications controllers for the purpose of adapting the specialized and/or limited addressing facilities of the attaching subsystems to that of the common network. It is primarily an address-translation function. The terminal that attaches to the COMC may, for example, rely on the COMC to transform the destination address to and from a local form. Each of the units attaching to a COMC might, in turn, have a set of its own attachments, whose local addresses are not known to the COMC. Thus, the extended concept permits a hierarchy of addressing knowledge and an associated hierarchy of knowledge of physical connections. Each attached unit might have a lower-level network whose particulars were unknown to the higher-level units.

Another boundary function is needed regarding the *pacing* of flows along the final leg of the path, from the COMC to the destination node. Pacing refers to the sending of messages only when the buffers (or other resources) of the receiving node are capable of receiving further transmissions. The pacing of the data flows from the COMC to a destination node may be different from the pacing desired for flows between the host and the COMC (see Fig. 3.7). The boundary functions in the COMC therefore provide buffers to allow two stages for pacing: a first stage of pacing from the origin node to the boundary function, in the COMC, and a second stage of pacing for flows between the COMC and adjacent cluster controllers or terminal nodes.

3.5.4   COMC Queueing and Editing

Bulk storage, such as that available from rotating disks, is available on hosts, advanced cluster control units, and minicomputers attached to hosts. Many communications controllers economize in this regard and provide only moderate amounts of storage for buffering and minimum amounts of disk storage for initialization, test purposes, and diagnostics. On the other hand, at those points in the network where bulk storage exists, traffic can be extensively queued. Such queueing may be advantageous in case of a line failure or in case of excessive load on the connecting links. Of course, the very presence of bulk storage in a COMC potentially introduces a source of overhead, which may reduce COMC throughput.

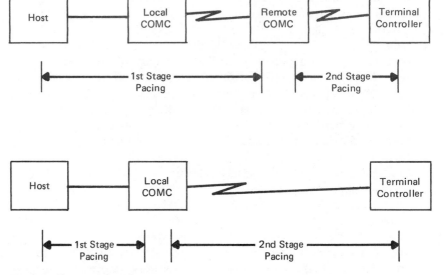

Fig. 3.7 Two-stage pacing.

Testing to see if data is to be stored on disk and managing the stored data do not come free. Nevertheless, there are situations in which the gain in function is worth the price.

A wide variety of competing front-ends, with a broad range of function, have been offered by different companies. In many cases, a general-purpose data processor has been employed as a front-end COMC [3.9]. Programming for these equipments spans a wide range. In some cases, single-task-oriented executives service communication lines and terminals, with user-supplied terminal-dependent code. In other cases, multitask operating systems are capable of coordinating diverse functions, like preliminary data reduction, message store and forward, spooling of data to I/O devices, and communications-circuit load leveling. The more complex operating systems provide such services as task scheduling on a priority basis and time-dependent task scheduling.

When there was sufficient processing capacity and storage in the front-end communications controllers, a variety of other useful purposes were found, particularly if the COMC was readily programmable. Preliminary editing of incoming information could be done there; validity checks on message content (such as all numerics in a numeric field) could also be done. The rejection of an erroneous message at this point is more efficient than after an extensive amount of handling in the main host. Similarly, very elementary types of query or attention signal could be accommodated in the front-end COMC. However, as the cluster controllers became more capable, it was then found advantageous to move such editing and validity checks to the programmable cluster controller, which was still closer to the source of the input.

3.5.5 Summary of COMC Functions

Thus, some of the important functions that the communications controllers (whether local or remote) absorbed included the following:

1. To provide data link control for the diverse link disciplines involved

2. To act in concert with the network manager in network start-up, varying on or off links or connected nodes, and network shut-down

3. To route messages acting as an intermediate node

4. To assist adjacent cluster control nodes in boundary functions, such as address translation

5. To support minimum function terminal nodes, in other boundary functions, to make it possible for them to connect to and use the common network

The future of the COMC will be influenced by three major developments:

1. The shift of more functions to terminals and cluster controllers, reducing the need for data editing, and other transformations in the COMC.

2. The wider use of broadband lines, which will reduce the need for feeding large numbers of low-speed lines. (Examples of this would include CATV, satellite, fast-connect digital, and packet-switching transmission systems.)

3. The lower cost of hosts. As this cost continues to decrease, the use of multiple hosts per site will tend to increase. Then either the local COMC may serve as a central distribution point for multiple hosts, or the COMC functions may be distributed and integrated again in each host.

The architecture for a distributed system must allow for the possible redistribution of this function and for the alternative options of function packaging.

It also appears that some future COMCs will have to address the requirements of interfacing to new data networks (see Chapter 17) and the issues of more complex routing (see Chapter 16).

3.6   CLUSTER CONTROLLERS AND SUBHOSTS

3.6.1   Introduction

At the same time that the separate COMC was evolving, a family of programmable cluster controllers for groups of diverse input/output devices, such as keyboards, printers, displays, diskettes, and cards, were also under development. As technology advanced, the functions in these cluster controllers expanded.

3.6.2   Basic Cluster Controller

Devices can be made somewhat less expensive by sharing some of the controls for that device in a common controller. Hence, the concept of the cluster controller is a natural one. In addition, the transmission lines can be used more efficiently when the relatively infrequent messages from each of a number of devices are multiplexed on a common line from the cluster controller to the host machine.

The device-related functions in the basic cluster controller are shown in Fig. 3.8. The implementations of these functions, of course, can vary widely, often with most or all of this function in microcode or other hardware. The data link controls in the cluster controller cooperate with the data link control in the COMC in the management of the links in the path to the host. The cluster path control serves to route messages to the proper device that is attached to the cluster controllers; more precisely, path control routes the message to the microcode that serves the session for a particular device (see the definitions of half-session and logical unit in Chapter 7). The cluster transmission control serves to keep track, at that end, of the logical connections between various devices in the cluster and various programs in the host. Each device (or group of devices) has device controller functions, which provide the appropriate activating signals for each device in accordance with the data or device commands that were received. Emanating from the cluster is a subnetwork for the distribution of information to the cluster's devices. These subnetworks have their individual data link controls.

The data-processing capability of the basic cluster controller could be very modest. The basic cluster controller might, for example, have only a very basic support for DASD (direct access storage devices). Data formats could be fixed to avoid the overhead of variable fields. Space allocations could be predefined for specified data sets, and new allocations for newly created data sets need not be available. The user interface could be at the simple READ/WRITE level, where the user

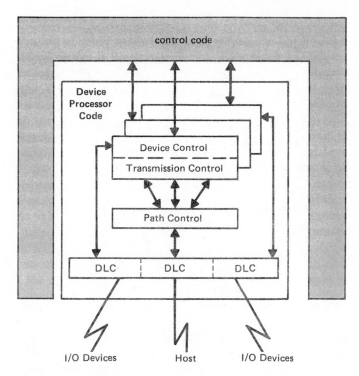

Fig. 3.8 Functions in basic cluster controller.

must specify data location on the particular storage device, with no attempt to provide device independence or logical views of the data. This would be consistent with the role of a basic cluster controller to do a specific, predetermined type of job, rather than to be a more general-purpose data processor.

Together, Figs. 3.6 and 3.8 show how the layers of communication function began to be distributed among the host, the communications controllers, and the basic cluster controllers. Note that the path control layer has a component in each of these nodes—the originating node, the destination node, and the intermediary (COMC) node. Data link control, on the other hand, is concerned with the management of each link as an independent entity. The DLC components at the endpoints of a data link are a mutually dependent function pair.

The *terminal node* (an SNA term) is like a basic cluster controller but has very limited function and is more dependent on a boundary function, in an adjacent COMC, for its operation. (The SNA view of a terminal node is given in Chapter 12.)

3.6.3 Advanced Cluster Controller

As logic and storage costs have decreased, it has become possible to consider a further utilization of the cluster controller. A part of the application that was particularly pertinent to the interaction with the cluster of devices could be executed within the cluster controller itself. The addition of more processing power and more storage then found the cluster controller with capability in all three of the primary functions:

- Data storage and data management
- Application processing
- Input/output management

Therefore, the cluster controller became more and more capable of operating in a stand-alone data-processing mode, at least for long periods of time.

The elementary operations, such as message editing, formatting for data entry, simple inquiry, and preliminary processing of a transaction, were followed by more generalized control code and a capability of performing at least basic data processing, along with the ability to control the devices attached to the cluster. This was accompanied by expanded data-storage services, such as the storage of records of variable length and index structures associated with random storage. Figure 3.9 portrays some of the functions of a more advanced cluster controller, which takes on many of the aspects of a general-purpose subsystem.

In many applications, then, the number of interactions necessary between the operator and the local cluster controller is many times more than the number of interactions needed between the cluster controller and the host. In a typical transaction, for example, two interactions with the host might be needed: one to obtain a pertinent record, and a second to return the updated record. In between, there can be a series of simple steps between the locally stored application and the terminal operator. In some cases, the local application can aid the dialogue with prompting techniques that need not be transmitted over the longer distance from the host. Freed from the expense and time delay of the longer transmission to the host for every interaction, the system designer can design local conversational languages and techniques that promote the local dialogue. (An example of this is the entering of an order entry at a display console. Filling in the necessary information in different fields of the screen may involve, say, ten exchanges of prompted messages to the operator ·before the order can be sent to the central computer.)

The movement of the specific device controls outboard to the cluster controller was followed by the residence in the cluster controller of those

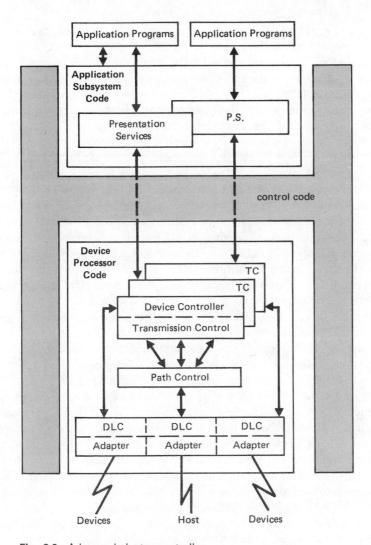

Fig. 3.9 Advanced cluster controller.

special format controls that were closely associated with the devices of the cluster controller. A partnership was formed between presentation services in the host (which might apply to a variety of terminals and cluster controllers) and presentation services in the cluster controller (which uniquely serviced its own devices).

To illustrate such presentation services, consider the problem of display-image formation. If there is a form to be displayed, then a normal approach is to transmit the many blanks between the characters of the display as well as the characters themselves. In many cases, the number of blanks transmitted far exceeds the desired information. If the cluster controller, on the other hand, is programmable, its data can be sent in a compressed form. In fact, only the character information need be sent if the form itself has been prestored in the controller of the display. The marriage of the fresh information coming down the line and the display format stored in the controller then provides the desired display. Other formatting functions might include the removal of leading zeros or blanks from fixed length fields and the insertion of decimal points and dollar signs where needed, along with field descriptors such as "collected funds available." Thus, formatting logic can be another versatile function within the presentation services of the advanced cluster controller.

Function key expansion is still another example of presentation services. This involves a program that will accept a single key depression and expand it into a multicharacter code via a table lookup routine. The expanded code is then sent to the destination for interpretation and action. The advantage of function key expansion lies in its reduction of the number of key strokes required in repetitive operator actions. Besides the control functions, such as "cancel," "transaction," "end of message," and "display next screen," any translation-related function, such as "credit card cash advance" or "withdrawal–debit," can be defined as a keystroke.

Graphics, in general, can also take advantage of local storage and processing. The generation of curves and some of the manipulation of images can be performed essentially as applications running on the advanced cluster controller. Short response times are particularly important in such work, and avoiding the need for transmitting large blocks of information to the host can be significant to complex interactions.

Application development facilities have often been more effective at some locations than at others. In the case of some cluster controllers, such as the IBM 3600 and 3790, application programs can be prepared on a host and then sent via channel or TP line to be stored on a diskette in the cluster controller. Alternatively, the diskette could be loaded at one installation and carried to a remote stand-alone cluster controller. These cluster controllers, however, did not themselves have stand-alone application development capability.

Thus, the functional possibilities within the advanced cluster controller multiplied, and its capabilities were generalized. It became, in fact, a data-processing subsystem that was capable of two modes of operation: as a stand-alone unit for long periods of normal operations, and as a satellite to the host for periodic interactions with host applications and data bases.

Application subsystems within cluster controllers were designed to acilitate distributed processing and distributed data. One example of this s the Display Management System (DMS) of the IBM 3790 cluster ontroller. DMS provides a linkage service which establishes, via a set of nacros, standard interfaces and communications protocols among distrib-ted modules of application programs. The linkage services locate the unction (invoked by name) and, if in the host, will transmit the data here, and will subsequently store the reply in a prespecified location. This service also allows programmers to request data by name against ocal or host resident files. If the data resides on the host system, the ransaction will be sent to the host. Replies from the host are then stored n 3790 user buffers, in work area files, or in catalogued data sets.

Remember that the differences between basic cluster controllers, dvanced cluster controllers, and hosts lie in the functions performed in hese nodes. It turns out that a common network architecture applies, whether the end-user in a node is an application program, a system ervice program, an application subsystem, a device operator, or a storage nedium. In every case, the objective is communication between pairs of ietwork addressable units. The telecommunications architecture can be argely independent of the breadth of function in a node. The protocols, uch as control commands and transmission headers, can be either the ame or functional subsets of one another. The architecture then can have certain unity, independent of function breadth in a node, even though mly subsets of the architecture may, for economy, be used in the simpler iodes.

3.6.4 Subhosts

Sometimes a host (that is, a general-purpose data-processing system) perates in a distinctly subordinate role to another host. The application programs in the subhost might, for example, pertain to specialized sensor-base operations, which in turn are coordinated by an application program n a parent host. This, however, is only an application relationship. From he viewpoint of systems architecture, there is nothing new here. The ubhost may appear to the network exactly as any other host would; in other cases, the subhost may appear to another host as if it were an idvanced cluster controller, depending on which subset of the network irchitecture is chosen.

3.7 GROWTH OF REGIONAL NETWORKS

Tree configurations. A tree configuration is illustrated in Fig. 3.10. A orporation might, for example, have a central data-processing center for ach of several regions. Each central complex might have one or more

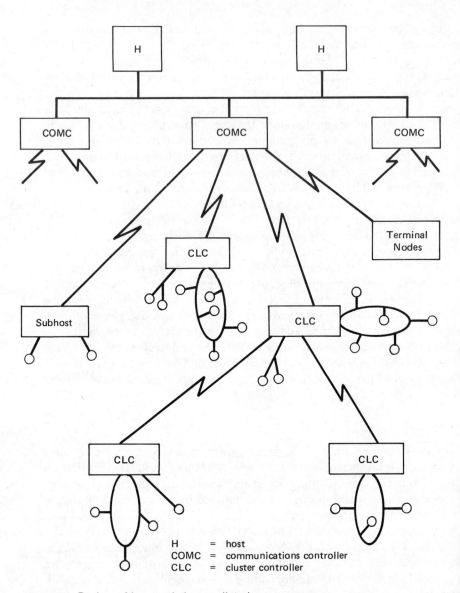

Fig. 3.10 Region with cascaded controllers in tree structures.

processors, with one or more communications controllers. Thus, a tree structure of simple terminal nodes, cluster controllers, and subhosts could be configured in each region. The lines connecting these nodes would be utilized more efficiently to the extent that messages would be multiplexed in the communications controller, cluster controller, or subhost.

Subsystem autonomy. Many cluster controllers and subhosts became more or less self-sufficient subsystems. The autonomy of these subsystems was usually constrained in such areas as application development (done on a host) and program load (done from a host). Nevertheless, the ability to install parts of a growing complex is facilitated by the ability of the advanced cluster controllers and subhosts to stand alone, at least for an extended period of time. These can be installed in local departments, initially for applications that require little dialogue with the host. As the applications become more fully developed, the dialogue with a central host can become as frequent as necessary. The reliability of the system as a whole is at the same time improved by the ability of the cluster controller/subhost to operate independently during those time periods when either transmission lines are inoperative or the central host is out of action.

Remote communications controller. If several cluster controllers were cascaded, the simpler design might be to operate with direct addressability only to the first cluster controller which, in turn, by examining the message content, establishes a second echelon of addressability to the lower-level cluster controller and its devices. This second echelon of addressability would really be a private arrangement between cluster controllers and is not part of the network architecture.

While this design is often satisfactory, it is not always so. It is sometimes desirable that we have a concentration of messages from a remote area and still retain direct network addressability to all terminal nodes and cluster controllers in that area. This can be achieved by having a remote communications controller, as shown in Fig. 3.11. This has a single line to the local COMC, and provides direct network addressability to all of its attaching units.

The remote communications controller is usually designed with the ability to drive higher-speed lines than a cluster control unit can. Its design can be optimized for the multiplexing function, thereby obtaining the benefit of efficient multiplexing or concentration, and high utilization of higher-speed lines between remote complexes.

Configuring for system availability. For most customers, a nonredundant configuration gives sufficient system availability, because many of the

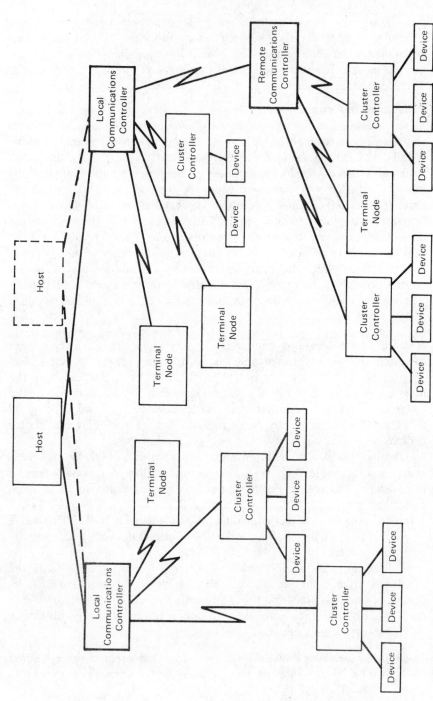

Fig. 3.11   Region with local and remote communications controllers.

units, if they fail, do not bring the whole system down. Key components, however, may merit special consideration. In Fig. 3.10, for example, if one must have very high system availability, it is desirable that

1. The operation of key cluster controllers and subhosts be possible, for extended periods of time, despite failure of the host or the link to the host.

2. Key remote communications controllers and cluster controllers have an alternate dial-in capability in case of failure of nonswitched lines.

3. Each local COMC be switchable among more than one host.

4. The direct access storage of the central complex be dynamically shareable between several hosts.

5. Software recovery programs exist in the host to provide for at least semiautomatic switchover of operations from one host to another in a warm-start fashion.

3.8 MULTIDOMAIN NETWORKS

Multihost configurations. In the foregoing discussion, we have seen the evolution of fairly complex tree structures, illustrated in Figs. 3.10 and 3.11, with increasing amounts of function being distributed to multiple levels of this structure. The nature of a tree is that there is only one path from the root to any other node. This permits a simple algorithm or set of tables to determine the path from the root to any node, or the path between any pair of nodes. On the other hand, a strict tree structure precludes the use of parallel paths between nodes, and alternate paths, in case of line failure, must be considered to be an alteration of the tree. When these tree structures are connected together, however, we may get mesh structures involving more possibilities for alternate paths.

It has been natural that tree structures should develop within a geographic region or a part of a larger organization such as a corporation. (Trees are not necessarily geographically separate; they often will overlap geographically.) The logical next step is to provide for the interconnection of these tree complexes. Referring back to Fig. 3.2, for example, we see that each of the plants, branches, and regional offices could themselves be complexes of the type illustrated in Figs. 3.10 and 3.11. Generally, considering each tree to be a domain, the domains might be interconnected in a mesh structure as suggested in Fig. 3.12, where again each domain could have the configuration complexity illustrated in Fig. 3.11.

An operator at a given terminal, in such a multihost network, may always want to communicate with the same host; or he or she may want

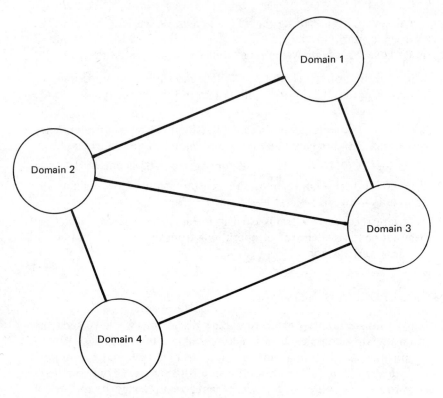

Fig. 3.12 Multiple regions in mesh.

to communicate with any application in any of the various hosts. A terminal can either

1. Dial up to any host,

2. Obtain its own private nonswitched line to that other host, or

3. Go via the communications controller at its parent host (that is, the one it uses most frequently), which can have a trunk to an adjacent host.

The first approach is more attractive if fast-connection facilities are available, but if the usage exceeds a certain amount, it is more expensive than a nonswitched host–host line. The second may lead to many lightly loaded nonswitched lines over relatively long distances. Therefore, one is often interested in sharing nonswitched facilities for cross-domain communication.

As indicated earlier, it has been helpful to have one resource manager in each domain that has responsibility for the logical connections among programs and devices in its domain of responsibility. These resource managers have been called, in SNA, system services control points (SSCP). An SSCP temporarily "owns" the terminals and programs assigned to it, in the sense that

- It alone can authorize a logical connection (a session) between programs, device operators, and storage media in its domain.

- It thus controls access and allocates resources in its domain.

In addition, the SSCP performs, for its domain, the network-manager functions of system bring-up, system shut-down, configuration adjust-ment, and some levels of system recovery (this is discussed further in Chapter 7).

On the other hand, communication systems can be built without a central control point, and it is then up to each end point to have all the information necessary to establish sessions and resolve contention for access. One can imagine, in fact, various degrees of control distribution, with levels of control (see Section 6.13).

Four classes of networking. Let us consider the case in which there is one control point per domain, and each domain has a host at the root of a tree configuration. One of the questions in multihost networking is the role of SSCPs in arranging a cross-domain connection. Assuming for simplicity that each host contains an SSCP, there are four different classes of multiple host operations that can be defined. These are illustrated in Figs. 3.13 and 3.14.

In class 1 (see Fig. 3.13), the purpose of networking is to economize on the use of transmission lines, sharing lines regardless of which host is being addressed by a terminal. The common network has sufficient addressing and routing capabilities to share transmission facilities among all messages, and it routes each message to its correct host or terminal destination.

In class 1, however, each terminal normally works (in a given time period) with only one host. A system services control point (SSCP), located in one host, "owns" a terminal for that time period in the sense that it alone can make a logical connection to that terminal, and thereby allocates all work to that terminal. Each terminal goes to the SSCP in its "parent" host for session initiation or authorization, and all dialogues are between a terminal and programs in its parent host. A change in owner-ship to a different host requires a disconnection, a removal from the resource manager in the old host, and an addition to the resource manager in the new host. There is no direct cooperation between the two resource managers, however. Each connection is explicit in the sense that

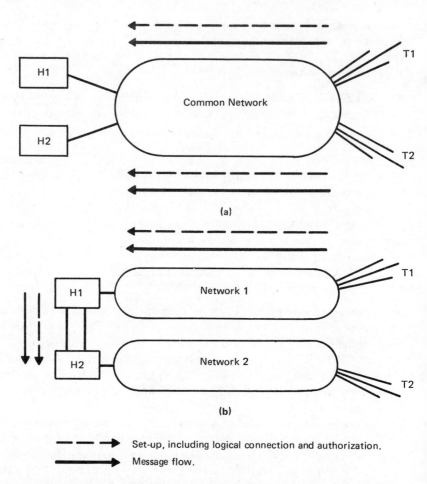

Fig. 3.13 Two lower forms of networking: (a) class-1 networking—shared communications network and exclusive host-terminal affinity; (b) class-2 networking—parent host involved in both setup and message flows.

the initiator must know the physical location of the service desired, and must know the network address for that service. In general, class-1 networking can be implemented by installing controllers, supplied by the common carrier or PTT, that establish the route from origin to destination.

Classes 2, 3, and 4, on the other hand, involve several degrees of direct cooperation between SSCPs, so that terminals can more easily work with multiple hosts.

In class 2 (see Fig. 3.13b), each host has a distinct local network such that all terminals in the local network communicate only with that one host. Hosts, however, are joined together by another network. A terminal, then, always works through its "parent host." *The parent host arranges the logical connection and authorization clearance with the other host, and all traffic passes through the parent host on its way to the destination host.* The destination host then routes messages to its own terminal. The connection may be implicit, in that *the service may be requested by name and the SSCP may determine the physical location and the network address of the desired service.* SSCP-SSCP services might also include queueing of requests for sessions when one party is busy, arranging a session by a third party, cross-domain network start-up/shut-down facilities, and cross-domain status monitoring, measurement, or recovery.

In class 3 (see Fig. 3.14a), the logical connection and authorization are arranged via the parent host, as in class 2. However, once this is done, *the actual data transmissions go directly between the origin and the destination via a network that is shared among hosts.* For example, the traffic between a terminal and a remote host need not enter that terminal's local (parent) host. SSCP-SSCP services could be the same as in class 2.

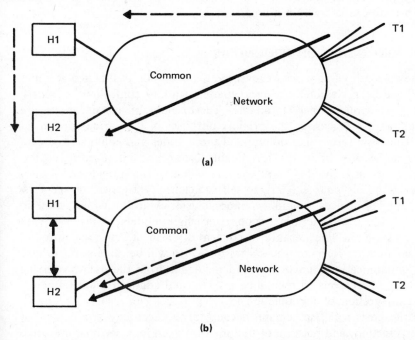

(a)

(b)

Fig. 3.14 Higher forms of networking: (a) class-3 networking—parent host only involved in setup; (b) class-4 networking—setup and message flow direct to destination host.

In class 4 (see Fig. 3.14b), it is not necessary for the originating terminal to work through its parent host for either logical connection, authorization, or data transmission. The terminal always goes directly to the destination host. Any coordination needed between resource managers in the several hosts is taken care of by them.

Classes 2, 3, and 4 raise the architectural question of the need for protocols to permit multiple SSCP coordination. The architectural requirement is to create, in effect, a single working network, with multiple control domains and SSCPs distributed to each control domain. The architecture for this will be addressed in Chapter 15.

The natural connection points for linking the multidomain network are the communications controllers, both local and remote. Thus, messages need not be routed through multiple hosts. They can pass, for example, from the originating node, via communications controllers, to the destination. A basic network of two control domains is illustrated in Fig. 3.15, and a mesh connection among four control domains is illustrated in Fig. 3.16. Interdomain communication can also be provided via local links, such as channel-to-channel connections, special ring networks, and private "links" within a host.

3.9 CONFIGURATION PROGNOSIS

In the above discussion, we have traced the evolution of function in nodes that have been classified as hosts, communications controllers, subhosts, cluster controllers, and terminals. These different classifications are useful, since they convey the primary purposes of the various designs.

The basic forces that determined these nodes and configurations are likely to be present in the foreseeable future as well. Continuing improvements in technology will encourage more widespread use of subhosts as loosely coupled, largely self-sufficient, data-processing centers. Clustering of devices around a common cluster controller will continue to benefit from shared terminal support, a single modem to the host, and better use of the line because of concentration in the cluster controller. The communications controller's raison d'être will be, as before, to give the communications function an independence from the data-processing function, for reasons of reliability, growth, and administration (although some integration of the function in other nodes can also be foreseen). And the hosts will also remain, because of the economy of a center for richer function, and because of the practical need for coordination of the domain, including the functional coordination of distributed applications.

On the other hand, we have also seen that processor power, storage, and programming services are increasingly being distributed among all

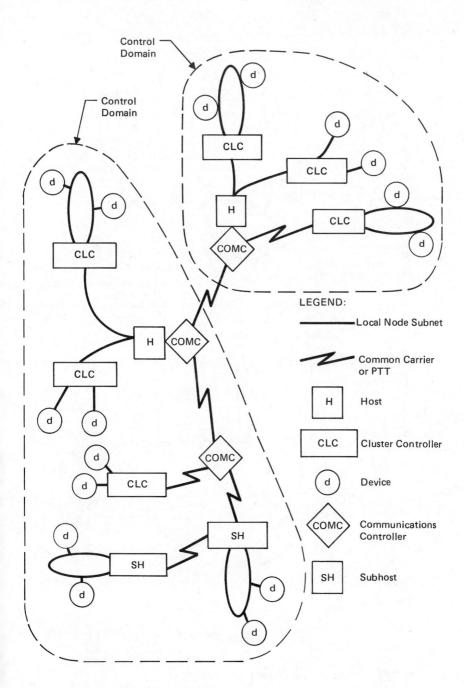

Fig. 3.15 Multiregion network with two control domains.

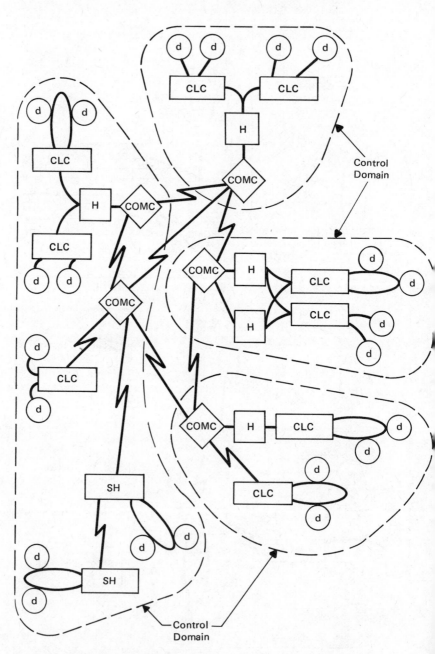

Fig. 3.16 Illustrative four-domain network.

types of node. The distinctions among these types are often only in the degree of function provided.

Experience also indicates that every node can be structured so as to have a subset of a common communications architecture. The commonality in that architecture must be able to provide communicability among all types of program, device operator, and storage medium, in all types of node.

3.10   EXERCISES

3.1 Explain why the practice of embedding line controls and/or network controls in the code of an application can increase system operating costs and retard system growth.

3.2 Why should a properly structured system architecture reduce the number of personnel devoted to system maintenance? How does this affect system growth rate?

3.11   REFERENCES AND BIBLIOGRAPHY

See also [6.5].

3.1 *IBM Systems Journal* **14,** No. 1 (1975), Special Issue on Supermarket and Retail Store Systems.

3.2 J. P. Gray and C. R. Blair. "IBM's Systems Network Architecture." *Datamation* **21,** No. 4 (April 1975): 51–56.

3.3 *O. S. TCAM Concepts and Facilities,* IBM Form No. GC30-2022.

3.4 *VTAM Concepts and Planning,* IBM Form No. GC27-6998.

3.5 *IMS/VS System/Application Design Guide,* IBM Form No. SH20-9025.

3.6 *An Introduction to the IBM 3790 Communications System,* IBM Form No. GA27-2767.

3.7 *COMTEN CNS, Communications Network System, General Description Manual,* COMTEN Publications No. MB 2013.

3.8 I. Cotton. "Network Management Survey." *NBS Tech. Note 805,* United States Department of Commerce (February 1974).

3.9 *Introduction to Computer Networks.* Maynard, Mass.: Digital Equipment (1974).

3.10 J. H. McFadyen. "System Network Architecture: An Overview." *IBM Systems Journal* **15,** No. 1 (1976). (Figure 3.1 reprinted by permission of *IBM Systems Journal.*)

3.11 *Customer Information Control System,* IBM Form No. GH20-1280.

3.12 *Introduction to the IBM 3704 and 3705 Communication Controllers,* IBM Form No. GA27-3051-3.

3.13 H. B. Becker. *Functional Analysis of Information Networks.* New York: John Wiley (1973).

3.14 G. D. Forney, Jr., and J. E. Vander Mey. "The Codex 6000 Series of Intelligent Network Processors." *Computer Communication Review* **6,** No. 2 (April 1976).

3.15 S. M. Ornstein, F. E. Heart, W. R. Crowther, H. K. Rising, S. B. Russell, and A. Michel. "Terminal Imp for the ARPA Computer Network." *AFIPS Conference Proceedings* **40** (Spring 1972): 243–254. Joint Computer Conf. AFIPS Press, Montrale, N. J.

4

Improving
Line
Utilization

4.1 INTRODUCTION

A variety of techniques are used to share transmission lines so as to improve their utilization, or to permit the use of better price performance and broader bandwidth lines. The primary techniques are

- Polling
- Multiplexing
- Concentration
- Combinations of these with line switching

Message switching and packet switching can be looked on as extended forms of concentration. All of these affect the distributed-systems architecture to some degree. A quick review of these means for improving line utilization is provided. However, the first four sections of this chapter are rather basic and are surely well known to some readers; in that case, these sections should be skipped.

4.2 MULTIDROP LINES

4.2.1 Polling and Multipoint

In multipoint operation, a line can be shared among many nodes. Each node has a "station" on the line to perform the line control function. One station on the line (called a primary station) governs the sharing of the line. The primary permits each secondary station, in turn, to transmit to the primary, by sending an authorization message to each secondary station. This procedure is called *polling*. The line-control protocol format includes an address with each message. Multiple messages for different destinations can be sent serially by the primary down the line, depending on each station, in turn, to examine the address and accept only those messages belonging to it. In addition to the savings in line costs, the multipoint circuit needs only one modem for each secondary station and one for the primary station. In contrast, point-to-point connections require two modems for each connection.

One way of maximizing the use of the line and its stations is to use full-duplex capabilities at the primary station to accommodate simultaneously many half-duplex secondary stations on a duplex line. In this mode (called multi-multipoint, or duplex multipoint), the less expensive secondary stations operate in half-duplex mode; however, the primary station keeps the lines full by sending to one set of stations while simultaneously receiving from another station. The primary station again directs the transmission from each secondary station, in turn, by polling.

4.2.2 Line Sharing

Multidrop lines permit the sharing of a given line by many similar terminals designed for the same line discipline and line data rate. Multidrop configurations are practical when the line capacity is many times greater than that required for any one terminal, so that the prospect of delay for any terminal, while the line is in use by others, can be made controllably small.

Line usage is very application-dependent. To illustrate a point, suppose that a conversational terminal transmits and receives messages containing 100 characters or 800 bits. Allowing for framing, addressing, checking, and control bits, each message might then involve 850 bits. Now, there may be a substantial "think time" or preparation time associated with each message so that the message rate from each terminal may be on the order of one message per 100 seconds. Thus, the average bit rate from that terminal is only 8.5 bits per second. Such an example demonstrates the fact that, in actual usage, burst rate is very often many times greater than the average rate at which a given terminal sends data. From statistics on teletype, graphic consoles, and remote batch stations, it appears that this ratio of burst to average rate per terminal may often be as high as 100:1; hence, the attractiveness of trying to share a transmission resource among many terminals.

There is, however, a probability of one terminal encountering a delay if other terminals happen to wish to transmit at the same time. The number of terminals actually attached to a multipoint line may, in fact, be dictated by the desired response time. In the above example, each terminal requires seven-tenths second to transmit its 850 bits on a 1200-bps line, and half that time on a 2400-bps line. If, then, several terminals desired to transmit at exactly the same instant, some would have to wait. First they would wait for the polling operation, which includes the time to process the polling list of the primary station and the time to send the polling messages to each station in turn. In addition, they would wait for other stations to transmit. Only four other transmissions, for example, would take 2.8 seconds on the 1200-bps line and 1.4 seconds on the 2400-bps line (for transmission alone, exclusive of polling). Thus with this type of line sharing, response time is very much a probabilistic question that depends directly on the line data rate, the message size, and the message rate per terminal, as well as the number of terminals on the line. Response time is further dependent on line reliability, since retransmission of any message affects traffic volume, which determines delays.

The above discussion assumes that there is a buffer in the terminal so that the message can be sent at the maximum data rate of the line. If no buffer is available at the terminal, then the line is utilized by that terminal for the entire duration of the key-in of the message. The buffer may be electronic storage or a physical medium (such as paper tape used for teletype transmission). If we were to assume that the operator keys data at a rate of one and one-half characters per second, the time consumed per message is 66 seconds rather than the fraction of a second previously assumed. Therefore, the operation of multidrop lines, with reasonable response time, is really feasible only with buffered terminals.

Another factor ignored in the above is the round-trip propagation time for polling commands and responses. If this is not small compared to the response-time requirements, we cannot stand the time needed to poll each station. The assumption of small propagation time may not be valid in either satellite transmission systems or in networks using store-and-forward switching. Therefore, polling may have to be eliminated, or performed very carefully, with those transmission systems.

4.2.3 Altering Polling

As the terminal loads shift, it may be desirable to alter the polling sequence so as to minimize inbound and outbound delays. This is usually done by means of operator commands, which either specify the new polling sequence or designate an alternative sequence that is already stored in the communications controller. If extreme load conditions occur, hence threatening an overload of the central processor or some other unit, it may be desirable to reduce the frequency of polling as well [3.13].

4.2.4 Hub Polling

The overhead in polling each station and the line turnarounds involved can significantly increase response times when one has a large number of terminals on long lines. An improvement can be obtained by a "round-robin" technique called hub polling on a duplex line.

As shown in Fig. 4.1, two data paths with simultaneous transmissions in both directions are required. Each station has an extra feature on its modem (or an additional modem) enabling it to receive signals from the adjacent (upstream) station, as well as from the primary station. In the process of hub polling, the primary station first polls the most remote station via the output line. The primary says, in effect, "I am ready; do you have any data to send?" The most remote station then transmits all the messages it has accumulated since its preceding transmission. Then the transmitting station sends a "go-ahead" to the adjacent station via the input line. Each station repeats this sequence, until the closest station has sent all of its messages. When the primary station receives the "go-ahead" from the closest station, the primary again polls the most remote station. All during the process of hub polling, the primary can be sending data to any of the stations. No confusion can exist on the output line, since only the primary uses it.

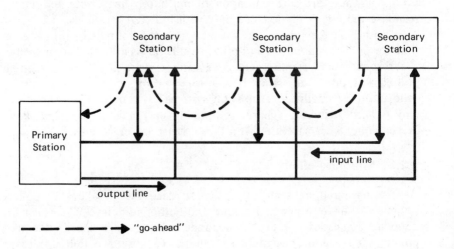

Fig. 4.1 Hub polling.

4.2.5 Loops

Another way of reducing polling overhead is through the use of a loop. An open-loop configuration is shown in Fig. 4.2. The primary station controls the loop, which passes serially through a number of secondary stations. Each secondary is a repeater for those messages destined further along the loop. The loop poll is achieved by a single command, which is passed along until a station needing to transmit is reached. Repetition of the loop poll by each station, in turn, continues until all stations have been relieved of their ready-to-send messages. There is an implicit priority determined by the position on the loop. The upstream station is always polled first when a poll is circulated around the loop. In addition, however, polling can be done by addressing a particular station.

In the loop, there is greater danger that a failure in one terminal will affect transmissions to other terminals. Various approaches, such as double loops and automatic bypass of a defective terminal or a defective portion of the loop, have been proposed. These, however, materially add to the cost of the loop, reducing its price/performance advantage.

Messages on the loop can be multiplexed, using either synchronous time-division multiplexing (STDM) or asynchronous time-division multiplexing (ATDM). These forms of multiplexing are discussed later in this chapter. A particular form of loop ATDM is discussed in Section 11.5.7.

4.2.6 How Polling Affects Architecture

Multidrop line capability, using polling, affects the architecture only at the data link control level, where protocols must be provided to give each station on the line its go-ahead signals. A discipline must be established, with appropriate protocols, to ensure that each device transmits only when it is its turn to transmit, and to fully coordinate the traffic of the

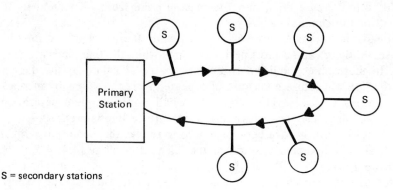

S = secondary stations

Fig. 4.2 Loop configuration

multiple stations on the line. The architecture must provide the structure for the necessary terminal addressing, indicators to transmit (polling), indicators for an end of transmission, and so forth. Every station on the multidrop line must conform to that architecture.

4.2.7   Contention Mode

In 1969, Abramson [4.3] described an alternative to polling, when a broadband transmission link serves multiple users. The technique was developed for use in satellite transmission, but could be applied in any case where the actual utilization will be a small percentage of the available bandwidth. In the ALOHA technique, no attempt is made a priori to coordinate the transmissions of the terminals. Each terminal transmits when it has something ready to be transmitted. There is, therefore, a probability that a collision will occur, and a retransmission will be necessary. The need for the retransmission, hopefully, is indicated by a failure of the check sum or a lack of an acknowledgment. If a check sum is incorrect, the receiver discards the message and the sender, after a time-out, retransmits that message.

This technique has been studied for use with broadcast repeaters in satellites or in regional radio stations. In these cases, since each transmission is repeated, the sender reads its own transmission and therefore knows if there was a conflict. If the probability of collision is low enough, then retransmissions will be infrequent and this contention mode will be satisfactory.

Abramson's analysis indicated that the channel becomes saturated when the actual load on the channel is about 18 percent of the channel capacity. This could be improved if all messages were of a fixed packet size and were synchronized to start with a common clock. The result would be to increase the channel saturation point from 18 percent to 36 percent of the channel capacity.

Loads do fluctuate, however, so that while the average load may be very small, there can be short periods of time when the line loads are very high. In these times, collision is more probable and there is the danger that the line will saturate because of repeated retransmissions by increasing numbers of users. The effects snowball until complete saturation exists. This obviously occurs when the need for a line is greatest.

Various controls have been proposed to reduce this cumulative effect and to allow a higher utilization of the channel capacity [4.4, 4.5, 4.7]. The proposal made by Binder involves a distributed control mechanism, whose purpose is to allocate time slots not in use by their owners. These available slots are assigned one at a time to each active node in a sequential round-robin manner, so that any particular node will not receive a second assignment until all the other active nodes have received one Furthermore, each node must always use its own slot before it can acquire dynamically assigned slots. Use of dynamically assigned slots may encounter conflicts, when an inactive node decides to use the slot it owns. The rule, then, is that when a conflict arises, the node assigned a slot relinquishes it.

One other conservative approach to the use of contention in multi-drop terrestrial lines is to limit the privilege of operating in contention mode to a very few users of a line, perhaps even to only one user who has a special need for operating asynchronously. The remaining users then await their polling authorization to transmit.

4.2.8 Digital Multipoint

In analog circuits, the number of stations on a multidrop line and the length of the line are limited by the noise on the line. With digital transmission (and signal regeneration rather than amplification), noise problems are greatly reduced. Accordingly, longer multidrop lines with more drops on a wider range of line speeds (for example, up to 56 kbps) will be possible.

4.3 MULTIPLEXING VERSUS CONCENTRATION

Communications controllers are frequently referred to as multiplexors or concentrators. The functions of multiplexing and/or concentration are also found in cluster controllers. This deserves clarification, along with a sorting out of different types of multiplexing and concentration and their architectural implications.

These two terms have often been used rather loosely and sometimes synonymously. In the following, we adopt the definitions given by Doll [4.1]. Multiplexing generally refers to static channel derivation schemes in which given frequency bands or time slots on a shared channel are assigned on a fixed, predetermined basis. (For example, a given terminal may always use time slot three in a cyclically repetitive arrangement of twenty time slots.) A multiplexor has the same instantaneous total input and output rate capacities. Concentration, by contrast, refers to sharing schemes in which some number of input channels dynamically share a smaller number of output channels on a demand basis. Concentration thus involves a traffic smoothing effect not characteristic of multiplexing. Since the aggregate input bit rate and output bit rate need not be matched in a concentrator, statistics and queueing play an important role.

Two examples of multiplexing are frequency-division multiplexing and synchronous time-division multiplexing. Examples of concentration include message switching, packet switching, and line switching. A hybrid sharing scheme referred to as asynchronous time-division multiplexing combines features of both multiplexing and concentration. Sometimes, in addition, polling is used to limit the inputs, so that the instantaneous input rate to the concentrator does not overrun its traffic smoothing capabilities. The common purpose of all of these processes is to efficiently share the use of a line among many messages, arriving at the multiplexor or concentration point along multiple lines.

4.4 SYNCHRONOUS TDM AND FDM

Straightforward synchronous time-division multiplexing and frequency-division multiplexing are relatively inexpensive, when compared to concentration techniques. Moreover, they cause no increase in the response time, whereas concentration can introduce a delay depending on the ratio of output capacity to aggregate input capacity.

Synchronous time-division multiplexing can be on either a bit basis or a byte basis. The basic principle of STDM is illustrated in Figs. 4.3(a) and 4.4(a), which illustrate moderate and heavy loads, respectively. With STDM, each station is assigned one time slot in each time cycle. That slot cannot be used by anyone else. In the examples of Figs. 4.3(a) and 4.4(a) there are, then, time slots that are wasted. Waste occurs when the assigned station has no data for its slots, and no other station can use them, since a time slot is reserved for each station. In newer applications [4.1] bit interleaving is used with a complete disregard for the content of the message. Thus, data transparency is an essential requirement for this type of multiplexing. The only nontransparency that can practically be accommodated is for framing characters that simply establish the beginning and end of each message.

In frequency-division multiplexing, the bandwidth of the trunk is divided into frequency channels. This is analogous to the division of the radio and television spectrum into channels for each broadcasting station. In data systems, each channel is usually assigned to a single terminal for its use in communicating to the central host. The channel may be used in half-duplex mode or in duplex mode, depending on the system design. Each channel can use independent modems and, hence, continue to operate despite failures in other channels.

It appears that time-division multiplexing can, in practice, be more efficient in the use of bandwidth than frequency-division multiplexing. The latter requires guard bands between the channels to prevent a

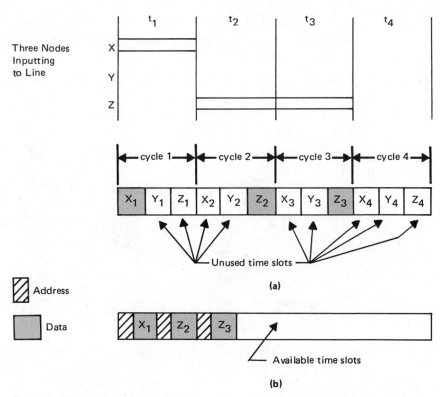

Fig. 4.3 Time-division multiplexing, moderate load: (a) synchronous; (b) asynchronous.

cross-channel interference, which imposes a practical limit on the efficiency of FDM. FDM is accordingly best suited for those situations (like satellites and CATV) where relatively large bandwidths are available and the allowable aggregate bit rate for FDM is not a constraining factor.

How synchronous multiplexing affects architecture. FDM is used in those configurations in which stations with special FM modems are multidropped on a voiceband or broadband line. The channel selection is unique to the particular link being used. A different channel could be used between each pair of nodes. FDM can thus be made part of the data link control for that link, and can be transparent to the rest of the distributed-systems architecture. For example, the logic in the intermediate nodes, which selects a particular outgoing link, can be made independent of the physical nature of the line and of the protocols of the link control, even though the end result is the selection of one FM channel on a given line.

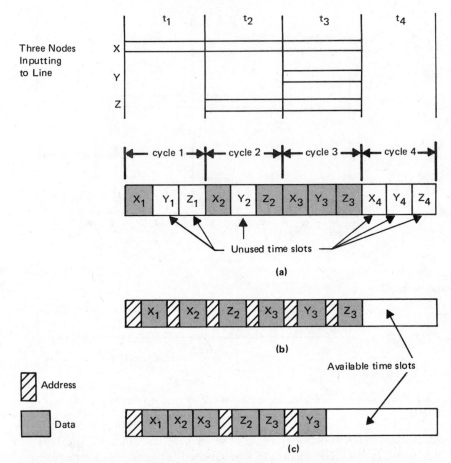

Fig. 4.4 Time-division multiplexing, heavy load: (a) synchronous; (b) asynchronous, fixed small packets; (c) asynchronous, messages of variable size.

Synchronous TDM is usually part of a point-to-point data link control. As such, its architectural effects can also be limited to that link, and not allowed to propagate into higher-level functions. If cascaded links employ STDM, then a further coordination of clocking among the data link controls for the several links is needed. Otherwise, some buffering would have to be provided to avoid a buildup of data, due to slight differences in rates of independent clocks. Since the effects of STDM are thus localized to the particular links and affect only the two end points of those links, STDM is also transparent to the rest of the system. It has no effect on the higher levels of the distributed-systems architecture.

4.5 ASYNCHRONOUS TDM AND CONCENTRATION

Many a remote terminal will actually be transmitting data less than 10 percent of the time that it is on-line. Therefore, with either frequency-division multiplexing or synchronous time-division multiplexing, the channel remains very inefficiently utilized. Asynchronous time-division multiplexing takes advantage of this fact by allocating the available time slices among only the users that are actually transmitting messages at that time (see Figs. 4.3b and 4.4b). In ATDM, addresses must accompany each message or message segment, but the sequence of stations using the line is not fixed. Any station can use the next available time on the line. Thus, the entire line capacity could be used, even when only a few of the stations are active. This, for example, might be of great use when a computer wants to send batched programs during off-peak hours.

Figures 4.3(b) and 4.4(b) illustrate the use of fixed-size packets, each containing a message or a message segment and each having an address. All transmissions can be bunched together, leaving room for any other transmissions that may also be ready. Figure 4.4(c) illustrates the same messages, bunched asynchronously, but with messages of various size. Additional buffering and buffer management are the prices that must be paid with ATDM for the better utilization of the communication line. ATDM is a form of concentration and suffers from a possibility of delay, as does all concentration. As the load and the delay build up, however, some information can still be exchanged with every station, if each station is given a turn and no packet is above a reasonable size.

4.5.1 Buffer Management

The buffer management in the concentrator must allow for the fact that at some times many devices will be transmitting on different lines simultaneously. Buffer management may also have to accommodate varying message lengths from different devices. If the concentrator itself is on a multidrop line, perhaps along with other concentrators on that same line, then the concentrator must accumulate messages and transmit them in bursts when it is polled. Thus, the amount of buffering and the complexity of the buffer management can vary considerably depending on the diversity of terminal types, line speeds, and message lengths. Therefore, it is practically necessary to place limits on the sizes of the transmitted messages and the line protocols that will be accommodated. For example, the SNA way of accommodating the variable message lengths from different types of work stations is to provide a facility for segmenting longer messages into more manageable segments. These segment sizes would be selected to fit the buffers along the path, and might also be tailored in accordance with line-reliability problems or response-time requirements. The architecture then must provide the controls necessary to identify this segmentation and to permit the reconstruction of the entire messages at the destination point.

Reassembly of segments that could arrive out of sequence, because they can take different paths, poses another set of problems. Either this out-of-sequence arrival must be prevented (as in SNA) by routing via the same physical path for each source/destination pair, or additional segment headers and buffer management must be used to reestablish the correct sequence.

4.5.2 Message and Packet Switching

In *message switching*, an entire message is sent to a centrally located node, where it is stored for as long as necessary, until an appropriate connection can be made with the destination. In the process of *packet switching*, on the other hand, the source and destination first agree to a logical connection. The message is segmented into smaller parts if that is needed to avoid monopolizing a line, and the segments, or packets, are routed through intermediate nodes in real time to the destination. Destination tables in each intermediate node permit a given message to "find its way" at each such node toward its destination. Packet switching is usually defined to require only one or two standardized packet sizes in the entire network.

A packet switching carrier may require that the user of that service do the segmenting of messages to conform to the carrier's standard-sized packets. Outside of the packet carrier, the user may still want to segment, but the user then chooses the segment size to suit his or her needs (for example, to suit buffer sizes, line reliability, or response-time requirements). Some algorithms used by packet carriers for routing segments of messages by different paths can result in segments arriving out of order at the destination.

Message switching and packet switching are functional extensions of ATDM involving the multiplexing of entire messages or segments of long messages, respectively. While there is a technical relationship among ATDM, message switching, and packet switching, the primary design objectives for each are distinctly different and the functions provided differ accordingly.

The primary objective of ATDM is efficient utilization of links. The availability of digital channels makes possible, through ATDM, the allocation of variable bandwidth on demand. The primary objective of message switching systems usually is to ensure the ultimate delivery of a message in a reasonable time which may be minutes, hours, or even days, depending on line availability and line-loading conditions. The primary objective of packet switching is to preserve fast response time, on the order of a few seconds, while reducing costs through the shared use of the lines, which can be high-speed trunks.

In line with these differing objectives, we find different amounts of message storage and different algorithms for their transmission in the three types of concentration. The message switching system, in particular, has very large amounts of secondary (usually disk or tape) storage to permit the accumulation of relatively large queues of messages. This might be appropriate, for example, to take advantage of lower transmission costs by using lines that become available only in the small hours of the morning. It might also be necessary in the event of a catastrophic line failure to one or more destinations. In the message switching system, the intermediate node that has the message switching function accepts the responsibility for the ultimate delivery. It acts as a "recovery node" in that the message is assumed to be safe and recoverable once it reaches the message switching node. In contrast to this, the packet switching system first ensures that a source-to-destination connection exists, that protocols are pre-established for an effective dialogue between source and destination, and that buffering and pacing are agreed to beforehand for efficient data flow. The buffer sizes and the queue management in multiple intermediate nodes can then be more economical. Regulations on the users can be imposed to limit segment size so as to help ensure an adequate response time for all. Response time is also aided by a link scheduler which alternates among segments of different messages. And finally, the responsibility for successful delivery of the message can be built into the protocols linking source, destination, and intermediary nodes, rather than recovery responsibility being placed on a central message switching node.

Packet systems have been implemented in two rather different configurations. Computer systems in close proximity to one another have been linked by packet-oriented ring networks [4.11]. In the ring configuration, no routing decisions are needed. Packets travel around the ring and are picked off by the addressed destination. The ARPANET, on the other hand, is an example of a mesh configuration, in which routing decisions for each packet are made at node junction points [4.12]. SNA also uses packets (though they are not called that) and also makes routing decisions at node junction points.

4.5.3 Line-switching Concentration

Not to be forgotten is the most frequently used form of concentration, involving the switched network [1.3]. This is a form of concentration only in the sense that a connection is established between a group of X-inputs to a group of Y-outputs on a demand basis, where X is typically much greater than Y. In this case, the burden of buffering, pending the availability of a connection, is placed completely on the sources. A variation of this process is obtained when one has a limited number of nonswitched lines from the central host to a remote private exchange. The many terminals connected to this remote exchange dial their connection to the central host and wait their turn (on a busy signal) if it happens that a channel to the host is not available.

4.5.4 Delay

All forms of concentration involve an exposure to delay when the aggregate inputs exceed the capacity of the line for a period of time. The delay, of course, approaches infinity if the oversubscription lasts an indefinite length of time, and is usually minimal, so long as the average utilization of the line is less than 60 percent. Beyond this point, even short periods of overload expose one to substantial delays. The approach to the saturation condition is illustrated by W. W. Chu [4.13] in Fig. 4.5, which shows the dramatic rise in delays.

In addition to this load-sensitive delay, of course, there is the delay caused by simply buffering and retransmitting (even if lines are immediately available) at each intermediary node.

4.6 POSITIONING MULTIPLEXORS OR CONCENTRATORS

Practical design experience [4.1] suggests that the cost of a network tends to a J-shaped function of the number of multiplexors and/or concentrators that are used, as shown in Fig. 4.6. In some networks, of course, it may cost more to use one multiplexor or concentrator than none.

Multiplexing and/or concentration is often readily provided as a complement to other functions, sharing resources with other functions in both the communications controller that is a front-end to a host and in the cluster controllers. These are at points of every network where it is most likely that we will have multiple inputs and will have an economic opportunity for multiplexing and/or concentration. Beyond these points, each additional multiplexor or concentrator must be carefully evaluated, and would not be used unless it produces net cost savings.

The only practical approach to a total configuration design involves an exhaustive search procedure. This must examine the alternative transmission services and successively search for the next most economic location for a multiplexor/concentrator, in the light of the tariffs for each of the alternative transmission services.

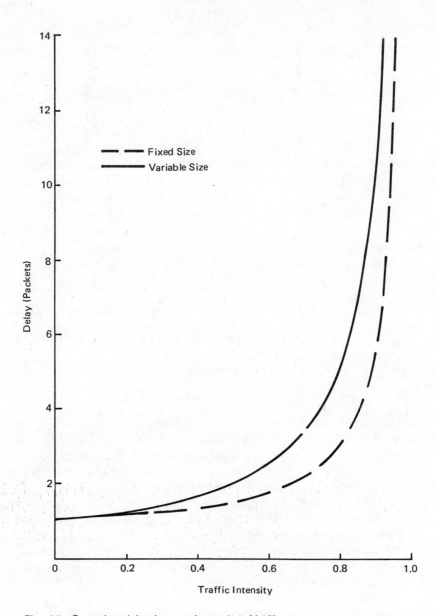

Fig. 4.5 Queueing delay in a packet switch [4.13].

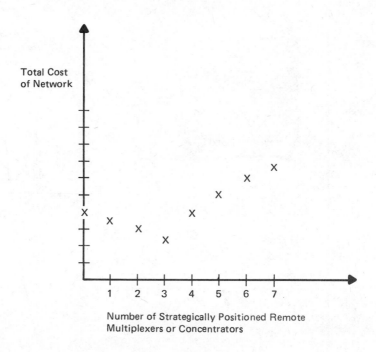

Fig. 4.6 Typical cost curve of network with multiplexers or concentrators [4.1].

Intracarrier concentration. In Fig. 3.16, for example, any of the common-carrier or PTT links shown there may, in fact, be an extensive carrier mesh network or a value-added network that employs the carrier mesh. Regardless of the complexity of that mesh or the number of intermediary nodes, with or without multiplexing or concentration that the mesh may contain, the net effect should be a transparent link in the overall system. To achieve this, most carriers have designed their networks to accept a total transmission, including all of its frame indicators, addresses, control headers, and checking bits, and to treat it simply as a bit stream, with no concern for its semantic content, once a circuit or a logical path through the common-carrier mesh has been established. This transparency is also a characteristic of newer nonswitched or switched digital data networks and of satellite systems.

4.7 EFFECTS OF DIGITAL TRANSMISSION

The tariffs of common carriers and PTTs have been such that one could realize a large reduction in the cost per bit transmitted as one moved from a low bandwidth line to a high bandwidth line (assuming good utilization of both). This cost delta provided the opportunity for gain by the use of a wide variety of techniques to improve line utilization, described above. With the introduction of digital transmission techniques (see Chapter 2), this cost delta is decreasing. It appears that, in general, there still will be a difference between the low-speed cost per bit and the high-speed cost per bit; however, the delta is decreasing, judging from proposed tariffs for new digital systems. If this trend continues, it will reduce the price that can be paid for equipment or services (external to the carrier) that improve line utilization. The result will be a need for further technology advances to reduce the costs of the techniques described in this chapter, if these techniques are to remain as attractive as they are.

The long-term effects of digital transmission will probably be in the sharing of communications facilities for voice, video, facsimile, and data. We seem to be in a period when it is advantageous to optimize ATDM systems on the assumption of data only and on the assumption of certain characteristics of data. On the other hand, the increasing diversity of the nature of information (see Section 2.3) will require that transmission capacity be rapidly switched in a time-varying manner among different types of user. This includes both users that need synchronous time division, such as voice or video, and users that benefit from asynchronous time division, such as data with high peak-to-average ratios. Digital transmission, coupled with a combination of synchronous and asynchronous time-division multiplexing, may provide the answer as digital technology progresses further.

4.8 REFERENCES AND BIBLIOGRAPHY

4.1 D. R. Doll. "Multiplexing and Concentration." In *Computer Communication* (eds., P. Green and R. Lucky). New York: IEEE Press (1975). (Figure 4.6 reprinted by permission of IEEE Press.)

4.2 N. Abramson and F. F. Kuo. *Computer Communications Networks.* Englewood Cliffs, N.J.: Prentice-Hall (1973).

4.3 N. Abramson. "Packet Switching with Satellites." *AFIPS Conference Proceedings* 42 (June 1973): 695–702.

4.4 W. Crowther, R. Rettberg, D. Walden, S. Ornstein, and F. Heart. "A System for Broadcast Communication: Reservation ALOHA." *Proceedings of the Sixth Hawaii International Conference On System Sciences* (January 1973): 371–374.

4.5 L. Roberts. "Dynamic Allocation of Satellite Capacity Through Packet Reservation." *AFIPS Conference Proceedings* 42 (June 1973): 711.

4.6 L. Kleinrock and S. Lam. "Packet Switching in a Slotted Satellite Channel." *AFIPS Conference Proceedings* **42** (June 1973): 703.

4.7 R. Binder. "A Dynamic Packet Switching System for Satellite Broadcast Channels." *IEEE 1975 Communications Conference* **III** (16–18 June 1975): 41-1.

4.8 E. V. Stelmah. *Introduction to Minicomputer Networks.* Maynard, Mass.: Digital Equipment Corporation (1974).

4.9 "A Microprocessor-based Packet Switching System." *Mini Micro Systems* (May 1976): 34–36.

4.10 S. M. Ornstein, F. E. Heart, W. R. Crowther, H. K. Rising, S. B. Russell, and A. Michel. "The Terminal IMP for the ARPA Computer Network." *Proceedings AFIPS 1972 SJCC* **40:** 243–254.

4.11 J. F. Hayes. "Performance Models of an Experimental Computer Communications Network." *Bell System Tech. J.* **53,** No. 2 (February 1974): 225–259.

4.12 S. R. Kimbleton and G. M. Schneider. "Computer Communications Networks: Approaches, Objectives, and Performance Considerations." *ACM Computing Surveys* **7,** No. 3 (September 1975).

4.13 W. W. Chu. "A Study of Asynchronous Time-Division Multiplexing for Time-shared Computer Systems." *AFIPS Conf. Proc.* **35** (1969): 669.

4.14 W. R. Crowther, F. E. Heart, A. A. McKenzie, J. M. McQuillan, and D. C. Walden. "Issues in Packet Switching Network Design." *AFIPS Conference Proceedings,* 1975 National Computer Conference, **44:** 161–175.

4.15 F. Diamond, R. Johnson, and D. McAuliffe. "Some Recent Applications of Automatic Data Processing in Telecommunications." *IEEE 1974 National Telecommunications Conference,* San Diego, California.

5
System
Objectives
Summary

5.1 INTRODUCTION

This chapter summarizes basic system objectives and design questions in the light of the preceding chapters. These amount to a set of value judgments on what is important in system design and in the formulation of an architecture for distributed systems. A discussion of migration objectives then completes the chapter and Part 1.

5.2 GENERAL DESIGN OBJECTIVES

From the preceding chapters, it is possible to establish a set of general design objectives. The key points are summarized in the following discussion.

Dependability. Data-processing systems have become increasingly essential to the day-by-day and even hour-by-hour operations of corporations. The architecture must provide for the following.

1. A very high probability of continuous availability for a specified subset of the total network functional capability

2. Autonomous recovery from errors at the lowest functional level feasible, with no effect on higher functional levels

3. A systematic passage of error/status information to higher levels for those cases where recovery is not achievable at the lower level and must be handled at a higher functional level.

Examples of specific facilities aimed at these objectives are the automatic retransmission at the data link control level, an alternate path capability at the path control level, and a definite-response capability at the level of the network addressable unit.

Price/performance.   Continued emphasis will be placed on total cost and on performance in its broadest sense of the value to the user. System structures that help to reduce costs for systems development, operation, and maintenance are particularly important to the improvement of overall price/performance.

Accessibility and usability.   Encouraged by the decreasing cost of compute-power, new classes of users find data processing and network services economical and useful. The growth in the number of users depends, particularly, on the usability of the system, because of a limited skill level among new users. Complexity of the system that is irrelevant to the use of the system must therefore be shielded from the user. The use of the system, for example, should be completely independent of system configuration and destination location. Well-defined user interfaces should have subsets for users with different skills. Of importance also are services that (1) prompt the user (on request), (2) minimize the amount of information the user must have about the network and the service being employed, and (3) accommodate the language that the user is accustomed to using.

Changeability.   DP/C systems are characterized by growth and change. The systems structure must facilitate the tailoring of the system design, in both hardware and programming, to meet the evolving needs of the individual installations. Applications must be permitted to be independent of the communications system and, to a large extent, independent of the peculiar characteristics of the remote end-users. Communication function and protocols should be largely independent of box architecture (hardware and software) and independent of the user-interfaces employed in individual products.

Each major level of the systems structure should be able to be changed without substantially affecting other layers of the structure. For example, data link control should be independent of path control and each of these, in turn, should be independent of the application and its presentation services. More of the changes should be possible via operator command, providing a more dynamic rebuild, rather than by a completely new systems definition.

Diversity of function.   Different application areas, system configurations, and device types will require increasingly diverse communications facilities. The large number of necessary options must be organized in a systematic hierarchy to avoid unnecessary proliferation of options. To promote more general communicability (ideally, an ability for any unit to talk to any other unit), common sets of options must be established, at least within product and/or user groups.

Distributed function. Improving hardware costs permit an increase in the amount of distributed function, including both compute power and data storage, in high-function terminals, in cluster controllers, and in remote subsystems in general. Simplified subsets of a total network architecture can facilitate a more economic growth of smaller, independent subnetworks. Subsequent coalescence into larger networks will be facilitated if the architectural subsets are chosen with this eventuality in mind.

Multiple domains. Different portions of a network can be expected to grow autonomously, for a time, with a subsequent coalescence. Even in a united network, there will always be justification for a degree of uniqueness within subnets of the whole. The total network architecture must be prepared to accommodate the following.

1. *Different addressing domains:* Where simplified or specialized addressing may be appropriate for a subnet.
2. *Multiple control domains:* Where resource control is regionalized and a coordination among peer control points is therefore required.

Diversity of transmission facilities. The structure must permit the exploitation of different transmission services in different parts of the same network and must readily change that service as the circumstance warrants it. The primary choices to be anticipated include:

1. Choice of communications carrier (for example, a terrestrial voice carrier, a terrestrial digital-service carrier, a satellite carrier, a packet carrier, or a value-added special-service carrier).
2. Choice of service of a particular carrier (for example, nonswitched or switched service), and a particular bandwidth depending on tariffs, geographic dispersion of destinations, and anticipated traffic.
3. Private, in-house transmission systems.

Important to this freedom of choice is the development of a minimum number of common interfaces for physical connections to a variety of transmission services, such as nonswitched, switched, packet, and value-added networks.

5.3 KEY DESIGN QUESTIONS

The preceding chapters highlight the concept of general communicability. The need for general communicability among multiple programs, operators, and storage media at many nodes raises the following design and architectural questions.

1. What end-to-end protocols will provide for *communication of data* between programs in nodes having different processor architectures, different user languages, and different programming support? The communication protocols must be independent of these node characteristics.

2. What common formats and protocols, independent of end-user peculiarities, are desirable for *selecting* and *controlling* devices, data sets, and programs?

3. Since diverse devices, data sets, and programs will have unique control protocols, how can the necessary translations, *from common network terms to unique end-user terms*, be accommodated? How can data be *mapped* to the presentation space of each end-user?

This must be done in a way that will not burden the writers of application programs or needlessly restrict the creation of new devices. Such a service must itself be readily changeable. Moreover, the insertion of a new presentation service should not affect transmission services.

4. How can *agreement* be reached, between two parties desiring to communicate, on the common message structures to be used and on the complementary facilities each will use to regulate the conversation and achieve recovery when needed?

5. Who *owns* the various resources in the network and who has responsibility for their allocation? Should this responsibility be centralized, or distributed, or a combination of both?

6. What *system services* should be provided for the establishment of physical connections, in configuring and reconfiguring the system, for starting up and shutting down the system, for establishing logical connections, for system recovery, and for monitoring the operations of the network so as to permit its optimization?

7. What transmission protocols will provide adequate *path finding* and *sharing* of links and parts of the same route, so that many different conversations can be simultaneously conducted between pairs of end-users? (This should permit one end-user to conduct multiple conversations simultaneously with multiple other end-users.)

5.4 MIGRATION OBJECTIVES

Data-processing/communication networks usually grow over a period of many years. It is inevitable, therefore, that many networks will consist of combinations of old equipment and new equipment, with old line disciplines alongside the new and, therefore, old protocols alongside the new. Older systems [5.1], for example, frequently grew to contain a number of distinct and logically separate subnetworks such as those illustrated in Fig. 5.1. Different access methods, different communication protocols, and

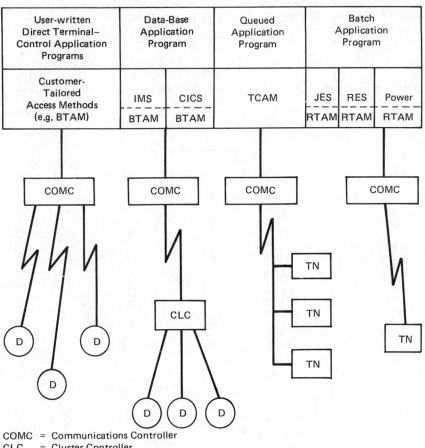

User-written Direct Terminal–Control Application Programs	Data-Base Application Program		Queued Application Program	Batch Application Program		
Customer-Tailored Access Methods (e.g. BTAM)	IMS	CICS	TCAM	JES	RES	Power
	BTAM	BTAM		RTAM	RTAM	RTAM

COMC = Communications Controller
CLC   = Cluster Controller
TN   = Terminal Node
D   = Device

Fig. 5.1 A pre-SNA network might involve several different, isolated, TP access methods, as many as six communication-line protocols, plus terminals and lines that are dedicated to specific application programs.

terminals and lines that were restricted to specific application programs characterized this conglomerate.

The goal is to move toward a common communications protocol, and to permit sharing of communications facilities among application programs and among terminals, as illustrated in Fig. 5.2. The common architecture would permit any terminal to obtain the services of any

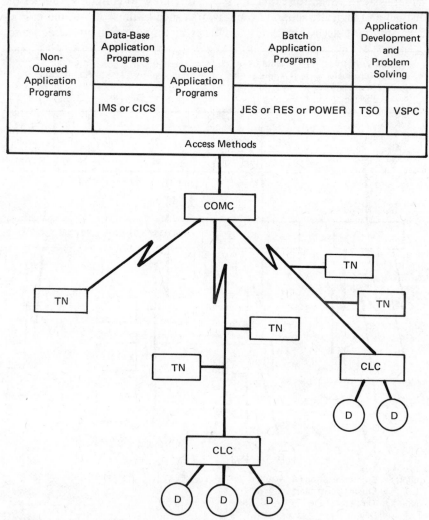

Fig. 5.2 Migration to a system that logically appears as shown, with the ability to share lines and communications controllers, and with the ability for any end-user to have access to any program.

application. Of course, any combination of communications controllers and either point-to-point or multidrop lines might be used. If multiple access methods (for example, TCAM and VTAM) are used, then interdomain coordination is necessary to achieve this accessibility.

Moving to a structure wherein all lines and terminals are accessible to all applications could mean major rewrites of those applications that have the specifics of the communications network imbedded in the application program itself. In the case where direct terminal control is deeply incorporated in the application program, or where custom-tailored access methods are used, one must either maintain separate networks for those applications or rewrite the applications.

On the other hand, for the remainder of the applications, application-rewrites can be avoided. With the advent of intermediary service programs, which absorb the specifics of lines and terminals, it is possible to make such a transition by replacing the intermediary programs without requiring any modification to the interface between these programs and the applications. Thus, one rewrite of an intermediary program permits us to leave intact a very large number of application programs. This is the case, for example, when using application subsystems such as IMS, CICS, JES, etc., which contain presentation services and shield the user from line and device characteristics [2.32, 3.5, 3.11].

The sharing of lines and terminals can be coordinated by a common access method. For example, an access method such as VTAM can provide sharing among application subsystems and applications. [Old applications that embed direct control of devices (for example, those using BTAM) are necessarily excluded.] The application subsystems shown using a common access method (and hence sharing lines) in Fig. 5.2, for example, include a data-base subsystem, a remote job entry subsystem, an application development subsystem, and a problem-solving subsystem. Alternatively, different access methods such as TCAM and VTAM can coexist side by side, in which case line sharing needs a coordination between the two resource managers (in effect, a multiple domain networking capability).

In addition, communications controllers can be designed to accommodate multiple line disciplines. In some cases, these diverse disciplines can be converted there, to a common form, so as to shield the remainder of the system from this diversity. In still other cases, simple coexistence with different subnets having different protocols is the proper solution.

On the one hand, the architecture must provide a more unified total structure so that, in time, we can achieve a reduction of the unnecessary architectural proliferation that has characterized many evolving systems. On the other hand, realistically, a degree of coexistence must be designed into the structure in order to provide a practical set of migration paths toward the desired architectural integration. Coexistence is needed for multiple control points, and coordination among at least the newer forms of control points is a growing requirement.

For the future, also, the architecture must facilitate a type of sub-function coexistence in recognition of the fact that different options will be optimum in different circumstances. The future type of coexistence, however, should be organized as part of the new architecture's layering concepts, with different functional subsets coexisting within the appropriate layers.

5.5 REFERENCES AND BIBLIOGRAPHY

5.1 J. P. Gray and C. R. Blair. "IBM's Systems Network Architecture." *Datamation* **21,** No. 4 (April 1975): 51–56.

Part 2
The Architectural Layers

Many of the principles of architecture for distributed systems are presented in this part by describing the basic concepts and facilities of a specific architecture, namely, the Systems Network Architecture (SNA). Comparisons to other architectures are included. The material reflects the fact that SNA is continuing to evolve by integrating the better elements of the experience to date and through the provision of structure that permits growth into newer areas.

In Chapter 6, the systems network architecture is described first in terms of basic concepts: network addressable units, sessions, functional layers, peer protocols, function subsets, and control domains. In Chapters 7 and 8, the outer layers of the SNA network are described, along with their relation to the end-users. The higher-level services—to match end-users to one another, to establish logical connections among end-users, and to regulate the data flows for the end-users—are examined.

Chapter 9 then studies the protocols (i.e., agreements between two parties) and the headers used in the transmission control layer. These protocols serve to coordinate the operation of a session. In concert with network services, these protocols also help to execute the session initiation and termination procedures. Chapter 10 describes the path control function which provides for a duplex path between transmission control elements. Path control, operating in all intermediary nodes as well as source and destination nodes, controls routing and address translation. Chapter 11 then describes how data link control manages the use of the line, maximizes line efficiency, and copes with a basically error-prone line to provide reliable transmission.

6
Basic Concepts of Systems Network Architecture

6.1 INTRODUCTION*

First, let us consider the communication between two persons. There, we can easily recognize an interaction at three levels:

1. *The cognitive level,* involving knowledge and understanding.
2. *The language level,* involving syntax and semantics of the language used, such as French or German.
3. *The signal level,* involving a transport mechanism, such as acoustics or writing.

Note first that these levels are largely independent of one another. Hence, one can use the same transport mechanism with either French or German, and alternate transport mechanisms could be used with a given language.

Note also that the sender and the receiver establish a match at each of the three levels. There are, in effect, a set of agreements (or protocols) that sender and receiver abide by at each of the three levels. *The lower levels are used by the upper levels and there is a sender-receiver dialogue at each of the three levels.*

In person-to-person communication, in the same room, there are a variety of languages and signals in use. Eye, facial, and body movements augment the spoken word, which can have many tones and variations. The

---

*The author is indebted to E. M. Thomas for the benefit of his writings on SNA structure, and his comments on the material in this chapter.

dialogue proceeds with two-way flow of information, including immediate acknowledgments and other signals of understanding or concern. It can be a fairly broadband, noise-free, and well-paced interchange.

In remote communication between persons, the bandwidth becomes more limited, noise on the channel increases, the transmission error probability increases, acknowledgment techniques are more limited, and delay in transmission may become an important factor. A more constrained dialogue discipline and a more explicit acknowledgment are needed. Greater care must also be exercised that the rate of information flow is not too great.

One or both ends of the communication may be a program, a storage device, or an operator at a device such as a display or printer. *Then additional protocols between sender and receiver must be explicit even to the smallest detail.* Serving the end-user are an explicit set of communications-related functions dealing with:

1. *The language,* possibly including formatting, translation, or editing services.

2. *Dialogue discipline,* to control the data flow (e.g., taking turns, waiting for responses).

3. *Transmission control,* including (a) *flow rate control* to suit end-to-end flow handling capabilities, and (b) *sequence control,* to ensure error-free end-to-end transmission.

4. *Transportation,* including passage of signals through a more or less complex transmission network, between units that are addressable.

Multiple dialogues, or sessions, may exist concurrently between any one addressable unit and others. Network services (analogous to the telephone operator) are needed to facilitate controlled use of the network. Other network services, normally invisible to the end-user, are needed for system maintenance, configuration change, etc.

The systems network architecture defines sets of communications-related *functions* that are distributed throughout a network; it also defines the *formats and protocols* that relate these distributed functions to one another. The objective is to achieve a general ability to communicate reliably among programs, device operators, and storage media, which may be located anywhere in the network. An implemented system that complies with the systems network architecture is called an *SNA network.* This may be implemented by a wide range of products in different combinations. Sufficient parts of such a system must be formally architected to allow proper communication between different participants in the network. However, it should not be inferred that *everything* within an

SNA network is defined completely by the architecture; some functions and/or adaptors are best left to be defined by product designers or users. It is primarily the key formats and protocols, needed for general communicability, that are architected. SNA seeks to provide a structure for communication having the following attributes. The SNA network should appear to be highly transparent. Any bit stream should be allowed, and the end-users should not normally be concerned with network topology, route selection, or media used. The characteristics of the end-users may be very diverse and changeable; still, the SNA network should facilitate the masking of characteristics (such as device peculiarities and codes used) that are not relevant to the other user. The network should facilitate the provision of important services, including safeguards for data integrity, end-to-end recovery, end-to-end data security, end-to-end flow rate control, and user-specific data formatting. Services should be optionally selectable; and it should be possible to subdivide the responsibility for SNA network management to suit the organization of the users.

The architecture can be understood in terms of six concepts:

1. Network addressable units
2. Sessions
3. Functional layers
4. Peer protocols
5. Function subsets within each layer
6. Control domains

In this chapter, an overall SNA perspective is first obtained by generally defining and describing these concepts as a base for more specific descriptions in subsequent chapters.

Typical nodes of one domain of an SNA network are shown in Fig. 6.1. Each node will contain an instance (or element) of some of the SNA functional layers. The elements of each layer in one node communicate with their peer elements for that same layer in other nodes. Within each of these layers, there may be available a number of alternative function subsets. Nodes of the SNA network, furthermore, are grouped into control domains for the coordination of network operations. There may be many such domains with users in different domains communicating with each other.

6.2 NETWORK ADDRESSABLE UNITS

We must be able to configure the system with a wide variety of nodes and distributed functions. This calls for an architecture of general communicability among programs, device operators, and storage media. General

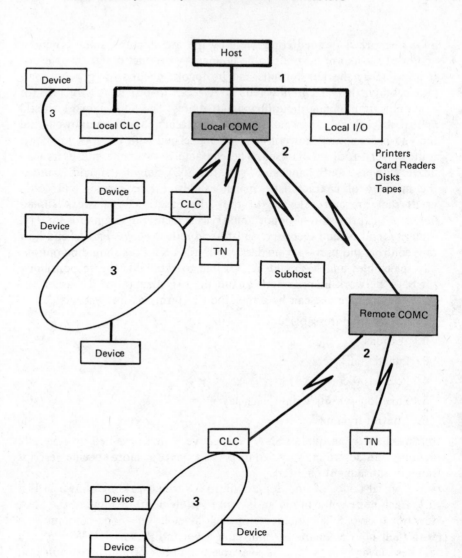

COMC = Communications Controller
CLC   = Cluster Controller
TN   = Terminal Node

Fig. 6.1 Three subnetworks, emanating from (1) host, (2) communications controllers, and (3) cluster controllers.

communicability can be expressed in terms of communication among coded entities that are directly addressable, that is, among what SNA calls the network addressable units (NAUs).

The NAU may be thought of as *a location in the SNA network that supports one or more ports for communication via the network.* The NAU is a relatively fixed thing, although new ones may be dynamically added. The outermost layer of each NAU is called *NAU services* and the outermost component in NAU services, at the boundary to the end-user, is called the *NAU services manager* (see Fig. 6.2). *Each NAU has a network address.* By definition, the NAU services manager provides a boundary to the SNA network. All end-users of the SNA network theoretically interface to one of these NAU services managers. (In practice, however, the NAU services manager may be transparent for some logical connections.) An end-user may always interface to the network through the same NAU, or the end-user may move from one NAU to another. In more sophisticated situations, an end-user might interface to several NAUs concurrently.

To reiterate, the NAU is a set of functions that provides one or more ports in the SNA network; the outermost layer of the NAU is NAU services; and each NAU is associated with a network address.

The network address is used internally within the SNA network to route messages between NAUs. It may be changed at the discretion of the network manager, without affecting the end-user operation. Each NAU also has a network name. Some implementations also provide for the use of alternate names which can be convenient identifiers for the users of the network. The network addresses can be changed without changing the names, but the correlation of name and network address

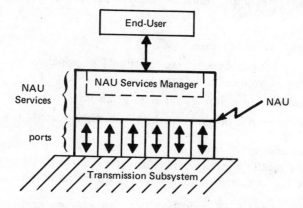

Fig. 6.2 The NAU, providing one or more ports in the SNA network.

must be known to the network services. (The network services are described in Chapter 7.) Different end-users may know an NAU by different names. These alternatives to the network name need not be understood by the NAU in question, but again the correlation of names must be known to network services. The NAU user requesting establishment of a network connection must know (or be told) the network name (or a recorded alternate name) of the destination NAU.

This three-level structure of alternate names, network names, and network address provides an advantageous freedom. As we shall discuss in Chapter 15, alternate names need to be unique only among users of a NAU; coordination across domains can be done using network names, and network addresses can change independently as configurations change.

Two NAU services managers (each within the NAU services of a different NAU) interact with each other through a set of functions called a session. The functions of the session define a logical connection between two NAU. One session exists per pair of NAU. Each NAU, however, can support multiple sessions, each session being associated with an NAU of a different destination. Thus, as shown in Fig. 6.3, the NAUs provide multiple ports for access to the inner layers of the SNA network. The objective is to achieve general communicability among end-users via the NAU services. In some cases, however, communication may be between a pair of NAU services with no involvement of end-users.

Communication among NAUs must encompass all of the situations described in the configuration evolution in Chapter 3. These configurations require NAUs to exist in different types of node, such as hosts, cluster controllers, subhosts, and terminal nodes (see Section 3.6). Different NAUs, for example, must be able to provide ports for any of the following:

- An application program
- An application subsystem (see Section 3.4), which in turn represents a group of application programs and/or devices
- An operator or a storage medium at an input/output device
- A system service program, such as data management

As we saw in Chapter 3, multiple application programs, multiple devices, and multiple service programs can exist in a single physical node. The desire for general communicability requires an architecture that

1. Facilitates the communication between any two end-users that are connected via network addressable units (NAUs) in the network.

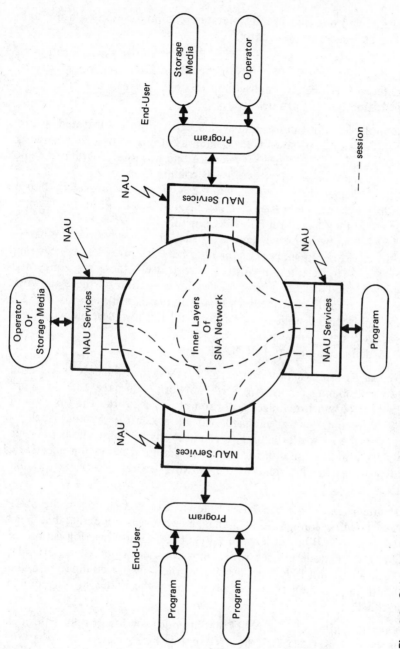

Fig. 6.3 Objective of general communicability among end-users via network addressable units.

2. Permits any one end-user to maintain communication with multiple other end-users, concurrently.

3. Provides this communication regardless of the physical location of the end-user or of the network configuration, regardless of the existence of one or more intermediate nodes, and regardless of the number of links involved.

The general communicability that is desired is simply illustrated in Fig. 6.3 by the existence of concurrent communications among four network addressable units. Each NAU may service one or more programs, or one or more operators at devices, or a combination of programs and operators. *Whether simple or complex, the NAU is a named entity that is addressable by any other NAU of the SNA network.* A given physical box (or node) may have multiple NAUs within it.

The SNA network serves end-users that are considered to be external to the network. In support of this, the network provides services that are considered to be internal to the network itself; these are concerned with management of the network. For the execution of these network services, the transmission facilities of the network will be needed [6.9]. Network addressable units are therefore needed for these network services, as well as for end-users.

SNA defines three types of NAU.

1. *System Services Control Point (SSCP):* A special-purpose NAU used for network management. An SNA network can have one or more SSCPs, each of which manages a portion of the network. The function of the SSCP is the general management of a control domain, such as bringing up the network, helping to establish logical connections between other NAUs, and helping in recovery and maintenance, when necessary. It also provides the interface to the network operator services for that domain.

2. *Physical Unit (PU):* An NAU that acts as a companion to the SSCP in SNA network configuration management. Each node that has been defined to an SSCP has at least one PU. The PU provides a location for configuration-related services which must be performed at a particular node. An SSCP and PUs together control the network configuration and the data-transportation resources provided by the nodes in the domain of the SSCP.

3. *Logical Unit (LU):* An NAU that provides windows or ports through which the end-user accesses the SNA network. The LU is also the port through which an end-user accesses SSCP-provided services to help in establishing logical connections between LUs. The LU may support

communication between end-users (or LUs) by editing or transforming the requests, grouping requests, correlating responses with requests, and otherwise bridging from the environment of the end-user.

Though structurally similar, each NAU type has a distinct network service in its NAU services layer. The relationships among SSCPs, PUs, and LUs will be discussed in Section 7.3. The functions of the PU depend on the nature of the transmission services in the node that the PU serves. The functions in LUs depend on the nature of the end-users they serve. In the following chapters, sets of architected functions which may optionally be in NAUs are described.

The number of LUs in a node is implementation-dependent. The process for creating or deleting an LU and the procedure for associating a given end-user with an LU can also be product-unique.

6.3 END-USERS

We reserve the term *end-user* for that source or destination of information that is external to the SNA network. As shown in Fig. 6.3, it may be a program, or an operator at an input/output device, or a storage medium such as cards, disks, or tapes. *Often, however, any of these can be represented by code or logic which then appears to be the end-user.* Any end-user should be able to establish communication with another end-user via the SNA network if the originating LU knows (or can be told) only the network name of the LU supporting that other end-user, or some alternate name that is also known to the SSCP of the originating end-user. (The name of the destination end-user is sometimes used as an alternate LU name.)

Program end-users. The most general form of end-user is a program. It may be a simple application program, or, on the other hand, it may be complex, having multiple levels that are not apparent to the SNA network. These might, for example, consist of functions within an application subsystem that serve multiple message processors. The program end-user may also interface to other input/output devices that are not visible to the SNA network. An example of this is a data-management program that interfaces via its private services to storage devices. Another example is a program in a cluster controller which, in turn, privately manages local devices.

Whether the program is simple or complex, each program end-user interacts with the NAU services. This interaction includes data exchange and also the occasional exchange of commands and indicators for control of SNA functions. The format of that control interaction can be product-unique; however, SNA specifies the information needed for this control (depending on the SNA functions selected).

Operator end-user.   The second possible form of end-user that interfaces to the SNA network is a human operator. In this case, certain functions within the work station, terminal, or device are considered to be logically part of the SNA network.

When dealing with a device, we must distinguish between the function being performed and the mechanism being used. For example, the function to select a particular item may be implemented using a light pen, a function key, a joystick, or numerous other electromechanical operations. The selection function has a place in the architecture; the means for its implementation is not architected. In this case, where the operator is to be the end-user, a boundary exists between a human operator and the NAU services, and that boundary may also be product-unique. Again, code or logic may be an intermediary and thus act as the end-user.

Media end-users.   The third possible form of end-user is a storage medium, such as tapes, disks, cards, etc. This may operate directly via a network addressable unit and SNA protocols, or, as noted above, it may be hidden from the network but accessed via a program that acts as the end-user of the network. If the medium operates directly via an NAU, then a boundary exists, for that product, between the medium and the NAU services. Otherwise, it is a program that has a boundary to the NAU services.

End-user components.   A single end-user may have multiple components. An application subsystem (like IMS), as an end-user, includes multiple message-processing programs as its components. An operator at a work station, as an end-user, may use multiple I/O mechanisms, such as a printer, a display, or a card punch. A data-management service, as an end-user, may define its components as data sets or other data structures. Hence, the architecture must also provide for *distinctive handling of a message depending on the selection of components that are within or available to an end-user.* The architecture must, accordingly, facilitate the addressing of end-user components in a manner appropriate to the end-user. (The related subjects of FM headers and presentation services will be covered in Chapter 7.)

End-user content and packaging.   As seen above, the end-user can have a wide variety of forms and components. The architecture of the SNA network puts no restrictions on the functions within the end-user or on the format of the interface to the end-user (though standards among groups of end-users are, as usual, advantageous). Therefore, *the key concept must be an architected definition only of the protocols and formats for message flows between NAUs;* the remainder (the end-user and its interface) is not architected.

The end-user is external to the NAU, even though the end-user and the NAU may sometimes be physically packaged together. Figure 6.4(a)

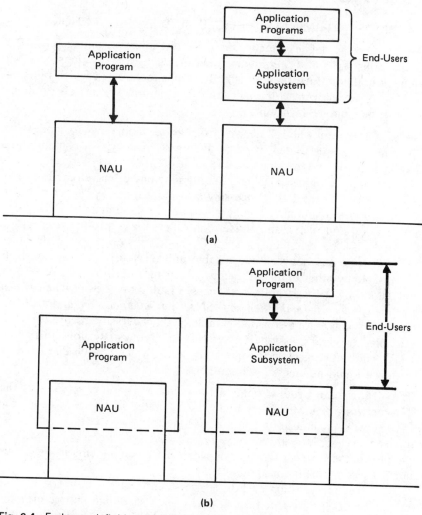

Fig. 6.4 End-user definitions: (a) NAU shown as separate from application subsystem and application program; (b) implementations where application subsystem or application program provides some of the NAU functions.

shows the idealized relationship between an end-user and the NAU, where the application program and the application subsystem are separate from the NAU. *In practice, the implementation often packages a portion of the NAU functions within the application subsystem or within the application program, as shown in Fig. 6.4(b). Such packaging does not affect the functional definitions or structure of the architecture and the inter-NAU protocols remain the same.*

6.4 NODES, TERMINALS, DEVICES, AND WORK STATIONS

An architecture defines function and the relationships among functions. Such terms as nodes, terminals, devices, and work stations are not architectural concepts; they are simply names for units in which function resides. A key concept is the fact that SNA permits various distributions of functions among such units.

Nodes. The term "node" derives from graph theory, where nodes are the junction points joined by links. Figure 6.1 is a typical configuration diagram showing connections among nodes.

The node is a physical package containing one or more functions that are important to the data-processing/communications system. Examples are host nodes (containing a general-purpose, self-sufficient CPU), communications controllers, and cluster controllers for controlling a group of terminals. To be classified as an SNA node, however, the node must house at least one network addressable unit (NAU). That is, it must be addressable by other units in the network, using a network address that is understood by the transmission services. In addition, *an SNA node must use the protocols established by SNA for internode communication.* Specifically, these are associated with defined headers and record formats. Examples are Transmission Headers (THs), Request/Response Headers (RHs), and network service commands, all of which will be discussed in Section 6.8 and defined subsequently.

SNA-defined and product-defined interactions. Various services of the SNA network reside in every node, as illustrated in Fig. 6.5; hence the SNA network includes a portion of each node, as well as the actual links between nodes. *SNA-defined commands and indicators flow across the interface between nodes,* flowing between SNA components in one node and SNA components in another node.

The boundary within each node, between the SNA network and the remainder of each node, is necessarily *product-unique;* therefore, the *format* of that boundary is not defined by SNA. This is the boundary between the end-user and the NAU services mentioned previously (see Section 7.2).

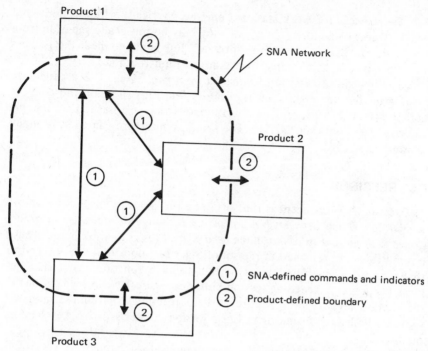

Product 1

2

SNA Network

1

Product 2

2

1

1

1

SNA-defined commands and indicators

2 Product-defined boundary

2

Product 3

Fig. 6.5 SNA defines commands and indicators that flow (primarily) across inter-node interfaces.

SNA services draw on the resources (such as storage or processor power) of the node in which they are housed. This may, for example, occur as a consequence of the receipt of an SNA command. These resources may be statically or dynamically assigned in different products. If the assignment is dynamic, requests for these resources are by non-SNA protocols that are unique to the product.

Terminal, device, or work station. These are units that contain a physical I/O mechanism, such as a keyboard, display, printer, or badge reader, that is serviced by a network addressable unit. However, these mechanisms may depend on a physically separate node, such as a controller or a CPU, for their operation. Different implementations may divide function differently between terminals, devices, or work stations, on the one hand, and controllers or CPUs, on the other hand. That is, the function of the network addressable unit (NAU) may be either wholly contained within terminals, devices, or work stations, or may be split between these and their associated controllers or CPUs.

The devices (or work stations) may be physically within a node that provides network addressability, or they may be physically separate from that node. In the latter case, a "private" link must connect the devices and the network addressable unit that is within the node.

Thus, again, *architecture is distinct from packaging.* The architecture focuses on the commands and indicators that must flow on the connections between NAUs, and on the functions that are needed to support message flows between NAUs. The same architecture can exist in many different packages.

6.5 SESSIONS

The second basic concept is that of a session. *The session is a temporary logical connection between NAUs for an exchange of messages in accordance with ground rules that have been agreed to for that exchange.* These ground rules are reflected in the set of SNA functions that are devoted to that session. The ground rules pertain to such functions as pacing the ,flows (to prevent exceeding session buffer capacities), recovery facilities at the session level, waiting for responses, groupings of requests and responses, and data formatting. *Each session connects two NAU services managers.*

The execution of a session is analogous to a human conversation, which consists of a dialogue between two people who are equipped to understand each other. Eventually, one of the two parties decides to terminate the conversation and perhaps start a conversation with someone else. An example of this is the case of a bank official who initiates a session with an application program for a new account. The official processes a whole series of new-account transactions over an extended period of time. The official might then terminate that session and initiate a different one, dealing with a loan or investment application. Another series of transactions may proceed within the second session. (It should be mentioned, however, that a new session is not always required in this situation. In some cases, an application subsystem such as IMS or CICS provides access to multiple application programs without requiring the establishment of a new session. In that case, the single session is between the LU supporting IMS or CICS and the LU supporting the bank official.

Architecturally, the session is the set of SNA functions that are used to support the interaction between two NAU services managers. The session is composed of two half-sessions, each being the user-oriented functions at one end of the interaction. This is illustrated in Fig. 6.6. There, we see two sessions; each session connects two NAU services managers and is composed of two half-sessions. The pair of half-sessions

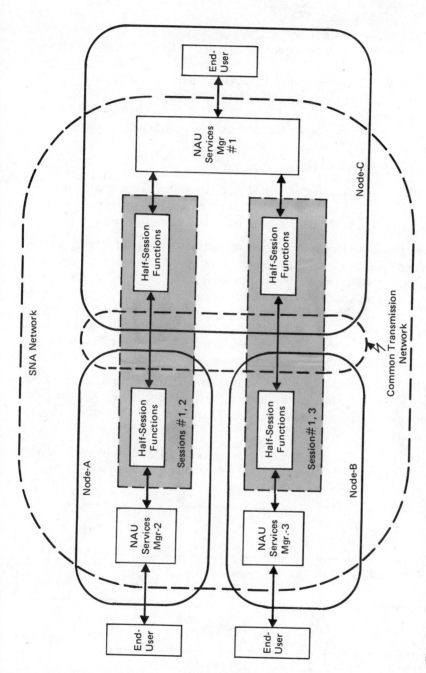

Fig. 6.6   Basic session structure in an SNA network.

provide *end-to-end services*, which may be tailored to serve end-users or NAU services managers. *A pair of half-sessions thus is a pair of matched ports.*

A session is uniquely identified by the pair of network addresses for the NAUs engaged in a session. This pair (for example, session 1,3 in Fig. 6.6) is called the Session ID (SID). That ID can also be used to reference all of the various elements that are part of a particular session.

6.6 DISTRIBUTED SNA SERVICES

An SNA network provides sets of distributed services to facilitate meaningful dialogues between pairs of users. First let us distinguish between two kinds of service: transmission services and end-to-end services.

Transmission services.   Having to do with the passage of messages along a route from origin to destination, these services include (among other things) the *management of links between nodes and the routing of messages, at every node,* so as to place each message on the right link or at the right half-session within a destination node. Such transmission services are distributed to adjacent nodes (see Fig. 6.7), and the functional interaction is between processes in adjacent nodes. Transmission services serve all who may share the use of a given link or route.

End-to-end services.   These services, on the other hand, cater to the needs of the origin and destination, and are distributed primarily between origin and destination nodes. There are two types of end-to-end services:

1. User-oriented end-to-end services are tailored to suit the needs of two end-users whose LUs are in session with each other.

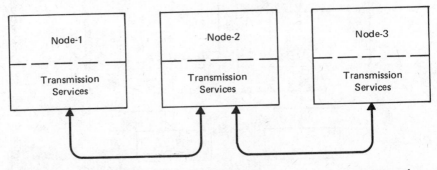

Fig. 6.7 Transmission-services function distribution requires complementary functions in adjacent nodes.

2. System services exist for the benefit of the network as a whole, and they too operate as origin-destination pairs.

As shown in Fig. 6.6, end-to-end services reside in the half-sessions and in the NAU services managers. Per-session end-to-end services reside in the half-sessions; per-NAU services, on the other hand, reside in NAU services managers.

One example of per-session user-oriented end-to-end services is called presentation services. These may format or otherwise manipulate the data in a message, so as to make the data more meaningful to the end-users. End-to-end services are distributed as a matched pair (see Fig. 6.8) with function in the origin NAU, the destination NAU, or both. The functional interaction is between processes in the origin and destination NAUs, irrespective of the number of intermediate nodes in between. As shown in Fig. 6.8, the distribution of function in these two NAUs is variable and need not be equal.

The best example of system services is called network services. These are distributed throughout the network for purposes of network/resource management. Examples are services for session establishment and physical configuration activation. Some network services are located in SSCPs; some may be distributed among multiple SSCPs; others are distributed to logical units (LUs) and physical units (PUs) throughout the network. Network services are an example of end-to-end services, existing as function pairs among SSCPs, PUs, and LUs.

6.7 FUNCTIONAL LAYERS

6.7.1 SNA Layering Structure

The third basic concept is that of functional layers. The SNA services are organized into layers, so that functions that are logically independent may be designed, implemented, and invoked independently. Remembering that end-to-end services may be in the NAU services manager or in a half-session, we first have three subdivisions:

1. NAU services (end-to-end services)
2. Other end-to-end services (in half-sessions)
3. Services of the common transmission network

These, in turn, exist as five layers in the SNA structure [6.4], as shown in Fig. 6.9. The five layers, in three sets, are as follows.

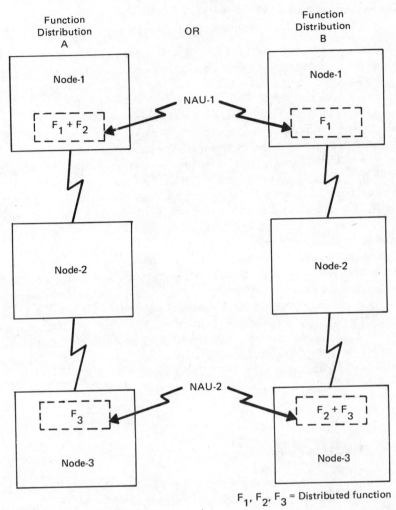

Fig. 6.8 End-to-end services, such as presentation services, operate as a matched pair, with function in origin NAU, destination NAU, or both.

1. *NAU services layer*, a grouping of outer components of the SNA network, including:

   ■ *NAU services managers* for each NAU, for interfacing to the end-users and providing common (*per-NAU*) end-to-end services. An example of a per-NAU service is *network services*, which in LUs assists in establishing a logical connection between that NAU and some other NAU.

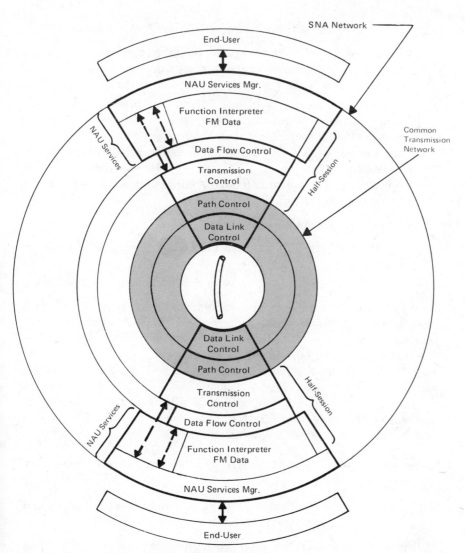

Fig. 6.9 Concentric layers in an SNA network.

■ *Function Interpreters for Function Management Data* (FI.FMD)
There is one FI.FMD for each session. Each FI.FMD contains one
or more *per-session* services either (a) in direct support of the
NAU services manager or (b) involving an interpretation of the
data being exchanged. An example of the former is a part of
network services that is dedicated to only one session. An example
of the latter is *presentation services* (PS) for editing and mapping.

2. *Other end-to-end services* (these are per-session)

  ■ *Data flow control layer*, to regulate the user's send/receive flow and the request/response flows and to ensure flow integrity. (Note that the SNA term "data flow control" does *not* pertain to rate of flow.)

  ■ *Transmission control layer*, to coordinate each session's transmissions, including sequence numbering and rate control between half-sessions. Transmission control functions exist at each end of a session. (They are not included in intermediate nodes of the transmission subsystem. Supplementary TC functions can exist, however, in a boundary node that is adjacent to a cluster controller or terminal node (see Section 9.5).)

3. *Common transmission network*

  ■ *Path control layer*, to route all messages to links and destination half-sessions.

  ■ *Data link control layer*, to control the flow of data on the links.

For end-user to end-user communication, the messages flow from each end-user to its NAU services manager within the NAU services layer. Then the messages flow, in sequence, from layer to layer toward the other end-user. The dashed lines in Fig. 6.9, from NAU services to data flow control and transmission control layers, indicate the flow of control commands to these two layers.

Messages of many different sessions can traverse the common data link control and path control layers. These layers are therefore part of what is called the *common transmission network*.

Properties of layers. The SNA layers are structured to attempt to meet two basic objectives:

1. Each layer should be functionally self-contained so that changes to it do not require comparable changes at other layers, and

2. Inner layers (inside NAU services) should be transparent to data sent from an outer layer.

By choice of functions and boundaries, layers are made logically independent in the sense that one can be changed, in either its functional content or in the way in which it implements its function, without greatly affecting other layers. Furthermore, the choice of the functions that are grouped into layers must be influenced by the search for simple boundaries between layers which, nevertheless, permit a wide variation of function within the layers. Well-chosen boundaries divide the total operation into manageable parts, whose development, alteration, maintenance, and operation can be largely independent for each part.

A second, very important reason for the layering structure stems from the recognition of the distributed nature of communication functions. Presentation services, data flow control, and transmission control each involve a dialogue between the originating NAU and the terminating NAU. The layered structure, with logically independent functions in each layer, gives one the freedom to shift end-to-end functions, within a layer, from one NAU to another; that is, to redistribute the function within a layer without affecting function in other layers.

The logical independence of layers is a condition that is difficult to achieve and can never be complete. Parameters for one layer are naturally generated in or passed from other layers. For example, the path control layer must be given the destination address by other layers. Nevertheless, a valuable degree of separation and independence can be achieved.

6.7.2 Session-Oriented Functions

A set of functions is assigned to each session that is established between a pair of NAU services managers. The functions assigned will vary from session to session; the maximum structure of the session is shown in Fig. 6.10. A layer, such as the DFC layer, will have an element (i.e., a DFC element) in each half-session. The half-session is thus composed of elements from different layers (e.g., TC, DFC, and FI.FMD). These are the half-session "team." For many sessions, the NAU services manager will be essentially transparent. Other elements may, in some cases, be nearly null. However, all sessions will have some transmission control and data flow control.

Some end-users can use concurrent sessions to communicate with other end-users at multiple network addresses. For example, an application program for a new account may be connected to three different bank officials at one time. To achieve this, there are multiple teams of functions, each team being logically distinct from the others and devoted to the operation of a single session. Each such session-team can include different function subsets of the layers shown in Fig. 6.10. For each session, there is a half-session at the origin NAU and another half-session at the destination NAU.

Each element of a session is a logically separate entity. One should remember, however, that this logical separation can be implemented in various ways—for example, as physically separate code, serially reusable code, or reentrant code.

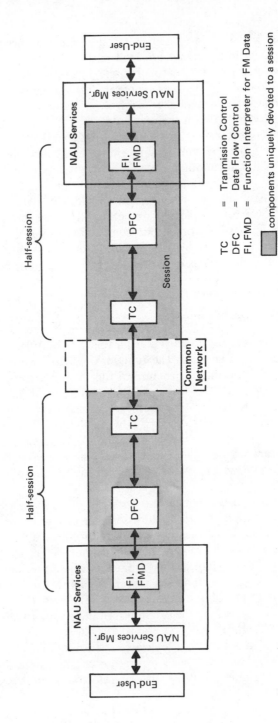

TC   = Tranmission Control
DFC   = Data Flow Control
FI.FMD   = Function Interpreter for FM Data

▨ components uniquely devoted to a session

Fig. 6.10 Elements of a session.

6.7.3 Layer Content of Session and NAU

Figure 6.11 illustrates two half-sessions serving a common NAU services manager at a single network address. The common transmission network (more specifically, the path control element of the node in question) serves this pair of half-sessions.

The NAU has been defined to include the functions in the shaded area of Fig. 6.11. It can be argued that the NAU might have been defined to also include the transmission control elements (TCE).

Optional content of the NAU. As already noted, the NAU content can vary greatly. First, the NAU services manager may be only a thin interface for LU-LU sessions, but that outer layer must contain service request handlers for sessions with the SSCP. Second, the NAU may contain a variety of services (in FI.FMD and data flow control) for each session.

Some implementations might also identify different interfaces for different sessions. Four possible interfaces are illustrated in Fig. 6.12. (The shaded area there represents an implementation-dependent transformation to and from the format expected by the SNA layer.) For example, the interface (4) to the NAU services manager might be used for the LU-SSCP session, but the interface (3), (2), or (1) might be used for LU-LU sessions. Although these options exist, commonality of all protocols is necessary if general communicability is to be encouraged. The number of possible modes of data flow control is very large, so the architecture for DFC must structure these options and define a limited number of function subsets for general use. In the case of the NAU services, some commonly used protocols are also necessary. First, there must be common services for establishing logical connections. There must also be common services for physical activations, that is, the loading and/or initializing of units to make them an active part of the network. And, in normal operations, it has been found advantageous to adopt common data formats so that application programs can be freed of some of the variations in device and/or program characteristics. The concept of sessions between NAUs having these common functions, *with common protocols*, provides a way of talking among many kinds of distributed service. This is the prime purpose of the architecture.

The NAU thus will normally contain versions of network services, presentation services, and data flow control. These are chosen to suit the character of the users being represented (or the network service being provided), but are nevertheless *subsets of architecturally defined functions*, so that they are understood in other parts of the network.

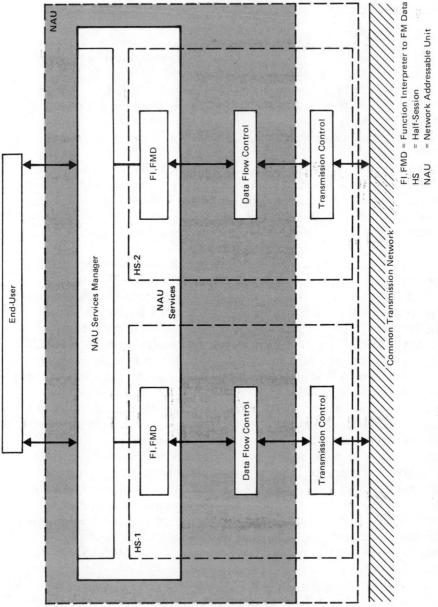

Fig. 6.11 Two half-sessions at one NAU.

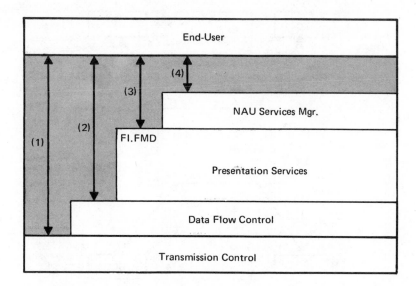

Fig. 6.12   Possible interfaces into the SNA network.

6.7.4 Different Views of SNA Structure

Everyone knows the story of the blind men who had different views of the elephant. The one holding the tail said it was a rope; the one feeling a leg said it was a tree. Similarly, one can have different views of the SNA layered structure.

The half-session view tends to focus attention on the elements of FI.FMD, data flow control, and transmission control, as the managers of what is sent or received. This view sees the half-sessions as the users of the common transmission network (that is, path control and data link control).

Another viewpoint groups layers so as to focus on the transmission process, as follows. Remember that path control performs a routing function. In origin and destination nodes, path control routes messages between one or more data link control elements and one or more transmission control elements (TCEs). This is illustrated in Fig. 6.13(a). Though not shown, the transmission control elements are each part of a half-session. On the other hand, in intermediate nodes, such as a communications controller, the routing is from one data link control element to another data link control element, as illustrated in Fig. 6.13(b). In some nodes, both of these types of routing may be performed, depending on the session being handled.

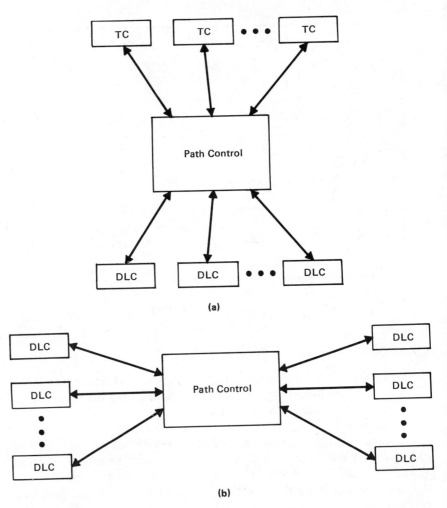

Fig. 6.13 Path control shown as a routing function: (a) lower layers in an origin or destination node; (b) lower layers in an intermediate node.

A collection of such configurations (such as those in Figs. 6.13a and 6.13b) involving an origin node, a destination node, and one or more intermediate nodes, can be looked upon as a network or a subsystem. A message can originate at a transmission control element in an origin node, make its way through one or more intermediate nodes, and arrive at another transmission control element in the destination node. This network has been called the *transmission control network* or the *transmission subsystem*. It involves only the transmission control, path control, and data link control layers. Each network addressable unit (NAU) has a boundary to this transmission subsystem. This is shown in Fig. 6.14, which compares the two views of the SNA network. Note that the transmission control elements are part of both the transmission subsystem and a half-session. The transmission control elements contain end-to-end services but also serve as a bridge between the NAUs and the common transmission network (path control and data link control).

6.8 FORMATS AND PROTOCOLS

In our usage, *format and protocol* mean a set of agreements involving three things:

1. The syntax (or format) of commands and headers to be exchanged
2. The semantics (or meaning) of these commands and headers in terms of what shall be done upon the receipt of each
3. The time sequence in which the commands and headers may be sent

The SNA network and each layer of the network are defined by the services they provide and the formats and protocols used to achieve those services.

As shown in Fig. 6.15, communication takes place between components of the same layer that possibly are in different nodes. To achieve this peer communication, data is sent via inner layers that provide a transparent transportation service for the outer layers. At the same time, an outer layer will pass parameters (that are needed for inner-layer operations) to an inner layer. Each layer defines the parameters that outer layers must provide to obtain its services. These parameters, and the data that will be passed transparently, constitute the boundary between layers.

We have referred to the SNA network. We now can define that network as the aggregate of functional elements such as those shown in Fig. 6.15 (but excluding the end-users) involving two or more NAUs in one or more different nodes of the network, *with functions at each level interrelated by sets of formats and protocols.*

6.8.1 Peer Protocols

The fourth basic concept is that of peer protocols. A peer, according to Webster, is one who is in equal standing with another. We refer to functions in the same layer, though possibly in different nodes, as *peer functions.* Peers can be operationally independent, such as two unrelated applications, or they can be operationally dependent, such as a cluster-

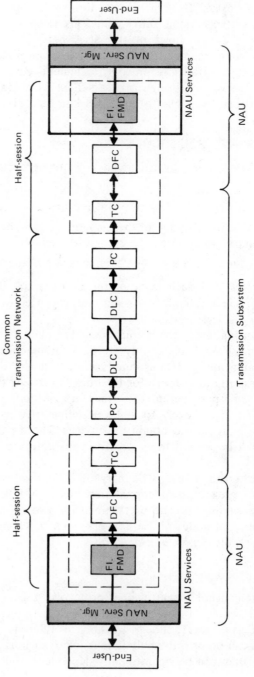

Fig. 6.14 Two views of the SNA layered structure (showing only one session).

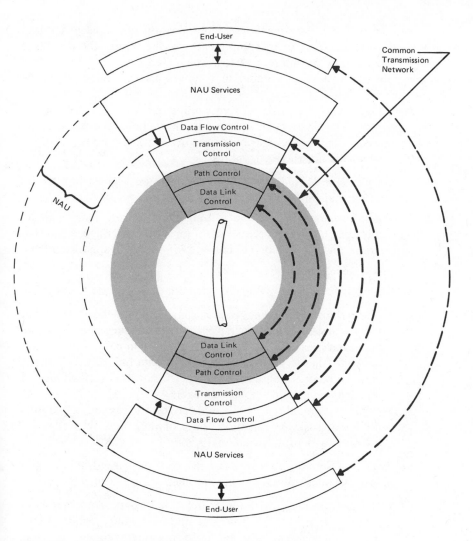

Fig. 6.15 Intralayer communication.

controller application program logged on to a host application program. Both the cluster-controller application program and the host application program are parts of the data-processing system and are considered peers of one another. Both of these appear as end-users to the communications system. Similarly, there can be peer functions, in different nodes, in each of the layers shown in Fig. 6.15.

Peer protocols determine how communication takes place within a layer, that is, between peer components of the layer, though these components may be in different nodes. The coded commands or control headers of that protocol are understood within a layer and need not be understood by inner layers.

Each layer may be distributed across multiple nodes. The peer protocols serve to coordinate the operations throughout the layer even though the components are distributed among multiple nodes.

Peer protocols must exist as follows.

1. *Data link control protocols:* To control flows on a given link for all stations on that link.

2. *Path control protocols:* For the routing of messages, at each node, onto the right links or ports, so as to direct the message toward its destination, and to the correct half-session in the destination node.

3. *Session-oriented protocols*

   a) *Transmission control protocols:* Including both of the following.

      ■ *Connection point manager protocol:* To route the data within the session-oriented layers; to convey all messages, for one particular session, into and out of the common transmission network (that is, the path control and data link control layers); and to control these flow rates to suit the capabilities of receiving connection point managers.
      ■ *Session control protocols:* To manage for one session the coordination of session activation, start of data flow, clearing, sequence resynchronization, and session termination.

   b) *Data flow control protocols:* For the control of send-receive and request/response flows, to suit the needs of users of the session.

   c) *FI.FMD protocols:* For the interpretation of data. An example of a service within FI.FMD is *presentation services* to format, edit, or translate the data so as to be more meaningful to the receiving end-user.

4. *Per-NAU protocols:* For dialogues between two NAU services managers. An example of this is the dialogue between network services in two NAUs (e.g., for session or configuration establishment).

Figure 6.16 portrays the operational span of four types of protocol in a network. *Data link control protocols relate functions in adjacent nodes,* and the DLC protocol for each link can be independent of that for any other link. Path control protocols relate pairs of PC functions in adjacent

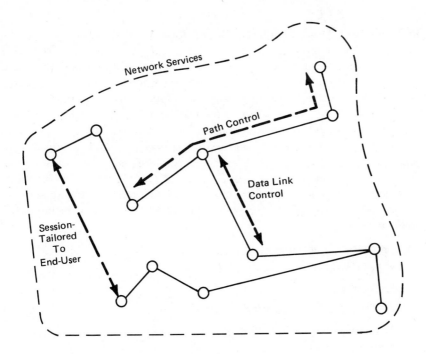

Fig. 6.16   Operational span for four types of protocol in a network.

nodes, but each pair of path control elements along a path exchanges some control information with the preceding pair of path control elements along the path. *Hence, that path control operation spans an entire path. The session protocol relates function in an origin NAU and function in a destination NAU.* Network services protocols relate pairs of functions in origin NAUs and destination NAUs; however, *many network service pairs, all centering on the SSCP, provide an operational span that includes all SNA NAUs in the domain of the SSCP.* Moreover, by SSCP-to-SSCP sessions, the operational span of network services can extend across a multiple-domain network.

A part of each of these protocols (and their associated formats) must be devoted to the maintenance of integrity and the provision of information for recovery from error.

The session team protocols. The half-session helps to ensure that the exchange between NAU services managers is transmitted correctly and has the proper format. Communication with understanding is more than bit transmission. If one user understands English only and the other understands Spanish only, they can transmit to each other all day, but this will not constitute an exchange of information or communication with understanding [6.6]. Similarly, if the format of the message or the device-control characters in the message are not what the receiving end-user can interpret there is no understanding. Also, if the sequence of messages in one direction, the sequence of responses to requests, or the rate of messages is such that messages appear to be garbled to the receiving end-user, there is no understanding of the messages sent, even though transmission of each message is perfect.

One of the purposes of the session protocols is to help avoid such problems and thus contribute to understanding of the transmission. Because each session may serve very different users, the functions that help comprehension often need to be unique for each session. A partial list of such options (for which protocols are needed) includes the following.

1. Presentation services
   - Formatting
   - Editing
   - Mapping to a presentation space
   - Compression and compaction
2. Data flow control
   - Brackets around a work scope (e.g., a transaction—see Section 1.2.3)
   - Chaining of requests
   - Request/response correlation
   - "My turn, then your turn" send/receive controls
3. Transmission control
   - Sequencing
   - Pacing (that is, flow-rate control)

These will be discussed further in Chapters 7, 8, and 9, respectively.

6.8.2   Interlayer Communication

SNA is concerned primarily with communication between NAUs. This has been expressed, as seen above, in terms of peer protocols for the communication between elements of the same layer. The format for this communication, at various levels, is well defined in SNA with a family of nested headers, as we will discuss later.

All this, however, is distinct from interlayer communication. SNA does define functional relationships between adjacent layers, and does specify the information that must be passed between layers. However, in order to perform its communication architecture job, *it need not, and hence should not, uniquely define all the formats for every interlayer communication within a node.*

SNA does not, for example, define user macroinstructions that the application program uses to access the network. These should not be constrained by SNA but should be left to evolve separately, meeting the application requirements and the design needs of the separate products. SNA does specify the *information* that must be supplied by the end-user to control the SNA functions, but those *formats* are not specified.

For similar reasons, SNA specifies the control information that must pass between layers but not the format for that information. Performance could be adversely affected by too great a formalization of the boundaries between layers. Design trade-offs will sometimes dictate one or another technique, such as control tables, commands, or macros, to implement the boundary. In some implementations, several layers may best be built with no visible boundary between them. In any case, whether or not the interlayer boundaries are visible, the separation of function and the use of the peer protocols can be adhered to.

We need a well-defined interface at any product boundary, such as at the data link control (DLC) level. Visibility of the DLC interface on the line side is a matter for international standards, because this is the point at which many products (from many different vendors) must *physically* connect.

6.8.3   Requests and Responses

Every message entering or exiting the common transmission network is referred to in SNA as a *request* (RQ) or a *response* (RSP). For each request there *may* be a response. Ordinarily, the response message only acknowledges receipt of a request; it does not reply to a request. The reply to the request (if there is one) will take the form of a new request, sent back to the originating NAU. This is illustrated in Fig. 6.17 for the case in which an application subsystem issues and coordinates the responses. (The reply is in the form of a new request traveling back to the end-user.) In some cases, the application itself (or the "message control" portion of the application) would issue the responses and correlate received responses with sent requests.

The acknowledgment (positive or negative) is not limited to an acknowledgment of mere reception by the half-session. Further checking may be involved at higher levels prior to sending a response. Some responses must await authorization from NAU services or the end-user. The checks made at these levels are open-ended. In some cases, for

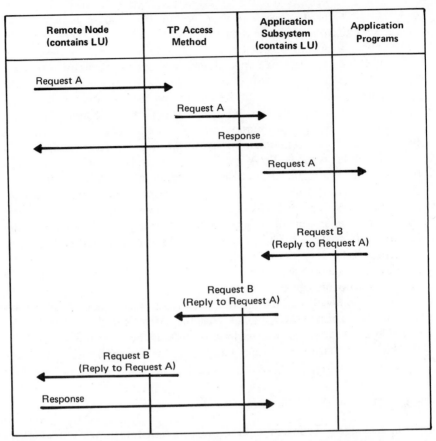

Fig. 6.17 Example of requests and responses with an application subsystem.

example, validity checks on the format might be made; in other cases, the response may be negative because of an inability to accept a command. The response, therefore, is used as a general-purpose acknowledgment from the receiver that the sender of the request may (or may not) proceed.

The request or response traveling in the transmission subsystem includes a number of headers that have been added to ensure proper routing and end-to-end coordination. Within the request or response, there also is the original unit of information that is intended to flow between the function pairs FI.FMD to FI.FMD, DFC to DFC, or TC to TC. In SNA this original unit of information is called the *request/response unit* (RU). The *decision* to send an RU is always made in one of the upper layers by either

1. the end-user, for normal data flow;
2. a service within NAU services, for session establishment, etc.; or
3. FI.FMD services, as when they form many RUs from a large end-user record.

The RU is actually *formed*, however, in either

1. FI.FMD services, for information flow between NAU services or end-users;
2. data flow control, for the exercise of DFC functions; or
3. transmission control, for the exercise of TC functions.

The format of the data may be modified by FI.FMD services. *It is convenient to assume that all such data units, whether they originate from an end-user or an NAU services manager, are processed by FI.FMD services (although in some cases the function of FI.FMD services may be essentially null).* All RUs to or from either of these two sources, therefore, are seen as products of FI.FMD services; we refer to them as FMD–RUs. Moreover, FI.FMD services may form multiple RUs from a block of information given them by upper layers. These too are FMD–RUs.

In addition, control RUs can be generated and received by the data flow control and the transmission control elements. These are referred to as DFC–RUs and TC–RUs, respectively.

Responses may be positive or negative. A negative response returns sense data (identifying the reason for a negative response). That sense data is followed by the SNA-defined request code (which identifies the type of request) if a request code was used (see Appendix C.3 for further details). Five special commands (see Appendix C.4) have data in the RU of a positive response.

6.8.4 The Protocol Headers

Each request unit and each response unit (RU) are accompanied by a number of control headers, which are used by the various SNA layers in the execution of their peer protocols (see Fig. 6.18).

Link headers. The data link control layer has its own peer protocols and so generates its own headers (actually, a link header and a link trailer). This controls the physical flows on the link, which may have multiple stations on a single link with distinct station addresses. Each link type provides specific header definitions. (Link headers are defined in Chapter 11.)

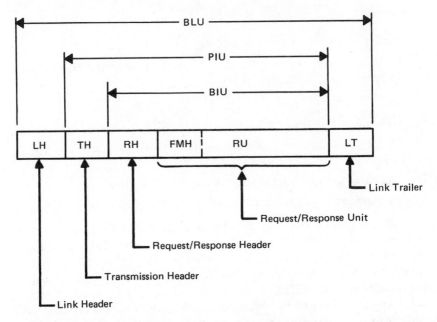

Fig. 6.18 The components of a basic link unit (without blocking or segmenting).

Transmission header. The path control layer generates its own header—the transmission header, or TH. The TH indicates the physical manipulation of the message (blocking or segmenting) and is used to control the physical routing of the message to the correct series of links toward its destination. (The TH is further defined in Chapter 10.)

Request/response header. The components of a half-session operate as a team. A single header type, called the request/response header (RH), is used to manage the flow of all RUs, whether they be FMD–RUs, DFC–RUs, or TC–RUs. The RH contains indicators for data flow control, such as send/receive and response-expected. It also contains indicators for transmission control, such as the pacing indicator. (The content of the RH will be further defined in Section 9.2.)

FM headers. The preceding protocol headers (link, TH, and RH) are required for all SNA requests and responses. A fourth, optional header is defined *within the RU*, called the FM header, and is used to support FI.FMD services. One of its uses to date is to make it possible for multiple components, such as printers, punches, operator consoles, and removable cassettes, to employ a single session. The FM header can be used to identify for which of several components the RU is intended, and *to select the appropriate FI.FMD services for that particular component.*

Remember that an end-user may be an operator, a storage medium, or a program (the latter includes system programs such as data management). Each may have different types of components, such as devices, data sets, and subroutines. In each case, the meaning of editing, formatting, and mapping may be somewhat different (for example, the positioning of data on a display screen, a scatter load into memory, a rearrangement or deletion of fields, an addition of new titles, etc.). In general, the FM headers can be used to select the FI.FMD service that is appropriate for particular data or for the destination component. In some implementations, this tool is used to provide separate data streams for the several components. (FM headers are described in Section 7.4.)

For sessions involving the SSCP, the RUs are strictly formatted, and the header (within the RU), which identifies a command and its format, is called the Network Service (NS) header.

Assembled RU and headers.   It is sometimes convenient to talk about the request or response as it is passed from layer to layer. At any given boundary, it will have more or fewer SNA headers. The principal groupings of RUs and their headers are illustrated in Fig. 6.18, and defined as follows.

The *Basic Information Unit* (BIU) is the unit of data and control information passed between the transmission control and path control layers. It consists of a request/response header (RH), followed by a request/response unit (RU):

$$BIU = RH + RU.$$

The *Path Information Unit* (PIU) is a unit of data and control information passed between path controls in different nodes. It consists of a transmission header and a basic information unit (or a segment of a BIU, as we will discuss in Chapter 10):

$$PIU = TH + RH + RU \qquad \text{(without segmenting)}$$
$$= TH + \text{segment of a BIU} \qquad \text{(with segmenting).}$$

All the necessary end-to-end and SNA path-finding information is packed into the RH and TH headers that are in a PIU. One or more PIUs may be in a *Basic Transmission Unit* (BTU) which is passed between path control and data link control layers.

The *Basic Link Unit* (BLU) is the unit of data and control information that is transmitted over a data link by data link control. The BLUs are also the data packages that the carrier must deliver intact to the destination. Using SDLC (Synchronous Data Link Control), the BLU consists of a link header and a link trailer, enclosing a BTU—i.e., one or more PIUs. (The SDLC structure is discussed in Section 11.5.)

The various headers are described further in Chapters 9–11. A preview can be obtained by examining the summaries in Appendix A.

6.8.5 Message Sizes

The physical sizes of units of information will vary in different parts of the network.

1. The *user record* that flows between the end-user and the NAU services may be of any size, depending on the application. It may be a few bytes in an interactive application or millions of bytes in file transfers (except for item 2 below).

2. In accordance with an agreement reached at session establishment (BIND) time, each end-user *or* NAU services will limit the size of the request/response units (RUs) that it sends to some *maximum RU size* for that half-session. This can be selected to match the buffer capacity at the receiving half-session.

3. Path control (at one or more nodes of the network) may optionally subdivide the BIU (i.e., RH + RU) into smaller *segments* or packets. The size of the PIU is therefore that of the TH plus that of the BIU segment if a segment size is set by the network manager. Segmenting is discussed in Section 10.4.

4. Data link control may package one or more PIUs into a *frame* for transmission on the link. The BLU usually is a single PIU plus link headers, but with blocking of PIUs, it could be of any length.

6.9 APPARENT PEER FLOWS

As shown in Fig. 6.19, a typical message will pass from an end-user via the NAU services manager to the half-session, then to path control, then to data link control, and then back through these same levels to another end-user.

As the transmission control (TC) layer (of the half-session) and the path control (PC) layer and DLC layer each receive data from an outer layer, *they each prefix that data with a header that conveys information pertinent to their own protocols.* These protocols are understood by the peer components in each layer. At the receiving node, the DLC, PC, and

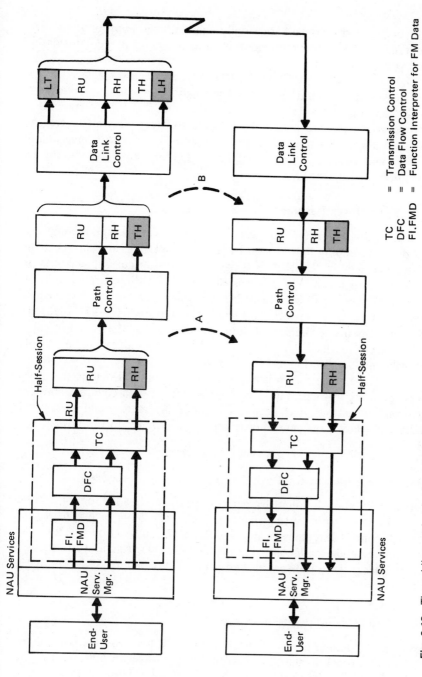

Fig. 6.19 The adding and stripping of headers at three levels.

TC   = Transmission Control
DFC   = Data Flow Control
FI.FMD = Function Interpreter for FM Data

TC layers, in turn, strip off (or simply examine) the appropriate control header and process the remainder in accordance with the information found within its header.

Figure 6.19 illustrates how the RH, TH, and link/trailer are successively added and deleted as the message passes from end-user to end-user. In addition to the RU and headers, shown in Fig. 6.19, certain other control parameters are passed from layer to layer. Examples are the passage of destination network address to path control, for its inclusion in the TH, and passage of station address to data link control, for its inclusion in the link header.

6.9.1 Peer Flows Between Half-Sessions

The format for the protocol between half-sessions is the RH. Note in Fig. 6.19 that the sending half-session transmits an RH-RU and the receiving half-session gets an RH-RU. It is as though a shortcut, labeled "A" in Fig. 6.19, were taken. The effect is the same as a direct transfer of the RH–RU between half-sessions. The RU may contain an FM header (FMH) or a network services (NS) header. Within the RH–RU, then, the different elements of the session find the information they need to carry out the NAU services-NAU services, DFC-DFC, and TC-TC protocols that were indicated in Fig. 6.15.

To achieve this effect, it is necessary to pass the RH–RU to the inner layers (path control and data flow control), along with some parameters (such as destination) that permit the inner layers to build their own headers. However, the inner layers are "transparent" to the flow of the RH–RU.

6.9.2 Peer Flows in the Path Control Layer

A similar situation is found by path control. The header for use by the protocol among path control elements is the TH. Note in Fig. 6.19 that the path control layer passes the TH-RH-RU combination to DLC. At the receiving node, path control gets a TH-RH-RU. Again, it's as though the DLC layer were transparent and a shortcut, labeled "B" in Fig. 6.19, were taken.

6.9.3 Peer Flows in All Five Layers

Figure 6.20 summarizes the flows between two half-sessions. The physical flow is vertical, in that figure, from layer to layer in both nodes. The intralayer communications are shown horizontally. Dashed lines pertain to data flow control or transmission control requests and responses.

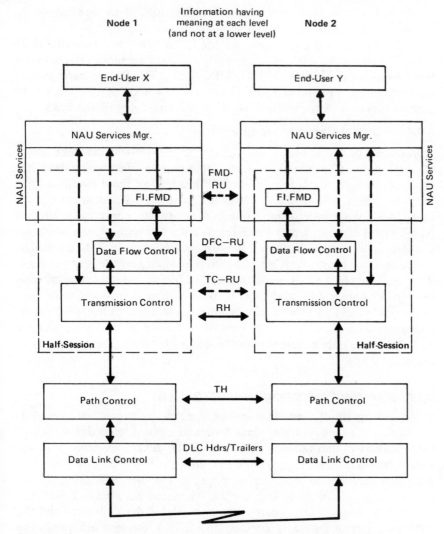

Fig. 6.20 Interlayer and intralayer communications (single-session case).

The RUs can flow between FI.FMD functions, between DFC functions, and between TC functions in the two half-sessions.

All RUs are accompanied by an RH for the protocol between half-sessions; the construction of the RH is done by transmission control as a service to the three layers in the half-session. RUs have no meaning at levels below where they are shown. Meaningful THs are exchanged at the path control level, while meaningful link headers and trailers are exchanged at the data link control level. Thus, there are intralayer communications at five layers of the communications system.

The figure shows a single session. The functions labeled "half-session" exist, at least logically, for each session. Peer flows exist between function pairs (FI.FMD–FI.FMD, DFC–DFC, TC–TC) *in each pair of half-sessions.* On the other hand, all sessions at a node share a single path control function. Also, multiple sessions can share any of the links.

6.9.4 Protocol Changes along a Path

A variation of the above is the change of protocols at different places along a path. Consider Fig. 6.21, for example. Two data links are involved. The protocols (hence, the link headers) of these two data links could be different, since the two links are completely independent of each other. Also, the transmission protocols to relate path control of node 1 to path control of node 2 may be different from the transmission protocols to relate path control of node 2 to path control of node 3. In particular, the addressing conventions may be different in different legs of the path. This will be clarified as we study the different types of transmission header in Chapter 10. Parameters of transmission control also may vary, in that the pacing parameter may be different in different legs of the path. However, such changes in path control or transmission control along a path are made only at nodes with "boundary functions," as described in Chapters 9 and 10.

6.10 ASYMMETRIC SESSION PROTOCOLS

When talking about symmetric and asymmetric functions, one must first distinguish between ordinary data flow and control procedures such as setup/takedown and recovery. *SNA facilitates either symmetric or asymmetric function pertaining to ordinary data flow.* (Presentation services and such facilities as chaining of requests together, obtaining certain responses, pacing of flows, etc., can be symmetric if so desired, but they usually are not and are tailored to the needs of the end-users and the NAU pair.) With regard to control, one should distinguish between the initiation of a control procedure and its execution. *It is often desirable, or necessary, for either party to be able to initiate a procedure,* such as initiating a session or calling for a recovery procedure. *Once initiated, one or the other partner may have a greater role to play in executing the procedure.* The current SNA policy, with exceptions, is the following.

1. Either symmetric or asymmetric facilities can be used for data flows.

2. Either end may initiate (or request) control procedures.

3. One end may take the lead in procedure execution.

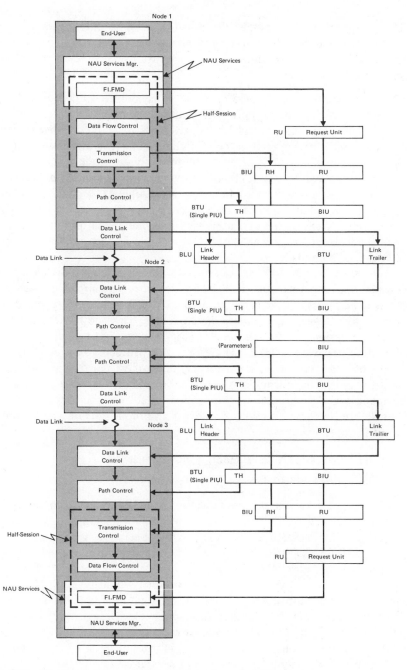

Fig. 6.21 Header changes with three nodes in path [6.8].

Thus (regardless of whether or not the session data flows may be symmetric) one half-session (called the primary half-session) is given special control responsibilities regarding overall session setup, takedown, recovery, and cleanup.

Recovery from error. A good example of asymmetric protocols is in the area of recovery. The common transmission network (that is, the path control and data link control layers) attempts to maintain message synchronism and to recover from certain classes of error that it can handle. However, for some types of error, there is no substitute for the higher-level message synchronization and recovery. Only the levels of transmission control and above can handle certain problems, because they have the sequence counts to check responses against requests. In some cases, the NAU services or the end-user itself must be called on for assistance. When necessary, they can direct DFC and TC to generate specific recovery commands.

In some of the difficult jobs of straightening out problems in synchronization and recovery, *it has been found to be simpler to let one of the two half-sessions take the lead in executing the recovery procedure, even though either might initiate the procedure.* The one having that kind of lead is designated the *responsible half-session,* and it must be capable of certain recovery actions. Therefore, the protocols between the two halves of the session are, for recovery (and other) reasons, asymmetric.

At session establishment time, a choice of recovery procedures can be made via a parameter in the session establishment commands. Responsibility for the correction of an error and the restart of a session may be given to either

- The half-session that is sending the request, or
- The half-session that is designated "primary."

If the sender is given the responsibility, then when the sender is the secondary, it will handle some error conditions by itself and will call on the primary half-session for assistance (via a special SNA command called REQUEST RECOVERY) when only the primary has a needed recovery capability.

A typical recovery situation, for example, would be the recovery of message synchronism (loss of synchronism might be due to a lost message or a message that arrives out of sequence). Though the secondary half-session may be the one to request recovery, the primary half-session is the one that would take the lead in proposing a new, sequence-synchronized, starting point. The use of special commands for this recovery will be described in Section 9.3 on session control, which is a function in the transmission control layer.

Asymmetric implementations. In general, any LU should be considered primary or secondary only in the context of a session. A single LU may act as a primary LU (PLU) in some sessions and as a secondary LU (SLU) in other sessions. A host LU, for example, may be the secondary in SSCP–LU sessions and the primary in LU–LU sessions. A given NAU could be built with only primary, or only secondary, or both primary and secondary session capabilities. Some economy can be gained by building an NAU with only primary or secondary capability. For example, it has been practical to build many hosts with only primary capabilities for LU–LU sessions when only a single domain and no host-to-host communications are required, and to build cluster controllers and terminal nodes with only secondary capabilities. NAUs in such nodes, however, can only communicate with NAUs in nodes having the opposite asymmetry. *In such cases as multihost networking (discussed in Chapter 15), it is necessary for hosts to have both primary and secondary capabilities for LU–LU sessions, as well as for SSCP–SSCP sessions.*

Thus, whether a particular node has capabilities for both primary and secondary half-sessions, or only one of these, has been an economic consideration. It's less expensive without both; however, this consideration fades as technology advances or general communicability is desired, and both capabilities can be provided.

Chapter 11 describes a comparable asymmetry at the data link control level. Here, too, cases have arisen in which a combination of primary and secondary station capabilities is desired at some stations. The International Standards Organization has, accordingly, simply defined a balanced mode where a combined station includes the capabilities of both a primary station and a secondary station (see Section 11.7.4).

6.11 NETWORKS AT VARIOUS LEVELS

The term "network" deserves some further discussion. It can be defined very generally as *any interconnected set of functional elements, which are interrelated by a common set of protocols and are managed by a common set of controls* [6.6]. The entire system shown in Fig. 6.1, as one example, qualifies as a network. Its functional elements could be interrelated by the SNA peer protocols and managed by the set of controls in an SNA system services control point. *The peer protocols are the essential bonds, and they serve to define the extent of the network.*

Figure 6.1 shows a network that has a single control domain. Most of Part 2 addresses this type of system. When there are multiple control domains, each control domain may operate as a network. Also the multiple domains become a multidomain SNA network if they are bound by a common set of protocols and are managed jointly by a higher level of common controls. A session in such a network may span more than one control domain. This multidomain network will be discussed in Chapter 15.

We also speak of the common transmission network, consisting of the path control and data link control layers. This, too, may be considered to be a network within the SNA network. Half-session functions use the common transmission network. The latter may also span more than one control domain.

Occasionally, one also refers to the network that exists at the data link control level, as we did regarding the subnetworks of Fig. 6.1. They are each part of the broader network that encompasses all nodes in the figure. Within a DLC network, one can, moreover, have a self-sufficient media network managed by the carrier, using its own internal set of protocols.

Each network that becomes part of a larger network must define the services that it is to render to its "users." The server network, in general, will also need to define the "user-server" procedures that can be used to obtain the services provided by a given network. With this concept of networks within networks, it is often best to use modifiers, as in SNA network, common transmission network, and link network. Otherwise, the context must be examined to identify the level of network under discussion.

6.12 FUNCTION SUBSETS

The fifth basic concept is that of function subsets. Function subsets are prescribed families of options that exist within each layer and each NAU type. For example, the data flow control for one session need not be the same as the data flow control for another session. Even within a given node, one end-user (in one session) may employ one function subset of a given layer; a different end-user (using another session) may employ a different function subset in that same layer.

Why function subsets? The ability to select function subsets within layers for any session is necessary in order to avoid the problem of having every user forced into a rigid function standardization. One very important subset is the null; that is, an entire element (such as presentation services) may be absent (except for a possible connection through the layer) for a particular half-session. On the other hand, unnecessary proliferation of function subsets can reduce general communicability, and must be regulated.

An example. The configuration in Fig. 6.1 is for a typical, tree-structured, single-domain SNA network. Every node (or box) in that configuration contains elements of some of the SNA layers. Each layer, moreover, can have different functional subsets as follows.

In Fig. 6.1, we can see three distinct physical networks at the data link control level. Each of the three DLC networks could use a different line discipline without affecting higher-level layers. The data link controls of the communications controller and cluster controller networks (2 and 3), however, could be (and are) functional subsets of a common DLC architecture. In SNA, these are subsets of the synchronous data link control (SDLC) (see Section 11.5.7).

At the path control layer, the sophisticated communications controllers can afford to have a richer path control function than the more primitive cluster controllers and terminal nodes. Hence, along a given path, end segments of the path could employ different function subsets of path control, again without affecting other layers. A current example is the use of more abbreviated addresses for terminal nodes than for cluster controllers (see Section 10.2).

At the transmission control and data flow control layers, each session uses functional subsets that suit the connected end-user and the facilities available. Examples are different ground rules for waiting, in an application program, for responses (see Section 8.4), and different commands that might be built in to affect resynchronization (see Section 9.3.2).

Finally, presentation services can be different for each session because different kinds of device control, formatting, and mapping may be needed in a particular session. On the other hand, the presentation services used in a given session can often be a subset of a common presentation services architecture, because many different end-users have basically common needs (see Section 7.4).

The architectural approach. Looking at the five functional layers (see Fig. 6.15) and the variety of functions that can be offered in each layer, we see that the total number of possible function combinations is extremely large. The architecture needs to provide a unifying structure for all these situations; it must also specify a limited set of common functions, so as to permit a growing degree of general communicability among all programs and devices in the combined network.

Some subsets, such as those for path control and data link control, are usually *built into the products at design time. Products that have common subsets of transmission facilities are identified as PU types.* These are defined in Sections 12.2 and 12.3. Other subsets, namely, those pertaining to the session-oriented functions (FI.FMD, data flow control, and transmission control), *may be selected at the time of session establishment.* That selection is done via parameters in the BIND command (and similar commands), which are used to establish the session.

The commonly used options that can be selected via these session establishment commands are grouped together in what are called profiles.

Profiles (i.e., commonly used sets of options) are defined for FI.FMD, data flow control, and transmission control (referred to as PS, FM, and TS profiles, respectively). These profiles continue to evolve as common usage dictates. (Some of the profiles established to date are listed in Appendix B.)

Then, only a particular combination of these profiles is supported by what is called an *LU type*. *A given LU type will only support sessions that draw from its allowable PS, FM, and TS profiles.* A product is thus identifiable by the LU type (or types) that it supports. All sessions should subscribe to one of the common LU types if general communicability is to be promoted. For a given session, these LU types and the selected profiles are specified in fields (of the BIND and similar commands) called *profile and usage fields.* This selection process is discussed more fully in Section 9.7.

The combination of *layering*, the availability of *options for function subsets* within each layer, and the *grouping of commonly used functions into LU types* are all steps toward the goal of permitting systems to be tailored, but also promoting broad communicability.

6.13 CONTROL DOMAINS

The sixth basic concept is that of control domain. This concept pertains to two things: first, the grouping of NAUs and nodes that must act in concert in the allocation of SNA resources, and second, the degree of centralization by which the resource managers will effect this coordination.

SNA resource management. Every SNA resource is managed in the sense of controlling access and sharing. The control of these resources corresponds either to their ownership or to special agreements among the owners. Different organizations may establish their own control domains, which then must be coordinated to permit cross-domain communication among peer domains. (See Figs. 3.15 and 3.16.)

The primary types of SNA resource allocation, of concern in any domain, involve

1. The activation (or deactivation) of the SNA configuration of physical units (PUs) and links
2. The activation (or deactivation) of SNA logical units (LUs)
3. The logical connection (or disconnection) of a pair of NAUs (e.g., LUs) by the setup and takedown of sessions

It is often useful to distinguish, as SNA does, between configuration services (for example, to provide NAU-to-NAU physical paths) and session services (for example, to connect NAUs to each other logically). A control domain contains both types of network service. Note, however, that in either case *we are really referring to activations (or deactivations) of functions in the SNA-defined layers.* This type of resource management, for the purpose of network control, is separate and distinct from the management of each node's processor and storage resources. Any call for these node resources may be a consequence of an SNA command, but is an implementation matter within each node, using product-unique procedures, and is not treated in the network architecture. The interface between these node resource managers and SNA is generally via the PU or the LU.

Degree of centralization. Theoretically, there are at least four possible classifications for network control:

1. A single, centralized, control for management of SNA resources that exist in all nodes within a control domain
2. Local control in all nodes
3. Local control in all nodes, operating hierarchically with a centralized control for a domain
4. Multiple-control domains (types 1 or 3) operating as peers of one another

A central point for domain resource control and for the provision of universally available system services appears to be the most efficient mode when (1) one node is clearly the focal point for the domain, and/or (2) the centralized system services to be provided are more elaborate than can be supported by each node, or (3) it is highly preferable to change evolving services in one place rather than in multiple places.

On the other hand, local control points, in each node, are useful to coordinate each node's operations and to interface to the various resource managers in that node. Following this reasoning, a hierarchical system of control can be established (see Fig. 6.22). *The first resource-management level consists of functions that are located in each SNA node.* The NAU that is called a physical unit (PU) contains a PU services manager that interfaces to resource managers for the inner layers in the node. These manage the resources within the data link control and path control layers, such as links, paths, etc. The NAUs that are called logical units (LUs) contain a logical unit services manager that interfaces to resource managers for the outer layers. These arrange resources within the node for session connectivity. *The next (second) level of management is at the central SSCP* for the domain, which is in session with each PU and each LU at the first level. This two-level distribution of control in a single domain is discussed further in Chapter 7.

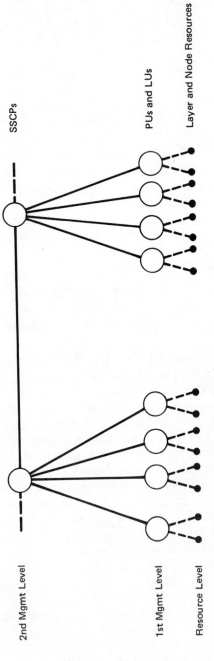

Fig. 6.22 Levels of control, with two control domains.

The size of each such domain may, however, be limited. More than one such domain, possibly in different geographic areas, may be needed by a given enterprise. Then there may be a need to form one SNA network, including multiple peer control domains. (The growth of multidomain networks was introduced in Section 3.8.) With coordination of the multiple SSCPs, one then has a distribution of network resource control at the SSCP level (see Fig. 6.22). The sharing of resources among SSCPs may be partial or full. For example, some NAUs may be limited to sessions in one domain, or to sessions between some but not all domains. *The coordination of resource management among SSCPs constitutes a third level of management* for the system.

The operational control of the network, as done by a network operator with the aid of network operations programs, is another distinct and important aspect of network control. This is potentially *another (i.e., fourth) level of management in the sense that certain responsibilities of this type may be further centralized or redistributed* (see Section 15.4.3).

Individual nodes (such as cluster controllers and subhosts—see Sections 3.6.3 and 3.6.4) may also arrange *private pseudosessions among their own attachments, without the knowledge of other nodes in the network.* This, too, is a form of hierarchical control when such nodes also participate, to some degree, in network communications.

Because all of these requirements are valid in different cases, growth paths may need to be provided, involving either

- One control domain, with centralized control, but also with distributed control functions in the PUs and LUs of each node
- One hierarchical control domain, with private pseudosessions in cluster controllers and subhosts
- Multiples of the above with cross-domain coordination.

Multidomain architectures are discussed in Chapter 15.

6.14 PARALLEL DEVELOPMENTS

6.14.1 ARPANET Structure

Recall first that the SNA layers are organized by logical function and not necessarily by physical entities. A given layer is distributed among nodes of the network, and the protocols are between like functions in the same or in different nodes.

A different example of a layered structure is that developed for host-to-host communication in the ARPANET. This is a highly successful experimental packet switching network, having almost a hundred network nodes and three satellite channels. The levels of protocol, shown in Fig.

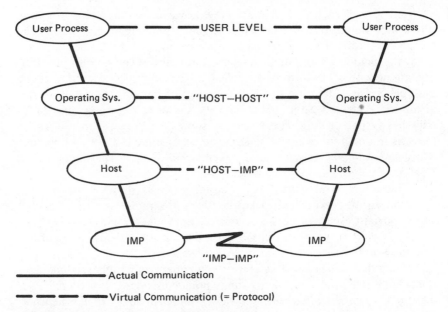

Fig. 6.23   Layers of protocol in ARPANET [6.2].

6.23, are related to common physical entities. The four levels there are as follows [6.2].

1. *IMP–IMP protocol:* The Interface Message Processor (IMP) is a "stand-alone" product that performs a store-and-forward function and supports interconnection of a host to the packet-switched network. The

IMP–IMP protocol provides communication among IMPs, and handles transmission error detection and correction, flow control to avoid message congestion, and routing among IMPs. It has functions analogous to both link control and path control.

2. The *HOST–IMP protocol* is path-independent, permitting the host to send messages to specified other hosts and to be informed of the status of those messages.

3. The *HOST–HOST protocol* is the set of rules that links the two host operating systems for starting user jobs in a remote host and for maintaining communications between jobs in two hosts. This protocol relates specially built adjuncts to the operating systems in each host that are called Network Control Programs (NCPs).

4. The *User Process–User Process protocols* relate networking functions that operate at the application or privileged application-subsystem level.

This includes protocols between specially built subsystems to handle requests for file transfer.

The ARPA projects have included experimental efforts at many of the levels addressed by SNA. However, the dominant effort has concerned the development of the packet switching network as a transmission system. Less effort has been made in the areas of higher-level functions and protocols.

A blend of the SNA and ARPANET development that would probably make best use of both would use the ARPANET as a service operating at the link level. Special connection procedures, similar to those of making a dial connection in SNA, would be involved. This subject, as it applies to commercial new data networks, is discussed further in Chapter 17. See also other discussions of ARPANET facilities in Sections 7.8, 9.8, 15.11, and 16.5.

6.14.2 DECNET

The Network Services Protocol (NSP) of the digital network architecture for the Digital Equipment Corporation [6.17] also uses a layered structure. Its philosophy roughly parallels that of SNA, but the structure is different.

Levels.   Four major DECNET levels are defined as follows.

1. *Hardware level:* Concerned with the actual transmission of data bits over a link, using techniques such as synchronous, asynchronous, or parallel transmission and the associated modem operations.

2. *Physical link level:* Corresponding more to the data link control level of SNA, concerned with message sequencing, message recovery, and line sharing.

3. *Logical link level:* Including parts of what SNA places in path control, and the half-session levels.

4. *Dialogue level:* Conversation built from the messages sent over a logical link. This level of exchange corresponds roughly to the end-user exchange in SNA using FM and NS headers. It can occur between user processes including application programs, system programs supporting I/O devices, or system programs supporting access to files.

Function breakdown.   The functions provided by DECNET NSP and the somewhat analogous SNA functions are further identified in the following.

1. Functions at the dialogue level
   - Create or destroy a logical link. The dialogue level issues commands for each; functions at lower levels handle these user-commands. (This corresponds to the establishment or termination of an SNA session. Such user-commands are handled in the NAU services layer, the outermost layer of the SNA network.)
   - Transmit or receive data over a logical link (where each transmission follows a receive request)
   - Interrupt over a logical link (where a transmission is made without a prior receive request)

   In order to minimize system buffer occupancy, the lower levels of NSP do not normally move any data over the link until a transmit request has a corresponding receive request, implying that a user buffer has been reserved for the incoming data. (This can be contrasted with the SNA pacing procedure within transmission control—see Section 9.2.4.)

2. Functions at the logical link level
   - Multiplex logical links into physical links (analogous to SNA path control—see Chapter 10)
   - Control traffic over logical links (analogous to SNA data flow control—see Chapter 8)
   - Ensure end-to-end delivery of data in proper sequence (analogous to SNA transmission control—see Chapter 9)
   - Segment/collect long messages over the logical links (analogous to segmenting and blocking in SNA path control—see Section 10.4)

3. Functions for network supervision
   - Route messages through net (analogous to SNA path control—see Chapter 10)
   - Detect node/link failures and maintain routing paths (see Sections 12.4, 15.10.1, and 16.3)

4. Functions for network maintenance
   - Trace message paths through the net
   - Maintain error logs
   - Measure network performance and delays
   - Test network operation

   (These roughly correspond to the maintenance services and measurement services that might be built into an SNA systems services control point (SSCP), as described in Section 7.3.)

See also the DECNET naming conventions in Section 7.8.2.

6.14.3 UNIVAC Intelligent Network

Another layer-like structure can be seen in the "intelligent network" described by Rodgers and Darling of UNIVAC [6.10]. The upper layers, associated with each end of a logical connection, are called *terminal handlers* or *inverted terminal handlers*. A lower layer is called a *message router*.

Terminal handlers are software modules that interface directly to terminals and satisfy all communication requirements that are unique to a type of terminal. Asynchronous as well as synchronous flow may exist between terminals and terminal handlers. The terminal handler contains a queue structure that communicates with the lower-level message handler, using transmission protocols that are common to the network. The transmission subsystem supports duplex message flows between terminal handlers.

6.14.4 UNIVAC DCA

The later "distributed communications architecture" of Sperry Univac [6.18] defines a more complete layered structure, as follows. Two end-users communicate with one another via a logical connection termed a session path. An end-user is connected to the network via a control environment [called *communication system user* (CSU)] which provides the interface logic to the inner layers of the system. A particular CSU may support single or multiple sessions on behalf of its end-users. (The CSU corresponds very roughly to the SNA LU.) DCA does not define how end-users interact or how they are addressed; this is considered to be a function of the particular CSUs connected to the paired end-users. The CSUs are the control environment in which the end-users are embedded and which provide the logical interface to the inner communications system.

Between the CSUs and the *transport network*, there is a layer called the *termination system* (TS) which provides the logical ports into the transport network (see Fig. 6.24).

The transport network, in turn, is divided into the following three levels.

1. Data unit control is responsible for segmenting and blocking, address transformation between transport network and termination systems, and flow control.

2. Routing control is responsible for determining over which route particular messages will travel.

3. Trunk control manages the communications resources, the queues to and from them, and recovery.

See the other discussion of DCA in Section 7.8.3.

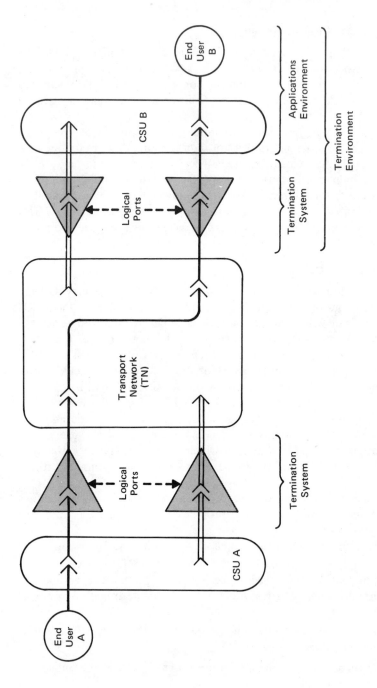

CSU = Communications Systems Use

Fig. 6.24   A session path in the Sperry Univac Distributed Communications Architecture [6.18].

6.15 EXERCISES

6.1 The following are examples of control commands and control indicators that form part of various communication system protocols.

a) Link station address number 3

b) Printer line feed command

c) Polling command to link station number 5

d) Request retransmission of last page

e) Printer tab command

f) Application program A's turn to send

g) Command to initiate a session

h) Typewriter carriage return command

i) Sequence number sent from half-session A to half-session B

j) Confirmation by link station number 3 of receipt of link message number 5

k) Application program information format identifier

l) Redundancy check-error on link message number 6

m) Notification of missing message for program B

n) Activate link number 32

Separate all of the above into the following five classes.

1. *Link controls:* Concerning the management of message flows on one transmission link

2. *Device controls:* Concerning the operation of input/output devices

3. *Other end-user or end-to-end controls:* Including commands (other than device controls) exchanged between two half-sessions

4. *Path controls:* Concerning the management of flows over a path composed of multiple concatenated links and intermediary nodes

5. *Network services:* Concerning the activation or deactivation of parts of the network

6.2 Which of the following statements concerning a response to a request are true?

a) It is, by definition, a reply to the query contained in the request.

b) It is mandatory for every request.

c) It may contain status information if an error condition exists.

d) It is differentiated from a request by a bit in the RH.

e) It must always be received before another request is sent.

6.3 Which of the following statements concerning peer protocols are true?

a) They involve syntax, semantics, and sequence of commands to be sent between nodes.

b) Their format can be either in headers or in control RUs.

c) They are sets of agreements between elements in the same half-session.

d) They are sets of agreements between components in the same layer, though in different half-sessions and/or different nodes.

e) They must be made at system generation time.

6.4 Name three elements usually present in a half-session.

6.5 What are the components of the following?

a) The Basic Information Unit (BIU)

b) The Path Information Unit (PIU)

c) The Basic Link Unit (BLU)

6.6 Which of the following statements are true?

a) Each NAU services manager may have multiple sessions with many other NAU services managers.

b) Each session exists for the duration of one message between a pair of end-users.

c) Each session may serve multiple end-user components (for example, display, keyboard, printer).

d) The NAU services manager contains some network services to help establish sessions.

e) The session can exist only with nonswitched lines.

f) The functions offered by a half-session are fixed by the transmission services to be used.

6.16   REFERENCES AND BIBLIOGRAPHY

See also [5.1].

6.1 H. B. Becker. *Functional Analysis of Information Network*. New York: John Wiley and Sons (1973).

6.2 S. D. Crocker, J. F. Heafner, R. M. Metcalfe, and J. B. Postel. "Function-Oriented Protocols for the ARPA Computer Network." *Proc. AFIPS 1972 Spring Joint Computer Conference*. Montvale, N.J.: AFIPS Press, 1972, pp. 271–280. (Figure 6.23 reprinted by permission.)

6.3 J. H. McFadyen. "Systems Network Architecture: An Overview." *IBM Systems Journal* **15,** No. 1 (1976).

6.4 J. H. McFadyen and E. M. Thomas. "Concepts of Systems Network Architecture." *Communication Networks*. Uxbridge, England: Online Conferences, Ltd. (September 1975).

6.5 *Document X3S34/589*, "Proposed American National Standard for Advanced Data Communication Control Procedures." Prepared by Task Group 4, Subcommittee X3S3, ANSI (15 October 1976).

6.6 B. D. Moldow. "Networking, a Layered Approach." Presented to *SHARE XLVI*, San Francisco (February 1976).

6.7 L. Pouzin. "Network Protocols." In R. M. Grimsdale and F. F. Kuo (eds.), *Computer Communication Networks.* Noordhoff, Leyden (1975).

6.8 *Systems Network Architecture—General Information.* IBM Form No. GA27-3102.

6.9 L. Pouzin. "Network Architecture and Components." Presented at the first European Workshop on Computer Networks, Arls, France (April–May 1973).

6.10 R. E. Rodgers and L. J. Darling. "Intelligent Communications Network." *IEEE 1975 Region Six (Western U.S.A.) Conference.* Salt Lake City, Utah (7–9 May 1975).

6.11 J. P. Gray and C. R. Blair. "IBM's Systems Network Architecture." *Datamation* **21,** No. 4 (April 1975): 51–56.

6.12 "SNA." Field Engineering Education Student Self-Study Course SR23-4208, Course 57290.

6.13 A. J. Keumann. "A Basis for Standardization of User-Terminal Protocols for Computer Network Access." *National Bureau of Standards NBS TN-877.*

6.14 ARPANET Protocol Handbook, *NIC 7104.* Stanford Research Institute (April 1976).

6.15 N. A. Teichholtz. "Digital Network Architecture." EUROCOMP, Brunel University (September 1975): 13–24.

6.16 L. Pouzin. "Virtual Circuits in Datagrams—Technical and Political Problems." *AFIPS Conference Proceedings,* Vol. 45. 1976 National Computer Conference, New York (7–10 June 1976).

6.17 *DECNET—Digital Network Architecture, Design Specification for Data Access Protocol.* Maynard, Mass.: Digital Equipment Corporation (1975).

6.18 *Sperry Univac Distributed Communications Architecture, Systems Description.* © 1976 Sperry Univac, Blue Bell, Pa.

6.19 T. F. Piatkowski, D. C. Hull, and R. J. Sundstrom, "Inside IBM's Systems Network Architecture," *Data Communications* (February 1977), pp. 33–48.

6.20 J. P. Gray, "Network Services in Systems Network Architecture," *IEEE Transactions on Communications,* Vol. Com-25, No. 1 (January 1977).

7

Higher-level
Services of
SNA Network

7.1 INTRODUCTION

This chapter* focuses on the use of the upper layers of the SNA network to provide higher-level services. Primary attention is given to the *NAU services layer*, which contains services of two very different kinds:

1. First, there are *network services* for either session establishment, configuration control, or maintenance. Network services are active in SSCP–LU, SSCP–PU, SSCP–SSCP, and PU–PU sessions. However, network services also support *all* sessions at the NAU where they are located and, therefore, are considered to be *per-NAU* rather than *per-session* services.

2. Second, there are higher-level services that support *each* LU–LU session. Examples of these are (a) *presentation services*, which may provide for the interpretation or modification of the data entering or leaving each end-user (these services may tailor the size, format, or content of that information to the needs of the receiving end), and (b) *session recovery services*, which may direct the resynchronization of a session or other recovery actions.

---

* Acknowledgment is given to the following principal contributors to the SNA designs reflected in this chapter: T. F. Piatkowski, G. A. Plotsky, J. R. Babb, and E. M. Thomas for the definition of network services; J. R. Babb, E. E. Cobb, and J. H. Jones for the structure of presentation services; and W. A. Bernstein, M. D. Froelick, and J. P. Gray for the material on FM headers.

NAU services are called LU Services (LUS), PU Services (PUS), and SSCP Services in those specific types of NAU. The NAU services have been among the most rapidly evolving parts of SNA; and (as of this writing) a complete internal structure has not yet been formally documented as part of SNA. It is clear, however, that the functions of NAU services can be thought of as having a structure such as the one shown in Fig. 7.1. The *NAU services manager* performs per-NAU services for all the half-sessions of that NAU. Hence, we will show network services located primarily within the NAU services manager. The NAU services also *provide a limited number of ports for sessions with other NAUs.* For each of these sessions, there will be a session-related FI.FMD element. This per-session FI.FMD element within the NAU services layer may contain an aggregate of services, including the above-mentioned presentation and recovery services. It may also contain per-session appendages to per-NAU services that are in the NAU services manager. The title FI.FMD comes from the ungainly name, *Function Interpreter for Function Management Data.*

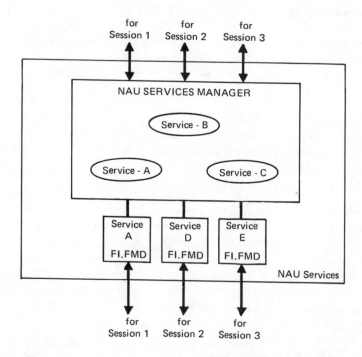

FI.FMD = Function Interpreter to FM Data

Fig. 7.1 NAU services.

The discussion of the other session-related end-to-end services—namely, data flow control and transmission control—is included in Chapters 8 and 9, respectively.

7.2 USE OF NAU SERVICES

7.2.1 End-User to LU Services Boundary

As indicated in Fig. 7.1, the information flowing across the boundary between the end-user and LU services may include sets that are associated with each half-session. One set of information must pertain to the SSCP-LU session for the purpose of establishing and terminating LU-LU sessions which that LU supports. Other sets would pertain to the information flow for each LU-LU session.

SNA puts no restrictions on the format of this end-user information, requiring instead that the product designer provide any necessary translations between the user format and the SNA-defined headers and control RUs. Common languages are certainly desirable among groups of end-users and/or groups of products, and common FM headers, NS headers, and control RUs for DFC and TC are major steps in this direction. Nevertheless a product design can still use product-unique commands so long as the translations to SNA formats are provided.

In theory, the *boundary* between the end-user and LU services may contain information (for each session) flowing to or from:

1. A per-NAU service (in the NAU services manager);
2. A per-session FI.FMD service (e.g., presentation services);
3. Data flow control (e.g., occasional quiescing commands); and
4. Transmission control (e.g., for occasional recovery situations).

The per-NAU services that are thus far best defined are network services, which cooperate in the management of the network. (All SSCP–SSCP, SSCP–LU, SSCP–PU, and PU–PU sessions use network services.)

Today, *in normal LU–LU data flow between end-users, the NAU services manager is essentially null.* In effect, presentation services (in FI.FMD) appears at the boundary between the end-user and NAU services.

7.2.2 Asynchronous Signaling

Different implementations may use different techniques whereby parts of the SNA network can asynchronously signal the code in NAU services. TCAM, for example, makes extensive use of user-specified *message handlers.* These special programs are packaged as part of the TP access method (TCAM), and are scheduled by TCAM on specified occasions. VTAM, similarly, will schedule *exits* for many of these purposes. These exits are programs that are packaged as part of an application program or application subsystem, but they are distinct from the normal instruction sequences. To illustrate, VTAM can include signals for the following exits (among others).

- LOGON: An exit that helps accede to a request of a remote NAU to begin a session
- LOST-TERMINAL (LOSTERM): An exit that helps in the withdrawal of a remote NAU from a session
- RELEASE REQUEST (REL REQ): An exit that considers a request from another NAU for release of a current session, so that a different session can be set up
- TPEND: An exit that helps in the network shutdown procedures
- SYNAD: An exit that handles negative responses and hardware malfunctions
- SCIP: An exit that handles requests for recovery assistance
- DATA-FLOW-ASYNCHRONOUS (DFASY): An exit that handles requests from other NAUs for the quiescence of flows and preparation for shutdown

SNA defines the control commands that are sent between NAUs in order to activate such exits or message-handling routines. (There is not always a one-to-one mapping between exits and the SNA control commands, however.) Such exits may be considered to be logically within the NAU services layer. However, the exits are currently implementation-dependent; these are *not defined by SNA,* nor are any control tables or other form of interface that may be needed between the exits and the end-user (i.e., the remainder of the application program or application subsystem).

7.3 NETWORK SERVICES

7.3.1 Introduction

This section describes the *functions performed by network services and its distribution among SSCPs, LUs, and PUs.* The placing of some network services in the SSCPs provides an opportunity for a degree of centralization where this is desirable. This permits simpler products to use these services without providing the full support themselves. The degree of centralization depends on

1. The number of SSCPs and the size of each control domain
2. The division of function among each SSCP and its associated LUs and PUs

The number of SSCPs in a multihost network is a user option; in current SNA implementations it is one or more per host; the special protocols among SSCPs are described in Chapter 15. In SSCPs, LUs, and PUs, *network services are primarily a per-NAU function within the NAU services manager.* However, there is a small portion of network services that is session-unique and is therefore part of a half-session. That portion is a sort of appendage (sometimes called an NAU services session appendage), which is located in the FI.FMD element of a half-session. The role of this appendage is rather limited, but may include storing the status of a command pertaining to a particular session. NAU services supporting multiple half-sessions, each of which contains an FI.FMD, data flow control, and transmission control element, are illustrated in Fig. 7.2.

7.3.2 Distribution of Network Services

As stated earlier, network services are included in each NAU services layer. However, the network services differ depending on the type of NAU in which they are located.

1. *SSCP Network Services* (SSCP.NS) are located in the SSCP services in one or more SSCPs (see Fig. 7.3a). The SSCP.NS are functions that serve other NAUs in each control domain, providing both physical and logical resource management. These include services for control of network configuration and session establishment and termination. The SSCP.NS coordinate the distributed network services and act as manager of a control domain.

2. *LU Network Services* (LU.NS) are located in the LU services (see Fig. 7.3b). The primary function of the LU.NS concerns logical connections, such as session establishment. These services are present in all LUs; that is, those NAUs that serve end-users of the SNA network.

In SNA, each of these LU network services can call on the SSCP network services for assistance. LU.NS interacts with SSCP.NS, using architected protocols and formats. That concept is illustrated in Fig. 7.4.

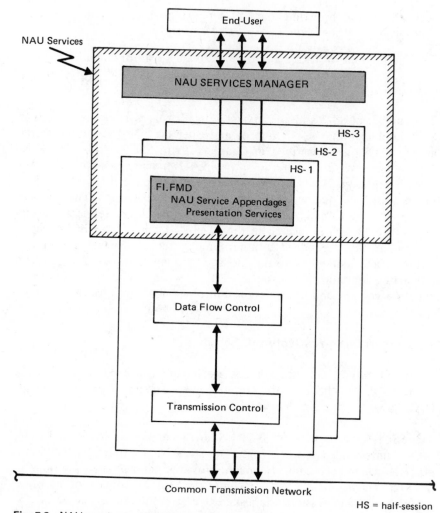

Fig. 7.2 NAU services with multiple half-sessions.

In general, the LU services may receive a request from an end-user, and then either

a) Provide the total service requested

b) Simply pass the request on to the SSCP

c) Transform the request into an architected form and then forward it to the SSCP

d) Perform a part of the service requested and then forward the remainder of the request to the SSCP for further processing.

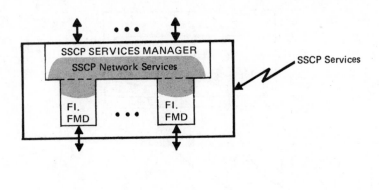

(a)

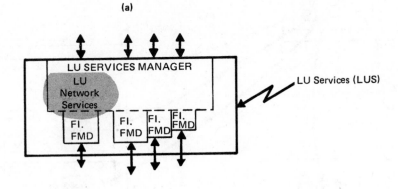

(b)

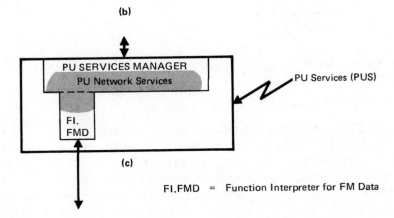

(c)

FI.FMD = Function Interpreter for FM Data

Fig. 7.3 Typical sets of higher-level services in the three types of NAU: (a) in SSCP; (b) in LU; and (c) in PU.

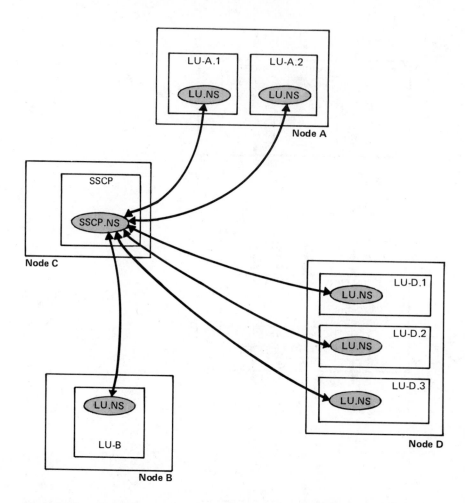

Fig. 7.4 Concept of having some network services distributed among the LUs and the SSCP.

Each LU, therefore, has two kinds of service available to it. When an LU is first activated, perhaps at the beginning of the day, its session with the SSCP is established. Thereafter, the LU services provide the end-user with *immediate services* from that LU and from the SSCPs in the network. Any number of LU–LU sessions can then be established and terminated by that LU's end-user. The LU–LU sessions are said to provide access to *connected services*. Immediate services and connected services are illustrated in Fig. 7.5.

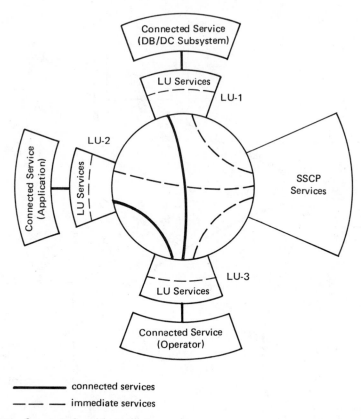

connected services

— — — immediate services

Fig. 7.5 Connected and immediate services.

3. *PU Network Services* (PU.NS) are located in the PU services (see Fig. 7.3c) and are concerned with SNA configuration resource management, including configuration establishment.

In most networks, a central coordination point is desirable (for one or more domains) for functions such as network bringup, network shutdown, reconfiguration in the event of a line or node failure, and coordination of network tracing or testing. To make this possible, a session is established between an SSCP and a PU in each node. That session links SSCP network services and PU network services, so they can operate cooperatively.

The concept of this distribution of network services among the PUs in the nodes and their tie to SSCP network services is illustrated in Fig. 7.6. (The connections shown are logical connections—i.e., sessions between the SSCP and each PU; the physical connections are less direct.)

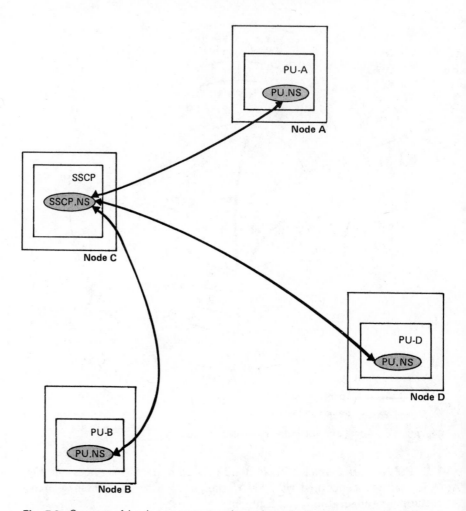

Fig. 7.6 Concept of having some network services distributed among the PUs and the SSCP.

NAU–NAU sessions. There are five kinds of session commonly used between NAUs. Four of these concern network services. The five kinds are:

1. LU-to-LU sessions, for data flow between end-users

2. SSCP-to-LU sessions, for network services primarily concerning session establishment or termination

3. SSCP-to-PU sessions, for network services primarily concerning physical configuration

4. SSCP-to-SSCP sessions, for cross-domain network services
5. PU-to-PU sessions for network services concerning notification of path interruptions.

SSCP-to-SSCP and PU-to-PU sessions will be discussed in Chapter 15. The other conceivable combination, PU–LU, has not been found to be necessary.

Every LU has capability for at least two sessions (see Fig. 7.7): one session with the SSCP, and one session with another LU. Architecturally,

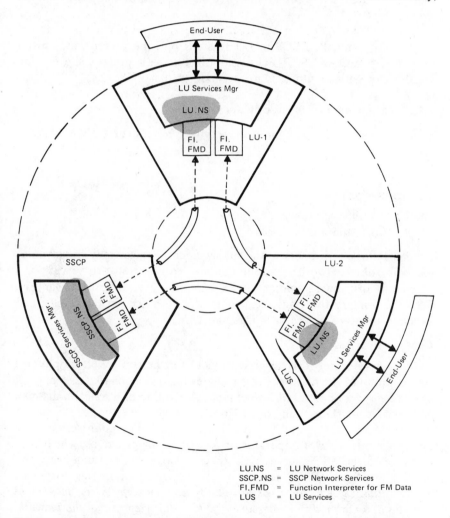

LU.NS   =   LU Network Services
SSCP.NS =   SSCP Network Services
FI.FMD =   Function Interpreter for FM Data
LUS   =   LU Services

Fig. 7.7 Network services and FI.FMD services in LU-LU and LU-SSCP sessions.

an LU can have many sessions with different LUs (one session with each other LU). However, an implementation may limit the number of sessions an LU can have. For example, each host LU can usually have many sessions, but cluster controllers are often limited, by implementation, to one LU–LU session per LU. (Particular COMC implementations may also expect only one LU–LU session per LU in a cluster controller; however, this is not an architectural requirement.) *Terminal nodes*, using a simpler address in the transmission header than that used by cluster controllers, *are architecturally limited to one LU–LU session per LU in the terminal node.*

Current configuration services require that, within a domain, the SSCP-to-LU and the SSCP-to-PU sessions both be prerequisites to an LU–LU session. An SSCP–PU session, in turn, is a prerequisite for any SSCP–LU sessions (with LUs in the node of that PU).

7.3.3 Categories of Network Services

There are four major categories of network services currently defined by SNA:

1. Configuration services
2. Session services
3. Maintenance services
4. Network operator services

Other network coordination and management services may be advantageous in some networks, as requirements evolve. Network services are potentially distributed among SSCPs, LUs, and PUs, as indicated in Fig. 7.8. The primary functions are configuration services in the SSCPs and PUs and session services in SSCPs and LUs.

Configuration services

This category of network services provides for the control of the physical configuration of the network. This includes the *activation and deactivation of links, physical units, and logical units.* Activation of physical units may be preceded by the sending of programs or microcode to those locations not capable of storing and loading their own. Configuration services are invoked by the network operator or by operations programs (which may interface to the SSCP services via special "box-services" unique to the node in which the SSCP resides or via a regular LU). *The distributed configuration services are used to initially configure the SNA network at start-up time, to modify it subsequently, to restart elements of the network, or to shut down the network.*

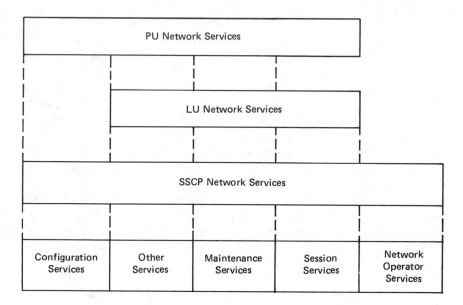

Fig. 7.8 Potential distribution of network services among the SSCP, PU, and LU.

Now it would have been possible, in principle, to put the controls for activating a box or activating a link, exclusively, in each box. Then when a line was supposed to be activated, the operator would run around and push buttons and switches to enter commands. If one had a network of ten boxes, one would need ten operators or one operator on roller skates. Clearly, that would be a little clumsy, so *what was done in SNA was to collect the control of a reasonable group of boxes and links in each system services control point.*

In the VTAM implementation [7.5], for example, configuration services can be invoked to activate a specific resource, or they can be requested to activate a symbolically named resource group, as defined by the installation. Resources can be defined at system-generation time, or at any time thereafter, but prior to their first use by VTAM.

When a specific installation is defined (that is, when the characteristics of all nodes and links are entered into the system's definition tables), each NAU is assigned its network address. However, NAUs that are connected via switched links are assigned their address by configuration services at the time when the connection is made.

To perform all these functions, configuration services can maintain tabular information relative to the symbolic name, network address, and activation status of all NAUs, as well as the status of links and sessions related to network services, that are within the domain of the SSCP. Most physical units are active in only one domain at a time, even though they may be defined in more than one domain. For example, a cluster controller with switched line support can dial into a domain and be assigned the network address associated with the port. The cluster can dial into any domain in which it has been defined as a resource. In other cases, more than one SSCP can interact with a resource as though each has exclusive control of that resource. An N-tail communications controller is an example of a node that can be active in multiple domains concurrently (see the discussion of cross-domain connections in Section 15.9).

One of the design trade-offs is whether such resource-definition information should be obtained early, at system definition time, or should be obtained later and more dynamically. In the ACF/VTAM implementation, the SSCP obtains considerable information as part of the system-definition process, including the following:

1. The link stations that are associated with a PU. If the SSCP can gain access to a station via the public switched network, the telephone number of the station and the ID to be returned by the station are also provided.

2. The name and characteristics of each LU associated with the PU load module (number of LUs, allowable session types, network names).

3. The name and characteristics of each link supported by the PU load module (line speeds, modem parameters, line retry parameters).

4. The connectivity of the physical network; that is, which links connect the node of the PU to which other nodes.

Some feel that there is a requirement [6.20] to reduce the amount of this system definition in favor of some more dynamic definition on the occasion of use. SNA also defines the *RU formats* for those requests that are sent between pairs of network services, such as between configuration services in SSCP.NS and configuration services in PU.NS. These formatted NS commands generally involve

1. Activation and deactivation of links

2. Contact of nodes prior to activation

3. Initial program load of nodes (the actual text that is transmitted is product-specific and is not architected)

4. Dump (that is, transfer) of stored data to the SSCP (similarly, the actual data transferred is product-specific)

5. Setting of control tables, such as path control's routing tables, in nodes

6. Dial-in and dial-out, using the switched network

7. Reports from each PU.NS on the status of a portion of the network

Many of the procedures involve interactions with transmission services in the data link control and path control layers. Further discussion of these is therefore deferred until Sections 12.4–12.6, after the transmission layers have been described. A list of the NS commands used for configuration services and their details can be found in Appendix C.

Session services

These *support the activation of a logical connection (called a session) between two logical units*, so that the ground rules for their subsequent dialogue are clearly established. Also, session services support the orderly takedown of sessions. To achieve this, session services are located partly in SSCP.NS and partly in LU.NS, for all SSCPs and all LUs. The session services in SSCP.NS include a variety of auxiliary services such as the translation of LU names into network addresses and the verification of the authority of one requesting a session.

Each logical unit may be built with a capability for only a limited number of simultaneous sessions. Session services in the SSCP allocate that capability (of an LU) when some other LU wants to establish a session with that LU. At each LU, each session becomes realized by the creation of a set of functions (called a *half-session*) that is dedicated to only one of an LU's sessions.

SNA defines the *RU formats* for requesting that a session be initiated or terminated, and also for the formal binding of the session between the LUs with ground rules that have been agreed on.

LU–LU sessions can be initiated in three ways:

1. By either of the two LUs that are to be joined in a session

2. By a third LU

3. By the network start-up or restart procedures in accordance with system-generation and configuration-status information

Particular implementations (for example, VTAM) may queue requests for a session with a given LU, if the latter is already in session and cannot handle another session. A further useful service can be provided if the waiting LU desires to interrupt another session. Suppose that LU-1 and LU-2 are in session, LU-3 wants a session with LU-1, and LU-3 wants LU-2 to give up its session. Following a request from LU-3, the SSCP can so notify LU-2. VTAM can direct that an exit be taken by LU-2 in order to consider the request of LU-3.

Functions in the transmission control layer, called session control, also play a key role in establishing each session. Therefore, the detailed discussion of procedures for establishing and terminating LU–LU sessions are deferred until Section 9.7, after a discussion of transmission control. Chapter 12 then gives an overview of session establishment and termination, after all the layers have been discussed. Section 12.5 illustrates the establishment of SSCP–LU and SSCP–PU sessions, and Section 12.7 illustrates the establishment of LU–LU sessions. Some readers may prefer to scan these illustrations before proceeding with the more detailed study of each layer in the intervening chapters. Session setup and takedown in multidomain networks are described in Sections 15.7 and 15.8, after a discussion of multiple-domain concepts.

Maintenance services

Maintenance services provide for the testing of network facilities. Traces can also be requested. The exact facilities offered depend on the various product capabilities. As an example, however, in the VTAM implementation, the tracing capability allows the network operator to specify, on a node or a session basis, that transmitted RUs and/or buffer areas are to be recorded. For each RU, information on its origin and destination are provided.

SNA defines the RU formats for function requests that are used by maintenance services. These RUs concern the following:

1. Execution of a test on a link, LU, or PU (with the type of test specified in the RU)
2. Beginning or end of a trace of activity in a resource (for example, link or LU) that is specified by the network address in the RU
3. Return of maintenance statistics or the results of specified tests or traces to the SSCP

The defined commands for maintenance services are discussed in Section 12.6, and details can be found in Appendix C.

Measurement services

Little has been architecturally defined in this area. However, the SSCP is a logical place to provide domain–wide coordination of measurement services. Any such coordination would have to involve defined RU formats for commands that start, stop, and record prespecified measurements in nodes of the SNA network.

Network operator services

These support communication with the network owner (that is, the owner's authorized representative). This service can be implemented so the network owner can access configuration, maintenance, and session services (via the SSCP services manager or an LU) and optimize network operations.

Operator commands, in VTAM for example, enable the operator to

1. Start up the SNA network
2. Shut down the SNA network
3. Activate and deactivate parts of the network, such as links, LUs, and PUs
4. Display status information
5. Control traces of message activity in some parts of the network
6. Collect network statistics

Implementation may permit these operator commands to be used by selected programs, as well as by the network operator at the console. Network operation support, in multidomain networks, is discussed in Section 15.4.3.

7.3.4 Network-Services RU Formats

Network services only understand SNA-architected RUs. If an unformatted RU is sent to SSCP network services, a preprocessor must convert the unformatted RU into the SNA-architected, formatted RU.

Many formatted requests going to or from SSCP.NS, LU.NS, or PU.NS have common fields, as illustrated in Fig. 7.9 and described below.

NS header. This header (like the FM headers that are used in LU–LU sessions) appears at the beginning of an RU. The first two bytes of this

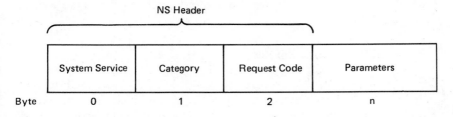

Fig. 7.9 Common format for NS requests.

NS header identify the service that the request is coming from or going to. The first byte is hexadecimal '01' to indicate network services. The second byte identifies the category of service within NS as either configuration, maintenance, network operator, or session service. The third byte of this header is the request code. This field specifies one of the possible commands used by the identified service category.

Parameters. Different NS requests have different numbers of parameters, depending on the request code. One of the parameters will frequently be the network address of the LU, PU, or link involved. Other examples of parameters also in common usage are:

1. *NAU or link name*
   - The first parameter byte identifies the name as belonging to either a PU, an LU, or a link.
   - The second parameter byte gives the byte length of the name.
   - The remainder gives the symbolic name in character-string form.

2. *Control vector* is a structured field used to update tables pertaining to characteristics of a PU, an LU, a link, path control functions, or data link control functions.
   - The first and second parameter bytes give the network address of the element to which the control vector applies.
   - The remainder gives the specific control vector data.

3. *Requestor ID* (a nonarchitected byte string for identification purposes), *password*, and *user field* (another nonarchitected byte string for supplementing user data). Each has the same format, as follows:
   - The first parameter byte gives the byte length.
   - The remainder gives the character string or bits for either the requestor ID, the password, or the user-specific data.

Further information concerning NS requests and responses is given in Appendix C.

7.3.5 SSCP Network Services

The substructures of the SSCP are shown in Fig. 7.10. An SSCP request may be *formatted*, where each field has a predetermined meaning. Alternatively, it may be *unformatted*, where a nonarchitected but product-defined or owner-tailored byte string conveys the command. The latter is

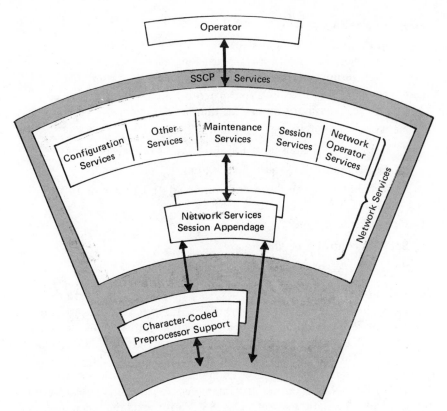

Fig. 7.10 Types of services within the SSCP.

useful for terminal operators, who key in the appropriate word format on a terminal keyboard. These byte strings must first be preprocessed by the SSCP to transform the character-string command into a field-formatted command. Thus the fields in character form must be able to be mapped to formatted form.

Conceptually, the SSCP services are an open-ended facility to aid in the coordination of the network operations. Four categories of the basic services were described above. Different implementations may add a variety of features to the basic SSCP capability. Though not fully architected, some of the possible extended uses of the system services control point are the following.

1. Start-of-day procedures

   ■ Affirming that all locations are fully operational

   ■ Reinitiating applications (probably at user request) with a cold or a warm start, as appropriate to each

2. End-of-day procedures
    ■ Shutting down segments of the network in an orderly sequence with adequate forewarning, permitting each node to initiate application termination or "save" procedures, as appropriate
    ■ Providing (to an application program) the data needed to compile statistical summary reports of the day's traffic

3. Network routing changes, occasioned by
    ■ Assessment of long-term link error rates or link outages
    ■ Assessment of long-term link loadings
    ■ Terminal node shutdown or failure, and designation of an alternate terminal for continuation

4. Network testing and diagnostic procedures

5. Security control procedures

7.3.6 PU Network Services

The distribution of some network services among the SSCP and the PUs of several nodes is illustrated in Fig. 7.11. Two sessions are shown. Actually, node C would also have a PU, and a third session would exist for it. Each PU contains a set of PU network services (PU.NS) within its PU services. The PU.NS are sets of procedures that are implemented as coded instructions. The PU services manager provides an interface, for PU.NS, to the SNA-layer resource managers, particularly those for data link control and path control. The SSCP, for example, can use that interface (via PU.NS) for link activations, for dial procedures, and for "bootstrap" start-up operations, such as the initial program load of a remote node. The SSCP can use the PU's interface to path control to change configuration tables and routing tables. The PU may also have an interface to the node's physical-resource manager (for example, the node's operating system, if it has one), which has control over resources such as storage and processor power.

As an example, configuration services in the SSCP may want to activate a cluster controller that is attached to a communications controller (see Fig. 7.12). This would involve the following interchange.

1. The SSCP sends a command, CONTACT, to the PU of the communications controller (COMC) because the COMC controls the link on which the desired cluster controller is attached. The CONTACT causes the PU of the COMC to initiate link-control procedures to establish contact with the cluster controller, confirm that power is on there, set the remote link station to a normal response mode, and confirm that the remote node is IPL'd.

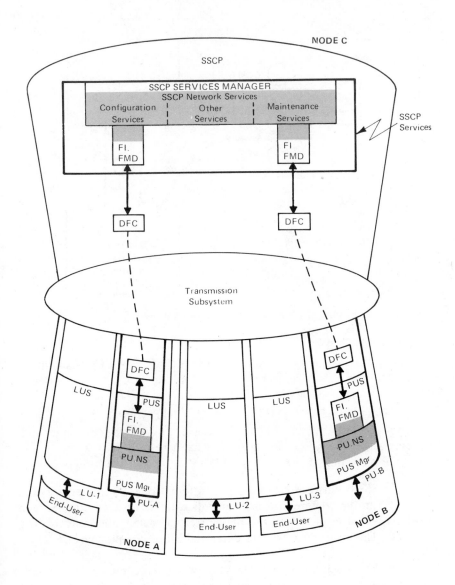

NS   =   Network Services
FI.FMD   =   Function Interpreter. FM Data
PUS   =   Physical Unit Services
LUS   =   Logical Unit Services
DFC   =   Data Flow Control

Fig. 7.11 Distributed network services (shaded areas) among the SSCP and PUs in multiple nodes.

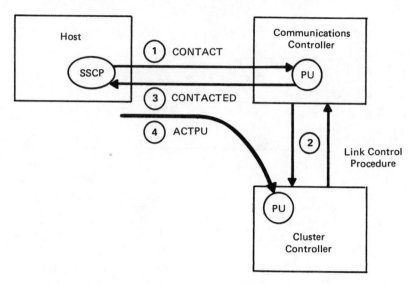

Fig. 7.12 Activation of physical unit in cluster controller.

2. The communications controller PU sends a CONTACTED command back to the SSCP, indicating that the link-level CONTACT procedure has been successfully completed.

3. An ACTPU (ACTIVATE PHYSICAL UNIT) command is then sent from the SSCP to the PU in the cluster controller. This command causes the SSCP-PU session to be established, thereby allowing the SSCP to communicate with the PU in the cluster controller.

Thus, the SSCP network services work through one distributed service, the PU.NS in the communications controller, to set up a path to another distributed service, the PU.NS in the cluster controller; the latter is then activated. This procedure will be described more completely in Section 12.4.

The PU in each node (in conjunction with path control and data link control) is also in a position to note failure of any of the attached links or attached nodes; in some nodes, like the COMC, the PU also has the responsibility of keeping the SSCP informed of such conditions. Link errors, for example, are usually recoverable at the data link control level; however, whenever they cannot be successfully recovered, the inoperative condition of that link and the affected nodes attached to that link must be reported by the PU to the SSCP. Notification of adjacent nodes may also be achieved (see Section 15.10.1).

7.3.7 LU Network Services

The distribution of other network services among the SSCP and multiple LUs in several nodes is illustrated in Fig. 7.13. Each LU.NS may have procedures for session, maintenance, and other services, corresponding to those in the SSCP. Of these, the basic ones are those that help in the establishment and termination of LU–LU sessions, in cooperation with the session services of the SSCP.NS.

The actual connection between any two logical units could theoretically be established by a dialogue directly between the LU network services of the two logical units. However, conflicts can arise if both LUs initiate a session simultaneously. Also, any services, such as name resolution or the matching of characteristics between the two ends of the session, would have to be done at each LU. Therefore, it sometimes becomes a more practical procedure for either of the logical units to first contact a third party (the SSCP) which, aware of all network status, then directs the logical connection (or BIND) between the two LUs (see Fig. 7.14). The details of the process of activating a session and the assistance provided by the transmission control layer are described in Section 9.7.

Throughout the SNA network, therefore, there can exist two sets of network services. There must be a PU network service (in a PU) in each node. Each PU is in session with the system services control point. Also, there must be an LU network service in every LU that represents an end-user. These services also are in session with the SSCP.

Coupling of logical and physical services. As described above, the LU network services (associated with each LU) and the PU network services (associated with a group of physical resources) are architected as separate entities. In LUs and PUs, these services are accessed by a separate network address. In using the system services control point (SSCP), the NS header denotes which category is involved; thus even here the logical and physical services can also be identified as separate entities, even though they are accessed by the same network address. There are circumstances in which the distributed logical services need to communicate with the distributed physical services, however.

An example would be the interaction in the SSCP between processes concerned with setting up a session (for example, processing the INITIATE command), and processes that establish physical paths for that session—e.g., those that (1) contact nodes to bring them into the network, (2) establish dial connections, and (3) recover physical paths.

Illustration of the use of both logical and physical network services are given in Sections 12.4 through 12.9. These illustrations are deferred to that later chapter in order to incorporate the roles of other layers as

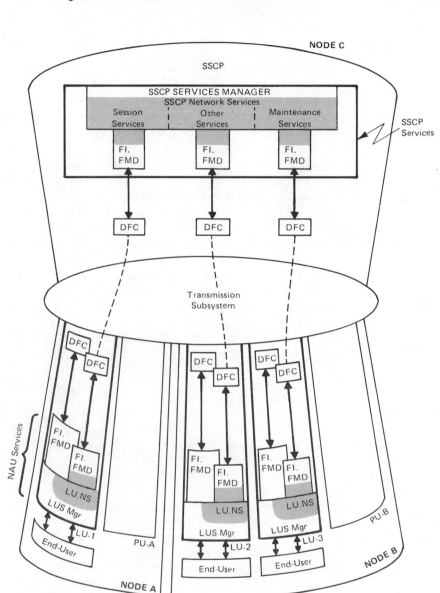

NS   = Network Services
FI.FMD = Function Interpreter for FM Data
DFC   = Data Flow Control

Fig. 7.13 Network services (shaded areas) distributed between LUs and the SSCP.

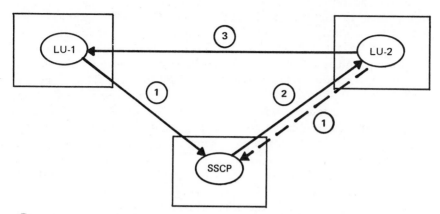

1 LU-1 (or LU-2) asks SSCP to initiate a session between LU-1 and LU-2

2 SSCP directs LU-2 to establish session (LU-2 has the primary half-session)

3 LU-2 "binds" the session with LU-1

Fig. 7.14 The three steps of activating an LU-LU session.

well. However, some readers may prefer to scan these illustrations at this point.

7.4 PRESENTATION SERVICES

7.4.1 Types of Presentation Services

A pair of presentation services (within the FI.FMD layer) matches a particular end-user (or NAU service) to the needs of another, and insulates one end from unnecessary details of the other. Each end-user (or NAU service manager) has specific requirements on formats and on commands that it understands. These may be different from those understood at the other end of the session. A pair of presentation services (one in each half-session) effectively *changes the view of the information so as to better match the needs or the language of each end-user or NAU service manager. To do this involves an interpretation of the RU itself or a transformation of the end-user's data to an RU.* Examples of these services are found in application subsystems such as CICS and IMS, and they can be provided for individual applications as well.

Different implementations of presentation services will provide different services. This may involve *transformation* of the RU (as in compression or compaction of data); it may involve the *addition* of information to the RU (as in the addition of column headings when formatting a display); it may involve *translation* of an RU (as in the translation of common commands, like data management or program activation commands, into the local language); or it may involve *formation* of RUs, such as changing one user record to many RUs, many user records to one RU, or many RUs to one user record. The presentation services may also interpret the FM header (within the RU) so as to *select* a particular type of presentation services that is appropriate for one end-user component (for example, printer, punch, console, one of many data sets, or one of many subroutines).

On the other hand, some end-users will require no presentation services at all. In that case, the end-users have a private understanding between the two of them of the data structures and semantics to be used, and no intermediary interpretations are needed.

Many of the existing presentation services use *common FM headers and/or RU formats* that are applicable to a class of end-users. The common formats and protocols serve as the "common language," through which paired presentation services interact, for a class of end-users or NAU services managers. The presentation services at each end then interpret the common formats to suit the needs of a particular end-user or NAU service manager. These purposes require presentation services having four kinds of facilities:

1. *Mechanisms for the selection of appropriate presentation services* for particular end-user components (for example, printers, subroutines, data records) *and subsequent routing* to and from those components

2. *Common commands* for end-user functions, such as those for database management and task management

3. *Data-record structures*, such as field formats and control characters in the data stream

4. *Mechanisms for editing and mapping RUs* in a flexible fashion

Different sets of presentation services can be expected to evolve to meet the needs of different application environments. For example, one set, using the type-1 and type-2 FM headers, has been developed to meet the needs of selection, control, and data set transfer in the remote job entry and data entry environment. Another set of presentation services is needed for the information display environment. That environment has needs in the areas of mapping and formatting of messages to the two-dimensional presentation space of a display.

In all cases, presentation services can and should be independent of other layers, including those used for information transport. The presentation services protocols must likewise be independent of any specific communications carrier if the user is to be free to take advantage of different transport facilities.

7.4.2 Location of Presentation Services

Presentation services can be physically located in both ends of every session. However, they may be predominantly at one end or the other. Host support requirements are reduced if the LU associated with a device contains all the presentation services that are unique to that device, as illustrated in Fig. 7.15. In this case, NAUs in any source node can use a common format that need not reflect the unique device characteristics of the destinations. *The transformation from the common format to the device format can be performed in the destination NAU. Then the device itself may change, and its local presentation services may have to change also, but the rest of the system can remain unaffected.* On the other hand, economy sometimes dictates a centralization of some presentation services for similar NAUs in different destination nodes. In this event, the partial location of presentation services in a host or in some

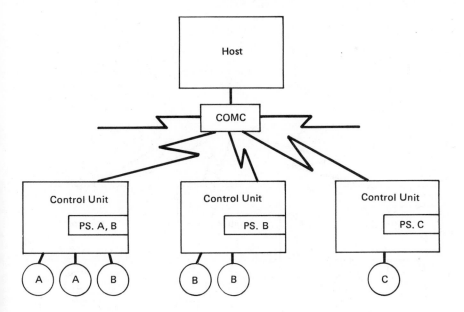

Fig. 7.15 Presentation services that are primarily decentralized.

other common node is needed (see Fig. 7.16). *The architecture must permit the distribution of presentation services between source and destination NAUs* and a cooperation between the presentation services in the two NAUs.

Figure 7.17 illustrates the various transformations that may be provided by presentation services at either end of the session. The transformations, in general, convert the user-specific data to or from the chain of RUs that is sent between NAUs. The transformations may or may not make use of stored data at one or both ends. In any case, the RU formats sent by one presentation-services element must be understood by its peer presentation services in the other half-session.

Different presentation services may be needed for different sessions of a given NAU. For example, some terminals as well as host subsystems can tailor their operations, depending on whether the work is job entry (to a job entry subsystem) or is data-base inquiry (to a DB/DC system such as CICS or IMS). Suppose that one logical unit (LU-1) wants to establish two LU–LU sessions, one with LU-2 and another with LU-3 (see Fig. 7.18). Within each session there must be logically distinct instances of presentation services. Each half-session (of which the presentation services are only a part) is identified with a common session ID consisting of the NAU address pair—for example, (1, 2). A component of

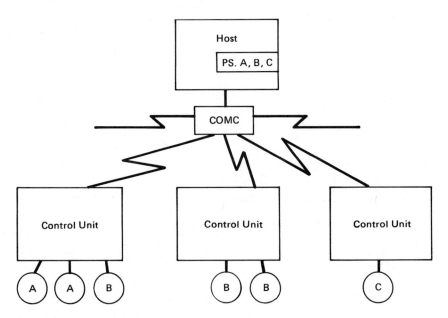

Fig. 7.16 Presentation services that are primarily centralized.

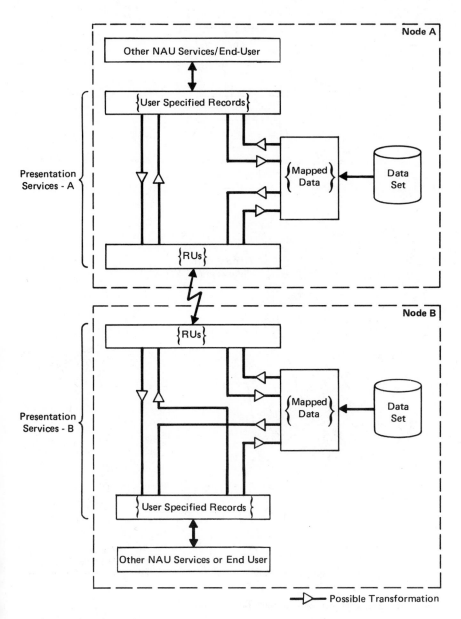

Fig. 7.17 Pair of presentation services with points of possible transformations.

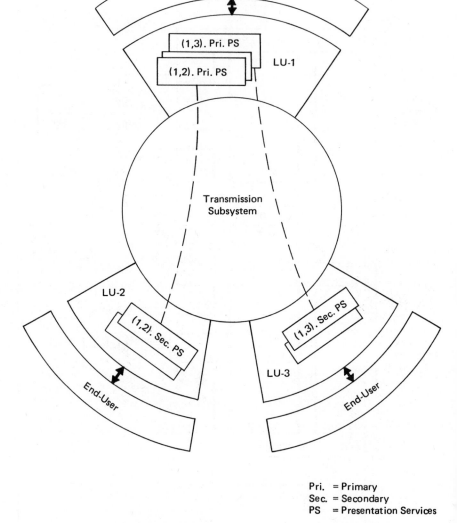

Pri. = Primary
Sec. = Secondary
PS = Presentation Services

Fig. 7.18 Presentation service pairs per session.

the half-session, such as presentation services, is similarly identified with
that session—for example, (1, 2).PS.

If, moreover, a given session serves multiple components, such as a
printer and a display, then *within that session there must be a selection of
the appropriate presentation service for the component. This selection, within
a session, is done by means of FM headers* in the leading edge of the RU
(immediately following the RH).

Note that only logically is there a distinct set of presentation services
for each LU–LU session or end-user component. An implementation may
achieve this distinction, by serially reusing one set of code or by using
reentrant code, if parts of the same presentation service are needed by
more than one session.

7.4.3 Use of FM Headers

Protocols are needed to communicate between presentation services at
each end of a session. One of the techniques for expressing these
protocols in LU–LU sessions is the use of the FM header within the RU.
The FM header is a format for the presentation-service protocol (see
Section 6.8.4). SNA has established a set of rules for the use of FM
headers, as follows.

Two LUs in a session agree at session initiation (BIND) time whether
or not they will use FM headers (FMH). This is done via the BIND
command, whose parameters indicate whether an FMH *may or may not
appear* once the session is bound (see Section 9.7.2 for details). If the
BIND command indicates that an FMH may appear, then each request
and each response must indicate, via a bit (the format indicator bit) in the
RH, whether or not an FMH is present in the RU. If an FMH is present,
it will be positioned immediately following the RH.

One format for the FMH is shown in Fig. 7.19. Seven bits are
allocated for FMH type, allowing up to 128 different types to be developed. The length field in the first byte of each FMH permits the overall
length of the FMH to vary. Generally, a variable length field within an
FMH will contain a length count of its own (as its first byte). However,

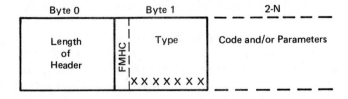

Fig. 7.19 FM header format.

one variable length field per FM header can have its length inferred from the length field of the FMH itself.

FM headers can also be used in combinations. It is often advantageous to define commands as a hierarchy, where one command modifies or supplements another. The concatenation of modifying FMHs is made possible by the use of an FMHC bit (the FMH concatenated bit) in the second byte of each FM header (see Fig. 7.19). The presence of a "one" in this bit position indicates the presence of another FM header following this one.

In some cases, presentation services must deliver *every* RU in formats that are unique to the recipient. An example of this is the network services commands, whose format was shown in Fig. 7.9. The format indicator bit in the RH is used there to indicate to the presentation services whether or not a properly formatted command is in the RU. If that bit is "off," then the presentation services in the SSCP must convert the unformatted RU to the format shown in Fig. 7.9. The SSCP only sends properly formatted commands to the LU network services, the PU network services, or another SSCP.

Other formatted commands can, however, be built on the header format shown in Fig. 7.19. A wide range of FM headers can be conceived containing commands for device control, data-set manipulation, task initiation, etc. In general, presentation services can be used to convert unformatted or formatted commands to a format that is acceptable to the recipient.

Illustrative uses of FM headers in job entry and interactive environments are given in the following sections.

7.5 PRESENTATION SERVICES FOR DATA TRANSFER

Two types of FM header have been developed in SNA for use with job entry subsystems (JES) and data base (DB/DC) subsystems such as IMS and CICS. These are called type-1 and type-2 FMHs. These headers are currently used for printer, card reader/punch, console, and data-base support.

A type-1 FMH is used to *select a special presentation service* for one or more blocks of data. These might be destined for different end-user components (for example, a printer, console, card unit, data set, or subroutine). This may be an initial selection or a resumption of a prior selection that had been suspended. Another type-1 FMH is needed to indicate completion of the selection. This may be a temporary or a final completion. In some implementations, this selection of a presentation service may be accompanied by the use of separate data streams for each end-user component (although the architecture in no way defines the end-user components or the interfaces to them). In other cases, the different presentation services might be applied to different data going to the same destination. The type-1 FMH also can be used to signal the use of compression or compaction of data.

A type-2 FMH is used to *provide more information on, or to request some action pertaining to, the component that was previously selected* by a type-1 FMH. This type of FMH might, for example, be used to request that forms be mounted on a printer or to request transfer of a data set. A type-2 FMH may occur only when an end-user component is already active (that is, only when a component has been selected, and that selection is not suspended or ended). The type-2 FMH applies to whatever end-user component is currently active at that time for that session.

7.5.1 The Type-1 FM Header

The format for the type-1 FM header (FMH-1) is shown in Fig. 7.20. Details are given in Fig. D.1 of Appendix D. Either the select field, the component name field, or both fields can be used to identify a presentation service for a particular end-user component. Strictly speaking, the FM header only identifies an FI.FMD *service* even though in implementations that service may be associated with a particular *end-user component.*

The type-1 FM header also contains control information (in the properties field) relative to the starting, suspending, resumption, and ending of a component selection, as described below.

Repeated component selection. In a given session, the action may shift continually from one end-user component to another. For example, the requests may be aimed first at one printer, then at another, then back to the first printer, etc. To facilitate this, and to avoid processing a complete

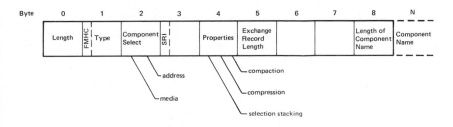

Fig. 7.20 Type-1 FM header format.

FM header with each change in selection, a technique of stacking selections has been adopted. The destination selection field can specify either

1. BEGIN component selection,
2. END component selection,
3. SUSPEND component selection, or
4. RESUME component selection.

With the SUSPEND, RESUME, and END commands, the parameters other than the component selection field are not acted on. Receipt of SUSPEND, in effect, pushes the selection down in a stack of selections, making room at the top for a new selection. If more than one component is in the stack, then the SUSPEND pushes down all such entries in the stack by one element. Receipt of a RESUME, in effect, pops up all entries in the stack by one element. An illustrative sequence of requests, using type-1 FM headers, is given in Fig. 7.21.

Only one component (and its selected FI.FMD services) are active for a given half-session at any one time. All requests apply to the active component (or the component then being made active). No type-1 FM header may be concatenated to another type-1 header.

Sometimes it is necessary to refer, in a request, to one of the sender's components rather than one of the receiver's components. This is made possible by the Stack Reference Indicator (SRI) (see Fig. 7.20) in byte 3 of a type-1 FMH. A zero in this bit position says that the FMH pertains to the receiver's component (selected by the sending LU); a one says that it pertains to the sender's component. For example, one can use the SRI to identify a message as one being sent from a display console, even though the prior series of messages was received on a printer (both being components of one end-user).

Thus component selection may be pictured as two pairs of stacks, with two stacks at each end of a session. The two stacks at each half-session keep track of the selection: One pair remembers the selections begun by the primary LU, while the other pair remembers the selections begun by the secondary LU. At session initiation (BIND) time, the depth of each stack is agreed to; this fixes the number of components that can be suspended and later resumed. With this component selection information, the presentation services can perform the particular services that are appropriate for the components that are active.

Another type-1 control bit (the demand select bit of the component select field) permits operations, that are normally transparent to the sender, to be inhibited. An example of such operations is the use of any one of several alternate components.

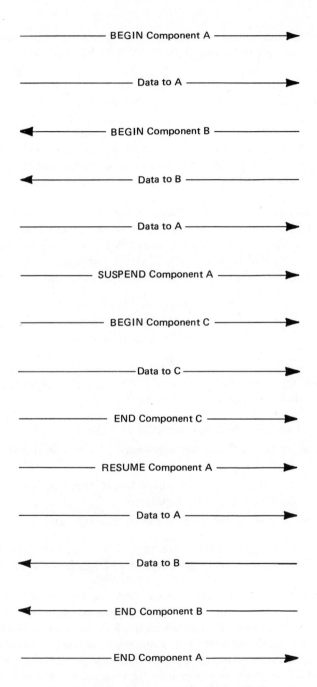

Fig. 7.21   Illustrative sequence using type-1 FM headers.

Compression/compaction. In the type-1 FM header, a compression indicator (CPI) and a compaction indicator (CMI) indicate whether compression and/or compaction are being used (see Fig. D.1 in Appendix D).

Compression involves the recognition of repeated characters, either blanks or some other character designated as a *prime character.* A code is sent instead of the repetitious string of prime characters. Compaction refers to a recoding to pack more than one character in a byte, by taking advantage of the fact that only a subset of the allowable 256 characters is frequently used. The particular compaction algorithm and the compaction tables that represent it are not architected, but some basic facilities are provided.

If either the CMI or the CPI bit is on, the data in each RU begins with a *String Control Byte (SCB).* The SCB follows the FMH if an FMH is present, unless FMHs are concatenated. Each SCB contains a count that locates the next SCB or completes the particular SCB code definition. The first two bits of the SCB specify the following information:

> 00 = no duplicate characters
> 10 = repeated prime character
> 11 = repeated next character
> 01 = compact code

The last six bits of the SCB give a count. This count, corresponding to the four cases above, respectively, is for the

- Number of bytes between the SCB and the next one
- Number of prime characters represented by this SCB (the next byte is the next SCB)
- Number of times the next character is repeated (the next SCB follows the character to be repeated)
- Number of compacted bytes between this SCB and the next one

For compaction, the sender must supply a compaction table to the receiver. This can be done via a type-2 FM header (see the following section).

With these facilities, the presentation services at the sender can compress or compact the data, and the presentation services at the receiver can decompress or decompact the RU. In some implementations (such as the JES3 Remote Job Processing support), compression or compaction may be selected by the operator at the time of log-on; user-specified compaction tables may be selected by data set, job entry station, or class of SYSOUT (i.e., by categories of job output).

7.5.2 The Type-2 FM Header

The type-2 FMH always acts as a modifier of a type-1 FM header; it applies to the active component selected by a preceding type-1 header. It either provides further information on, or requests that operations be performed on, the previously selected component.

A type-2 FM header may occur within an RU either

1. Immediately following a type-1 or another type-2 FMH, whose FMHC (concatenated) bit is on (there is the restriction, however, that a type-2 FMH cannot be concatenated to a SUSPEND or END type-1 header).

2. Immediately following the RH of a first element of a chain of RUs. (Chains will be discussed in Chapter 8.)

3. Following another RU (in the same chain) whose last FMH has its concatenated bit on.

The format for the type-2 FM header is shown in Fig. 7.22. Its key characteristic is a seven-bit operations code, plus parameters for that code. There are presently defined four classes of type-2 codes:

1. Device control
2. Compaction/compression
3. Data management
4. Data management extensions

More precise definitions of these codes are given in Appendix D. Their purposes are roughly as follows.

1. Device Control
   - PERIPHERAL DATA INFORMATION RECORD (PDIR): Requests the forms mount, electronic-forms control load, train mount, and copy functions, which are features of many line printers.

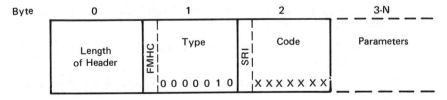

Fig. 7.22 Type-2 FM header format.

2. Compaction/Compression

- COMPACTION TABLE: The parameters of this code contain the number of master characters (those that are frequently used) and a representation of the compact-code table that is to be used by presentation services.
- QUERY FOR COMPACTION TABLE: Requests that the receiver send the named compaction table.
- PRIME COMPRESSION CHARACTER: Allows a specific character to be designated as the prime compression character.

3. Data Management Codes (The concerned data sets are named in a preceding type-1 FM header.)

- CREATE DATA SET: Causes the creation of a data-set entry in a directory.
- ERASE DATA SET: Erases the records within a data set, but leaves the data-set entry in a directory intact.
- SCRATCH DATA SET: Causes (1) the deletion of the data set from a directory, and (2) the freeing of space associated with the data-set name.
- SCRATCH ALL DATA SETS: Destroys all data-set entries for the specified component and volume ID (volume ID is sent in a supplementary FMH).
- QUERY FOR A DATA SET: Requests that the data set be sent to the requestor.
- ADD: Causes the addition of a record to a data set.
- ADD REPLICATE: Causes the replication of a record to a data set.
- REPLACE: Causes a logical record to replace another logical record at the specified record ID (record ID is sent in a supplementary FMH).
- REPLACE REPLICATE: Causes a record to replace a number of records within the data set. The record ID header (see the discussion on data management extensions below) indicates the starting point of the operation.
- ERASE RECORD: Causes the erasure of a record or records from a data set.
- NOTE: Requests the record ID of the next available record in the data set.

- NOTE REPLY: Provides the record ID of the next available record, in reply to the sender of the NOTE.

4. Data Management Extensions (These are qualifiers of the preceding type-2 data management codes, regarding data sets named in a preceding type-1 FM header.)
   - RECORD ID (RECID): Selects a particular record within the data set.
   - PASSWORD: Validates the authority of the requestor to reference and change data sets and data-set records.
   - VOLUME ID (VOLID): Specifies a volume ID to be associated with the data set (VOLID precedes other type-2 headers).

Commands such as these are intended to be independent of particular node implementations. If necessary, presentation services can provide the translation between the common forms and the forms that are understood by particular end-users.

7.5.3 Illustrative FMH Sequences (Type-1 and Type-2)

The following three sequences of commands illustrate the ways in which a series of FM headers can be used.

1. Erase multiple records within a data set:

BEGIN	(Type-1, selects a data set)
ERASE RECORD	(Type-2, defines the operation)
RECID	(Type-2, identifies record to be erased)
RECID	(Type-2, identifies another record)
END	(Type-1, ends data-set selection)

2. Replace multiple records within a data set:

BEGIN	(Type-1, selects a data set)
REPLACE	(Type-2, defines the operation)
RECID	(Type-2, identifies the record)
data	(provides data for second identified record)
END	(Type-1, ends data-set selection)

3. Add records to a data set:

BEGIN	(Type-1, selects a data set)
ADD	(Type-2, defines the operation)
data chain	(provides data to be added)
data chain	(provides more data to be added)
END	(Type-1, ends data-set selection)

7.6 PRESENTATION SERVICES FOR TEXT PROCESSING

Text processing is another example of the use of common control codes for a variety of end-users. Device control codes (which, for example, might start a new line) can be made common for the network. The presentation services element, associated with a given half-session, can serve to convert either to or from that common form so as to match the particular end-user of that half-session. In this case, *presentation services scans each RU to locate the control codes and then processes the control codes.* (Note that this is done at an upper level and not, as formerly, at the data link control level.)

In a text-editing application, for example, we may need the host compute-power to do the line formatting, word hyphenation, page formatting, etc. At the host, then, we would have to insert into the data stream each indication that a new line or a new page should be started, etc. If we can adopt a common indication for these line and page starts that all NAUs would recognize, then a valuable flexibility results. We can then introduce new devices, or a new cluster controller with new devices, more freely. By programming those new units to take those common line and page indicators, we can add new facilities without having to upgrade or in any way recode the centralized application in the host. At each destination, each page is mapped to the dimensions of that device's presentation space. The prior system remains operational.

The common codes are needed at the interface between nodes. Within a given node, on the other hand, a particular device may need a conversion from the common form to its particular form. Presentation services are the area of the structure that performs such conversions.

A more ambitious use of presentation services would be to omit "next-line" and "next-page" indicators from the transmitted byte stream, and to leave that formatting to a presentation service in the destination half-session. This would permit different numbers of characters per line and different numbers of lines per page in different devices. These are only a few examples of how presentation services can be used to promote device independence.

Text processing naturally deals in coded byte strings. The byte is the unit of data, and a sequential scan (for example, a standard left-to-right scan) is appropriate. The byte code is also necessarily a standard, like the *EBCDIC or ASCII codes.* As explained above, presentation services can convert to common device-control characters and information delimiter characters, so that many types of device can accept the common exchange record.

The *SNA graphic character set* is shown in Fig. D.2 of Appendix

D. True subsets have been defined so that products may employ 48-, 63-, or 94-character graphic sets. The eight-bit EBCDIC code has the capacity for a limited number of device control codes. Those referred to as the *SNA character string (SCS)* controls are shown in the code chart of Fig. D.3 of Appendix D, and each of the corresponding commands is briefly defined in Appendix D. The ASCII set is shown in Fig. D.4.

An FM header may precede character-string data within an RU. *If the RU contains text data (rather than formatted fields), the text data must be scanned by the presentation services. Control codes in the text are there interpreted and executed (if in the allowed set) so as to map the text data to the presentation space of the intended device.* This might, for example, be the space for a large or small-screen display, a line printer with a large page, or a typewriter with a small page.

7.7 PRESENTATION SERVICES IN AN INTERACTIVE ENVIRONMENT

7.7.1 Use of Field-Formatted Data

Presentation services also evolved in the interactive environment, which is characterized by display terminals connected to DB/DC subsystems such as IMS and CICS. Mapping services of DB/DC subsystems have been developed in a type of presentation service that deals with data organized in fields and treats the various fields as data objects. *Mapping of these fields to the display space* is often done in the host LU. The LU in the cluster controller then receives a byte string with special positioning controls that are recognized by the display unit. In theory, however, *mapping can be done at either end or both ends of a session.* The following somewhat theoretical discussion will assume this generality, although particular implementations may not use it.

DB/DC applications deal not only with byte strings per se but with groups of bytes called *fields*. The data objects may, for example, be a person's name, Social Security number, or home address. The records (an SNA-RU chain; see Chapter 8) being exchanged between nodes may be composed of a set of fields whose sizes are predefined, and whose meanings are known to the end-users. Furthermore, the position of a field in the visual presentation is often significant. For example, the first column may be reserved for name, the second column for Social Security number, etc.

In field-formatted data we take advantage of positional significance in the RUs; a given field has a predetermined position in an RU chain. Different field sizes and positional groupings of fields can be identified by a header (the FM header) which accompanies the RU chain.

The fact that the *data within a field is transparent* is an important property of field-formatted RUs; any bit pattern may occur, subject only to the constraints of the data type that the field contains. Examples of valid data types are

- Characters (for example, eight bits per character)
- Packed decimal (for example, four bits per numeral)
- Binary
- Floating point
- Noncoded bit strings

The fact that the RU is structured in fields eliminates the necessity for the receiver to scan a character string for separators or other controls.

Presentation services may have a different role to play with field-formatted records. The device receiving a field-formatted RU may have a narrow carriage or a wide carriage; it may be a printer or a display; and *a particular field may need to be positioned at a particular place in that two-dimensional space.* The arrangement of the visual presentation of fields may have to be different for different devices. Supplementary headings may or may not need to be added to make the visual presentation more readable. Also, the sequence in which the fields are presented may best be tailored to the functions performed by that operator. *The presentation services, therefore, have the job of taking the field-formatted RUs and mapping their fields to a particular presentation space in a format desired by the particular destination end-user.* This mapping requires that the format of the RUs be identified and also that the destination NAU be somehow advised of the desired visual format.

The basic mapping support (BMS) of CICS is an example of presentation services performed at the sending end. This relieves the application program of having to construct the control information for each display image. The layouts of the data on the screen are specified by the application programmer beforehand, in a set of definitions known as *maps.* Then, during execution of a transaction, the application program supplies the name of a map, along with the output data. The BMS constructs the RUs containing a merger of the output data and the fixed data from the selected map, together with any necessary control information in order for the appearance on the screen to match the map specification [7.10].

Instead of transmitting all details of the desired format with the data (as was also done by character insertion in the case of the coded byte stream), it may sometimes be more practical to *store the desired field formats in the destination node.* With a display, for example, the stored information could specify the position on the display for each field of the RU chain. It could also provide whatever supplementary information needed to be merged with the incoming data. The presentation services could then use that remotely stored map to generate the particular format desired for the newly received data.

Transformations such as these can be better organized by using the concepts of logical presentation spaces and format descriptors, which are discussed in the following sections.

7.7.2 Logical Presentation Spaces

Whether we are concerned with a line printer, a display, or any other output device, there is an address space for the creation of the image. For example, the unit of addressability of that space might be lines and columns (as on a printer or alphameric display). The unit of addressability for a graphic (line) display or an image (picture) display might be the coordinates of points or picture elements.

A degree of device independence can be obtained by thinking in terms of a corresponding *logical presentation space* (LPS) that is not tied to particular physical sizes or characteristics; the same logical presentation space then could represent, for example, either a display or a plotter. An LPS has an address space (for example, lines and columns), without specifying the physical distances between points of addressability. The LPS must also have a defined extent (for example, the number of lines or columns) in each dimension. The LPS does not, however, define such things as character size, line spacing, or page size. Because of this factor, a given LPS can be transformed to physical images of different sizes on different devices. Figure 7.23 illustrates a simple logical presentation space for alphamerics; the coordinates are columns and lines rather than a unit of measurement such as centimeters.

Obviously, different devices might use the same or a different LPS. They might use the same type of LPS (alphameric, graphic, picture) but of a different extent. Also, one can readily imagine many needs for combinations of LPSs—for example, an alphameric LPS of one extent in one area (or window) of a display, and another LPS of different extent in another area. Or, conceivably, combinations of graphic constructions and alphameric data may be desired, again calling for more than one LPS per device.

One would first map a given RU chain to an LPS that is appropriate for a class of devices, and then apply a final transform to suit the particular dimensions of one device. Paging and scrolling could be used to map a large LPS onto a smaller physical presentation space.

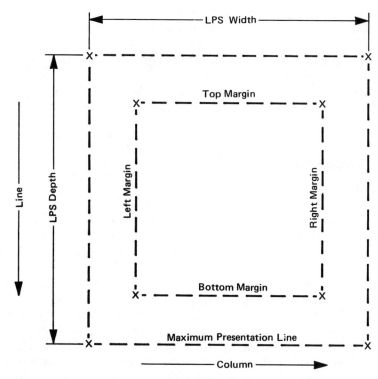

Fig. 7.23 Alphameric logical presentation space, in rows and columns.

7.7.3 Separation of Formatting Function from Application Processing

Another example of the separation of application programs and formatting function is the IMS message format service. First, control blocks are generated during execution of the message/format utility program, using control statements specified by the application analyst. Four sets of these control blocks describe the message input/output formats:

- Application program input
- Application program output
- Device input
- Device output

Information in such control blocks is used, by the separate IMS message format service, to relate fields in an application message to fields of a device message. In an obvious generalization of this concept, rather than any particular implementation, we refer to *descriptions of field formats and the code to achieve transformations to or from an LPS,* collectively, as *format transforms.* In general, the format transform must include a definition of the field structures in both the RU chain and the LPS.

If more than one format transform were to be used for a given device, they would also need to be identified, perhaps by name. Note that more than one format transform might be needed even for a single LPS. Hence, we see that what is involved, in general, is a transformation of a given RU chain, by a specified format transform, to a specified logical presentation space (or vice versa). Then there is the further transformation to the dimensions of a particular device. All of these processes logically would be the responsibility of the presentation services.

The transformations that are made in accordance with the format transform can, in theory, be implemented at either end of a session. In general, one can think in terms of a pair of format transforms (in the presentation services), one at each end; whatever transformations are not provided by one must be provided by the other. The division of work between the two is implementation-dependent, which in turn depends on what kind of common language is desired for multiple attachments. If any common transmission language were used, then the role of the format transforms would amount to that of translators to and from that common transmission language.

In theory, then, the sending-end presentation services may either:

1. Transform the field-formatted application data to a byte string with embedded field delimiters, adding formatting control characters in the case of printers or displays, or

2. Transmit a field-formatted RU chain to the destination presentation services, together with a header identifying the format of the data.

In the first case, the receiving presentation services would scan the byte string for delimiters and formatting information, and, accordingly, write the data to the presentation space. In the second case, the receiving presentation services must have a predefined *format transform.*

As processing power becomes available at remote sites at lower costs, this second alternative becomes more attractive because

- The data transmitted is reduced;

- Response time may be improved;

- Host cycles are off-loaded;

- Host application programs and application subsystems become more independent of the characteristics of devices to which data is sent.

7.7.4   Perception of Models

The evolution of classes of presentation services is related to the attempts to create common models of users of a common transmission network. The term *virtual terminal* is sometimes used for such a model, and the proposed models can take on many structures [7.9, 7.11, 7.12, 7.13, 7.14].

Most models are a simplification of reality. The logical presentation space is, obviously, a simple model that partially represents an actual device. The SNA character string (SCS) controls, or formatted records, are used with a particular LPS "model" in mind. Command interpreters for SCS controls and/or format transforms must interpret the input and control a particular device. Similarly, the data-base commands in type-2 FM headers are used with a particular "model" of the data-base subsystem in mind. Different data-base models could have different needs for data-base commands. Each of the protocols (SCS controls, FM headers, etc.) in effect defines an aspect of a model of the user of a common transmission network.

Different models will prove to be more appropriate for different classes of devices, data-base organizations, operating system control functions, and applications. One hopes that, with time and experience, a modest number of such models and their protocols will prove to be applicable to a broad variety of end-users. The set of models, however, must be somewhat open-ended, to meet increasingly diverse and evolving requirements.

We have, in this chapter, considered only protocols for the upper layer. These are the most variable. However, other disciplines that need to be assumed for such models should be reflected in the lower layers of each half-session—namely, data flow control and transmission control, which are examined in the next two chapters. The aggregate of the function subsets chosen in each of these layers (and, more specifically, their protocols) then define a particular model seen by the common transmission network. Thus, one can begin to see a convergence of the concept of common models for users, on the one hand, and the SNA concepts of function subsets and LU types (introduced in Section 6.12).

7.8   PARALLEL DEVELOPMENTS

7.8.1   Higher-level Protocols Used in ARPANET [6.2]

The *user-process to user-process* protocols that were developed for AR-PANET are related to the foregoing and include the following.

1. Initial Connection Protocol (ICP) provides a method for establishing a logical connection between processes in different hosts.

2. Data Transfer Protocol (DTP) specifies methods of formatting data for passage through the network.

3. File Transfer Protocol (FTP) endeavors to shield users from the peculiarities of different filing systems, and to make it possible to exchange sequential fields among different file systems. It involves the logical connection of FTP programs in the two hosts [7.4, 7.6].

The Initial Connection Protocol is very roughly comparable to the SNA session services (see Section 7.3.3), which is a part of network services. The Data Transfer Protocol and the File Transfer Protocol, on the other hand, currently have no clear counterpart *within SNA*. Both SNA and ARPANET are evolving sets of primitive commands for cross-processor operations (for example, the data management commands in FM headers; see Section 7.5.2), but some of the processing involved in DTP and FTP would seem to be in the nature of an end-user (which might be in an application program, application subsystem, or system service) outside the SNA network.

ARPANET file transfer.   Recall that in SNA, a set of data management commands has been defined as part of the type-1 and type-2 FM headers. A somewhat comparable set of commands exists in the file transfer protocol of the ARPA network [6.7, 7.6]. A sampling of these commands (which are divided into three classes) follows.

1. Class A: USER, PASSWORD, ACCOUNT

2. Class B: MODE, STRUCTURE, TYPE

3. Class C: RETRIEVE, STORE, APPEND, DELETE, RENAME, LIST, ALLOCATE

Class-A commands set up a user context, class-B commands set up a file context, and class-C commands are instructions. The byte strings in these commands must first be handled (at a host) by a language interpreter (syntax analyzer) *which transforms the commands to a locally executable form*. The interpreted command is then sent to a subsystem in the host that is designed to execute the file transfer commands.

7.8.2 DECNET Naming Conventions

A large number of conventions have been devised for naming things, places, organizations, etc. SNA has left the LU naming convention undefined. Each SNA installation or network may seek a naming structure that best meets its needs. One of the interesting naming structures is that offered by DECNET [6.17]. There, the name of the object on the destination system (to which connection is desired) has the structure: OBJ-TYPE,DSCRIP,GROUP,USER.

- OBJTYPE is the object type being referenced. This binary number is the encoding of commonly referenced objects on computer systems, such as processes, file systems, line printers, etc.

- DSCRIP is the character-coded descriptor field of the object. It describes the object being referenced.

- GROUP is the group code referencing this object. This, together with the user field, defines a qualifier for such uses as protection during execution, directory name for object search, etc.

- USER provides another level of qualification when used with GROUP code.

7.8.3   UNIVAC Network Control

The Sperry Univac Distributed Systems Architecture [6.18] distributes the network control function as follows. (DSA was introduced in Section 6.14.4.) An end-user connects to the network via a *Communication System User* (CSU) that is somewhat analogous to the SNA LU. Then, within each termination environment (which includes the end-users), there is a special CSU (called *application management services*) whose responsibility it is to link that environment with the network control elements of the system (see Fig. 7.24). These application management services *provide network control services to the end-users.* (Contrast these separate CSUs with the SNA practice of incorporating session services in the outer layer of each LU.)

These special CSUs for application management services are connected via preestablished paths to an *area network management services* (see Fig. 7.25). All of the latter, in turn, are interconnected with each other. In addition, there are lower levels of network management services in special CSUs that reside *within each major physical component* in the network. (Compare these with the SNA physical units.) Groups of these physical component CSUs are connected to an area network control CSU. All of the area network management services may also be connected to a master controller called the *global* network management services.

7.8.4   UNIVAC Presentation Services

The port presentation services in the Sperry Univac DCA [6.18] serves to transform the data, address, and control information into a form suitable

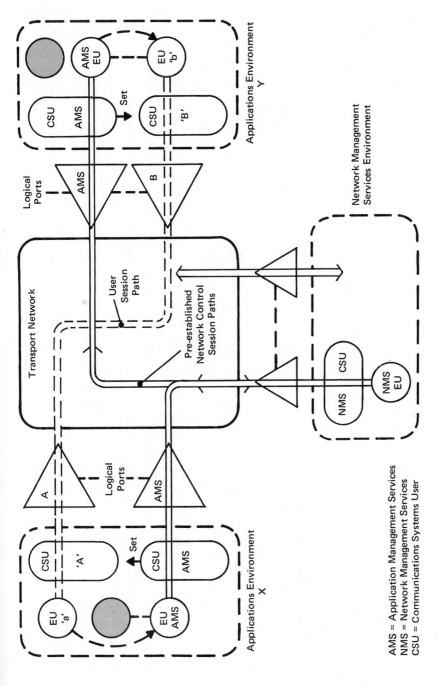

AMS = Application Management Services
NMS = Network Management Services
CSU = Communications Systems User

Fig. 7.24 Network control paths of the Sperry Univac Distributed Communications Architecture [6.18].

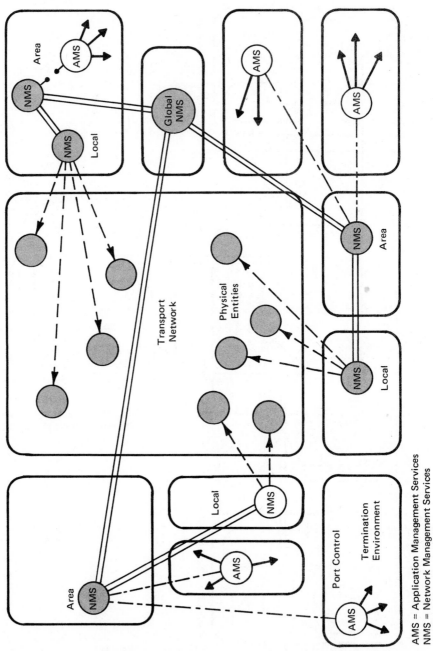

Fig. 7.25 Network control CSU hierarchy of the Sperry Univac Distributed Communications Architecture [6.18].

AMS = Application Management Services
NMS = Network Management Services

for the transport network and the remote port with which it is paired. The binding of a specific port presentation service can be done in one of three ways:

1. System generation or system initialization time,
2. Session establishment time, or
3. Specially implemented interaction between a pair of logical ports.

7.9 EXERCISES

Which of the following statements are true?

7.1 Common device-control characters and information delimiter characters can help to

a) make application programs oblivious to all device capabilities.
b) make devices more interchangeable (though each device may need a somewhat different presentation service).
c) make applications independent of the network configuration.
d) reduce changes to the application when devices with completely new features are provided.

7.2 Presentation services for field-formatted data can

a) rearrange fields of a record to suit a particular display.
b) add headings and supplementary characters.
c) provide a different format for a given set of data to suit each application.
d) do the mapping of the RU chain (into a presentation space with a new format) in a remote controller; but it cannot do this mapping in the host.

7.3 In the SSCP, configuration services

a) can be used by an NAU only if a session exists between the NAU and the SSCP.
b) control the activation and deactivation of links, physical units, and logical units.
c) do not apply to dial-up connections.
d) provide an IPL for every node in the network.

7.4 In the SSCP, session services

a) must, by their very nature, always reside in a host.
b) issue the BIND command to the secondary logical unit.
c) arrange for the transformation of LU name to network address.
d) send the CONTROL INITIATE command to logical unit services of the primary LU.

7.5 Using Appendixes C and D, construct the bit pattern for a type-1 FM header, as follows.

- A type-2 FM header is to follow this type-1 FM header.
- No alternate destination is allowed.
- The destination is a data set on disk number 15 at the receiving LU.
- This is a beginning selection.
- No compression, expansion, or "exchange-media" is involved.
- The name of the desired data set is TOM.

7.6 Using Appendix D and Fig. 7.22, construct the bit pattern for a type-2 FM header, requesting that the data set selected in a previous type-1 header be sent immediately to the requestor.

7.7 Using Appendix C, construct the INIT-SELF NS-RU for the following circumstances.

- The name of the destination, known to the originating end-user, is the name of the destination application program, called BANKBALANCE.
- The originating end-user is a teller (operator) whose identification, known to the SSCP, is TELRAKJONES.
- The destination application program is protected by the SSCP, and only those operators supplying the current month's password (which is DECEMBER41920) are connected to the application.
- The application is designed so that it expects to receive, as part of the connection process, a designation from the teller as to whether the interaction is "normal" or is to be processed on a "priority" basis. The desired connection is for normal processing.
- The installation has defined two types of session, which have been labeled XXXBATCH and INTERACT. The system definition provides information on the session characteristics for each of these two modes. The BANKBALANCE application program must operate in the INTERACT mode.

7.10   REFERENCES AND BIBLIOGRAPHY

See also [6.6, 6.7, 6.8, 6.17, 6.18, and 8.2].

7.1 *Information Management System/Virtual Storage (IMS/VS) Advanced Function for Communication.* IBM Form No. SH20-9054-0.

7.2 E. M. Aupperle. "Merit Computer Network Experiences." *IEEE 1975 Communications Conference* **III** (16–18 June 1975).

7.3 C. S. Carr, S. D. Crocker, and V. G. Cerf. "Host–Host Communication Protocol in the ARPA Network." *Proc. AFIPS 1970 Spring Joint Computer Conference* **36:** 589–597. Montvale, N.J.: AFIPS Press (1970).

7.4 G. M. Schneider. "DSCL—A Data Specification and Conversion Language for Networks." *Proc. ACM, SIGMOD Conference* (San Jose, California, May 1975). New York: ACM (1975): 139–148.

7.5 H. R. Albrecht and K. D. Ryder. "VTAM: A Systems Network Architecture Perspective." *IBM Systems Journal* **15,** No. 1 (1976).

7.6 N. Neigns *et al.* *"File Transfer Protocol."* NIC 17759, ARPA Network Information Center (July 1973).

7.7 H. Zimmerman. "The CYCLADES End-to-End Protocol. *Fourth Data Communications Symposium,* Quebec (October 1975).

7.8 *Digital Network Architecture: Network Services Protocol.* Maynard, Mass.: Digital Equipment Corporation (July 1975).

7.9 A. S. Chandler. "Network-Independent High-Level Protocols." EURO-COMP, Brunel University (September 1975): 583–601.

7.10 D. J. Eade, P. Homan, and J. H. Jones. "CICS/VS and Its Role in SNA." *IBM Systems Journal* **16,** No. 3 (1977).

7.11 D. L. A. Barber. "The Role and Nature of a Virtual Terminal." *Computer Communications Review* **7,** No. 3 (July 1977).

7.12 P. Schicker and H. Zimmerman. "Proposal for a Scroll Mode Virtual Terminal." *Computer Communications Review* **7,** No. 3 (July 1977).

7.13 V. G. Cert, A. McKenzie, R. Scantlebury, and H. Zimmermann. "Proposal for an International End-to-End Protocol. *ACM Sigcomm. Comp. Comm. Review* **6,** No. 1 (January 1976).

7.14 Design Specifications for Data Access Protocol, DAP, Digital Equipment Corporation, Maynard, Mass. (July 1975).

8
Data
Flow
Control

8.1 INTRODUCTION*

Once the session is established, the end-users must be able to maintain the integrity and order of the flow of RUs between them. Various factors make it certain that one or the other end-user will tend to fall behind in the handling of messages. Processor-power mismatches, varying loads on shared processor power, transmission delays, and storage access delays all contribute to a loss of synchronism. Also, different applications are structured to expect responses under different conditions, and various groups of RUs need to be treated as entities by the application.

Different aspects of keeping order in flows are handled in the transmission control and data flow control layers of a session. The transmission control elements (TCEs) control the actual rate of flows between TCEs by a pacing mechanism. The TCEs also check that the common transmission network maintains FIFO sequence and does not lose any normal flow requests. The remainder of the complex job of maintaining integrity and order in the data flows is handled in the data flow control layer.

As shown in Fig. 8.1, the DFC lies between the FI.FMD and the transmission control elements. Each session contains a DFC element that is tailored to that session. DFC works in concert with a transmission

---

* Acknowledgment is given to W. A. Bernstein, J. C. Broughton, P. S. Cullum, A. H. Jones, and K. Soule for their contributions to the data flow control portion of SNA, reflected in this chapter.

265

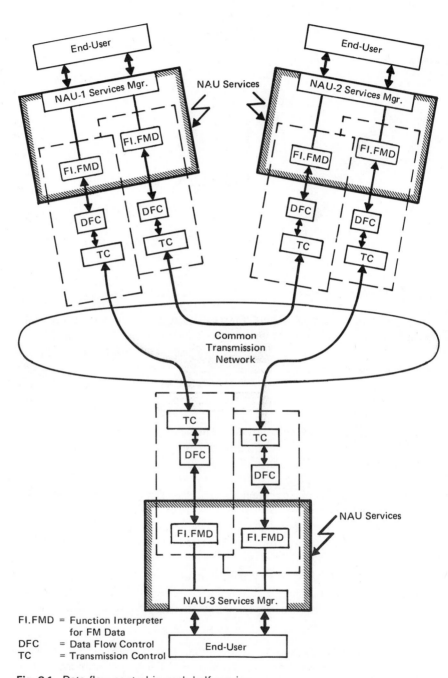

FI.FMD = Function Interpreter
         for FM Data
DFC   = Data Flow Control
TC   = Transmission Control

Fig. 8.1 Data flow control in each half-session.

control element to control the flows associated with that session, polices the adherence to DFC agreements, reports to the end-user DFC errors that cannot be corrected, and assists in error recovery. To do this, DFC monitors and generates commands (DFC-RUs or indicators in the RH) for the following:

1. Having an end-user withhold sending, if necessary, while the other end-user is sending

2. Grouping a number of requests going in one direction into an entity called a chain, for response or recovery purposes

3. Having several sets of conditions (for example, definite response and exception response) under which responses are sent for certain chains of requests

4. Waiting for responses and the ordering of responses

5. Grouping bidirectional exchanges into a work scope by delimiters called brackets

6. Quiescing and/or shutting down the transmission of normal data flow in one direction of a session

The SNA data flow control is thus end-user–oriented, rather than transmission-oriented.

These controls are applied to the requests and responses to and from the FI.FMD element. These RUs are part of the *normal flow* between half-sessions. Other requests and responses (for control purposes) terminate in the DFC and TC layers. Some of the latter also flow in sequence, intermixed with FMD–RUs (in the normal flow). Other DFC–RUs and TC–RUs, however, travel in a separate flow, called the *expedited flow*. The latter do not necessarily stay in sequence with normal flow RUs; they may be expedited (in the TC layer) by moving ahead of normal flow requests waiting to be processed (see Section 9.2.4). DFC policing functions do not apply to expedited RUs.

8.2 SEND/RECEIVE MODES

Data flow control maintains one of three send/receive modes between the two NAUs, depending on the agreements set at session initiation time. These modes address the question, Does the application have to "shift gears" when the direction of flow of requests reverses, or can bidirectional flows of requests occur concurrently? The flows in question appear mostly at the boundary between FI.FMD and data flow control. This flow of FMD–RUs is joined by some DFC–RUs so the send/receive modes pertain to the total normal flow requests between half-sessions. These send/receive modes are, however, completely independent of the transmission modes at the link control level (where the terms half-duplex and duplex are also used).

SNA defines three send/receive modes, as follows.

1. *Half-duplex flip-flop* (*HDX–FF*). In this mode, the two NAUs take turns being the requestor (that is, the sender of requests). Whichever NAU is the requestor of the moment can permit the other NAU to become the requestor by sending a *change-direction indicator* in the request/response header (RH). The half-duplex flip-flop mode is a natural conversation mode for a person at a keyboard. For example, while printing is being received, the keyboard is locked. The change-direction signal unlocks the keyboard and it is then the operator's turn to key in a message. *The HDX–FF protocol applies only to requests on the normal flow.* Responses and expedited RUs are, in effect, in duplex flow. An expedited DFC–RU, called SIGNAL, can be used by either NAU to request the other to send the change-direction indicator.

2. *Half-duplex contention.*   In this mode, either NAU can begin sending a request. If the other does not simultaneously want to send, the requestor and responder relationship is established until the requestor completes a chain of requests (that are related by chain indicators in the message headers). At that point, they again are in contention. Contention must be resolved if a request is received by an NAU that is currently sending a request or a chain of requests. Resolution of contention is decided in accordance with an agreement that is made at session initiation. One LU always wins the contention, whichever the agreement specifies.

3. *Duplex* (*FDX*). In this mode, requests flow in both directions simultaneously. Flows in both directions are independent of each other. Correlation of flows is done at a level above DFC. An example of a duplex flow is a session that services many similar requests from a large pool of identical terminals, such as those for credit verification. In these applications, a large number of simple transactions are processed in parallel, so duplex flow is more efficient.

Figure 8.2 illustrates two of the send/receive modes: (1) half-duplex flip-flop, and (2) duplex. It is the DFC layer that keeps track of the state of each flow, polices the rules, and reports any violations of the rules. In CICS/VS, for example, if the application program erroneously attempts to WRITE before the other logical unit has sent the change-direction indicator, then the DFC in CICS/VS will send the SIGNAL command to

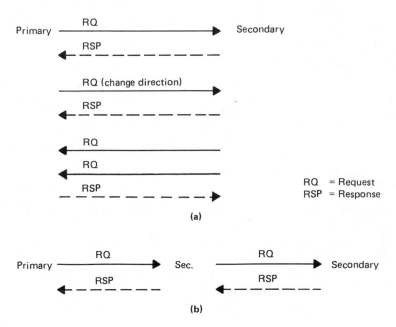

Fig. 8.2 Send/receive modes between one pair of half-sessions: (a) half-duplex flip-flop; (b) duplex.

request change of direction. Only when the other LU sends the change-direction indicator will CICS/VS honor the WRITE request [7.10]. Remember that these send/receive modes have meaning only at the end-user and half-session levels. The common transmission network is oblivious to these modes, providing, in effect, a duplex point-to-point flow between each pair of TC elements.

Note too that the send/receive modes control only what is called the "normal flows" in both directions. In addition, there are "expedited flows," which are used for control purposes rather than data transfer.

8.3 CHAINS

The chaining protocol permits one to send a chain of requests through the network, as an entity, and to manage the recovery of the chain, as a unit, when that is necessary. Breaking a large message into a chain of RUs can also serve to match the RUs to the buffers of the receiving application or application subsystem. (Note that at this DFC level, however, there is no concern for details of the transmission subsystem and, in particular, no concern for link station buffers.) Breaking a long message into a chain of smaller RUs also may permit processing or printing to overlap with transmission.

A chain may have only one element (one RU), or it may have many elements. All RUs of a chain are sent sequentially and in the same direction.

Chaining is used for recovery and must coincide with a recoverable unit. Consider, for example, that this is a page for a printer. The sending end-user (or an application subsystem) would have to provide the indication that this page is a recovery unit. The indications would be

1. A *begin-chain* (BC) indicator with the request containing the first line of the page

2. An *end-chain* (EC) indicator with the request containing the last line of the page

3. A *middle-of-chain* (MOC) indicator for all other lines of the page

The receiving end-user may not be aware of the use of chains. The data flow control function within CICS/VS, for example, issues RE-CEIVE requests to VTAM to obtain each RU; and only when the whole chain has been assembled by presentation services (within FI.FMD) will it be passed to the CICS/VS application program to satisfy an outstanding READ request [7.10].

Operator's actions at a keyboard can also control the use of chains. For example, if the transmission of a message is requested by the use of an EOB (end-of-block) key, this signifies that other related transmissions are to follow. Then the LU can insert either a BC (begin-chain) or MOC (middle-of-chain) indicator in the RH, depending on whether this is the first use of EOB since the last end-of-chain. If, on the other hand, a transmission is requested by the use of the EOM (end-of-message) key, then the LU can insert an EC (end-of-chain) indicator in the RH.

Different request/response regulations are appropriate for different applications. These regulations have been defined for chains, including the single-RU chain as well as the multi-RU chain. One obvious kind of protocol, for example, is something that SNA calls the *definite-response chain*. In that protocol, *A* sends a chain to *B*. *B* responds to confirm the receipt of the chain by the receiving end-user. *A* then sends another chain, and *B* responds, etc. This mode of operation is useful when the application environment demands that before an additional piece of information is sent from one end-user to another, the previous transfers of information must have been completed. As an example, when a chain represents the transfer of money from one institution to another, the banking industry demands that a definite response from the second institution must be received before additional transfers are accomplished.

A positive response to each element of a chain is not required (and is, in fact, forbidden by the architecture). A positive response is reserved for the final request in the chain. It is sufficient from a recovery standpoint to send responses to the other requests only if they are in error, in which case a negative response would be sent. Thus, with a *definite-response chain*, only the last request in the chain calls for a definite response; all other requests in the chain call for exception response (see Fig. 8.3). In this manner, the sender can be notified of the successful or unsuccessful transmission of an entire chain with minimal network overhead for acknowledgments [7.5].

There are other environments where, for efficiency or performance reasons, an exception mode of operation can exist for the entire chain. There an entire chain of RUs can be sent from one end-user to another without any acknowledgment from the receiving end-user, except when an error has occurred. Every RU in that chain would have an exception-response indicator in its RH. Typical of that mode of operation is the situation where a user may have multiple inquiries against a static data base. The user requires responses only if there has been an error, in order to identify which inquiry is in error.

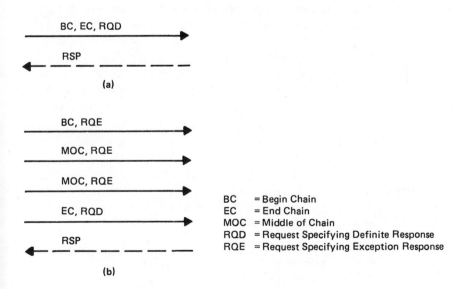

(a)

(b)

BC   = Begin Chain
EC   = End Chain
MOC = Middle of Chain
RQD = Request Specifying Definite Response
RQE = Request Specifying Exception Response

Fig. 8.3 Definite-response chains: (a) single element; (b) multiple element.

In other applications, even the exception response is unnecessary. For example, status-updating messages may arrive at fixed intervals and replace previous data, so the dialogue to correct any one message may be a waste of time. In this case (no response mode), every request of the chain would specify "no response." Thus three modes are needed:

1. *Definite-response chains:* The last request in a chain specifies "definite response"; all others specify "exception response."

2. *Exception-response chains:* All requests in a chain specify "exception response."

3. *No-response chains:* All requests in a chain specify "no response."

The choice of the request/response protocol for each RU in the chain is indicated by setting preassigned bits in a message header (the RH).

One of the DFC functions is to police the adherence to the chain regulations, and to alert the end-users to any violations of these regulations. This includes checking to ensure

1. Proper sequence of first-of-chain, middle-of-chain, and end-of-chain

2. That only the last element of a chain calls for a definite response

3. Receipt of one definite response for each definite-response chain

The DFC function has been implemented partially in application subsystems and partially in TP access methods. Today, the majority of the DFC function is implemented in application subsystems like IMS. The trend is toward the provision of this function outside the application. The VTAM record interface includes a format for specifying, for each request, whether it is first-of-chain, middle-of-chain, or end-of-chain, so that the proper request/response header (RH) can be constructed within VTAM.

Types of response. It may be desirable to have more than one degree of assurance conveyed by a response. In some installations, for example, acknowledgment by the NAU is deemed to be distinct from acknowledgment by the end-user. To permit such distinctions, SNA permits multiple codes for the definite response and exception bits. Three bits (bits 0, 2, and 3 in the second byte of the RH of each request) are used to code the type of response desired, as follows:

0 0 0	no response (RQN)
1 0 0	definite response type-1 (RQD)
0 1 0	definite response type-2 (RQD)
X Y 1	exception response, if X and/or Y = 1 (RQE)

The definitions of *type-1 definite response* and *type-2 definite response* are determined by the end-users. When used by IMS, for example, the sender is assured that a request can be recovered, in case of some failure, only if (1) the request specifies a type-2 definite response; (2) the sender of the request maintains the sequence number (see Chapter 9); and (3) the receiver of the request logs the data before returning the response. The definite response is usually returned before the request is fully processed to avoid delay. An appropriate time might be, for example, after an initial examination of the data, after a positive conclusion can be reached as to the processibility of the data, and after assuring possible recovery in case of error. In CICS/VS, if a definite-response chain is received to satisfy an application READ request, then CICS/VS delays sending a response until the transaction issues its next READ or WRITE request. This thereby indicates that the prior request has been successfully received by the application program.

The definite response to a chain of FMD–RUs has an RU of zero length. Positive responses to five control commands return additional data (see Appendix C.3). The exception response carries the reason for the error in the RU. (See Appendix E for exception codes.)

In the case of an exception response, DFC may call on the end-user (e.g., an application program or an application subsystem) for handling. In the VTAM implementation, for example, VTAM will schedule an application exit (called SYNAD) to handle the exception response. An *application exit* is a routine that is coded by the application or systems programmer and receives control when specified events occur. A special command called CANCEL has been defined as a DFC–RU to terminate a partially sent chain of requests. The receiver of a negative response (for example, the application exit) could CANCEL the previously sent portion of the chain by directing that this command be sent by DFC.

8.4 CONTROL MODES (WAITING FOR RESPONSES)

Given definite or exception responses for each chain, there are further questions on *whether the sending NAU must wait for responses* before sending additional requests. The SNA control modes define the type and number of chains that can be sent before waiting for a response.

1. In *immediate-control mode,* only single RU chains are allowed, each chain specifies definite response, and only one chain requiring definite response may be outstanding.

2. In *delayed-control mode,* multiple RU chains are allowed, and one of the following rules applies: (a) Only one chain requiring definite response may be outstanding (this is called *immediate-request mode*), or (b) multiple chains, even those requiring definite responses, may be outstanding (this is called *delayed-request mode*).

These are illustrated in Fig. 8.4. These different control modes apply to normal flows. Expedited flows, on the other hand, generally use immediate-control mode.

The waiting ground rule for normal flow is selected at the time when the session is established (and is included as a parameter of the FM profile in the BIND command).

The data flow control element correlates received responses with sent requests, and polices the waiting ground rules established at BIND time. DFC will alert the end-user to any violations and will reject the violating request.

To illustrate, the SSCP–PU sessions to cluster controllers have low traffic rates and so run in immediate control mode; each request is acknowledged by a response before another request is sent. Also multi-element chains are not allowed. All SSCP–LU sessions similarly use immediate control mode. In contrast, SSCP–PU sessions to communications controllers and hosts have a requirement to support high traffic rates and some delay in responses. These sessions, therefore, are run in delayed control mode; multiple requests can be sent before a response is received [6.20].

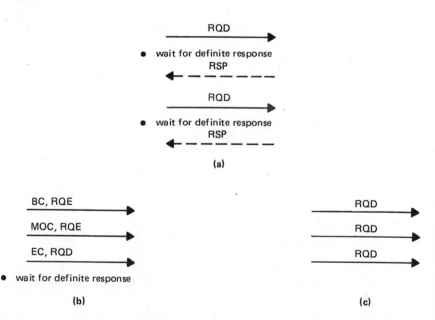

Fig. 8.4 Waiting ground rules for requests: (a) immediate-control mode; (b) immediate-request mode, i.e., only one definite response outstanding; (c) delayed-request mode, i.e., multiple definite responses may be outstanding.

8.5 RESPONSE ORDER

The above control modes regulate the sending of requests. Response modes are also selected (as parameters of the FM profile and the FM usage fields) at session BIND time. Two response modes affect the *order in which responses must be sent,* as follows.

1. In *immediate-response mode,* responses are sent in the order in which the corresponding requests were received.

2. In *delayed-response mode,* the responses may be sent out of order. The requestor cannot, therefore, assume that a response to one request (or chain) implies anything about any previous request (or chain).

Each response carries an indicator (that is, a sequence number or a unique ID) of the request it matches.

Delayed-response mode is illustrated in Fig. 8.5. As an example, SSCP–PU sessions use delayed-response mode because that traffic concerns the management of independent resources (e.g., lines and adjacent nodes).

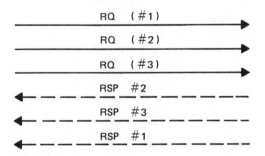

Fig. 8.5 Delayed (out of order) response mode.

8.6 RESPONSE SYNCHRONIZATION

An application program (or application subsystem) may or may not continue processing while it waits for a response. Though the ground rules for having the application wait are not a part of the data flow control layer, the DFC policing helps to preserve the integrity of the waiting procedure. A brief digression to examine some synchronization techniques will help complete the response-handling picture.

The way in which one maintains synchronism with expected responses varies with the implementation. To illustrate, several options offered by VTAM will be described briefly.

Responded output. The program can indicate (by a parameter on the SEND macro) that VTAM is to consider the response to be the completion of the I/O operation. The output data area is not to be reused until the response has been received.

If the option of the SEND macro further specifies "synchronous" request handling, VTAM returns control to the next sequenced instruction only after the response has been received (see Fig. 8.6a). If, on the

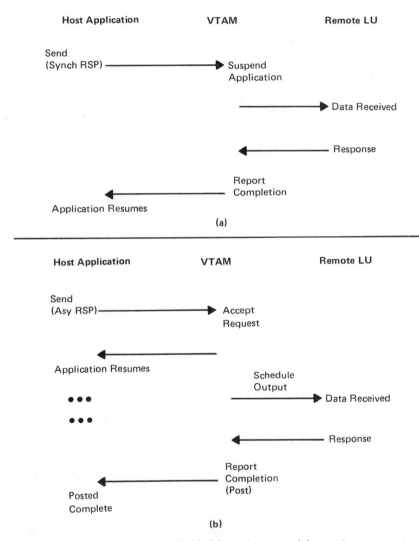

Fig. 8.6 Responded output in VTAM: (a) synchronous; (b) asynchronous.

other hand, the option of the SEND macro specifies "asynchronous," then VTAM returns control to the next sequential instruction as soon as VTAM has accepted the request. VTAM later notifies the application that the response was received by posting an event control block, which the application can check (see Fig. 8.6b).

Scheduled output. The application can indicate (by a parameter in the SEND macro) that, as soon as the message has been scheduled for transmission and the output data area is free, VTAM is to consider the operation completed.

Then, with both synchronous and asynchronous request handling, the application proceeds before the response arrives (see Fig. 8.7). However, with synchronous scheduled output (Fig. 8.7a), the application does not proceed until VTAM gets through its work to the point of scheduling the output. On the other hand, with asynchronous scheduled output (Fig. 8.7b), the application resumes as soon as VTAM accepts the request. When the response arrives, it is queued by VTAM, which schedules the RESPONSE exit. Note that one of the differences between the processes shown in Fig. 8.6(b) and 8.7(b) lies in notifying the application.

8.7 BRACKETS

Brackets are indicators within the RH that are used to embrace a series of requests and responses (in both directions) that together comprise a unit of work. An example of this is the process of seat-reservation applications in the airlines industry, where the terminal operator may perform a number of operations that all relate to allocating a seat on a given flight to a given individual. The brackets identify all the requests and responses as belonging to one transaction, and serve to prevent other, unsolicited RUs from appearing within that seat-allocation transaction.

The brackets can enclose any series of chains in both directions. The bracket is delimited by the use of (1) the *begin-bracket* (BB) indicator in the RH of the first request of the first chain, and (2) the *end-bracket* (EB) indicator in the RH of the first request of the last chain.

A typical bracket communication is illustrated as follows. Suppose that an NAU (NAU-2 in Fig. 8.8) receives an inquiry from one of its input devices. Then, as shown in Fig. 8.8:

1. NAU-2 transmits a request to an application program, NAU-1, indicating the begin-bracket indicator in the RH of that request.

2. The application program processes the request and replies with a chain of requests, which receives a response from NAU-2.

3. NAU-2 then sends a request asking for more data.

4. This is supplied by NAU-1 as a single request chain, which also gets a response.

5. NAU-2 then sends a single request chain containing the end-bracket indicator.

When the session is first activated, an agreement is reached between the two NAUs (via the BIND command) whether or not brackets will be

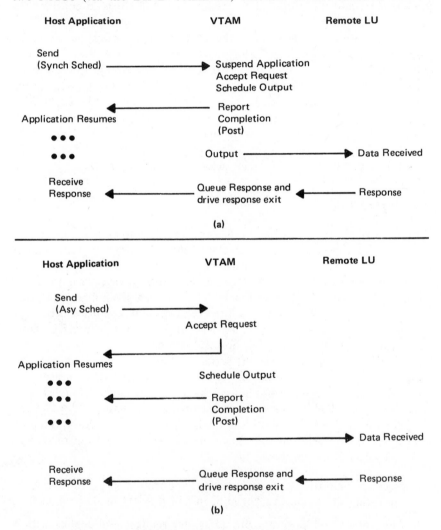

Fig. 8.7 Scheduled output: (a) synchronous; (b) asynchronous.

used, and, if so, which rules will be followed concerning the operation of brackets. One of the NAUs is designated as the "*first speaker.*" That NAU has the freedom to begin a bracket without first asking permission from the other NAU to do so. The other NAU is called the "bidder," which must ask permission of the first speaker to start a bracket.

The bidder can use a DFC command, called BID, to request permission to begin a bracket. A positive response to the BID indicates that the first speaker has granted permission to begin a bracket, while a negative response denies permission. The decision by the first speaker to allow a new unit of work may be dependent on a number of factors. This might include availability of resources, an application program decision, or an operator decision. When permission has been denied, the first speaker might subsequently advise the bidder to begin brackets by using another DFC command called READY TO RECEIVE (RTR). The negative response to the original BID will carry a code telling whether or not an RTR will follow. That sequence is illustrated in Fig. 8.9.

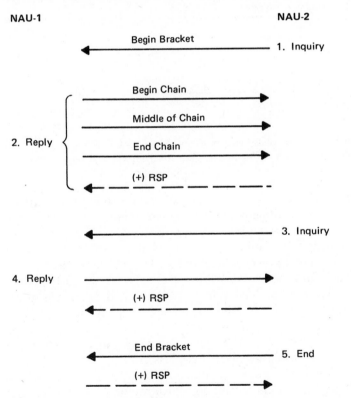

Fig. 8.8 Bracket communication, when NAU-2 is the first speaker.

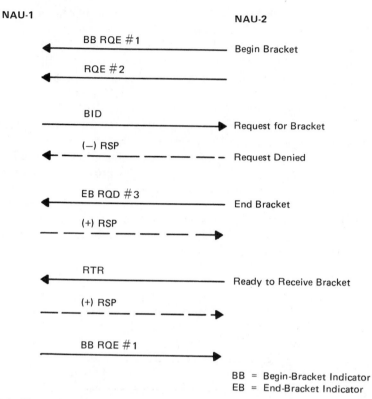

BB = Begin-Bracket Indicator
EB = End-Bracket Indicator

Fig. 8.9 Illustration of BID for brackets, when NAU-2 is the first speaker (NAU-1 might send a BID after NAU-2 sends BB but before NAU-1 receives BB).

Either NAU might attempt to begin a transaction by starting a bracket. If both attempt this at the same time, one NAU, specified at session initiation as the first speaker, is allowed to begin the bracket and the transaction. The other NAU, the bidder, must wait until the end of the bracket before again attempting to begin its bracket.

Some subsystems (like IMS) routinely use the BID command to notify some remote NAUs that an unsolicited request is pending. As described above, the positive or negative response to the BID indicates whether or not the NAU is ready to receive the unsolicited request. If not, then a subsequent RTR command can be used to indicate that it is ready to receive the unsolicited request.

In some environments (like remote job entry), the probability is very high that a BID would receive a positive response. In these environments, the bidder may bid by simply attempting to initiate a bracket (that is, by sending an RU–RH with the begin-bracket bit on). The first speaker views this attempt as a BID. The positive or negative response and the use of RTR are as described above.

At session establishment (BIND) time, it is agreed that one or both NAUs may end a bracket. The end-bracket (EB) indicator is sometimes used to unlock the terminal keyboard at the end of a transaction (when the send/receive mode is half-duplex flip-flop).

The bracket protocol has also been used to share a single I/O device, such as a printer, among several logical units. In one instance, a printer is principally used by one LU as a bulk printing device; however, after an end-bracket indicator (and before a begin-bracket indicator), the bulk print LU releases control of the printer, which may then be used by other LUs that need a printer for only a short time (e.g., for display of hard copy). The printer is reacquired by the bulk print LU when it receives the BID command.

8.8 DFC–RUs

When directed to do so by a higher level, DFC generates its own request/response units (RUs) for the exchange of "special-situation" control commands with the DFC function in the other NAU. The DFC commands that may thus be sent (depending on agreement at session initiation) may include the following:

1. *Error management.* The chain is the unit of recovery, but what do we do when an error occurs in the middle of a chain? We need to reset the tracking of the chain states, as follows.

    ▪ CANCEL: "Purge chain elements already received." The CAN-CEL command is requested by an error-recovery program (in NAU services or the end-user) when the NAU receives a negative response while the chain is still being sent. The destination NAU that generated the negative response while receiving the chain discards the remaining elements of the chain until the receipt of an end-of-chain or a CANCEL command.

2. *Quiesce series.* For a variety of reasons, one end-user or one NAU may need to ask the other to pause for a while. The end of the chain is a logical place to pause. Three commands serve to achieve this pause.

    ▪ QUIESCE AT END OF CHAIN (QEC): "Cease all transmissions of requests on the normal flow, at the end of the data chain currently being sent" (see Fig. 8.10). QEC is on the expedited flow. As soon as the NAU replies to the QUIESCE AT END OF

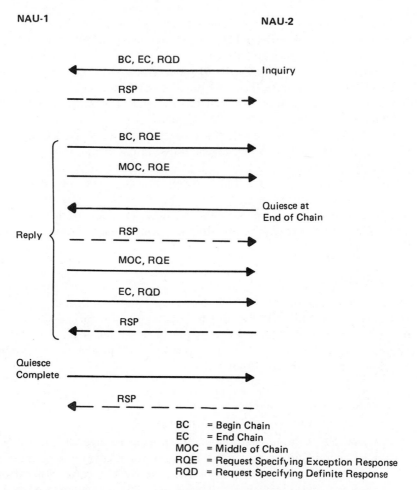

Fig. 8.10 Quiesce at end of chain (which is expedited and requires a response).

CHAIN by sending a QUIESCE COMPLETE command, that NAU can no longer send requests on the normal flow. It can only receive requests and send responses on the normal flow, although it can still send and receive requests and responses on the expedited flow.

- QUIESCE COMPLETE (QC).

- RELEASE QUIESCE (RELQ): "You may send requests now." Upon receiving the RELQ, the NAU may again send requests on the normal flow.

3. *Cleanup set*

   ▪ CHASE: "Return all outstanding responses, and send a response when this is done." The CHASE command can be used when preparing to shut down or quiesce (see Section 9.7.5) to ensure that all preceding requests and responses have been processed prior to termination. It can be used at any other time as well. For example, if an NAU has been transmitting multiple requests with only exception responses specified, then the CHASE command (coupled with the check by the receiving TCE of sequence numbers) can be used to verify their receipt.

   ▪ SHUTDOWN (SHUTD): "The work is done; complete end-of-session processing and quiesce when ready to end the session" (sent from primary NAU to secondary NAU). The DFC commands SHUTDOWN and SHUTDOWN COMPLETE serve to arrange an orderly termination of a session. A secondary NAU can use the CHASE command after receiving SHUTD. After the secondary sends the SHUTDOWN COMPLETE command, processing can be completed in the primary, if that is appropriate. After the primary has completed its cleanup operations, it may end the session.

   ▪ SHUTDOWN COMPLETE (SHUTC): "Preparation for shutdown is complete" (sent from secondary NAU to primary NAU). SHUTC indicates that the secondary has completed session processing and has placed itself in the quiesce state. RELQ may be used to release SHUTC.

   ▪ REQUEST SHUTDOWN (RSHUTD): "My work is done; send me an UNBIND or a CLEAR and UNBIND" (sent from secondary NAU to primary NAU). Note that RSHUTD, despite its name, does not call for the SHUTD command.

4. *Expedited signaling.* As the architecture develops, a limited number of expedited information messages will be formatted. The information can be carried as prescribed fields of the expedited command SIGNAL, which serves as a general-purpose carrier.

   ▪ SIGNAL (expedited message using predefined codes). An example of such a code is the request-to-send code, which can be used in the send/receive mode called half-duplex flip-flop. Processing an attention key at the terminal, for example, can result in the DFC element sending a SIGNAL command with the attention parameters. This, in effect, requests that the other NAU pass the change-direction indicator to the requestor as soon as possible.

5. *Brackets set*
   - BID: "May I issue bracket?"
   - READY TO RECEIVE (RTR): "You may initiate bracket."
6. *STATUS*
   - LOGICAL UNIT STATUS (LUSTAT): "Here is some status information of the type specified in the second and third bytes." For example, if an LU detects that one of its components or work stations is not functioning, the LU can use the LUSTAT command to notify the other LU of the condition. The LU can also use the LUSTAT to notify when the component is operable.

Note that QUIESCE AT END OF CHAIN (QEC) and SHUTDOWN have a difference in force. QEC requires a quiesce at the end of the current chain or at the end of a subsequent CHASE, at the latest. SHUTDOWN, on the other hand, requires a quiesce only when the secondary is ready.

Architecturally, all the DFC commands, except the trio SHUTDOWN, SHUTDOWN COMPLETE, and REQUEST SHUTDOWN, can be sent either from the primary NAU to the secondary NAU or vice versa. However, BID may be sent only from the NAU bound as bidder, and RTR may be sent only from the NAU bound as first speaker. Particular implementations may not include facilities for all of these commands.

Only six of the DFC commands are sent on the expedited flow. These are

1. QUIESCE AT END OF CHAIN
2. RELEASE QUIESCE
3. SIGNAL
4. REQUEST SHUTDOWN
5. SHUTDOWN
6. SHUTDOWN COMPLETE

The other DFC commands are sent on the normal flow. For further details of these DFC–RUs, see Appendix C. The information that flows between DFC and NAU services is summarized in Section 12.10.

8.9 INTERACTING WITH DATA FLOW CONTROL

The data flow control layers execute DFC procedures when ordered to do so by the end-user or by the NAU services. These procedures affect the setting of proper control bits in the request/response header (RH) and the transmission of special DFC–RUs when special DFC commands must be sent. The way in which one orders the DFC to perform these services may vary with TP access methods and the application subsystem employed. Nevertheless, the result of the DFC action, whether in RH content or in special DFC–RUs, is common for the entire network. That is, the RH and the DFC–RUs are architected and can therefore be understood by every NAU that elects to incorporate them. To illustrate, we might have the following correspondence between user commands and DFC action.

User Command	DFC Action
Start of Transaction	Begin Bracket
Start of Page	Begin Chain
Stop Program	Quiesce at End of Chain
Resume Program	Release Quiesce

The user commands may be different in each node, but the DFC actions can be common and the same for all NAUs.

As a further example, consider the relation of VTAM to DFC. VTAM does not fully police the adherence to the DFC protocols. Additional policing is done in application subsystems like IMS and CICS. However, the VTAM RECORD interface offers the SEND macro, which can include the following key parameters:

1. Designation of the unit as a request or a response

2. For a response, identification of the response (ID number)

3. For a request, specification of chaining information that identifies this unit as the first, middle, last, or only element in a chain

4. For a request, designation of the unit as user data or control information. This control information (in the SEND macro) is expressed via a set of *control indicators* that correspond to DFC indicators or commands.

VTAM permits the inclusion of the following control indicators in the SEND macro:

1. CANCEL

2. The three quiesce commands: QUIESCE AT END OF CHAIN, QUIESCE COMPLETE, and RELEASE QUIESCE

3. The cleanup commands that are sent from the primary NAU: SHUTDOWN and CHASE

4. SIGNAL (change-direction request)

5. BID

6. LOGICAL UNIT STATUS

ACF/VTAM allows secondary LUs (i.e., those supporting the secondary of an LU–LU session) to be located in a host. ACF/VTAM, accordingly, also permits the SEND macro to indicate the DFC commands—REQUEST SHUTDOWN, SHUTDOWN COMPLETE, and READY TO RECEIVE. Control indicators for any of the above, in the SEND macro, result in the generation of the corresponding DFC–RUs.

In addition, the SEND macro can include parameters for change direction, begin bracket, and end bracket. Each of these results in bits being set in the RH of the request they accompany.

When VTAM receives certain DFC commands, it will schedule an exit to process the command. For example, the expedited DFC commands QUIESCE AT END OF CHAIN, RELEASE QUIESCE, REQUEST SHUTDOWN, SHUTDOWN COMPLETE, and SIGNAL will be processed by the exit known as Data Flow Asynchronous (DFASY). In ACF/VTAM, that exit will also process the SHUTDOWN command, and another program, DFSYN, will process any BID that is received. Most *normal-flow* DFC–RUs, however, simply pass with FI.FMD data to the VTAM-user (being flagged as DFC–RUs).

Thus, the RECORD interface of VTAM is a relatively explicit, low-level interface, in the sense that all these control commands are visible at that interface. Application subsystems like IMS and CICS, on the other hand, shield the application programs that use the subsystem from much of this control detail.

8.10 SUMMARY OF DFC FUNCTIONS

The DFC layer is concerned with eight sets of protocols:

1. Send/receive modes
2. Chaining
3. Required response to a chain (that is, definite-response, exception-response, and no-response chains)
4. Waiting for responses (i.e., control modes)
5. Order of responses (i.e., response modes)
6. Brackets
7. Quiescing
8. Shutdown

DFC maintains the integrity of the flow with regard to responses that indicate errors and also responses that confirm reception of a request.

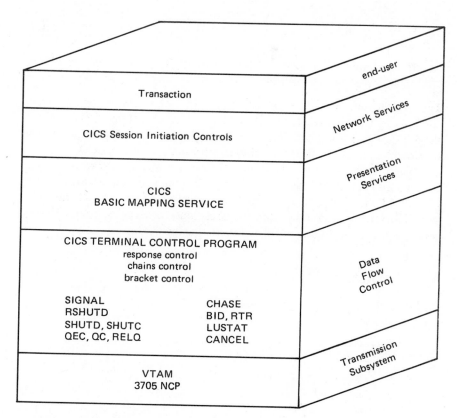

Fig. 8.11 Illustrative mapping of implementation and SNA structure.

Once the end-user decides whether to ask for a response and, if so, how many requests will be sent before waiting for a response, the DFC checks that response rules are followed.

If the transmission control element for the session contains a message queue for incoming messages, then the data flow control element must have a corresponding dequeueing function.

In performing these control functions, DFC completes four types of action.

1. It passes, intact, the request/response unit (RU) that it receives from either NAU services or the transmission control element.

2. It generates or passes along the correct indicators for each RU such as chaining, bracketing status, and the form of response expected (none, exception, or definite).

3. It enforces the data flow protocols and may generate error indicators when a violation occurs.

4. It generates its own control RUs when directed to do so by the end-user or NAU services.

The architecture precisely defines the DFC–RUs containing the DFC commands, the coding of the RH which reflects the state of each RU in the DFC regulations, and the state transitions that must accompany the receipt of each DFC–RU and DFC control bit.

The data flow control functions are often implemented within application subsystems, such as IMS, CICS, JES, etc. This is illustrated, in the case of CICS, in Fig. 8.11, which also shows a mapping of the transmission subsystem, data flow control, presentation services, and network services to corresponding parts of a system using CICS.

8.11 EXERCISES

Which of the following statements are true?

8.1 Concerning chaining:

a) Every request must have either an exception response or a definite response.

b) Every chain may have one and only one definite response.

c) Responses must always be returned in the same sequence as the requests received.

d) More than one definite response may be outstanding if this is agreed to at BIND time.

e) If one request of a chain is a definite-response request, then all requests of that chain must be definite-response requests.

8.2 Concerning brackets:

a) Ordinarily, only one half-session may initiate brackets without seeking the permission of the other half-session.

b) In some situations, the begin-bracket indicator will be accepted as a BID for brackets.

c) Only one NAU may terminate a bracket in all sessions.

d) Brackets only identify a unit of work flowing by requests in one direction.

e) The change-direction indicator (CDI) may not be used within brackets.

f) The ready-to-receive (RTR) command advises the bidder when it can begin brackets.

8.3 The change-direction indicator (CDI) is part of the RH and

a) CDI indicates that the receiving link station can now send.

b) CDI indicates that the receiving half-session can now send requests and that it cannot send responses.

c) CDI indicates that the receiving half-session can now send requests as well as responses.

d) The SIGNAL command can be used to request the change-direction indicator.

e) CDI is essential to the operation of half-duplex link flows.

8.4 At session initiation time, each half-session can be specified to permit either

a) Only one definite response to be outstanding.

b) Multiple definite responses to be outstanding.

c) Multiple exception responses to be outstanding.

8.12 REFERENCES AND BIBLIOGRAPHY

See also [7.5].

8.1 J. H. McFadyen. "Systems Network Architecture: An Overview." *IBM Systems Journal* **15,** No. 1 (1976).

8.2 *Advanced Function for Communication—System Summary.* IBM Form No. GA27–3099.

8.3 *ACF/VTAM Concepts and Planning.* IBM Form No. GC38–0282.

8.4 *ACF/VTAM General Information.* IBM Form No. GC38–0254.

9
Transmission
Control

9.1 INTRODUCTION*

Transmission control is the lower layer of each half-session and is located between data flow control and path control (see Fig. 8.1). The instance of transmission control for one session is sometimes called a transmission control element (TCE). One transmission control element is assigned to each half-session. The TCE is the "front office" for the half-session, providing a session-oriented entry to the common transmission network.

Whenever two NAUs wish to establish a session with each other, they must each use a transmission control element for that session. It then becomes a connection point for that session to the common path control layer, which is shared by all sessions. Thus, each TCE is a "user" of the common transmission network.

From data flow control (DFC), transmission control (TC) receives all the RUs generated by the FI.FMD services and also any control RUs generated by data flow control. Like DFC, transmission control generates some of its own RUs, which are for the exchange of control commands with its paired TC in the opposite half-session. These control RUs (which are usually sent at the direction of the end-user or the NAU services) flow with the simplest of data flow control—that is, only single-element chains, a response for each request, no brackets, no pacing, and duplex flows.

---

* The transmission control part of SNA, which is reflected in this chapter, is due primarily to the work of J. C. Broughton, P. G. Cullum, A. H. Jones, and R. J. Sandstrom.

Within the transmission control element, there are three components dedicated to the one session.

1. *Connection point manager* (*CPMGR*): Performs most of the transmission control jobs once the session is established; these concern routing within the half-session, sequencing, pacing, checking, and other support functions.
2. *Session control* (*SC*): Helps by keeping track of the session status, coordinating activation/deactivation for that one half-session, and providing support for starting, clearing, and resynchronizing session-related data flows.
3. *Network control* (*NC*): Helps in some special situations relating to network services, particularly the notification of status of links attached to communications-controller nodes (the lost subarea notification is discussed in Section 15.10.1).

The relation among these three components, and the layers above and below transmission control, are shown in Fig. 9.1. These components of TC are described in the following sections.

9.2 CONNECTION POINT MANAGER

The connection point manager (CPMGR) is the coordinator of all the flows for one half-session and the interface for the half-session to the common network. The CPMGR has the following four primary jobs:

1. Routing of incoming RUs (those entering the half-session from the common transmission network) to different functions within the half-session (using indicators in the RH)
2. Construction of the RH for all RUs that leave one half-session (on their way to the common transmission network)
3. Generation of sequence numbers or identifiers for each request that leaves the half-session (on its way to the common transmission network)
4. Controlled sending of normal-flow requests, using pacing

9.2.1 Routing

The first job of the CPMGR is to perform a routing function within the half-session, sending the incoming RUs to (1) session control, (2) network control, (3) data flow control, or (4) FI.FMD. *This routing is done in accordance with the indicators in the RH of the incoming RU*, which specify what within the half-session should get each RU (see Fig. 9.2).

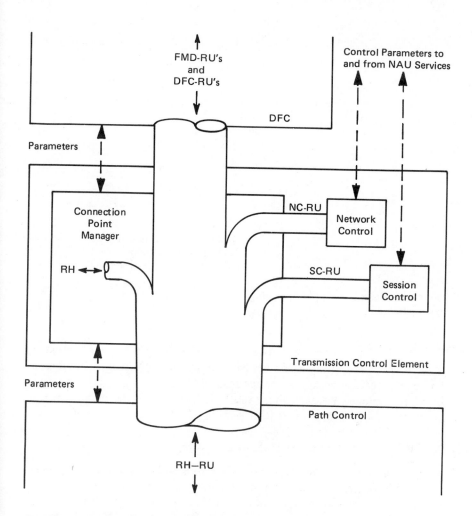

Fig. 9.1 Flow-routing and header addition in transmission control.

Thus, the CPMGR for each session acts as a sort of mailman for each session, with a part of the RH telling who in the session is to get each letter.

The output side of the CPMGR (called CPMGR.SEND) is responsible for merging the flow of RUs from session control, network control, data flow control, and FI.FMD into one flow to the path control layer.

In some implementations, data flow control will issue a command to receive the next normal-flow RU when the end-user is ready to receive it. Since this command might not be issued until long after the RU arrives in

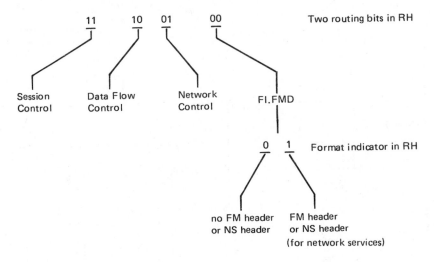

Fig. 9.2 Routing bits of RH (for routing within half-session) and the format indicator in the RH.

the CPMGR, the interface between the CPMGR and the DFC must be queued. Such queues must be logically organized by session. (Implementations can, of course, use a common physical store for multiple sessions.) In other implementations, where the DFC can handle the maximum rate at which RUs arrive, no CPMGR queuing is necessary.

9.2.2 Request/Response Header

The second job of the CPMGR is to construct the RH for all RUs emanating from the half-session on their way to path control. (The complete format of the RH is shown in Fig. A.1 of Appendix A.)

The connection point manager receives outgoing RUs from the NAU. These may have originated either in the FI.FMD or DFC. The CPMGR also receives other RUs from the TC functions, session control, and network control (see Fig. 9.1). Along with each RU come control parameters. The CPMGR uses this control information to build a request/response header (RH) for each RU. In effect, the CPMGR packages the given control information into a standard form, and sends the combination, RH–RU, to path control, along with some of the leftover control parameters. The RH–RU combination is called a basic information unit (BIU) (see Fig. 9.3).

The FM header (see Section 7.4.3) and the RH contain almost all the control information needed by the TC, DFC, and FI.FMD elements in the receiving half-session. (Some parameters from the TH, like sequence numbers and the expedited flow indicator, are also passed to upper layers.) Every RH is three bytes. Each request includes at least the following in its RH:

1. *Identification* as either a request or a response (one bit)

2. *Routing information* (two bits) to direct the RU to either FI.FMD, DFC, SC, or NC (see Fig. 9.2)

3. *Format indicator* from FI.FMD (one bit), to indicate a formatted RU or an FM header within the RU (see Fig. 9.2)

- In the case of a session with the SSCP, the format indicator bit tells whether the RU contains highly compact coded (formatted) information or whether it contains more loosely structured (unformatted) information that an operator would key in.

- In the case of the LU-to-LU sessions, the format indicator equal to one in the first RU of a chain tells that there are FM headers within one or more contiguous RUs at the beginning of the chain. The FM headers, in turn, can then specify a format for the RU data.

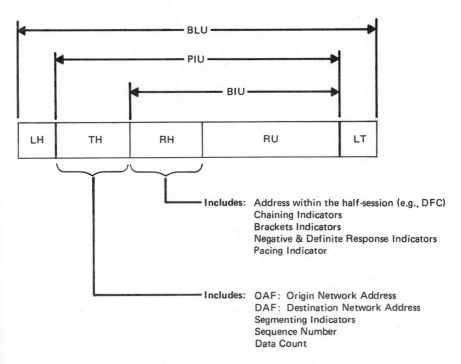

Fig. 9.3 SNA message format.

4. *Sense data indicator* (one bit) to tell whether a four-byte sense data field is included in this RU, immediately following the RH.

The sense bit can be set by a CPMGR that detects an error (for example, a sequence error) so as to advise its NAU of an error condition. It can also be set by a boundary-function connection point manager (BF.CPMGR) in a communications controller that detects an error in a request, so as to notify the destination NAU of an error condition. The CPMGR or BF.CPMGR can insert sense information in place of the data in the request, describing the error condition. However, the request code, in formatted RUs, is not discarded; the sense code is followed by up to three bytes of original RU (as described for negative responses in Appendix C). This modified request (see Fig. 9.4) is then called an EXCEPTION REQUEST (EXR).

When the destination NAU receives the EXR, it can send an appropriate response to the originator, including the sense data provided. The use of the EXR technique (rather than sending back a negative response from the CPMGR or the BF.CPMGR) enables the destination NAU to keep track of the data flows. It can keep all responses in order and also ensure that at most one response is provided per chain.

The EXR is also used within a half-session as an internal signal, generated by request-receiving protocol machines and sent to response-sending protocol machines to indicate that the error denoted by the sense data has been detected for the received request. Currently defined SNA exception codes can be found in Appendix E.

5. *Chaining information* from FI.FMD (two bits). These two bits tell whether this RU is the (1) beginning of a chain (BC code 10), (2) middle

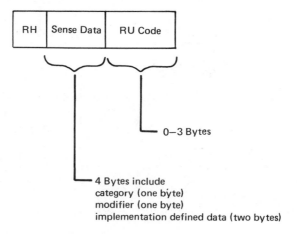

Fig. 9.4 Sense data and RU code in exception request.

element of a chain (MOC code 00), (3) end of a chain (EC code 01), or (4) only request of a chain (code 11).

6. *Response indicators* (three bits) to tell whether the sender desires no response, an exception response (that is, response on error only), or a definite response (see Section 8.3).

7. *Pacing indicator* (one bit) to regulate normal session flow. In a request header, the pacing indicator says that the sender is soliciting a pacing response indicator. Receipt of the pacing indicator in a response tells the sending CPMGR that an additional group of requests may be sent.

8. *Brackets indicators* (two bits from FI.FMD. Begin Bracket (BB) code (10), indicates that the current chain is the first chain in a bracket. End Bracket (EB), code (X1), indicates that the current chain is the last chain in a bracket. Bracket indicators may be set to a "1" only in the RH of the first request in a chain. (Thus BB/EB applies to chains within a work scope just as the BC/EC applies to RUs within a chain.)

9. *Change-direction indicator* (one bit), for change of direction of request flow (when the relationship between NAUs is half-duplex). Receipt of the change-direction indicator (CDI) tells the receiving NAU that it may send. Only a request on the normal flow that is marked "end-of-chain" may carry the CDI.

10. *Code indicator* (one bit) from presentation services (in FI.FMD) for code selection (for example, EBCDIC, ASCII, etc.).

The RH of the current version of SNA requires three bytes, some bits of which are as yet unassigned and thus available for future requirements (see Appendix A for a full definition of RH bit positions).

The combination RH + RU, which is called a basic information unit (BIU), is normally only a string of bits to the common transmission network, that is, path control and data link control. The BIU is intended for the opposite half-session, and so the BIU is not "understood" by the intervening path control and data link control layers.

Response RH. The RH of a response has a slightly different format from the RH of a request. The first bit of the RH indicates whether this is a request or a response, and so defines the format of the RH.

The RH of each response omits the bracket, change-direction, and code-selection indicators, and includes indicators of whether the response is positive or negative. If an error has occurred, the response will be negative, the "sense-data-included" bit will be set, and the response will contain four bytes of sense information plus the RU request code if there is one. (See Section C.3 in Appendix C for sizes of the request codes.) A summary of the process of assembling and disassembling the RH is given in Section 12.10.

9.2.3 Sequence Numbers

A third important job for the CPMGR is to associate a sequence number (or other identifier) with each request that it sends to path control. It is a BIND option (in TS profile) whether sequence numbers or identifiers chosen by the originators are to be used in normal flow. However, most profiles include the use of sequence numbers. The CPMGR may also check that normal-flow requests are being received in the proper sequence. *If the CPMGR detects an out-of-sequence incoming request, it converts it to an EXCEPTION REQUEST,* inserting sense data that identifies the type of error (exception 2001). The DFC element then turns this around by generating a negative response containing that same error indicator.

With current TS profiles, all outgoing FMD requests, in LU–LU sessions, use the normal flow and get a sequence number. Some DFC and TC commands use an expedited flow, which go out of the normal sequence. These, therefore, do not get a normal-flow sequence number, but get a separate numerical ID. The sequence number or ID generated is returned to the issuer of the request (FI.FMD, DFC, or SC), so that the issuer or some higher level can keep track of requests.

The boundary between the TC element and the upper layers of a half-session is shown in Fig. 9.5. Note that when sending a request, the

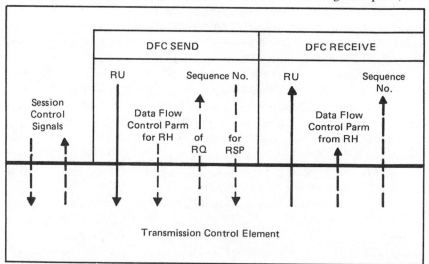

Fig. 9.5 The boundary between the transmission control element and the upper layers of a half-session.

sequence number is returned from transmission control; when sending a response, the sequence number is sent to transmission control. If the RU is in the expedited flow, an ID would be sent across the boundary in place of the sequence number. The session control signals pass to NAU services, which may pass them on to the end-user.

Each response keeps the same sequence number (or ID) as its request. *This permits a check to be made (by the request sender's DFC) to correlate responses with requests and to wait, when appropriate, until the response arrives.* When a response is being sent, the DFC element sends the sequence number, with the response, to the CPMGR. (If the request flow is between session controls (SC) in the two half-sessions, then SC or a higher level has the role of correlating expedited responses and requests by unique identifiers rather than by sequence numbers.)

If path control segments an RU into smaller segments, the sequence number of the RU stays with each segment, thus preventing an association of a segment with the wrong RU.

In the originating node, the sequence number is passed by transmission control, as a parameter, to path control, which packages it within the transmission header (TH). It remains within the TH until the destination node is reached, where it is passed up to the destination half-session. Terminal nodes (see Sections 3.6.2 and 12.3.1) have no capability to handle a sequence number. In that case, the sequence number is retained by the boundary function in the COMC, which performs some of the TC functions for the terminal node.

Since the terminal node does not understand sequence numbers, it is necessary to send only one RU at a time from a COMC to that node and to wait for a pacing-response confirming receipt of that message each time. Otherwise, if more than one RU were sent and an error indication came back from the node, there would be no way of determining which particular RU was in error.

Sequence numbers are of less value when operating in immediate control mode; that is, when only one request is sent at a time (see Section 8.4), and the sender waits until a response is received for each request. Then any unique identifier suffices to correlate the response with the request. *RUs on expedited flow operate in this immediate control mode and use only a unique ID instead of a sequence number.* If positive response is not received, the same request, with the same unique identifier, can be retransmitted.

9.2.4 Pacing

As a fourth major job, the CPMGR also can ensure, by a protocol among CPMGRs, that it does not send RUs at a rate greater than the receiving CPMGR can handle. This *flow rate control*, called *pacing*, is achieved by a protocol between a pair of CPMGRs. The agreement made at the time of session establishment (BIND) may specify no pacing, pacing in one stage, or pacing in two stages (see Fig. 3.7). The first stage is from the CPMGR in the originating node to that in the boundary node. The second stage is from the CPMGR in that boundary node to the CPMGR in the destination node. This permits different pacing parameters to be used in the two stages.

By prior agreement, a host CPMGR will send only up to n RUs until it receives a go-ahead signal from the boundary node CPMGR to the effect that another n RUs may be sent. A similar agreement is made (as a parameter at session establishment) between the boundary node CPMGR and the destination node CPMGR. The value of n can be different for the two agreements. For many terminals, the value of n, today, is one.

The SNA protocol involves having the sending CPMGR send n requests and also (by setting the pacing bit in an RH) ask permission to send another n requests. Ordinarily, the go-ahead signal from the receiving CPMGR, authorizing another group of n requests, is a pacing response. This is obtained *by simply setting the pacing indicator in the RH of the next response* sent by the receiving CPMGR. Sometimes, however, the receiver wants to send a pacing indicator, but there is no handy response in which to set it. (This certainly is the case when the requests are sent under no-response protocols.) In this case, an *Isolated Pacing Response* (IPR) is sent instead. The IPR is a unique response, identified by the fact that (1) the response bit is set to one; (2) both the definite-response 1 and the definite-response 2 bits are zero; and (3) the pacing bit is set to one. The isolated pacing response does not correspond to any prior request, and it is discarded when it has served its function as a pacing response.

In addition, a *maximum RU size* is agreed to, for each session, at session establishment (BIND) time. Therefore, a receiving CPMGR can time the sending of a pacing response, knowing that for each pacing response, no more than n RUs of a specified maximum RU size will be received for that particular session.

Figure 9.6 illustrates the idle time on several lines when the definite response is used with each message as an OK to send the next message. Figure 9.7 shows how even a pacing with $n = 1$, coupled with chaining, can increase utilization of the line to the terminal. One can readily see, then, how the increase in pacing with larger values of n would further increase the utilization of both lines.

Pacing is particularly useful in preventing one or a few sessions from overloading the resources (especially half-session storage) of a node while increasing the line utilization. It is also useful in speeding up recovery, because a large amount of data in the network might cause long recovery

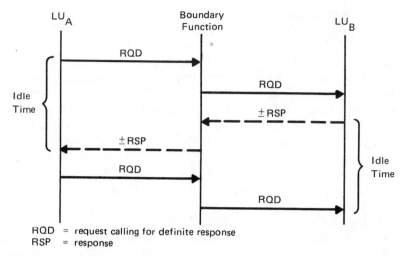

RQD = request calling for definite response
RSP = response

Fig. 9.6   Idle time from waiting for definite response.

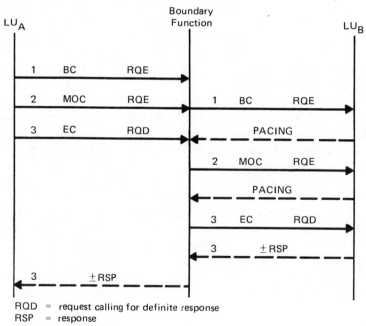

RQD = request calling for definite response
RSP = response
BC = Begin Chain
MOC = Middle Of Chain
EC = End Chain
RQE = request calling for exception response

Fig. 9.7   Pacing with $n=1$ and chaining.

times. All normal flows can be paced (when pacing is selected at session establishment). This includes all FI.FMD requests and most DFC requests.

The receiving CPMGR, in the boundary and destination nodes, must be made aware of those node-dependent characteristics that limit the node's ability to receive RUs. SNA provides no restrictions on what considerations will affect the decision to issue a pacing response (thus authorizing transmission of another group of requests). This decision is implementation-dependent. Typically, the limiting resource is the amount of storage available to a half-session. The inability to empty the buffers at a faster rate may be due to a limitation in the processing power, print speed, etc. As RUs arrive, they consume any available buffering in the CPMGR, and are passed to the FI.FMD, DFC, SC, NC, or the output CPM for boundary function. In many implementations, buffering is not dedicated, but is pooled for use by multiple sessions. In any case, when available buffering falls below a certain point, the CPMGR must withhold pacing responses. As more buffering is freed and rises above another point, CPMGR can again return pacing responses.

Ordinarily, pacing is only needed in one direction—from the powerful host to the terminal or cluster controller. There are situations, however, such as host-to-host communication, in which bidirectional pacing is required. In general, therefore, the SNA provides for one- or two-stage pacing in either or both directions, as selected at session establishment (BIND) time.

In current implementations of SNA, each SSCP maintains a table of pacing counts for all LUs defined in its domain. In two-stage pacing, the SSCP maintains an additional set of pacing values for the boundary function. If two-stage pacing is used in both directions, there are four pacing counts per session. Currently, up to three of these are selectable at session establishment time and are inserted by the SSCP into the BIND image (see the BIND command in Appendix C).

Expedited RUs are urgent RUs going from data flow control to data flow control, from session control to session control, or from network control to network control. These RUs flow independent of the normal flow, out of the normal sequence. For example, expedited RUs can move ahead of a normal flow of RUs that are waiting in a CPMGR queue for pacing. RUs from FI.FMD services to FI.FMD services travel in the normal flow.

Some commands in the expedited flow can proceed even when the normal flow is blocked. For example, after a CLEAR (and before a START DATA TRAFFIC) it may be necessary to send an STSN command to set sequence numbers and resynchronize. On the other hand, expedited DFC commands are blocked after CLEAR.

9.3 SESSION CONTROL

Session control, as part of transmission control, helps to control one particular half-session. It's a "front-office" type of function that acts as a control point to coordinate the work of others.

1. It manages the activation and deactivation of that one half-session.
2. Given that a session is activated, session control can open and close the flow gate; that is, it can start data traffic and clear data traffic, as directed by the end-user at the primary NAU.
3. If the session gets in trouble, particularly if an RU gets lost or out of sequence, then session control is available to help a higher level resynchronize.

More specifically, session control is characterized by the commands it can issue or to which it can respond. For each command, session control maintains a record of the various states (for example, reset, pending, active) associated with each command. It changes these states in response to certain inputs, and it provides certain outputs on the occasion of each state change. The recorded state, in turn, is referred to by the other members of the session team, and by path control, to guide their operations.

9.3.1 Session Control Commands

All session control commands are expedited. They include the following.

1. For session activation:
   - ACTPU: Activate a session between the SSCP and a PU (only sent by SC in the SSCP to TC elements assigned to a PU).
   - DACTPU: Deactivate that SSCP–PU session (also sent by an SC in the SSCP).
   - ACTLU: Activate a session between the SSCP and an LU (sent by an SC in the SSCP to a TC element of a half-session in an LU).
   - DACTLU: Deactivate that SSCP–LU session.
   - BIND: Activate a session between two LUs (sent by the SC of a primary half-session at an LU).
   - UNBIND: Deactivate that LU–LU session (sent by the SC of a primary half-session at an LU).
2. For data traffic initiation and termination:
   - START DATA TRAFFIC (SDT): Enable the transmission of FI.FMD and DFC traffic in both directions (sent by the SC of a

primary half-session). The user may delay giving this command, after a session has started, in order to first perform some further initialization or resynchronizing procedures before entering normal operation.

- CLEAR: Purge all requests and responses that may be flowing in a session and inhibit further normal-flow traffic until a START DATA TRAFFIC is issued (sent by the SC of a primary half-session). CLEAR will reset the sequence number count in the CPMGR of the secondary to zero. CLEAR can thus be used after a catastrophic error, as a first step in a data-traffic recovery sequence.

3. For recovery:

- REQUEST RECOVERY (RQR): The secondary half-session wants the primary half-session to direct a data-traffic recovery procedure. The subsequent recovery procedures are not defined; they are left up to the primary. In particular implementations, CLEAR and STSN are available as options to be used in the recovery procedure.

- SET AND TEST SEQUENCE NUMBER (STSN): Sent by the primary to resynchronize the sequence numbers of the end-users and connection point managers at both ends of the session in the course of recovery and resynchronization procedures. This command can be used to resynchronize either the PRI-to-SEC flow, the SEC-to-PRI flow, or both flows. Action codes can be set independently for each flow. The synchronization of sequence numbers is essential to obtaining transmission assurance between pairs of logical units.

Action codes of the STSN command (applicable to each flow) are as follows.

> Set: The connection point managers' values for sequence numbers (in both half-sessions) must be set to the values in the STSN–RU.

> Sense: The secondary end-user (or NAU services) must return its sequence number for this flow in the response to the STSN command.

> Set and Test: The connection point managers' values for the sequence numbers must be set to the STSN–RU values, and the secondary end-user (or NAU services) must compare that RU value against its own value and respond accordingly.

> Ignore: One of the flows (primary to secondary or secondary to primary) is to be ignored while the other flow is resynchronized.

The data traffic and recovery commands, though generated by session control, can be initiated by NAU services or the end-user. In the VTAM implementation, the two data traffic commands, START DATA TRAFFIC and CLEAR, and the recovery command, SET AND TEST SEQUENCE NUMBER, can each be specified as a parameter in the VTAM SESSIONC macro. ACF/VTAM also allows the SESSIONC macro to generate a REQUEST RECOVERY command. When certain session control (SC) commands are received, VTAM will schedule an exit known as session-control input process (SCIP) to process that command. The SCIP exit is driven when a primary LU receives an RQR. In ACF/VTAM, this exit is also given control when CLEAR, SDT, STSN, BIND, or UNBIND commands are received. The parameters of these commands are made available, via control tables, to a VTAM RECEIVE macro.

For further details concerning session control commands, see Appendix C.

9.3.2 Use of STSN for Flow Recovery

If the messages are not in precisely the sequence that the end-users assume, chaos often results. Therefore, once a connection point manager detects an RU that is out of sequence, recovery procedures must immediately be invoked to avoid a catastrophic series of errors. One of the recovery facilities, which can be selected at session establishment time, is the SET AND TEST SEQUENCE NUMBER (STSN) command introduced above.

The best recovery procedure will depend on the nature of the application. In some cases, it is sufficient for the primary half-session to simply back off to a safe sequence number and then, via the STSN, reset the secondary connection point manager to that safe sequence number. The data traffic would start again from there.

In other cases, it is best to determine the last valid message received by each side. It may be dangerous to assume that the connection point manager records are correct, since the error may have occurred in the CPMGR. In this situation, the safest check is with the end-users themselves (or NAU services) if they have kept a record of the sequence numbers. Though SNA uses the CPMGR to assign the sequence numbers and to check that incoming requests are in sequence, it is felt that in an emergency, the higher-level sequence numbers are probably the more basic source, if they are available.

Thus the complete protocol associated with STSN requires that two versions of the normal-flow sequence numbers be kept. The first version is kept at the connection point managers of both the primary and secondary half-sessions. This includes sequence numbers for both the last sent and the last validly received normal-flow requests. The second version is kept by NAU services or by a program outside the NAU at the end-user level. Often, the second version is kept by either the application program or by an application subsystem that serves applications and/or devices.

Either or both the primary-to-secondary and/or the secondary-to-primary sequence numbers can be set, sensed, or set and tested at the secondary half-session. The "set" of the CPMGR version is done by session control of the secondary half-session. At the same time, the session control in the primary half-session can reset the primary's sequence numbers, too.

Only the version of NAU services or the end-user is "sensed," and the "test" involves a comparison of that version and the version carried in the STSN command.

To recover the secondary-to-primary flow, all that is required is for the primary to arrange to

1. Send the SC command CLEAR, which first resets the secondary CPMGR version of sequence numbers to zero, and also removes any RUs that are still in transit. CLEAR also resets flow controls dealing with chaining, brackets, send/receive controls, etc., in both primary and secondary half-sessions. A successful CLEAR action will result in a positive response from the secondary.

2. Send STSN with the "set" action code and the sequence number of the last validly received secondary-to-primary request. This will set the CPMGR sequence number and also direct that the secondary end-user (or NAU services) be notified of the sequence number with which it will resume.

To recover the primary-to-secondary flow, the primary end-user or NAU services can

1. Send CLEAR as above.

2. Send STSN with "sense" action code to determine the last RU that was processed successfully by the secondary end-user or NAU services.

3. Purge its recovery queue of the RUs successfully received by the secondary.

4. Send STSN with the "set" action code to set the CPMGR version (for each CPMGR in the session) to the values at which recovery will begin, and to direct that the secondary end-user or NAU services be notified of this value.

The series of requests and responses for this recovery are shown in Fig. 9.8.

If it is the secondary half-session that discerns a sequence number problem, then *a negative response, indicating sequence number error, will start recovery action at the primary.* In other situations, it may be necessary for the secondary to send a REQUEST RECOVERY command to the primary so that the above series of steps will be undertaken, since only the primary can issue CLEAR and STSN commands.

An example of how resynchronization can be handled is given by CICS/VS [7.10]. There, *atomic units of work* (AUWs) are defined such that resynchronization may be done at the beginning of any AUW. An AUW is either a complete transaction or a part of a transaction that is delimited by safe *resynchronization points,* such as after a data base has been read and the associated update sequences are complete.

If the end-user or NAU services does not maintain a version of the sequence numbers, then the STSN can only set the CPMGR numbers and notify the secondary end-user of the setting.

Some applications (and application subsystems such as IMS) prefer to terminate the session when sequence number mismatches are detected. The STSN resynchronization procedure then can be used to guarantee the

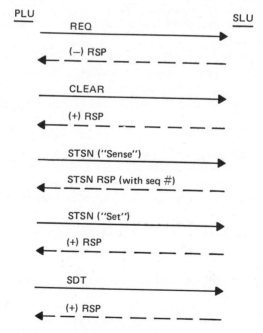

Fig. 9.8 Requests and responses for sequence number recovery.

integrity of messages across sessions, if message resynchronization is always made to occur at the start of a session. In that case, the STSN is issued by the primary after the BIND command, but before the START DATA TRAFFIC command.

9.4 PRE-SESSION ROUTING

As discussed above, path control normally routes to a specific connection point manager (CPMGR), which is identified with a specific session. But what if no session yet exists? Path control then has an RH–RU to deliver, but the network address pair (in the OAF/DAF) does not correspond to any known session. This situation occurs when three commands are sent to an NAU for the purpose of first establishing a session, namely,

- ACTPU: To establish an SSCP–PU session
- ACTLU: To establish an SSCP–LU session
- BIND: To establish an LU–LU session

In these three cases, no CPMGR is active there as yet. In fact, one of the purposes of establishing the session is to activate a CPMGR for that session. In SNA, the job of doing this rests with a transmission control function called common session control, which, by the nature of its job, is not part of any session.

When no connection point manager exists for the network address pair in the TH, path control routes the request to common session control in the TC layer for the destination node. (If the destination address is unknown, a negative response will be returned with an appropriate exception code.)

If the request is not ACTPU, ACTLU, or BIND, the common session control component will reject it with "no session" in the sense data. If, however, the request is one of these three session-generation requests, common session control arranges the activation of a half-session and directs the request to the session control of the "new" transmission control element.

DACTPU, DACTLU, or UNBIND will deactivate the associated transmission control element.

9.5 TRANSMISSION CONTROL BOUNDARY FUNCTIONS

Boundary functions are performed in a host or communications controller for directly attached cluster controllers and terminal nodes. At the transmission control level, there are three boundary functions, as follows.

1. Providing pacing of the data flows for half-sessions in adjacent cluster controllers and terminal nodes
2. Providing sequence number management for terminal nodes
3. Performing some session control functions in cooperation with the half-sessions that are in the adjacent cluster controllers and terminal nodes

Other boundary functions concerned with address translation are performed at the path control level.

To illustrate, let us examine a sequence of operations for the boundary function, using Fig. 9.9. It starts at the path control element of a communications controller (or host), when that element determines that the destination address is that of an NAU in a cluster controller or terminal node directly attached to that communications controller (or

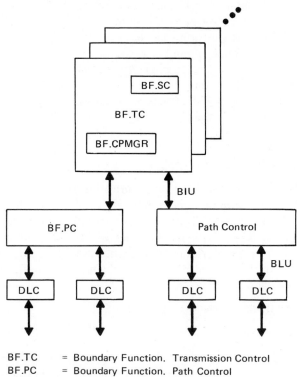

BF.TC   = Boundary Function. Transmission Control
BF.PC   = Boundary Function. Path Control
BF.SC   = Boundary Function. Session Control
BF.CPMGR= Boundary Function. Connection Point Manager

Fig. 9.9 Boundary functions.

host). Path control then routes the basic information unit (BIU) to the boundary function connection point manager (BF.CPMGR) for that session (that is, for the NAU pair identified in the transmission header).

The boundary function connection point manager examines the RH of the BIU received from path control. If the BIU contains a session control (SC) RU (for example, STSN, SDT, or CLEAR), then it is forwarded to the associated BF.SC element. BF.SC also maintains control tables on session status in accordance with session-activation and session-termination commands that pass through it. After processing by BF.SC, the BIU is returned via the BF.CPMGR to path control. If, on the other hand, the BIU does not contain a session control RU, the BF.CPMGR performs its pacing function and returns the BIU to the BF.PC function.

Not all sessions employ pacing, but if they do, a pacing queue for that session will exist in the sending CPMGR doing the pacing. An RU on the expedited flow, on the other hand, need not wait for pacing; it can be advanced (in the CPMGR) ahead of normal-flow requests that are waiting for a pacing indicator in a response.

The BF.CPMGR performs the total sequence number function for terminal nodes. A sequence number is generated for all requests from the terminal node. The sequence numbers are also checked for all requests to the terminal node. Since only one request is forwarded at a time to the terminal node, the BF.CPMGR can save the sequence number of each such request and insert that same sequence number in the subsequent response, if there is one.

9.6 NETWORK CONTROL (NC)

This component within transmission control also issues its own requests and transmits them without benefit of an NAU's DFC or FI.FMD. As yet, little use is made of the NC facility. As networks evolve, however, it is expected that the NC flow will meet the needs of the node's physical unit. It might be used, for example, for communication among physical unit services in multiple nodes in order to handle problems in reconfiguration, path alteration, slowdown, etc.

9.7 ESTABLISHING AN LU–LU SESSION*

9.7.1 Introduction

Having noted the ability of session control in the transmission control element for each session to handle certain session-generating commands,

---

*The portion of SNA that is described here is due primarily to the work of J. R. Babb, T. F. Piatkowski, and G. A. Plotsky. The BIND protocol is due to P. G. Cullum, J. P. Gray, and J. Oseas.

and having seen also the role of common session control in activating a TCE when needed, we are now in a position to examine further the sequence of commands used to initiate an LU–LU session.

A session involves a definition of the characteristics of the communication between two end-users (or, more precisely, between the two NAUs that are used by the end-users). Now, the session characteristics could be identified in the headers associated with each and every data unit to be transmitted. Some teleprocessing systems have been built largely on this principle. It has been recognized, however, that most of the communication characteristics do not change from message to message and can be recorded at the initiation of the session. Certain other characteristics that do change from time to time can still be included within message-control headers. Thus, the design of the session mechanism depends on the judgment as to which communication characteristics can appropriately be established at the beginning of a session and which need a flexibility for modification during the conduct of the session. The data flow for a given session, then, is directed by the set of control tables that contain the agreements made at session initiation time, augmented by a supplementary degree of control from the bits in the headers.

9.7.2 The BIND Command

Let us assume that two LUs exist and that one wants to initiate a session with the other. A single command, called BIND in SNA, must be sent by one LU to the other, proposing the session and requesting agreement on a set of ground rules for the session. An RU format for the BIND command is illustrated in Fig. 9.10.

There could be more than one type of BIND contract, so the initiator of the BIND must advise what type of BIND contract it has in mind. The format (FMT) field specifies the format of the BIND RU, and so tells the other LU what meaning to give to the various fields in the RU. A type field further specifies whether the BIND is a cold start (the only one thus far defined) or some other type (such as a warm start, which does not reset everything but uses information from a prior session).

The RU format for the BIND command that is illustrated in Fig. 9.10 is more general than is needed by some products. Specific products may ignore some fields.

Request Code for BIND	Format	Type	FM Profile	TS Profile	FM Usage	TS Usage	PS Profile	PS Usage	Length of PLU Name	Primary LU Name	Length of User Data Field	User Data
1 Byte	1 Byte		1 Byte	1 Byte							1 Byte	

Fig. 9.10 An RU format for the BIND command.

BIND options. Because it also serves to pull together some of the material explained earlier, a summary of the principal options that might be selected for a session and proposed in a BIND command is given in the following.

1. Transmission control facilities:
   - Pacing on normal flow will be one of the following:
     > no pacing,
     > primary to secondary only,
     > secondary to primary only, or
     > primary to secondary and secondary to primary.
   - Pacing parameters will be
     > primary pacing count $= n_1$ (for requests flowing from the primary),
     > secondary-send pacing count $= n_2$ (for requests flowing from the secondary), and
     > secondary-receive pacing count $= n_3$ (for requests flowing to the secondary).
   - A maximum RU that will be sent this session (and policed by TC) is
     > K bytes from the primary half-session, and
     > L bytes from the secondary half-session.
   - Sequence numbers (or IDs) are used on the normal flow.
   - Only some transmission control RUs will be used. Examples that are currently architected are shown in the following table.

	Case A	Case B	Case C	Case D	Case E
START DATA TRAFFIC	No	No	Yes	Yes	Yes
SET AND TEST SEQUENCE NUMBERS	No	No	No	No	Yes
CLEAR	No	Yes	No	Yes	Yes
REQUEST RECOVERY	No	No	No	Yes	Yes

2. Data flow control facilities pertaining to both half-sessions:

   ■ Normal-flow send/receive mode will be either

   > duplex (FDX),

   > half-duplex (HDX) contention, or

   > half-duplex flip-flop (HDX-FF).

   ■ Contention resolution: One half-session speaks first in HDX-FF mode and wins contention in the HDX contention mode. This will occur when either

   > the secondary speaks first and wins, or

   > the primary speaks first and wins.

   ■ Recovery responsibility will be in either

   > the primary half-session, or

   > the sender of the RU in trouble.

   ■ Brackets will be used (or not).

   ■ First speaker (one having the freedom to begin bracket without first asking permission of other half-sessions) will be either

   > the secondary half-session, or

   > the primary half-session.

   ■ Bracket termination will be either by

   > rule number 2 (terminated on last request of last chain), or

   > rule number 1 (termination depends on response to end-bracket indicator).

   ■ Only certain data flow control RUs (see Section 8.8) will be allowed in this session. Examples might be one of the following:

   > none,

   > CANCEL, SIGNAL, LOGICAL UNIT STATUS, CHASE, SHUTDOWN, SHUTDOWN COMPLETE, and REQUEST SHUTDOWN,

   > the above plus QUIESCE AT END OF CHAIN, QUIESCE COMPLETE, and RELEASE QUIESCE, or

   > the above plus BID and READY TO RECEIVE.

3. Data flow control facilities for each of the two half-sessions (each half-session may be different):

- Chaining use—either
    > multiple RU chains are allowed, or
    > only single RU chains are allowed.
- Waiting rules—either
    > only one definite response can be outstanding, or
    > multiple definite responses can be outstanding.
- Chain response protocol will be one of the following:
    > no response,
    > exception response,
    > definite response, or
    > definite response or exception response.
- Responses will be in the same order as requests received (or not).
- End-bracket indicator may (or may not) be sent by this half-session.

4. Presentation services facilities:

- Identification of matched pair of services (though presentation services may be different in each half-session).
- FM headers may be used (or not).
- Alternative codes will be used (or not) (for example, ASCII and EBCDIC).
- Data compression will be used (or not) when sending (may be different for each half-session).

New requirements can be expected continuously. As new facilities are provided, new bind formats can be defined accordingly. On the other hand, some implementations have no need of all the options listed above. Moreover, the number of possible combinations of these many options is very large. Hence, a relatively small number of *PS profiles, FM profiles,* and *TS profiles* have evolved that are commonly used subsets of the above. Each profile identifies a prescribed subset of the architecture. In the BIND command, six fields defined the session: three profile fields and three usage fields that provide information on the profiles.

- *TS profile and TS usage fields* specify facilities that are primarily in the transmission control layer. These include pacing counts, maximum RU sizes, and information as to whether sequence numbers (or IDs) and certain TC commands will be used.

- *FM profile and FM usage fields* specify facilities that are primarily in the data flow control layer. These include the request/response mode (e.g., definite or exception responses), the send/receive mode (e.g., HDX–FF or duplex), chaining, brackets, and the allowable DFC commands.

- *PS profile and PS usage fields* specify the characteristics of the FI.FMD services (including presentation services) in each half-session.

Different profiles will be defined as necessary, but the desire for general communicability among NAUs fosters use of a small number of common profiles. Some of the common FM profiles and TS profiles thus far defined in SNA are listed in Appendix B. For other details of the BIND command, see Appendix C.

Different profiles have been found to be appropriate for different categories of sessions. For example, current practice in the use of TS profiles is as follows:

- TS Profile No. 1: SSCP–LU sessions and SSCP–PU sessions for PUs in cluster controllers and terminal nodes

- TS Profile Nos. 3 and 4: LU–LU sessions

- TS Profile No. 5: SSCP–PU sessions for PUs in communications controllers

A particular combination of TS, FM, and PS profiles is sometimes referred to as a *session type*. This may be used effectively to characterize a session or a product that supports such sessions. One sometimes hears the term *virtual terminal*, meaning one that appears to the network to have certain prescribed characteristics. A session type (i.e., specific combination of TS, FM, and PS profiles) is a very effective way of characterizing a virtual terminal. In general, commonly used session types, composed of commonly used TS, FM, and PS profiles, will evolve as effective ways of characterizing products.

The NAU-to-NAU protocols could be greatly simplified if we had only one type of device and one rigid profile. Henry Ford is famous for having said, "You can have any color car you want, so long as it is black," and certain production economies did result. However, we now find it possible to contract with the dealer so that we get almost any car model that we want. It is important to be able to get the stripped-down, minimum-cost model when that is what is needed, and also to be able to get the air-conditioned, more automatic, and safer model, with extra horsepower, when that is what meets the requirement.

A wide diversity of end-users and modes of operation exists in today's networks and this will increasingly be the case in tomorrow's networks. Therefore, we need this ability to "make a contract" at the beginning of a session and to pick from a reasonably wide but still definitely limited set of session types in order to obtain those session services that meet the requirements of the end-users. The request/response header (RH) then can provide the further flexibility of control needed from request to request.

9.7.3 SSCP Assistance

The session-establishment agreement reflected in the BIND command can, in theory, be established by direct communication between the two concerned LUs, without the help of a third party. This is more feasible in a portion of a network where simple uniformity can be imposed. In general, however, it is less efficient for every end-user to have the knowledge and capability to set up a session, unassisted, with other end-users that are somewhat different. First of all, a good deal of the information on the characteristics that may be selected by each LU can be kept in one place to economize on storage and speed the formulation of the BIND parameters. Second, conflicts can develop, where two end-users simultaneously call on one another, with transmission delays confusing the true state of affairs. To avoid the necessity of unscrambling misunderstandings, one can establish this session through a third party, which easily can resolve any race and would initiate only one session between a pair of LUs. A third reason (perhaps the more enduring reason) for using the third party is that there are a number of system-type services that can be provided, such as name resolution and authorization checks, if this third party is the system services control point.

Name resolution.   One of the services provided by the SSCP is to make it possible for the end-users to address each other using easily remembered names rather than coded addresses. The network owner can establish whatever conventions are most appropriate to his or her network environment. The names may be completely arbitrary. They may have a mnemonic correlation with the function performed. They may utilize major and minor names or name modifiers in order to associate certain end-users with others. They may also need synonyms in different organizations.

These names must be translated into network addresses; thus, at the beginning of each session, the initiating logical unit must obtain the appropriate translations. This could in theory be done by broadcasting a query to all other network addressable units (or perhaps to all PUs) in a general search for an NAU that is able to make that particular translation. In SNA, this is handled more simply, however, by calling an SSCP, which maintains a central directory of the names for all the LUs within its control domain. Since the SSCP makes the translation, the network addresses need not be fixed. The network addresses can change, as the network changes, without affecting the names or the applications. (Name resolution, and the use of alternate names in a multidomain network, are discussed in Section 15.4.2.)

Log-on modes. To avoid the necessity of each LU having to specify all of the BIND parameters at the initiation of each session, these parameters can be *predefined to the SSCP, at system generation time, as log-on modes.* The log-on process then merely has to refer to one of these log-on modes by name in the INITIATE SELF command. The SSCP can maintain a list of log-on modes for all LUs in the system and can provide the information derived from the log-on mode to the primary LU for inclusion in the BIND command. In the VTAM implementation, the proposed log-on mode can be examined by the host application via the INQUIRE macro. The application can either accept the proposed log-on mode, pick a new mode, or create a new mode (subject to acceptance by the other LU when the BIND is sent).

9.7.4 LU–LU Session Initiation

Two prerequisites to any LU–LU session are as follows:

1. The SSCP first establishes a session with the PU of each LU's node (this can be done with the ACTPU command).
2. The SSCP then establishes a session with each of the LUs (this can be done with the ACTLU command). In the following, we assume that these prerequisites have been completed. (The process of "bringing the system up" is described in Section 12.5.)

Each node may have its own macros or other protocols for the end-user to employ in the initiation or termination of an LU–LU session. These must be open-ended to suit the product or the application. Whatever they are, LU services must receive control as a consequence of the issuance of that end-user command. Then the standard sequences described below would follow.

Either of the two LUs may be able to initiate a session with the other one. This can be done by an INITIATE SELF (INIT) command sent from the LU services of the initiating LU to the SSCP, as illustrated in Fig. 9.11. The INIT request parameters indicate the name of the other LU in the session to be activated.

A mode name can be supplied with the INIT command. This will identify a predefined set of BIND parameters (for example, the PS, FM, and TS profiles) that the initiating LU desires for the session.

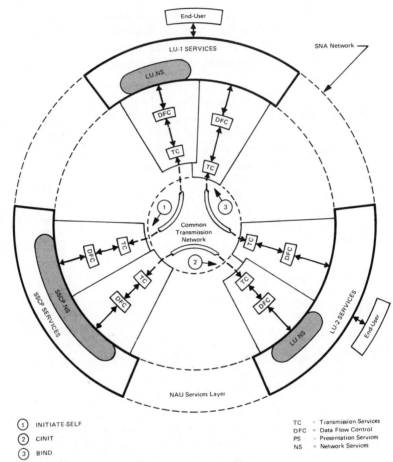

Fig. 9.11 Using the SSCP for session initiation.

The session services (within SSCP network services) receive the INIT request and check the command for syntax errors. If the request is valid, the SSCP services manager may do the following:

- Determine the authority of the initiating end-user to request a session activation. The SSCP may know that the desired LU is reserved for sessions with only selected LUs.

- Resolve the requested LU name (carried on the INIT) to a network address (or to a network name, if multiple SSCPs are involved, as described in Section 15.4.2).

- Activate the SSCP session with the requested LU, if this has not already been done. This may require link and PU activation procedures to activate connections between the SSCP and the requested LU. (However, in some implementations, notably VTAM, failure to find the requested LU already activated results in a termination of efforts to activate the session.)

- Ascertain the availability of any other network resources needed for the requested session. (For example, the desired NAU might already be in session and not able to support another one.)

- Resolve the mode name carried on the INIT to a set of BIND parameters for the requested session.

- Select one of the NAUs to be the primary LU for the session (i.e., to support the primary half-session).

- Request, via another command called CONTROL INITIATE (CINIT) that is sent to the LU services of the primary LU (PLU), that the PLU attempt a BIND for the specified session. CINIT will carry the BIND parameters resolved from the mode name.

When the SSCP services manager receives an INIT command, it may reject the request for a variety of reasons, depending on the implementation of the services manager. For example, the SSCP might return one of the following sense codes:

- 0803 Missing password;

- 0804 Invalid password;

- 0805 Session limit exceeded: The requested half-session cannot be bound, since one of the LUs is at its session limit;

- 0806 Resource unknown: The LU or PU name or address is not recognized;

- 0810 Missing requestor ID;

- 0812 Insufficient resource;

- 0821 Invalid session parameters: Session parameters are not valid or are not supported by the requested LU;

- 080E LU not authorized: The requesting LU does not have access to the requested resource;

- 080F End-user not authorized: The requesting end-user does not have access to the requested resource.

Observe that an architect has a choice of where such session-initiation functions could be performed, with varying degrees of centralization. One could consider trying to perform them in

- The LUs of the proposed session
- The PUs, which have resource responsibility for a node
- The SSCP for a single control domain
- A single control point for a multidomain network

Some functions require knowledge concerning elements in more than one node. Some functions can gain in efficiency by having all their storage in one location with somewhat more efficient execution paths. *The choice made in SNA is to use an SSCP for each control domain* (usually centered in one host but encompassing multiple nodes), *to coordinate among SSCPs when necessary in a multiple-domain network, and to work via extensions to the control points in* (1) *one or more PU services for each node, and* (2) *the LU services for each LU* (see Section 7.3.2). The three-step SNA process for session initiation in a single domain is illustrated in Fig. 9.11, as follows:

1. INIT is from the LU network services of LU-1 to the SSCP network services.
2. CINIT is from the SSCP network services to the LU network services of LU-2 (which is the primary LU).
3. BIND establishes a new session between LU-1 and LU-2 (the BIND command is at the TC level).

The LU services manager of LU-2 responds to the CINIT command by causing a transmission control element (TCE) to be activated for the LU–LU session. The LU services manager then works with session control (within TC) for that new half-session to issue the BIND command.

At LU-1, the BIND command enters via common session control (as discussed in Section 9.4) because there is no active half-session at LU-1 to receive the command from path control. Common session control passes the BIND command to the session control function in the transmission control element of the desired half-session. Session control generates a response to the BIND command.

Once a positive response to the BIND command is received by the primary half-session from the secondary, the PLU will confirm to the SSCP that the session has been started (via a SESSION STARTED command). The primary half-session can then issue a START DATA TRAFFIC command to permit LU–LU traffic to flow.

Rather than starting the LU–LU session by an INITIATE SELF command from one of the LUs as described above, it is also possible to start the session from other sources, as illustrated below for a VTAM/IMS environment.

1. Logical units in remote nodes can be defined to VTAM (which contains an SSCP) as "belonging to" an application subsystem, like IMS. Then *when the application subsystem is started*, VTAM can schedule a LOGON application exit for each LU so defined.

2. The VTAM network operator can request that a session be initiated (by using the OS/VS VARY command with the LOGON option). VTAM processes that request and passes it to the host application program for which the session was requested.

3. The master terminal operator of an application subsystem (such as IMS) can also request session initiation for a remote LU by entering a session-initiation command for that subsystem (for example, the IMS/VTAM/OPNDST command).

Regardless of how the session initiation is requested, the same NAU-to-NAU protocols can be used, and identical processing can occur when the SSCP receives the requesting RUs. For further details on the session-initiation and session-termination RUs, see Appendix C.

After the LU–LU session has been activated, the LUs can maintain the session for as long as communication between the two LUs is possible. In the event of a temporary network outage, the session can continue, although there may be no physical connection between the two LUs. The session also persists whether or not contact with the SSCP is maintained.

9.7.5 LU–LU Session Termination

Either LU may send a TERMINATE SELF (TERM) command to the SSCP. The SSCP would then send a CTERM command to the LU services (LUS) in the primary LU, which in turn would arrange for the deactivation of the LU–LU session. This now requires a dialogue between the session control (SC) elements in the two halves of the LU–LU session. The LU services of the primary LU would direct the session control (in TC) of the primary half-session to send the UNBIND to the secondary half-session.

Various unformatted log-off commands can, of course, also be devised. Each of these must be converted (by either the LU or the preprocessor of the SSCP) into the formatted termination commands. A log-off command acceptable to VTAM, for example, includes supplementary parameters that specify

1. Whether the log-off is unconditional or whether it is conditioned on approval by the other LU in the host
2. Whether this termination of an LU–LU session should also be accompanied by a termination of the LU-SSCP session

If the primary LU decided to terminate the session, it would be well for it to alert the secondary LU to prepare to shut down, prior to sending the UNBIND. The sequence of commands would then be as shown in Fig. 9.12. In this case, the primary LU has proceeded with the UNBIND before advising the SSCP; no CTERM is involved. The PLU subsequently would advise the SSCP via a SESSION ENDED command.

The CHASE command is used to obtain confirmation on the completion of processing of the outstanding requests and responses. Once the response to the CHASE is provided, the recipient is assured that all requests preceding the CHASE have been received (no sequence errors reported), and their responses (if any) have been sent.

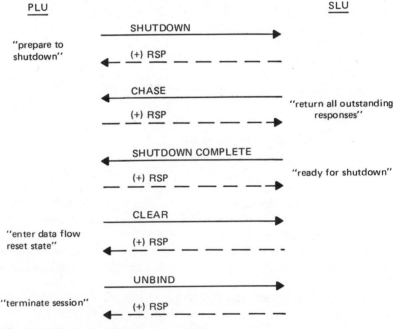

Fig. 9.12 Illustrative shutdown sequence.

The CLEAR is not absolutely required for session termination. It can be used at any time to purge all primary-to-secondary and secondary-to-primary requests and responses on the normal flows in the indicated session, and to reset data traffic. An indication that CLEAR has occurred is given to both the primary and secondary NAU services managers. They then cannot generate any further FMD or DFC requests until another START DATA TRAFFIC command is given. Thus, the CLEAR puts the session in a state ready for termination, but the PLU could decide at that point to either unbind or to start data traffic again. If this option is not desired, the CLEAR command is not needed prior to the UNBIND.

Instead of terminating the LU–LU session by a TERMINATE SELF command from one of the LUs, as described above, session termination can also be invoked by operator commands. In the VTAM/IMS environment, for example, session termination can be invoked by either the VTAM network operator or the IMS/VS master terminal operator. The termination procedure, once the request is received by the SSCP, can be the same as when the SSCP receives a TERMINATE SELF command.

9.7.6 Control of Sessions

Ordinarily, both end users (or NAU services) must be consulted prior to the activation of a session, and both must also be notified once the session is established. The complete session-activation sequence, with end-user consultation, is shown in Fig. 9.13. Consider, for example, that LU-1 requests a session and that LU-2 represents an application program (or an application subsystem); in that case, LUS of LU-2 would have to get the concurrence of the application program (or subsystem) to establish the session. If LU-2 used the TP access method, VTAM, then the procedure would be to drive an exit, the LOGON exit. In considering the LOGON request, the application program (or application subsystem) may want to first examine the proposed BIND parameters that were provided in the CINIT. This can be done via the VTAM INQUIRE macro. The application program (or application subsystem) may accept, modify, or substitute for the proposed log-on mode.

Assuming that it desires to establish the session, the application program (or subsystem) will so indicate by another VTAM macro designed for that purpose called Open Destination (OPNDST) [8.2, 8.4]. The OPNDST macro might be issued as part of the LOGON exit. Other nodes, of course, could have their own private means of conducting this dialogue.

Session termination may also involve consultation with the end-user. The TERMINATE SELF command may be designated as either "forced" or "orderly." The orderly request permits an end-of-session

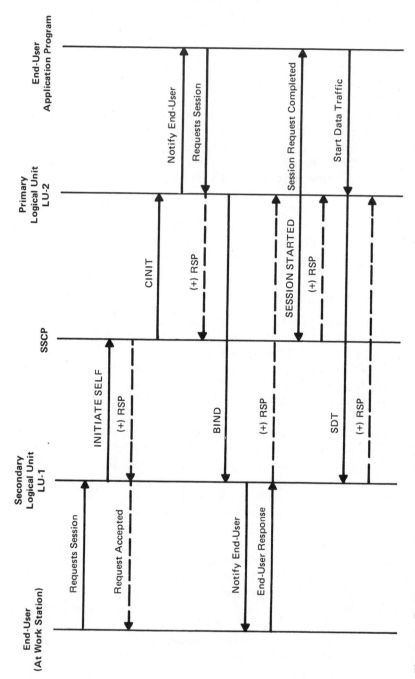

Fig. 9.13   End-user participation in session activation.

procedure to be executed at the primary LU before the session is unbound. One possible sequence for an orderly termination is shown in Fig. 9.14. The forced request requires the primary LU to unbind the session immediately and unconditionally, without the prior permission of the primary end-user.

If LU-2 again happened to use VTAM, then the receipt of an "orderly" CTERM by the LUS of LU-2 would cause it to drive an application exit, the LOSTERM exit, to notify the application program of the request to end the session. (Such exits are logically within the NAU services layer.) NAU services then could use another VTAM macro, called Close Destination (CLSDST), to signal that session termination should proceed. Prior to issuing the CLSDST macro, the application program may want to complete the processing of some pending requests. After that, it could initiate the shut-down sequence shown in Fig. 9.12. The final CLEAR and UNBIND commands are finally triggered by the Close-Destination macro.

Each product may have its own unique interface for this consultation between the end-user and the LU services. In the 3790 Communication System (a cluster controller), the statement used in the 3790 application program to establish a session (between a 3790 program and a host application program) is called Open Session (OPNSESS). The corresponding termination statement is CLOSESS. The SNA architecture does not constrain this, but SNA defines the consequent internode commands, as described above.

9.8 PARALLEL DEVELOPMENTS

9.8.1 Address Spaces and Session Establishment

Recall that in SNA sessions are established between logical units (LUs) that have global network addresses. The session is established between LUs by the use of special commands, notably the BIND command. LU–LU sessions are set via the network services function of each LU. This is done with the assistance of the SSCP (see Section 7.3). A special session links the network services in the SSCP with the network services in the LU. Somewhat similar connection problems have been faced in the experimental packet switching systems, where a "call" has to be established between two users of the carrier. We will note some of their approaches in the following discussion.

In the ARPA network [1.7], the end-users of the network employ port-to-port connections with port addresses called *sockets*. The sockets are identified by a 32-bit *host number* with 24 bits specifying a user

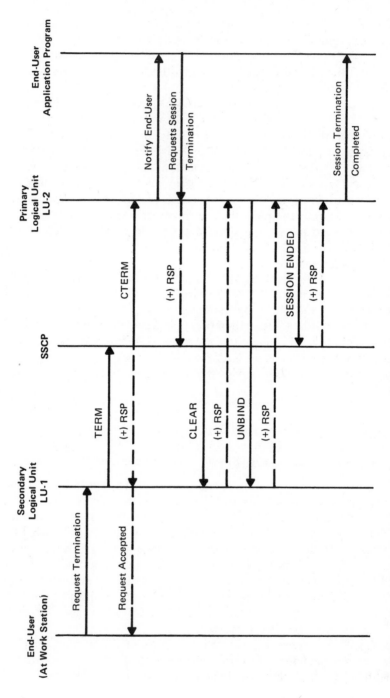

Fig. 9.14 Session termination (note, however, that CLEAR is optional prior to the UNBIND).

identification. These sockets must be allocated to end-users; and a preliminary dialogue takes place, following the initial connection protocol (ICP) [6.2], to exchange socket names before setting up a normal message flow. When a connection is set up, the receiving host allocates an eight-bit *link number* which is used together with the host number to identify the connection.

A *network control program* (NCP) in each host is responsible for establishing connections and maintaining a correspondence between end-users and sockets. The NCPs thus work together to carry out distributed network services functions. A special "link zero" channel is available for NCP-to-NCP communication. This channel is independent of the end-user to end-user channel.

In the CYCLADES network in France [9.2], subscribers (for example, a human user, a device, a subsystem, or a software processor) use permanent names known throughout the network. A hierarchical name space is used: geographic region and transfer station. Each node of the carrier must know region names and the names of transfer stations within its own region. Usually, subscribers are attached to a particular host software package called a transfer station (which is analogous to the ARPANET's network control program, except that there may be more than one of them per host). The subscriber can apply to its transfer station for port names. These port names, then, can be exchanged between transfer stations as part of the initial protocols to set up links between subscribers.

Another experimental packet switching network has been developed at the National Physical Laboratory (NPL) in England [1.7]. The setting up of calls in the NPL scheme is done by using special message types, rather than by having a special channel for the host network control programs (NCP), as with the ARPA network.

9.8.2 Acknowledgments, Ordering, and Pacing

Recall that in SNA the request/response protocol provides a high-level acknowledgment (when it is called for) that a chain of requests has been successfully received at the destination NAU (see Section 8.3). Ordering of requests so as to detect and remedy missing requests or out-of-sequence requests is done by the use of the sequence number field in both requests and responses. The SNA pacing mechanism (see Section 9.24) authorizes the sending half-session to transmit a prescribed number of requests so as to avoid overrunning the destination. Comparable problems have been addressed within experimental carrier systems—these will be reviewed in the following discussion.

Throughput considerations. In the ARPA network, entry and exit from the ARPANET take place via ARPANET nodes called Interface Message Processors (IMPs). There may also be intermediary IMPs for routing between the entry and exit IMPs. In the early ARPANET implementation, an acknowledgment system was used between the exit IMP and the entry IMP that was called "ready for next message" (RFNM); it told the entry IMP that the exit IMP had received the message. The entry IMP could then advise the originating ARPANET user that the ARPANET was ready for the next message. Therefore, the limitation was one message at a time *between end-users of the network*. The RFNM was actually sent after a multipacket message (up to 8063 bits) had been reassembled, the first packet had been delivered, and the exit IMP had sufficient free buffer space for another multipacket message of maximum length. Thus, the ARPANET regulated how much traffic entered the network.

The analysis by Cerf [9.3] showed that, originally, the ARPANET throughput dropped hyperbolically if the users of the ARPANET were separated by multiple IMPs. By that analysis, the throughput of a 50-kbps line, for example, dropped to 14–35 kbps for messages of 1–8 packets, when faced with three inter-IMP hops. Satellite transmissions, with longer delays, would aggravate the problem. This distance (hop) dependence was due in large measure to the original RFNM "one-message-at-a-time" protocol.

In Version 2 of the ARPANET, flow control was implemented by setting a maximum number of four messages that could be outstanding *between any pair of entry-exit IMPs*. Multiple hosts attached to an IMP competed for the four "tokens." One now had to invent methods that guaranteed the proper sequencing of messages. Also, in Version 2, no multipacket message could enter the network until storage for that message had been allocated in the destination IMP.

In Version 3 of the ARPANET protocols, the network permits up to eight messages in flight *between any host-host pair*. If n messages are in flight, then the next one may not proceed until an RFNM is returned back at the entry IMP for any one of the n outstanding messages. Kleinrock [9.5] observes that if the round-trip delay is greater than the time it takes to feed the n messages into the network, then the source will be blocked while the entry IMP awaits RFNMs.

9.9 EXERCISES

Which of the following statements are true?

9.1 One transmission control element is assigned to each

    a) logical unit

    b) transmission subsystem

    c) session

    d) half-session

9.2 The RH is attached to all RUs generated within a half-session by

    a) logical unit services

    b) session control

    c) connection point manager

9.3 To avoid buffer overruns, pacing controls the flow of requests by

    a) always requiring a separate authorization from the destination half-session for the transmission of each successive request.

    b) requiring authorization from the destination node for transmission of a number of segments.

    c) requiring authorization from the receiving connection point manager for transmission of another block of request units (RUs).

9.4 If path control does not find a connection point manager to accept an incoming request (for a known destination NAU), then path control will

    a) generate an error response.

    b) route the request to common session control for that node.

    c) route the request to logical unit services.

9.5 The format indicator, in the RH, indicates

    a) whether a message to the SSCP is formatted or unformatted.

    b) whether an FM header is included in the RU.

    c) whether format conversion is provided by presentation services.

9.6 An RU on the expedited flow

    a) can be placed ahead of normal-flow requests at the host and at boundary nodes.

    b) cannot be delivered if all normal-flow traffic is stopped.

9.7 Sequence numbers are generated by the connection point manager

    a) for all normal-flow requests being sent by the CPMGR.

    b) for all responses and requests being sent by the CPMGR.

    c) and the assigned sequence number is returned to the originator of the RU (i.e., to FI.FMD, DFC, or TC).

    d) and the CPMGR checks to see that requests being received are in the correct order.

    e) and responses are given the same sequence number as that of the corresponding request.

9.8 The BIND command enables one to tailor each session; options in this command permit one to select

a) whether a particular sequence of requests will be chained together.

b) which NAU will normally speak first to begin brackets.

c) which station will win contention in half-duplex contention mode on the link.

d) whether multiple RU chains will be allowed.

e) whether pacing will be provided on expedited flow or on normal flow.

f) which DFC–RUs and TC–RUs may be used.

g) which presentation services may be used.

h) whether FM headers may be used.

9.9 Match the following elements with their function.

Elements	Function
a) Connection point manager	1. Manages the activation and deactivation of one half-session
b) Session control	2. Supports SSCP–LU sessions
c) Data flow control	3. Adapts two end-users to each other in an LU–LU session
d) Logical unit services	4. Generates the RH for a half-session
e) Presentation services	5. Supports initial network start-up
f) Session services	6. Gets network names translated into network addresses
g) Configuration services	7. Provides facilities for testing nodes and links
h) Maintenance services	8. Assists in controlling the flow of requests and responses in a session

9.10 Create the bit pattern for the RH for the following circumstances.

- A request is generated by FI.FMD.
- The RU contains an FM header, and no sense data is included.
- The RU is the only element of a chain.
- A response is desired only if there is an error condition.
- Permission is being requested to send another group of requests to the destination.
- The sender is the first speaker and wishes to begin a bracket with this request.
- This is a duplex send/receive mode.
- There is no code selection.

9.11 A violation of bracket rules has occurred in a request that originated in the FI.FMD services in an LU–LU session. The begin-bracket (BB) bit was set on middle of chain. An RH usage error is to be indicated in a negative response. Give the RH and the two coded bytes of sense data (i.e., category and modifier exception codes) in the negative response, assuming the following.

- There is no FM header.
- A definite-response type 1 had been requested.
- A pacing response is not appropriate.

9.12 Using Appendixes C and D, construct the byte pattern for the INITIATE SELF command in the following situation.

- The mode name to identify the desired BIND parameters is 000000HI.
- The name of the destination LU is JO.
- The originating end-user is not identified; there are no password and no user data.

Use hex codes throughout.

9.13 Using Appendixes C and D, construct the bit pattern of the BIND command for the following situation.

- FM profile 4
- TS profile 2
- Multiple RU chains are allowed from both half-sessions.
- Multiple chains requiring a definite response may be outstanding from both half-sessions.
- Chains from primary and secondary will ask for definite or exception response.
- Compression will be used in both directions.
- Primary or secondary may send end-bracket (EB) indicator.
- FM headers are allowed.
- Brackets will be used, with bracket termination rule number 1.
- No alternate code will be used.
- Normal flow will be duplex.
- The sender of each request will have recovery responsibility.
- The secondary is the first speaker for brackets.
- All pacing counts are one.
- Maximum RU size is 256 bytes for both half-sessions.
- The primary LU name is MO.
- No user data accompanies the BIND.

9.10 REFERENCES AND BIBLIOGRAPHY

See also [7.8, 8.2, 8.4, and 15.7].

9.1 P. G. Cullum. "The Transmission Subsystem in System Network Architecture." *IBM Systems Journal* **15,** No. 1 (1976).

9.2 L. Pouzin. "Presentation and Major Design Aspects of the CYCLADES Computer Network." In *Computer Communication Networks* (eds., R. L. Grimsdale and F. F. Kuo). Noordhoff, Leyden (1975).

9.3 V. G. Cerf. "An Assessment of ARPANET Protocols." *Proc. Second Jerusalem Conference on Information Technology*, Vol. 1 (July 1974).

9.4 L. Pouzin. "The CYCLADES Computer Network." *Data Networks: Analysis and Design, Third Data Communications Symposium*, St. Petersburg, Florida (November 1973): 80–87.

9.5 L. Kleinrock. "ARPANET Lessons." *Proc. IEEE 1976 Communications Conference*, Philadelphia (June 1976).

9.6 W. L. Price. "Simulation Studies of an Isarithmically Controlled Store and Forward Data Communication Network." *IFIP Congress* (August 1974): 151–154.

10
Path
Control

10.1 INTRODUCTION*

The path control element in each node acts like the cargo dispatcher in a trucking firm. It packages the cargo and routes it to the next node.

Path control is needed, first of all, within the source and destination nodes to route BIUs to and from the multiple half-sessions in those nodes, and it serves the connection point managers (which are within transmission control elements). *It is the responsibility of path control to route to the correct active half-session* or to common session control in the destination node if the appropriate half-session is not active. (If the destination address is unknown, a negative response will be returned.)

A sending connection point manager communicates with a receiving connection point manager. The intervening layers of path control and data link control are the transportation mechanisms that must be transparent to the information being communicated between the two CPMGRS. (An exception to this transparency is made in the case of a path error, when the message is not deliverable. In such a case, path control does examine the RH to determine whether it is a request or a response, which affects its recovery action.) What is sent between CPMGRs is the BIU (RU plus the RH), which provides both the data and the logic to control the dialogue between the two half-sessions. Path

---

* Acknowledgment is given to W. F. Emmons, T. B. McNeill, and J. Murdock for their contributions to the development of the path control portions of SNA that are reflected in this chapter.

control adds the TH to the BIU (or segments of the BIU), forming one or more Path Information Units (PIUs).

Path control has the responsibility of routing the BIU, perhaps along multiple data links and through multiple nodes, from the originating CPMGR to the destination CPMGR. Each path control element in each node provides duplex, point-to-point flows. This is true at the path control level, even though connecting links at the data link control level may restrict these flows in half-duplex link operations, and even with multipoint flow controls on the link. The common network (consisting of all path control and link control functions in the path between two half-sessions) maintains order (First-In, First-Out) for all normal-flow requests between a pair of TCEs. *The path control finds the route, from node to node, always routing to the next proper link and station, toward the destination of the PIU.* Address transformation, in boundary-node path control, permits diverse attachments to operate in their private addressing worlds, and still participate in the network.

Each path control element routes individual PIUs, or a block of PIUs forming a BTU, on and off the appropriate links; it also routes individual BIUs to and from transmission control elements. Information on different sessions from the same NAU may use different links; also, individual links may handle requests flowing on different paths.

The originating end-user and the functions of its half-session need have no concern about the physical location of the destination or of the route to get there. Path control is given the BIU and parameters for the transmission header (TH), including the addresses (of both the destination and the originating NAUs). The rest is up to path control, to select the path, using various links along the way as necessary, and to deliver the BIU to the destination CPMGR.

In Chapters 7 and 9 the SNA facilities for binding a session and for pacing the flows were discussed. Binding and pacing functions are done within half-sessions, and so permit a simpler path control function. The degree of storage needed in intermediate nodes also depends on the expectation that messages can be delivered promptly rather than stored to await the availability of resources. Low storage capacity tends to be a corollary to minimum store-and-forward delay; overcoming congestion by simply increasing storage would tend to increase delay. Message switching nodes, for example, anticipate long delays and provide correspondingly large storage. A more economical design with only modest buffers results when

1. The originator of the message uniquely "owns" a part at the destination (by prior agreements and this ownership assures him or her of a degree of buffer space in the destination.

2. A pacing discipline is followed, with feedback from the destination, to ensure that the expected buffer spaces are not overrun.

A relatively "lean" path control is the design objective in SNA. Today's implementations, therefore, depend for the most part on *per-session end-to-end flow rate controls* to avoid buffer depletion and overrun (actually two-stage pacing—see Section 9.2.4). Path control adds only gross controls (e.g., slowdown) to this. In complex networks, others have found it advantageous to provide controls over total (*multisession*) flows. If and when such requirements develop, path control would be a logical place to support such controls.

Note that configuration considerations have not appeared in earlier discussion of the half-session. Any configuration restrictions, like having only tree structures, are visible at the path control layer (e.g., in routing tables) but not at higher levels.

10.2 ADDRESSING

A consistent addressing structure is essential to network operations. SNA assigns network addresses to each SSCP, PU, and LU that communicates via the common transmission network. The specific address either is assigned at system definition time or is assigned dynamically as part of a dial connection using the switched network.

The network address is the basic unit of addressing. It is distinct from station addresses on a particular link (at the data link control level), which must be associated with the desired network address.

Addressing by subareas and elements
The set of network addresses within an SNA network is called an *area*. This addressing area is divided into a number of *subareas*. Each addressing subarea is further divided into *elements*.

An area may contain one or more SSCPs, that is, one or more control domains. A particular node may contain one or more subareas (although implementations usually assign only one subarea to a node). A particular network addressable unit (NAU) is identified by the combination of subarea and element addresses.

Subarea addressing. Routing through the network is facilitated by subdividing the 16-bit network address into two parts, as shown in Fig. 10.1. The *subarea address* is comparable to the area code of the telephone system and the *element address* corresponds to the subscriber's telephone number. With this arrangement, *much of the routing can be handled by examining only the subarea address*. A node that provides services dealing with the full 16-bit address is sometimes referred to as a *subarea*

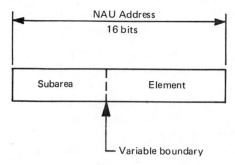

Fig. 10.1   Division of network address.

node. When the PIU finally arrives at the correct subarea, the element address is examined. (Note that the element address pertains to a portion of the NAU address and should not be confused with implementations of layers such as TC element, PC element, etc.).

The fraction of the 16-bit network address that is devoted to the subarea address has been a variable to be decided by each network owner. One network may choose to have only four bits in the subarea address, so that only 16 subareas are allowed. Another may allocate eight bits of the network address to the subarea address, in which case that network could have up to 256 subareas. Within a given network, however, the division is fixed and is selected at system generation time; that is, the time when all the nodes in the network are defined. The usual implementation is for a subarea address of eight bits.

Hosts and communications controllers have one (or possibly more) subarea address assigned to them. *All NAUs in cluster controllers and terminal nodes adopt the subarea address of the host or communications controller to which they are attached.* Three such subareas are shown in Fig. 10.2.

To illustrate, let us trace the passage of a request in Fig. 10.2, from an application program in a host, through a local communications controller (COMC) to a remote COMC, and then to a cluster controller or terminal node. The local COMC, performing an intermediate function, routes only on the subarea address. In effect, this COMC asks, "Is this PIU for my subarea or not?" Since the subarea addresses do not match, the next question is "What is the link-level address of the next adjacent node, in order that I can send it on its way toward the correct subarea?" This might, for example, be a link address and a link station address. There are various ways of obtaining these addresses. Assume for now that they are in one of the local COMC's tables *that relate destination subareas to link-level addresses of the next adjacent node along the route.* Path control

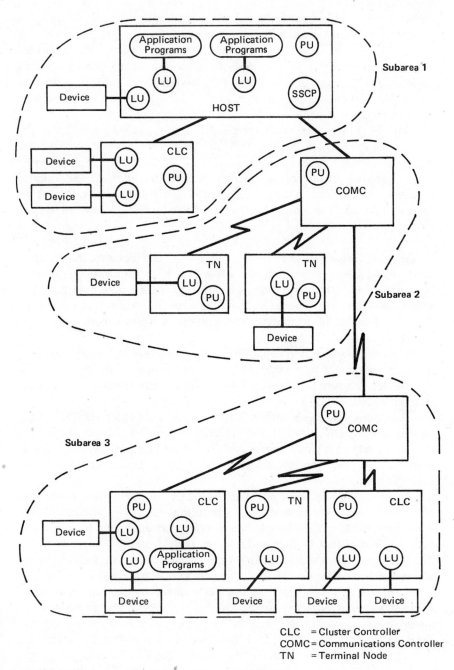

CLC   = Cluster Controller
COMC= Communications Controller
TN   = Terminal Node

Fig. 10.2 Three subareas within one control domain.

places the PIU, along with the link address and link-station address, on an appropriate link-station outbound queue. Then, when the data link control for that queue is ready, the PIU is sent to that link and then to the right station, which in this example is at the remote COMC. When the remote COMC determines that this PIU has the same subarea address as that COMC, then and only then must the element portion of the address by examined.

The PC function in the local communications controller is an example of an *intermediate function* (IF), an SNA term used to describe the capability of routing received messages onward to the destination, based on the subarea portion of the destination network address, and keeping the same transmission header (TH). Hosts and communications controllers can have an IF in which they route received messages onward to their destination subarea.

Element addressing. The 16-bit address of the network addressable units would allow up to 64,000 addresses, if the address space were efficiently used. Ordinarily, only a fraction of these would ever be active at any one time. Moreover, the NAUs in a given destination node, like a cluster controller or terminal node, will be in session with only some subset of the available NAUs at any one time. Therefore, some economy in the element-addressing capabilities of destination nodes can be made; one certainly needs fewer than 16 bits of addressing for the NAUs within one cluster controller or terminal node. How many fewer is a subjective question.

Any node that deals with a shortened address (which may be unique to that node itself) is sometimes referred to as a *local node*. It requires that some adjacent node provide address transformation services for it. Two types of local nodes are currently defined, type-1 and type-2, as described below.

In the case of cluster controllers, it seems reasonable that fewer than 256 NAUs need ever be addressed within that one node. Therefore, only 8 bits of address, rather than 16, seem more than adequate; so only 8 bits need be transmitted to that node, which is designated as a *type-2 node.* The TH used with a type-2 node requires 8 bits for an origin address and another 8 bits for a destination address. The shortening of the address from 16 bits to 8 bits can and does take place in the communications controller that is adjacent to the cluster controller. The adjacent communications controller performs a *boundary function* in doing this address translation, so as to reduce the burden on the cluster controller.

In the case of other, less complex nodes, often called terminal nodes, a still smaller number of logical units is anticipated. So only 8 bits of address (conveniently, one byte) are used for both the address of the NAU in the terminal node and other indicators. Nodes receiving this very short form have been designated as *type-1 nodes*.

Short forms of both the origin address and the destination address are exchanged between the communications controller and a type-2 node (for example, a cluster controller). This allows (architecturally, at least) each logical unit of the cluster controller to have multiple simultaneous sessions, with a different destination address for each session of that logical unit. However, this ability to conduct multiple sessions per logical unit is a luxury that the simpler type-1 node probably can do without. Since there is only-one session per logical unit, there is no need to keep passing both addresses back and forth between the boundary node and the type-1 node. On this assumption, the address of the LU that is in session with a type-1 node LU is not even sent by the boundary node to its adjacent type-1 node. The boundary node remembers what the other address is, but does not transmit this to the type-1 node.

Note that address transformations (to and from local address) are made in an adjacent node having a boundary function. However, this applies only to addresses contained in the transmission header (TH). Some network service RUs contain network addresses; since they are in the RU, these addresses are not transformed by the boundary function. Such network service RUs, therefore, are used only with subarea nodes that deal with full 16-bit addresses.

Link addresses

For convenience, the current SNA network services also utilize network addresses to identify links between nodes. A link is activated via the PU services of the node that contains the primary station for that link.

When using the switched network, the physical link is provided via the dial procedure. In this case, the dial number may be considered a special link address. The dial address is used to establish the physical connection. Once the dial connection is established, the same addressing discussed above is used for communication among network addressable units (NAUs).

10.3   BOUNDARY-FUNCTION ADDRESS TRANSFORMATION

The communications controllers (COMCs), in the example shown in Fig. 10.2, are performing a *boundary function* (BF). The position of this boundary function, in the SNA structure, is shown in Fig. 10.3. The job of a boundary function at the path control level is the *transformation of*

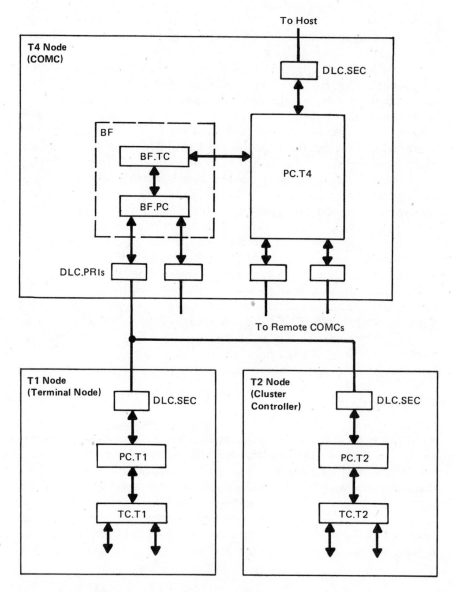

BF.TC = Boundary Function. Transmission Control
BF.PC = Boundary Function. Path Control

Fig. 10.3 DLC/PC/TC structures.

network addresses to local addresses, and vice versa, for cluster controllers and terminal nodes that are directly attached to the COMC. (Other jobs of the boundary function pertain to session control and pacing at the transmission control level—see Section 9.5.) Hosts by definition understand subarea addresses and do not need boundary-function support from some adjacent node.

The possible diversity of function is extremely wide in cluster controllers and terminal nodes. Regarding addressing, the manufacturer may have reason to build in a very simple address that is unrelated to the SNA network address. The address may be hard-wired and unchangeable, or it may be in read-only storage, which is also set as part of the manufacturing process. A single short address for all instances of that type of terminal can also ease installation and facilitate maintenance.

In short, the addressing world of the attaching nodes may be quite different from that of the network, calling for a transformation between the two addressing conventions. This address transformation is one of the services that must be provided by the path-control boundary function in either a communications controller or a host.

For an illustration of address transformation, consider Fig. 10.4. The end-users may think best in terms of mnemonic *names*. These are translatable (by a system services control point) to unique numeric *network addresses*, which in SNA are 16 bits long. Each of these, in turn, may have a smaller *local address* that is unique when associated with a particular location, such as one station on one link in a particular subarea. For example, network address 3400 translates to subarea 3 local address 25 on station 1 of link 2.

The cluster controllers and terminal nodes in SNA can communicate with the communications controller in terms of their short local addresses. The COMC, knowing their link and station for each attachment, can always relate these local addresses to the corresponding network address, and vice versa. The network address pair forms the origin address and destination address fields (OAF/DAF) in the TH that is sent between subareas. This pair is established when a session is first initiated.

In the case of the type-2 nodes (such as cluster controllers), which receive a short form of both the origin address and the destination address in each transmission header, the short local form of these addresses is referred to as an OAF'/DAF' pair, which is only two bytes long. This is half the size of the OAF/DAF pair.

In the case of the type-1 nodes (often called terminal nodes), which never receive an origin address, the local address is called a Local Session ID (LSID). It consists of only one byte, as shown in Fig. 10.5. Six bits of the LSID are used to indicate a session with one of 64 possible

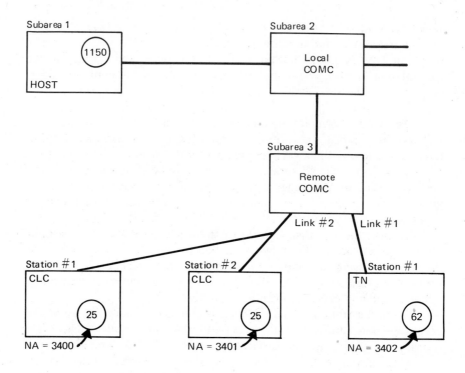

Fig. 10.4   Names and addresses of NAUs.

Network Name	Network Address	Subarea Address		
		Local Address	Link	Station
Teller 5	3400	25	2	1
File Q	3401	25	2	2
Tom	3402	62	1	1
HDQTRS	1150			

0	1	2-7
SSCP or LU	PU or LU	LU address

Fig. 10.5   Local session identifier (LSID).

LUs in the type-1 node. One bit is used to indicate a session with the node's physical unit. Since each LU can be in session with one other LU and with the SSCP, one bit is reserved to tell whether this particular message is for an LU–LU session or an LU–SSCP session.

One must be able to set up and change these transformations. In SNA, the relating of an element address to a link, station, and node type is usually established during system generation, but may be established dynamically by means of SSCP commands that instruct the physical unit services of the COMC (see Section 12.4.3). The correlation of a local OAF′/DAF′ or LSID with the network OAF/DAF is performed during session initiation when the BIND command is passed through the COMC.

Referring again to Fig. 10.4, let us say, for example, that LU-1150, in the host, establishes a session with LU-3401, in the cluster controller. As part of the system-generation process (or a dial-in process to be described in Section 12.6), the boundary COMC is advised of both the network addresses in the attaching cluster controllers and the local short forms of those addresses. As part of the session-initiation process (via the TH that accompanies the BIND command), the boundary COMC is advised of both network addresses (1150/3401) for that particular session. The short form of the addresses, the OAF′/DAF′, then consists of

1. The local address 25 understood by the cluster controller, and
2. Some short form for LU-1150 (like 50) that can be selected by the communications controller, which can tell the cluster controller (via the TH) to use that short form for this session.

The only address that the cluster controller needs to understand for that session is the OAF′/DAF′, which is 50/25 for host-to-cluster-controller messages and 25/50 for cluster-controller-to-host messages. The COMC, however, must also remember that session 50/25 is found at station 2 on link 2. It is this combination of information (local address plus link/station) that provides a unique designation.

The same cluster controllers that attach to communications controllers via TP lines may be attached directly to hosts via the host's I/O channels. In that case, the boundary function for the cluster controller is located in the host.

10.4 SEGMENTING AND BLOCKING

In any transportation process, the size of the package to be carried may be a problem. The post office, for example, has a maximum size that it will handle. Also it is often more economical to put many small items into a single box, rather than wrap and pay the freight for a large number of very small packages. The shipping lines also give attractive rates if all packages are in containers of a standard size, because their handling is then more efficient. The transportation company may package smaller containers into large standard-sized containers, or it may choose to handle individually the convenient smaller packages in a large shipment. We have similar considerations in transporting the BIU through the network. Buffer sizes are usually limited in each node. If the PIU is very long, it ties up the buffers in intermediate nodes and the receiving node for a long time while the entire message dribbles in. If the message is exceedingly short, the data unit itself will be dwarfed by the size of the headers necessary to carry it, and the overhead to be paid for transporting a large number of very small data units will be unnecessarily high.

In SNA, therefore, another function of the path control layer is a repackaging job. This is called *segmenting*, if the BIU is to be broken up into smaller packages (i.e., multiple PIUs), or *blocking*, if a number of PIUs are to be combined in a single package. Segmenting and blocking are illustrated in Fig. 10.6.

Segmenting considerations. Response time is a major reason for segmenting. Consider, for example, a network of three nodes with the requirement to transmit a 2400-bit message from node 1 through node 2 into node 3. Consider that the data links have a capability of 1200 bits per second. Assume that propagation time is negligible, and that transmission time is determined largely by message-serializing time (see Section 1.3.5). The transmission of the entire 2400-bit message from node 1 to node 2 would require two seconds. The transmission of that same 2400-bit message from node 2 to node 3 would require another two seconds with no overlap between the two. The total transmission time, therefore, from node 1 to node 3 is four seconds (see Fig. 10.7a).

If, on the other hand, the 2400-bit message is segmented into four equal segments (or packets) of 600 bits each, we then have the potential for the overlap shown in Fig. 10.7(b). Transmission of each of the 600-bit segments from node 1 to node 2 requires $\frac{1}{2}$ second for a total transmission time (as before) of two seconds. However, as soon as node 2 has received the first segment, it begins to transmit that first segment to node 3. Similarly, as soon as it receives the second segment, it begins to transmit that second segment to node 3. The transmission from node 2 to node 3 again takes two seconds for the four packets. However, three of the segments transmitted from node 2 to node 3 are overlapped with the transmission of segments from node 1 to node 2. The total time of transmission from node 1 to node 3, therefore, is the transmission time for five segments, or 2.5 seconds. The overall improvement is $1\frac{1}{2}$ seconds

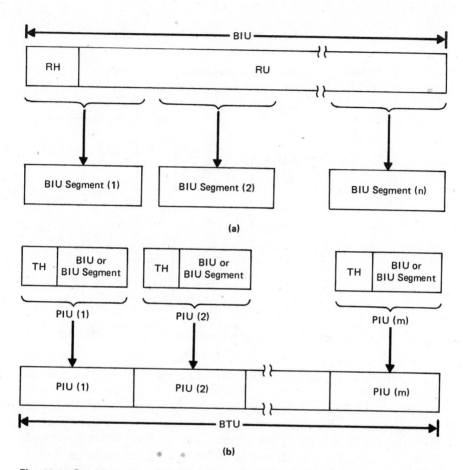

Fig. 10.6 Segmenting and blocking. (Reprinted by permission from *Systems Network Architecture—General Information,* IBM Form No. GA27-3102. Courtesy of International Business Machines Corporation.)

out of the original four, or an improvement of 37 percent in this particular example. The benefit, of course, is greater for larger records and larger numbers of segments.

Segmenting of larger messages also can be an aid in reducing the amount of retransmission on the occasion of a line failure. Depending on the error rate of the link, line efficiency can be improved by imposing a maximum message size for each link.

The segmenting algorithm allows larger BIUs to be sent along high bandwidth or higher reliability links (e.g., between communications controllers) and still have smaller BIUs sent over the lower bandwidth or

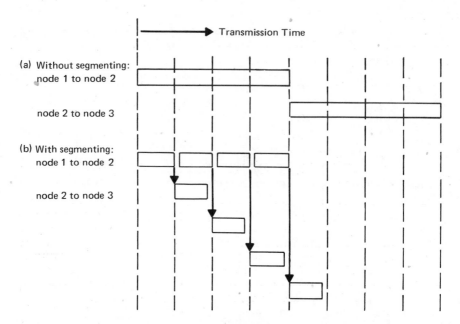

Fig. 10.7 Potential for shortened delay in intermediate node, with segmenting.

lower reliability segments of the path (e.g., the final link to a cluster controller).

Path control in each node must know what segment size is appropriate for each message. This will be the smaller of (a) the maximum size permitted in the light of system response time and link reliability considerations, or (b) the maximum link buffer size of the receiving station. Note that segmenting accommodates buffers in the common transmission network, including those at the DLC level. This is separate and distinct from any use of chaining to accommodate buffers at the application or application-subsystem level, or the designation of a maximum RU size in accordance with half-session buffer capacities.

The network owner may find it advantageous from a performance standpoint to fix the maximum segment size for all or some paths in the total network. This can help to guarantee response times along those paths, while giving the opportunity for efficient use of buffer space.

Note that every BIU and every BIU segment gets a TH header; thus at each stage of path control, the destination address for every BIU and every BIU segment can be examined. Path information units (PIUs) containing BIU segments may be forwarded unchanged by path control. Alternatively, each intermediate path control may segment a whole BIU or further segment a BIU segment, prior to forwarding. The repeated segmenting, in successive nodes, is rarely advantageous. In most cases, the entire path is known a priori, so a fixed segment size for each route can be selected.

Blocking considerations. The information in the block consists of a string of path information units (PIUs). This string is called the *basic transmission unit* (BTU). It is the unit of information passed between path control and data link control. The BTU can consist of one or more PIUs, depending on whether path control does blocking (see Fig. 10.8).

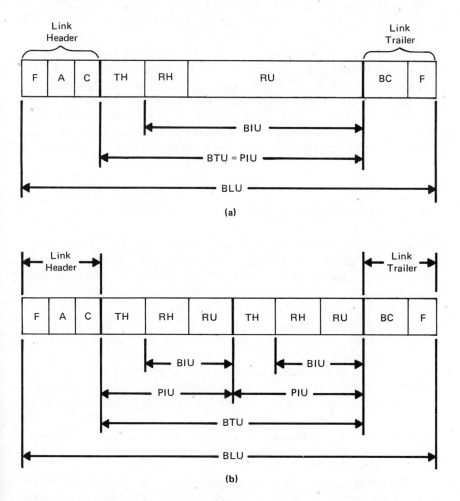

Fig. 10.8 (a) Basic link unit with no blocking; (b) basic link unit with blocking.

At each node, path control must examine the block, because it may be that some of the messages in that block are destined for one line while other messages in that same block are destined for a different line. The path control examines the first TH, and then the Data Count Field (DCF) in that TH; by comparing the data count field (for that PIU) with the bit count (for the entire information field) provided by the receiving data link control, the path control can determine whether or not there is another PIU within that block. From the DCF it can determine where to find the next TH in the bit string. After disassembling the block, path control proceeds to route each PIU according to its ultimate destination. If a number of small PIUs are again headed down the same line, a reblocking of those messages can take place.

When blocking, we group together PIUs within a single set of data link control headers, thus saving some header overhead on the links. On the other hand, too much blocking forces longer queues to a specific data link, and it implies that a delay exists until a sufficient number of BIUs are assembled to fill a block. Thus, blocking must be used with discretion to avoid effects on response time. Blocking has seldom appeared to be necessary. and it therefore is not usually implemented as a path control option.

10.5 TRANSMISSION HEADER

The protocol at the path control level concerns the jobs of packaging (that is, segmenting or blocking) and routing. The format for those protocols is the transmission header, which accompanies a BIU (or BIU segment) in the common transmission network (see Fig. 10.6). The TH accompanying each BIU (or BIU segment) can vary in size and content. For example, as seen in the above discussion of addressing, the job of path control can be simplified in the final leg of the path, depending on the nature of the destination node. In the case of the cluster controller, the address can be shortened. In the case of the terminal node, the origin address need not be sent to it at all. As another simplification, blocking is seldom advantageous on the final leg because buffering in the destination node is more often in short supply; therefore, the data count field, needed for blocking, can sometimes be dispensed with. Thus, there are good reasons for subsetting the transmission protocols to suit the lesser needs of different destination nodes.

In the current SNA, the TH can be from two to ten bytes in length, depending on which TH format is used. However, all of the THs thus far defined are subsets of the general form shown in Fig. 10.9.

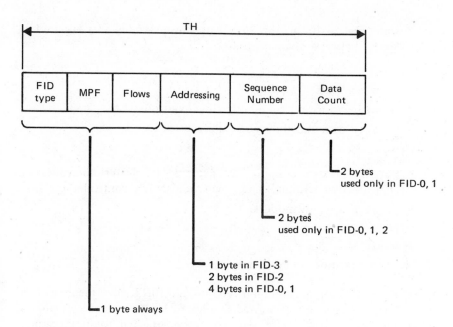

Fig. 10.9 Transmission header (TH).

Format identifiers. The function subsets in the path control layer are identified by what is called a Format Identifier (FID). The first four bits of the transmission header (TH) are used for the format identifier, thus allowing up to 16 FID types. To date, SNA has defined only four, leaving the rest for future needs.

A node is somewhat characterized by the sophistication of the transmission header (TH) that it is able to handle, and particularly by the size of the address field involved. As shown in Fig. 10.10, there are three THs corresponding to three sizes of addressing as follows:

1. Hosts and communications controllers can handle the full TH, including two bytes for the origin address field (OAF) and two bytes for the destination address field (DAF). This TH contains a format identifier (FID) of type 1.

2. Type-2 nodes, such as most cluster controllers, can handle a reduced TH, including a one-byte OAF' and a one-byte DAF'. This TH includes an FID of type 2.

3. Type-1 nodes, usually called terminal nodes, can only handle a still smaller TH, including only one byte for both origin and destination. This TH includes an FID of type 3.

As shown in Fig. 10.10, the three types of transmission header are used to communicate between nodes as follows:

1. FID-1
   - Between hosts
   - Between hosts and communications controllers
   - Between comunications controllers

2. FID-2
   - Between a type-2 node (for example, a cluster controller or high-function terminal) and a communications controller
   - Between a type-2 node and host

3. FID-3
   - Between a type-1 node (for example, a terminal node) and a communications controller.

These three formats are summarized in Fig. 10.11, and the places in which they are used are illustrated in Fig. 10.10. Note, however, that a given line can have different types of node attached to it; therefore, messages with different FID types can be interleaved on the same line. FID-0 is the same as FID-1, but is reserved for non-SNA attachments.

Mapping field (MPF). After the four bits for FID type, every TH contains two mapping field bits, which tell the PC whether that PIU contains a whole BIU or only a segment of a BIU. If the latter, these two bits tell whether we have the first segment, a middle segment, or the last segment of a BIU. These are necessary in order for PC to be able to recombine segments into a whole BIU before passing it to a CPMGR. Note, however, that this mechanism does not guard against out-of-sequence segments or lost segments (see the discussion of segment sequence below).

Flows. Each of four logical flows is potentially used by each PIU. The four flows arise because we have (1) two directions of flow (primary-to-secondary and secondary-to-primary), and (2) two independent flows in each direction (normal and expedited).

The OAF/DAF field of the transmission header indicates the direction of flow (the first address always being the sending NAU). Another bit in the TH, the expedited flow indicator (EFI), designates whether the associated PIU is on normal or expedited flow. Both the OAF/DAF fields and the EFI are given to PC, as parameters, by the originating CPMGR.

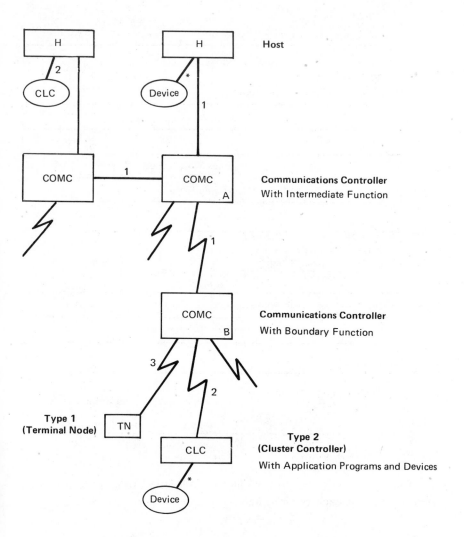

1 — Four bytes OAF/DAF network address within transmission header (TH); (FID-1)
2 — Two bytes local form of OAF/DAF network addresses within TH; (FID-2)
3 — One byte local form of session ID within TH; (FID-3)
* — No network addressing on this connection

Fig. 10.10 Transmission header (TH) usage and addressing fields between various node types.

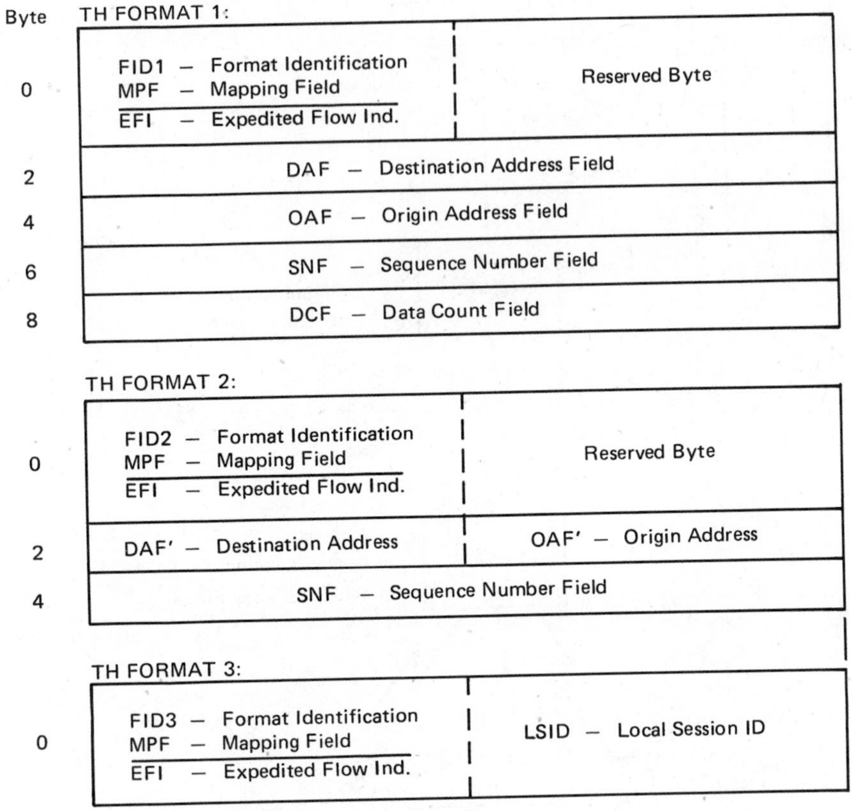

Byte   TH FORMAT 1:

FID1 — Format Identification MPF — Mapping Field EFI — Expedited Flow Ind.	Reserved Byte

0

2	DAF — Destination Address Field
4	OAF — Origin Address Field
6	SNF — Sequence Number Field
8	DCF — Data Count Field

TH FORMAT 2:

FID2 — Format Identification MPF — Mapping Field EFI — Expedited Flow Ind.	Reserved Byte

0

2	DAF' — Destination Address	OAF' — Origin Address
4	SNF — Sequence Number Field	

TH FORMAT 3:

FID3 — Format Identification MPF — Mapping Field EFI — Expedited Flow Ind.	LSID — Local Session ID

0

Fig. 10.11 Three TH formats.

With these, path control could keep PIUs in order in each of four logical flows for each session, namely:

1. Primary to secondary—normal flow
2. Secondary to primary—normal flow
3. Primary to secondary—expedited flow
4. Secondary to primary—expedited flow

Ordinarily, implementation of path control does not give priority to expedited PIUs. Current PC implementations recognize only two flows, one in each direction, with all RUs in each flow obeying FIFO order. (The boundary function CPMGR does give priority to expedited flows.) On the other hand, the expedited flow indicator is there, so special path control protocols could make use of the expedited flow indicator, in the TH, to also give priority within path control to the expedited PIUs.

Addressing and sessions. Path control must deliver each PIU to the transmission control element that is assigned to that session. How does PC know to which session a PIU belongs? It is determined from the pair of NAU addresses in the origin address field (OAF) and destination address field (DAF) sent in all THs of FID-0 and FID-1, or from the short versions (OAF' and DAF') in the TH of FID-2. This is one reason for sending both the origin and the destination addresses.

In the case of FID-3, there are at most two sessions for each LU in the type-1 node; the path-control boundary function, in the adjacent COMC, must remember the OAF/DAF for each of these sessions from the time that the session is first initiated.

The other purpose of sending the OAF with each PIU is for notification of an inability to deliver the message. Say, for example, that a link breaks between an intermediate node and the destination node; the intermediate node, in that case, can examine the OAF and can send a status message back to the originator. It has been found, in general, that recovery from failures is facilitated if both the origin and the destination are immediately known.

Sequence number field (SNF). SNA requires that (1) all normal-flow requests be kept in order (first-in, first-out), and (2) all expedited requests be kept in order. To enable the system to maintain order for all requests of a session and to permit the correlation of responses with requests, each BIU has a sequence number field, provided by the originating connection point manager (CPMGR). The sequence number field is carried in the transmission header (TH), when we have FID-1 or FID-2.

All requests and responses, on both normal and expedited flows, carry a sequence number field. Most normal-flow requests and responses carry a sequence number. Expedited-flow PIUs and some normal-flow PIUs do not participate in that same numbering sequence; they contain, instead, an identification number that is distinct from the normal-flow sequence number. Whether normal-flow requests use sequence numbers or another ID is selected at session establishment (BIND) time.

All responses carry the same sequence number (or ID) as the request to which the response belongs. Since the sequence numbers of requests from the two ends of the line are generated independently, these sequence numbers could conceivably coincide. That is, a request from A to B could have a sequence number of 18, while a request from B to A could also have a sequence number of 18. Moreover, the return responses would also have a sequence number of 18. In order to keep these separate, it is necessary to know from which end the request originated. The implementation has no difficulty determining the direction of flow.

Together with the request/response indicator in the RH, the sequence number (or ID) eliminates any confusion in the CPMGR as to whether a BIU is out of sequence.

Segment sequence. Segmenting introduces some special problems. When segmenting, the SNA path control puts the same value in the sequence number field (SNF) for each segment of a given BIU. The destination path control uses the OAF/DAF pair and the mapping field to identify the segments when recombining the BIU, prior to passing it to the destination connection point manager.

However, keeping the same sequence number on all segments of a BIU means that a lost segment will not be detectable above the data link control level. If that segment is being transmitted at the DLC level, and that frame is lost or out of sequence, then that error *can* be detected at the DLC level because DLC has its own sequence number for each transmission (or frame). This fact, and the preservation of correct order by data link control, will prevent a misassembly of a BIU.

It can be argued however, that the preservation of order (FIFO, or first-in, first-out) at the DLC level should not be relied on. The maintenance of FIFO solely at the DLC level can become complicated, particularly if one had parallel links or an ability to selectively reject one message (for retransmission) at the DLC level. It has been argued, therefore, that path control may need a further assist to guard against lost or out-of-sequence segments. It appears from some studies that if parallel links or alternate paths were present, the receiver of the PIUs should either re-FIFO or reject any out-of-order PIUs. This is an area in which further work may have to be done to meet new requirements.

Data count field (DCF). This field in the TH contains a count of the number of bytes in the BIU or BIU segment that is associated with the header. As we noted in the discussion of blocking considerations (see Section 10.4), path control uses the DCF to locate the beginning of the next PIU when a string of PIUs has been blocked together.

10.6 PARALLEL DEVELOPMENTS

10.6.1 Option Selection

As we saw in Section 9.7.2, the SNA BIND command offers the user an opportunity to select from a wide range of options for each session. Other options, like FID type, can be set at system definition time. Options may be suited to the end-user or suited to the transmission subsystem. Another illustration of the use of options can be seen in the way that the DECNET architecture offers its choices.

The DECNET architecture [6.17] defines some of its options accord-ing to whether the communications network guarantees (a) message delivery or return to sender, or (b) that delivery will be sequential. The options are correspondingly selected as follows:

1. *Network guarantees sequential messages and delivery or return:* Option involves no sequence numbers for messages.

2. *Network guarantees sequential messages but not delivery or return:* Option involves sequence numbers for messages and sequential acknowledgment of each message.

3. *Network guarantees delivery or return but not sequential messages:* Option involves sequence numbers for messages but allows nonse-quential acknowledgments.

4. *Network guarantees neither delivery/return nor sequential messages:* Option is the same as in (3) above.

These options are comparable to several of the SNA options. These are first of all the immediate or delayed control modes and the immediate or delayed response modes, which specify (among other things) both the number of acknowledgments that may be outstanding and the required order of acknowledgments. This control is exercised in the data flow control layer (see Section 8.4). Second, SNA allows either the use of sequence numbers or the use of some other message identifier. That control is exercised in the transmission control layer and is discussed in Section 9.2.3. Then the FID-3 option in path control allows simpler terminal nodes to operate without any sequence number field at all, as discussed in Sections 9.2.3 and 10.5.

10.6.2 Data Units

Recall that SNA permits one to specify a *maximum RU size* to suit half-session buffer capabilities. RUs can also be *chained* together to form a recovery unit. Then, in the path control level, RUs may be *segmented* into smaller units (or packets) to suit the transmission subsystem. Also, with blocking, the *frame* at the data link control level may contain multiple PIUs. Along these lines, the description of the data units used in the Sperry Univac distributed communications architecture [6.18] is in-structive. These are defined at five levels:

1. *User data set:* The record as seen by the end-user, whose size varies enormously depending on the application. It may be a few bytes in an airlines reservation system or millions of bytes in a file control application.

2. *Acknowledge set:* The chain of transmitted units that constitutes the unit of recovery. Acknowledgments from the destination can be made on the basis of these acknowledge sets.

3. *Port data unit:* The maximum size of data unit that can be handled by the destination port, depending on the buffering capabilities there. A terminal, for example, might be limited to 1000 bytes for one screen or to 80 bytes for one line.

4. *Network data unit:* The segments into which the transport network may subdivide the port data units. The network data units are of a fixed maximum size for a given transport network.

5. *Frames:* The units handled by data link control. A frame may contain multiples of the network data units.

10.6.3 Alternate Paths and Parallel Links

A great deal of study and experimentation is under way on advanced routing techniques incorporating alternate paths and parallel links. These are discussed in Chapter 16.

10.7 EXERCISES

Which of the following statements are true?

10.1 Addressing is necessary for path control, and

a) every NAU and every nonswitched link is given a 16-bit network address.

b) every destination node must be able to recognize 16-bit network addresses.

c) different logical units at different link stations can have the same local address.

d) the path control function in an intermediate node examines only the subarea portion of the destination network address.

e) the boundary function that supports nonswitched lines does require that address transformation tables be at least partially defined at system generation time.

10.2 Segmenting of BIUs and PIUs is done by the path control elements

a) to improve response time.

b) to reduce the amount of retransmission on error-prone links.

c) to better utilize parallel paths.

d) to match modem capabilities.

e) to match the buffer capability of destination nodes.

10.3 Match the following LU address sizes with the nodes that can accept that address.

a) 16 bit   1. Type-2 (cluster controller)

b) 8 bit   2. Type-5 (hosts)

c) 6 bit   3. Type-1 (terminal nodes)

                                4. Type-4 (communications controllers)

10.4 The following hexadecimal data stream (four bits per character) represents a TH+RH+RU.

   1E0030001000000700080B8900001020A300A

The first character transmitted is on the left. Using the formats in Appendix A, answer the questions below.

a) What format of transmission header (FID type) is used?
b) List the contents of the transmission header (TH), the request/response header (RH), and the request/response unit (RU).
c) What is the sequence number of this message?
d) Is this message on the normal or expedited flow?
e) What is the address of the origin of the message?
f) Is this a request or a response?
g) Which element is involved in this message?
   i) FI.FMD
   ii) data flow control
   iii) session control
   iv) network control
h) What is the one-byte request code, and where is it located in the RU?
   i) X'01' in byte 0
   ii) X'02' in byte 1
   iii) X'OA' in byte 2

10.5 Construct the bit pattern of the transmission header for the following conditions:

- FID type 3
- Last segment of an RU destined for an LU
- Expedited flow
- Local address of LU = 32

10.8   REFERENCES AND BIBLIOGRAPHY

See also [6.10, 6.17, 6.18, 8.2, 9.1, and 9.4].

10.1 W. S. Hobgood. "The Role of the Network Control Program in Systems Network Architecture." *IBM Systems Journal* **15,** No. 1 (1976).

10.2 D. W. Davies and D. L. A. Barber. *Communication Networks for Computers.* New York: John Wiley and Sons (1973).

10.3 J. McQuillan. "Adapter Routing Algorithms for Distributed Computer Networks." Report 2831. Cambridge, Mass.: Bolt Beranek and Newman (May 1974).

10.4 "Systems Network Architecture." IBM Field Engineering Education Student Self-Study Course, SR23-4208-1, Course 57290.

10.5 P. J. Nichols. "General Purpose Protocol Integrates Different Networks." *Data Communication* (September/October 1976).

10.6 J. M. McQuillan. "Throughput in the ARPA Network-Analysis and Measurement," Report No. 2491. Cambridge, Mass.: Bolt Beranek and Newman.

11
Data
Link Control

11.1 INTRODUCTION

This chapter* addresses the management of a data link connecting two or more nodes (like a cluster controller or host) and/or devices (like a keyboard work station) (see Section 6.4). In SNA, each data link control element (DLC) serves a path control element (which can use multiple DLCs). The DLC executes the orders of the path control element by delivering the BTU to the link address specified.

Teleprocessing data link controls are analogous to the communications conventions used between the locally attached I/O and the host, or between independent programming processes in a multiprogramming system [11.5]. They involve the physical transfer of data from one input/output station to another input/output station. There are two complications, however. The first complication is that the serialization of information and the delay and distortion accompanying transmission over long distances necessitate a more complex bit-synchronization technique. Synchronization is facilitated if the bit transmission rate is known a priori to the receiver. (The serialization is necessary not only for economy but also to avoid the serious skew problems when one attempts to transmit bit-parallel over long distances.) The second complication is the error rates experienced on many teleprocessing links, and the consequent

---

* Acknowledgment is given to W. D. Brodd, R. A. Donnan, W. F. Emmons, and J. R. Kersey for the SDLC developments reported in this chapter, and to P. E. Boudreau, R. C. Dixon, C. Peck, and R. F. Steen, who did the supporting reliability and performance analysis.

need in many applications for fairly comprehensive error-detection and recovery techniques.

Basically, the job of the data link control layer is to establish and terminate a logical connection between stations, to handle the transfers of data between them, and to ensure message integrity in those transfers. The stations on the link may be only two (point-to-point) or many (multipoint). The physical connection may be switched or nonswitched.

The structure that has evolved, and is now becoming an international standard [11.10, 11.20], has the characteristics of being code-independent and fully transparent to the bit pattern being handled, uses a single format for a combination of data and control, efficiently combines a number of control functions in a single transmission, uses improved error-control techniques, is application-independent, and is independent of path control. This DLC is known in IBM as *SDLC* (Synchronous Data Link Control) [11.1]. *ADCCP* (Advanced Data Communications Control Procedure) is a very closely related draft American national standard [11.4, 11.10] and *HDLC* (High Level Data Link Control) is a very similar draft before the International Standards Organization (ISO). The portion dealing with frame structure is an approved ISO standard [11.20]. Other related disciplines are the BDLC (Burroughs Data Link Control) [11.2] and the DDCMP (Digital Data Communications Message Protocol), which is a byte-oriented protocol of the Digital Equipment Corp. [11.3]. The universal data link control (UDLC) of Sperry Univac is said to encompass SDLC, HDLC, and ADCCP.

11.2 HISTORY OF DATA LINK CONTROL

Data link controls have had a natural evolution; thus (for those not familiar with it) a brief review of its history should help to explain the present protocols.

A series of data link controls has been developed since 1960 that has added facilities as the breadth of the data communications applications grew. As might be expected, the early growth tended to optimize for specific known needs, which then proved to be less appropriate for the broader requirements.

Start-stop. The principle of start-stop transmission was developed in the electromechanical era of early teleprinter systems. The *start pulse* released a clutch to allow a shaft to produce one revolution; the shaft stopped as it produced the final *stop pulse*. During this one revolution, between start and stop pulses, the bits for one character were generated. The start-stop mode, with transmission of one character at a time, is still widely used today, although the electromechanical rotation has been largely eliminated. The start-stop sequence is illustrated in Fig. 11.1.

The start and stop bits serve to bit-synchronize and character-synchronize the receiving station with the transmitting station. The importance of synchronization is illustrated in Fig. 11.2. In place of the rotating mechanism, most modern receiving stations have a clocking device that starts when the start pulse is detected, and continues for as many pulse periods as there are bits in the character. Note that every bit string (or character) handled in a start-stop mode must have the same number of bit positions. The stop pulse provided the character synchronization; in the electromechanical era, it was made 1.42 times as long as a bit pulse to allow for differences between the sending and receiving mechanisms. *Devices with keyboards but without a message buffer require this asynchronous mode of operation, sending one character at a time.*

The General-Purpose Discipline (GPD), developed by IBM in the early 1960s for start-stop control, used the binary-coded decimal code to provide two unique DLC control characters and three additional multiuse characters. These five control characters could be dispersed within the message. The receiver had to scan the message for them in order to pick

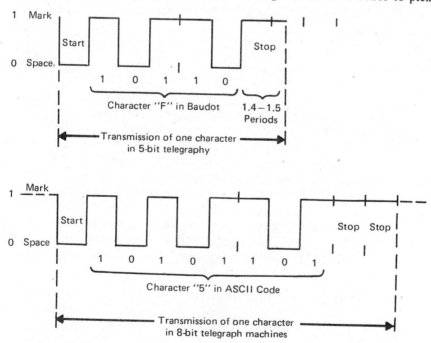

Fig. 11.1 Start-stop transmissions, one character at a time.

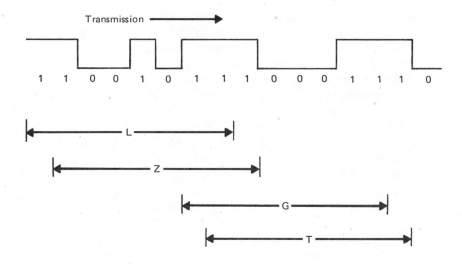

Fig. 11.2 Bit synchronization: Starting at the wrong place gives a different character.

out the control intended [11.6]. Within the message, one might find an assortment of line-control, device-control, and device-addressing characters (see Section 3.2.2).

Synchronous. To improve line efficiency by the elimination of start and stop periods for each character, the next stage of development used "synchronous" transmission. In this type of transmission, a buffer served to collect the characters from the keyboard asynchronously. It could then transmit the entire message synchronously. Instead of relying on the start/stop bits to provide bit synchronization, another source of timing had to be used. Some modems transmitted a master clock signal for this. It was desirable, however, to derive the bit-synchronizing signal from the 0-to-1 or 1-to-0 transitions in the data stream itself. Such self-clocking avoided the consequences of any tendency of the modem clock to drift. It was performed with the aid of special characters in the message, whose coding ensured sufficiently frequent 0-to-1 transitions. Once the bit clock had been started, it was not stopped until some end-of-transmission indicator was received.

STR. An early example of synchronous DLC was IBM's Synchronous Transmit/Receive (STR). STR's four-out-of-eight code provided six uniquely defined control characters and 64 data characters. It had no addressing structure; hence it was limited to point-to-point configurations (see Fig. 11.3), with only two stations on the link.

BSC. In the early 1960s, two codes in particular had to be accommodated (without conversions for transmission). These were the eight-bit
EBCDIC used on IBM's S/360, and the seven-bit plus parity ASCII (see
Appendix D). These codes, rather than four-out-of-eight codes, were
used in the next DLC development called Binary Synchronous Communications (BSC).

The addressing deficiency of STR was also remedied in this next
development, so that half-duplex multipoint configurations, as shown in
Fig. 11.4(a), could be handled.

In BSC, synchronization was aided by special characters called PAD
and SYN. PAD was a set of alternating 0's and 1's used to help establish
bit synchronization in business-machine clocks. The SYN character,
whose code pattern is 001100010, also served to help synchronize by
character. To assist in initial synchronization (for example, following a
line turnaround), each transmission was prefaced by a control-character
sequence of PAD SYN SYN (see Fig. 11.5). Then, in addition, the DLC
caused SYN characters to be inserted periodically into the data stream.
Thus, one was assured of sufficient transitions for the self-clocking
mechanism to stay in bit synch, and for alignment of the characters as
well. The message itself was framed by another set of control characters:

- SOH for Start of Header
- STX for Start of Text
- ETX for End of Text

Another character, ETB, provided a blocking function for a message
segment.

Control characters can, however, be variously interpreted. For example, in many instances, the ETX was interpreted not just to delimit a

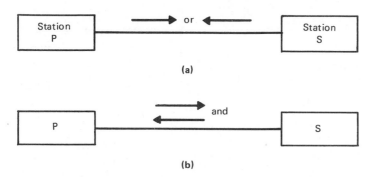

Fig. 11.3 Point-to-point link flows: (a) half-duplex; (b) duplex.

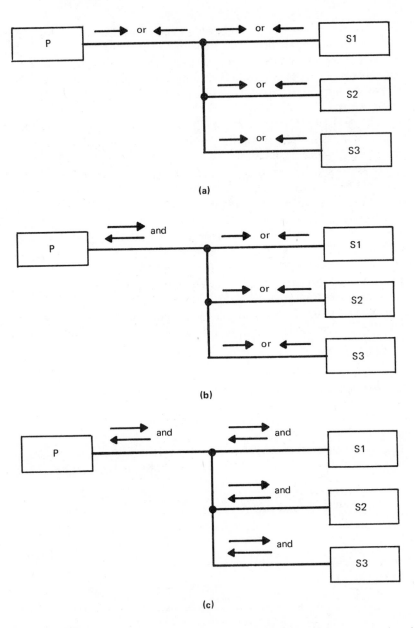

(a)

(b)

(c)

Fig. 11.4 Multipoint link flows: (a) multipoint half-duplex—only one secondary is active at a time; (b) multi-multipoint—e.g., P sends to S1 while receiving from S2; (c) multipoint duplex—P sends to *any* one S and receives from *any* one S.

Fig. 11.5 BSC message format.

block of information on the line, but also to indicate a higher-level grouping, such as the completion of a larger message or the completion of a transaction. Different interpretations were built into devices and programming systems. As a result, different types of equipment sometimes could not be attached to the same communication line and be able to communicate with the same application program, without having a separate portion of the application program for each device [11.13].

A problem arises when control characters may inadvertently appear in the data. When sending programs, for example, when almost any bit pattern is possible, control characters might very well be formed without the sender's knowledge. To get around this problem, another DLC feature was created to ensure that any inadvertent control characters in the data were not taken seriously by the receiving DLC. This feature was called *transparent mode*. If the data in the text is to be transparent, to be treated only as a bit pattern without any control characters therein, then it is delimited by DLE STX and DLE ETX (or DLE ETB). Then such control characters as STX, ETB, or ETX could appear in the text, yet be treated as data. If a DLE character appeared in the text, another DLE was inserted by the sending station. The receiving station then had to strip one DLE from each pair of DLEs. Other uses of DLE, such as DLE ETB, were detected as such and not passed as data.

The format for a BSC transmission is shown in Fig. 11.5. The header contains information provided by the user and is not solely a data link control field. *Line control commands for polling, addressing, etc., are provided in separate control messages, rather than contained in a header.*

Figure 11.6 illustrates the various codes that have been used for data transmission and the nomenclature used by each code to identify bit positions. The bit that is furthest to the right is the least significant bit. Note that with some codes the most significant bit of each character was transmitted first. With both ASCII and EBCDIC, the least significant bit of each character is sent first (even though the most significant character precedes the less significant character).

Thus, *the stations on the line had to be built to scan for control characters in a way that depended on the code used.* The code determined the number of bits per character, the order in which bits were transmitted, and whether a parity (checking) bit, as well as the bit patterns for each character, was included with each character.

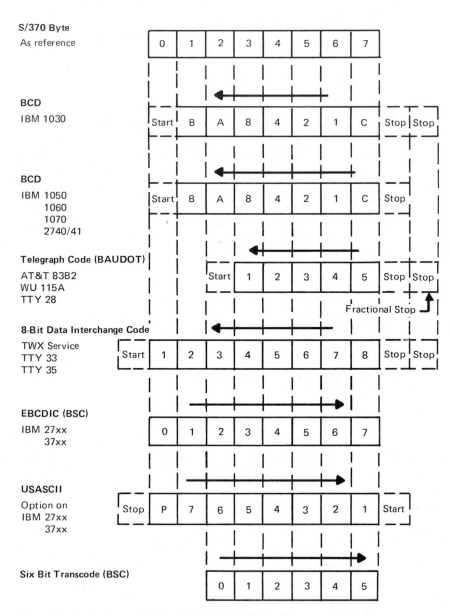

First ◀━━ Last: Arrow indicates order in which binary bits are transmitted

Fig. 11.6 Different codes may have different bit meanings, different directions of transmission, different use of parity, and different bit storage in memory.

The evolution of data link controls was partly tied to the codes used. As the code set expanded from five-bit Baudot to six-bit Binary Coded Decimal (BCD) to seven-bit ASCII to eight-bit EBCDIC, *each new code prompted a new data link control. There was a need to divorce data link controls from the codes used.*

With BSC, line control was again somewhat mixed with device control and end-to-end (e.g., half-session) controls used line control facilities. Error detection in BSC was also incomplete, since block error control was applied to data characters but not to control or address characters.

The 24 DLC control characters offered in BSC, using EBCDIC code, are shown in Fig. 11.7. Thus, at this point, instead of a few basic DLC control characters, *we had a growing need for control characters and control-character sequences for data link control, device control, and formatting of messages.* Each station had to be built to recognize these characters and character sequences at the link control level. On the other hand, there is no limit to the growth of new requirements; character coding proved to be expensive; upward compatibility, as new functions were added, proved to be impossible; and such richness of control

SOH	Start of heading
STX	Start of text
ETB	End of transmission block
ETX	End of text
EOT	End of transmission
ENQ	Enquiry
NAK	Negative acknowledgment
SYN	Synchronous idle
ITB	End of intermediate transmission block
DLE	Data link escape
ACK0	Even positive acknowledgment
ACK1	Odd positive acknowledgment
WACK	Wait before transmit, a positive acknowledgment
DISC	Mandatory disconnect
RVI	Reverse interrupt
TTD	Temporary text delay
XSTX	Transparent start of text
XETX	Transparent end of text
XITB	Transparent end of intermediate block
XETB	Transparent end of transmission block
XSYN	Transparent synchronous idle
XENQ	Transparent block cancel
XTTD	Transparent temporary text delay
XDLE	Data DLE in transparent mode

Fig. 11.7 Data link control characters defined for BSC using EBCDIC.

characters and sequences of control characters in the data complicated both the hardware and the software.

Other concerns developed for the limitations of BSC. Duplex operation of the line was not provided, and the line turnaround time of half-duplex operation significantly affects line efficiency. This was aggravated by the fact that in BSC, as in the start-stop mode, *every message transmitted was individually acknowledged.* The protocols did not provide for acknowledgment of some group of messages, which could improve efficiency. BSC also proved to have a severe problem in highly interactive applications on multidrop lines. *With BSC, a sending station could continue to send indefinitely, thus monopolizing the line and impacting the response time of other stations on the line.* An enforced rule was needed so that each station would be limited (e.g., to a certain number of finite transmissions).

The reliability of BSC was also hampered by its *lack of checking on addresses and short control sequences.* Another limitation was the assumption that device control was exclusively a host function, with certain device-control codes detected at the link control level. An approach was needed that would facilitate the placement of device controls (like the formatting of presentations and the conversions of device control codes) either in the host or in the remote attachments, depending on system designs, and independent of link control.

11.3 DATA LINK CONTROL REQUIREMENTS

Taking a hard look at the job of data link control, one finds that the minimum requirements for a data link control are the means to

1. Bracket the information being sent, thus distinguishing the information from other (noise) signals, and indicating the bits to which the checking mechanism should apply
2. Identify and thus permit addressing of the sender and receiver
3. Detect errors and to provide recovery
4. Manage the sharing of the link among multiple stations

Different applications and system configurations can impose many other requirements that tend to be open-ended and subjective. A number of them, however, have great apparent value. Among these are the following:

1. The DLC should be transparent to the data being sent. Any bit pattern should be allowed.

2. The DLC architecture should be subsettable for diverse modes, including

   ■ Half-duplex, sometimes called *two-way alternate* (see Fig. 11.3a)

   ■ Duplex, sometimes called *two-way simultaneous* (see Fig. 11.3b)

   ■ Hub polling (see Fig. 4.1)

   ■ Loop configuration (see Fig. 4.2)

   ■ Point-to-point (see Fig. 11.3)

   ■ Multipoint (see Fig. 11.4a)

   ■ Multi-multipoint (see Fig. 11.4b)

   ■ Leased or dial

3. Preservation of data integrity and sharing of the link should be managed efficiently, avoiding a large amount of traffic uniquely for these purposes.

4. Recovery actions should be localized where possible, so that stations not affected can continue operations while another station is recovering.

5. Addressing and control structures should be open-ended to permit growth in both without affecting earlier installations.

6. Interactive operations, as well as batch operations, must be efficient.

Somewhat more controversial is the belief that control of the data link should be the responsibility of one primary station in order to

1. Permit efficient management, such as hub polling and loop operation

2. Simplify recovery procedures by having one clearly in charge

3. Economize by having such responsibilities in one rather than all stations.

11.4 POSITIONAL SIGNIFICANCE

An alternative to using an extended control character set, whose characters may be sprinkled among the data, is to rely on positional significance and a coded control field [11.7].

A structure is positionally significant when one can take the next k bits as having a particular meaning. For example, one specific field (say, bits i through j in a sequence following a unique delimiter) may be dedicated to coded control commands. The unique delimiter might provide synchronization and transmission block delineation.

The size of this control field ($n = j - i$) should be fixed for a given link, but may need to be extendable as the link configuration evolves.

Within this one control field, it is theoretically possible to define 2^n different data link control operations, dealing with making and terminating logical connections, managing the sharing of the link, and assuring message integrity. Another specific field can similarly be positionally reserved for addressing. Also, a specified number of bits preceding the ending delimiter can be reserved as a checking field.

Positional significance is the approach adopted throughout SNA for the nested series of headers, shown earlier in Fig. 10.8. The acceptance by the national and international standards groups of positional significance, rather than control characters, for the data link control level makes possible a nesting of independent headers used for all four levels of SNA control, that is:

1. Data link control headers and trailers

2. Transmission header (TH)

3. Request/response header (RH)

4. FM header or NS header

A generalized structure for data link control, based on positional significance, can take the form of

$$F[A][C][Information][FCS][F],$$

that is,

$$[Link\ Header][Information][Link\ Trailer]$$

where F = the flag, the unique delimiter to synchronize and delineate the transmission; A = the station address field; C = the control field; and FCS = the frame check sequence for error detection.

The entire sequence (FAC, I, FCS, F) is called a *frame*. With positional significance, each field other than the information field is of a known length. Its position, relative to the flag delimiters, is therefore also known. Data link control functions that were formerly performed with special characters are coded in the control field. Non-DLC functions are excluded from the link header and the link trailer.

In theory, the lengths of the control field and the block check field could be different, within different address domains, on the same link. One set of stations, for example, might be operator-attended and use clear text; for these, the size of the frame check sequence might be zero. In other cases, a check sequence of length 16, 24, or 32 might be desirable. In theory, the primary could operate at these different levels of implementation, based on the addresses of the secondary stations. In practice, however, this complexity does not seem to be justified, and fixed field sizes for a given link are used.

11.5 DLC STRUCTURE

This section describes the SDLC structure, along with notes showing those instances where further extensions are indicated under the ANSI- and ISO-draft link control standards. The particular format for SDLC transmission blocks is shown in Fig. 11.8. The information field is variable; all other fields are fixed. If we have a contiguous series of frames, then the trailing flag of one frame is also the lead flag of the next frame.

The efficiency of transmission of information depends on the total data link control procedure, but a partial figure of merit is the ratio of information field size to total frame size. If the information is 25 bytes, that ratio for SDLC is 83 percent; if the information is 256 bytes, that ratio is 98 percent.

In HDLC and ADCCP, the control field is potentially extendable in those links where it is needed [11.10, 11.20]. This would, for example, be advantageous in satellite links, where a larger sequence number would correspond to the longer transmission times. In the draft ANSI and ISO standards, the control field is extendable to two bytes.

In Fig. 11.9, the SDLC format is compared with the corresponding Binary Synchronous (BSC) format. The improved efficiency is apparent. In this illustration, the acknowledging station has no information to send. If it did, then the SDLC acknowledgment would be contained within the control field of that information frame. The illustration uses duplex flow for SDLC. However, with the addition of a turnaround, the example applies to half-duplex as well.

The frame going from the primary station to a secondary station is called a *link command;* the frame going from a secondary station to the primary station has been called a *link response.* These terms should not

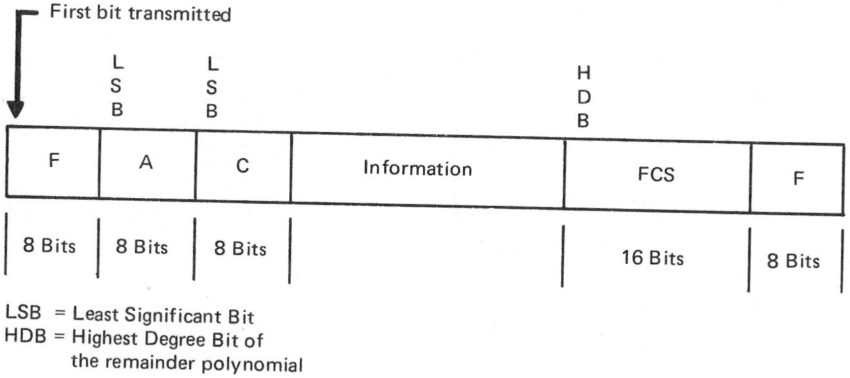

Fig. 11.8 The SDLC format.

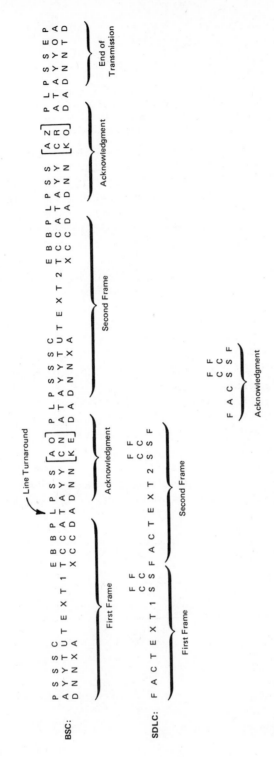

Fig. 11.9 Illustration of BSC half-duplex and SDLC duplex flows, involving two successive inquiries from a link station.

be confused with the completely separate requests and responses discussed earlier, which are exchanged between half-sessions.

11.5.1   SDLC Objectives

The positionally significant structure was adopted for SDLC as the best way of meeting the DLC requirements enumerated above, and also of achieving separation of function. The SCLC protocol was carefully limited to link level functions only. This DLC architecture, then, has no dependence on device characteristics or data structures.

The information field contains the data that is to be carried by the DLC level. That data is meaningless at the DLC level, even though it contains headers (for example, TH, RH, and FMH) that are meaningful at higher levels. No restrictions are placed on the information field because it is transparent to the DLC. Link headers and link trailers pertain only to DLC.

If non-DLC information is to be carried, including any device control messages, it must be included within the information field, and DLC will be unconcerned with it. Structure of the information and delineation of information such as start or end of message for contextual reasons (similar to the sentence and paragraph of a text) are not DLC functions.

A second objective is to give the effect, so far as the other layers of the communication system are concerned, of a highly reliable link, even though retransmissions because of errors at the DLC level may be needed. This requires that the DLC level itself be able to detect errors and to correct those errors without outside assistance.

A third objective is that the link be fully able to be shared so that there can be many stations on the same line, even though the higher-level protocols may be different for each station.

11.5.2   Flag

Although the SDLC structure avoids the use of special characters within the transmission, SDLC does use a unique bit sequence for the start and termination of each variable-length frame.

The *flag* used by SDLC is a unique sequence of bits, namely, a zero, six one bits, and a zero (01111110). All receiving stations will continuously scan for this sequence, which signifies the beginning or end of a frame. SDLC uses the same flag byte for beginning and ending the frame as do HDLC and ADCCP.

Bit stuffing. To avoid an occurrence of this flag bit pattern anywhere else in a frame, a technique called *bit stuffing* is used. When transmitting, the sending station monitors the stream of bits being sent. Any time a contiguous string of five bits occurs, there is a possibility of an unintentional flag developing; therefore, the sending station will automatically insert an extra zero into the bit stream.

This "zero bit insertion" prevents more than five contiguous ones from ever appearing between the flags. Note that this applies to the address, control, and frame-check-sequence fields as well as to the information field, but not to the flag fields.

Then, when receiving, the station again monitors the bit stream. Whenever five consecutive ones appear, the sixth bit is examined. If it is a zero, *the receiving station deletes it from the bit stream prior to presenting the information to a higher level.* If the sixth bit is a one, then the sequence may be a flag or an error (or, in the case of a loop configuration, a go-ahead signal). If the seventh bit is a zero, the station accepts the combination (01111110) as a flag; otherwise, it rejects the frame (or, in the case of a loop, accepts the combination (0111 1111) as a go-ahead; see Section 11.5.7).

Thus, the flag is kept unique to the beginning and end of a frame. Synchronization can be established based on the appearance of the flag, and the positional significance of each field can be established relative to the flag.

NRZI.   Recall that bit synchronization must be maintained during the entire frame, which may be quite long (limited by the buffers available at the receiving station and the ability to clear these buffers in time). Since bit synchronization is maintained by the pace of the bit stream itself, it is necessary that there be an adequate number of signal polarity transitions occurring periodically. This is achieved by a combination of the aforementioned bit stuffing and the use of nonreturn-to-zero inverted (NRZI) coding. The NRZI coding is illustrated in Fig. 11.10.

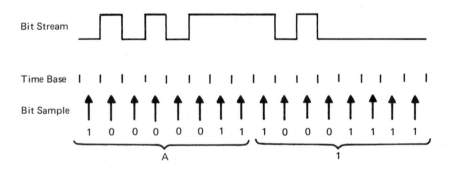

Fig. 11.10   NRZI transmission coding.

In NRZI, *a polarity change occurs every time there is a binary zero in the message. Now, since bit stuffing ensures that there will never be more than six contiguous ones, we are assured of a zero, hence a polarity change, at least every six bits.* This will guarantee bit synchronization, regardless of the length of the message. At the receiver, a differentiation extracts impulses that are used to repeatedly trigger a timing circuit, which emits a zero bit, for one bit time, when triggered. This restores the data to true data form.

Thus, by a combination of techniques, there is assurance of establishment and maintenance of synchronization. The flag itself provides message synchronization and character synchronization, while the combination of bit stuffing and NRZI ensures sufficient polarity transitions to maintain bit synchronization.

Abort. Some error (hardware or programming) may occur in the sending node during the transmission of a frame. In that case, it may be best to abort and ignore the partial frame that was sent. To do this (on any SDLC link other than a loop), the sending station ends the frame in an unusual manner by transmitting at least eight (but fewer than fifteen) contiguous one bits, with no inserted zeros. Receipt of eight contiguous one bits is interpreted by the receiving station as an *abort*. (The loop is different, as is described in Section 11.5.7.)

Idle link state. A link is defined to be in an *idle state* when a continuous one state is detected that persists for 15 bit times.

11.5.3 Address Field

Distinct from the destination address of the network addressable unit (NAU), a station address at the link level is necessary to allow for the possibility of more than one station (that is, more than one input/output point) on a given link. Stations may be nodes (such as cluster controllers or hosts) or devices (such as a keyboard work station).

The SDLC address field is one byte long, permitting up to 254 stations on a given link. (All zeros are reserved for null—e.g., testing—and all ones are reserved for all-stations.) Each station address pertains to only one station on one link, and it is completely separate from the network address of the logical unit. The RU, traveling between half-sessions, may have to traverse many links on its way to the NAU.

The station address always pertains to a secondary station on a particular link. The primary station is that one on the link that directs the multiple use of the link. The primary station also has responsibilities dealing with initial link activation, link deactivation, and recovery from error situations (see Section 12.4). All dialogues take place between the primary and a secondary. *The address field tells which secondary the frame is going to or coming from.*

A secondary may, however, have more than one address for receiving. It will always have its own unique address for sending; but in addition, it may be part of one or more groups and have to recognize one or more group addresses. A special case is the "all-stations" address which all secondaries must recognize.

In normal polling, on multidrop lines, the primary will accept frames from only that address that has been polled. However, in hub polling and in loop configuration using a nonsequenced poll, the primary must accept any secondary station that responds to the poll. In addition, in the case of a switched environment, the primary station must be prepared to accept a multiplicity of valid addresses (or a noncommitted address) when a station first dials in.

The ISO standard (HDLC) and the ANSI draft standard (ADCCP) include provisions for an extended address field. *In extended mode, its address field would consist of a chain of bytes, with another address byte following so long as the first bit in any address byte is a zero* (the first bit of the address is the least significant bit). An example of an application where this mode might be useful would be the use of long aircraft IDs as the address, which could be displayed directly without address to ID translation.

11.5.4 Control Field

The control field provides the personality of the data link control. It permits a single information transfer to serve multiple control functions. For example, one frame sent from the primary station to a secondary station may be used

1. To *send information* from a primary station to a secondary station
2. To *acknowledge* to the secondary that one or more specified frames, previously sent by the secondary, have been validly received, error-free
3. To *poll* the station, authorizing it to send any frames that it has ready

Similarly, a single frame sent from a secondary station to the primary station may be used

1. To *send information* from the secondary to the primary
2. To *acknowledge* to the primary that one or more specified frames, previously sent by the primary, have been accepted as error-free

3. To *indicate whether this is the final frame* of a transmission or if more frames are to follow immediately

Control field formats. There are three different formats for this field, with a few bits assigned to identify which format is being used [11.1]. The three formats, shown in Fig. 11.11, are the following.

1. *Information transfer format* (I), having full sequence control (with a send sequence count, Ns, and a receive sequence count, Nr), and (optionally) an information field.

2. *Supervisory format* (S), having a receive sequence count (Nr) but not a send sequence count, and used to manage the link in normal operation.

3. *Nonsequenced format* (NS), having no sequence counts at all, and used primarily for setting operating modes, exchanging identification, and other miscellaneous operations. (The HDLC and ADCCP terminology for this format is *Unnumbered* rather than Nonsequenced.)

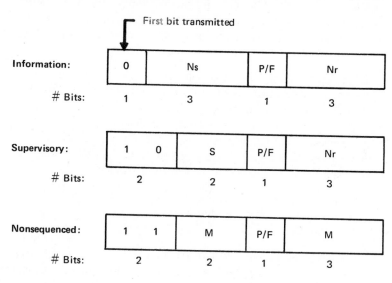

Where Ns = Send Sequence Count (bit 2 = low order bit)
      Nr = Receive Sequence Count (bit 6 = low order bit)
      P/F = Poll Bit for Primary Station Transmission
          = Final Frame Bit for Secondary Station Transmission
      S = Supervisory Function Control Bits
      M = Modifier Function Control Bits

Fig. 11.11 Three formats for the basic DLC control field [11.10].

Note that if the first bit of the control field is a zero, the I format is used; if the first bit is a one, then the second bit tells whether an S format or an NS format is used. In all three formats, one bit is used as a poll/final (P/F) bit. The primary station can use this bit to poll a secondary station. The poll bit also *demands an acknowledgment* (via the receive sequence count, Nr) of frames accepted by the secondary. The secondary station can use the same bit position to indicate the last frame to be sent (in response to a poll).

Supervisory format (S).   In the S format (see Fig. 11.11), two bits of the control field permit encoding of up to four control commands and responses for the purpose of controlling information flow. Three such link commands and responses have been defined (to be sent by either the primary or the secondary) as follows [11.1]:

1. RR (Receive Ready): Confirms sequenced frames through Nr-1 and indicates that the originating station is ready to receive.

2. RNR (Receive Not Ready): Indicates a temporary busy condition in which no frames that require buffer space can be accepted. RNR confirms sequenced frames through Nr-1 and indicates that frame Nr is expected next.

3. REJ (Reject): May be transmitted to request retransmission of sequenced information. REJ confirms frames through Nr-1 and requests Nr and following frames. REJ is an error control frame that may (optionally) be sent by a duplex station that has detected a sequence error in the received Ns count. Only one reject exception condition is established at any given time. An REJ may be interspersed in the sequence of transmitted frames.

Another command, called Selective Reject (SREJ), is included in both HDLC and ADCCP. This command would reject only the one frame indicated by the Nr.

Nonsequenced format (NS).   When the first two bits of the control field are ones, the nonsequenced format is used, in which there are no Ns or Nr sequence count fields. In the nonsequenced format (see Fig. 11.11), five bits are available for encoding link control commands and link responses.

Currently defined nonsequenced commands and responses include the following [11.1]:

1. NSI (Nonsequenced Information): An NSI frame is the vehicle for nonsequenced information. It can be sent by either the primary or the secondary station. (NSI is called UI in HDLC and ADCCP).

2. SNRM (Set Normal Response Mode): This command subordinates the receiving secondary station to the transmitting primary station. No unsolicited transmissions are allowed for a secondary station that is in normal response mode. NSA (see below) is the required positive response upon acceptance of SNRM by the secondary station. The SNRM causes the Nr and Ns counts of the secondary station to be reset to 0. The SNRM also causes the Nr and Ns counts in the primary (those counts pertaining to that same secondary) to be reset to zero.

The secondary station in normal response mode must initiate transmission as the result of receiving a frame with the poll (P) bit set to 1, and may respond after receiving an optional response nonsequenced poll (NSP) with P equal to 0. Then the secondary station would respond with one or more frames.

3. DISC (Disconnect): This command places the receiving secondary station effectively off-line. The required link response is NSA. A disconnected secondary station is logically disconnected and cannot receive or transmit information frames. It may, however, respond to mode setting commands (for example, SNRM), and it may respond to the Exchange Identification (XID) command. If appropriate, DISC may be used to perform a physical as well as a logical disconnect.

4. NSA (Nonsequenced Acknowledgment): This is the affirmative link response to SNRM, DISC, or SIM link commands (and none other). No I field is permitted with the NSA response. [The HDLC and ADCCP term is Unnumbered Acknowledgment (UA).]

5. RQI (Request for Initialization): An RQI frame is transmitted by a secondary station to notify the primary station of the need for an SIM command. Any command other than SIM can cause repetition of RQI by the secondary station at its next response opportunity. (The HDLC and ADCCP term is RIM.)

6. SIM (Set Initialization Mode): This command initiates system-specified procedures at the receiving secondary station. It can be used to alert the secondary station to the fact that subsequent frames will contain control information. The architecture does not specify what the system procedures are, but, to illustrate, SIM has been used to precede frames containing the configuration services RUs: IML TEXT, DUMP TEXT, and REMOTE POWER OFF (see Sections 12.4.4 and 12.6). No I field is permitted in the SIM frame. NSA is the required link response. The Nr and Ns counts of the primary and secondary stations are reset to 0.

7. DM (Disconnected Mode): This link response is transmitted by a secondary station to indicate that it is in a disconnected mode.

8. XID (Exchange Station Identification): This link command or link response is used when establishing a switched network connection to verify the identity of the nodes being connected. An information field may be included in the command sent from the primary station to provide the primary-station identification. The secondary-station response is the vehicle for identifying the responding secondary station to the system. XID may be used on nonswitched lines also. The information field is transferred to the PU services in each node (see Section 12.6).

9. NSP (Nonsequenced Poll): This command, with no P bit, invites transmission from the addressed secondary station(s); with the P bit on, it demands transmission from the addressed secondary station(s). An I field is not permitted. The response to an NSP command requires an F bit only if the command had the P bit on. [The HDLC and ADCCP term is Unnumbered Poll (UP).]

10. CMDR (Command Reject): This link response is transmitted by a secondary station when it receives a frame that has a good FCS, but is invalid for one or more of the following reasons.

- The command is not implemented at the receiving station. This category includes unassigned commands.
- The I field is too long to fit into the receiving station buffers.
- The command received does not allow the I field that was also received.
- The Nr that was received from the primary station is incongruous with the Ns that was sent to it. As an example, an incongruous Nr received by a station would be one that has been previously transmitted and confirmed. Another would be an Nr that confirms a message that has not yet been transmitted.

The secondary station cannot release itself from the CMDR condition, nor does it act on the command that caused the condition. It repeats the CMDR whenever it responds, except to an acceptable mode-setting command: SNRM, DISC, or SIM. The secondary station sends an I field containing status information as part of the CMDR response frame. This I field provides the secondary-station status data that the primary station needs to initiate appropriate recovery action. [The ADCCP term is Frame Reject (FRMR).]

11. TEST: As a command, a TEST frame may be sent to a secondary station to solicit a TEST response. If an I field is included in the command, it is returned in the response (unless the I field cannot be stored in the secondary station buffer). TEST is part of SDLC and is under consideration for HDLC and ADCCP.

12. RD (Request Disconnect): This link response is defined as an optional function in HDLC and ADCCP but is not currently implemented as a part of SDLC. It is used by the secondary station to request that it be placed in a logical and/or physical disconnected state via a DISC command.

13. SARM and SABM: In addition to the normal response mode currently used by SDLC, both HDLC and ADCCP provide for two asynchronous response modes, with two nonsequential commands for mode setting. An SARM (Set Asynchronous Response Mode) command places a *secondary* station in a mode where it can initiate transmission without receipt of a frame with the poll bit set to 1. The SABM (Set Asynchronous Balanced Mode) command is used when two stations are *combined* stations in that they have identical link command and link response abilities. The asynchronous balanced mode also permits asynchronous transmission and promises to be the more important of the two; it is described further in Section 11.7.4.

11.5.5 Acknowledgments and Retransmissions

In BSC, as in most previous link controls, the receiving station responded with a negative acknowledgment (NAK) when an error was detected. Then the sending station, which had stopped sending while waiting for an acknowledgment to that one message, retransmitted the message. One alternative to this "stop-and-wait" procedure is to *number the frames, store a number of them at the sender for possible retransmission, and send all those frames without waiting for an acknowledgment on each.* Then an acknowledgment for the group can be contained within a single subsequent frame from the other station. This is usually more efficient, so long as error rates are reasonable.

Because duplex operation is a required capability, SDLC (like ADCCP and HDLC) adopted two independent sets of sequence numbers, one for each direction of flow. This permits the recovery of one flow to proceed independent of the sequence numbers of the other flow and avoids some possible timing ambiguities [11.5]. Only information frames are sequence checked.

Two sequence number counts are therefore maintained by each station. The send sequence count (Ns), operated modulo eight, provides a count for each information-transfer frame that is transmitted from that station. The receive sequence count (Nr), also modulo eight, is incremented once for each valid, in-sequence, error-free, information frame that is received by that station. A secondary station, since it always transmits only to the primary, needs to keep only one pair of these sequence counts. The primary station, on the other hand, needs to keep one such pair for each secondary station to which it is transmitting. *When one station sends its receive sequence count (Nr) to the other station, it will serve to indicate the next frame that is expected and to acknowledge all the frames received up to (but not including) the value indicated by the receive sequence number.* Each subsequent Nr thus sent reconfirms that all preceding messages have been accepted. Multiple frames can be acknowledged in a single frame.

In the SDLC discipline, an acknowledgment is required at least once every seven requests. Otherwise, with modulo-eight, ambiguity in the response could result. The required verification also avoids buffer saturation. If too many frames are kept pending verification of their receipt, it could develop that too many buffers are full, leaving insufficient room for the receipt of data from the other end of the line. A lockup then would be possible.

If the receiving station has only a few buffers, then these must be emptied rapidly enough for the frames that are following. The sender, on the other hand, must have enough buffers to hold all frames sent until the receiver has acknowledged them. The waiting time for the acknowledgment is at least twice the delay in the transmission path, which is quite long in satellite transmissions.

In the extended modes of HDLC and ADCCP, the counts for Ns and Nr are 128, which (with larger buffers) increases the ability to operate efficiently with high data rates on satellite links. The two-byte control field for this extension is shown in Fig. 11.12 [11.10]. Note that the nonsequenced format has P/F bits in bit positions 5 and 9. A receiver in extended control field format interprets the P/F bit in bit position 9. A receiver in basic control field format (one byte) interprets the P/F bit in bit position 5.

The performance of the line (in terms of the number of useful data bits transmitted per second) is dependent on the number of retransmissions that take place. The progress of the RU through the network is held up while the retransmission takes place. The transit times (hence, the response time) of that RU, and of the others that might otherwise have gotten on the line sooner, are affected.

Because of the uncertain reliability of the links, a very positive and definite acknowledgment is called for at the link level. This sequence number correlation at the link level is applied to each of a possible series of links in the path between network addressable units. It is intended to establish reliable transmission on each link without undue recourse to higher levels.

The link-level sequence number correlation is separate from the RU sequence numbers established for the dialogue between connection point

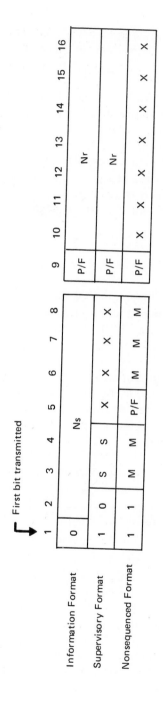

S = Supervisory function bits
M = Modifier function bits
X = Reserved and set to zero

Fig. 11.12 Three formats for extended control field [11.10].

managers in the origin and destination nodes. *Note that a given BIU (RH + RU) with one RU sequence number may be segmented into several basic link units, each of which would then have a unique link sequence number for a particular link.*

Note also that at the link level acknowledgments are mandatory, even though delayed. The send and receive counts must each be verified at least every seven transmissions. On the other hand, acknowledgments at the NAU level are optional and can be either (1) none at all, (2) exception response only, or (3) definite response. Thus, a wider range of response correlation techniques is needed at that higher level to match different application needs. This correlation is independent of the multiple link level correlations, which may be only on segments of higher-level requests.

11.5.6 Polling

As discussed in Section 4.2, polling is one of the means used to coordinate multiple stations on a line and to increase the line utilization. However, the overhead occasioned by the sending of polling messages has often been wasteful of line capacity. The newer line control disciplines, therefore, have the capability of combining polling operations within frames, which also perform information transfer.

When in normal response mode, the poll bit is used by the primary station to authorize the addressed secondary station to begin sending. Once a secondary station has begun sending, it may continue to do so until one of the following occurs:

1. The secondary station has sent a maximum of seven frames without receiving acknowledgments from the primary. More than seven are not permitted because, with a modulo-eight sequence count, ambiguity will result if more are uncorrelated.
2. The secondary station has no more messages to send.
3. The primary station commands the secondary to stop sending (applicable only to duplex secondary stations).

That same P/F bit is used by the secondary station to advise the primary whether or not each frame sent by the secondary is the final (last) one for that transmission. The efficiency of SDLC in multidrop lines, compared to BSC or start/stop, usually proves to be substantial. This results in a higher number of transactions per terminal per hour, for a wide range of terminals per line [11.11].

11.5.7 SDLC Loop

As described in Section 4.2.5, the loop has secondary stations connected in serial fashion and returns to the primary station as an input channel. All secondary stations monitor the traffic on their loop connection and act as a repeater station. The repeater action is suspended when a secondary station receives a *go-ahead* signal following a poll of that station.

A poll frame may poll a particular station by specifying one station's address and requiring a station response. Another type of poll is an optional response poll for which the secondary station's response is optional. This is commanded by a *nonsequenced poll* (NSP) command (containing no sequence numbers); it is called UP in HDLC and ADCCP. That polling command may be used with either a specific station address or a broadcast (all stations on the loop) address.

A go-ahead pattern is defined as a zero bit followed by seven one bits, that is, 01111111. Go-aheads are generated on the loop (after a poll frame) by the primary station transmitting the ending flag and then continuous one bits. That string of one bits is continued until all second-ary transmissions, if any, are complete. This sequence follows each poll frame.

The go-ahead signal, following a poll frame, must be propagated down the loop. If a secondary receives the go-ahead and wishes to transmit, *it converts the go-ahead to a flag (01111110) by simply chang-ing the seventh bit to a zero.* The station then appends the standard SDLC format of address, control field, information, frame check sequence, and ending flag. The secondary station then permits the primary station's one bits to be propagated down the line. The ending zero bit of the final flag followed by the stream of one bits also creates the go-ahead (01111111) for the next station.

The primary knows that all secondary stations have been polled when it receives a go-ahead.

11.6 ERROR DETECTION

11.6.1 Introduction

In Chapter 1, the wide variations in line reliability were discussed. Despite these variations, high transmission reliability must be assured. The inevitable errors must be corrected. There are two basic approaches to the correction of transmission errors. These are

1. Forward error correction, where enough redundancy is sent with the message not only to detect an error, but also to correct the error at the destination.

2. Error detection at the destination, followed by a request for retransmission.

The amount of redundancy needed with each message is greater if correction, as well as detection, is to be achieved at the destination. On the other hand, retransmissions can also be expensive of line bandwidth, if many retransmissions are needed. Response time may also suffer with retransmission. In most studies, the conclusion has been that the use of detection and retransmission is the preferred approach [11.9], so long as the error rate on the line is moderate. Besides the added bits needed per message, forward error corrections suffer from the fact that

1. Data communication facilities available today have widely varying error characteristics, and error correcting codes need to be designed rather precisely to the error characteristics of the link. A single correction code will generally be effective on fewer types of errors than a single detection code.

2. The hardware needed for correction is more costly than that for detection. Therefore, if the error rate is not high (say, better than a 95-percent probability of sending a correct message) and if the occasional time for retransmission can be tolerated from a response-time viewpoint, then the use of detection and retransmission is preferred over forward error correction. However, there are some situations (such as in satellite systems) where the time for retransmission is a major factor. In these cases, forward error correction merits further consideration.

11.6.2 Early Detection Codes

One of the simplest kinds of redundancy is the *parity check* across some groups of bits. A common practice is to add a parity bit to each character transmitted. This has been referred to as *vertical redundancy checking* (VRC). It provides an excellent check against single-bit errors, but it does not protect against burst errors, which are common in today's communications facilities. Additional protection can be obtained by adding a parity bit for each bit position of all the characters in the message. This is called *longitudinal redundancy checking* (LRC). With both VRC and LRC, errors will be detected in all messages having one-, two-, or three-bit errors, all messages with an odd number of errors, and some with an even number of errors. Other patterns, however, are not detected. Parity checking can be viewed as performing an arithmetic operation on the data. Using the vertical parity check, we add the bits of a byte, modulo-two; with longitudinal parity check, we add the corresponding bits in successive bytes, modulo-two. Since in modulo-two arithmetic, *without carries*, addition and subtraction are the same, we could look at this as a succession of subtractions, too.

Another redundancy technique, common in radio telegraph circuits, is to use character codes of N bits per character, of which precisely M bits will be ones for every character. In a four-out-of-eight code, for example, four bits of every character would be ones. If noise effects were always of the same type (for example, always changing zeros to ones), then the M out of N codes would be very secure. Unfortunately, this is not the usual case; the oscillatory nature of noise can cause zero-to-one changes and one-to-zero changes in the same message. Experiments [1.3] reportedly found that a four-out-of-eight code, used on a 1200-bps line, was only about twice as good as a simple parity check per character.

11.6.3   Cyclic Codes

Extensions to the LRC technique, which detects most multiple-bit error patterns, are the burst-error-detecting cyclic codes, sometimes referred to as polynomial codes. If the successive subtractions in longitudinal parity check work so well, then the successive subtraction in long division, by a polynomial, may be even better—and it is. This cyclic checking has been recommended by the CCITT and is used in SDLC, HDLC, and ADCCP.

To understand cyclic codes, it is convenient to think of the bits of the message to be sent as the coefficients of a polynomial in the dummy variable X [11.8]. Then a message 110111 is represented by the polynomial

$$G(X) = X^5 + X^4 + X^2 + X + 1,$$

where the coefficient of the term of the highest degree is sent first. Such a message polynomial $G(X)$ would, with SDLC, include the address field, the control field, and the information field as coefficients of the polynomial. Such polynomials are then treated according to the rules of algebra, except that modulo-two arithmetic is used. This uses binary addition with no carries.

Examples of modulo-two addition and multiplication are the following.

$$
\begin{array}{l}
X^4 + X^3 + X^2 + 1 \\
\underline{X^4 + X^2 } \\
 + X^3 + 1
\end{array}
\qquad
\begin{array}{l}
X^4 + X^3 + 1 \\
\underline{X + 1} \\
X^5 + X^4 + X \\
\underline{ X^4 + X^3 + 1} \\
X^5 + X^3 + X + 1
\end{array}
$$

The cyclic code is defined in terms of a so-called generator polynomial, $P(X)$. $P(X)$, say, is of degree n, which must be less than the degree of the message and equal to the size of the frame check sequence that we want to use. Many good generator polynomials have been proposed. The now widely accepted CCITT V.41 polynomial, for example, is

$$P(X) = X^{16} + X^{12} + X^5 + 1,$$

which is of degree 16; thus, in this case, $n = 16$.

What we are going to send is the message and the frame check sequence. We represent the frame check sequence by another polynomial $B(X)$ also of degree n. Then the representation of the frame check sequence alongside that of the message looks like the frame check sequence plus the message shifted left by the amount of the frame check sequence. The equivalent polynomial of the combination is simply

$$M(X) = X^n G(X) + B(X).$$

The original basic idea concerning polynomial codes was to *choose the representation of the frame check sequence $B(X)$ such that the transmitted $M(X)$ is exactly divisible by the generator polynomial, $P(X)$. Thus when we divide the received message at the destination by the same generator polynomial $P(X)$, we should get a clean zero.* Anything other than a zero would indicate an error.

We determine $B(X)$, therefore, as that which when added to $X^n G(X)$ will make $M(X)$ exactly divisible by $P(X)$. In other words, $B(X)$ is the remainder, $Rs(X)$, that results when we divide the shifted message, $G(X)$, by $P(X)$.

$$\frac{X^n G(X)}{P(X)} = Q(X) + \frac{Rs(X)}{P(X)}$$

$$B(X) = Rs(X)$$

Let us say that an error has occurred in transmission. What is received is not $M(X)$, but $M(X) + E(X)$, where $E(X)$ is the pattern of erroneous bits. The only time that we would not detect an error is when the error pattern $E(X)$ happens to be also exactly divisible by the generator polynomial $P(X)$. This turns out to be a rare event indeed. It can be shown [11.8] that all of the following are not divisible by the polynomial $P(X)$, and hence, are detectable:

1. All single-bit errors
2. All double-bit errors, so long as $P(X)$ has a factor with at least three terms
3. Any odd number of errors, so long as $P(X)$ contains a factor $(X + 1)$
4. Any burst error for which the length of the burst is n bits (the size of the block check) or less
5. Most of the burst errors for still larger bursts

A variation on this basic idea is to further modify $M(X)$ so that at the receiver the remainder [after dividing by $P(X)$] is not always zero, but is always some other unique polynomial. Then any deviation from this unique remainder indicates an error.

11.6.4 Compensating for Flag-induced Errors

We have seen that the theory of cyclic codes appears sound, and the use of these codes should be extremely effective. However, there is a weakness. We do not send merely the message and the frame check sequence; we also add a flag at each end. What happens if there is an error in the flag? *The flag is not a random sequence of bits, like the data is;* it is always 01111110; *so its sensitivity to errors deserves special attention.* The probability of the flag being hit and causing an undetected error was enough to justify some special precautions.

The next idea, then, was to further operate on the first and last group of bits in $M(X)$ to reduce the chance that a hit flag could cause an undetected error. Many solutions to these boundary problems are possible. The solution adopted by SDLC (and included as solutions by ANSI and ISO) was chosen for ease of implementation, and centers on simple inversions of the beginning and end groups of bits in a special sequence, as follows [11.10]:

1. The 16-bit shift register, into which the original message $G(X)$ is to be shifted, is preset to all ones rather than to all zeros.
2. Next, the resulting 16-bit frame check sequence is inverted before sending.
3. Then the receiving 16-bit shift register is also preset to all ones before shifting in $M(X)$.

At the receiver, two classes of checking equations have been proposed [11.4], one to normally provide a zero remainder and one to normally provide a unique nonzero remainder, respectively. The implementations for these alternatives are slightly different, but the bits on the line and the checking effectiveness are the same for both.

A shift register implementation can be used for either class of checking [11.10]. On the other hand, many products have found that microcode can best be used [11.13].

Thus, using the CCITT V.41 generator polynomial and some inversions to guard against a boundary problem caused by flags, the cyclic code is the redundancy technique that was chosen for SDLC and was also adopted by both ANSI and ISO for line control standards. Undetected block errors are still a possibility, even with the cyclic-code frame check sequence. However, they are predicted to be in the range of one every 10^{10} to 10^{11} frames (with short frames, even on today's commercial voice-grade lines) an occurrence that is very rare indeed [1.3].

The result is that data link controls that employ such checking as part of an automatic retransmission protocol create the effect of an extremely reliable link, so far as higher levels are concerned.

11.7 ILLUSTRATIVE SDLC SEQUENCES

To understand the various SDLC protocols and the use of the various SDLC commands, it is best to simply examine the commonly used sequences of commands in SDLC operations. The purpose and use of the link commands then become more evident. Illustrative sequences of supervisory, nonsequenced, and information frames are described below. A summary of the link commands, link responses, and their codes is provided in Appendix A.

The DLC operation begins when path control puts a message for a particular secondary station on a queue. Data link control would find on that queue the station address and the information field. It would not find either the flag, the control field, or the block check. Data link control would add the beginning flag, the control field, the block check, and the final flag.

11.7.1 Error-free Sequence

The normal sequence of polling and responding is very simple and relatively efficient. A sequence of transmission might occur as follows:

- The primary would send a series of frames to station X and to other stations. Each station would update its receive counters with each accepted frame. At some point in time, one of the frames that is sent to station X would have a control field with the P bit on. Thus, in one frame, we have both an information transfer and a request for a response from that station. After receiving the frame with the P bit on, station X must respond.

- If it doesn't respond immediately, the primary will initiate a time-out and then enter recovery mode.

- If the secondary has some information to transmit, it will do so.

- In transmitting that information, station X would, at the same time, be confirming the receipt of the previous frames from the primary by the transmission of the Nr field. It also transmits the Ns field, thus enabling the primary to check whether its understanding is the same as that of station X. When station X has no more frames to send, it sends its final information frame with the F bit on.

Because the sequence count field is normally only three bits, corresponding to eight frames, there is a rule that no station may send more than seven frames without turning the P/F bit on and requesting a confirmation. Figure 11.13 illustrates the send (Ns) and receive (Nr) counts in successive frames with duplex (two-way simultaneous) operation. Note that acknowledgments are made without having to stop data transmission in either direction.

11.7.2 Retransmission Sequence

Since we expect errors to appear on the line, the retransmission sequence also must be simple and automatic. If the frame check sequence is not all right, the receiving station will freeze its Nr counter and simply throw away succeeding frames, even if they are correct. [With duplex (two-way simultaneous) operation, the "receiving" station could also be sending.] If the receiving station is a secondary in half-duplex procedure, it will wait until it receives a poll request. Then it will advise the primary station of the next expected frame (and thus of the last correct frame received). When transmitting, Nr would repeatedly report the expected frame, until that expected frame is received. The primary station would have to retransmit the expected frame and subsequent frames.

Figure 11.14 illustrates a retransmission by a terminal in duplex operation. The CPU finds an error in frame number one, but does not send an Nr to that terminal until sometime later. When the terminal gets the message that the CPU is still waiting for a correct frame number one, it backs up and retransmits beginning with that frame.

Another problem would be the absence of a link response after an extended time. At the end of a time-out, one or more frames are retransmitted by the primary, starting with the last Nr sequence number that has been received.

11.7.3 Supervisory Frames

The SDLC supervisory commands and responses are very effective in promoting the flows. They are described below.

Receive Ready (RR). This supervisory frame is sometimes used by the primary station for polling. The RR is sent to a particular station with the P bit on; this, in effect, says, "I am ready to receive; you will send information if you have any; else respond without information." The

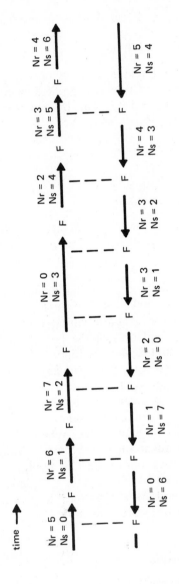

Fig. 11.13 Illustration of send (Ns) and receive (Nr) counts in successive messages with duplex (two-way simultaneous) procedure.

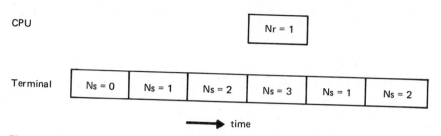

Fig. 11.14 Retransmission with duplex (two-way simultaneous) procedure.

receiving station will respond with information frames if it has those. If it has no information to transmit, it will send back a supervisory response (such as an RR frame) with the F bit on. This would indicate a final transmission, saying, "I have nothing more to send." The primary station can then send a Receive Ready command with the P bit on to another secondary station, asking it, in turn, whether it has anything to send. The RR frame, like all supervisory frames, contains the Nr field. Thus, the exchange of supervisory frames is an occasion for confirming a number of messages received.

Figure 11.15 illustrates some of the alternative link responses to a Receive Ready (RR) command. Figure 11.16 illustrates two uses of the Receive Ready command in a half-duplex (two-way alternate) operation. In one case, the primary polls station number one and subsequently station number two. In the other case, secondary station number two informs the primary station that station number two is ready to receive but has no I frames to send at this time. Note that the number of line turnarounds is reduced when

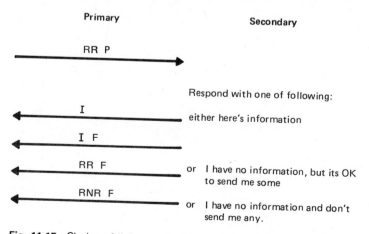

Fig. 11.15 Choice of link responses to an RR command.

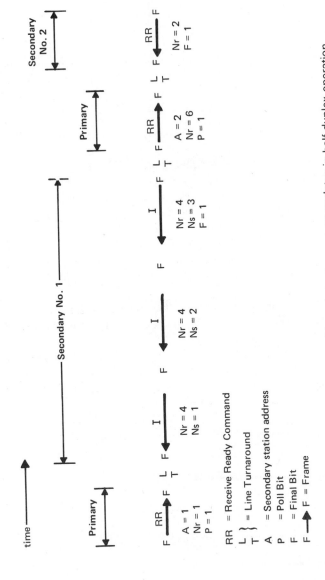

Fig. 11.16   Receive Ready (RR) commands and sequence count updates in half-duplex operation.

multiple (up to seven) information frames can be sent in response to a single polling frame. In this example, the primary advises that it is looking for frame numbers one and six from secondary station numbers one and two, respectively. These secondary stations, in turn, advise the primary that they are looking for frame numbers four and two, respectively, from the primary. (Remember that, at the primary, sequence numbers for each station are independent of those for another station.)

Receive Not Ready (RNR).   Stations can advise one another that they are alive without asking for the transmission of an information frame. The primary can send a Receive Not Ready (RNR) with the P bit on; the secondary station thus knows that the primary station is active even though it is not authorizing the transmission of I frames. When receiving this, the secondary station must respond, and can return a Receive Ready (RR) with the F bit on, indicating to the primary station that it too is alive. The accompanying Nr also acknowledges previously received frames. Alternatively, the secondary station could return a Receive Not Ready, thus indicating to the primary that, though it is alive, it is unable to receive frames containing an information field at this time.

The RNR condition of a primary can be terminated by sending an RR I, or REJ with the P bit on, thus inviting transmission at the frame number of the accompanying Nr.

Clearing the buffers.   Since these two supervisory frames (the RR and RNR) contain the Nr count, they are, in effect, authorization to a station to clear their buffers if their Nr counts check. Each station must maintain the information of sent frames in their buffers until they get a validation from the other station of correct reception. Therefore, the exchange of the Nr counts is important to the efficiency of buffer usage. For example, even though a primary does not desire any further information from a particular secondary station because its buffers may be full, the primary can nevertheless send a Receive Not Ready command, thereby enabling that secondary to clear its buffers. Alternatively, the primary could send an RR with the P bit off in order to release the secondary buffers.

Reject (REJ).   When there are two duplex stations on a duplex line, both may be transmitting simultaneously. They can continue doing this so long as each sends no more than seven frames before getting a sequence count validation (see Fig. 11.13). The returning Nr's tell which frames are expected next. If one of the stations discerns that there is an error in the Ns sequence count, it can take immediate and positive actions to advise the sender via the supervisor command (REJ). Let us say that a station receives frames with sequence numbers 1, 2, 3, and 5. After the receipt of sequence number 5, the receiving station transmits the Reject

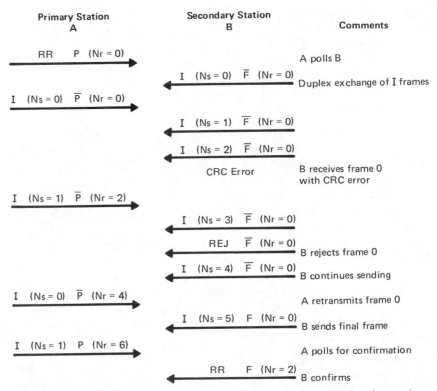

Fig. 11.17 Use of REJECT command with duplex (two-way simultaneous) procedure.

command containing the Nr count field, advising the sender that something is amiss and the next frame that it expects to receive is number four.
It is then up to the sender to retransmit frame number four and succeeding frames. The use of REJ is illustrated in Fig. 11.17.

The Selective Reject (SREJ) command is included in HDLC and
ADCCP. With SREJ, only the one frame indicated by the Nr that is with
SREJ is to be retransmitted. Those frames following Nr that are already
transmitted need not be retransmitted. In Fig. 11.17, for example, use of
an SREJ instead of an REJ would have caused the primary to retransmit
frame 0 but not frame 1.

11.7.4 Mode-setting Sequences

A station might be in one of the following response modes [11.10]:

1. Normal Response Mode
2. Asynchronous Response Mode

3. Asynchronous Balanced Mode
4. Normal Disconnected Mode
5. Asynchronous Disconnected Mode
6. Extended modes (with extended sequence numbers for the first three)

Normal Response Mode. When a station first powers up or is first connected via a switched network, it assumes what is called a disconnected mode. If the primary station sets the secondary station into normal response mode, that secondary station will be in a position to exchange frames when addressed by the primary station or polled by the primary station. To do this, the primary will first send the Set Normal Response Mode (SNRM) command to the secondary station with the poll bit on. The secondary station must respond to the polling request. It will send back an Unnumbered Acknowledgment (UA) with the final bit on, saying, in effect, "Yes, I'm OK; we can proceed to communicate."

If the primary sends a Disconnect with the P bit on to a secondary station, then the secondary station must logically disconnect from the line. But prior to disconnecting, it sends an Unnumbered Acknowledgment with the F bit on. If the line is a switched line, then, in addition, the secondary will actually drop the line and a re-dial will be necessary.

Asynchronous Response Mode. The normal-response mode requires polling; that is, the secondary station may not speak until the primary polls it. In asynchronous-response mode, one station could respond without being polled. The primary could enable that station by sending a Set Asynchronous Response Mode (SARM) command. That secondary would put its frame on the line to the primary whenever it is ready. *The principal use for asynchronous response mode is for point-to-point connections (where there is only one secondary). With duplex lines, there will then be no collisions.*

Asynchronous Balanced Mode. This mode in the draft international standard [11.18, 11.19] avoids the primary-secondary asymmetry and has two main objectives:

1. Each station on a point-to-point link would have equal ability to perform error recovery, including resetting the mode.
2. On a dial-up link, there would be no inability to communicate because of unworkable primary-primary or secondary-secondary relationships.

A station operating in asynchronous balanced mode (ABM) is called a *combined station* (rather than a primary or a secondary station).

A balanced configuration consists of two combined stations using point-to-point, half-duplex (two-way alternate), or duplex (two-way simultaneous) procedure, switched or nonswitched. Both stations have identical responsibility for exchanging data and control information and initiating recovery functions. Each combined station maintains one Send Sequence Number (Ns) and one Receive Sequence Number (Nr) on the information frames it sends and receives. Link commands are transmitted with the remote station address, while link responses are transmitted with the local station address. A Set Asynchronous Balanced Mode (SABM) command is used to place the addressed station in ABM.

The command/response repertoire of the combined station includes the sum of the basic repertoires of primary commands and secondary responses. The Frame Reject (FRMR) is used by a combined station to report the receipt of a frame having the same reject conditions as specified for the CMDR link response, but FRMR may be sent as a command or a response, as appropriate at the time of transmission. A Reset (RSET) command is also included. The addressed station confirms the acceptance of the RSET by transmission of a nonsequenced acknowledgment, and sets its Nr count to zero. If the acknowledgment is received correctly, the initiating station resets its Ns count.

Equipment may be efficiently constructed with the capability of alternately operating as a primary station, a secondary station, or a combined station because (1) there is consistent definition of the commands and responses, and (2) there is supersetting of the repertoires.

11.7.5 Broadcast

Let us say that we want to broadcast a frame to all secondary stations. For example, it might be, "Prepare to shut down in 10 minutes." We cannot simply send out a broadcast frame in an I frame because an I frame has sequence number fields, and these will not likely correspond to all of the secondary stations at the same time. We can send out a broadcast frame by using a nonsequenced information frame (NSI). The NSI is sent out without sequence number fields and without the poll bit being on. The address of eight one bits is reserved as the broadcast address. The broadcast address should be used, therefore, only in those cases where failure to receive the frame would not involve a breach of system integrity.

An alternative, more complex, but safer procedure would be to

1. Send SNRM to all stations to reset all frame counts

2. Send the broadcast message, in an I format, without the P bit

3. Poll each station in turn for a response

11.7.6 Node Initialization

Assume that the node that we wish to contact has its power on and has a bootstrap capability, but the node is not fully initialized and the initialization must come from an adjacent node having the primary station. Then when the primary tries to set the secondary station into normal-response mode, that secondary will respond with a Request Initialization (RQI).

When the primary station receives the RQI, the primary station passes the RQI to the physical unit of its node. The physical unit is in session with the SSCP, who establishes what IPL text is needed for the initialization. The primary station then sends Set Initialization Mode (SIM) to the secondary. Following commands from the SSCP, the PU of the adjacent node will then send (via DLC) a series of frames to the secondary—either information frames or nonsequenced information frames—containing the text for the initialization. Once this is complete, the primary station again sends the Set Normal Response Mode (SNRM) command to return the secondary station to that operating mode.

An illustration of this initialization sequence is given in the first three commands from the primary station of Fig. 11.18 (which also illustrates the subsequent operation of several stations on one multipoint line). (See Section 12.5 for a more complete initialization description.)

11.8 CLASSES OF PROCEDURE

The data link control can be described as having one of three classes of procedure with optional functions. The classes stem from the facts that:

1. There are three types of stations: primary stations, secondary stations, and combined stations.

2. There are two types of configurations: unbalanced (for primary and secondary stations) and balanced (for combined stations).

3. There are two types of transmission response: normal and asynchronous.

The three fundamental classes are therefore:

1. Unbalanced operation, asynchronous response mode.
2. Unbalanced operation normal response mode.
3. Balanced operation, asynchronous transmission.

The basic repertoire of commands and the proposed optional functions for these classes of procedure (as cited by the International Standards Organization and reflecting ISO/CCITT committee recommendations on

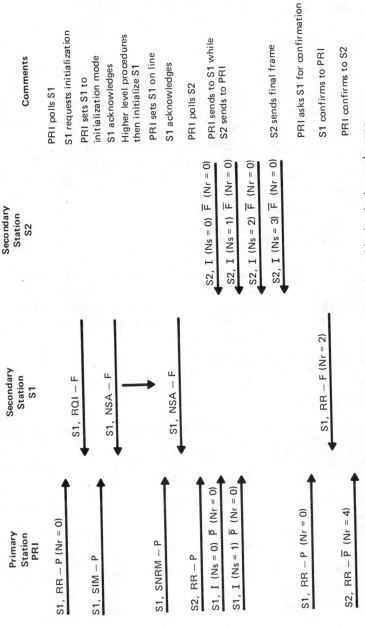

Fig. 11.18 Use of request initialization, and bidirectional flows in multipoint duplex exchanges.

balanced mode as of April 1977) are summarized in Figs. 11.19 and 11.20 [11.21, 11.22]. Evidently, the standards groups are close to achieving a single set of options common to the three basic repertoires.

A given data link control may support one or more of the three basic repertoire plus any subset of the optional functions. *SDLC, for example, as currently implemented, supports the basic repertoire for unbalanced*

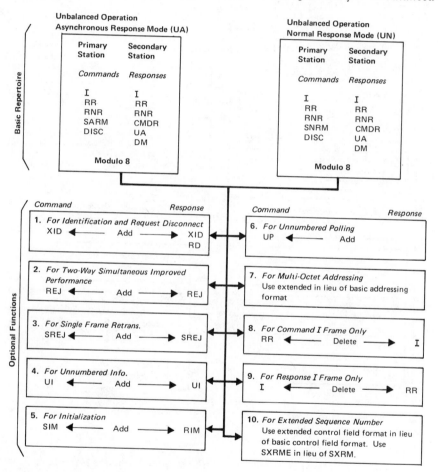

Note: Corresponding SDLC terms are:

UA = NSA (Nonsequenced Acknowledgment)
UP = NSP (Nonsequenced Poll)
UI = NSI (Nonsequenced Information)
RIM = RQI (Request Initialization)

Fig. 11.19 HDLC proposed unbalanced classes of procedure (subject to further change pending final approval by ISO) [11.22].

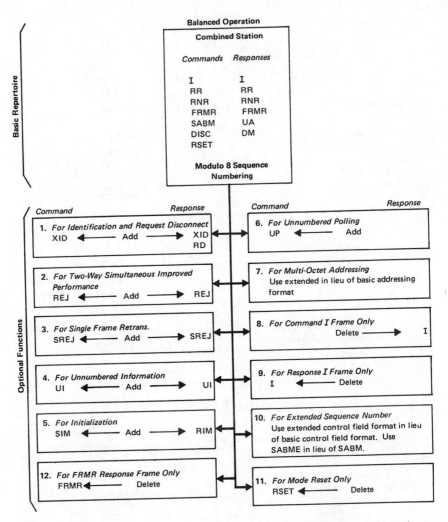

Fig. 11.20 HDLC proposed balanced classes of procedure (subject to further change pending final approval by ISO) [11.21].

operation, normal response mode, plus the optional functions numbers 2, 4, 5, and 6. SDLC also supports option 1 except for the Request Disconnect (RD) link response, which current implementations of SDLC do not support. Other data link controls currently support different subsets of the optional functions. As requirements develop, however, one would expect each data link control to adopt those additional standardized functions that become justified.

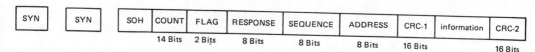

SYN	SYN	SOH	COUNT	FLAG	RESPONSE	SEQUENCE	ADDRESS	CRC-1	information	CRC-2
			14 Bits	2 Bits	8 Bits	8 Bits	8 Bits	16 Bits		16 Bits

Fig. 11.21   DDCMP message format [11.15].

11.9 PARALLEL DEVELOPMENTS

Digital Equipment Corporation provides a data link control called DDCMP (Digital Data Communications Message Protocol) which parallels the operating features but only some of the architecture of SDLC, HDLC, and ADCCP [11.3]. DDCMP is byte-oriented, rather than bit-oriented.

DDCMP is designed to operate over synchronous duplex or half-duplex channels, switched or dedicated links, point-to-point or multipoint networks, and parallel links. In addition, DDCMP will also accommodate asynchronous, start-stop modes.

DDCMP uses a data count field to determine the length of the data, whereas SDLC uses the trailing flag (and a fixed-length frame sequence check) to locate the end of the data field.

The format of a DDCMP transmission block is shown in Fig. 11.21 [11.15]. DDCMP uses one control character as the first character of a frame to distinguish between data, control, and bootstrap frames (SOH, ENQ, and DLE, respectively). The link header contains a count of the number of bytes in the information field, a response field for positive acknowledgment of received frames, a sequence number field (modulo-256), and an address. Unlike SDLC, DDCMP sends a separate negative acknowledgment frame when an error occurs.

11.10 EXERCISES

11.1 What would be the bit pattern placed on the line if data given to the data link control layer were 01111111, assuming zero bit insertion was in effect and NRZI was not.

11.2 Which of the following SDLC commands or responses cause the send/receive counts, that are retained in a station, to be incremented?

  a) RR

  b) SNRM

  c) I

  d) NSA

11.3 Which SDLC command or response, sent by either a primary or secondary station, indicates that its buffers are full and it cannot accept any more frames with information fields for the time being?

11.4 From the list below, select those items that are synchronous data link control activities.

a) Synchronizing the receiver to the transmitter

b) Selecting a station that serves an I/O device

c) Detection and recovery from transmission errors

d) Controlling when sending and receiving will occur

e) Specifying the original source (for example, the end-user) of a frame

f) Reporting improper data link control procedures

g) I/O device control

11.5 The primary reason for using NRZI coding is which of the following?

a) To provide ample transitions when receiving long streams of zero bits

b) To provide ample transitions when receiving long streams of one bits

c) To invert all zeros to reduce the power consumption on the communications channel

11.6 Assume that the primary SDLC station has sent six frames to a secondary station. All frames are in the information transfer format and the primary's Ns count was three (011, binary) prior to sending the six frames. If the poll bit was on in the sixth frame, what will be the Nr count sent back to the primary from the secondary? (Assume normal, no-error operation and half-duplex communications channel.)

11.7 In those secondary SDLC stations that have a local IPL/IML capability, what does the SIM command do?

11.8 Which of the three SDLC formats (information, supervisory, or nonsequenced) can never have an information field within the frame?

11.9 Which SDLC command/response may be used during duplex operation to indicate a sequence error?

11.10 Assume that the SDLC primary is transmitting information-type frames to a secondary and a frame check error occurs. How does the secondary inform the primary of this error condition?

11.11 Listed below are some statements regarding the purpose of various SDLC commands or responses. Match the statements to the appropriate command or response.

_____1. A command that puts a second-   a) NSA
           ary in normal-response mode

_____2. Indicates that a station is not   b) NSP
           ready to receive (busy)

_____3. Indicates that the sequence   c) RNR
count is in error and a transmit
or retransmit is required

_____4. A response used to acknow-   d) NSI
ledge mode setting com-
mands

_____5. A response indicating that the   e) SNRM
secondary requires initializa-
tion

_____6. A command that will put a   f) RQI
secondary off-line

_____7. A command that allows an   g) REJ
optional response from an
addressed station

_____8. Command or response that is   h) DISC
used to move data (informa-
tion) but does not cause a
change of or testing of the Nr
or Ns counts

11.12 From the list below, arrange the listed events in the correct order as they
would occur, assuming secondary-station to primary-station transmission of one
frame on an SDLC loop.

a) Secondary changes the go-ahead pattern into a flag

b) Primary issues a nonsequenced poll (NSP) command

c) Secondary transmits its own address

d) Secondary transmits an information field

e) Secondary transmits a frame check sequence

f) Secondary transmits a control field

g) Primary transmits a zero bit followed by a continuous stream of one bits
(go-ahead pattern)

h) The secondary transmits the ending flag.

11.13 Construct the bit pattern for the link header for an SDLC frame as follows:

- Station address 16
- Supervisory command: Receive Ready
- Last validly received sequence number at the sending station was 2
- A response is demanded from the receiving station

11.11 REFERENCES AND BIBLIOGRAPHY

See also [1.3 and 10.6].

11.1 *IBM Synchronous Data Link Control, General Information.* IBM Form No. GA27-3093.

11.2 M. J. Bedford. "BDLC—A Link Control Method That Can Handle Up To 127 Unacknowledged Frames." *Data Communications* (November/December 1975).

11.3 S. Wecker. "Dialog on Digital Data Communications Message Protocol." *Data Communications* (September/October 1974).

11.4 D. E. Carlson. "ADCCP—A Computer-Oriented Data Link Control." IEEE 11th Computer Society Conference (COMPCON 75), **1**: 110–113. Washington, D.C.: (9–11 September 1975).

11.5 J. P. Gray. "Line Control Procedures." *Proc. IEEE* **60** (November 1972): 1301–1302.

11.6 J. R. Kersey. "Taking a Fresh Look at Data Link Controls." *Data Communications* (September 1973): 65–71.

11.7 R. A. Donnan and J. R. Kersey. "Synchronous Data Link Control: A Perspective." *IBM Systems Journal* No. 2: 1460–162 (1974).

11.8 W. Petersen and D. Brown. "Cyclic Codes for Error Detection." *Proc. IRE* (January 1961).

11.9 H. O. Burton and D. D. Sullivan. "Errors and Error Control." *Proc. IEEE* **60** (November 1972): 1293–1301.

11.10 Sixth Draft, Document X3S34/589 *"Proposed American National Standard for Advanced Data Communication Control Procedures."* Prepared by Task Group 4, Subcommittee X3S3, ANSI (15 October 1976).

11.11 "Communications Clinic—SDLC," *Modern Data* (February 1975, March 1975, April 1975, June 1975, September 1975).

11.12 D. Farber. "Data Ring Oriented Computer Networks." *Courant Computer Science Symposium* 3, *Computer Networks*. Englewood Cliffs, N.J.: Prentice-Hall (1972).

11.13 E. Sussenguth. "Systems Network Architecture." *Interface '76*. Miami, Florida (29–31 March 1976).

11.14 P. E. Boudreau and R. F. Steen. "Cyclic Redundancy Checking by Program." *AFIPS 1971 Conference Proc.* **39**: 9–15.

11.15 *Introduction to Minicomputer Networks.* Maynard, Mass.: Digital Equipment Corp. (1974).

11.16 "Synchronous Data Link Control." IBM Field Engineering Education Student Self-Study Course, SR23-4130.

11.17 A. K. Bhushman and R. H. Stotz. "Procedures and Standards for Inter-Computer Communication." *AFIPS Proceedings, 1968 Spring Joint Computer Conference,* **32** (30 April–2 May 1968), Atlantic City, New Jersey.

11.18 HDLC Proposed Balanced Class of Procedures, ISO/TC97/SC6 N1444 (March 1977).

11.19 HDLC Proposed Enhancement to DIS 4335, ISO/TC97/SC6 N1445 (March 1977).

11.20 International Standard ISO 3309, Data Communications High-Level Data Link Control Procedures—Frame Structure. Ref. no. ISO 3309–1976 (E).

11.21 HDLC Proposed Balanced Class of Procedures. Document ISO/TC97/SC6 N1444 (revised). Geneva (April 1977).

11.22 HDLC Proposed Unbalanced Classes of Procedures. CCITT document ISO/TC97/SC6 N1339 (November 1976).

Part 3
Overview
of Operations

In Part 2, the functions of each of the SNA layers were examined in some detail. Part 3, then, describes the combined operations of all the layers. It also describes techniques for precise definition of the architecture and some of the finer structures within layers.

Chapter 12 traces, step by step, a number of important multilayer sequences. The boundaries between the layers are summarized. Chapter 12 thus serves to illustrate operational aspects of a complete single-domain network.

Chapter 13 shows how the communication protocols can be more precisely defined in terms of finite state architecture. By this more detailed definition, it also takes the reader a step closer to the structures within layers, and illustrates in more detail both intralayer and cross-layer operations.

Chapter 14 provides an overview of the operations of recovery, integrity, and security.

12
Putting
It Together

12.1 INTRODUCTION*

In this chapter we bring together many of the pieces described in the previous chapters. The purpose is to review the relations among the parts and to illustrate the total network operation. Each of the major node types, and the SNA layers involved therein, are first reviewed (for those desiring further node overviews). Then a series of step-by-step discussions of network operations is presented. The network start-up sequences, to bring the nodes and logical units on-line, and the dial sequences, involved in making a connection in switched network operations, are described. Key physical-unit functions that coordinate communications in a given node are illustrated. Then the log-on sequence to connect a remote user to a host application is reviewed. The actions of NAU services and the interface to the end-user are illustrated, and the information flows across boundaries between layers are summarized. Though somewhat tedious, this series of detailed illustrations and summaries should help to clarify the network operations and the interrelationships among layers.

12.2 SNA NODE TYPES

We now briefly review the various types of SNA node and their distinguishing characteristics in the light of the layered structure and distributed

---

* The author is indebted to J. M. Cavin for the benefit derived from his work in portraying overall SNA sequences, and to W. A. Bernstein and G. A. Plotsky for consultations on this chapter.

services described in Part 2. Remember that a node is not an architectural concept (see Section 6.4); it is simply a place that houses function. Cost and/or design efficiencies have a lot to do with each node's design and the establishment of a hierarchy of node types. (See Section 3.9.) We will examine the SNA functions in current node types and illustrate that a description of each node, in terms of SNA functions, is a description of a subset of a single SNA node structure. (Readers who are less concerned with the somewhat arbitrary node types should proceed to Section 12.4.)

12.2.1 Node Types by Dominant Function

First recall that the principal types of SNA node in use today are

1. Subarea nodes (dealing with 16-bit network address)
   - Hosts
   - Communications controllers
2. Local nodes (dealing with addresses understood only by the node and transformed to the network addresses by an adjacent boundary function
   - Cluster controllers (including some high-function terminals) and subhosts
   - Terminal nodes (having simpler transmission protocols than those of a cluster controller)

These node titles imply the *main functions* of the node; however, this does not necessarily exclude other functions from that node. The cluster controller, for example, can include application processing, which is a main function of a host node. Also, the host can include the intermediate node function, which is a main function of a communications controller. Also, there are no restrictions architecturally as to which types of node may have end-users and logical units.

Note too that all four examples of node may contain a data processor. This processor in the host is, by definition, of general purpose; the processors in the other three might be either of general or special purpose, but are relatively limited in capability. Devices may be attached to hosts, communications controllers, cluster controllers, or terminal nodes.

In SNA, these four examples of nodes—hosts, communications controllers, cluster controllers, and terminal nodes—are designated as types T5, T4, T2, and T1, respectively. The architectural distinctions among them are in the layers and function subsets that are used for each type. Informally, these type numbers correspond to each node's PU-type (see Appendix B.3), which denotes the capabilities in the lower layers, particularly in data link control and path control.

12.3 SNA LAYER CAPABILITY IN EACH NODE TYPE

In the following discussion, the essential characteristics of each node type are first reviewed, and then an illustration is given of how the SNA layered structure applies to that node type.

12.3.1 Type-1 (Terminal) Node

A terminal is a node of lesser function to which one or more I/O devices can be attached, and which depends on the boundary function of the adjacent host or communications controller for (1) transforming network addresses to local address form, and vice versa, and (2) handling normal-flow sequence numbers. The terminal-node path control always uses the FID-3 transmission header.

The terminal node, as it relates to the SNA network, is shown in Fig. 12.1. The node has a physical unit and up to 64 logical units. Logical units serve devices. Note, however, that SNA does not architect the devices or the device drivers, or their interface to the NAU services. Each implementation provides the necessary information for the SNA headers and the transformations to and from the SNA header formats. Each logical unit has only one session with the SSCP and one session with another LU. Any data links to the devices are not visible to the SNA network; these are often unique to the device (and the device drivers). The type-1 path control permits segmenting but not blocking capability (it cannot receive or send blocked RUs). In some implementations, the PU activation is handled by a boundary function in an adjacent COMC.

12.3.2 Type-2 (Cluster Controller) Node

A cluster controller (CLC) node can control a wide variety of devices and may have a data-processing capability. It depends on the boundary function of the host node or of the communications controller to which it is attached for assistance in pacing data flow within a session, for transforming network addresses to local address forms and vice versa, and for some assistance in session control for its PU and LUs. The path control of a cluster controller always uses the FID-2 transmission header when communicating with a communications controller or a host.

A cluster controller can have up to 256 NAUs. Some cluster controllers (like the cash-dispensing unit) have only a PU and one logical unit. They still use FID-2 and appear to the network as a type-2 node, exactly as a small cluster controller would.

The layers and NAUs in the cluster controller are shown in Fig. 12.2. Logical units support both application programs and devices. Remember

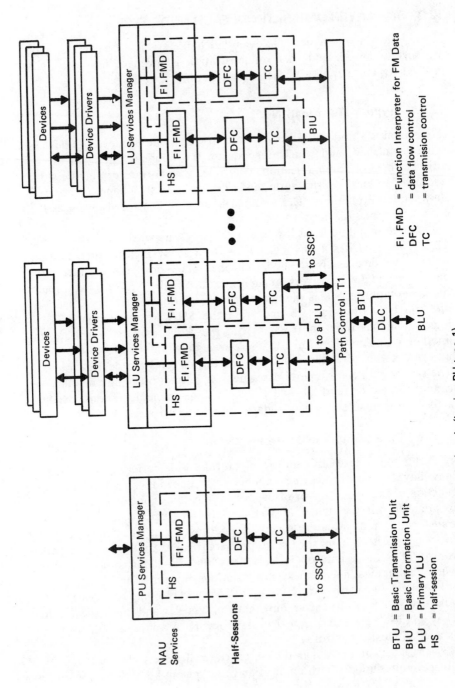

BTU = Basic Transmission Unit
BIU = Basic Information Unit
PLU = Primary LU
HS = half-session

FI.FMD = Function Interpreter for FM Data
DFC = data flow control
TC = transmission control

Fig. 12.1   Possible structure of terminal node (having PU-type 1).

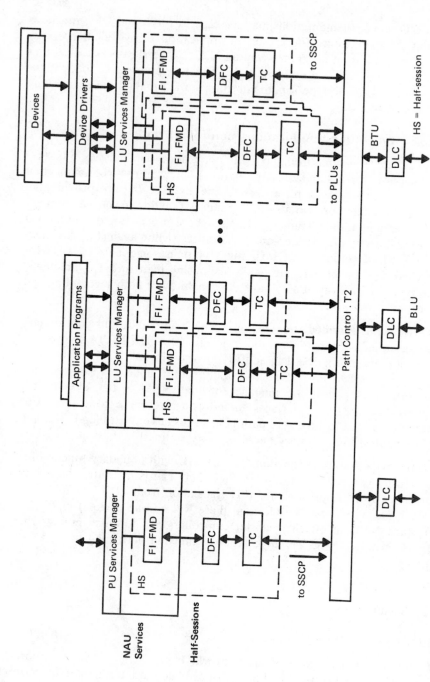

Fig. 12.2   Cluster controller node (having PU-type 2) as seen by the SNA network.

that different implementations may package FI.FMD and DFC functions within an application program or an application subsystem that serves multiple application programs. Multiple LU–LU sessions per logical unit are permitted architecturally (but this is not supported in today's implementations). The type-2 path control has the capability of segmenting but not of blocking.

12.3.3 Type-4 (Communications Controller) Node

A communications controller (COMC) is a node that handles transmission services for a subarea of the network and controls communication lines and such related resources as line buffers. It may provide the intermediate function and also the boundary function for cluster controller nodes and terminal nodes. Usually, there are no logical units in a COMC; however, there is no architectural restriction against it. Architecturally, for example, a COMC might contain some part of LUs for attached devices that are incapable of housing their own LU functions. The type-4 path control may have the capability of both segmenting and blocking.

COMC with intermediate function. The communications-control unit with intermediate functions is shown in Fig. 12.3. The PC.T4 involves no FID translation. It's FID-1 in and FID-1 out. The sole NAU in the node is the physical unit for controlling the node's resources for transmission services; the manager of that NAU is the PU services manager. This NAU interfaces to individual resource controllers (for example, the link-control and path-control resource controllers). Multiple DLCs control both primary and secondary stations.

COMC with boundary function. The COMC with boundary function for the cluster controller is shown in Fig. 12.4. The path control boundary function (BF.PC) performs the FID translation from FID-1 to FID-2 or FID-3, and vice versa. In addition, there will be one element of BF.TC for each NAU in attached cluster controllers and terminal nodes. The BF.TC in the COMC has three types of function pertaining to

1. Pacing
2. Sequence numbers for T1 (terminal) nodes
3. Session control

12.3.4 Host (Type-5)

A host is a type-5 node of the network. It provides a general-purpose data-processing function, and may also provide the intermediate function

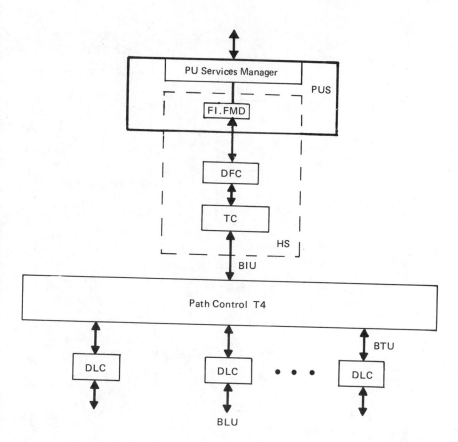

HS = half-session
PUS = physical unit services

Fig. 12.3 Communications controller (having PU-type 4) with intermediate function.

and boundary function (for example, the boundary function for channel-attached cluster controllers is located in the host). The system services control point function for a control domain of the network is often located in a host. A host that houses an SSCP is sometimes referred to as a *control host*. The type-5 path control may have the capability of both segmenting and blocking.

Implicit in the host are all the processing engines, storage devices, and management functions needed to carry out its role. Also implicit are those locally attached devices, such as card machines, disks, and tapes, that are not SNA nodes. If any such attached device is to be used by another SNA node, it is done via a logical unit in the host.

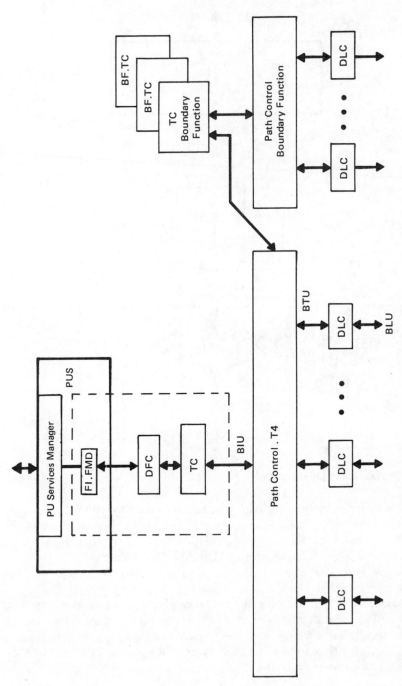

Fig. 12.4 Communications controller (having PU-type 4) with boundary node function.

The layers and NAUs found in hosts are shown in Fig. 12.5. The three NAU types, PU, LU, and SSCP, are permitted in this node. Logical units in hosts have full addressability to any other LU in the network via the full 16-bit destination address. The host always uses the FID-1 transmission header when talking to another host or a communications controller. Each logical unit is capable of conducting concurrent sessions with multiple other LUs. Logical units in the host can represent either programs or attached devices, and may support either primary or secondary half-sessions.

Section 3.6 discusses the subhost, which is a general-purpose processor whose application programs are subordinate to application programs in a host. Architecturally, however, the subhost is not different; it can appear to the SNA network as either a type-5 node (like a host) or a type-2 node (like a cluster controller).

12.3.5 Layer Involvement

Figure 12.6 summarizes the layer involvement for SNA session flow between NAUs. Any message to an end-user traverses all levels, and the interface to the end-user is handled by the NAU services. The boundary functions reside in the path control and transmission control layers; therefore, RUs served by boundary function in a node do not pass above transmission control for that node. Intermediate function is entirely within path control. Therefore, requests receiving intermediate function in a node use only the two lowest layers in that node.

12.4 BRINGING THE SYSTEM UP

12.4.1 Introduction

This is the first in a series of step-by-step discussions to help the reader grasp the interrelationships among the functions in the SNA layers as they appear in different types of node in a network.

In the beginning, one should ask, "*What* network?" It must somehow be defined. *In each communications controller and in the SSCP, pertinent parts of the network must be defined* in terms of tables that are organized for the efficiency of the product. For the convenience of the network definer, products like the IBM 3705, VTAM, and TCAM provide high-level *macro instructions*, whose parameters, when filled in, give the product the information it needs. For example, the macros for a definition of a communications controller may contain parameters for types of connection (point-to-point, multipoint, or switched), line discipline (e.g., SDLC, BSC, or start/stop), and line speed (e.g., 1200, 2400, or

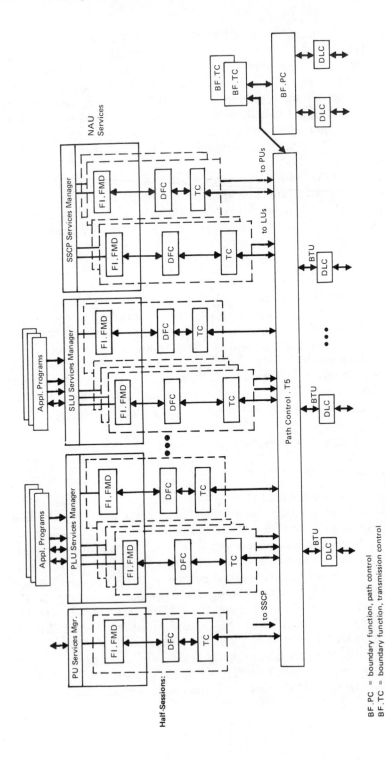

BF.PC = boundary function, path control
BF.TC = boundary function, transmission control

Fig. 12.5 Possible structure of host node (having PU-type 5) as seen by the SNA network.

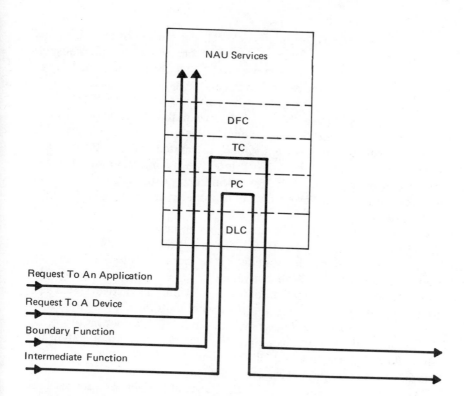

Fig. 12.6 Layers used for various functions.

4800 bps). Parameters of other macros define the type of node attached to each line. Logical units and the physical unit for each attaching node are described. Some of the same information, along with network operating rules and other characteristics of the control point, must be provided for a definition of the SSCP.

A set of macros for each product is then expanded by an assembler into tables that are suited to that product's design. The output of the assembler is then submitted to another program called a *linkage editor*, so that a linkage can be established between the generated tables and the control code of the product. (Subsequent alteration of the definition and the use of alternate definitions are also feasible.)

Let us assume that this system definition has been completed. Now, how do we activate all or only part of the network? An assortment of warm boxes distributed over the landscape is still not an SNA network or a system. It becomes one only *when the appropriate SNA functions in each node are operational and there is a confirmed relationship among these functions in the various nodes.* We call the process of initializing the SNA functions and of establishing and confirming the relationships among functions "bringing the system up." This involves the interplay of the SSCP, the communications controllers, and the PU and LUs in all destination nodes.

The first question usually is, "Who turns on the electrical power in all the nodes of the network?" Safety considerations may make it inadvisable to automatically turn power on in widely distributed nodes of the network from a central control point. Therefore, we assume that this is done manually by operators in each location, perhaps at the beginning of each day. Any automatic power-on facility is properly the responsibility of the network owner.

Bringing the system up then involves the activation of the physical units of the node, the logical units that are to be active at that time, and the links that connect these nodes. It is both a "wake-up" and an interconnection process. The activation of a link involves merely the setting of the primary station of that link into the active state. *The activation of the physical units and the logical units involves the establishment of a session between those units and the SSCP.* The activation of the physical units may require, as a preliminary step, the setup of station-to-station flow and the loading of the control code for the node by a transmission of text from the system services control point.

The current sequence in which the nodes of the network are brought up is like a wave emanating from the system services control point. First the nearest adjacent nodes are activated; they, in turn, are then used to activate the next most adjacent nodes, and so on. This allows the SSCP to understand, from the "bring-up" process, what paths are available to various NAUs.

All network service flows use relatively simple protocols. Each sender is responsible for the retransmission of requests, which are currently single-element chains only. The use of single-element chains eliminates the need for reset operations such as CLEAR (used for LU–LU sessions). The flow uses IDs rather than sequence numbers for request/response correlation. The "bring-up" processes described in the following section are illustrated in Figs. 12.7–12.10.

As shown in Fig. 12.7, the illustrative configuration includes a host, a local communications controller, a remote communications controller, a cluster controller, and its attached devices. This is part of a typical tree structure. There are three physical units outside the host: PU 1000, PU 2000, and PU 3000 (whose short-form address is 30). The cluster controller contains a logical unit, LU 3101 (whose short-form address is 31). The host contains the SSCP (address 0101) and an LU whose address

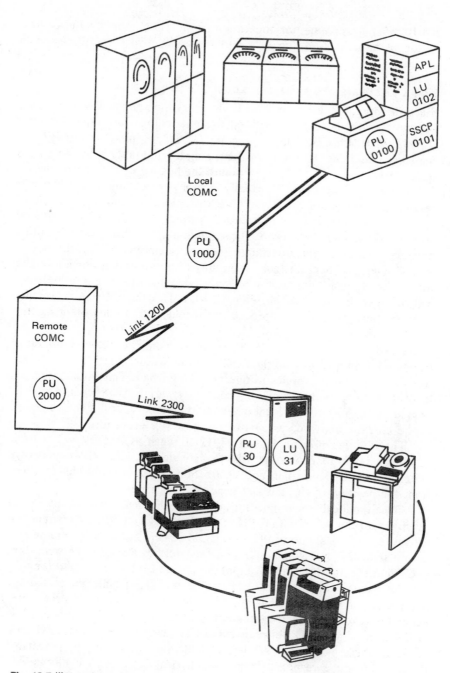

Fig. 12.7 Illustrative configuration.

is 0102. (The supplementary operation support programs for the coordination of network bring-up in a multidomain network are discussed in Section 15.4.3.)

12.4.2 Activate the Host and Local COMC

Since the operator does not want to do everything personally in bringing the system up, he or she will need some help. *The system operator therefore first loads the control program (initial program load or IPL) of the node containing the SSCP.* In this example, that node is the host. The operator loads the operating system into the host by means of a bootstrap program there. This host IPL usually includes an activation of the system services control point, the host PU, and the local channels.

Once the host is up, the *network operator can enter a command to bring up the rest of the network.* This command may bring up the entire network according to a prearranged network definition within the SSCP. Alternatively, an operator command may bring up only a portion of the total network or, in some cases, only a single node or string of nodes. We will consider, in Figs. 12.7 through 12.10, only a single string emanating from the host, but the same procedures would apply to any other part of the network.

The first action by the SSCP, resulting from the network operator command, would be to load the local communications controller (COMC) to which the string of nodes in question is attached. This initial machine load of the local communications controller may be a procedure that is unique to the host and its local (channel) data link control. (The channels of the host are activated as part of the host IPL procedure.)

The notation used in Figs. 12.8–12.10, such as ACTIVATE LINK 1200, is meant to direct the PU to activate the link whose network address is 1200. The origin and destination of a command can be seen from the position of the tail and head of each arrow.

Once the local communications controller has been loaded, the SSCP can transmit the ACTIVATE PHYSICAL UNIT (ACTPU) command to activate the physical unit of the local COMC. This ACTIVATE command is similar to a BIND command, and it establishes a session between the SSCP and the physical unit. The parameters and rules to be used for this session are indicated by the FM profile and TS profile contained as parameters of the ACTPU command. However, there is no procedure needed to reach a bilateral agreement on proposed control parameters (as in the case of a BIND between two LUs). In the case of ACTPU and ACTLU, these parameters are less variable and can readily be preestablished. A positive response from the Physical Unit 1000 confirms the success of the activation of the SSCP–PU session (see Fig. 12.8).

Now that the session to PU 1000 has been activated by the ACTPU, it can be called on to do some work. The bring-up activity can be extended to each of the next adjacent nodes. In our example, we have only one, the remote COMC, so the next step in our example is to ask PU 1000 to activate the link that connects the local COMC to the remote COMC. The ACTIVATE LINK command serves this purpose. It is an RU sent by the SSCP configuration services to the PU managing a link. The PU services manager can then send a corresponding function request to the proper DLC (determined by the address of the physical link that is to be activated). The purpose of this request is to ready the DLC function and condition the link for operational use; that is, it resets and initializes the port to the data link. (The DEACTIVATE LINK from the SSCP, later on, causes the PU services manager to issue a corresponding deactivating request to DLC.) The positive response from PU 1000 (back to the SSCP) confirms that the link activation will be undertaken.

12.4.3 Attempt to Contact the Remote COMC

Before proceeding to use the activated link, a probing action is needed to set up a station-to-station connection and to determine whether the remote COMC is indeed ready for action. This is an example in which PU services must communicate with an adjacent node whose SNA capability may or may not be fully operational. More specifically, *PU services, in one node that is already active, can comply with NS requests from the SSCP to contact and load another, nonoperational node.* In this case, there is no session yet in operation with the other node. PU services in the operational node must rely on link-level procedures, which are not part of any session, to achieve contact with the adjacent node, to confirm its identity, and perhaps to assist in providing it with an initial machine load. The CONTACT command starts this sequence; its objective is to activate a particular station-to-station flow. Thus, in our example, the configuration services of the SSCP send a CONTACT command to Physical Unit 1000 in the local COMC (see Figs. 12.8 and 12.9). This generates a contact procedure at the data link control level from the local COMC station to the remote COMC station.

For SDLC links, the primary station at the local COMC sends a Set Normal Response Mode (SNRM) command down the line to the secondary station at the remote COMC. Special functions in the adjacent node must interpret the link procedure, and must be operative even though the full SNA capability in that node is not operative. If the power is on at the remote COMC, the secondary station will respond with one of two link-level responses. If the remote COMC is not initialized (i.e., program- or microcode-loaded), the secondary station will send back a Request

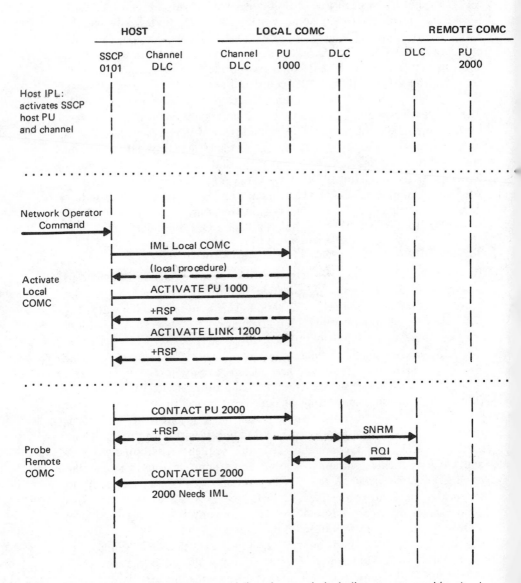

Fig. 12.8 Activation of first and second tier of network, including remote machine load.

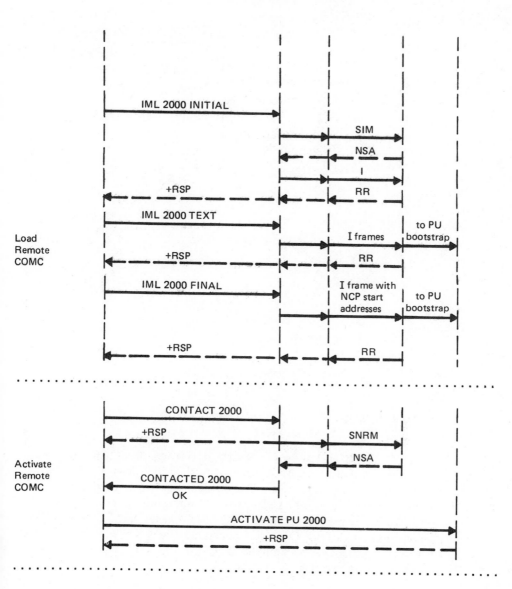

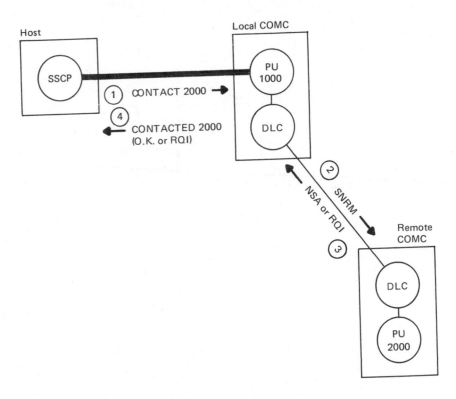

Fig. 12.9 SSCP asks PU 1000 to CONTACT PU 2000.

Initialization (RQI) link-level response. If, on the other hand, no initialization of the remote COMC is necessary, then the secondary station will send back a Nonsequenced Acknowledgment (NSA) link-level response. In Fig. 12.8, it is assumed that initialization is required and the initialization request is returned to PU 1000 in the local COMC. (*Note*: Upon receiving a DISCONTACT command from the SSCP later on, the PU services manager will direct DLC to send a link-level disconnect command to the secondary station.)

12.4.4 Load Remote COMC

Upon receipt of the requirement for a load, (RQI) PU 1000 will notify the configuration services of the SSCP by sending a CONTACTED command, with parameters indicating that Physical Unit 2000 needs an initial machine load. The SSCP then will proceed to initialize the PU in the remote COMC by a series of steps (see Fig. 12.8). First, the secondary station at the remote COMC must be put into an initialization mode, so that the text to follow will flow to the node IML routine (bootstrap function). For this purpose, the SSCP sends an IML INITIAL command to the physical unit in the local COMC. Upon receipt of this, Physical Unit 1000 directs its primary station to send a DLC-level command—Set Initialization Mode (SIM)—to the secondary station of the remote COMC. In some cases, the SIM may trigger a local "load" of code, using facilities in the destination node. In this example, however, it is an alert to the secondary station that the information sequence to follow is special control information. The SIM is acknowledged with an NSA link response. Once the initialization mode is established, the SSCP will proceed to send a series of IML TEXT commands containing the actual text for the initialization of the physical unit in the remote COMC. This text is sent first to the adjacent physical unit, in the local COMC, which in turn directs its primary station to transmit those "I frames" to the secondary station in the remote COMC. There, these frames are handed to the bootstrap function in the remote COMC. For each of these transmissions, Physical Unit 1000 sends a positive response to the SSCP as soon as it initiates the transfer of the I frames at the link level. Also, the secondary station sends a confirming RR frame to acknowledge its receipt of the frames as they are sent. Finally, to complete the transfer, the SSCP sends an IML FINAL command which contains the starting address for the control code in the remote communications controller.

12.4.5 Activate Remote COMC and Remote CLC

After this lengthy process, the remote COMC should be more cooperative. At any rate, it is worth a try. Having received positive responses from Physical Unit 1000 for each of these initialization steps, the SSCP will try again to contact the station for Physical Unit 2000 in the remote communications controller (see Fig. 12.8). The SSCP sends the CONTACT command to Physical Unit 1000 in the local COMC, which, as before, orders DLC to send a Set Normal Response Mode (SNRM) link-level command to the secondary station at the remote COMC. At this point, that secondary station should be able to return a Nonsequenced Acknowledgment (NSA) response to the local COMC, which will then trigger Physical Unit 1000 to send a confirming CONTACTED command back to the SSCP, indicating a successful contact.

Thus, a series of steps has been accomplished: The SSCP has successfully activated the local communications controller; the link between the local COMC and the remote COMC has been activated; via the local COMC, the SSCP has loaded the remote COMC; and the SSCP has gotten confirmation that a path is complete to the PU in the remote COMC. The SSCP, therefore, then sends an ACTIVATE PHYSICAL UNIT (ACTPU) command directly to PU 2000 (via the path control in the local COMC but without passing through the PU in the local communications controller). A positive response from PU 2000 to the SSCP then confirms that the PU in the remote COMC has also been activated and that a session now exists between that PU and the SSCP.

Figure 12.10 illustrates how an analogous procedure is then followed to activate the physical unit in the cluster controller that is attached to the remote communications controller. The physical unit in the local COMC is now out of the picture. The SSCP uses PU 2000 in the remote COMC to first activate the link to the cluster controller; then it sends a contact procedure to the cluster controller. Finding the cluster controller already loaded [by the receipt of a CONTACTED (loaded) command], the SSCP then is able to send the ACTIVATE PHYSICAL UNIT command directly to the PU in the cluster controller. The boundary function in the remote COMC was established at system generation time for nonswitched lines, or as part of a dial procedure (see the following section) if a switched line is to be used from the remote COMC to the cluster controller.

Once the session with the PU in the remote cluster controller is activated, it is then possible for the SSCP to activate sessions to all the logical units in the cluster controller that are to be brought on-line. This is done by the ACTIVATE LOGICAL UNIT (ACTLU) command, sent directly to the logical units in the cluster controller.

12.5   DIAL SEQUENCES*

12.5.1   Introduction

In the foregoing discussion, we assumed that each link was in place, as would be the case if nonswitched (leased) lines were arranged beforehand. Let us now look at the switched network and the sequences for the creation of a link by the dial-out and dial-in procedures.

The switched network (as distinct from nonswitched, or leased, lines) has a larger role to play in future networks. Today, these connections are often used for (1) infrequent calls, or (2) backup, in case of failure of a leased line. As we indicated in Chapter 2, however, fast

---

* Acknowledgment is given to F. Banks, M. Bastion, H. K. Philips, T. P. Taylor, and W. R. Wheeler for the material in this section.

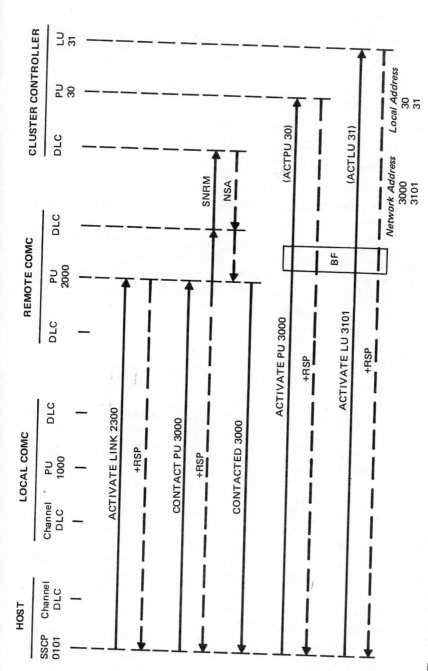

Fig. 12.10 Activation of logical and physical units in remote cluster controller.

call-establishment services (less than one second) are appearing throughout the world. This will increase the use of switched networks for data in
the future.

Common-carrier companies and PTTs throughout the world offer a
variety of switched services at different tariffs. Examples of these are

- Direct Distance Dialing: DDD
- Wide Area Telephone Service: WATS (USA)
- Foreign exchange (USA)
- Tieline networks
- New data networks, particularly switched digital transmission systems
  (see Section 2.4)

Normally a dial port (that is, a link with access equipment to a public
switched network) is not dedicated to only one type of switched network
service. The telephone number used to reach a given station determines
the type of service. In some cases, where access to the switched network
is allowed from a private branch exchange extension, the selection of
service can be made by a prefix access code (such as 8 for tieline and 9 for
DDD in the United States) preceding the seven-digit telephone number.

*The difference between a dial and a nonswitched connection is not
visible to the logical unit.* The transmission network, with the aid of the
SSCP and its associated physical units, masks that difference from all
sessions.

In keeping with the concept of the separation of functions in SNA,
the dial-oriented network service commands between the physical unit in
the attaching node and the SSCP are largely independent of the particular
data link control procedure used. However, the dial sequence includes the
use of the SDLC link-level Exchange Station ID command for identification of the attaching node.

The connection problem can be visualized in terms of connecting two
nodes, one of which is already a part of an SNA control domain and
houses a physical unit (PU) that is in session with the SSCP (see Fig.
12.11). We will say that that node has the *switched-network access facility*
(SAF). The other node, which we will call the *entering node*, is not initially
physically connected to the same control domain as the SAF node, and its
physical unit (PU), accordingly, is not in session with the SSCP. Both
nodes, however, must have some capability (auto-call or manual-dial
capabilities) that enables them to connect to the switched network. The
connection procedures are essentially the same whether we use a manual-
dial or auto-dial technique. A call that is initiated by the SSCP on behalf
of a logical unit that is active within the SNA control domain is referred

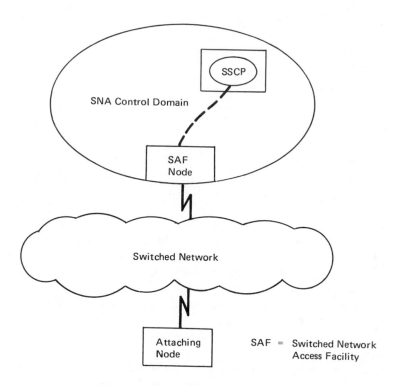

Fig. 12.11 Attaching via the switched network.

to as a *dial-out* procedure. Call initiation from a physical unit on behalf of a logical unit in the entering node is referred to as a *dial-in* procedure.

For every link there will usually be one station that is designated as primary to control the link. (See also the discussion of balanced mode in Section 11.7.4.) Some stations are built with only secondary-station or only primary-station capability. Others are built so they could be either primary or secondary. The capabilities of the called station must be known at the calling station, and the calling station must operate accordingly. Ordinarily, a station that is calling a primary-only station will assume secondary status, and vice versa. If the called station is capable of operating as a primary,then it will do so, and the calling station will operate as a secondary. In our examples, we will dial out from a primary station and dial in from a secondary station.

To have a dial capability, a node must have a more complex set of physical unit services. The SSCP, too, must have the additional capability to

1. Dynamically set up the communications controllers with necessary control information
2. Establish the connection
3. Ensure the network integrity by exchanges of identification

Also, as part of the process of bringing the network up, the SSCP should be able to activate groups of ports for switched lines (for example, all WATS lines or lines to selected nodes) as specified by the user.

It is important that *all path and link considerations, whether we use switched or nonswitched facilities, be transparent to the NAU–NAU session and also the end-use application programs or operators*. Since a station can be connected to the system on different links, and NAUs can therefore appear as different network addresses at different times, the system should remember the network address currently in use for a symbolically named NAU, and provide the translation from name to network address. In SNA, the SSCP provides this service.

There are two main circumstances for using dial facilities. One is the dialing of a connection between stations in subarea nodes, such as between two communications controllers (COMCs). The other is the dialing of a connection between a station in a subarea node and a station in a local node. An example of this is a connection between a COMC and a cluster controller or terminal node. The subarea-to-subarea dial is somewhat more complex, and is less frequently used. Therefore, in the following discussion, we will confine our detailed descriptions to the dialing of a connection between a subarea node and a local node.

12.5.2 Four Stages of Connection

When using the switched network, the physical circuit (path) is first established; then logical connections (sessions) are activated between the SSCP and the physical unit of the node and the logical units. Once these steps are completed, any LU-to-LU session can be established in the same manner as with a nonswitched line.

But let us break this down further. One can see four stages to this establishment of the switched connection, as follows:

1. First we must have a path to the node containing the switched-network access facility (SAF). This involves link and PU activations, as discussed in Section 12.4. For some reason, then, the SSCP must be called on to establish a switched network link that terminates in the SAF node. This may be a scheduled part of the process of bringing up the

network. Or, it may be a later operator request for that link. Or, it may be on the occasion of an INITIATE command to establish an LU–LU session—one that the SSCP knows requires a switched network connection. The station to be used by the SAF must then be selected and activated by the SSCP.

2. In accordance with a sequence of network service commands between the SSCP and the PU of the SAF node, the SAF will either initiate a dial-out sequence or will be conditioned to receive a dial-in sequence. The common carrier or PTT must actually establish the switched network connection. This will follow the signaling, via a standard dial interface (for example, RS 366), of either (a) a DIAL OUT from the SAF node in the SNA network, or (b) a DIAL IN from an entering node.

3. An exchange of identification must be made to verify the identity of the physical nodes that have been connected. (This is either a one-way or a two-way identification, depending on implementations.) The exchange of identification must verify either that (a) the entering node is one that is anticipated, or (b) any necessary table updates or other accommodations can be made.

4. Configuration information must be sent to the physical unit (PU) in the SAF node. The entering node must be contacted and its NAUs must be activated.

These four stages will be examined in still more detail, for those who need it, in the following section.

12.5.3 Dial-out Sequence

Figure 12.12 illustrates the steps involved in establishing the physical connection when dialing out. In this case, the node with the switched-network access facility (SAF) is the *calling node*. In this example, we will assume it is a COMC. The seven sections in Fig. 12.12 are numbered to correspond with the following paragraphs. The procedure is as follows.

1. Link selection

The initial action is taken by a network operator or a program, which submits a command to the SSCP that either directly or indirectly requires the SSCP to establish a session with a particular remote logical unit. One such command (which is implementation-dependent) is a so-called vary-on command, which is designed to bring on-line a unit that has been previously defined to the system.

Upon receipt of the vary-on command (or other instigating command), the SSCP will select a path through a node or nodes to the desired

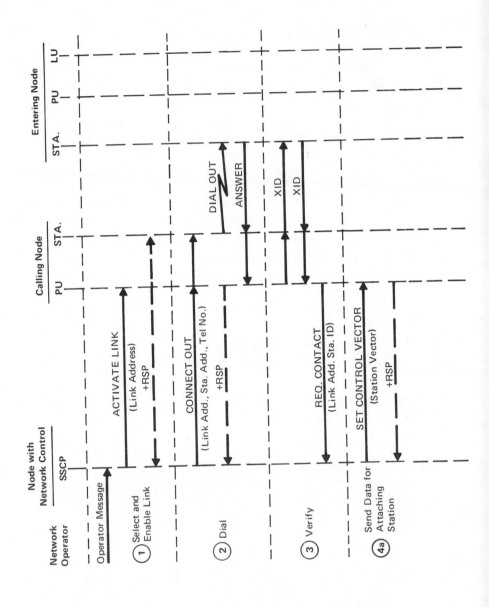

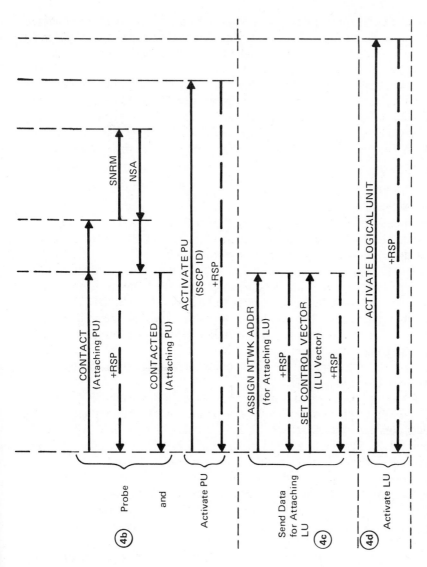

Fig. 12.12 Dial-out sequence, and activation of an attaching node and logical unit.

station. The SSCP will determine what links and nodes must be activated in order to fulfill the vary-on command. In this example, the SSCP must establish a link that uses the switched network between two nodes.

Upon determining that the switched link is to be established, the SSCP will first send an ACTIVATE LINK command to the physical unit (PU) of the node having the calling link station. This places the addressed link station in the active state and sets up the basic control for the link. The ACTIVATE LINK command contains the network address of the link. A positive response from the PU confirms the link activation in the calling node.

2. Dial step

The SSCP then directs the SAF PU (in the calling node) to execute the dial procedure by sending a CONNECT OUT (CONNOUT) command to the PU. The CONNECT OUT command requests that PU to establish a connection with the station in the entering node.

The CONNECT OUT command includes the network address of the link, along with an indication of whether the called station is primary or secondary and the telephone number to be dialed (in EBCDIC digits and separator characters). The number of times that the dial operation is to be retried (if the line is busy) is also included. Upon direction from the PU, the calling station will then dial out the specified telephone number. The answer is a tone detected by the modem and signaled to the data link control in the calling node.

If the calling node does not contain an auto-dial capability, then the CONNECT OUT command will not contain the telephone number to be dialed. Instead, the CONNECT OUT command-type field will specify manual-dial. The calling node will then enable the link for the dial operation and monitor the establishment of the physical connection. In the meantime, the SSCP will issue a command to the network operator indicating the telephone number and either some identification of the manual access arrangement or the actual telephone set associated with the selected dial port. Assuming that the physical connection is manually established, the procedure follows as in the case of auto-dial. If the network operator does not succeed in establishing the connection, the network operator enters an INOPERATIVE command to the SSCP, including an identification of the manual access arrangement. (*Note*: The ABANDON CONNECT OUT (ABCONNOUT) command, issued later, directs the PU to terminate an outbound switched connection to the specified link station.)

3. Verification

As a third step, the calling station then solicits station identification from the addressed entering station, and, if appropriate, also provides calling station identification. The Exchange Station Identification (XID) link-level command of SDLC is used for this purpose (see Section 11.5.4.). The station ID contains a unique box identification and information that indirectly identifies the SNA transmission facilities (such as FID type) in the node.

The parameters accompanying the link response to the XID are a station ID, which includes three types of information:

- It identifies (with eight bits) the type of node (for example, whether it is a cluster controller, a terminal node, or a communications controller).

- It identifies (with twelve bits) the subclassifications of function. For example, if it is a cluster controller, it can be identified as a banking system node, or an in-store controller type, or a general-purpose cluster controller.

- It contains (in 20 bits) a unique binary number that is associated with the entering station.

Upon receipt of the link response to the XID from the entering station, the calling PU will notify the SSCP that a physical connection with a station has been established on the indicated link, and will request a CONTACT of that station. This request is done via the REQUEST CONTACT (REQCONT) command. *Both the link network address and the entering station ID are sent as parameters with this request.*

4. NAU activation

The fourth stage is to contact the entering station and activate the physical unit and logical units there. Prior to attempting to contact the newly dialed entering station, the SSCP will first *set up necessary tables, via the PU of the SAF node, that are needed for data link control, path control, or boundary functions* in the SAF node. Each attaching network component, such as NAUs, links, and link stations, must have its pertinent data sent to the PU of the SAF node. This is achieved by sending one or more SET CONTROL VECTOR commands from the SSCP configuration services to that PU.

It may not be necessary for the SSCP to explicitly assign a network address for the attaching physical unit. When the network configuration involves a one-to-one relationship between the link (really the dial port) and the entering station, the physical unit address can be one greater than the link network address, by convention.

If the entering node may connect to different communications controllers, then the attaching LUs get different network addresses, depending on the COMC used.

In this dial-out example, ASSIGN NETWORK ADDRESS and SET CONTROL VECTOR commands must be sent to the PU in the SAF mode to provide (1) network addresses for the LUs in the entering node, and (2) control vectors for the link station of the entering node and the boundary function capability for the LUs in the entering node.

The ASSIGN NETWORK ADDRESS (ANA) command is a configuration-services RU sent via the PU in order to update the path control routing tables for BF.PC. The RU contains fields for (1) each destination LU, and (2) the address of the PU for the adjacent node, which represents the cluster to which these LUs belong. This information, in combination with the control vector information, permits a correlation of each destination LU with the next link and station addresses on the route to the destination.

The SET CONTROL VECTOR (SETCV) RU is sent from the SSCP configuration services to a PU in order to update node control tables. It can contain control information for such network components as NAUs, boundary functions, links, and link stations. Different control vector formats have been defined, depending on the nature of the network component being described (see Appendix C for details).

- If the component being described is an entering link station, the control vector would include (1) the maximum segment length for that station, (2) link-error recovery control information, and (3) the link station address and the network address of the physical unit at that station.

- If the component being described is a boundary function for an NAU, then the control vector would include (1) pacing information, (2) the local transform of the network address, and (3) the network address itself.

- If routing to a subarea were involved, then the control vector would include (1) that subarea address, (2) the link station address, and (3) the network address of the link that is to support the path to the next node enroute to the subarea.

In our example, the remaining sequence is in four stages, as shown in parts 4a, 4b, 4c, and 4d of Fig. 12.12 and described below.

4a. Station data

The SSCP sends to the SAF node the control vector for the entering link station.

4b. CONTACT and ACTIVATE PU

The SSCP tells the PU in the SAF node to CONTACT the entering station. This results in the sending of the SDLC link-level Set Normal Response Mode (SNRM) command to the entering station.

If we assume in this case that the entering node is already loaded, this fact is confirmed by the return of an NSA (Nonsequenced Acknowledgment) command. Upon receipt of the NSA, the SAF PU confirms the satisfactory probe by sending a CONTACTED command back to the SSCP.

With a satisfactory contact, the SSCP can then send an ACTIVATE PHYSICAL UNIT (ACTPU) command directly to the attaching PU. A positive response to the ACTPU will include an eight-character EBCDIC symbolic name of the load module currently operating in the node. This serves to update the SSCP's information on the capability of the node.

4c. Addresses and data for boundary function

The SSCP then sends to the SAF node (1) the network addresses for the attaching LUs via ASSIGN NETWORK ADDRESS commands, and (2) one control vector for the boundary function for each attaching LU. (These SET CONTROL VECTOR commands carry pacing information and the local address of the LU.)

The LU address will contain the subarea of the COMC into which it has dialed. All intermediate routing for that LU will be based only on that subarea address. Recall that the entering station ID from the link-level Exchange Station Identification (XID) command is included as a parameter of the REQUEST CONTACT command, which is sent from the PU of the SAF node to the SSCP. The SSCP can therefore correlate this station ID with information obtained at system generation time to determine the number of LUs in the entering node and their characteristics.

4d. ACTIVATE LU

The SSCP can then send the ACTIVATE LOGICAL UNIT (ACTLU) command directly to the LU in the entering node. As in the case of the ACTIVATE PU command, the ACTIVATE LU is handled in the entering node by its common session control function, which arranges for the activation of the appropriate transmission control element and half-session. The positive response from the session control of the newly established half-session then completes the procedure for "varying on" the logical unit.

12.5.4 Abnormal Conditions

Procedures must also be established for a variety of anticipated abnormal conditions. Among these are the following examples.

1. An incoming call is ringing at the time when the CONNECT OUT is received for that same link: The reasonable procedure is for the concerned physical unit to send a negative response to CONNECT OUT, indicating that the resource is not available. The ring is then accepted, and the call proceeds.

2. An incoming call arrives on the same link that has just been enabled by a CONNECT OUT command: A reasonable procedure would be to provide a positive response to the CONNECT OUT command rather than a RING on the link, and proceed with the dial-out.

3. Invalid ID of the entering node is detected by the SSCP: A reasonable procedure would be for the SSCP to issue a disconnect command, which places the receiving secondary station effectively off-line.

12.5.5 Dial-in Sequence

Dial-in is very similar to the dial-out procedure described above. The fourth stage of the dial-in sequence is identical to that shown in parts 4a, 4b, 4c, and 4d of Fig. 12.12. There are small changes in the first three stages for the dial-in case. The SSCP will send an ACTIVATE CONNECT IN (ACTCONNIN) command (instead of the CONNECT OUT command shown in Fig. 12.12). The ACTCONNIN command is received from the SSCP configuration services by the PU in the SAF node. The command contains the link network address and information as to whether the link station is primary or secondary. This information permits the PU services manager to forward the command to the correct DLC. DLC accordingly enables that station to accept an incoming call. (The DEACTIVATE CONNECT IN (DACTCONNIN) resets the CONNECT IN state for the indicated link.)

Subsequently, a remote station dials the telephone number of the port that was activated. The modem then sends a signal to data link control, alerting it to the fact that a station has dialed in. The called station will then send out the nonsequenced command Exchange Station ID (XID), which asks for further information from the entering station. The address field sent along with the XID command contains the broadcast code (all ones) since, at this point, the called station does not know the address of the station that has dialed in. When the secondary station receives the XID command, it will respond with its station address plus the parameters that describe the nature of the secondary station.

The called station may (as an option) send its ID to the calling station when it transmits the original XID command. (The XID is required on the establishment of a connection to switched lines; it is optional in the case of nonswitched lines, where the security problem is not as great.) The remainder of the sequence is as shown in Fig. 12.12.

12.5.6 The Final On-hook Sequence

In order to terminate a connection via the switched network, a series of disabling commands is required, as shown in Fig. 12.13. The disconnection may be requested by either end of the line. When a node is severing a link to the SNA network, its physical unit issues a REQUEST DISCONTACT (REQDISCONT) command to the SSCP. On the other hand, the SSCP may decide to go on-hook (for example, all LU–LU sessions with LUs in the attached node may have been terminated). In either case, the SSCP sends DEACTIVATE LOGICAL UNIT (DACTLU) commands to each of the logical units in the severing node. The FREE NETWORK ADDRESS commands (one per logical unit) are then sent to the physical unit in the SAF node, telling the PU to discard the vectors pertaining to the terminated logical units. Then the physical unit is deactivated in the severing node, and the SSCP tells the physical unit in the SAF node to direct the sending of a link-level command to disconnect the station at the severing node. With this done, the SSCP formalizes the abandonment of the connection with an ABANDON CONNECTION command to the physical unit of the SAF node.

12.6 OTHER PHYSICAL NETWORK-SERVICE RUs

Most of the important NS–RUs have been introduced as part of the preceding discussions and illustrations. There are some others that deserve brief mention to give the reader a further acquaintance with the breadth of network services that is possible. Details of these commands (and those used in the illustrations) are in Appendix C.

DUMP INITIAL/TEXT/FINAL. Three types of command from the SSCP configuration services are used to cause a dump (that is, a transfer of stored information) from a remote node, and a return of this information to configuration services as data on the response. As in the IML series, DUMP INITIAL is sent by the SSCP to a PU in the node adjacent to the one being dumped (because the node being dumped may not be fully operational). We will call this adjacent node the "helper" node. The PU services manager in the helper node directs the primary data link control there to send the SIM link-level command. As before, the SIM

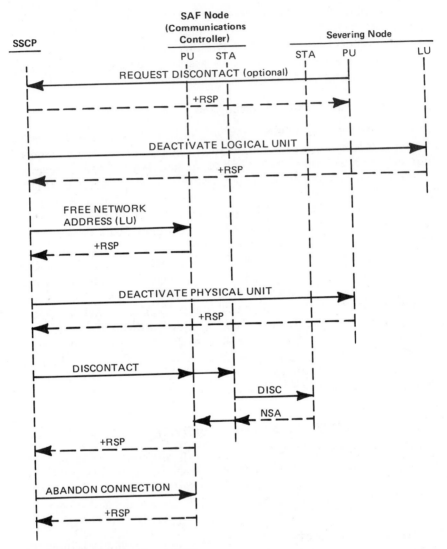

Fig. 12.13 Final *on-hook* sequence.

alerts the secondary DLC (in the node being dumped) to the fact that subsequent information will be control information.

The DUMP INITIAL command is followed by one or more DUMP TEXT commands and then the DUMP FINAL command from the SSCP to the PU in the helper node, thence to the secondary DLC in the node being dumped, which passes these commands on to its node dump routine. (The request codes within the NS–RUs distinguish them from the IML series of commands.)

Each DUMP TEXT command contains a starting address and a length count in order to permit only a portion of the load modules to be dumped. DUMP FINAL terminates the dump sequence, after which the primary DLC station will send a link-level disconnect command to the secondary station. (A CONTACT is required from the SSCP after DUMP FINAL, if the secondary station is to be contacted again.)

Asynchronous link reports.   Special asynchronous events, such as reporting an outage, may need to be sent from the DLC to the PU services manager, which must be prepared to receive the asynchronous reports. The PU services may then send an INOPERATIVE (INOP) RU to the SSCP specifying (1) the network address of the inoperative link or station, and (2) whether the report concerns (a) loss of contact with a link station, (b) failure of a link, or (c) failure to establish connection with a switched link.

Diagnose link/station.   Some PU services managers are able to direct a DLC to execute a predefined test with specified parameters. This might be in accordance with an EXECUTE TEST NS–RU which the PU received from the SSCP maintenance services. The types of test are not currently part of the architecture, and may be product-specific. The test, for example, might involve only DLC station operation, or it might include link-level activity and remote station operation. Depending on implementation, test results could be returned via the PU to the SSCP maintenance services upon completion of the test.

Start/stop line traces.   Similarly, some PU services managers can direct a DLC to start and stop a predefined line trace function. This might be in accordance with ACTIVATE/DEACTIVATE TRACE NS–RUs which the PU received from the SSCP maintenance services. Predefinition would have to include the types of information to be recorded, the format of the information, and the amount of data to be recorded.

RECORD MAINTENANCE STATISTICS/RECORD TEST DATA. These two RUs have been defined to permit the passing of maintenance statistics and test results from a PU or from an LU to a centralized recording facility at the SSCP. A RECORD TRACE DATA RU returns data collected during a trace of the indicated resource from a PU to the SSCP maintenance services.

ENTERING/EXITING SLOWDOWN. These two commands can be sent by a PU to the SSCP configuration services to advise the SSCP that the sender has entered or exited a state called SLOWDOWN. This state is generally associated with buffer depletion in the sender's node. It may require that the SSCP take some steps to get the traffic through the unit temporarily reduced or suspended until the state is exited. The PU services must be made aware of the buffer depletion state (for example, by path control and/or transmission control) via a private (product-unique) means.

LOST SUBAREA (LSA). This RU is used to provide notification, from one PU to another, that a malfunction has occurred and the path to a subarea has been broken. This command assumes greater importance in multidomain networks; its operation is discussed in detail in Section 15.10.1.

12.7 LOG-ON SEQUENCE

12.7.1 Introduction

So the system is up and running; now some useful work can be done if we set up an LU–LU session. Let us consider now what happens when an operator approaches a terminal attached to the cluster controller and wishes to log-on to (i.e., establish a session with) an application program (which we will call APL) in the host. In such a process, the operator commands and some of the node facilities may be unique to that product. At some point, however, *the conversion is made to the defined SNA RU formats, and the communication between NAUs proceeds according to the architecture.* Assume, for example, that the cluster controller employs a local loop for communication between the cluster controller and multiple devices. When the operator turns power on to his or her terminal, that terminal may begin searching for a Nonsequenced Poll (NSP) and then for a go-ahead signal on the loop (see Section 11.5.7). Once the go-ahead signal is received by that terminal, it will create a frame and send in a Disconnected Mode (DM) response. In reply, the control code of the cluster controller will direct that a Set Normal Response Mode (SNRM) command be sent to that device, which should respond with the Nonsequenced Acknowledgment (NSA) link response. At the same time, an element of the application subsystem is assigned (by the cluster's control code) to talk with the device that is requesting to be on-line. Other products will have different, but somewhat equivalent procedures.

The operator provides his or her password and account number, and *requests the application subsystem to activate a particular application program for execution in the cluster controller.* A dialogue then can proceed between the newly activated cluster application program and the attached device. Let us follow the action in Fig. 12.14 in three stages. The circled numbers in Fig. 12.14 correspond to the following numbered steps. (There is a lot of detail in the following discussion, but the reader is encouraged to plow through it since it serves as an excellent summary and review of much that went before.)

12.7.2 Stage One of Log-on

The first stage is to get an INIT SELF command to the SSCP. We will track one possible sequence for that in the first six steps, illustrated in Fig. 12.14, as follows.

1. *Log-on request.* The operator wishes to log-on to an application program (APL) in the host. To do this, the operator enters the log-on command (unique to the cluster controller product) to the cluster application program. To fulfill this request, the cluster application program must then attach one of the logical units that had previously been activated within that cluster controller. This is done via the services of the cluster's control code.

2. *Cluster application opens.* Each product may also have its own macros that an application program can use to request a session. Let us call this OPEN SESSION. The OPEN SESSION command is issued by the cluster application program to ask for a session with APL in the host.

3. *INIT SELF to COMC.* The OPEN SESSION command is handled by the logical unit services of the attached logical unit, which builds an INIT SELF command. At this point, the SNA commands and protocols begin to be used. The RH and the TH are added by the transmission control and path control elements and the request is placed on a queue available to the secondary station on the link between the cluster controller and the remote COMC. The short-form origin address field (OAF') of the TH contains the local address for the LU that was assigned. The destination address field (DAF') in the TH is the short-form address for the SSCP, which had been conveyed to the cluster controller at the time when the logical unit was activated (that is, at the time when a session was first established between the SSCP and this LU).

When the remote COMC sends a Receive Ready (RR) command to the cluster controller with the poll bit on, the secondary station will reply with a frame containing the INIT SELF command and an FID-2 transmission header. The link header will contain the secondary station address.

4. *Boundary function.* The information field of the frame is passed to the path control element (PC) and then to the boundary function in the

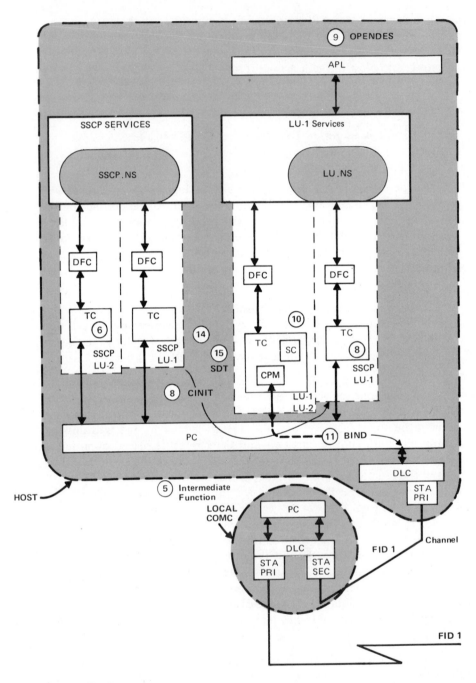

Fig. 12.14 The log-on sequence.

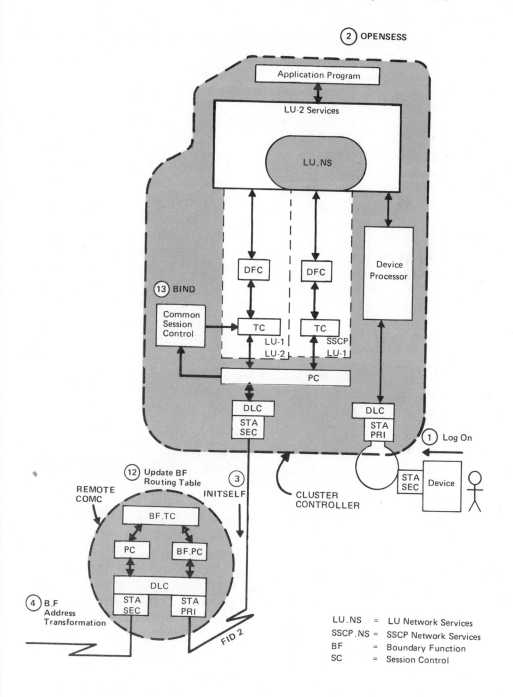

LU.NS = LU Network Services
SSCP.NS = SSCP Network Services
BF = Boundary Function
SC = Session Control

remote COMC, where the address transformations are made to permit further transmission as a FID-1 request. (If the origin node were a terminal node, rather than a cluster controller, the BF.TC would have to provide the contents of the sequence number field in the TH at this point. A BF.TC would also be involved if two-stage inbound pacing were used.) That request is then made available on a path control queue to the data link control element (DLC) in the remote COMC. The frame is transmitted on the link between the remote and local COMCs when a Receive Ready, with the poll bit equal to 1, is received by the secondary link station.

5. *Intermediate function.* The local COMC's path control element examines the TH, determines that the request is not destined for its subarea, and therefore performs only the intermediate function of routing it onward to the host. The local COMC operates on the host channel by sending an Attention command to the host, which responds with a Read command. By this mechanism, the request is obtained by the data link control in the host, which passes it to the host's path control element.

6. *To the SSCP.* The path control element in the host examines the TH, and (based on the OAF/DAF there) passes the request to the particular transmission control element (TCE) for the session between the SSCP and the LU in the cluster controller. The transmission control element routes the request to the session services, a part of the network services in the SSCP.

12.7.3 Stage Two of Log-on

The second stage of the log-on process occurs when the SSCP does its work, gets the primary half of the session set up in an LU in the host, and gets a BIND command sent from that half-session. We will track that process in the next four steps (7 through 10) in Fig. 12.14, as follows.

7. *SSCP network services.* The SSCP determines whether the initiating logical unit has the appropriate authority and whether the requested APL application is up and running. If both of these are OK, the SSCP sends a positive response to the initiating logical unit. The SSCP, in addition, converts the names of APL and the initiating logical unit into network addresses, and puts together appropriate BIND parameters for a session between these two logical units.

8. *To APL's LUS.* The SSCP then sends a CONTROL INITIATE (CINIT) command to the LU network services in the LU services for APL. The SSCP does this by using the session between the SSCP and the

LU for APL. Again, the path control element, using the OAF/DAF, routes the command to the correct transmission control element.

9. *Check with APL.* The LUS of APL will probably first determine whether or not the APL application program is willing to accept a new session. LUS does this by driving a log-on exit to notify APL of the session request. Then the LU services will send a positive response back to the SSCP, indicating its receipt of CINIT. If APL is willing to have another session, it so indicates (by an OPEN DESTINATION command, if VTAM is being used).

10. *New half-session.* With its approval from the APL application, the LU services will arrange for the activation of a transmission control element for the desired LU–LU session; LUS will then work with the session control in that new TC element to send the BIND command to the LU in the cluster controller.

12.7.4 Stage Three of Log-on

The third stage and the completion of the log-on process is to get the BIND command to the cluster controller, to get the second half of the session set up there, and then to start data traffic. We will track that part of the process in the next five steps (11 through 15) in Fig. 12.14, as follows.

11. *BIND to COMC.* The request containing the BIND command passes via the local COMC to the remote COMC, which sees its own subarea in the TH and so passes the request to the TC boundary function.

12. *More boundary function.* The connection point manager in the BF.TC examines the RH, sees that this RU is destined for session control (as are all BIND commands), and so routes the request to the session control portion of BF.TC. Session control (BF.SC) checks that a session does exist between the SSCP and the destination LU, and then assists in the setup of the new session's boundary function by establishing session-control tables for it.

The request is then sent back to BF.CPMGR. Since the BIND command is expedited, it is not queued to wait until a pacing indicator is received; the request, instead, is sent directly to the boundary function of path control (BF.PC). The BF.PC then updates its routing table to include the APL network address and an arbitrary short form (OAF'), along with the network address and the local address for the cluster LU, for this new session. BF.PC then sends the request, now having a FID-2 TH, to the cluster controller.

13. *Common session control.* Since no session with APL yet exists, the BIND command is handled by the common session control for the cluster controller, which arranges for the activation of the new half-session in the cluster controller.

14. *Confirmation.* A positive response to the BIND request is then returned all the way back to the session control for APL, which advises its LUS, which, in turn, advises the SSCP that this session has been started.

15. *SDT.* When the application, APL, is ready, it can advise its session control to issue the START DATA TRAFFIC (SDT) command, which formally opens the flow of requests and responses between the two logical units.

12.8 LOGGING OFF

Some time later, when the operator has completed the interaction with the host APL program, he or she issues a log-off command (that may be unique to the cluster product). This is handled by the cluster application program, which then may follow one of two courses, as follows:

1. The application program may direct its DFC to issue a REQUEST SHUTDOWN command to the primary LU in the host. The primary half-session is then required to send the CLEAR and UNBIND commands.

2. Alternatively, the cluster application could have issued a product-unique command that directs its LUS to terminate the session. The cluster LUS would translate this to an SNA TERMINATE SELF command, which it would send to the SSCP. Then the SSCP would forward a CTERM to APL's LUS, which would advise APL of the request to terminate via an application exit. The CLEAR and UNBIND sequence would then follow as before.

3. In either case, the positive response to the UNBIND is noted in the remote-COMC boundary function, which then removes this session from its tables. After being advised (by the primary half-session) of a positive response to the UNBIND, the primary LUS will send a SESSION ENDED command to the SSCP.

12.9 EXAMPLE OF LU SERVICES IN OPERATION

In Chapter 7, the role of the NAU services was described in general terms. The NAU services manager (within NAU services) exchanges data and control information with the end-user and with components of the SNA network. Now that we have also reviewed the functions of the inner layers of the SNA network (particularly the DFC and TC layers), the following discussion will provide a more specific illustration of the operation of LU services.

In general, the LU services will

1. Provide network services for session establishment and termination, working in collaboration with the SSCP. This includes monitoring these sequences for proper adherence to the protocols.

2. Set up and take down the FI.FMD services, data flow control, and transmission control functions for each session supported by the LU.

3. Manage the communication between sessions at that LU, particularly between the LU–SSCP session and the LU–LU sessions.

4. Provide a single interface to the end-user, for exchanging control information as well as data. The controls may include commands for session establishment or termination, and also commands pertaining to the operation of presentation services, data flow control, and transmission control. With regard to these controls for lower layers, however, LU services may be essentially transparent, serving only to pass the commands via a common interface to the end-user. The particular lower-level control commands that may appear at the boundary between the end-user and LU services depend on the subsets of function that are chosen at BIND time for each session and on the optional functions (such as recovery aids) that may be implemented within the LU.

There is a wide range of SNA options in the various layers, hence a wide range of possible inputs to an NAU services layer. Our purpose is not to provide an all-inclusive discussion; probably no example of NAU services would ever have to accommodate all possible SNA options. It is, however, instructive to consider the specific roles of NAU services for at least one possible situation, since that will serve to review network operations as well as to illustrate one possible set of end-user interactions. This section then provides only one example of simple LU services. The one chosen can have a session characterized by

- FM profile 3: CANCEL, SIGNAL, LUSTAT, CHASE, SHUTD, SHUTC, RSHUTD, BID, and RTR are allowed; the send/receive mode is HDX-FF.

- TS profile 2: CLEAR is required; SDT, RQR, and STSN are not allowed.

In the following discussion, we will also assume (for generality) that the LU of the example can support either primary or secondary half-sessions (for LU–LU sessions). Illustrative inputs to and actions taken by this particular example of LU services are then as follows.

Inputs pertaining to session establishment or termination

1. ▪ Input: The end-user requests communication to a specified destination.
   ▪ Action: LUS sends INITIATE SELF command, or an unformatted equivalent, to the SSCP.

2. Input: CONTROL INITIATE command from the SSCP (when the LU is to support a primary half-session).
   ▪ Action: LUS passes the parameters in CONTROL INITIATE to the end-user.
   > If the end-user indicates that the parameters are satisfactory, then LUS sends a positive response to the SSCP, sets up the presentation services, data flow control, and transmission control for the half-session, and directs session control to send a BIND command to the destination LU.
   > If the end-user indicates that the parameters are unsatisfactory, then LUS sends a negative response to the SSCP.

3. ▪ Input: A BIND request (when the LU is to support a secondary half-session).
   ▪ Action: LUS will pass some of the BIND parameters to the end-user.
   > Then if the end-user indicates that BIND parameters are unacceptable, LUS will send a negative response.
   > Otherwise, LUS will set up the half-session and advise session control (of the appropriate half-session) to send a positive response.

4. ▪ Input: A positive response to a BIND (received via an attached primary half-session).
   ▪ Action: LUS indicates "session active" to the end-user; then LUS sends SESSION STARTED to the SSCP.

5. ▪ Input: A negative response to BIND and an indication from session control (in the TCE) that the session is reset.
   ▪ Action
   > If certain codes are indicated in sense bytes, then LUS so indicates to the end-user.

⟩ Otherwise, LUS terminates communications and sends BIND FAILURE to the SSCP.

6. ▪ Input: The end-user requests "shutdown" (when LU supports the primary half-session).

   ▪ Action: LUS will direct the DFC to send SHUTDOWN.

7. ▪ Input: SHUTDOWN COMPLETE (from the DFC of an attached primary half-session).

   ▪ Action: LUS will pass parameters to the end-user. If the end-user then calls for an unbind, LUS will direct session control to send CLEAR and UNBIND.

8. ▪ Input: The end-user requests termination of the session.

   ▪ Action: LUS will send TERMINATE SELF to the SSCP.

9. ▪ Input: CONTROL TERMINATE (from the SSCP when LU is supporting the primary half-session).

   ▪ Action: LUS will indicate "end of session" to the end-user and direct session control to send CLEAR and UNBIND.

10. ▪ Input: UNBIND.

   ▪ Action: LUS will direct session control to send a positive response, indicate "unbind" to the end-user, and terminate communication.

11. ▪ Input: A positive response to UNBIND (received via an attached primary half-session).

   ▪ Action: LUS will send SESSION ENDED to the SSCP.

Inputs pertaining to controls used during an LU–LU session

1. ▪ Input: Change-direction indicator (received via DFC).

   ▪ Action: LUS will indicate "send mode" to end-user.

2. ▪ Input: SIGNAL (request to send) (received via DFC).

   ▪ Action: LUS will pass contents to the end-user.

3. ▪ Input: CANCEL (received via DFC).

   ▪ Action: Indicate "cancel" to the end-user.

4. ▪ Input: LUSTAT (received via DFC).

   ▪ Action: LUS will indicate "LU status" and pass the status code to the end-user.

5. ▪ Input: The end-user requests "change direction."

   ▪ Action: LUS directs the DFC to send SIGNAL (request to send).

6. ■ Input: An indication that an error was detected in data being sent, or the end-user requests "cancel."

   ■ Action: LUS will direct DFC to send CANCEL (which will be done if DFC is in the "In-chain" state).

12.10 HEADER ASSEMBLY AND DISASSEMBLY

Finally, in this series of multilayer overviews, we should have a look, in Figs. 12.15 through 12.18, at the anatomy of header production—that is, at how the parts of requests and responses, particularly the ingredients of their RH and TH, are collected from and/or distributed to various layers. At the same time, we can then see what information the boundaries between layers may contain.

The packaging and analysis of the SNA headers take place in four different layers:

1. FMH (or NS header) in NAU services.

2. RH in transmission control.

3. TH in path control.

4. LH and LT in data link control.

Request/response units (RUs) can be generated at the three levels of FI.FMD, data flow control, and transmission control. The NAU services manager may communicate with all three of these RU-generating layers, and provides the common interface to the end-user.

The notation used in Figs. 12.15–12.18 is consistent with that used in the RH and TH definitions in Appendix A. In particular, note the following:

BBI, EBI	= begin- and end-bracket indicators
CDI	= change-direction indicator
BCI, ECI	= begin- and end-chaining indicators
DFC	= data flow control
DR1, DR2, ERI	= response forms (definite or exception)
EFI	= expedited-flow indicator
FI	= format indicator
NC	= network control
PC	= path control
PS	= presentation services
R/R	= request or response indicator
RTI	= response-type indicator (positive or negative)
RU	= request/response unit

RUC	= RU category (FI.FMD, DFC, SC, or NC)
SC	= session control
SDI	= sense-data indicator
SID	= session identifier
SNF	= sequence number field
{RU}	= information pertaining to the RU

Some observations on Figs. 12.15 through 12.18 follow.

From the viewpoint of the end-user, there are three paths for request and response information, those to or from

1. FI.FMD services (concerning FMD–RUs),
2. Data flow control (concerning DFC–RUs), and
3. Transmission control (concerning TC–RUs).

The first path is for normal message flow; the second and third paths are for (DFC and TC) control commands, and are indicated by dashed lines in the figures.

All three of these paths may terminate at NAU services. For sessions involving network services (for example, SSCP–LU, SSCP–PU, SSCP–SSCP sessions), the RH header content is simplified (i.e., never any chains or brackets) and the RUs are processed by the NAU services layer (see the discussion of network services in Section 7.3). In LU–LU sessions, the FMD–RUs may be interpreted by FI.FMD services (see the discussion of presentation services in Section 7.4) within the NAU services layer. For LU–LU sessions, the programs for processing the DFC–RUs and TC–RUs can be implementation dependent and are not currently defined by SNA. The DFC and TC layers have defined functions to perform in connection with these control commands; however, invoking the command and guiding the larger procedure is done by message handlers or exits that can often be considered to be in the NAU services layer (see Section 7.2.2).

In all three paths, the information is in three parts: (1) TH information, (2) RH information, and (3) RU information.

The circles around RH (in TC) and around TH (in PC) signify only that these headers are assembled or disassembled at those locations. Note, however, that the information in these headers often comes from or is distributed to other locations. The circle around SNF (in TC) signifies that the sequence number field is generated there; that information then flows in two directions, as indicated.

The processes of *sending requests and responses* are shown in Figs. 12.15 and 12.17. The information needed for the RH comes mostly from

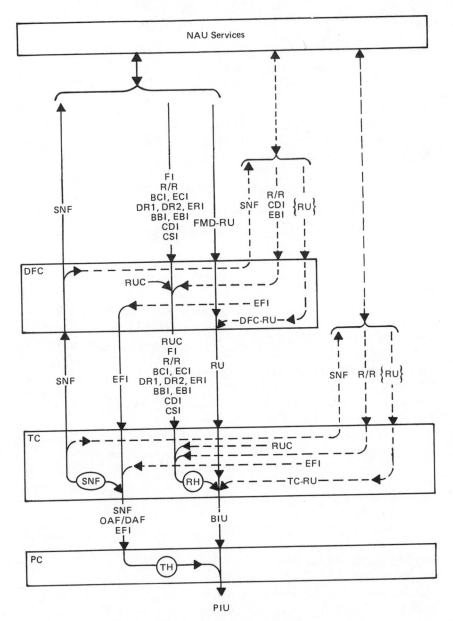

Fig. 12.15 Assembly of headers when sending requests.

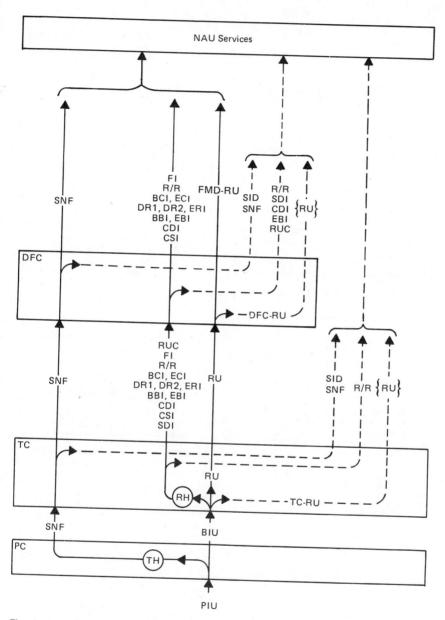

Fig. 12.16 Distribution of header information when receiving requests.

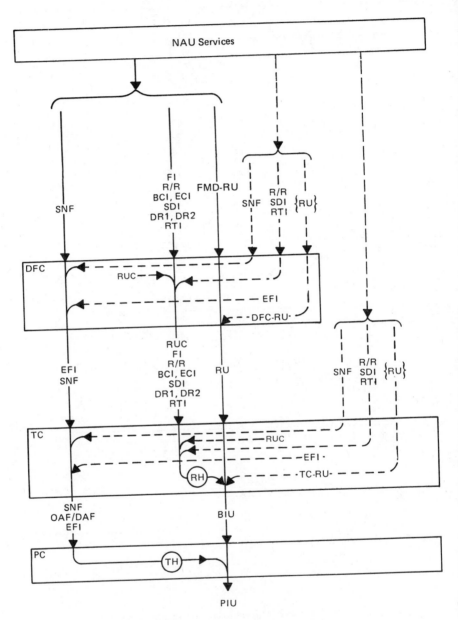

Fig. 12.17 Assembly of headers when sending responses.

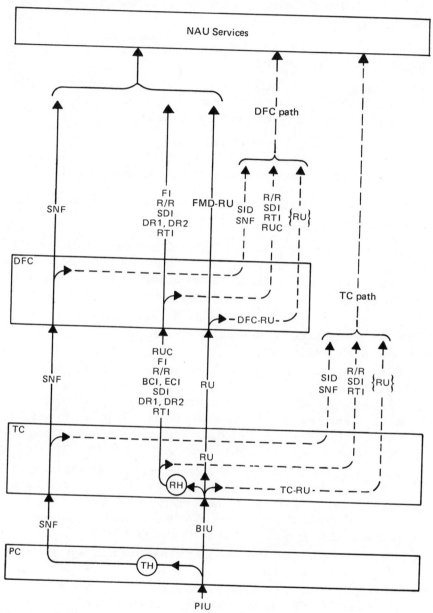

Fig. 12.18 Distribution of header information when receiving responses.

NAU services or the end-user, via one of the three request/response paths. Note also that

1. The RU category (RUC), to indicate FI.FMD, DFC, SC, or NC, is added by DFC or TC, as appropriate.

2. The change-direction indicator (CDI) can be provided for normal-flow requests that flow from NAU services. The CDI is not used for expedited flows (all transmission control RUs are expedited).

3. Bracket information can be provided on the normal flow to or from NAU services. The end-bracket (EB) information can also be in the DFC flow as a cleanup operation with some DFC commands (like CLEAR).

4. The DFC and TC elements provide the expedited-flow indicator (EFI) when appropriate.

5. The sequence number field (SNF) for all sent requests is returned from the TC element to higher levels. The sequence number field (SNF) of all received requests is also forwarded to higher levels so that they can provide the SNF if any subsequent responses are sent.

6. The origin address field (OAF) and the destination address field (DAF) are implicit to that session and are provided to path control by the transmission control element.

Receiving requests and responses are shown in Figs. 12.16 and 12.18. All or parts of the TH, RH, and RU information are routed to one of the three request/response paths (concerning FMD–RUs, DFC–RUs, or TC–RUs). Within transmission control, the flow is either to session control (SC) or to network control (NC). All of this routing is in accordance with the settings of the RU category bits in the RH. Note that

1. The sense-data-included (SDI) indicator and the associated sense data can be included in the FMD–RU flow on the occasion of a negative response. The SDI also occurs in exception requests (EXRs) when an error in a request is detected prior to its destination. In this case, the SDI and sense data are sent by DFC to higher levels.

2. The sequence number fields for all received requests and responses are passed to higher levels.

3. NAU services may handle more than one session. If that is the case, the session ID (SID) must accompany each received RU.

4. Though not illustrated, the flow to and from the end-user may be subdivided into separate flows for each component, if multiple end-user components are identified in the FM header.

This look at the anatomy of header production concludes our discussion of "putting it all together." It is hoped that this series of somewhat detailed compositions (the node diagrams, the sequences for set-up, dial, and log-on, the NAU-services example, and the RH/TH flow diagrams) will also serve as reference and summary material.

12.11 EXERCISES

12.1 Which of the following statements are true?

a) The CONTACT command can be used to get a remote link station set to the normal response mode.

b) The PU services act to interpret requests from data link control and to forward corresponding SNA commands to the network services in the SSCP.

c) The Set Initialization Mode command is sent directly from one PUS to another PUS.

d) The BIND command must specify whether a switched or nonswitched link will be used for that session.

e) A dial-in port must be enabled (by an ACTIVATE CONNECT IN command) before it will accept a dial-in.

f) The end-user and the logical unit need have no knowledge of the telephone number or any other parameters of a dial connection.

g) The network address for any attaching physical unit (in a dial-in) can be related to the link address associated with the dial-in port.

h) In dial-out or dial-in, the SSCP can send data that is needed by path control in a node via the PU of that node.

12.2 Which of the following are true?

a) In some implementations, an operator at a terminal attached to a cluster controller must first "connect" to the cluster controller before attempting to log-on to a host.

b) The cluster controller knows the network address of the SSCP even before the SSCP–LU session is established.

c) The session-control boundary function will pass a CINIT on to a cluster controller even if BF.SC has no record of an SSCP–LU session with the destination LU.

d) A BIND command will not be sent to a cluster controller until the boundary function receives a pacing indicator from the cluster.

e) A log-off command from an operator may be translated into a REQUEST SHUTDOWN to the primary LU or a TERMINATE SELF to the SSCP.

12.3 Which of the following statements are true?

a) The interface between the end-user and the NAU services can contain commands pertaining to network services, data flow control, and transmission control, as well as presentation services data.

b) When a "change direction" is received from the opposite half-session, the receiving DFC must go to the send state, but the end-user need not be advised.

c) The NAU services need and receive exactly the same amount of information from the RH of every incoming request.

d) The NAU services may have to forward (to lower levels) the information for the sequence number field in responses.

13
Finite
State
Architecture

13.1 INTRODUCTION*

As is evident from the foregoing discussion, the personality of any network architecture is determined by the protocols used to communicate at each of the layers. These protocols can be used with confidence, however, only if they are unambiguous and if they are complete. A protocol that permits uncertainty regarding the consequences of certain events or combinations of events leads to errors and premature session terminations.

Previous chapters have illustrated the architecture by means of sequences of commands. These are educational. Relying solely on such sequences can, however, be dangerous, because there is a very large number of possible sequences; thus, a definition by sequences tends to be incomplete.

An alternative approach (used in product design) is to express the architecture in terms of

1. Discrete state machines (which will usually be finite state machines, or FSMs), showing changes in state and outputs occurring on the occasion of input signals.

---

*The material in this chapter stems from the work of T. F. Piatkowski, which led to the precise description of SNA in terms of finite state machines. Acknowledgment is also given to J. R. Babb, J. C. Broughton, T. B. McNeill, G. Plotsky, G. D. Schultz, K. Soule, and R. J. Sundstrom for the development of particular FSMs reflected in this chapter.

2. The validity checks that are made when an input signal is received. These checks concern formats of the input and the presence of valid states in the concerned FSMs.

FSMs and associated validity checks can exist at all layers of the architecture.

This alternative, based on the need for a formal, unambiguous, and complete definition of communication protocols, has proven to be quite successful, and has led to the development of two complementary techniques [13.1–13.4].

1. *The finite state machine (FSM):* A logical device possessing a finite number of states (memory) and a simple set of rules, whereby the response (state transitions and output sequences) of the machine to input sequences is well defined.
2. *The block diagram:* A flow chart in which the blocks represent finite state machines and surrounding functions, such as validity checking and branching or routing.

The FSM, in practice, is a repetition of a very simple concept. It has a current state, an input and perhaps an output, and a next state. To illustrate, an FSM might have a total of three states: (1) an active state, (2) a reset state, and (3) a pending state (awaiting some confirmation). An activate command might be intended to change the state from reset to active; a deactivate command might cause the reverse; and the pending state might be an interim state until some condition is fulfilled (such as receiving a positive response) after which one of the other states would be entered. The pending state may also be used while waiting for the completion of an action (for example, the completion of a dial sequence). Pending states permit one to "back out" of a procedure before the procedure is completed, if an interim check is negative.

The purpose of this chapter is to

1. Introduce the concept of the finite state machine and to illustrate the power of the FSM in protocol definition, and
2. Use this tool in further illustrations of how the various protocols combine in total system operation.

It is not our purpose to give a definition of SNA in terms of FSMs. This becomes highly voluminous and is well beyond the objectives of this text. Detailed FSM-type definitions for SNA are available in the *SNA Format and Protocol Reference Manual* [13.2].

13.2 GRAPHICAL REPRESENTATION OF FSMs

Various techniques have been used to portray states of the FSM, the transitions between states, and the input and output signals that accompany a transition. Matrices and several forms of node graphs are commonly employed [13.1, 13.3]. One form uses circles for states and connects the circles by arrows that represent state transitions. We will use the simple graph technique illustrated in Fig. 13.1. In this diagram, states are represented by vertical lines, and transitions between states by horizontal arrows. The arrows have the following attributes:

1. The input signal causing the transition appears directly above the transition arrow.

2. The output signal that accompanies the transition appears directly below the arrow.

3. An input (and its associated output) that does not cause a state transition is shown with a returning loop.

4. The head of the arrow terminates at the new state; arrows may cross over state lines without implying that they are passing through that state.

It is assumed that a state transition takes place instantly upon the arrival of an input, and that the state remains unchanged until another input arrives. It is also assumed that only one input arrives at a time. In practice, it may be necessary sometimes to provide race resolution and possibly queueing in order to approximate these assumptions.

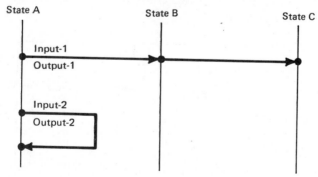

Fig. 13.1 The basic parts of the state diagram.

13.3 LOCATION OF FSMs WITHIN EACH LAYER

FSMs can be located in any layer of the SNA network. To understand the place of the FSMs in each layer, we must examine the structure of the layer itself. Figure 13.2 illustrates the fact that each layer can have two distinct elements, one called the primary and one called the secondary. Each element has two components, one devoted to sending requests and responses and one devoted to receiving requests and responses. Primary and secondary halves of every layer can be so organized.

Figure 13.3, then, shows a simplified sketch of the three basic functions in the send and receive portions of a given layer, as follows:

1. *Usage checker:* Checks the message for valid field usage, valid parameter values, and other state-independent factors. If an error is detected, an error message may be generated and either returned to the originator or sent on to the destination.

2. *Router:* Routes valid messages, or portions thereof, to a specific finite state machine (FSM).

3. *FSM:* Checks the validity of the message relative to its current state and changes state when appropriate, reacting with a transformed message or with new outputs when appropriate. If a state-dependent error is detected, an error message may be generated and either returned to the originator or sent on to the destination.

Within a given layer, in a given node, the send and receive FSMs may be coupled (that is, they may exchange signals); they might, in some cases, be so closely coupled as to appear to be a single FSM or a single set of FSMs.

As shown in Fig. 13.4, each protocol involves a dialogue between an FSM in the send portion of an element in one node and another FSM in the receive portion of an element in that same layer in another node.

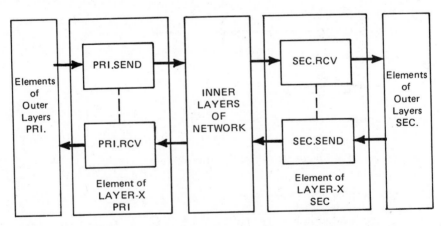

Fig. 13.2 Pairing of primary and secondary elements in a given layer [13.2].

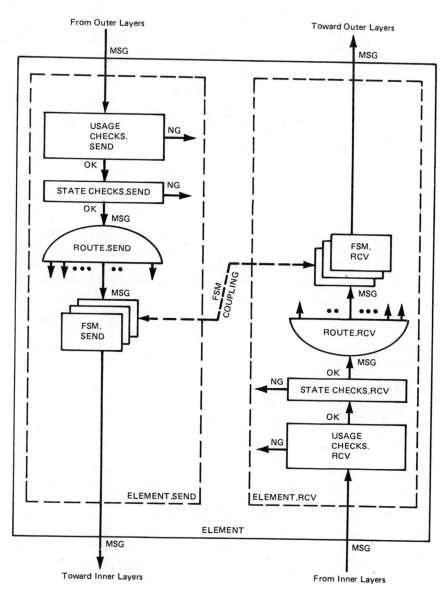

Fig. 13.3   Basic element structure [13.2].

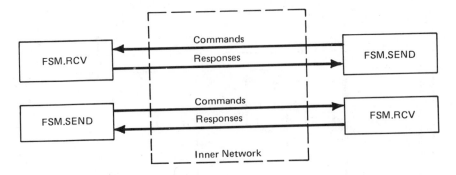

Fig. 13.4   The FSM SEND/RCV pairs [13.2].

Every protocol involves such matched, asymmetric, FSM send/receive pairs.

Some of the key SEND functions, RECEIVE functions, and FSMs in the transmission control and data flow control layers of SNA are shown in Fig. 13.5—the composite of a single node. Note that the CPMGR has a single RCV function, but the DFC element has one RCV function for responses and another for requests. The SEND functions are similarly structured. Thus, some layers find it advantageous to have separately identifiable components for

- Request.RCV
- Response.RCV
- Request.SEND
- Response.SEND

This groups functions in two ways—first those according to send or receive, and then, within each of these, those handling requests and responses.

The function interpreters in the TC and DFC layers (for example, FI.SC or FI.DFC) interpret header information and serve to select a particular FSM or SEND/RCV function within its area. (*The function interpreters in the TC and DFC layers do not interpret the RU.*)

13.4 BASIC FSM PAIRS

Most SNA FSM pairs are variations of three very simple structures. These three types of FSM pairs are shown in Fig. 13.6, and are referred to as one-cycle, two-cycle, and variable-cycle FSM pairs. If one understands these three basic structures, then one can readily use complex FSMs built from multiples of them. Each FSM pair consists of an FSM.SEND in one node and an FSM.RCV in another node.

One-cycle FSMs. These manage one-time actions, such as signaling, setting control vectors, etc. Figure 13.6(a) is an example of a one-cycle send/receive pair. The action is initiated somewhere at the node containing the FSM.SEND. The input causing the action is not shown; it might be the end-user or some layer between the end-user and FSM.SEND. In any case, an input causes the transition of FSM.SEND to the pending state, with the accompanying issuance of an output command (shown as "cmd" below the arrow). (The pending state is a way of remembering, for a time, that some prior event has occurred.) This output command might be a control RU, or it might be expressed by the setting of control bits in one of the headers. That same command then appears as an input to the FSM.RCV (in the other node), which drives the latter FSM into the pending state.

Next, some other input to FSM.RCV will either confirm that the action specified in the command (for example, setting the control vector) has been taken, or indicate that the action cannot be taken. This drives the FSM.RCV from the pending state back to the reset state, with the accompanying output of *a positive or negative response.* That same response then becomes an input to the FSM.SEND, driving it also back to the reset state. *Thus, the one-cycle FSM leaves the reset state and enters a pending state while the action is requested or in process; it returns to the reset state when the action is completed or when the action cannot be completed.*

Two-cycle FSM. This send/receive pair is illustrated in Fig. 13.6(b). The two-cycle moves to an active state in two steps. *The FSM does not enter the active state until after confirmation has been received that the action can or should be completed.* The two-cycle FSMs manage bistable actions such as activating and deactivating PUs, LUs, and links, binding and unbinding sessions, or starting and clearing data traffic. An illustrative sequence (Fig. 13.6b) is as follows:

1. Some action (unspecified) at the send node provides an input to FSM.SEND, driving it to the pending active state and causing the output of the command labeled "cmd (activate)."

2. The same command appears as the input of FSM.RCV, driving it also to the pending active state. This latter transition provides an output to inform some function at the receive node that an action is desired.

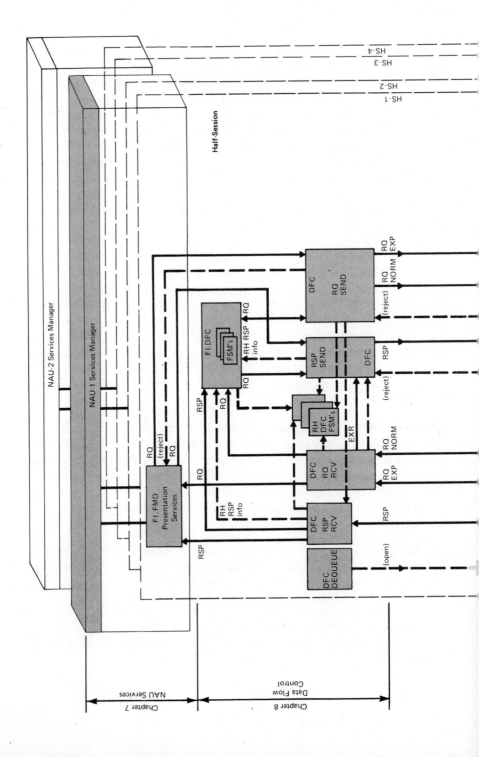

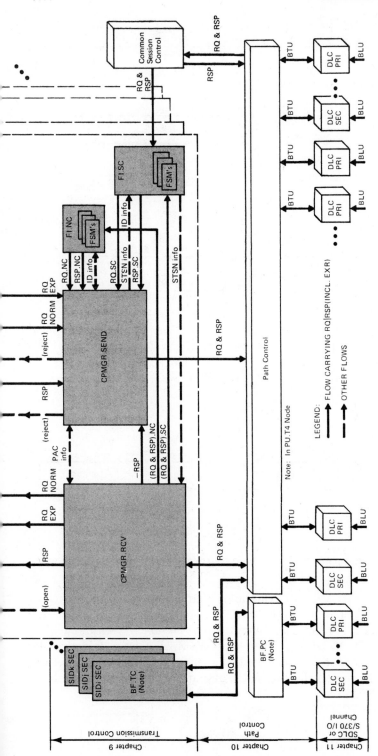

Fig. 13.5 Structural overview of a node with maximum SNA function [13.2]

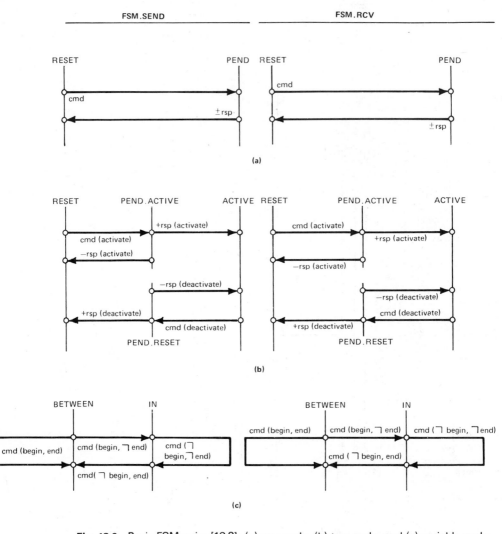

Fig. 13.6 Basic FSM pairs [13.2]: (a) one-cycle, (b) two-cycle, and (c) variable-cycle.

   3. When FSM.RCV gets confirmation that the desired action is complete, that input drives FSM.RCV from the pending state to the active state, causing an output of a *positive response* back to FSM.SEND. If, on the other hand, FSM.RCV were told that the action could not be completed, that input would drive FSM.RCV back to the reset state, causing an output of a *negative response* back to FSM.SEND.

4. The receipt by FSM.SEND of a positive response drives it to the active state. On the other hand, the receipt of a negative response drives it back to the reset state.

A similar two-stage sequence is involved in the reverse process, where a deactivate command drives the FSMs from the active state to the reset state after confirmation is received that the desired action can be completed.

Variable-cycle FSMs.   These FSMs, illustrated in Fig. 13.6(c), control the sending and check the receiving of request/response sequences, such as those occurring in chaining, bracketing, segmenting, initial program loading (IPLing), and dumping.

For example, a user action may call for a chaining of a string of requests. That input to an FSM.SEND causes a transition from the between-chain state to the in-chain state. The message "begin chain and not end of chain" outputs from the FSM.SEND and is packaged as the setting of the BC and EC bits in the RH. That same command then appears as input to an FSM.RCV in the other node, driving it too from the between-chain state to the in-chain state. Note also that some inputs do not result in a state change.

13.5 FSM-NAMING CONVENTIONS AND SYMBOLS

With a very large number of FSMs distributed among all the SNA layers, it becomes necessary to adopt a naming convention that definitely identifies and locates the FSM under discussion. While naming conventions can be cumbersome, it pays to make them complete and definite; otherwise, misunderstandings among designers can be disastrous. The convention adopted by SNA [13.2] is the *qualified name convention* that is illustrated in Fig. 13.7. Each term in the name identifies a further structural subdivision, and terms are separated by periods.

The format frequently used in SNA is

Session ID .PRI or SEC .Specific FSM .Receive or Send

The session ID consists of the pair of network addresses of NAUs that are in session; for example, NAU–X, NAU–Y.

The first two parameters identify a particular half-session. This combination is accordingly called the half-session ID (HSID), and those FSMs that can be assigned to any half-session are prefixed with the generic term HSID. The FSM title then is

HSID .title of the specific FSM .RECEIVE or SEND

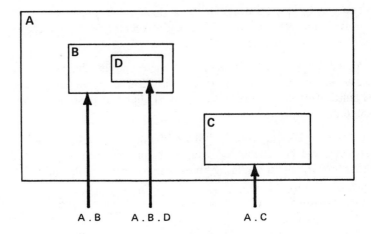

Fig. 13.7 Qualified name convention [13.2].

As an example, a hierarchy of terms, forming a name for the FSM that receives the INITIATE command in the SSCP, would be the following:

- (SSCP,ILU).PRI.—In the primary half of the session between the SSCP and the initiating logical unit.
- INIT(PLU,SLU).—The initiate FSM that is concerned with establishing a session between an addressed PLU and SLU.
- RCV—In the receive portion of the half-session between the SSCP and the ILU.

Thus, the fully qualified name would be

$$(\text{SSCP,ILU}).\text{PRI.INIT (PLU,SLU)}.\text{RCV}$$

A word of caution is needed regarding the use of the terms PLU and SLU. It has been convenient to refer to *the LU that manages a primary half-session* as the PLU (primary LU); similarly, the LU that manages a secondary half-session is often called the SLU. This causes no difficulty, so long as a given LU manages only primary half-sessions or only secondary half-sessions for all of its LU–LU sessions. There often are cases, however, in which an LU manages both primary and secondary half-sessions; thus the PLU and SLU names have meaning only with regard to specific sessions.

The broad arrow is often used for resets from any state; it is even used for resets in cases where only one other state exists.

13.6 ILLUSTRATIVE FSMs

There follow a number of examples of the use of FSMs to define protocols and, at the same time, examples of how the FSMs relate to one another. These serve as exercises to familiarize the reader with the use of FSMs and to clarify some of the concepts of SNA structures and protocols. Though it is somewhat tedious to go through, there seems to be no easier way to become really familiar with the technique of using FSMs and the architecture they represent. Because this technique is felt to be a significant advance in the art of system design, the reader is encouraged to invest the time needed to follow these illustrations.

13.6.1 FSMs for ACTIVATE LU

Our first illustration concerns the operation of the command, ACTIVATE LOGICAL UNIT (ACTLU). Every logical unit in an SNA network must first be activated by the SSCP. Such activation of the logical unit establishes a session between that logical unit and the SSCP. The process of generating and sending an ACTLU command from the SSCP to a logical unit is illustrated in Fig. 13.8.

The dialogue takes place between the half-session (SSCP,LU).PRI and the half-session (SSCP,LU).SEC. *Within each of these half-sessions there is a session control (SC) function in the transmission control element.* A part of each session control function is a set of FSMs, including two that are called SESS.SEND and SESS.RCV. One pair of these FSMs is shown in the upper half of Fig. 13.8. An illustrative sequence of state changes, as a function of time, is shown in the lower half of Fig. 13.8. We will trace this sequence, as follows.

Assume that both FSMs are initially (at time zero) in the reset state. Then

- (t$_1$) The network operator inputs a command to activate the logical unit (or some command that is unique to the product, but is equivalent). This is passed by the SSCP services to session control in the (SSCP,LU).PRI half-session; and this input immediately drives SESS.SEND into the pending active state, generating at the same time the ACTLU command.

- (t$_2$) The ACTLU command passes through the common network and is delivered (via common session control in the destination node) to the session control in the (SSCP,LU).SEC half-session. The ACTLU drives SESS.RCV into the pending active state, generating at the same time an "activate received" message for the end-user of the LU. The reply to this message will signify whether or not the

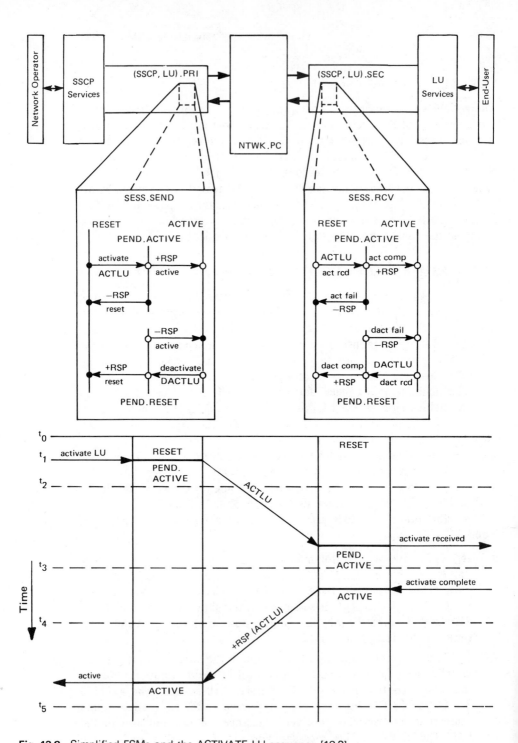

Fig. 13.8 Simplified FSMs and the ACTIVATE LU sequence [13.2].

activation can be completed. Let us assume that the reply from the end-user is affirmative, indicated by the "activate complete" message; this results in the driving of SESS.RCV to the active state and the generating of a positive response to the ACTLU command.

- (t_4+) The positive response to the ACTLU passes back through the common network to SESS.SEND. There the response drives SESS.SEND into the active state, generating at the same time an "active" message back to the network operator.

Thus, each FSM went first to a pending active state. Upon receipt of an OK from the end-user, both FSMs went to the active state.

If, on the other hand, the end-user of the LU had returned an "activate failure" message, this would have driven SESS.RCV back to the reset state, generating at the same time a negative response to the ACTLU. That negative response, in turn, would have driven SESS.SEND back to the reset state.

In a similar fashion, the deactivate process can be seen in the FSM state diagrams. The network operator's DEACTIVATE command drives SESS.SEND from the ACTIVE state to the pending reset state, generating at the same time the DACTLU command. The latter inputs to SESS.RCV. The process parallels that of the ACTLU, above, with the final state depending on the reply from the end-user of the LU.

13.6.2   FSMs for LU–LU Session Activation

This illustration (though a challenge to follow) shows the interaction among FSMs in different sessions that occurs when an LU–LU session is first activated. (Session establishment was discussed without FSMs in Section 9.7.4.) Figure 13.9 presents an overview of the activation sequence. (Readers more interested in LU–LU session operation, rather than its set-up, should proceed to Section 13.6.3.)

Four NAUs can be involved (see Fig. 13.9). In the case shown, the initiating logical unit (ILU) is not one of the two LUs that are to be bound in the session. The ILU requests the SSCP, via an INITIATE (INIT) command, to establish a session between two other LUs, referred to as the primary LU (PLU) and the secondary LU (SLU).

Recall from Section 9.7.4 that *three NS–RUs are involved in establishing a session.* Accordingly, three sets of FSMs are involved in this sequence:

1. INIT.—The FSMs that handle the INITIATE command in the ILU and the SSCP

2. CSESS.—The FSMs that handle the CONTROL INITIATE (CINIT) command in the SSCP and the PLU

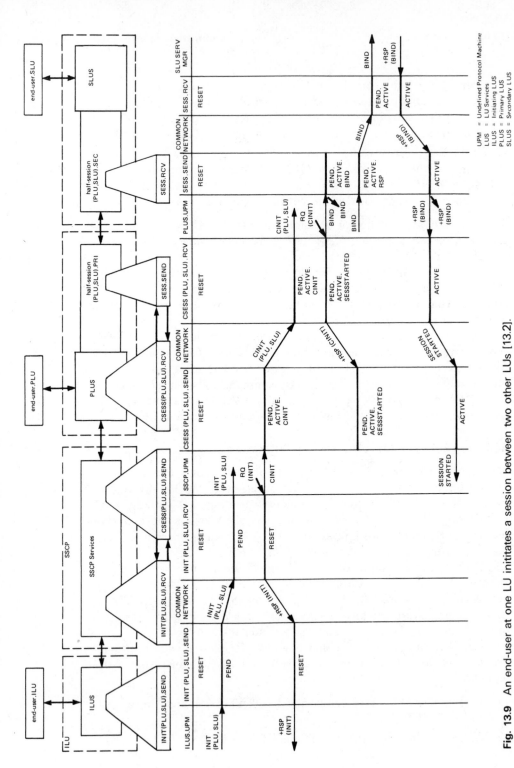

Fig. 13.9 An end-user at one LU inititates a session between two other LUs [13.2].

UPM = Undefined Protocol Machine
LUS = LU Services
ILUS = Initiating LUS
PLUS = Primary LUS
SLUS = Secondary LUS

3. SESS.—The FSMs that handle the BIND command in the PLU and in the SLU

Each of these exists as a send/receive pair of FSMs. Thus, there are the following FSM pairs:

1. For the session (SSCP,ILU):
   - INIT(PLU,SLU).SEND
   - INIT(PLU,SLU).RCV
2. For the session (SSCP,PLU):
   - CSESS(PLU,SLU).SEND
   - CSESS(PLU,SLU).RCV
3. In the session (PLU,SLU):
   - SESS.SEND
   - SESS.RCV

Each FSM pair handles one of the three commands involved in establishing a session. We will examine (in part) the sequence of commands between each pair of FSMs and also the commands from one pair to another pair.

The INIT sequence. The overall sequence begins when an end-user at the ILU issues a product-specific command to establish the session. An *undefined protocol machine* (UPM) at the user interface of the initiating LU services (ILUS) directs the input to the FMS called

$$INIT(PLU,SLU).SEND$$

There is a partner FSM called

$$INIT(PLU,SLU).RCV$$

in the SSCP services.

The input from the ILUS.UPM drives the INIT(PLU,SLU).SEND from the reset state to the pending state; at the same time, this generates the INIT command that is sent to the SSCP via the DFC of the ILU, the TCE of that half-session, and the common network.

This INIT command appears as an input to the FSM called INIT-(PLU,SLU).RCV (which is in the session services portion of the SSCP). This INIT command drives INIT(PLU,SLU).RCV to the pending state, generating at the same time an output to a UPM of the SSCP services manager which handles intersession communication within the SSCP. At this point, the INIT FSMs in both the ILU and the SSCP are in the pending state, awaiting the processing of the INIT by the SSCP services manager. The latter performs the various services described in Section 9.7.4.

A positive request from the UPM of the SSCP services manager then resets INIT(PLU,SLU).RCV. At the same time, that FSM sends a request to DFC.RSP.SEND, which generates a positive response back to the INIT(PLU,SLU).SEND in the ILU. Receipt of that positive response resets that FSM too.

The reset of the INIT(PLU,SLU).RCV also generates a CINIT command that is sent to another FSM in the SSCP, called control session or CSESS(PLU,SLU).SEND. This starts the CINIT sequence. The job of the INIT FSMs is now finished.

The CINIT sequence.   Within SSCP, the CINIT command is sent from INIT.RCV to CSESS.SEND (see Fig. 13.9).

The CSESS FSMs can have two pending states. The first (PEND.AC-TIVE.CINIT) *awaits confirmation at the PLU* that the validity check of the parameters in CINIT is OK. The second pending state (PEND.AC-TIVE.SESSTARTED) *awaits confirmation from the SLU* that the BIND is accepted there.

Note the chain of events in Fig. 13.9. The CINIT command arrives at CSESS.SEND from INIT.RCV. This input puts CSESS.SEND (in the SSCP) in the pending active state. That transition also generates a CINIT request that passes, via DFC, TCE, and the common network, to put CSESS.RCV (in the PLUS) in the pending active state, too.

When CSESS.RCV goes to the pending active state, *it passes the CINIT up to a UPM of the PLU services manager for an unarchitected validity check.* Assuming that the check is OK, the PLU services manager then drives CSESS.RCV to the second pending state. That sends a positive response to the CINIT, thus driving CSESS.SEND (in the SSCP) also to the second pending state. Thus a response from the validity check first drives CSESS.RCV (in the PLU) to the second pending state, which then sends a positive response to the CINIT to drive CSESS.SEND (in the SSCP) also to the second pending state.

The OK from the UPM of the PLU services manager and the transition of CSESS.RCV to the second pending state also result in the sending of the parameters for the BIND command to the FSM called SESS.SEND, which is in the TCE of the (PLU,SLU).PRI half-session. Later, when the PLU gets a positive response to the BIND command, CSESS.RCV (in the PLU) is finally driven to the active state. That FSM at the same time generates the SESSION STARTED command, which, in turn, drives CSESS.SEND (in the SSCP) also to the active state.

A negative response to the BIND command, on the other hand, should move CSESS.RCV from the second pending state back to RESET and should also cause the sending of a BIND FAILURE command to the SSCP via DFC.RQ.SEND.

The BIND sequence. Before the preceding sequence could be completed, the BIND command had to be sent and a positive response had to be received. The management of that sequence is done by the SESS.SEND and SESS.RCV FSMs, which are shown in Fig. 13.10.

In this case, the sending FSM (in the PLU) has two pending states, while the receiving FSM (in the SLU) has only one pending state. The sending FSM (SESS.SEND) first awaits confirmation from the end-user of the PLU (via the PLU services manager) that the BIND parameters are acceptable (or are suitably modified by the end-user). Only then is the BIND command sent to the SLU (via CPMGR.SEND). At the second pending state, the SESS.SEND FSM awaits word that a positive response (to the BIND command) has been received from the SLU.

Prior to that, SESS.RCV (in the SLU) is driven to the pending active state by the input of the BIND command, which results in a notification to the end-user of SLU. An OK from the end-user (again via the SLU services manager) then drives SESS.RCV from the pending active state to the active state, generating at the same time the positive response to the BIND command. That positive response is sent back to the PLU (via CPMGR.SEND).

The positive response to BIND drives SESS.SEND in the PLU to the active state also. At the same time, this generates the positive response from SESS.SEND back to the PLU services manager and CSESS.RCV to move the latter to the active state, as discussed earlier.

This permits the completion of the total sequence by the output of the SESSION STARTED command from CSESS.RCV (in the PLUS) back to CSESS.SEND (in the SSCP).

13.6.3 FSMs in LU-LU Operations

Next we will take a closer look at the structure involved in the LU–LU session. To gain perspective, refer first to Fig. 13.5 which depicts an entire half-session. Note that session control (SC) is part of the transmission control element, contains its own set of FSMs, and serves both CPMGR.SEND and CPMGR.RCV. Note, too, that the data flow control element has another set of FSMs, which serve both the SEND and RCV sections of the DFC element.

Figure 13.11, then, depicts a portion of two half-sessions and pairs of FSMs that are very commonly used. Two of these are in the transmission

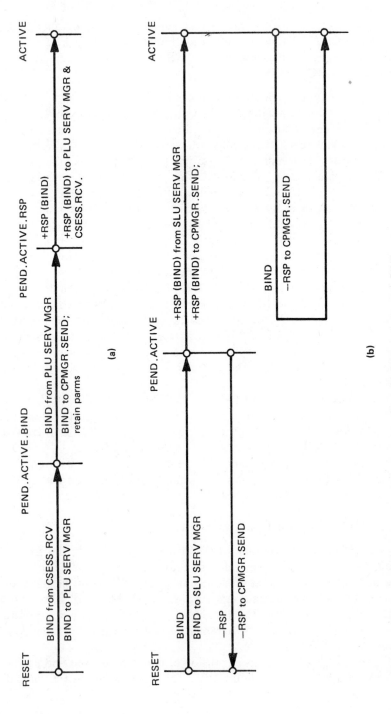

Fig. 13.10 Illustrative portions of the FSM called SESSION, which handles the BIND command [13.2]: (a) (PLU,SLU) PRI.SESS.SEND, and (b) (PLU,SLU) .SEC.SESS.RCV.

control layer—namely, session (SESS.), which handles the BIND command, and data traffic (DT.), which handles the START DATA TRAFFIC command. Two others are in the data flow control layer. One is the FSM for the half-duplex flip-flop (HDX–FF) mode, which reacts to the change-direction indicator in the RH. The other is the chaining FSM, which reacts to chaining indicators, such as begin-chain or end-chain, in the RH. Figure 13.11 singles out some of the pairs of FSMs that would work together, such as CHAIN.SEND in one half-session and CHAIN.RCV in the other. Each half-session has both SEND and RCV FSMs to handle chaining. The operation of the session FSM was discussed above (see p. 483). The other three FSMs will be discussed in Sections 13.6.4 and 13.6.5.

13.6.4 FSMs for START DATA TRAFFIC

Our next illustration of an FSM concerns the start of normal-flow data traffic between two logical units. The primary half-session has the responsibility of declaring the normal flow between the two LUs as being either "started" or "cleared." (This freedom to stop and start data traffic exists only when a session is bound.) The START DATA TRAFFIC (SDT) and CLEAR commands are *issued by session control (SC) in the transmission control element* of the primary half-session. The state of this normal-flow data traffic is managed by FSMs called DT.SEND and DT.RCV, located within session control for each half-session. The locations of these FSMs are illustrated in the upper part of Fig. 13.12. The FSMs themselves are shown in Fig. 13.13. Let's trace the action of the SDT command, using Figs. 13.12 and 13.13.

Assume that both FSMs start in the reset state. The end-user of the primary LU (PLU) issues an SDT macro, or its equivalent, which is passed to session control via the PLU services manager. This input drives DT.SEND to the pending active state, generating at the same time an SDT command destined for the secondary half-session. As shown in Fig. 13.13(a), that SDT command is first sent to CPMGR.SEND, which, in turn, will see that it is sent via the common network to the secondary half-session.

The SDT command enters the secondary half-session CPMGR and is routed to the function interpreter for session control (FI.SC). Then the SDT appears as an input that was sent from FI.SC to DT.RCV. This input drives DT.RCV *to the pending active state, generating at the same time a notification of the SDT command for the SLU services manager.* An OK from there drives DT.RCV to the active state, generating at the same time a positive response to the SDT command. That positive response is sent back to the primary LU via CPMGR.SEND.

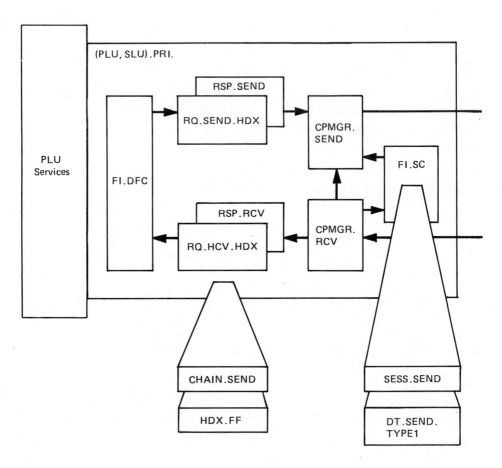

Fig. 13.11 Commonly used FSMs in LU-LU session [13.2].

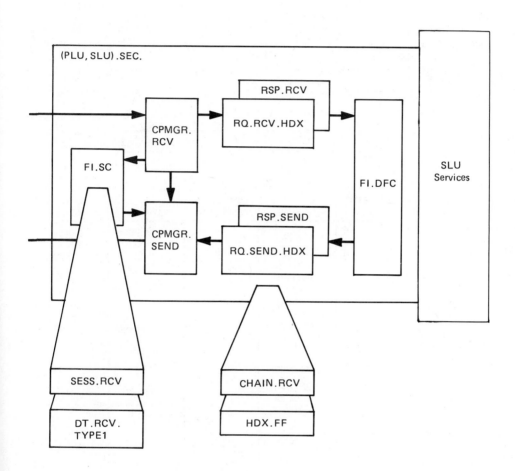

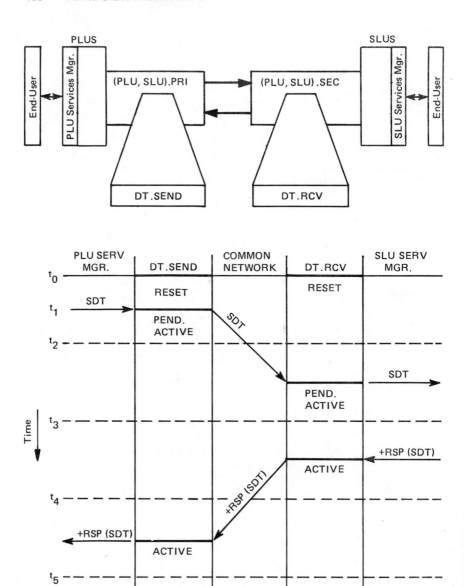

Fig. 13.12 START DATA TRAFFIC activation [13.2].

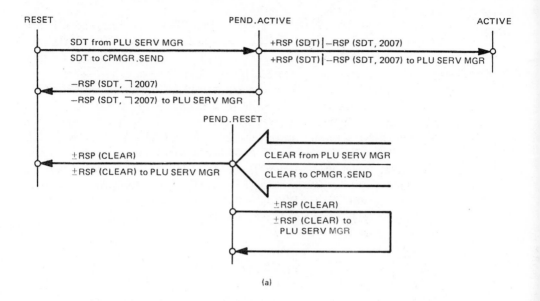

(a)

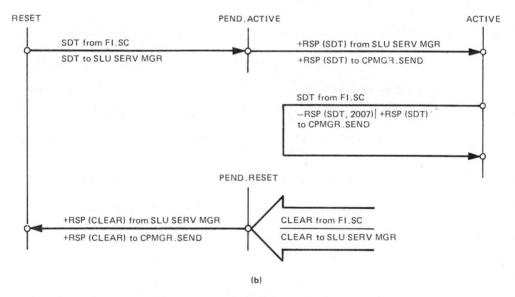

(b)

Fig. 13.13 Portions of the FSMs for data traffic [13.2]: (a) (PLU.SLU) PRI.DT.SEND.TYPE1, and (b) (PLU,SLU) SEC.DT.RCV.TYPE1.

Instead of the positive response to the SDT command, the primary LU might have received a negative response, with code 2007, which says that the data traffic was *not reset* when the SDT was received. In either case, the response drives DT.SEND to the active state.

If session control at the primary is told by higher levels to send a CLEAR command, that input will drive DT.SEND to the pending reset state, and will generate the CLEAR command for transmission (via CPMGR.SEND) to the secondary LU. That CLEAR command then appears from FI.SC as an input to DT.RCV, driving it too to the pending reset state. *Upon confirmation from the SLU services manager that the CLEAR command should be accepted, DT.RCV is reset,* and a positive response to the CLEAR command is sent back to the PLU (via CPMGR.SEND). That positive response, in turn, drives DT.SEND also to the reset state.

13.6.5 FSMs for HDX–FF Chaining

Our final illustration, showing the use of finite state machines to define the architecture, concerns the control of the flow of chains of requests in a half-duplex flip-flop (HDX–FF) mode.

Figure 13.14 shows the FSM that manages the HDX–FF operation in a reaction to the exchange of the change-direction indicator in the RH when no brackets are being used. Four sets of situations are illustrated.

1. If there is no definite request (RQD) (for example, if no response is required for a request unless there is an exception condition), *then the state changes whenever the change-direction (CD) indicator is on* and (a) is received while the FSM is in the receive state or (b) is sent while the FSM is in the send state.

2. No state change occurs if the change-direction indicator is off ($\neg CD$).

3. If a definite response is requested (RQD), situation (1) above is modified to include a *pending state, which awaits the return of a positive response* before the FSM goes to the new send or receive state.

4. Recovery actions can drive the FSM to either the send or the receive state, depending on which recovery options were chosen at session BIND time, and also on whether the half-session is performing recovery action for a received request (recovery r) or for a sent request (recovery s). In Fig. 13.14, the three BIND options pertaining to recovery are noted to the right of the FSM; and the corresponding state transitions are shown by broad arrows alongside.

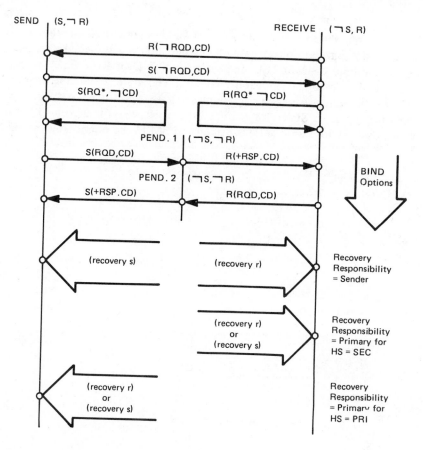

R   = Receive
S   = Send
RQ*   = Request of any type
RQE   = Request indicating exception response requested
RQD   = Request indicating definite response requested
recovery r = Recovery for received request
recovery s = Recovery for sent request

Notes:
1. This protocol machine is for half-sessions having normal-flow send-receive mode = HDX . FF and no brackets.
2. The following table shows the reset state of this FSM for each half-session:

HS	Contention Resolution	Reset State
.PRI	SEC	Receive
.PRI	PRI	Send
.SEC	SEC	Send
.SEC	PRI	Receive

Fig. 13.14 Portions of the FSM for half-duplex flip-flop (HDX.FF) [13.2].

The chain FSMs are shown in Fig. 13.15. These are very simple because even a single request can be a single element chain; that is, all requests are part of some chain. Any time that a half-session sends or receives an end-of-chain (EC) indicator, its SEND or RCV FSM (respectively) is driven to the between chain (BETC) state. Any time that the half-session sends or receives a request that does not have an end-of-chain indicator, its SEND or RCV FSM (respectively) is driven to the in chain (INC) state. Purge actions drive the FSM to the purge state, so that

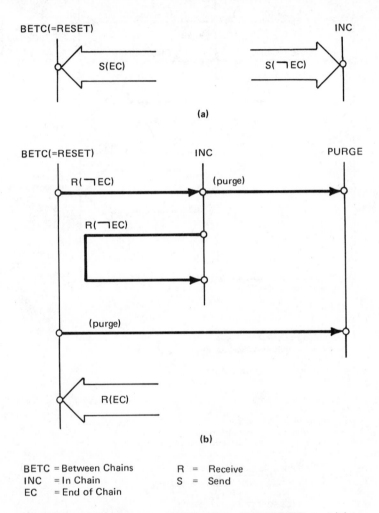

BETC = Between Chains	R = Receive
INC = In Chain	S = Send
EC = End of Chain	

Fig. 13.15 FSMs for chaining [13.2]: (a) for CHAIN.SEND. and (b) for CHAIN.RCV.

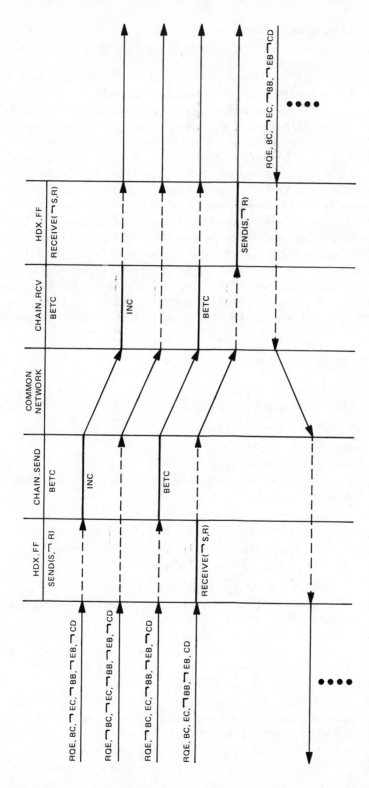

Fig. 13.16 Half-duplex flip-flop chaining example [13.2].

no other requests can be processed until an end-of-chain indicator is received (for example, with a CANCEL command).

Figure 13.16 depicts a chaining example, with the successive changes in state of the HDX-FF and chain FSMs. The first request, *with a begin-chain (BC) indicator*, drives CHAIN.SEND and CHAIN.RCV (in the sending and receiving half-sessions, respectively) to the in chain state. The third request, *with an end-of-chain (EC) indicator*, drives both back to the between chain state. The fourth request, *having both BC and EC indicators*, causes no state change in the chain FSM. However, since that request carries a change-direction (CD) indicator, it drives the HDX–FF FSMs in both half-sessions to their opposite states.

The last request, flowing now in the opposite direction from the preceding requests, contains a begin-chain (BC) indicator. However, it does not affect the chain FSMs shown. It does affect the other pair of chain FSMs that are not shown—namely, the CHAIN.SEND in the right half-session and the CHAIN.RCV in the left half-session—driving them to the in chain state.

13.7 EXERCISES

13.1 In the FSM convention
   a) what is the signal above an arrow?
   b) what is the signal below an arrow?
   c) what do vertical lines represent?

13.2 Which of the following are true?
   a) An output from a send FSM is often an input to a receive FSM in the opposite half-session.
   b) A pending state can be an interim state, pending validity checks, approval from a higher level, or completion of an action.
   c) Every FSM must have at least a reset and an active state.
   d). The send and receive FSM pair must have the same number of states.
   e) An input always moves the FSM to a new state.
   f) Send and receive FSMs in the same elements can be coupled, so that an output of one provides an input to the other.
   g) A positive or a negative response from an opposite half-session can determine whether an FSM moves from a pending state to an active or a reset state, respectively.

13.3 Which of the following are true?
   a) An FSM in the SSCP remembers that an ACTLU has been sent, and moves from a pending active state to an active state when a positive response is received from the LU being activated.

b) An INITIATE OTHER command moves the CSESS FSM in LU services to a pending state.

c) The LU services may support a primary half-session for a session with another LU and a secondary half-session for a session with the SSCP.

d) The BIND command immediately moves the session FSM (in session control) to the active state.

e) The DT FSM, which remembers whether data traffic is started or cleared, is located in session control in a transmission control element.

f) The HDX.FF FSM changes state whenever the change-direction indicator (in an RH) is on and is sent while the FSM in the sending half-session is in the receive state.

g) If the CHAIN FSMs are in the "between chains" state, then a request having both BC and EC indicator bits on will not cause any change of state.

h) There are no pending states in the chain FSM; a single request or response should affect both a CHAIN.SEND FSM and a CHAIN.RCV FSM in the same way.

13.4 Following the INIT sequence described in Section 13.6.2, construct an FSM pair to handle the INITIATE command. Two FSMs are needed:

- (SSCP,ILU) .SEC.INIT.SEND, and
- (SSCP,ILU) .PRI.INIT.RCV.

Each FSM needs only two states—reset and pending.

13.5 Following the CINIT sequence described in Section 13.6.2, construct an FSM pair to handle the CINIT command. Two FSMs are needed:

- (SSCP,PLU) .PRI.CSESS.SEND, and
- (SSCP,PLU) .SEC.CSESS.RCV.

The two pending states for both FSMs are

- PEND.ACTIVE.CINIT, and
- PEND.ACTIVE.SESSSTARTED.

13.8 REFERENCES AND BIBLIOGRAPHY

13.1 T. F. Piatkowski, "Finite State Architecture." Technical Report IBM TR 29.0133. North Carolina: Research Triangle (August 1975).

13.2 *SNA Format and Protocol Reference Manual*, IBM Form No. SC30-3112-0. Figures 13.2 through 13.16 reprinted by permission from this source, copyright 1976, by International Business Machines Corporation.

13.3 Z. Kohavi. *Switching and Finite Automata Theory*. New York: McGraw-Hill (1970).

13.4 M. Minsky. *Computation—Finite and Infinite Machines*. Englewood Cliffs, N.J.: Prentice-Hall (1967).

14
Reliability
and Security
Control

14.1 RAS STRATEGY*

It is well understood that reliability, availability, and serviceability (RAS) of a data-processing/communications system must be built into the total system design. The architecture should facilitate:

1. The validation of information content, where feasible, to minimize erroneous inputs to components of the system.
2. The enforcement of protocols (with detection of their violation) so as to maintain orderly exchanges and understanding.
3. The isolation of programming errors and hardware malfunctions to small parts of the system, so as to minimize their impact.
4. The bypassing or correction of problems close to where they are detected, when this is feasible, so as to reduce dependence on more complex global procedures.
5. The termination of the minimum unit of work, maintaining continuity of the remainder.
6. The distribution of some diagnostic aids to each node for local repair.

The approach to repair is to reduce the number of personnel that must be engaged in the repair. This follows from the decreasing costs of logic,

* Acknowledgment is given to W. A. Bernstein, E. E. Cobb, L. Loucks, and J. Oseas for the architecture of session recovery and to H. R. Albrecht, W. W. Blackwell, and R. Opdahl for their corollary work on general recovery, which is reflected in this chapter.

storage, and microcode in each node, relative to personnel service costs. Node repair, for example, may involve microcode diagnostics and maintenance statistics that are resident in the node, and can be used by the operator (or a customer service person). This can often verify that the node itself is functioning properly, thus suggesting that the problem is in the communications carrier equipment or in some other node [6.20].

The SNA network is only a part of the system that must be so designed. The network, however, could have severe problems because of the higher probability of loss of synchronism. Once the synchronism of message flow has been lost due to unanticipated failure or a protocol flaw, further exchanges are liable to be meaningless until a common agreement on the resumption of synchronism is reached [14.3].

14.2   ERROR RECOVERY HIERARCHY

Error-handling facilities can be very diverse and product-dependent. They can, therefore, be only partly defined as part of a systems architecture. Nevertheless, as a first cut, the error-handling facilities of a communications system can be grouped into the hierarchy shown in Fig. 14.1:

1. *Automatic retransmission* at the data link control level.
2. *Lost-path procedures* at the path control level. In some architectures this is independent of other levels; in SNA this requires a collaboration with higher levels.
3. *Message handlers and application exits.* These may be either user-written or system-provided recovery programs for specific situations. They are often tailored to an application or an operating environment. Recovery can pertain to a single session.
4. *Operator intervention.* Some problems that cannot be handled otherwise are referred to the network operator; others go to the terminal operator.

The first class, *link-level retransmission,* illustrates handling of *temporary* errors in a manner that is completely automatic, is performed by the system, and is executed at the level of structure responsible for the function in trouble. As discussed in Section 1.3.6, the data on the links are very susceptible to errors due to line noise, equipment malfunction, and conditions related to the movement of data over long distances. As described in Section 11.6, *the DLC level can include the capability* (like the polynomial redundancy check) *of checking the validity of the transmitted information, address, and control field.*

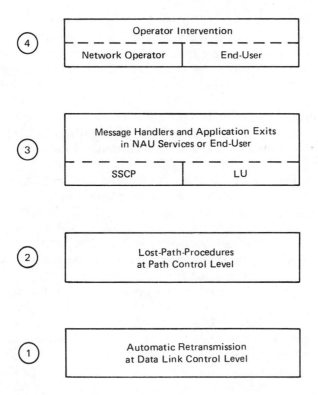

Fig. 14.1 Classes of error recovery.

Many line failures are of short duration and are self-healing. This may be due, for example, to servicing efforts at a switching center. It may also be a temporary carrier fade or a temporary burst of extraordinary interference. For this reason, SNA adopted a pause and retry algorithm at the primary station which can be used to ride over the short-duration failures [6.20]. The algorithm contains three parameters. R is the number of immediate retransmissions to be attempted before a pause of P seconds is entered. M is the number of times to repeat the retries and pause sequence before declaring the line to be inoperative.

The second class of recovery concerns *problems in finding a path* to the destination. In some architectures, the selection of an alternate route is distributed among the nodes of a network. In others, the selection is centralized or is done by the originator of the message. This problem is discussed further in Chapter 16.

In SNA, currently, *permanent* problems at the link and path control levels are referred to the SSCP and sometimes turned over to the originator of the request. For example, the detection by a communications controller (COMC) of a permanent link or link station failure (for example, no response after a time-out or continued errors after a maximum number of retries) can cause the PU services manager in the COMC to *place the link or link station in the inoperative state, and to notify the SSCP via the INOPERATIVE request.* The request contains the network address of either the failing link or the PU associated with the failing link station. This is followed by a RECORD MAINTENANCE STATISTICS command to report the final status of the COMC counters to the SSCP.

In addition, communications controllers may keep counts of the number of retries for each line. When the counters fill up, their contents can be reported, via RECORD MAINTENANCE STATISTICS commands, to the SSCP, where the statistics are logged. These logs may be scanned periodically to detect marginally satisfactory lines, modems, and interface hardware. Based on this, the network operator may declare a link or a station to be inoperative.

When a loss of physical connectivity occurs between adjacent subareas in complex networks, this information can be propagated throughout the network by the LOST SUBAREA command, so that all affected parties can be notified. This applies particularly to multidomain networks, and so is described further in Section 15.10.1.

When a link or a station is declared to be inoperative, path control in the COMC also modifies its own link and station status tables. Then, subsequently, if path control finds that a station to which a path information unit (PIU) is destined is inoperative, it *generates a negative response* (if requested in the RH), *reverses the OAF and DAF, and returns the request to the sender.* The response contains sense data defining the error as a lost contact. Without an alternate path capability (see Chapter 16), permanent link failures also result in returned requests, an unbind of the session, and notification of the network operator. This situation can, however, be corrected by activating a switched backup link (see Section 14.5).

The third class of error-handling facilities depends on *end-to-end recovery programs.* Such procedures are referred to by one of several mechanisms. In TCAM, the vehicle is the message handler, operating as part of the TCAM message-control program. In VTAM, the mechanism is usually the application exit, operating within the message-control portion of an application program or within an application subsystem (see Section 7.2.2). In SNA terms, these nonarchitected message handlers may exist within NAU services. These programs can exist in an LU to detect errors in message content as well as to direct recovery of error situations that were detected at inner layers of the SNA network.

Errors in message content. A common type of error encountered in teleprocessing systems occurs when message contents do not comply with some system requirement. Typical of this type of error, which lends itself to detection, are the following:

- Deviation from user-specified formats
- Absence of user-required fields
- Use of either numeric or alphabetic data when the other is required
- Incorrect or invalid FM header fields
- Field values outside a user-specified range

Errors of this type can be detected by specially written validity checks in message handlers at the NAU services level of the architecture. TCAM provides a structure in its message handlers containing detection facilities for many invalid-message error conditions. The TCAM macros also offer capabilities for rejecting the erroneous message before it is passed to the destination end-user. Responses that identify a detected error can be automatically generated and returned to the sender of the request.

Other content errors may be detected only with more elaborate analysis or comparisons with other stored data. These might best be performed by the end-user, or by an auxiliary application program to which the end-user has access.

DFC and TC direction. As described in Sections 8.8 and 9.3.1, a variety of DFC and TC commands are available for purging, quiescing, chasing responses, reporting LU status, requesting recovery, and resynchronization. While the DFC and TC layers have defined work to do in connection with these functions, invoking the function and guiding the recovery process is done by the nonarchitected message handlers and exits. As an example, those NAUs that support the SNA commands CLEAR, SET AND TEST SEQUENCE NUMBER, and START DATA TRAFFIC can contain end-to-end recovery programs that direct the use of these commands to resynchronize traffic after an error has been detected by an incorrect sequence number.

SSCP recovery routines. Nonarchitected recovery programs also can be implemented within SSCP services (see Section 7.3.5). While the trouble-reporting RUs, activation/deactivation RUs, and testing RUs are defined (see Chapters 7 and 12), the recovery procedures within the SSCP are open-ended and are not architected. In concept, *the malfunction information is made available; the testing and different reconfiguration commands are available; and different implementations will then use these commands to achieve different degrees of automatic testing and reconfiguration.* This may or may not be implemented so as to be completely under the direction of the network services manager in the SSCP. The general intent is to relieve the network operator of tedious operational tasks that do not require human decisions. Status reports to the operator may, of course, be required.

The fourth class of error recovery involves *operator intervention*, either by the network operator, an operator responsible for an application subsystem, or an end-user operator at a work station. The configuration control, session control, and maintenance facilities of the SSCP (see Chapter 7) are at the disposal of the network operator (through an operator interface that may be different in different product implementations). *These facilities include activation/deactivation commands for links, logical units, and physical units.* They may also include testing facilities. Queued subsystems (such as TCAM) and/or application subsystems (such as IMS) also may include operator commands to

1. Display information about queues in the network

2. Retrieve messages by time, by span of message sequence numbers, by destination, or by origin.

The network or subsystem operator thus has a growing amount of information and tools for problem analysis and recovery. Session-related problems, on the other hand, may be referred to a terminal operator. Physical problems such as paper jams are typical. In general, *this class of error recovery must include all the error types that cannot be handled at lower levels.*

A given problem may be solved by a low-level recovery procedure or may escalate to a higher level. In theory, the recovery of physical connectivity of a link, for example, might involve one or more levels, as follows:

- Automatic recovery by data link control of transient link errors
- Reporting to the SSCP of inoperative conditions, so as to simply inhibit future use of the link
- Preprogrammed replacement by the SSCP of a defective link with an alternate link
- Network-operator action to provide alternate links

In the face of this diversity, the architecture must (1) systematically provide for error detection and error reporting, (2) provide some measure of automatic error correction, (3) anticipate the major error recovery procedures to be used, and (4) provide a basic set of commands on which the anticipated facilities can be built.

14.3 SNA REQUEST RECOVERY

14.3.1 Introduction

The preceding was a broad discussion of failures and the major steps to be taken in coping with them. *Many of these malfunctions are evidenced as missing or erroneous requests and responses or as some violation of protocol* (see Section 6.8.3 for a discussion of requests and responses). A comprehensive system for enforcement of protocol and validity checking of requests and responses can greatly help in detecting malfunctions, correcting some, and preventing a cascading of error effects.

In SNA, each level of the architecture is responsible for detecting and reporting errors that affect the processing of the request. *Upon detection of an erroneous request, a negative response must report the error to the sender of the request.* The sender may complete the recovery procedure, or, if the sender is a secondary, it may call on the primary for recovery assistance. The BIND command establishes an agreement as to whether the sender or the primary has recovery responsibility.

The recovery procedure (at the sender or the primary NAU) must either

1. *Correct the error, select a restart point within the session,* and start data traffic there, or

2. *Unbind the session* and flag the problem for off-line correction.

14.3.2 Error Reporting

An error or malfunction can be reported by any one of four means:

1. An *exception request* (EXR), which is a forwarding of a request found to be in error. The request is truncated and identified as an EXR by setting the sense bit in the RH. The request is made to carry sense data that identifies the nature of the error. The EXR is the means by which errors detected on received requests by one layer can be signaled to other layers within the same half-session.

2. A *negative response.* An EXR may, for example, be converted to a negative response with the sense data obtained from the EXR. Or, in other cases, a negative response may be generated within a half-session without benefit of an EXR, but based on one layer's analysis of the request.

3. *Special error requests.* Certain requests are used for specific error situations (see Appendix C for details). These are as follows.

- BIND FAILURE and UNBIND FAILURE are sent from the primary LU to the SSCP to report rejections or errors in BIND or failures in UNBIND.

- NETWORK SERVICES PROCEDURE ERROR (NSPE) is a command sent from the SSCP to an LU to report failures in attempts to BIND or UNBIND.

- CONTACTED (ERROR) is sent with error-indicating parameters by a PU to the SSCP to report a failure on CONTACT.

- LOGICAL UNIT STATUS (LUSTAT) can be sent by one LU to another to
  - > indicate the sequence number of an RU that erroneously requested no response.
  - > indicate a function cancellation.
  - > report the status of an LU component.

4. Configuration failure requests, including INOPERATIVE (INOP) (see Section 12.6) and LOST SUBAREA (see Section 15.10.1).

Nonreportable errors. An error in a request is not reportable if the TH or the RH has been destroyed. If the nonreportable error is transient, the next request on the session will cause a sequence number error, which will trigger recovery. If the nonreportable error is permanent, the SSCP may be notified by the PU services manager, via an INOPERATIVE command, when an error count reaches a predetermined threshold.

14.3.3 Sense Data Codes

The means for reporting the error condition are the sense data codes that accompany the response. A listing of the sense codes is provided in Appendix E. They are divided into five major categories, which reflect the nature of the exception and the level of the communications system in which it was detected. These categories are as follows:

- *Path error:* for example, path outage, TH error, or destination LU not active

- *RH usage error:* for example, values of RH violate session rules (such as BB not allowed or definite response not allowed)

- State error: for example, a sequence number error, or an error in the sequence of chain indicators (BC, MOC, EC)

- *Request error:* for example, a mismatch in DFC or PS capabilities
- *Request reject:* for example, the delivery, but not the execution, of a request because of invalid pass-word or an unknown resource

With well-defined error conditions, for each SNA layer, the probability is much higher that a satisfactory recovery procedure can be anticipated. Recovery actions that are recommended by the network are likely to be accepted, and most users will not wish to modify this action. This is in contrast to BTAM-like support in which most errors (other than line errors) had to be handled by the user's program because recovery action was more dependent on data content, device type, or line connection.

14.3.4 In-session Repair

An algorithm to restart data flow after an error might choose to (1) resend the chain (or chains) for which a negative response was received, (2) send the next chain, or (3) resynchronize and then proceed. The latter is the most cautious of the three, but could have the following variations:

1. *Back up to the most recent prior chain that in effect begins a new presentation space.* Examples of this are chains that (a) form feed, (b) erase screen, and (c) create a data set.
2. *Rewrite the presentation space from a checkpoint.* This would require that the LU maintain an image of the presentation space; then when an error occurs, the current presentation space would be erased and the checkpoint would be used to rebuild the presentation space.
3. Use the SET AND TEST SEQUENCE NUMBER (STSN) command to determine a restart point.
4. *Query an operator* for a restart point.

This restart may or may not be preceded by other steps to correct the cause of the error. In-session recovery is possible when an error is caused by a temporary condition. This is generally the case of errors falling in the categories of "state error" and "request reject" (see Appendix E).

Recovery from state error.   A sequence-number error is a state error; it may indicate that one or more requests were lost, duplicated, or simply out of sequence. If the sender of the request is a secondary, it may send a REQUEST RECOVERY (RQR) command to the primary. Then, the primary NAU has the four options cited above.

1. If one of the first two resynchronization options is chosen, the primary may simply *resynchronize the request sequence numbers and*

proceed. CLEAR may be sent to clear the data flow and to set send and receive sequence counts to zero in both connection point managers. START DATA TRAFFIC (SDT) is then sent, if required, and the next chain can be transmitted.

2. If the request chains must be processed in a particular order, the primary may resynchronize the request sequence numbers and *continue with the chain that follows the last chain successfully processed by the receiver.* The primary may use the SET AND TEST SEQUENCE NUMBER (STSN) command to set and/or to determine the user sequence numbers at the secondary (see Section 9.3.2). Using implementation-dependent protocols, the primary NAU services or end-user can determine how to set the CPMGR sequence numbers so as to affect proper end-user recovery.

State errors can also be found in received requests in the data flow control layer, having to do with chains, brackets, direction, and quiesce protocols. These state errors do not imply that requests were lost or duplicated; the sequence number would have been checked previously in the transmission control layer. *DFC state errors often require the sending of a negative response (by the receiver) and then the canceling of the chain by the sender of the request.* If the sender has recovery responsibility, it may send an end-of-chain (EC) indicator (either in CANCEL or in another FMD request) to terminate an incomplete chain for which a negative response had been received. The next chain may then be sent or the failing chain may be resent (see chaining in Section 8.3).

Recovery from request reject. Recovery within an active session is also generally possible when the exception code is in the "request reject" category (see Appendix E). These causes are generally temporary in nature—they include the following:

- Operator errors
- Temporary equipment malfunction
- Out-of-forms condition
- Insufficient available resources
- Lack of authorization
- Contention or race conditions

In these cases, the receiver of the request, after returning the negative response, begins purging the remainder of the chain. Then, receiving an end-of-chain (EC) either in a CANCEL or in another FMD request, the receiver of the request ends the purging and causes a discarding of any request already received in that chain.

For failures involving possible manual intervention, the sender may

1. Continue the session by selecting another device of the destination LU (via an FM header; see Section 7.4.3) or

2. Await indication from the destination LU (via LUSTAT) that the error condition has been removed.

14.3.5 Session Deactivation

When in-session recovery is not possible, the NAU responsible for recovery may deactivate the session. This is generally the case for severe problems such as equipment outages, programming errors, or system-definition mismatches. Errors of this type are usually reported in the sense-code categories of

- Path control,
- RH usage error, or
- Request error.

Enforcement failures. Within an SNA session, certain rules and protocols must be observed by each functional level. Some of these are common for all sessions—for example, the rules for the use of segmenting bits in the TH or the use of chaining bits in the RH. Other rules, established at BIND time, may vary from session to session. The rules for bracket initiation and FM header usage, for example, may be different for different sessions.

Each level of the sender is responsible for enforcing the rules and protocols that it uses in communicating with its counterparts. For example, if the end-user is able to request begin-brackets and end-brackets, the data flow control level must verify that the bracket states are correct before permitting the BB or EB indicators to flow with a request. *Detection of a violation within a given layer of the sender can result in a rejection of the RU.* If a protocol error is due to a system-definition error, a program error, or some permanent hardware failures, the session is generally not recoverable, and an unbind will result.

System-definition errors. SNA facilities in each node must be somewhat aware of the characteristics of other nodes with which it communicates. These characteristics include the format identifier (FID type) used in the transmission header (TH), the maximum transmission length (BLU), and the supportability of segmenting. In addition, path control in each node must have the path tables required to route requests to the proper link stations. Such information must be defined at system-definition time; or, in the case of connection via the switched network, the information must be defined at the time when the connection is established and the entering node is recognized by the SSCP.

Errors in routing information may make transmission of a request to the next node impossible. Negative responses will be returned to the sender identifying the condition. Generally, the session must be unbound, and the system definition must be corrected.

NAUs also require knowledge of each other's characteristics if they are to communicate. LU characteristics are defined to the SSCP, which is responsible for making them available to the primary LU. That information is then used to help to establish agreement between the two LUs at BIND time. Any errors in this information will lead to mismatches in capabilities and will require the session to be unbound.

14.4 APPLICATION-PROGRAM/SUBSYSTEM FAILURE

Many designs aim to isolate application failures so that only one of many application programs need be affected. TCAM and applications subsystems (like IMS, for example) are structured so that a separate and relatively independent region of storage is allocated to each application program. Because of this and because of the operating system structure, *it is possible for an application program in one region to fail completely, without affecting other application regions or the message-control portion of the application subsystem.*

With some application subsystems that provide queueing services for their multiple application programs, remote terminal operators can even continue to enter messages for the failed application program; these messages are stored in the message-control portion of the application subsystem until the failed application is restarted [15.8].

If the messages for the failed application were queued on disks, none of these messages need be lost. If the input to the application was queued in main storage, then the one message that the application was processing when the application failed was probably lost. In either case, messages that had been processed by the application and had been given to the message-control portion of the application subsystem need not be lost.

Some application subsystems are designed to take periodic *checkpoints* and to restart from the last checkpoint. Messages received between the last checkpoint and failure time may have to be re-received and/or resent.

Implementations of queued systems, like TCAM, can also perform a *queue scan* as part of their restart processing [15.8]. This involves searching the queues from the time of the last checkpoint record to the time of failure. Previously sent messages are therefore not sent again, and completely received messages need not be reentered.

14.5   NETWORK OPERATOR RECOVERY AIDS

When an error is permanent, a message is usually sent to the network operator's console. The message may define the condition, indicate the probable cause, and suggest a course of action.

If further information is needed for problem determination, the operator may

1. Obtain printouts of any traces performed in connection with the error (for example, I/O traces, buffer traces, and storage management traces within the TP access method, or line traces in a communications controller).

2. Save any dumps that may have resulted from the error (for example, dumps from the TP access method or a communications controller).

3. Initiate diagnostic programs to test devices and lines involved in the error.

4. Reconfigure so as to substitute facilities or avoid part of the TP network.

Usually only a portion of the network malfunctions. This portion must be diagnosed (in many cases) while application programs continue to use the operable portions of the network. Test supervision programs [such as the IBM TP On-line Test Executive Program (TOLTEP)] allow multiple on-line tests to be run concurrent with application programs. Many on-line tests are designed to diagnose hardware problems and to verify the reliability of a device in the TP network.

Switched backup

One of the reconfiguration options available to an operator is to employ a new switched line on the occasion of a failure of a line from a communications controller to a cluster controller. Also, if the communications controller fails, a new switched line can be used between an alternate communications controller and the cluster controller.

This can be achieved by *multiple network definitions in the SSCP, involving dual definitions for the PU of the cluster controller.* In the normal definition, the PU of the cluster could be associated with its normal address on, say, a nonswitched line. In the backup definition, *the PU of the cluster can use a different NAU name,* and be associated with a switched line on the same or a different communications controller. *The LU names would remain the same.* In the case of a failure of either the nonswitched line or the communications controller, the backup definition is used by the network operator to generate the dial-out procedure described in Section 12.5.

In these circumstances, a simple and clear procedure, to date, is to terminate the session on the occasion of the line failure. The end-user can then establish a new session after the backup line has been put into place. Intermediary recovery programs can also be devised to perform the session establishment for the end-user, and application exits can be devised to establish appropriate resynchronization points for the application.

14.6   DATA SECURITY

14.6.1   Security Strategy*

Data security involves the protection of data from unauthorized or accidental modification, destruction, or disclosure. The security facilities of the communications system are only a part of an overall security plan for the total system; but the communications networks must do their part to help protect against wiretapping, generation of specious but apparently legitimate messages, masquerading as a legitimate network node, forged end-user identity, unauthorized access by legitimate end-users, and misrouting of messages.

To maintain perspective, it is well to remember that the major exposures probably exist outside the communications system. It is felt [14.10] that, in many cases, the unfortunate things that happen to systems and data have the following decreasing order of probability:

1. Errors and omissions in the normal course of job performance

2. Dishonest employees, using data and system functions that they have been authorized to use

3. Fire

4. Disgruntled employees

5. Water damage (floods, leaks, etc.)

6. Others, such as the unauthorized access of nonemployees

The protection of the communications system, therefore, only becomes meaningful when steps are also taken to reduce exposures and facilitate recovery from all of the higher probability events.

---

*The author is indebted to R. H. Courtney for the benefit of his writings on the subject of data security, and to J. Oseas and R. E. Lennon for the benefit of their studies on cryptography architecture.

The major objectives of a family of security measures should include

1. Positive unique *identification* of legitimate end-users, nodes, and other named resources of the data-processing and communications systems

2. *Authorization* of system activities, involving interactions among end-users and other named system resources

3. *Surveillance* of system activity, including the means of achieving strict personal accountability of people for their actions (keeping a journal of events is the common technique used)

4. *Strong system integrity*, including protection against wiretapping and eavesdropping

14.6.2 Identification

End-user identification

Most schemes for user identification fall into three classes, using

1. Something the end-user *knows*, such as a password;

2. Something the end-user *is*, such as a fingerprint or a voiceprint; or

3. Something the end-user *has*, such as a badge or credit card.

Usually, a combination of classes 1 and 3 can give a high assurance of correct identification. For example, a magnetic-stripe credit card containing an account number and expiration date can be used in conjunction with a password, end-user name, or end-user number that is *not* embossed on the card.

Assurance is needed that an input is really from a card rather than a keyboard. This is accomplished by the use of unique, nonkeyable, framing characters transmitted with the magnetic-stripe character string (see Secure String ID Reader in Appendix D.3). SNA specifies that *data that is dispatched as secure by the use of framing characters should not be printed or displayed, nor should it be edited in the buffers of the SNA network.*

Product-unique log-on procedures can incorporate card, password, name, or number identification techniques. The SNA command INITIATE SELF contains defined fields called Requester ID and Password for end-user identification and verification (see Appendix C), so these can be forwarded as part of a session-initiation procedure. Alternatively, many products employ the User Field in the INITIATE command to convey ID and password information to an application program.

Station identification

An auxiliary station identification procedure is useful *to guard against inadvertent transposition of link stations during transactions.* To this end, the Exchange Station Identification (XID) command in SDLC (see Section 11.5.4) contains an I field for node type and ID number. The REQUEST CONTACT command is used for the forwarding of this information to the SSCP (see Section 12.5.3). The station identification characters may be factory-assigned and hardware-generated. In addition, communications controllers can have circuitry to permit programs sensing loss of continuity of connection, so as to indicate the need to recheck the identification of the station before transmitting more data to it.

This facility has value in preventing the inadvertent loss of data. It is not considered a security facility, however, because it would not be difficult for a technically competent penetrator to circumvent the station ID, using an impostor terminal. Therefore, *a completely secure end-user identification is still the basic requirement.*

14.6.3 Authorization

Authorization mechanisms may be in (1) the SNA network, (2) the node operating system, and (3) the node data management subsystem. These all serve to enable only authorized users to perform only those functions that they are authorized to perform, upon only those data that they are authorized to access, using only those hardware and software resources that they are authorized to use.

As mentioned previously, *the password field or the user field of the INITIATE command can be used to convey identification and authority information to the SSCP.* This information may be checked both by the SSCP and/ by verification programs in application subsystems (such as TSO for time-sharing services, or a batch job-entry subsystem). Once a user is accepted on the system, the ability to access data can be further controlled by information previously entered in a special access-control program. In the IBM Resource Access Control Facility (RACF), for example, access to data is either granted or denied automatically; messages describing detected attempts at unauthorized access can be routed to a security console for immediate action; and an audit trail of access information can be generated for later analysis [14.11].

14.6.4 Cryptography Basics

Cryptography (crypto) is the transformation of data from a clear form to a coded one (enciphering) and the reverse process (deciphering), using a process intended to be fully known only to the cooperating proper communicators of the data. Protection can be provided either to data on communication lines or to data resident in a storage medium.

Data encryption standard.   The National Bureau of Standards (NBS) has established [14.8] a Federal Data Encryption Standard (DES) (effective July 1977). Characteristics of this algorithm [14.6] include the following.

1. The secrecy of the transformation is dependent only on the secrecy of the key, not the secrecy of the algorithm.
2. So long as the same key is used, position or time synchronization of enciphering with deciphering is not required.
3. When enciphering or deciphering, the change of a single bit in either the key or the input text has an unpredictable effect on the output text.
4. Analysis of clear/enciphered text pairs does not aid in determining the key used.
5. The DES algorithm is expected to be available as an LSI package. This should provide a relatively low-cost high-speed implementation suitable for use in network cryptographic devices.

In some systems, this DES algorithm may be a component of a larger algorithm.

Pipeline crypto [14.6].   In pipeline crypto, a unique key is employed *for each pipeline of messages or logical connection.* The key is generated randomly and is assigned to the specific pipeline of messages. If the pipeline key is transmitted over the network, it must itself be encrypted under some other key known to each of the communicating end-units. The pipeline key must be dynamically set in participating end-units. *A control point of the network must be able to control the setting of keys.* The network protocols must be able to, in effect, switch the crypto devices on and off. Pipeline crypto does not imply any crypto capability except at the ends of the communication path.

Link crypto.   As the name implies, link crypto protects only a link, rather than a path. When multiple cascaded links are used, the message must be deciphered and then enciphered at each intermediate node, introducing overhead and some security exposure at these points. Link crypto does not require that a control point for the network be able to set the keys.

Personal crypto.   Many variations of personal identification and crypto are possible. Some proposals employ both an individual's account number and a more carefully guarded *personal identification number* (*PIN*). In one approach [14.9], the PIN becomes a key used to encipher the account number. This text, in turn, is enciphered by another key for transmission. Using another approach, both the account number and the PIN are enciphered (by a key unique to the pipeline of messages or logical connection) before transmission to the central site. There, the enciphered values of both are stored and can be checked.

In a variation of this approach, the PIN is originally created by enciphering the account number. The PIN can then be checked for validity at the terminal by enciphering the submitted account number and comparing it to the submitted PIN. Both the account number and the accepted PIN would then be enciphered (by another key) before transmission. In all of these cases, the PIN need never appear in clear form at the central site; all validity checks can be made on enciphered PINs.

File security. This is the protection of data that is resident in a storage device. A convenient way to preserve the identity of the key used to encrypt the data in a storage device is to record a name for that key along with the enciphered data.

Handling keys. Keys must not exist within the network in the clear form except when they are actually being placed in one of the registers within the crypto device. The crypto device should be designed so that physical access to registers within it is destructive to its contents (so that any microprobing, for example, cannot succeed in disclosing any key).

14.6.5 Cryptographic Network Operations

The relationship of crypto to any architecture is straightforward. To illustrate, one approach to network security at the system design level, using crypto techniques, has been presented by F. R. Heinrich and D. J. Kaufman [14.6]. The following is an adaptation of some of that work.

Control point. Access to the network can be controlled through one or more control points, which can authorize a logical connection between any two addressable ports based on access-control information that is stored at the control point.

Before the two ports are connected, the initiating port engages in a dialogue with the control point, requesting assistance in establishing the desired connection. In this dialogue, *the initiating port identifies the requestor of the connection and authenticates that identity by a password.* The control point uses previously stored access-control information to verify the initiator's identity and to determine whether the desired connection is authorized.

All messages in this dialogue between the control point and the iniating port are enciphered, using keys that had previously been manually inserted at the two ends. *Creating the desired logical connection between two ports requires that a new key* (a pipeline key) *be established by the control point at each of the two ports to be connected.* The control point generates a random, distinct pipeline key to be sent to the encryption devices at both ports. As stated previously, the transmission of a pipeline key in the network requires that the pipeline key itself be enciphered by some other key known to each of the communicating end-units. One of the ports then proceeds to establish the logical connection with the other port. When the crypto devices at the two ports begin to use the new pipeline key, the two ports can communicate.

Security analysis. Besides the protection against wiretapping, the above procedures provide some additional benefits:

1. Pipeline crypto uses a distinct key for each logical connection. Therefore, misrouted messages are made unintelligible to unauthorized recipients.

2. Masquerading as a legitimate network node is impossible because the bogus node would not know an appropriate key. Spurious messages from a bogus node are therefore unintelligible.

On the other hand, care must be taken in several areas:

1. The validation of the initiator's identity and the authorization of the connection depend on the control point being tamperproof. This, in turn, depends on the design of the control point and its vulnerability to the environment in which it operates.

2. Protection is provided for communication between crypto devices. If these crypto devices are located in controllers or hosts, and if other links connect them to the actual work stations, then the security of these local links (really everything beyond the crypto devices) is a local responsibility. The involved controllers and hosts may need procedural and physical protection.

3. Alteration of enciphered text causes unpredictable results. Validity checks, therefore, may detect such alterations. To aid in this detection, it can be argued that it is valuable to *include an error detection field as part of the message to be enciphered.* Inclusion of both redundancy checks

and message sequence numbers as part of the message to be encrypted prevents alteration of the enciphered message and undetected playback of messages. If this is not done, a combination of other checks such as nonenciphered sequence numbers, request/response correlation, non-enciphered block checks, and validity checks by the end-user must be relied upon.

14.7 REFERENCES AND BIBLIOGRAPHY

See also [15.8], [3.5], and [6.20].

14.1 *VTAM Concepts and Planning.* IBM Form No. GC27-6998.

14.2 *Information Management System/VS: General Information Bulletin.* IBM Form No. GH20-1260.

14.3 L. Pouzin. "Network Protocols." In *Computer Communications Network* (R. L. Grimsdale and F. F. Kuo, eds.). Noordhoff, Leyden (1975).

14.4 F. Heart. "The ARPA Network." In *Computer Communications Network* (R. L. Grimsdale and F. F. Kuo, eds.). Noordhoff, Leyden (1975).

14.5 "Exploring Privacy and Data Security Costs—A Summary of a Workshop." U.S. Dept. of Commerce, National Bureau of Standards, August 1975. *NBS Technical Note* 876.

14.6 F. R. Heinrich and D. J. Kaufman. "A Centralized Approach to Computer Network Security." *AFIPS Conf. Proceeding, 1976 National Computer Conference,* Vol. 45. New York City.

14.7 D. J. Kaufman. "A Distributed Approach to Computer Network Security." System Development Corporation, SP-3848 (31 May 1976).

14.8 National Bureau of Standards. "Data Encryption Standard." FIPS PUB 46 (15 January 1977).

14.9 D. Kaufman and K. Auerback. "A Secure National System for Electronic Funds Transfer." *AFIPS Conf. Proceeding, 1976 National Computer Conference,* Vol. 45. New York City.

14.10 R. H. Courtney. "A Systematic Approach to Data Security." *Proceedings of U.S. National Bureau of Standards Symposium on Privacy and Security in Computer Systems.* Washington, D.C. (4–5 March 1974).

14.11 Resource Access Control Facility (RACF) General Information Manual, IBM Form No. GC280722.

Part 4
Advanced
Functions

This part addresses several advanced functions of an architecture for distributed systems.

Chapter 15 describes a generalization of the preceding structure to include multihost networks with distributed resource control points (SSCPs) and multiple control domains. Topics include the transparent establishment of sessions across domains and multidomain network recovery.

Chapter 16 discusses the techniques for routing messages and the topics of alternate paths and parallel paths. Particular attention is given to explicit routing with variable paths and distributed routing techniques.

Chapter 17 discusses the roles of new data networks, such as digital transmission systems and packet switching systems, in an architecture for distributed systems. Topics include interfaces and functional relationships to SNA.

15
Multidomain
Networks

15.1 INTRODUCTION*

The concepts of distributed control were introduced in Section 6.13. The distribution of network services among an SSCP, LUs, and PUs was discussed in Section 7.3.2; illustrations of that distribution were given under "Establishing an LU-LU session" in Section 9.7 and in the discussion of "Bringing the system up" in Section 12.4.

The architecture discussed thus far can be applied to a *single control domain, in which network services for all nodes in the domain are coordinated by a single SSCP.* (These network services include physical configuration services, as well as session, maintenance, operator, and other services.) That architecture provides for communication among NAUs that are distributed in tree configurations, whose root is a host. However, as noted in Section 3.8, a natural extension is to interconnect such single domain trees and to provide communication among NAUs in multiple domains. The advantages sought by such *multidomain networking* include the following.

1. Increased accessibility of data and application programs for different locations; the investment in an application can then be spread over more users and benefits can be extended.

---

* The SNA cross-domain networking services described in this chapter are due primarily to P. DeBacker, J. Eisenbies, R. Jueneman, L. Loucks, R. Rodell, J. Tell, and E. Thomas. I am particularly indebted to J. McFadyen and E. Thomas for the benefit of their writings and consultation on this subject, and to N. A. Bouroudjian for his helpful review.

2. Reduced development and maintenance costs; less duplication of data, application programs, and system programs in different locations reduce the total effort needed to develop, update, and repair them; competency centers in different locations can efficiently focus skills on particular subsystems (for example, IMS) or on particular classes of applications (for example, payroll).

3. Better availability; work can sometimes be handled by an alternate host when the originally intended host is inoperative.

4. Increased production beyond the capacity of a single host.

The extension to multiple domains should not, however, disrupt the operation of the single domain. If the objectives for ease of use (see Section 5.2) are to be taken seriously, then an architecture for distributed systems must be structured so as to facilitate extensions to multiple-domain operations, without affecting (a) existing applications, or (b) existing user interfaces. If a given function is performed in both single and multiple domains, the user interfaces for that function should be the same in both cases.

If (because of multiple-domain usage) a generalization is needed for any command seen by a logical unit, then that generalization should suffice, and the identical command should be usable for both single- and multiple-domain operations. This may lead, in some cases, to a dual form of a command, where either form can be used for same-domain or for multidomain operations, but where the newer form offers more function. The SSCP must in such cases be able to accept either form.

Specifically, it is highly desirable that an end-user (application program or operator) in a given domain use *one set* of interfaces and procedures that are applicable whether the work spans one or more domains. Ideally, so far as any LU is concerned, *the establishment of LU-LU sessions, the use of product-specific commands by the end-user, and the interaction with another LU should be no different whether one or more domains is involved.*

This transparency, with the same protocols at the LU whether one or more domains is involved, has sometimes been referred to as *transparent* networking. *Nontransparent* networking, on the other hand, requires that the end-user and/or the LU have some explicit knowledge and take some action that is different from single-domain actions whenever multiple domains are involved.

15.2 CONTROL DOMAINS AND NETWORKS

What is a network? One sometimes thinks of the *SNA network* as the total assembly of components that the end-user employs for communication purposes. More precisely, it is the aggregate of SNA functions, which

are distributed among all those physical components, with the understanding that

1. Elements of the network (such as a transmission control element or a
    path control element) are structured in relatively independent layers.
2. Elements at a given layer are interrelated via a set of protocols that
    are common for that layer.
3. Elements of the network are managed by a set of resource controls
    that are common across the network.
4. Elements of the network at each major layer are interconnected by
    some lower-level transmission facility.

The concept of control domains and the levels of the control were
introduced in Section 6.13. Each resource that is shared must have that
sharing managed. Requests to use the resource must be accepted or
rejected by some criteria. If the resource is not available, the request may
be rejected or queued. Thus the access to a shared resource, be it a
program, a device, a processor, or a communications facility must be
"controlled."

As explained in Chapter 7, we start with two levels of control within
a single domain. The first (or local) level is that of the PUs and the LUs in
SNA nodes. The PU services (PUS) manage the resource controllers in
data link control and path control. The LU services (LUS) manage
session-related resource controllers. The second (or domain) level of
control is that of the SSCP, which manages the PUs and the LUs and
exercises overall resource control for the domain.

A further generalization then is to recognize that resource control
may be distributed among domains. *We began by thinking of a network
as being managed by one common set of resource controls. We retain that
definition of a network, but allow these controls to exist in distinct control
domains (see Fig. 15.1), so long as a cross-domain resource control exists
as well.* A multiple-domain network exists when global resource management is effected across all the involved control domains. This is done by a
set of cross-domain protocols that are distributed across SSCPs.

As networks become more complex and multiple domains of control
need to be handled, it may be helpful to think in terms of an association
of networks in which (1) a given network can span multiple control
domains and (2) one network can "use" another lower-level or subordinate network, such as an SNA network using a media network provided
by a communications carrier. Still, we want to retain the same understanding that in each network the implemented elements are interrelated
via sets of peer protocols, the physically separate elements in each
network are interconnected via some transmission facility, and each
network is managed by a coordinated set of controls.

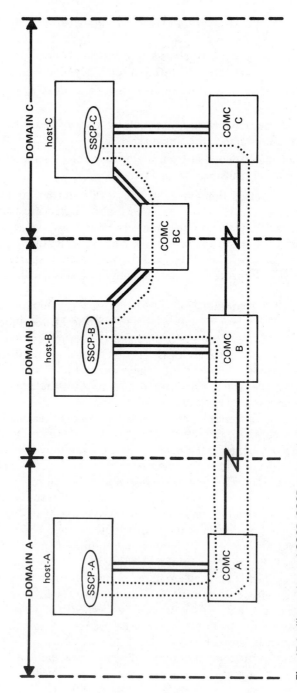

Fig. 15.1   Illustrations of SSCP–SSCP connections.

A coordinated set of controls is illustrated in Fig. 15.1, which shows a three-domain network (domains A, B, and C) each with its own system services control point (SSCP). Note, however, that *control domains are not necessarily one-to-one with hosts.* The SSCPs for domains A, B, and C could be in the same or different hosts; that is, the SSCPs for multiple domains may exist in a single host. Each domain could have its own extensive tree configuration (that is not shown in Fig. 15.1) similar to that, say, in Fig. 6.1.

Some of the possible SSCP connections today are illustrated in Fig. 15.1:

1. Via the communications controllers of adjacent domains.
2. Via a shared communications controller that has channel connections (twin tails) to adjacent domains.
3. Via a communications controller in an intermediate control domain.

Paths internal to a host between SSCPs in the same host are also feasible.

A second characteristic of a multidomain network is that elements in the several domains are interrelated via sets of peer protocols. Figure 15.2 shows the connection of two end-users in two different control domains, with transmission taking place via a third control domain. Note that *the apparent flows in the exercise of the peer protocols* (for example, NAU services-NAU services, DFC-DFC, TC-TC) *are between elements in the same layer but in different control domains.*

The path control and data link control levels in Fig. 15.2 exist in three control domains, since the PC and DLC protocols are executed in the intermediate node as well as the other two nodes. On the other hand, the upper levels involve an execution of protocols only between elements in two domains. These protocols are oblivious to the fact that the lower levels span three (or more) control domains.

The allocation of resources for this exchange (for example, the setup of the LU-LU session) must involve cooperation between the communication resource managers (that is, the SSCPs) of the two domains. This agreement between the two SSCPs for the setup of this particular session could be made at session initiation time.

The success of the transmission also depends on the cooperation of the resource manager (SSCP) for domain C. Since this cooperation is not necessarily session-unique, the agreements for this cross-domain cooperation could be made either at session initiation time or at an earlier time, such as system definition time.

Note in Fig. 15.2 that the path control layer extends across domains. It follows that network addresses must be coordinated across domains and

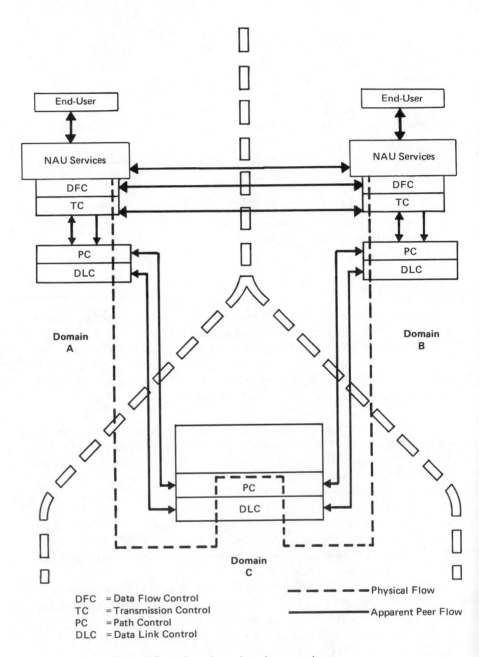

DFC = Data Flow Control
TC   = Transmission Control
PC   = Path Control
DLC = Data Link Control

— — — — — Physical Flow
——————— Apparent Peer Flow

Fig. 15.2 Apparent peer flows in a three-domain network.

that path outages must be reported across domains. Moreover, if new subareas are added to the network, then some of the routing tables in all domains of the network must be updated.

Figure 15.3 illustrates the fact that a server network may itself connect separate control domains. In this illustration, domain C may operate independently, since it uses protocols at the path control level that are confined to operations within domain C. *Note that in this example the facilities in domain C connect to domains A and B in the data link control level.* This is the case despite the fact that, within domain C, higher-level functions (that is, PC-2) are used.

In this illustration (Fig. 15.3), protocols for path control functions PC-1 are executed only in the two domains A and B. As in the previous example of Fig. 15.2, the success of the operation depends on agreements made by the resource managers of domains A and B with the resource manager of domain C. Again, these agreements to establish a path may be made dynamically (like a dial sequence) or they can be made at an earlier time (like setting up a "permanent" circuit at system definition time).

15.3 CROSS-DOMAIN CONNECTIONS

Multidomain architecture involves the following cross-domain connections:

- SSCP-to-SSCP session

- LU-to-LU session

- PU-to-PU session (for example, PU in COMC A to PU in COMC B in Fig. 15.1)

These logical connections in turn need to use transmission facilities that employ cross-domain links and cross-domain paths.

Cross-domain LU-LU sessions require (in addition to the SSCP-SSCP sessions) that each LU be in session with its SSCP, just as in the case of a single-domain LU-LU. The cross-domain LU-LU connections can then take many forms, some of which are illustrated in Figs. 15.4–15.7. In these illustrations, we assume the current SNA implementations, wherein (1) cluster controllers do not understand full network addresses and hence need the support of "boundary functions" in an adjacent node, (2) hosts do understand full network addresses, and (3) SSCPs are accordingly located in hosts. The illustrated connections are in three groups, as follows.

1. *LU-LU via switched line.* Data flows (see Fig. 15.4) between an LU in cluster controller (or terminal node) A/B and an LU in a host

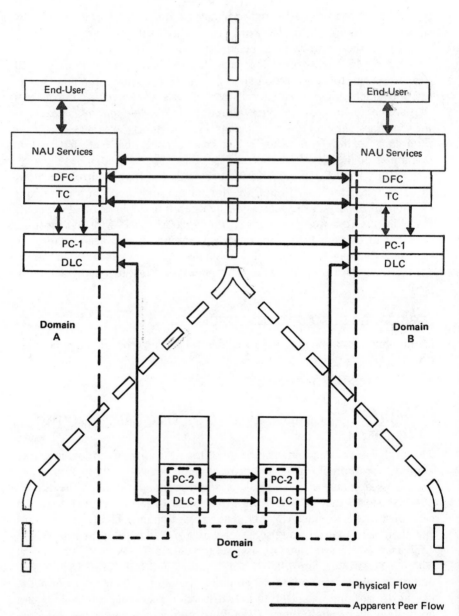

Fig. 15.3 Three-domain network, where third domain contains a path control network, but appears in the DLC network linking two other domains.

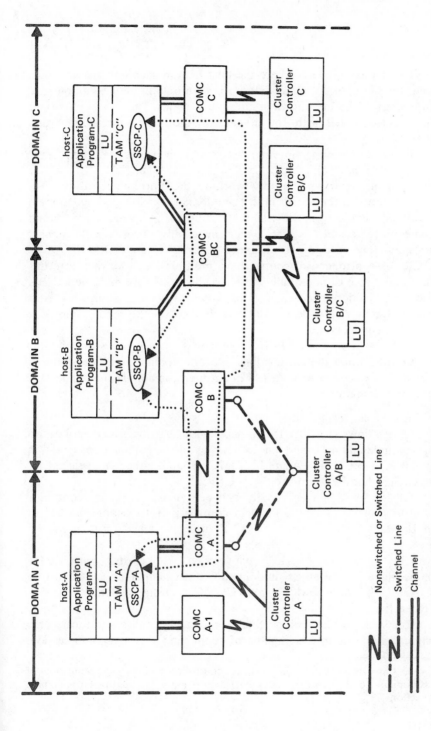

Fig. 15.4   Illustrative configuration of a multidomain network.

of domain A or domain B via a *switched* line and either COMC A *or* COMC B.

The simplest mode is where the host LUs in each domain (to which the cluster LU is to be connected) are known only in their own domains, but the cluster LUs are known in multiple domains. The cluster controller then associates itself with one domain or another by dialing into that domain.

The switched connection and the session in one domain are terminated before establishing a new session (for that same cluster LU) in the other domain. For this mode of networking, therefore, no coordination is necessary between the SSCPs in the two domains, so long as each domain has full information on the LU that is dialing in. (This mode should become more feasible as fast-connect switched networks with connect times below one second become more generally available.)

Cluster controllers, of course, have multiple LUs and therefore this node should, at least potentially, permit a cluster to have multiple LU-LU sessions with different domains. This, however, would require a cluster implementation whose design did not depend on the assumption of a single host connection.

The cross-domain SSCP-SSCP session becomes necessary, in this configuration, when the cluster dials into one domain and then wants to get an LU-LU session with an LU in another domain via the connection to the first domain.

2. *LU-LU via local COMCs*

a) Data flows (see Fig. 15.5a) between an LU for a host application program in domain A and an LU for a host application program in domain B via COMC A *and* COMC B and either a switched or nonswitched line between the two COMCs.*

b) Data flows (see Fig. 15.5b) between an LU in cluster controller (or terminal node) A and an LU in domain B (for example, an LU in host B) via COMC A *and* COMC B, using switched or nonswitched lines.*

c) Data flows (see Fig. 15.6) between an LU in cluster controller (or terminal node) A and an LU in domain C (for example, an LU in host C) via COMC A *and* COMC B *and* COMC C, using switched* or nonswitched lines.

Note that an LU supporting a secondary half-session can only communicate with an LU capable of supporting a primary half-session.

---

* SNA-3 supports automatic dial to cluster controllers and permits manual dial of cross-domain connections, but does not support automatic dial of cross-domain connections.

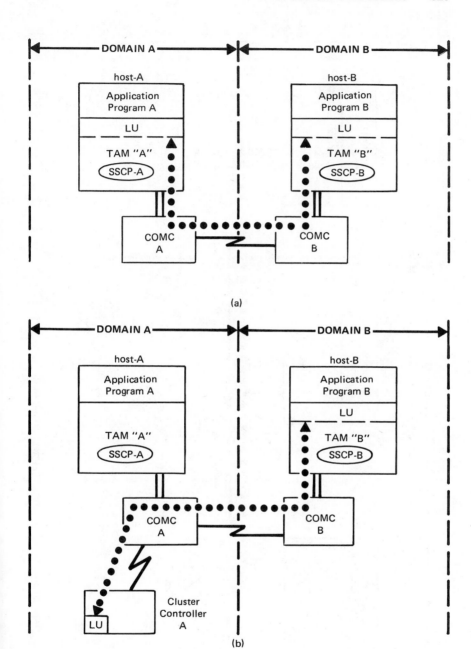

Fig. 15.5 Two-domain connections: (a) cross-domain connection: host to host; (b) two-domain connection: cluster controller to host.

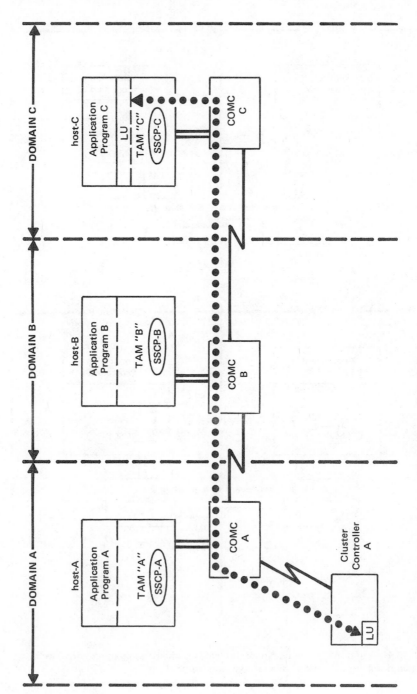

Fig. 15.6   Three-domain connection: crossing intermediate domain.

Current implementations of SNA have PLUs only in hosts. Therefore, so long as cluster controllers and terminal nodes are implemented with only secondary LU capability, those LUs only communicate (via COMCs) with PLUs in hosts.

3. *LU-LU via twin-tailed COMC:* Data flows (see Fig. 15.7) between LUs in cluster controllers (or terminal nodes) B/C and LUs for application programs in either domain B *or* domain C via the twin-tailed COMC BC (using switched or nonswitched lines).

The SSCPs in domains B and C jointly use the COMC resources. Architecturally, considerable sharing is possible. Application programs in domain B and domain C can share the SDLC lines on COMC BC. One terminal LU can access an LU on one CPU while a different terminal LU on the same or a different line, attached via the same COMC, can access LUs in a different CPU. Individual clusters and terminal nodes may also be connected to applications in either domain. Implementations of different access methods or controllers may, however, restrict the ownership of either lines or clusters.

If the cluster controller is on a switched line to the twin-tailed COMC, another mode of operation is possible. The PU of the cluster can be defined to SSCP B and to SSCP C, using different names. Each SSCP can (via ACTIVATE CONNECT IN) enable a different link station at the COMC. The cluster controller then receives a different PU address, depending on which port it dials into. The cluster (or terminal node) can therefore be connected to (dialed into or dialed out from) either control domain via the COMC without participating in cross-domain sessions.

The above connections appear to be the basic ones. Other cross-domain connections may also prove to be valuable. Some of these (not included in SNA-3) are the following:

1. A remote COMC in one domain connected directly to a remote COMC in another domain, and a local COMC in one domain connected directly to a remote COMC in another domain.

2. Parallel links between any two COMCs.

3. Multiple levels of remote COMCs (tandem remotes).

4. Direct CPU-CPU connection without use of COMCs (for example, private loop connection) for local CPUs.

5. An LU supporting a terminal connected to an LU supporting another terminal.

Note that links between COMCs can be very diverse, such as satellites, conventional telephone circuits, packet switching networks, etc. These may appear to the using nodes as switched or nonswitched links.

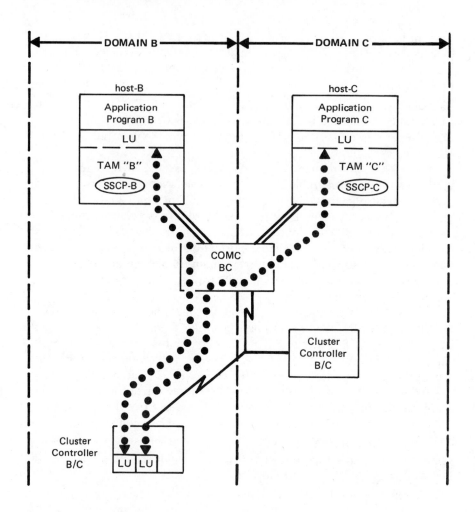

Fig. 15.7   Shared COMC, cross-domain connection.

Thus, in theory, links connecting cluster controllers to communication controllers and links connecting communications controllers may be switched or nonswitched. Product implementations, however, may restrict this. (In the ACF/VTAM implementation, for example, cross-domain connections can only be system-generated as nonswitched connections, although manual dialing by an operator may be used to actually achieve the connection.) In any case, by one type of link or another, *networking facilities have the objective of making any host application program accessible to any device or to any other application program in any of the connected domains.*

Variety of sessions. If hosts have both primary and secondary LU capabilities and both cluster controllers and terminal nodes have only secondary LU capability, then cross-domain sessions involve only the following varieties:

1. In sessions between LUs in hosts, either LU may be the primary LU.

2. In the session between two SSCPs, either SSCP may be primary.

3. In sessions between an LU in the host and LUs in cluster controllers or terminal nodes, the LU in the host is the primary.

The LUs and SSCPs in varieties 1 and 2 may be in the same or in different hosts. Missing from this list are sessions between LUs that are all in different cluster controllers or terminal nodes. Such sessions would require that one of the cluster controllers (or terminal nodes) have primary LU capability (and this is not provided by current architecture, SNA-3).

15.4   USE OF THE SSCP

15.4.1   Role of the SSCP

As discussed in Chapter 7, the SSCP performs a range of network services dealing with configuration, session, maintenance, network operator, and other services. Some of these services provide *control* functions; others do not. *These services can remain operative for each domain and, in addition, can serve cross-domain sessions.*

Conceivably, control points might be of at least three types. First, one could conceive of one super SSCP that manages communications resources in all nodes (even multiple hosts) that ever communicate with each other. This raises reliability concerns and the question of distance to that single central site. Second, at the other extreme, one could in effect put an SSCP in every node, eliminate all control points for multinode domains, and rely on capabilities distributed to all nodes to achieve network services. This may be satisfactory for small networks of a few nodes and minimum network services. However, as the network grows and as network services increase in scope and importance, this complete lack of service centers involves considerable duplication and may become uneconomical. A third alternative is to use an SSCP for multinode domains and coordinate among domain SSCPs. A distribution of network services then exists at the three natural levels:

1. The NAUs within nodes (by PUS and LUS).

2. The domain [by the domain resource manager (SSCP) for multiple nodes in that domain].

3. The multidomain network (by cross-SSCP resource management).

The fact that networks are often composed of a federation of previously autonomous domains that have grown independently, and the sometimes strong needs for local resource control, argue well for the third alternative. *The single domain thus is a component in a multidomain network, but each domain may contain multiple nodes.* That is the approach used by SNA.

In a philosophy of general communicability, a given LU might be connected via different sessions to LUs in different domains. Because such connection may be limited by capacity or capability, control involves the rejection of some requests for access and, preferably, queueing of requests for access. It would seem that the architecture should permit growth to a point where any logical unit could be accessed (after queueing) by any other logical unit in any control domain; and logical units in general could conduct multiple sessions simultaneously. This would promote resource sharing and application growth and would facilitate configuration change. Particular implementations, of course, may restrict that generality.

When we want an LU to be able to be in session with units in several control domains, it is necessary for that LU to be able to coordinate with the SSCPs of the several control domains. An efficient way of doing this is to *keep each LU in session with only one SSCP and then provide sessions among the (smaller number of) SSCPs.* This tends to reduce the complexity of each LU and also reduces the total number of connections that must be made. This is illustrated in Fig. 15.8. Each cross-domain LU-LU session is set up by using a session between the concerned SSCPs. *The existing sessions of each LU (with its managing SSCP) are used to formalize session establishment via the local SSCP, while the two SSCPs coordinate with each other.* Then after the session is established, the LU-LU RUs flow directly, without further concern of the SSCPs until session termination time.

The cross-domain facilities can then be *transparent* in the sense that so far as the end-user and the LU are concerned the cross-domain connections are no different from comparable single-domain connections and they require no special network knowledge or awareness. *Each LU works with its own SSCP in the same way, whether the session is in one domain or across multiple domains.* The SNA approach is to provide a range of fully transparent networking capabilities in matters such as LU-LU session setup and LU-LU operations during the session. Application programs or application subsystems can then also provide nontransparent networking capabilities where that is desirable.

Note that the same cross-domain links may be used to support data flows of both LU-LU sessions and SSCP-SSCP sessions. Both types of

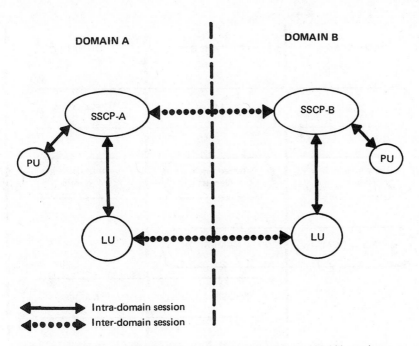

DOMAIN A

DOMAIN B

Intra-domain session
Inter-domain session

Fig. 15.8 Use of the SSCP–SSCP session to establish an LU–LU session.

sessions, for example, would use the transmission facilities linking COMC A and COMC B in Fig. 15.4.

15.4.2 Name Resolution

To facilitate change, SNA allows three sets—network address, network name, and alternate NAU name—to change independent of one another. One of the services provided by the SSCP is the resolution of the symbolic NAU names to network addresses.

The user of the network need not be aware of the network addresses and can work with symbolic names that are more meaningful in the context of the applications and terminal operators. First, each network address has a *network name*. All network names are unique within a domain, but are not necessarily unique across domains. A *subset* of the network names in each domain is used in cross-domain operations (see Fig. 15.9); *these are commonly known and unique across the domains in which they are used. Then alternate NAU names* may also be needed.The name used to identify a resource may vary because

1. Different users of the same resource may know it by different names that are better suited to the user's purpose.

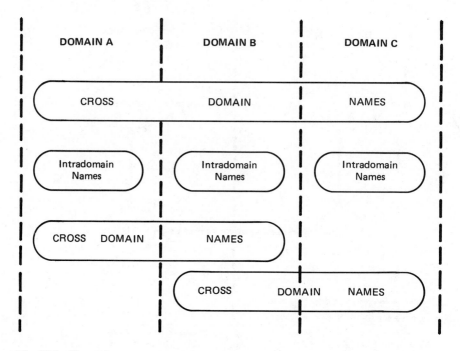

Fig. 15.9 Network name uniqueness.

2. The request may be for any resource in a pool of resources, each of which has a unique name; the pool may therefore need a name.

3. The requestor may have no way of knowing the true name of the resource and hence uses another symbolic name.

For these reasons, a resource name used by the issuer of a network service command can be different from the network name in a particular domain.

Within the SSCP of each domain, therefore, there is a need for translation between network names and alternate (or uninterpreted) names, and vice versa. There are no restrictions on the alternate names, so the use of end-user names as alternate LU names is not excluded. Several approaches are theoretically possible:

1. Each domain could have its set of aliases, and *each domain SSCP would have to "interpret" every other domain's aliases.* This would require that every domain have "interpreting" capability for every other domain, a capability that increases as the square of the number of domains.

2. Each domain could have its set of aliases; and *each domain SSCP would have to "interpret" only its own aliases,* translating them into a set of network names that is common across domains. This reduces the interpreting capability to one that increases linearly with the number of domains.

The second approach is the more practical and versatile, and is the one favored by SNA. However, in an architecture like SNA, *the "interpreting" capability can be product-specific:* It may not be needed in some products, simple in others, and sophisticated in others. *Alternate LU names may be mapped to network names, depending on the LU making the service request.* The current approach is to make it the responsibility of the "network owner" at system generation time to ensure that the network names to be used in cross-domain sessions are unique throughout the network. Aliases may then be related to those common network names in the SSCP of each domain as needed. Note that *this allows alternate names to change,* without affecting cross-domain coordinations (via network names).

In SNA, every domain has the capability of resolving network names into network addresses for those NAU that lie within that particular domain. The name-to-address translation for a resource outside a given domain cannot be done in that domain. For this, the SSCP of the domain requesting the resource must be able to communicate with the SSCP of the domain in which the requested resource resides. This second SSCP will then relay the associated network address back to the requestor. Each SSCP then needs to know where to send network names that are for resources outside its domain. Currently (in VTAM, for example) this total list of common network names and their associated SSCPs is developed at system generation time.

The network addresses must also be unique throughout the network because they are used for message routing. One could, in theory, attach additional "area codes" for each domain to insure this, allowing duplicate subarea codes in different domains. However, even without an area code the only addresses that need to be coordinated across domains are the subarea portions of the network addresses. As discussed in Chapter 10, element addresses can be duplicated in different subareas and (in some cases) even within a subarea. The number of subareas is sufficiently small that it usually should not be difficult to make all subarea addresses in the network unique. This is the SNA approach.

Note that configuration changes involving new network addresses do not affect network names. Hence, *configurations and network addresses can change* without affecting cross-domain coordinations via network names.

Thus we have two important consequences:

1. The actual translations of network name to network address and of alternate name to network name can always be localized to one domain, and

2. Alternate name changes do not affect the transportation environment, and network address changes do not affect the application environment.

15.4.3 Network Operations

Another major function of the SSCP in SNA is to provide services to the network operator. The network operator uses network services (for example, session, configuration, and maintenance services) provided by the SSCP.

An operator can be represented by an LU. Similarly, an LU can represent a "programmed operator" to provide network operation support. A combination of network operators and network-operation support programs can thus be in session with each SSCP. A network operator can also be in session with a network-operation support program, and two network-operation support programs can also be in session with each other (see Fig. 15.10).

Operator control can be distributed in current implementations. Each operator may be restricted to a subset of network resources, and

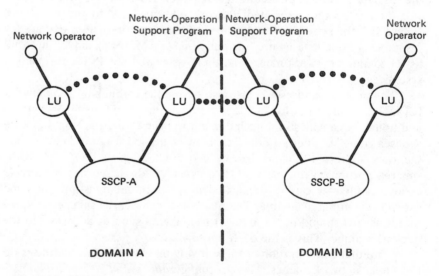

Fig. 15.10 LU-LU sessions for network-operator-support programs.

commands may be issued only against the SNA resources in that operator's span of control. These include any SNA resource defined to the SSCP, including cross-domain resource tables, lines, and resources in such nodes as communications controllers, local and remote cluster controllers, and terminal nodes, as specified in the system definition. In Fig. 15.10, for example, by using protocols between two network-operator support programs, a single network resource in domain B can be controlled in domain A, or all the network resources in domain B can be controlled in domain A. Commands submitted by an operator in domain A that affect resources in domain B are sent to the network-operation support program in domain B over the LU-LU session for the two network-operation support programs. The program in domain B then submits the command to the SSCP for domain B [15.8]. Note that in ACF/VTAM special facilities of a program operator interface are provided for the sessions between network-operation support programs and an SSCP. These are not provided for an ordinary SSCP-LU session. Hence, the network operator commands go first via the LU-LU session that connects a network operator to a network-operation support program. A combination of SSCP facilities and network-operation support programs [15.8 and 15.9] thus can provide

- Support of multiple (local and remote) network operators.
- Ability through the use of authorization facilities to limit each operator's control to specified portions of the network.
- Ability for multiple network operators to share network control responsibility, where each may control a portion (or one may control all) of the network.

Supplementary facilities in operation support programs offer

- Capability for user-written exit routines to screen and edit operator message traffic.
- Capability for user-written command processors to support customized operator commands or operands.
- Logging of operator messages which can provide a hard copy for later audit of network operations.

One other mode deserves mention. In a multihost establishment, multiple SSCP cross-domain services also allow one to consolidate the major part of network control in one host, thereby freeing other local processors for more application processing. *One of several processors, in effect, can take the role of a communications processor for the others, if one SSCP is assigned ownership of most of the establishment's network.*

Then the SSCP in each host would still manage the LUs in that host, but only one SSCP would manage all the cluster controllers and terminal nodes.

15.5 BYPASSING A HOST (FOR DATA FLOWS)

Current implementations place the SSCP in a host (although this is not a basic part of the architecture). Then, when several domains are involved, what is the involvement of the several hosts in the flow of normal traffic to an LU in a terminal? In particular, when using lines from a cluster controller or terminal node to the COMC of its local host (see Fig. 15.5b), a question remains. Does all traffic flow through each host to which a cluster controller or terminal node is connected (that is, through its "local" host)? Or does traffic flow to that local host only for SSCP functions?

Many networking systems are built on the premise that all traffic from a terminal passes through its local host. Often the local host to which a terminal is normally attached contains an application program (or application subsystem) that acts as the intermediary between the local terminal and an application in a remote host. Examples of this include IBM's TCS/TCAM, NRJE, and IMS/MSC. ACF/VTAM networking support also provides facilities so the user can write such an intermediary application for pre-SNA devices.

Teleprocessing performance and host utilization can be improved, however, if traffic from a cluster controller or a terminal node (or some other COMC) does not enter the local host (or any other local processor) for local process execution, but passes instead via the COMCs directly to the remote host (see Fig. 15.5b). A middle-ground solution, which was referred to in Chapter 3 as class-3 networking, *makes use of the SSCPs in each host for session activation and session termination and for other network services, but does not pass LU-LU session traffic through the local or intermediate hosts once that session is established.* That session traffic bypasses the local host, as shown by the dotted lines in Figs. 15.5(b), 15.6, and 15.7. VTAM and TCAM support provides this class-3 networking (bypassing hosts) for all SNA cluster controllers and terminal nodes that attach to communications controllers (COMCs).

15.6 NETWORKING FACILITIES

The practical achievement of this class-3 networking in the configurations of Figs. 15.5, 15.6, and 15.7 requires new facilities beyond those described in earlier chapters, particularly in hosts and COMCs. To sum up, these include the following:

1. Facilities for physically communicating between nodes in two domains, including cross-domain link activation.

2. Facilities for logically communicating between SSCPs in any two domains. To maintain the equality of the SSCPs, it is desirable that an SSCP can support either a primary or a secondary half of the sessions to other SSCPs.

3. Means for activating cross-domain LU-LU sessions, complete with cross-domain name resolution.

4. Transit node capabilities of COMCs, so that once an SSCP has assisted in setting up a session, subsequent traffic need not be routed through both hosts on its way to its destination.

5. Implementation of COMCs such that a host failure does not disrupt the transit (cross-domain) functions of local communications controllers: (a) A session whose LUs are not in the failing host, but whose flow passes through the domain of a failing host, should be able to continue without interruption; (b) moreover, sessions involving a nonhost LU should be able to continue even though that LU has lost contact with its SSCP. Such sessions should continue so long as new services are not needed from the SSCP. Session termination must also be possible without the SSCP. Reinstatement of the failing host should also not impair the COMC transit function.

6. Facilities for cross-domain reporting of failures that are brought to the attention of network services in a PU.

15.7 SSCP-SSCP SESSIONS

In order to achieve the above types of cross-domain coordination, it is necessary to have a session between the SSCPs of different domains. Each SSCP is, of course, a network addressable unit, so these cross-domain sessions are only special versions of NAU-NAU sessions.

Each domain usually grows autonomously, and each operates as the peer of any other domain. Any domain may need to take the initiative in cross-domain operations. It follows that a peer relationship should exist between SSCPs such that either SSCP can establish an SSCP-to-SSCP session. The SNA approach to these SSCP-SSCP sessions is described in the following.

Cross-domain resource managers

In Chapter 7, it was shown how network services are distributed in pairs between the SSCP on the one hand and LUs and PUs on the other. These services for a single domain were discussed under four headings: (1) configuration services, (2) session services, (3) maintenance services, and (4) network operator services. Each of these services potentially has a counterpart in each SSCP of a multidomain network to deal with multi-domain network services.

The portion of the SSCP that deals with cross-domain services has been called the *cross-domain resource manager* (CDRM). The portion of the SSCP discussed heretofore, concerned with only one domain, is accordingly referred to as the *domain resource manager* (DRM) (see Fig. 15.11). A summary of the potential distribution of the network services among the cross-domain resource managers, domain resource managers, logical units, and physical units in a two-domain network is shown in Fig. 15.12. Each SSCP is a single NAU; the DRM and CDRM share a unique network name and a unique network address. The NS header allows implementations to easily distinguish requests for CDRM services from requests for DRM services.

Chapters 9 and 12 illustrated the use of session activation commands—namely, the ACTLU, ACTPU, and BIND—for SSCP-LU, SSCP-PU, and LU-LU sessions, respectively. In like manner, another session activation command, ACTCDRM, is used to activate an SSCP-SSCP session which links two CDRMs in different domains. The ACTCDRM includes fields defining FM and TS profiles as in the BIND command described in Section 9.7.

Because the SSCPs are peers of one another, any SSCP must be able to initiate an ACTCDRM command. SNA permits this, with the ground rule that the first NAU to successfully complete sending an ACTCDRM (and getting a positive response) becomes the primary for the SSCP-SSCP session (see Asymmetric Protocols in Section 6.10). Thus either SSCP may become the primary NAU for a cross-domain session. The response to that ACTCDRM contains information about the peer SSCP. (This is one of the few cases where an SNA response carries information in addition to an acknowledgment.)

Resources are identified to the SSCP if they are to participate in multidomain sessions. In particular, in current ACF/VTAM implementations, if an NAU is to participate in multidomain networking, then it is defined as a *local resource* in its own SSCP and as a *cross-domain resource* in other SSCPs. In a given SSCP, an LU (with a given network name) may be either a local or a cross-domain resource, but not both at the same time.

Procedure correlation

A procedure, like a session initiation procedure, may involve a series of network service commands, such as INIT-SELF, CINIT, BIND, and SST.

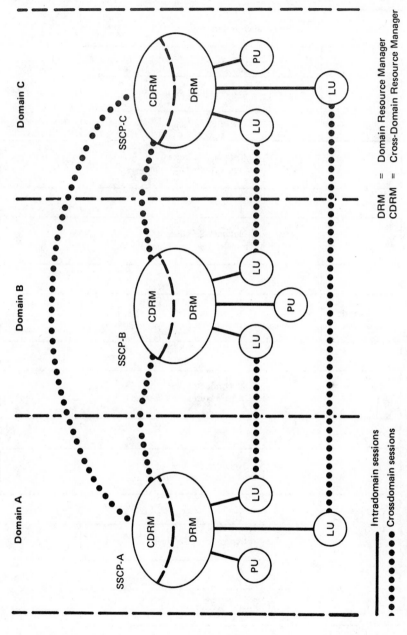

DRM   =   Domain Resource Manager
CDRM =   Cross-Domain Resource Manager

Intradomain sessions
Crossdomain sessions

Fig. 15.11 CDRM-CDRM and LU-LU cross-domain sessions.

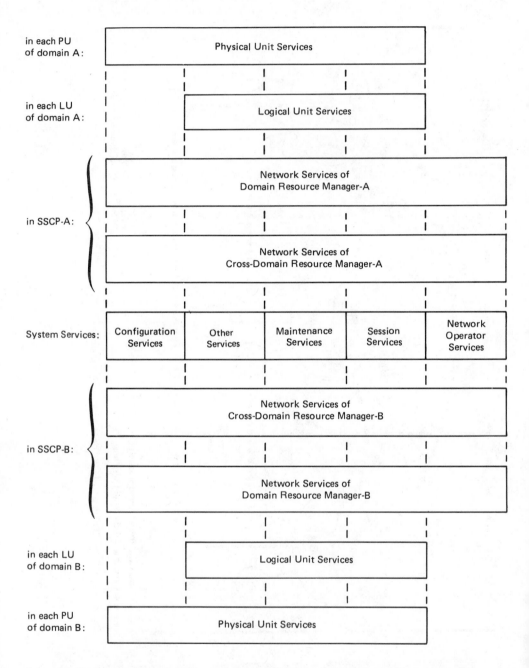

Fig. 15.12 Summary of the potential distribution of network services among the SSCPs, LUs, and PUs of two domains.

A cross-domain procedure is not simply between a pair of NAUs with the help of a single SSCP, as in the single-domain case. Often four NAUs (two LUs and two SSCPs) are involved as, for example, when an LU in one domain asks its SSCP to work with another SSCP in another domain to set up an LU-LU session with an LU in that second domain. In some cases (as with INITIATE OTHER commands) up to four SSCPs can be involved in the set-up procedure. Therefore, some care must be taken in correlating all requests in these multiple sessions that belong to one procedure.

The network services requests and responses used in SSCP-SSCP sessions correspond to those used within a domain. However, their capabilities have been expanded in two respects, as follows.

1. The responses in the CDRM-to-CDRM sessions may carry additional status information about the procedure being processed.

2. Requests in CDRM-to-CDRM sessions, which flow in either direction as part of a procedure (for example, an LU-LU session activation procedure), may carry a *procedure correlation ID* (*PCID*). This makes it easier for the two SSCPs to keep track of the multiple sequences of requests that they can have with regard to setting up multiple LU-LU sessions. The PCID is generated by the SSCP of the domain where the service request originates.

The PCID, for example, might contain two fields: the network address of the SSCP originating the cross-domain procedure and a unique identification number generated by the originating SSCP (for example, time of day might be used). A use of the procedure correlation ID (PCID) in requests is illustrated in Fig. 15.13. There the same PCID could appear in the three cross-domain commands—CD-INIT, CD-CINIT, and CD-SST. (These three commands extend the INIT, CINIT, and SST commands for cross-domain operations.)

Note that the INITSELF, CINIT, BIND, and SST commands appear as in single-domain operations so that the cross-domain operations are transparent. The cross-domain commands provide the necessary bridge between SSCPs. The existence of that bridge depends on the prior establishment of the SSCP-SSCP session.

Establishing the SSCP-SSCP session

The ACTCDRM command for the SSCP-SSCP session establishes rules for that session as follows.

1. Only single-element chains.

2. Multiple chains, each requiring a response, may be outstanding.

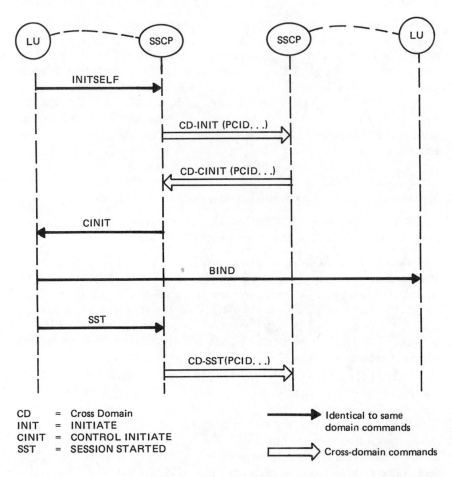

Fig. 15.13 Use of procedure correlation ID (PCID) to relate three cross-domain commands in the INIT sequence.

3. Recovery of flows is the responsibility of the sender of the request.

4. IDs will be used instead of sequence numbers.

5. CLEAR and RQR (REQUEST RECOVERY) are available.

6. Pacing is bidirectional (each CDRM specifies its pacing parameter when it sends or responds to the ACTCDRM command).

Establishing the SSCP-SSCP session is done by the sequence shown in Fig. 15.14. The enable commands are product-specific and are not architected. The purpose of the enable A and enable B commands is to add these particular CDRMs to the list of CDRMs from which each SSCP is willing to accept ACTCDRM requests. *This gives the network operator direct control over the extent of the network. Each domain can be enabled to participate with only some subset of the entire network, if this is desired.* The enabled CDRM table may be constructed at system generation time.

Note that the establishment of the SSCP-SSCP session requires the cooperation of an operator in both domains. The operator commands to set up the cross-domain session are not architected so they may be product-unique. (Standardization may be pursued independent of the network architecture.)

An ACTCDRM may be accepted or rejected, depending on the state of the receiving CDRM. Requests to CDRMs that have not been enabled, or for which parameters do not match, will be rejected by a negative

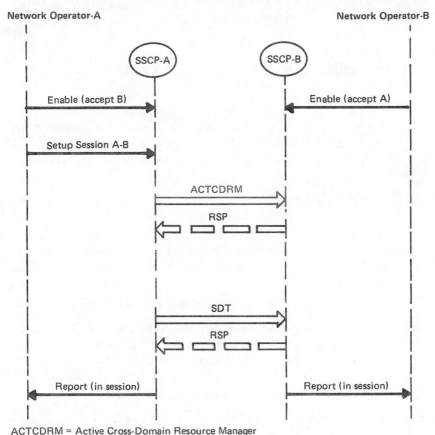

ACTCDRM = Active Cross-Domain Resource Manager

Fig. 15.14 Setting up an SSCP–SSCP session.

response with appropriate sense byte encoding. Even after a positive response, data cannot flow until the sender of ACTCDRM sends START DATA TRAFFIC (SDT). This allows the primary NAU to reject the ACTCDRM response by issuing a DACTCDRM before session flow begins. The DACTCDRM (Deactivate Cross-Domain Resource Manager) unbinds the SSCP-SSCP session. Either CDRM may issue the deactivation request.

Because no third party is the referee in the SSCP-SSCP session activation, a contention situation can occur if both SSCPs issue an ACTCDRM simultaneously (that is, within the transmission propagation delay). In this event, some algorithm in the SSCPs, based on SSCP IDs, can be used to arbitrarily resolve the contention in favor of one SSCP.

The only asymmetry currently existing in CDRM sessions is that the primary NAU issues CLEAR and SDT while the secondary sends REQUEST RECOVERY (RQR) to the primary, indicating that CLEAR must be issued.

15.8 CROSS-DOMAIN LU-LU SESSIONS/SETUP

15.8.1 Introduction

LUs have no perception of any difference between same-domain and cross-domain LU-LU sessions. As in the case of same-domain LU-LU sessions, there are three session-initiation situations to be handled, as follows.

1. One of the LUs to be connected requests a connection, and the other LU is able to enter into session immediately.
2. A session is requested between two LUs and one of them is temporarily occupied, requiring a queueing of the request for session. (The desired LU may already have as many sessions as it is capable of conducting at one time.)
3. An LU directs that a session be established between two other LUs.

Section 15.8.2 provides an overview that illustrates the procedures used in cross-domain LU-LU session setup. For those needing it, further detail and explanation are then provided in Sections 15.8.3–15.8.6.

15.8.2 Simplified Session Activation Sequences

Simplified sequences for the activation of cross-domain LU-LU sessions are shown in Fig. 15.15 for the three cases: (1) primary LU initiates session; (2) secondary LU initiates session; and (3) third-party LU

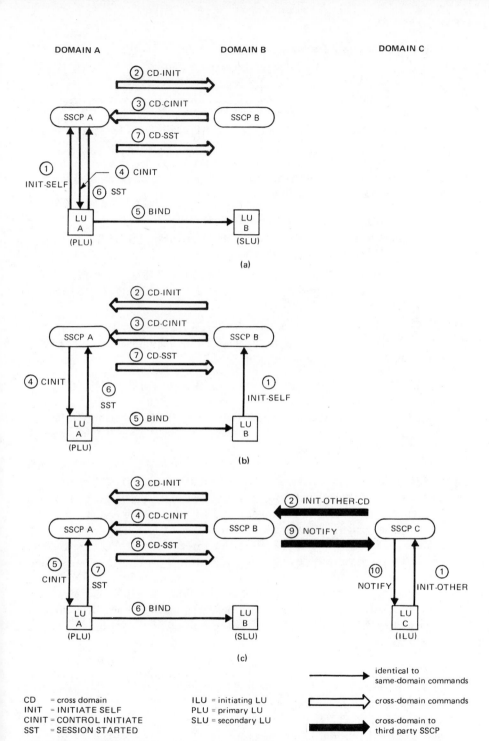

Fig. 15.15 LU-LU cross-domain sessions activation: (a) primary LU initiates cross-domain session; (b) secondary LU initiates cross-domain session; (c) third-party LU initiates cross-domain session.

initiates session. SSCP-LU sessions and SSCP-SSCP sessions are prerequisites to this cross-domain LU-LU session activation. The session initiating LU (ILU) is LU A, LU B, and LU C, in Figs. 15.15(a), (b), and (c) respectively.

A small number of additional NS commands are needed to initiate cross-domain sessions, corresponding to commands in same-domain sessions. These are the following.

1. CD-INIT (CROSS DOMAIN INITIATE): Transports an INIT request from the origin SSCP to the destination SSCP. The response to the CD-INIT returns resolved parameters to the origin SSCP.

2. CD-CINIT (CROSS DOMAIN CONTROL INITIATE): Passes secondary LU information from its SSCP to the SSCP of the primary LU.

3. CD-SST (CROSS DOMAIN SESSION STARTED): Notifies the secondary LU's SSCP that an LU-LU cross-domain session has been activated.

In each case of Fig. 15.13, the INIT-SELF (case a or b) or INIT-OTHER (case c) is followed by inter-SSCP commands, including a CD-INIT and a CD-CINIT between the origin and destination SSCPs. These are followed by a CINIT to the primary LU (PLU) from its SSCP. The PLU then sends the BIND to the secondary LU.

The establishment of the session is then confirmed by a SESSION STARTED (SST) from the PLU to its SSCP, and a CD-SST from there to the SSCP of the other LU. In the case of a third-party SSCP, it is also notified of the session establishment by a cross-domain NOTIFY command. The origin SSCP, which sends the CD-INIT command, is SSCP A, SSCP B, and SSCP B in the three cases of Fig. 15.15. The CD-INIT provides the destination SSCP with the network name of the destination LU. When sent by the SLU's SSCP, the CD-INIT also provides the *alternate LU name* of the destination LU if one was used since that alternate name needs to be recognized by the SLU when it receives the BIND command. This is the case when the initiating LU is a secondary.

Whichever SSCP controls the secondary LU then sends the CD-CINIT. It provides information about the secondary LU that will be needed by the primary LU's SSCP. The CINIT, sent to the primary LU, contains names for both the primary LU and the secondary LU. In the case of an INIT-OTHER request (Fig. 15.15c) both names are network names. On the other hand, in the case of an INIT SELF (as in Fig. 15.15b), the name of the destination LU used in CINIT will be the alternate name since that is the one that the initiating LU expects to receive in BIND.

15.8.3 Self-setup of Cross-domain LU-LU Sessions

The simplest form of a cross-domain LU-LU session setup is the case in which one of the LUs to be connected requests the session. This is the INIT-SELF case. Let us look further at it.

The sequence of commands for this case is shown in Fig. 15.16. Note that to preserve the transparent nature of the networking all requests and responses seen by either LU are the same as they were for the corresponding single-domain case.

INIT-SELF indicates whether the origin LU can operate as a primary LU, as a secondary LU, or as either. If the origin LU has both capabilities, the destination SSCP in the other domain specifies the relationship. The origin LU becomes primary when both LUs have primary and secondary capability.

The CD-INIT in effect transfers the request for the session to the other SSCP. After the response to the CD-INIT, both SSCPs have an awareness of

- The requesting user and its password
- The network name and network address of both LUs
- The PCID for this procedure
- The BIND mode requested
- Related queueing and LU status information

CD-INIT may flow in either direction, depending on which LU initiates the session request. The sequence starting with CD-CINIT is the same regardless of which LU initiates the session request. The CD-CINIT passes to the PLU's SSCP information about the secondary LU that is needed for the generation of CINIT. It includes the bind image maintained by the SLU's SSCP for its LU and selected by the mode parameter in the INITIATE-SELF. In this way, the PLU's SSCP can complete the CINIT request without maintaining complete information on all SLUs.

If a bind failure is encountered, the PLU notifies its SSCP, as in the single-domain case. A cross-domain SESSION FAILURE command (CD-SF) will then be sent to the SLU's SSCP. The other LU can be notified of the failure by its SSCP via a NETWORK SERVICES PROCEDURE ERROR command.

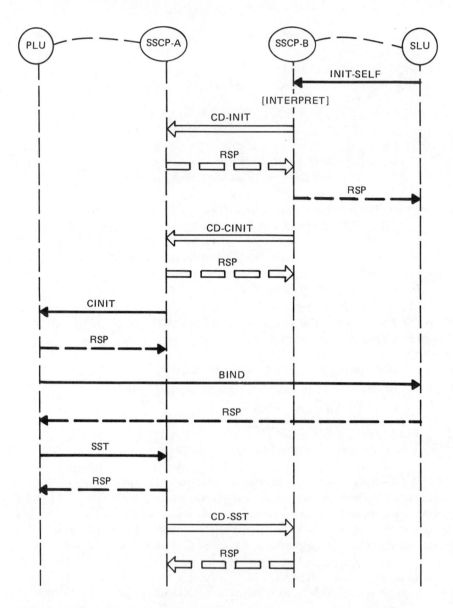

Fig. 15.16 One of the LUs to be connected requests a cross-domain connection.

15.8.4   Queued Setup of Cross-domain LU-LU Sessions

The INITIATE-SELF command (and the INITIATE-OTHER command) from an initiating LU to its SSCP may contain a parameter indicating that the request for a session may be queued. This parameter in INITIATE may be one of four options:

1. Initiate but do not queue.
2. Initiate if possible, and queue if the other LU is not available.
3. Queue, because the requesting LU is not available.
4. Dequeue a pending queued session request.

Either option (2) or (3) can result in a session request being queued, if the SSCP implementation provides queueing services.

     If both SSCPs support the queuing function, they both remain aware of the queued session request after the CD-INIT request and the response. The latter carries the status of the requested LU, and so can advise that an LU is unavailable for a session. The session request then remains queued until the needed resource becomes available.

     When the LU status changes, its SSCP must be so advised. That SSCP then issues the CD-INIT with the dequeue parameter. Let us assume that this time the CD-INIT is successful, as indicated by a positive response. The subsequent sequence is then the same as in Fig. 15.16, starting with the CD-CINIT.

15.8.5   "Other" Setup of Cross-domain LU-LU Sessions

Another situation arises when one LU requests that a session be set up between two other LUs. This might occur, for example, when an LU is ready to terminate its session and wishes to pass its partner LU, with which it has been in session, into another session with some new LU.

     Figure 15.17 illustrates the "other" setup, with the complication that one of the LUs for the requested session is already occupied in an existing session. In that example, LU_D requests that a session be set up between PLU_C and SLU_B. However, the latter is occupied in an existing session with PLU_A. (In Fig. 15.17, the parentheses indicate the presence of an information field.)

     Domains B and C will be directly responsible for the requested session, and the cross-domain exchanges between them are the same as those described previously. In addition, cross-domain RUs must be exchanged with domains D and A as shown by the darker arrows in Fig. 15.17. These are in three parts:

1. Domain D makes the setup request (via CD INIT OTHER),

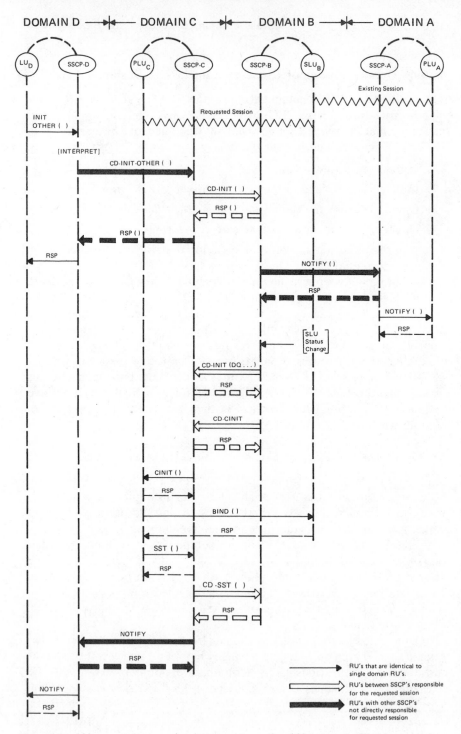

Fig. 15.17 LU_D requests a session between two other LUs, one of which is currently occupied.

2. Domain A is notified that its PLU_A is asked to give up its session with SLU_B, and

3. Domain D is notified when the session, which it requested, is finally started.

The CD-INIT OTHER could be sent by SSCP-D to either SSCP-C or SSCP-B, since both B and C will be responsible for the requested session.

The CD-INIT OTHER request arriving at SSCP-C can indicate which LUs are to be notified about the requested session and under what conditions. The CROSS DOMAIN INITIATE (CD-INIT) informs SSCP-B whether or not LUs in session with SLU_B are to be notified. SSCP-B notifies SSCP-A, which in turn notifies PLU_A.

All SSCP-LU exchanges and LU-LU exchanges can be identical to those used in single-domain operations.

As previously, the initiating LU (in domain D) may use LU names that are different from the common network names used for cross-domain sessions. Therefore (in current ACF/VTAM implementation), SSCP-D may have to interpret the names of the requested LUs, transforming them (for that particular initiating LU) to network names that are unique across the connected domains.

In the example, the first CD-INIT is unsuccessful because the SLU_B resource is not available. Queueing takes place as called for by CD-INIT. Following a status change of SLU_B, a retry of CD-INIT is successful, and this is followed by the CD-CINIT containing the SLU parameters. The normal BIND sequence follows, as in the single-domain case.

When the requested session is started, the CD-SST takes care of notifying SSCP-B. A cross-domain, third party NOTIFY command must be used to notify SSCP-D also.

15.8.6 Deactivation of Cross-domain LU-LU Sessions

Takedown

The takedown of cross-domain LU-LU sessions is likewise equivalent to that provided by the current single-domain services, and the takedown commands seen by an LU can be the same for both single- and multiple-domain operations.

As in the single-domain case, it is possible for a PLU to directly terminate a session via a CLEAR-UNBIND sequence, followed by a SESSION ENDED (SE) RU, sent by the PLU to its SSCP. This may be appropriate when the name resolution or dequeueing functions of the SSCP are not needed.

Alternatively, the TERMINATE SELF command can be used by either LU to obtain the ability to terminate a session using an alternate LU name. (As with the INITIATE services, either the network name or an alternate name may be submitted.) Figure 15.18 illustrates a termination sequence. The CD-TERM can flow in either direction, depending on which LU issues the TERM-SELF.

The end-user is consulted (via product-specific commands) if the option chosen is an orderly takedown rather than a forced takedown. The CTERM will carry an indication as to where the termination procedure was initiated (pri/sec/other) and why (normal/recovery), to facilitate reporting to the PLU end-user.

The completion of the CLEAR-UNBIND flow and user notification is reported back to the PLU's SSCP by the SESSION-ENDED, so that the SSCP may takedown its session knowledge. Similarly, the takedown of active session knowledge across domains is triggered by a CD-SESSION ENDED.

Single-domain takedowns include an "all" option in TERM-SELF which terminates multiple sessions of a given LU. In multidomain operations, this group termination must be transformed by the receiving SSCP into individual CD-TERM requests for each session, since different sessions may involve different domains.

Regarding queued setups, the terminate service may indicate that one of several forms of terminate be performed:

1. Active sessions only

2. Queued sessions only

3. Both active and queued sessions

As with the INITIATE-OTHER service, SNA also provides a TERMINATE-OTHER service, in which some third party can ask for the takedown of queued and/or active sessions between any two LUs. This operation must involve checking the identity of the third party. The ID of the requesting party and password fields are provided for this permission check. The "other" takedown involves sending the TERM-OTHER request (in a CD-TERM-OTHER) from the SSCP of the third party to the SSCP at one end of the affected session. This results in a CD-TERM between the responsible SSCPs, and the termination process proceeds as described before.

CLEANUP

When a session deactivation procedure does not complete properly, there is session information left in various NAUs that must be cleaned up.

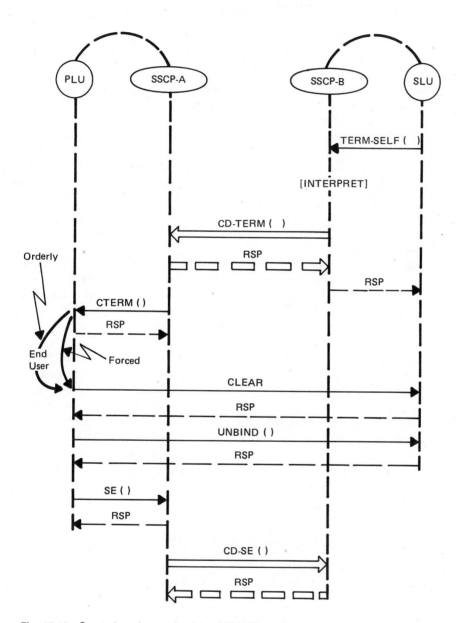

Fig. 15.18 Cross-domain termination of LU-LU session.

Information about a session exists in the PLU, the SLU, and the SSCPs managing their domains. In addition, for cluster-controller and terminal-node SLUs, there is also information in the boundary function of the communications controllers to which cluster controllers or terminal nodes are attached.

The cleanup for "self" type operations may be thought of as one NAU telling another NAU to clean up the session-related information; it also indicates that the sending NAU has done likewise. For this purpose, a "cleanup" parameter has been defined for a number of NS requests. Figure 15.19 shows various forms of cleanup requests that can be used. The CLEANUP request directed to an SLU or the CTERM (with cleanup parameters) directed to a PLU performs the same session-reset function as a CLEAR-UNBIND sequence without using the LU-LU path.

In the case of existing cluster controllers and terminal nodes, an expedient can be used, that of resetting the SLU and its boundary function by a DACTLU. The SLU can then be cleanly reactivated with an ACTLU. This is a simple near-term solution involving no change to existing products, but one that is satisfactory only so long as each SLU is limited to one LU-LU session (this is characteristic of present implementations, but is not an architectural limitation for cluster controllers). With multiple LU-LU sessions per LU, one would not want the cross-domain termination procedures to force termination of healthy sessions of that same LU.

The takedown commands, terminate-self, terminate-other, and the supporting functions of CTERM and CD-TERM can also play a role in cleaning up PLUs and SSCPs and in providing the stimulus for the above-mentioned SLU cleanup. Accordingly, each of these four takedown commands has been assigned a cleanup parameter that serves to set the cleanup actions in motion.

15.9 CROSS-DOMAIN LINK CONNECTION

Cross-domain paths include (1) TP links between communications controllers, (2) paths that use the computer channel connections (and the path control function) of an N-tail communications controller, and (3) private paths within a host that supports multiple control domains. The connection sequences will vary depending on implementation and the type of link involved. In any case, the procedures in the two domains are unsynchronized, except where both procedures become dependent on the same link-level activity. As an illustration, we will examine the connection between two communications controllers.

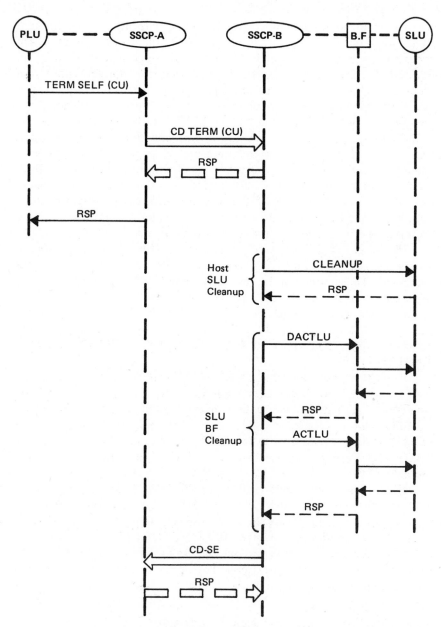

Fig. 15.19 Possible use of CLEANUP command and cleanup parameter, when deactivation of a session does not complete.

The connection between communications controllers in two different control domains is, in SNA-3, a point-to-point connection. To the system generation, it is a nonswitched connection, although manual dialing can be used. In any event, the setting up of the cross-domain connection requires the cooperation of the operators (or operations programs) in the two domains. Each SSCP, prompted by its operator (or a "bring-up" operations program), issues the ACTIVATE LINK request, followed by a CONTACT procedure to the PU in the local communications controller. CONTACT directs the PU to initiate a procedure to establish link-level contact with the station at the other communications controller. Both primary and secondary data link controls have the capability to handle CONTACT and DISCONTACT procedures in a cross-domain connection. This equality ensures the explicit cooperation of both domains and preserves the independence that some domains require.

Upon receiving the CONTACT, the PU for the primary station directs the sending of an SNRM (Set Normal Response Mode) link-level command. The secondary station will respond with the expected NSA (Nonsequenced Acknowledgment) only if prior to that time a CONTACT command was also received (from its SSCP) by the PU for the secondary station. If that is the case, then the primary station proceeds to send a polling command, and both PUs respond to their SSCPs with a CONTACTED request.

If, on the other hand, the CONTACT had not yet been received by the PU for the secondary station when the SNRM arrived, then no NSA would be returned. Instead, a Disconnected Mode (DM) link response would be sent or a time-out would occur on the SNRM. In that case, the primary station would repeat the SNRM. Eventually, the dual CONTACT will permit a connection or the operators must resolve the problem.

Either SSCP may initiate the DISCONTACT. If the PU at the primary station receives the DISCONTACT request, it will direct data link control to send a link-level Disconnect command. If the PU at the secondary station receives the DISCONTACT (from its SSCP) it will direct the secondary station to issue a link-level "Request Disconnect" signal as a response to the next poll. The primary station must then send the Disconnect link-level command.

15.10 MULTIDOMAIN NETWORK RECOVERY

The multidomain network offers some unique opportunities to provide recovery in the event of malfunction over and above those cited for the single-domain network in Chapter 14. A number of these opportunities are discussed in the following sections.

15.10.1   Notification for Network Integrity

When a loss of physical contact between adjacent subareas occurs, the affected SSCPs and the concerned sessions must be notified of resulting route interruptions and recovery strategies must be initiated. We will discuss several approaches to meeting this need.

A loss of contact can be the result of

1. A physical outage of link, link station, or subarea node.
2. A DISCONTACT request originated by an SSCP and carried out by a PU such that there no longer is any contact with a particular node at the link level.
3. A DEACTIVATE LINK request carried out by a PU such that the link to one or more nodes is no longer active.

At least three approaches to the notification problem are theoretically conceivable:

1. *Inoperative Notice.*   The detecting PU could advise its SSCP (via an INOPERATIVE command), which in turn could advise other SSCPs. The SSCPs would then need all routing information so as to determine which routes have been lost. The SSCPs in turn could advise all PUs and LUs in the network.
2. *Lost Subarea.*   The detecting subarea PU could advise its adjacent subarea **PUs,** which in turn could advise *their* adjacent subareas, thus propagating the knowledge throughout the network. Each subarea PU could then determine for which destinations it had a routing interruption.
3. *Blocked Path.*   The detecting PU could advise only the LU that originated a request when that request encounters the loss of physical connectivity. The originating LU could be advised via its own PU.

The first approach would make use of existing sessions between each SSCP and its PUs and LUs, as well as SSCP-SSCP sessions. It is a global approach, and the notification is centralized in each SSCP. Routing information would have to be both centralized for recovery and distributed to subareas for normal operations.

The "lost-subarea" approach would disseminate the routing interruption notification information like a ripple in a pond; the transmissions would be concurrent. This approach would require PU-PU sessions (or equivalent) between adjacent subarea nodes.

The "blocked-path" approach would be the most direct so far as the originating LU is concerned. Intermediary PUs need not be involved; therefore, the time to notify that LU would probably be the shortest of the three. Each originating LU in turn would discover for itself that a problem exists, so the time for total network awareness could be very long.

SNA-3 uses the lost-subarea approach plus an SSCP notification. This rapidly notifies the SSCP and all subarea nodes of the problem. Different recovery strategies can be built once this information is thus disseminated.

Lost subarea notification

The LOST SUBAREA command is propagated from PU to PU so that every subarea will rapidly become aware of a route interruption. It is originated by the PU services of a type-4 node (for example, a communications controller) or a type-5 node (for example, a host), which detects a loss of contact to an adjacent subarea. The LOST SUBAREA RU contains the subarea addresses of all lost subareas, and it is sent to all adjacent subarea PUs. The list of lost subareas is recompiled at each subarea; that is, if a subarea is not lost to a receiving PU, then that subarea is omitted from the list. Those adjacent subarea PUs, in turn, then propagate the RU to all of their physically adjacent subarea PUs (except the PU from which the RU was received), as shown in Fig. 15.20. This updated list is also sent by each subarea PU to its SSCP in a network services version of the LOST SUBAREA command.

The PU-PU sessions are designed to be implicit once the PUs themselves are activated; hence, separate activations of these sessions are not required.

Various procedures could then be devised to notify affected LUs. Since the pertinent information on route interruptions is known to every affected subarea PU, it theoretically could take steps to notify the session ends in its subarea that are affected by the outage. Another more expedient solution would take advantage of the fact that each subarea PU also notifies its SSCP concerning the lost routes for its subarea. The SSCP also knows the LUs per subarea and the address pairs for each session. The SSCP could therefore deduce the affected LUs and could then notify the PLU for each affected session.

To illustrate, consider the failure of subarea 06 in Fig. 15.21. This might be detected by a cross-domain link time-out in subareas 05 and 07. The subsequent actions might be as follows.

1. PU services in COMC nodes 05 and 07:

    a) Send INOPERATIVE command to SSCPs in 01 and 03, advising that link station is inoperative.

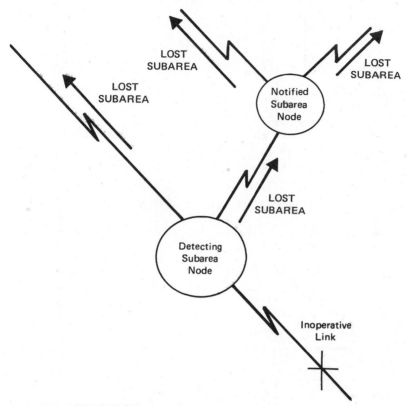

Fig. 15.20   LOST SUBAREA propagation.

b) Determine which subareas are lost.
- 05 has lost 02, 06, 03, 07, 04, 08, 10.
- 07 has lost 02, 06, 01, 05, 09.

c) Send LOST SUBAREA with subarea list to all adjacent subarea PUs.
- From 05 to 01 and 09
- From 07 to 03 and 08

d) Send network services RU containing the lost subarea list.
- From 05 to SSCP in 01
- From 07 to SSCP in 03

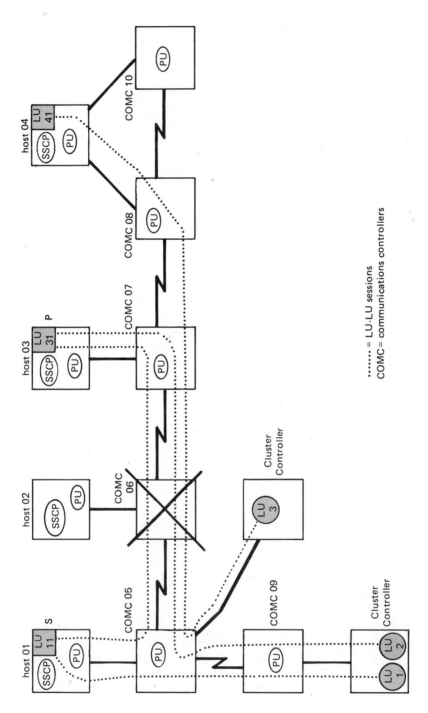

····· = LU-LU sessions
COMC = communications controllers

Fig. 15.21   Path failure.

2. PU services in COMC 08:

   a) Receive LOST SUBAREA from COMC 07 and propagate it to host 04 and COMC 10.

   b) Send network services RU containing the list of lost subareas to SSCP in host 04.

3. PU services in COMC 09 and 10:

   a) Receive LOST SUBAREA from 05 and 08, respectively.

   b) Do not propagate LOST SUBAREA.

   c) Send network services RU containing list of lost subareas to SSCPs in hosts 01 and 04, respectively.

3. In hosts:

   a) SSCPs in hosts 01 and 03 receive link INOP from COMCs 05 and 07, respectively, and advise network operators.

   b) Hosts 01, 02, 03, and 04 notify (for example, via user exits) their applications that are affected by the lost subareas.

   c) SSCP in host 01 may reset LU 2 and LU 3 whose sessions have been interrupted (for example, by sending a DACTLU followed by an ACTLU).

15.10.2 Host Failures

An important requirement for physical network integrity is that a host or channel failure not disrupt any cross-domain sessions in which the host does not contain the end-user. Sessions that use the local COMC of the failed host as a transit node should not be affected. In Fig. 15.22, for example, failure of host 3 will result in the termination of the LU-A to LU-C session, but it need not affect the other two sessions (LU-A to LU-B and LU-A to LU-D).

The host failures may be due to failure in the CPU hardware, the operating system, the TAM (Teleprocessing Access Method), or the channel. Detection of the failure by the local communications controller might result from either a channel time-out or an abnormal I/O response.

If the failure of the host is of short duration, no host backup procedures need be put into effect. Upon recovery of the host, the local communications controller can be activated (*warm*) so as not to result in a re-IML (initial machine load) of the communications controller. The cross-domain sessions using that communications controller as a transit node then need not be affected by the host recovery.

If, however, the host recovery involves an SSCP restart and a *cold* restart procedure [for example, an ACT-PU (cold) and ACTLU (cold)]

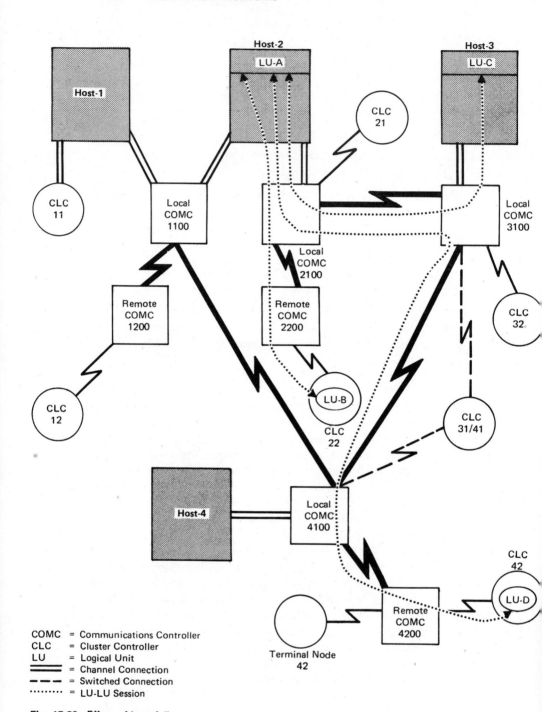

Fig. 15.22 Effect of host failure.

for all of its cluster resources, then all cross-domain sessions involving those cluster resources would be disrupted on the occasion of the host restart. To avoid this, the operator at the failed host might determine from other operators which resources were involved in cross-domain sessions and then wait for session termination, so as to avoid disrupting them in the bringup process.

A preferable solution, obviously, would be to have a "warm start" of the cluster controller similar to that provided for the communications controller. There an ACTPU with *error-recovery procedure (ERP)* indicated as a parameter would not involve a reset but would provide confirmation that the activation and establishment of a session with the new SSCP is complete.

Alternate host via twin-tail COMC

If, on the other hand, the host failure is likely to be of long duration, then several options for establishing a backup host can be considered *so as to transfer resources from the domain of the failed host.* If the local communications controller of the failed host has twin tails (like the COMC 1100 in Fig. 15.22) to another (backup) host, then the resources that are accessed via that COMC can all be put in the domain of that backup host. Whether or not this requires an IML of the COMC (with associated disruption of all sessions passing through it) depends on the teleprocessing access method design. For example, some resources accessed via COMC 1100 in Fig. 15.22 might be owned by host 1 but accessible as a cross-domain resource by host 2. Those same resources can also be defined, but not active, as local resources in host 2. Then upon failure of host 1, the definition in host 2 can be switched by operator command from that of a cross-domain resource to that of a local resource. Upon activation of those switched resources by host 2, sessions with these resources can be resynchronized (see Section 14.4) and proceed. *With this procedure, a re-IML of COMC 1100 is not required, so other sessions involving resources that were not switched are not affected.*

There may be more than two control domains involved. In general, when a resource is redefined as a local resource in one domain, then all other domains that are to treat that as a cross-domain resource must be advised of the new location.

Alternate host via TP link

There are situations in which a backup SSCP should be used but there is no twin-tailed COMC. Then *a local communications controller (without twin tails) might be defined as a local resource to two adjacent domain hosts.* COMC 3100 in Fig. 15.22, for example, could also be defined as a resource to host 2. The COMC would normally be activated by its channel attachment from host 3. If, however, host 3 is down and COMC 3100 remains operational, the network operations (that do not involve the down host) may proceed normally. At this point, the SSCP in host 2, after a VARY command from the operator, may take over COMC 3100. The attached PUs and their LUs can be similarly acquired. Again, however, if the acquisition commands ACTPU and ACTLU for the cluster controllers are "cold restart" (as often implemented) then sessions in those clusters are disrupted. *If needed because of a subsequent failure of COMC 3100, that COMC can be reloaded via its SDLC link to COMC 2100.* COMC 3100 then becomes, however, a remote COMC to host 2. (ACF/VTAM has a restriction that in such a case, COMC 3100 could not itself be connected to a remote COMC to produce cascaded remotes.)

In still other situations, manual dial can be used to connect a remote COMC to a local COMC in another domain. This requires, however, that the new controlling SSCP has been generated to accept the remote COMC as a resource in its domain.)

15.10.3 Communications Controller Failures

The communications controller has become a vital part of the multi-domain network. What can be done if one fails? If a communications controller node becomes inoperative, that can be detected by adjacent physical units. While node implementations of PUs can vary widely, it is architecturally the responsibility of the adjacent PU to detect the failure, drawing on information provided by each layer of the communication system in that node.

In Fig. 15.23, for example, consider that LU-F is in session with LU-B, LU-C, LU-D, and LU-E. A failure of local communications controller (COMC) 2100 will be detected by local COMC 3100, remote COMC 2200, and host 2. The LU-F to LU-B session is the only session affected.

The detecting PU services managers will notify their SSCPs of the inoperative condition. In turn, the SSCPs will notify their domain network operator. Further, the detecting PUs would also notify their physically adjacent subarea PUs (using the LOST SUBAREA command) as described above.

If, for example, LU-B in CLC-22 tries to send requests and if responses were called for, then a path error indication will be returned by COMC 2200.

COMC 2200 may also cease polling the cluster controller when the COMC decides that the SSCP has been lost. In some implementations

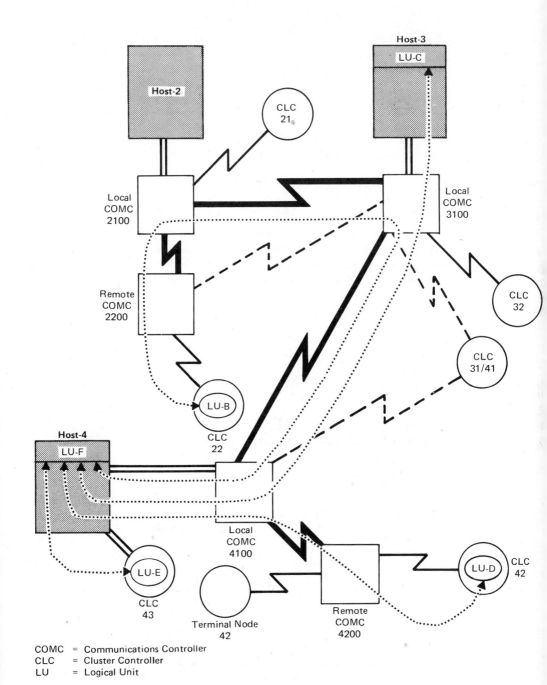

COMC = Communications Controller
CLC = Cluster Controller
LU   = Logical Unit

Fig. 15.23 Effect of communications controller failure.

this is always done for switched lines (to forestall needless billing) but is only done for leased lines if that option is chosen at system definition time. Some cluster controllers are designed to recognize the lack of polling (after a time-out) as a sign that the path is out and then to initiate LU cleanup.

The problem of a lost communications controller also raises the question of using alternate paths around the failed unit. This topic is discussed in Chapter 16.

15.11 PARALLEL DEVELOPMENTS

15.11.1 Networking via ARPANET

ARPANET provides communications among widely divergent hosts. In general, the user must be aware of the site of required resources and the command language instructions necessary to invoke them [15.5].

The ARPANET services are provided by interaction between user processes (at the application or application-subsystem level). In one mode, the user processes are in the two hosts. Figure 15.24, for example,

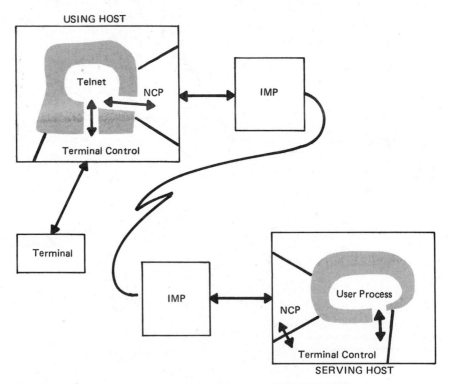

Fig. 15.24 Data flow for remote interactive use in ARPANET [15.6].

shows the data flow for remote interactive use. This requires that all traffic pass through the TELNET application [15.3, 15.6] in the using (local) host. In a similar way, jobs from a remote job entry terminal would flow in their entirety via an RJE process in the local host on its way to the remote host for processing there.

The network control program (NCP) shown in Fig. 15.24 interfaces between these user-level programs in the host and the network. The NCP establishes the logical connection and controls the data flow between the user-level programs in the two hosts.

In another mode, a special interface message processor (IMP) with a multiline controller can provide direct network access to terminals (switched, nonswitched, and hard-wired) by *providing both the TELNET function and NCP function* itself. This device is called the Terminal Interface Message Processor (TIP) [15.9]. With it, traffic need not pass through a local host.

The ARPA network provides multiple paths between an entry IMP and an exit IMP. If any failure occurs either in intermediary IMPs or in lines, alternate paths are automatically provided. (See further discussions of ARPANET in Sections 16.14.1, 7.8.1, 9.8, and 16.5.)

15.12 EXERCISES (pertaining to SNA-3 networking)

15.1 Which of the following statements are true?

   a) All elements of a given layer of the architecture must be in the same control domain.

   b) The transmission subsystem must be totally in the same domains as the half-sessions it serves.

   c) Cross-domain LU-LU sessions have as prerequisites both LU-SSCP and SSCP-SSCP sessions.

   d) The SSCPs for multiple control domains may reside in a single node.

   e) With networking architecture, an LU in one host can establish a cross-domain session with any LU in another domain's host, cluster controller, or terminal node.

   f) SSCP-SSCP sessions must use separate transmission facilities from LU-LU sessions.

15.2 Which of the following statements are true?

   a) All network names must be unique across all domains.

   b) Alternate names (other than network names) must be translated to network names by the SSCP owning the initiating (or terminating) NAU.

   c) Network names must be converted to network addresses by the SSCP owning the NAU to be converted.

d) Network operation support programs in different domains can cooperate to execute network operator commands. However, lines in one domain cannot be activated/deactivated by a network operator in a different domain.

15.3 Which of the following statements are true?

a) The network services commands to establish a session (that is, INIT-SELF, CINIT, BIND, and SST) can be the same for single-domain and cross-domain sessions.

b) The NOTIFY command can be used to advise an SSCP that one of its LUs that is already in session is asked to relinquish its session.

c) One can clean up an improperly terminated session by sending DACTLU followed by ACTLU. This will only affect the session needing cleanup, even if the LU has more than one LU-LU session.

d) The architecture can leave most user commands independent of whether same-domain or cross-domain LU-LU sessions are involved.

15.4 Which of the following statements are true?

a) The LOST SUBAREA command is sent only from the detecting subarea PU to the SSCP.

b) PU-PU sessions can be designed to be implicit once the PUs themselves are activated; hence, separate activation of these PU-PU sessions is not required.

c) If the system makes all the subarea PUs aware of lost subareas, one is in a position to execute programs for both session recovery and transmission subsystem changes.

15.13 REFERENCES AND BIBLIOGRAPHY

See also [6.2].

15.1 TELNET Protocol Specifications, NIC No. 18639 (August 1973).

15.2 *The Terminal Interface Message Processor Programs.* Bolt Beranck, and Newman, Inc., September 1975. (Report # AD-A01 6 281 distributed by National Technical Information Service, U.S. Dept. of Commerce, Washington D.C.).

15.3 A. A. McKenzie. "HOST/HOST Protocol for the ARPA Network." NIC No. 8246, Network Information Center. Menlo Park, Calif.: Stanford Research Institute (January 1972).

15.4 B. D. Moldow. "Networking—A Layered Approach." Presented at *SHARE XLVI*, San Francisco (February 1976).

15.5 H. S. Elovitz and C. L. Heitmeyer. "What Is a Computer Network?" *Computer Networks: A Tutorial*, IEEE Computer Security (October 1975).

15.6 S. D. Crocker, J. F. Heafner, R. M. Metcalfe, and J. B. Postel. "Function-Oriented Protocols for the ARPA Computer Network." *Proc. Spring Joint Computer Conference.* Montvale, N.J.: AFIPS Press (1972), pp. 271–280. (Figure 15.24 reprinted by permission.)

15.7 *Telecommunications Control System Advanced Function: Concepts and Facilities.* IBM Form No. GH20-1735.

15.8 "*Network Operation Support Program*, General Information Manual," IBM Form No. GC38-0251.

15.9 "*ACF/VTAM Design Objectives*," IBM Form No. GC38-0253.

15.10 R. R. Everett, C. A. Zraket, and H. D. Benington. "SAGE—A Data Processing System for Air Defense." *Proc. Eastern Joint Computer Conf.* (1957), pp. 148–155.

15.11 W. J. Luther. "Conceptual Bases of CYBERNET." *Computer Networks*, 1970 Courant Computer Science Symposium 3. Englewood Cliffs, N.J.: Prentice-Hall (1972), pp. 111–146.

15.12 B. Combs. "TYMNET: A Distributed Network." *Datamation* **19,** No. 7 (July 1973).

16
Routing
Techniques

16.1 INTRODUCTION*

We will use the word *route* to mean a defined set of elements that a path
information unit (PIU) traverses when sent *from path control in an origin
subarea to path control in a destination subarea.* This set of elements
comprises links, data link control layers, and path control layers. (We here
reserve the word *path* to mean the set of elements that a PIU traverses
when sent from transmission control of one half-session to transmission
control of the other half-session.)

Routing decisions may be made in four stages, as follows:

1. Selection of the carrier—that is, routes that employ, for example, a
   satellite carrier, a value-added carrier, or a common carrier/PTT. Some
   routes may involve the services of more than one carrier.

2. Selection of services within each carrier—that is, routes that use, for
   example, direct distance dial (DDD), WATS, leased, or digital services
   of one or more carriers.

3. Routing decisions along the path to, from, and between carrier services.

4. Routing decisions within carrier services.

Most of the traffic between nodes of a distributed data-processing
complex consists not of lone wandering packets but of messages involved in

---

* The author is indebted to R. J. Jueneman and M. W. Doss for input and helpful
comments on the material in this chapter.

sessions. In a typical session, many messages are sent. Examples are data-entry or data-inquiry sessions in which a sequence of messages is sent and file transfers in which many messages to form a data set are sent. With some forms of routing, the routing decision can be made once for the entire session (unless a malfunction or an unusually large shift in line loads occurs). In other forms, individual messages (or parts of messages) are rerouted during a session.

Route selection may have to be based on many factors in different circumstances. These may pertain to carrier selection, use of an alternate route on the occasion of link failure, or load balancing among routes to reduce congestion. To illustrate, consider the following. In certain situations, the lower cost of point-to-point satellite service may dictate use of that route for most traffic. During rain outages or eclipses of the satellite, on the other hand, terrestrial routes may be needed to ensure availability. A bulk transmission deferred to the early morning hours may best be routed via unused voice links for lowest cost. On the other hand, if the expected volume is higher than the voice links can handle, the use of a route via a broadband nonswitched digital trunk may be the least cost. If the bulk transmissions are few in number, then a switched broadband link may be less expensive. In most traffic, it is essential that FIFO order of all messages and all message segments be maintained. Some carriers will inherently maintain FIFO in their transmissions; others may rearrange messages at the destination to recover FIFO; but some routes may not ensure this. Local destinations may benefit from routes that use special carriers such as CATV. Some traffic may merit a route at a premium cost in order to obtain very fast response time. In some of these illustrations, it is desirable that the origin node have a role in the route selection. In other situations, the route selections are entirely within one carrier's domain (which appears as a link to the remainder of the network). These selections then may be based on workload distributions within that carrier, the objective being to optimize the performance (for example, throughput or average response time) of the carrier.

Different routing techniques may be employed by a common carrier or PTT, a value-added network, or a user of a carrier. In an SNA network, therefore, the user and/or the SNA network manager has routing control only over the portions of the network that are outside the carrier (or VAC) facilities.

SNA is not committed to any one route-changing philosophy. The literature now reflects a rapid development and critical evaluation of many techniques. Some important possibilities are reviewed in this chapter.

16.2 ALTERNATE VERSUS PARALLEL ROUTES

Alternate routes

We use the term *alternate routes* to mean those that are employed only in case of a failure of the route normally used, or in the case of a major change in loads. This amounts to a reconfiguration or a use of an alternate system definition that can be prestored in the communications system. The need for such a switchover should ordinarily be relatively infrequent. Therefore, it may be acceptable to terminate sessions on the normal route and reinitiate those sessions, with a resynchronization of RU sequence numbers, on the alternate route. (However, not all end-users and/or session facilities can easily handle resynchronization; see Section 14.4.4). The term alternate routing is reserved for support that permits selection of an alternate for some routes without any disruption of other routes. Then only some sessions passing through a node need be affected by the change.

The procedure for employing an alternate route can be partially manual or completely automatic. Some of the theoretical possibilities in increasing order of complexity are as follows.

1. The routing table in each node contains a series of entries for each destination subarea. They are ordered according to desirability, with the most desirable route first in the series. The use of a new entry to select a new route for a given destination requires a manual intervention on the part of the network operator.

2. The detection of the unavailability of the normal route and the selection of the next alternate route in the series is automatic. The alternate route selection may seek the highest order route that is available.

3. The order itself can be changed in accordance with link loadings or other criteria.

Whenever a route is changed, in any case, the system must either (a) perform the route change completely transparently with no effect on the message stream to the end-user, or (b) notify the end-user to resynchronize.

Parallel routes

Multiple parallel routes, on the other hand, involve the *concurrent use of more than one route between the same pair of subareas* (for example, between two hosts, a host and a communications controller, or two communications controllers). The objectives of parallel routes are two-fold:

1. Load leveling among two or more different routes as loads on the lines change. (The workload information, used to decide which route to take from a given node, may be global involving the entire network, or local involving only adjacent nodes and links.)

2. Incremental investment by the user who wants to gradually expand the bandwidth between adjacent nodes by adding parallel links. (Smaller lines can be added rather than going to a single line of much higher capacity.)

A possible exposure in the use of parallel routes is the loss of order of requests and responses within a session. Since path lengths and path characteristics differ, the order of RUs or RU segments arriving at the destination may be different from the order in which the source sent them. (SNA-3 does not guard against this possibility since all segments of a given request carry the same sequence number.)

This exposure can be eliminated by the expedient of keeping all RUs for a given session on the same physical route. Load leveling by having different parallel routes does not cause a loss of order so long as each session remains on one route. Shifting a session to another route in the middle of a session could be accompanied by (1) a temporary quiescing of the session, with all responses to outstanding requests completed before the route switch, or (2) a notification to the end-user and a resynchronization after the switch.

Carriers that employ parallel routes as part of their transmission may or may not accept the responsibility for maintaining order of messages within a session. If this is not done, then a higher level must reorder as necessary.

The existence of multiple routes between domains does not necessarily imply support for alternate routes or parallel routes. In the configuration of Fig. 15.22, for example, there are multiple routes between domains 1 and 4. Illustrative routes are

1. From host 1, via COMC 1100, host 2, COMC 2100, COMC 3100, and COMC 4100, to host 4.

2. From host 1, via COMC 1100, COMC 4100, and COMC 4200, to cluster controller 42.

These could all be used in, for example, an ACF/VTAM implementation without support in the sense of alternate or parallel routes. These multiple routes may be used only with a restriction that *one of these routes (and only one route) be used to go between each pair of origin and destination subareas.* With that restriction, the bandwidth of the multiple routes can be used, but a given route cannot be dynamically changed for only one session without affecting other sessions. To change routes on a session basis would require specific new support for that capability.

16.3   TYPES OF ROUTING TECHNIQUES

In each communications controller, path control must determine the next step along the route. Specifically, this is the next link address to be used in moving a message on toward its destination subarea. The routing algorithm determines how path control selects this next link in the path.

In practice, path control determines this next link from a routing table, whose ultimate purpose is to provide information of the form shown in Fig. 16.1. The means for generating this table may be simplistic or sophisticated, static or dynamic, but the result should be a correlation of destination subareas with a next station and link [9.1].

As shown in Fig. 16.1, the search argument of the routing table need only be the subarea portion of the destination address field (DAF) in the TH. This is true until the message arrives at the communications controller for the destination subarea. Then the routing table must point to a supplementary table whose search argument includes the element address portion of the DAF.

There are, of course, many ways in which to implement the table search. Using one approach, a routing table may first provide only an address to a control block for the next station along the route. At this

Destination Subarea	Next-Station (from this node)	Outgoing Link Address	Outgoing Station Address
1	C	1	1
2	F	1	2
3	E	2	5
4	A	3	1
5	D	3	2
6	*		
7	B	4	7

* local subarea, route to boundary function.

Fig. 16.1 Routing table.

point, the link to that next station may not yet be determined. The control block could then, in turn, provide the up-to-date pointer to the appropriate link address and the address of the station on that link (depending on the routing strategy then in effect).

In destination nodes, the routing-table search argument is the OAF/DAF (or DAF'/DAF') pair of origin and destination addresses, so that a unique transmission control element (and half-session) can be picked as the receiver.

Different routing strategies determine how the routing tables are generated and how they are used. For example, three approaches that have been proposed for the generation or use of the routing table are the following.

1. *Fixed centralized routing*, where the routing table is determined by some central agency and is distributed to all the nodes. This has been entirely adequate for simple tree networks. This approach may or may not provide a system for using alternate routes.

Tymnet [16.13] is an example of centralized routing. (This commercial network consists of over 160 nodes on two continents, with a prime time load of over 1000 simultaneous users [16.22].) There a single active supervisor called the Supervisor in Active Mode (SAM) establishes the circuit by selecting the appropriate intermediate nodes between the originating and destination nodes. Tymnet routes remain static for the duration of a session. A backup supervisor can become active in the event of a SAM failure.

2. *Explicit path routing* involves decisions at each node based on the content of headers that accompany each message. That information may be items like a route specification, which is transformed at each node and propagated along the route. The originating node (or its designee such as an adjacent communications controller) selects the route. An explicit route can be selected at an origin subarea such that all PIUs assigned to that route must traverse the same sequence of elements (DLC, links, and PC) to the destination subarea. This routing technique can also be made to be adaptive to changing conditions by the inclusion of alternate explicit routes in the routing tables of each node [16.1].

3. *Distributed stochastic routing* requires that each node dynamically gather information from its adjacent nodes concerning the workloads on links from there to the destination. The number of links along each route and the sizes of message queues at each link may enter into a calculation of route "costs." Based on this information (which described the situation a short time ago), each node makes an independent decision on which

link to use for the message at hand. The ARPA network is an example of distributed stochastic routing.

These and many other routing techniques can be classified according to three characteristics: the decision place, the information used, and the decision time (see Fig. 16.2). These characteristics can be subclassed as follows.

1. *Decision place.* The place where the route is selected may be centralized or distributed.

   a) In a centralized system (for example, TYMNET [16.9]), the routing table for each node is determined at a central location and sent to each node; each node is given the route for each destination.

   b) In one type of distributed decision (for example; Arpanet [16.10]), the selection of the route to a given destination is based on the workloads; and the decision is made at each node along the route.

   c) In another type of distribution decision (for example, explicit path routing [16.1]), the selection of a route is made at the originating node for the message.

2. *Information source.* The route selection may be based on information concerning either link characteristics (for example, cost and availability) or link workloads. The source of this information may be

   a) The originating node of the message, if the selection of the route is by link cost or the matching of link characteristics to the message characteristics.

   b) A node in the vicinity of an outage, if the selection of the route is by link availability.

   c) All nodes in the network, if the selection is based on workloads throughout the network.

   d) Those nodes immediately adjacent to the node making the decision, if the selection is by workloads in the local environment.

   Note that the current workload at any node can only be known precisely at that one node. Information about the workload at one node may be sent to another node, but that information is already somewhat out of date by the time it arrives. Global information in particular (being gathered from greater distances) is meaningful only in terms of averages over a period of time.

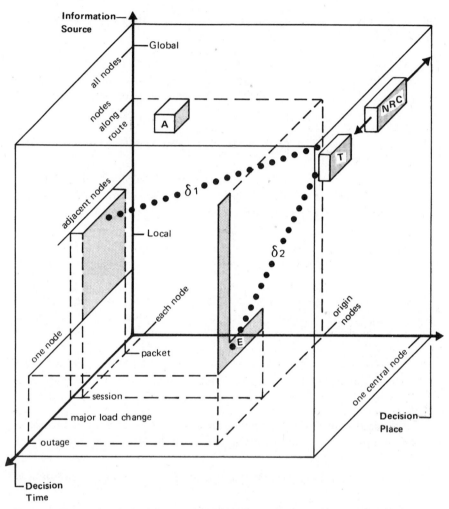

Fig. 16.2 Routing algorithms in the three-space of information source, decision place, and decision time.

3. *Decision time.* Selection of a new route to a given destination may be made frequently or infrequently. Occasions for route selection might be

   a) The start of a packet.
   b) The start of a session.
   c) Major shifts in workload patterns.
   d) Link or node outages.
   e) Major shifts in network configuration or use of carrier services.

   When multiple routes exist between a pair of nodes, the preferred route may change from time to time due to changing load conditions. How rapidly one should change the preferred route depends on the load characteristics themselves and the economic benefits to be derived, as well as the cost and difficulties one can encounter with too rapid a reoptimization. A conservative approach is to consider a reoptimization of routes on a relatively long-term basis. That can involve the employment of a slowly adaptive and largely heuristic optimization. The sending node could periodically sample the time delays encountered in the several available routes and could modify the route in accordance with this long-term sampling. However, shorter-term optimization will sometimes be advantageous.

   These three characteristics are shown as a three-space in Fig. 16.2. Tymnet is plotted there as using a centralized technique, using a great deal of global information, and making relatively infrequent changes in routing strategy. There a typical route is established essentially on a session basis at the beginning of each session. The ARPANET, on the other hand, is plotted as using a distributed decision technique with something less than global information and making frequent changes in routing strategy.

   Experience seems to indicate that centralized techniques yield a higher network throughput *if the traffic patterns are stable.* This follows from the fact that the route selections are based on global information of the entire network. A total network optimization is therefore possible, and there is no uncertainty about the condition of an entire route. Distributed decision techniques, on the other hand, have information on adjacent links and nodes immediately available; therefore, the distributed techniques can *respond more rapidly to local load changes.*

Combining techniques. A generalization of these techniques, admitting combinations of approaches, can be made. Following Rudin [16.8], the "delta routing" technique assumes a node routing center having global information (NRC in Fig. 16.2) and allows the route selection to be by either packet, session, or some other occasion. However, instead of having the NRC select the route to each destination, the NRC provides several such routes, leaving it up to a more local decision to choose among those several options.

In Fig. 16.2, δ indicates that local choices of the options provided by NRC make the decision technique more or less distributed. If there is only one choice available, the technique is centralized; if multiple choices are available, then a hybrid of central and distributed techniques exists.

In Fig. 16.2, δ_1 indicates multiple choices given by the NRC *to each node* in the network where these choices are then based on local information (for example, workloads); and the route selection, among the options given by NRC, may be on a packet or session basis.

In Fig. 16.2, δ_2 indicates multiple choices of explicit routes given by the NRC *to each originating node.* The route options given by the NRC may be selected on a session basis, depending, for example, on gross loading information or the need to match the characteristics of the message type to that of the link. Or an alternate route might be chosen from among the NRC options on the occasion of an outage. This plane of operation would be extended vertically if the source of information coming to the origin node were the nodes in the vicinity of the outage and the intervening nodes along the route (see Section 15.10.1).

Routing objectives.   As seen above, there is a wide range of techniques from which to choose. In general, it appears that the optimum routing mechanism external to carriers should be such that

1. Decisions can be made, sometimes by the originating node and sometimes by a control point with global information, on (a) selection of the carrier, (b) selection of carrier service, and (c) selection of the route to, from, or between carriers.

2. FIFO message ordering can be guaranteed when that is a requirement.

3. Parallel paths can be used in some other cases for load balancing or high bandwidth applications.

4. The routing mechanism requires only minimal space overhead in the message header and modest processing or storage in each node.

5. Uncertainties in pathing, such as unplanned looping and unpredictable meandering, can be minimal.

6. Isolation of the cause of an error and recovery from failure of a link or a node can be straightforward.

16.4   EXPLICIT PATH ROUTING

The proposal for explicit path routing made by Jueneman and Kerr [16.1] is a logical extension to the simple routing table of Fig. 16.1. It appears to meet the objectives stated above to a considerable degree. As shown in Fig. 16.3, the search argument in each node is still the destination subarea. However, instead of pointing to a single next link and station address (as formerly), the argument now points to a set of such addresses corresponding to multiple possible paths toward the destination subarea. There remains, then, a mechanism for selecting in each node one of the members of this set.

A straightforward approach might be (1) to use an ID for each path between the origin and destination node, (2) to send this path ID along with each message, and (3) to use this path ID to select, in each node, the correct member of the set referred to above. This, however, would require a path ID large enough to account for all possible paths between any two

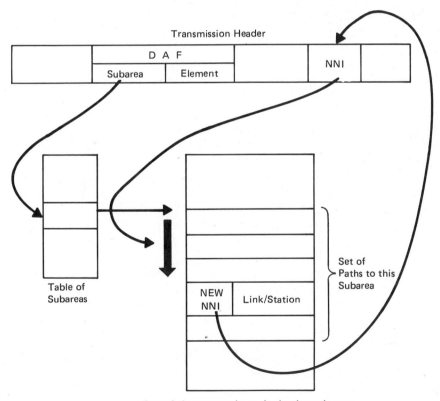

Sets of alternate paths to destination sub areas

Fig. 16.3   Use of next node index (NNI) in explicit path routing.

nodes. A smaller ID can be used, instead, if one uses at each node the ID of only those links at that node that lead *toward* the destination node. The way to do this is as follows [16.1].

Next node index.   As shown in Fig. 16.3, the transmission header for each message would contain not only the destination address field (DAF), but also a small field called Next Node Index (NNI), which is used to select one of the possible links emanating from that node toward the destination. If we allow up to 16 links at each node that *all lead toward one destination subarea,* then the NNI need be only four bits; three bits would allow eight links. The NNI is used to steer the table lookup so as to pick one member of the set that belongs to the destination subarea.

Thus the subarea portion of the DAF selects the set of table entries associated with that subarea. The NNI is then used to select a particular member of that set to get a particular next link/station to which the message should be routed next. At the same time, *the member selected provides a new NNI value for use at the next node* (see Fig. 16.3). The new NNI replaces the old NNI when the message is sent to that next node. That new NNI then is similarly used in that next node to steer the table lookup there.

This process is repeated in each node. At each node, the NNI retrieved from the previous node selects one node from among the possible next nodes. *Note that (for a given set of tables in each node) the entire route is determined by the selection of the first NNI at the origin node.* A different NNI in the origin node can result in a different NNI in any following nodes; hence a new route can be created that can be different in any one or all legs of some other route.

To change the route being used to a given subarea, the origin node need only change the NNI that it uses on the next message. The effect of using the first alternate NNI will propagate by the use of corresponding alternate NNIs in each successive node. Hence, path selection (as distinct from mere link selection), on a message-by-message basis, is possible with this technique.

In practice, to preserve FIFO, route switching must be done with care, either between sessions, or by quiescing a session during the route switch. Alternatively, one can lose FIFO and then restore order of messages at the destination.

Route switching on link failure.   One of the possible reasons for doing a route switch is because of a link or node failure in the route being used. In this event, since the message cannot be delivered via the indicated route, it is necessary that the originating node be advised so that it can select an alternate route. Some form of LOST-ROUTE message must be sent by the detector of the break to the originating node [16.2].

Other route selection. The loading of routing tables in each node could, of course, be a part of the system generation process. In addition, however, it would be desirable for the SSCP to be able to change the routing tables.

Jueneman and Kerr [16.1] further suggest that it may be desirable to implement a session-specific route selection to indicate which routes were allowable for that particular session. By this means, the load for different sessions might be distributed among different routes, and particular transmission media, such as satellites or digital terrestrial links, could be specified for particular sessions.

Also, since explicit routes are used from origin to destination, message transit times for entire routes could be gathered, which might also influence alternate path selection by the originating node. (In this instance, no information need be exchanged between nodes that are not presently communicating, so as to keep network overhead at a low level [16.1].)

As mentioned previously, the delta routing concept can be used to portray these variations in route selection (see Fig. 16.2). The network routing center (for example, an SSCP or a coordination among SSCPs) would use global information and would specify a number of explicit routes for each originating node to use to get to each destination. The originating node selects from among these explicit routes given by the NRC, perhaps to obtain a transmission service that suits the needs of that session. Or the selection may be based on outage information provided to the originating node by nodes along a route (see Section 15.10).

It has been speculated [16.23] that an extension to SNA-3 for handling the requirement of alternate paths might readily use the explicit routing technique. Such extensions are examples that could be made without affecting most elements of the architecture. Even changes such as new FID types and expanded THs, which would affect the path control layer, would not necessarily affect other layers because of the isolation provided by a layered structure. As emphasized in Section 6.12, an architecture for distributed systems must facilitate function subsets within each layer and the ability for new subsets (such as new FIDs and new commands) to coexist with prior functions.

16.5 DISTRIBUTED STOCHASTIC ROUTING

If the routing table in each node is dynamically modified to reflect changing traffic patterns, the routing technique is said to be stochastic. The algorithm used to determine changes to the routing table may be based on information in the node making the decision, plus information from (a) adjacent nodes only (for example, queue sizes), (b) all other nodes in the network, or (c) primarily the adjacent nodes, plus some information on the state of the network along the route to the destination.

Global algorithms, based on information from all nodes in the network, require either that all nodes exchange information with every other node or that all nodes exchange information with a central node. The former involves a very high overhead in traffic devoted to traffic optimization. The latter introduces the vulnerability of the central routing center plus possible delays in routing information via the center. The ARPANET algorithm is of type (c) above and is the best known example of distributed stochastic routing.

Distributed stochastic routing techniques use tables at each node to determine the next step in the route of a packet. The choice of the route possibilities, however, is based primarily on the traffic in each of the links concerned. Different criteria can be used to guide the construction of the routing tables. Among these [10.2] are

1. The best use of links at busy periods by spreading the traffic.

2. Minimizing the transit delay.

3. Minimizing the route miles traveled by packets.

4. Minimizing the number of nodes visited in transit.

In "minimum weight routing," a weight can be assigned to each of the last three factors. Then the routing criterion is to minimize the total weight when these weights are summed over all the links comprising a route.

The transit delay might be determined dynamically from observations of the performance of each link [16.12]. For example, the expected delay of a packet going from node I to node D might be estimated by observing the delay of another packet coming from that same node D to node I. That delay might be determined at node I by having the time of sending recorded in the packet and subtracting this from the current time. Under some traffic conditions, however, this may be a very poor estimate because flows in opposite directions may be of very different magnitudes. Other estimates of delays can be obtained as a function of queue lengths for each link. Special messages might be sent to adjacent nodes in order to carry transit-delay information, such as time of origin or queue lengths.

In synchronous updating, the delays are calculated and the tables are updated periodically by all nodes at the same time. In ARPA, this was first done every half second. Alternatively, the updates of the routing tables might be done only when transit delays exceed a prescribed level.

The ARPANET routing tables are updated by computations that take place in each network node called interface message processors (IMPs). Each IMP periodically exchanges information with its adjacent IMPs on the delay experienced in sending messages via the adjacent IMP to each destination. This is estimated based on the number of links involved and the recent queue lengths on each link. By periodic messages between adjacent IMPs, information can be propagated from IMP to IMP and each IMP can build up a weighting table for routes to each destination. On the basis of this information, each IMP periodically recomputes a new shortest-delay next link to use for each possible destination node.

The frequency with which routing control messages are exchanged between nodes should be a function of the line bandwidth and the expected stability of traffic patterns. Since there is a delay in the measurement and algorithm-calculation process, there is a possibility of oscillating control, as in any closed-loop control system. Instabilities, such as looping of packets, can occur. The very high frequency variations in traffic cannot be followed, some smoothing of the variation is necessary, and the frequency of correction must be related to the frequency spectrum of the pattern changes after smoothing.

In ARPANET, operating on 50 kbps lines, the routing control messages are exchanged between any pair of adjacent IMPs at least every 640 msec. The "I-heard" messages that are sent to test the status of the phone lines and the status reports that are sent by each IMP every 52.4 seconds to the network control center represent a much smaller fraction of the background traffic [16.7].

R. G. Gallager [16.14] has proposed another distributed stochastic algorithm for establishing the routing tables in the various nodes of the network. The proposed mode, however, is to keep the routes from each source to destination fixed over long periods of time, and to change them only when necessary *to reduce the long-term average delay* per packet. In the ARPA network, the objective is to route each packet in such a way as to minimize *its* delay, with no regard as to how that might affect the delay of other packets. In the referenced algorithms [16.14], the objective is to route each packet in such a way as to minimize overall delay in the network. Accordingly, long-term average delays are the criterion and routes need not be changed frequently.

The use of *different routing options* within a single communications architecture is illustrated by DECNET which allows the user to provide any one of three types of algorithms in path finding [6.17].

1. *Preset Manual Routing.* All routing information is preset within the nodes *at system generation time* (or entered by the network operator

if such a feature is implemented). "This is a very manual system, but for all but the largest complex topologies provides most of the needed mechanism for reasonable routing."

2. *Preset Dynamic Routing.* Routing tables are again preset at sysgen time, but are *occasionally* updated as paths change by the use of ROUTING PATH messages from node to node.

3. *Distributed Routing.* This technique uses relatively frequent ROUTING PATH messages to pass information between adjacent nodes on the current state of each other's routing table. These messages may be used as a means of balancing link loads.

This again illustrates the value of a layered approach where alteration within one layer (to substitute a new functional subset) need have no effect on other layers.

16.6 MULTIDOMAIN ROUTING

As noted in Chapter 15, domains of a network tend to grow autonomously with a subsequent growth of interdomain operations. What, then, are the requirements for a consistent routing technique across multiple domains?

First, it is evident that a carrier operates in many ways as an autonomous control domain. Though the carrier appears to the using half-sessions to be operating at the link level, the carrier may have within itself sophisticated routing techniques. These may operate at a path control level unique to the carrier. Clearly, the routing techniques employed in this manner, apparently within the link level, need have no relationship to the routing techniques used outside that carrier. For example, the routing technique within a given carrier might be primarily of the distributed stochastic type, using workload information within the carrier to optimize carrier performance. The routing in the remainder of the network, on the other hand, might use the explicit path routing technique aimed at optimizing carrier selection and at providing alternate paths on the occasions of link outages and major shifts in load patterns.

In the remainder of the multidomain network external to the carrier or VAC, routing techniques are active in the path control layer. The path control layer extends throughout all control domains that have participating half-sessions or through which sessions are routed, and a degree of compatibility is needed among them.

That routing technique can, however, be a superset of the basic path control protocols. An example of this is the explicit routing technique described above, in which several fields could be added to the existing fields in the TH (transmission header). Some domains, in a multidomain network, then might simply not use those extra fields. Portions of routes within that domain then would appear as fixed portions of a route in an otherwise alterable-route network.

Thus there appear to be no fundamental problems (but certainly practical ones) to the creation of multidomain networks in which

1. A consistent routing technique such as explicit routing extends across multiple control domains.
2. Some domains do not actively participate in route alteration, but appear as fixed portions of an otherwise alterable-route network.
3. One or more carriers may themselves have their own unique routing techniques for carrier operation and retain the appearance of links in the remainder of the network.

16.7 REFERENCES AND BIBLIOGRAPHY

See also [10.2].

16.1 R. J. Jueneman and G. S. Kerr. "Explicit Path Routing in Communications Networks." *Proc. Third International Conf. on Computer Communications*, Toronto (August 1976).

16.2 "Explicit Path Routing for Switching Network." *IBM Technical Disclosure Bulletin* **18,** No. 9 (February 1976).

16.3 H. Opderbeck. "Problems in the Design of Control Procedures for Computer Networks." *Computer Communications Review* **5,** No. 2 (April 1975).

16.4 L. Fratta, M. Serla, and L. Kleinrock. "The Flow Direction Method: An Approach to Store-and-Forward Computer Communication Network Design." *Networks* **3** (1973), pp. 97–133.

16.5 J. M. McQuillan. "Adaptive Routing Algorithms for Distributed Computer Networks." Report No. 2831. Cambridge, Mass.: Bolt, Beranek and Newman (May 1974). Available from the National Technical Information Service, AD 781467.

16.6 S. R. Kimbleton and S. M. Schneider. "Computer Communication Networks: Approaches, Objectives, and Performance Considerations." *Computing Surveys* **7,** No. 3 (September 1975), pp. 129–173.

16.7 L. Kleinrock, W. E. Naylor, and H. Opderbeck. "A Study of Line Overhead in the ARPANET." *Communications of the ACM* **19,** No. 1 (January 1976), pp. 3-13.

16.8 H. Rudin. "On Routing and Delta Routing: Techniques for Packet Switching Networks." *Proc. IEEE 1975 Communications Conf.*, San Francisco (June 1975): pp. 41-20–41-24.

16.9 L. R. Tymes. "TYMNET—A Terminal-Oriented Computer Network." *Proc. AFIPS Spring Joint Computer Conference* (1971), pp. 211–216.

16.10 F. E. Heart, R. E. Kahn, S. M. Ornstein, W. R. Crowther, and D. C. Walden. "The Interface Message Processor for the ARPA Network." *Proc. AFIPS Spring Joint Computer Conference* (1970), pp. 551–567.

16.11 H. Frank and I. T. Frisch. *Communication, Transmission, and Transportation Networks*. Reading, Mass.: Addison-Wesley (1971).

16.12 T. Baran, F. Boehm, and P. Smith. "On Distributed Communications." Series of eleven reports by Rand Corporation (August 1964).

16.13 R. P. Blanc. "Review of Computer Network Technology." NBS Technical Note 804 (January 1974).

16.14 R. G. Gallager. "Local Routing Algorithms and Protocols." *Proc. IEEE 1976 Communications Conf.* Philadelphia (June 1976), pp. 20-17–20-20.

16.15 J. Rinde. "Tymnet I: An Alternative to Packet Technology." *Proc. ICCC* (1976).

16.16 L. Kleinrock. *Queueing Systems*, Vol. II. New York: Wiley (1976).

16.17 D. W. Davies. "The Control of Congestion in Packet Switching Networks." *Proc. of Second ACM IEEE Symposium in the Optimization of Data Communications Systems*, Palo Alto, California (October 1971).

16.18 W. L. Price. "Simulation Studies of a Barithmically Controlled Store-and-Forward Data Communication Network." *IFIP Congress* (August 1974), pp. 151–154.

16.19 H. Rudin. "On Alternate Routing in Circuit-Switched Data Networks." Research Report RZ801, IBM Zurich Research Laboratory, Switzerland.

16.20 C. A. Sunshine. "Source Routing in Computer Networks." *Computer Communication Review of the ACM* **7**, No. 1 (January 1977).

16.21 D. G. Cantor and M. Gerla. "Optimal Routing in a Packet Switched Computer Network." *IEEE Transactions on Computers* **C-23** (October 1974), pp. 1062–1069.

16.22 J. Rinde. "Tymnet 1: An Alternate to Packet Technology." *Proc. ICCC*, Toronto (3–6 August 1976), pp. 268–273.

16.23 J. P. Gray. "Network Services in Systems Network Architecture." *IEEE Transactions on Communications* **COM-25**, No. 1 (January 1977).

16.24 K. Maruyama, L. Fratta, and D. T. Tang. "Heuristic Design Algorithm for Computer Communication Networks with Different Classes of Packets." *IBM J. Research Dev.* (July 1977).

17
Interfacing to New Data Networks

17.1 INTRODUCTION*

As we discussed in Section 2.4.5, data transmission systems using a whole new technology are emerging. Within the next two to five years digital public data networks will be providing more efficient and more reliable service to support rapidly growing distributed data processing systems. There exists then an opportunity before these systems are fully developed to establish common interfaces that will allow direct interconnection on a common worldwide basis.

Here we will focus our attention on two of the principal types of new data networks (see Section 2.4 for a broader view of transmission trends), namely, digital synchronous networks and packet switching networks. Examples of the former are the currently operating Dataphone Digital Service (DDS) of AT&T in the United States, the currently operating INFODAT and DATAROUTE in Canada, the DDX network planned for initial operation in Japan in 1977–1978, and the Nordic Public Data Network planned for initial operation in Norway, Sweden, Denmark, and Finland in 1978–1979. Some of these use older interfaces, but the trend for this type of network is to use the recently defined CCITT X.21 interface. Examples of packet switching networks are TELENET, now in operation in the USA, and TRANSPAC and DATAPAC, scheduled for

---

* The author is indebted to M. Levilion and A. Potocki of the LaGaude, France Laboratory for the benefit of their studies of packet switching systems. Acknowledgment is also given to R. A. Donnan for his input regarding the X.25 interface and to F. P. Corr for his comments on this chapter.

operation in France and Canada in 1977–1978. These three plan to use the CCITT X.25 interface.

In this chapter, we will adopt the terminology of the communications carriers shown in Figs. 17.1 and 17.2. The data terminal equipment (DTE) can be any type of user facility from a large computer system to a very simple terminal. The data circuit-terminating equipment (DCE) terminates the access line from the carrier's data switching exchange (DSE) and performs any signal conversions necessary to the operation of the carrier.

Real digital circuits (e.g., using the X.21 DTE/DCE interface) extend from one DCE, via the DSE network, to another DCE. In packet switching networks, on the other hand, a real circuit extends from each DCE to a DSE, and virtual circuits are provided among DSE's. This involves sharing of a broadband facility (e.g., 50 kbps) among multiple unrelated subscribers. The technique employs asynchronous time-division multiplexing on a message (that is, a fixed-size packet) basis (see Section 4.5).

Value-added carriers (VAC's) also use the DSE network, leasing facilities from another carrier. The VAC, in effect, provides an intermediary DSE, which understands the X.25 interface, at entry and exit points of the DSE network.

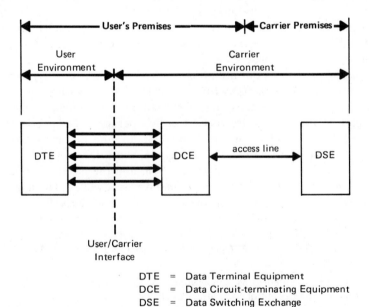

DTE = Data Terminal Equipment
DCE = Data Circuit-terminating Equipment
DSE = Data Switching Exchange

Fig. 17.1 Interfacing to new data networks.

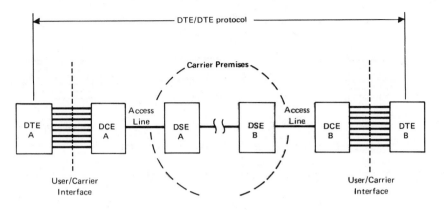

Fig. 17.2   DTE-to-DTE connection.

The CCITT view is of protocols that span the DTE/DCE interface. One should understand, however, that the carriers are free to, and usually do, locate their protocol functions in the DSE rather than in the DCE. The figures of this chapter illustrate that fact. These protocols operate at several levels and in several time phases. This introduction provides an overview of these levels and phases for both X.21 and X.25 interfaces. The specifics of these two interfaces then follow in subsequent sections.

The interface between the DTE and the DCE may be served by protocols at three levels, the third being added for packet switching networks. These are the following.

1. *Level 1.* For analog and for some early digital networks, this is the EIA RS 232-C or the equivalent CCITT V.24 electrical interface. For newer digital synchronous networks and for most new packet switching networks, this will be the CCITT X.21 interface (although some packet switching networks will use X.21 BIS, which is basically the same as V.24). X.21 includes protocols for call establishment and clearing, which are DTE/DSE protocols (see Fig. 17.3).

2. *Level 2.* The HDLC data link control provides a protocol for the simultaneous bidirectional flow of data blocks called "frames" (including an address field, a control field, and a frame check sequence, as well as an information field) (see Chapter 11). Note that in the case of new digital synchronous networks (Fig. 17.3a), a flow using HDLC (or some other data link control) will be between two or more DTEs. This DLC protocol is a DTE/DTE protocol and is *not* part of the X.21 DTE/DCE interface. However, in the case of packet switching networks (Fig. 17.3b), this

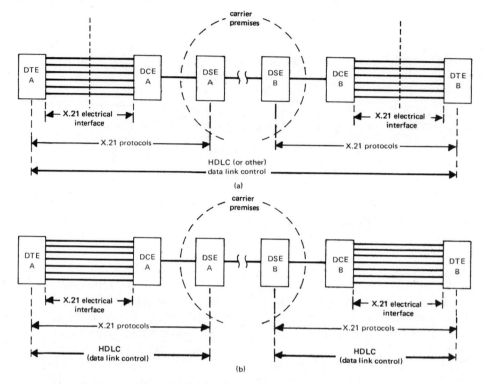

Fig. 17.3 (a) X.21 and DTE/DTE data link control in a synchronous digital network. (b) X.21 and the X.25 DTE/DSE data link control in a packet switching network.

HDLC flow is between a station in a DTE and a station in a DSE. This *is* part of the X.25 DTE/DCE interface.

3. *Level 3.* A third set of DTE/DSE protocols, at a third level, is needed in X.25 to support the DTE-DCE interface for packet switching networks in order to subdivide or form messages into packets with the appropriate packet headers and to provide DTE-DSE packet flow rate control.

Now let us look at how communication facilities perform in four time phases:

1. The call-establishment phase concerns the "setup" of the communications carrier facilities so as to provide communication between a calling DTE and a called station.

2. The data transfer phase is when the connection is established and data may be transferred.

3. The call-clearing phase concerns the release of the communications carrier facilities.

4. The idle phase equates to the *on-hook* condition in telephone networks, but may further indicate that the DTE is Ready or Not Ready to accept a call.

How do these time phases then relate to the aforementioned three levels?

We find three different situations regarding the call establishment and clearing phases:

1. These phases do not exist at level 1 *if the DTE uses a nonswitched circuit of an X.21 digital network*. They also do not exist if the DTE uses a nonswitched access line and a permanent virtual circuit of an X.25 packet-switched network. (There is, however, some sort of start-up procedure, at the start of the work day, for example.)

2. These phases do provide a *direct DTE-to-DTE* connection and disconnection *when the DTE uses an X.21 switched, digital network*. These too are at level 1.

3. When using an X.25 interface and switched virtual circuits, one can think of a combination of two networks, each of which has distinct time phases. *In packet-switched networks,* call establishment and clearing phases *for virtual circuits* are evidenced *by special packets formed at the third level.* In addition in packet-switched networks, there may be other completely separate call establishment/clearing phases at (the X.21) level 1 if the *access* to the packet-switched network is via a *real switched* circuit.

How do real and virtual circuits relate to SNA? First note that in case of circuit switching (of real circuits) between DTEs, *there is no protocol involving interaction between the DTE and the carrier network during the data transfer phase.* The only protocol during the data transfer phase is a DTE-DTE protocol spanning the entire real circuit [17.19]. Virtual circuits, on the other hand, do require a protocol between the DTE and the carrier network during the data transfer phase. This is illustrated in Fig. 17.4, which shows the higher level DTE-DTE protocols of SNA in a system using both (a) DCE/DCE real circuits and (b) DSE/DSE virtual circuits. The DCE/DCE real circuit is transparent to and independent of the data link control protocol. The use of the currently defined X.25 interface for virtual circuits, on the other hand, requires a specific DTE/network packet protocol and the corresponding functions in the DTE. (The level-1 interface is not shown in Fig. 17.4 but

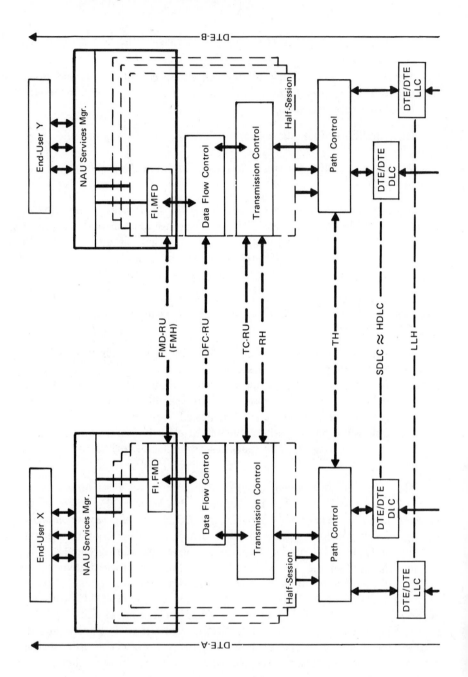

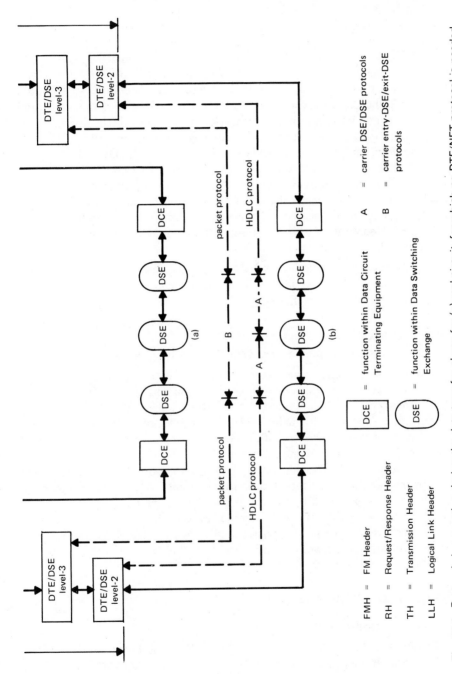

FMH = FM Header
RH = Request/Response Header
TH = Transmission Header
LLH = Logical Link Header

DCE = function within Data Circuit Terminating Equipment

DSE = function within Data Switching Exchange

A = carrier DSE/DSE protocols

B = carrier entry-DSE/exit-DSE protocols

Fig. 17.4 Protocols in operation during the data transfer phase for (a) real circuit, for which no DTE/NET protocol is needed, and (b) virtual circuit.

could be X.21 in both cases.) *The higher level DTE-DTE SNA protocols can be the same for either real or virtual circuits.* Note that (as with any link) the use of the TH and SNA path control enables one to have multiple NAU destinations per real or virtual circuit; the use of FM headers enables one to serve multiple end-user components in a given NAU, each having separate FI.FMD services (see Section 7.4). It should be remembered, however, that diagrams such as Fig. 17.4 show the total structure, and particular products may omit certain of the layers shown or may only use function subsets of each layer. In the case of real circuits (using, for example, an X.21 DTE/DCE interface), the DLC level is used for DTE/DTE data link control (using, for example, HLDC or SDLC). In the case of virtual circuits, Fig. 17.4 shows a reduced version of DLC (sometimes called logical link control) to provide *some* DTE/DTE link-level management for each virtual circuit. Discussion continues on the need and content of this function, but one implementation offers the options of:

1. packet counts (similar to Ns and Nr; see Section 11.5.5) for DTE detection of lost or out-of-sequence packets;
2. recovery functions that span DTE to DTE;
3. use of a DTE/DTE XID command sequence for complete station identification (see Section 11.5.4);
4. use of a test command for DTE/DTE testing purposes.

The first two assume some possibility of error within the packet network. The last two involve higher-level identification and testing services, which are not strictly DLC functions. While I thus indicate a probable need for some such functions (for DTE/DTE management of a virtual circuit), this will depend on experience with different packet switching networks and on further evolution of the X.25 interface [17.18].

Figure 17.5 further illustrates the transport portion of a hypothetical network containing both real and virtual circuits. Again, the path control elements can serve both, and the higher layers are unaffected.

In the following, we will examine the specifics of the X.21 interface for digital synchronous circuit-switched networks, the X.25 interface for packet-switched networks, and some of the current suggestions for further evolution of the X.25 interface.

17.2   X.21 INTERFACE

17.2.1   Introduction

During the 1968–1972 period, a Joint Working Party for New Data Networks studied the evolving circuit-switched data networks. This group

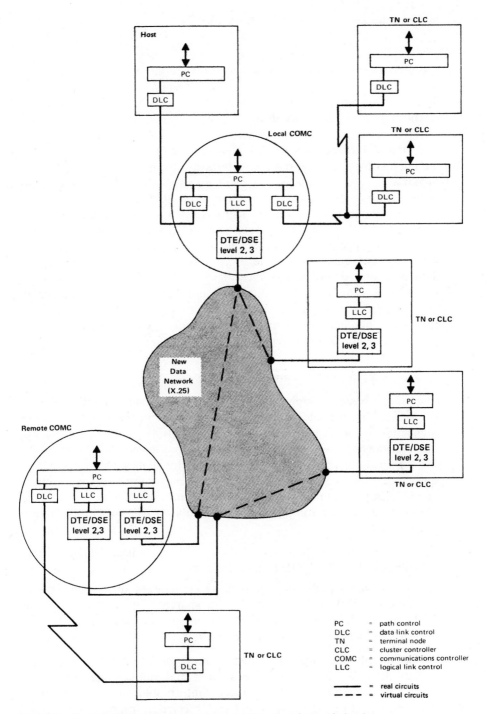

Fig. 17.5 Hypothetical network containing both real and virtual circuits.

prepared eleven draft recommendations (called the X-series), which were approved by the CCITT Fifth Plenary Assembly of December 1972. Since a considerable amount of work remained, Study Group VII was established by CCITT to develop further recommendations for data transmission over public data networks.

One of the resulting CCITT Recommendations, X.21, specifies the parameters for a general-purpose interface for synchronous operation on public data networks, and a revised Recommendation X.21 was unanimously approved by the CCITT at Geneva in 1976.

The application of digital technology to both transmission and switching was beginning to provide shorter call set-up times, lower error rates, higher speeds, and lower tariffs. It was apparent to the study group that important economic and technical advantages could be realized by defining a new simplified interface that would readily be accommodated by the new technology. In addition to improvements in cost and quality over interfaces in current networks, the new X.21 interface facilitates *fully automatic call establishment and clearance with a repertoire of call progress and malfunction signals.*

17.2.2 X.21 Structure and Facilities

One of the basic principles agreed to early in the development of X.21 [17.2] was that the interface should be transparent, that is, bit-sequence independent, for all user data in the data transfer phase. Simplicity was also a prime objective, as evidenced by the resulting circuits shown in Fig. 17.6. Two circuits (T and R) were provided for duplex data interchange, one circuit for each direction of flow. Since synchronous operation is specified, a third line provides bit timing from the network to the DTE. These three circuits comprise the "basic interface." Two other circuits were added:

1. Circuit C (control) is *used by the DTE* to indicate (among other things) ON/OFF hook to the network.

2. The circuit I (indication) is *used by the network* to indicate (among other things) the start of the transparent data phase. Thus the separate phases were indicated without special characters in the data stream and transparency was preserved.

An optional byte timing line is also allowed for use in some networks.

In X.21, a simple call-establishment and call-clearing protocol is used. The calling DTE sends the address information (selection signals or dial characters) to the network and may receive in response appropriate call progress signals (for example, number busy, out of order, etc.). The network signals (in effect, rings) the called DTE by sending "BEL"

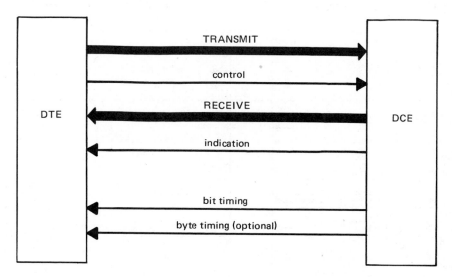

Fig. 17.6 X.21 interchange circuits.

characters on the R circuit. The called DTE would normally respond affirmatively.

The alphabet used to exchange control information is that of the International Alphabet No. 5 (CCITT Recommendation V.3). These control characters are sent on the T and R circuits preceded by two SYN characters (when not in the data transfer phase). *This use of code strings (rather than circuits) for control information is a major advantage of X.21 in that it provides a practically unlimited number of control signals.* ON and OFF conditions for circuits C and I refer to continuous ON (binary 0) and continuous OFF (binary 1) conditions.

An illustrative sequence of X.21 commands is shown in Fig. 17.7, where the changes in interface circuits are shown for each command as one proceeds from the idle phase through the call-establishment, data transfer, and call-clearing phases. Note for example, that:

1. The transition to the call-establishment phase occurs when $C \rightarrow ON$ and continuous zeros are sent on the T circuit.

2. DCE tells the DTE it is O.K. to proceed by sending "+" characters on the R circuit.

3. Selection characters are sent by the DTE, after which it waits, sending all ones.

4. The DCE returns call-progress signals (if necessary) on the R circuit.

5. The DCE confirms the connection by sending all ones on the R circuit.

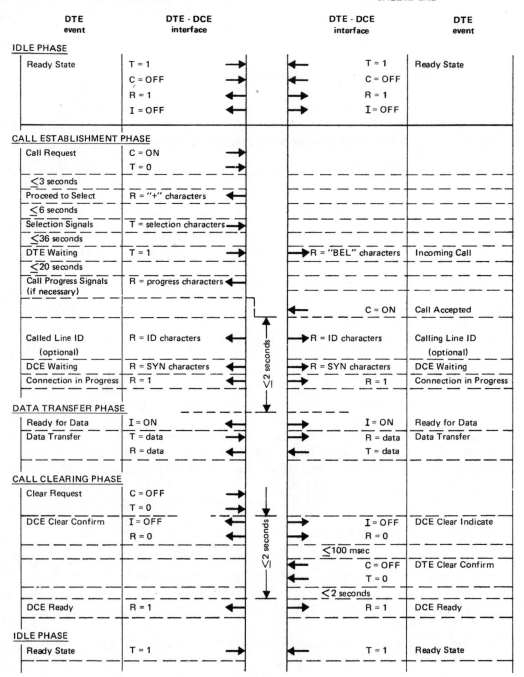

Fig. 17.7 X.21 basic sequence (normal operation) showing changes on interface circuits in different time phases.

The reader can step through each action in Fig. 17.7 at both the calling and called ends and appreciate the simplicity that has been achieved. (Of course, calling and clearing are not necessarily done from the same end, as shown in Fig. 17.7.) State diagrams that define the sequences more precisely can be found in [17.6].

Call-progress signals. Call-progress signals are comprehensively defined for interface X.21 so that predetermined action can be taken for each of a wide range of situations. Recommendation X.96 (Geneva 1976) [17.7] includes those shown in Fig. 17.8. Support of the X.21 interface involves the handling of these call-progress signals by the network services that manage the establishment and clearing of calls.

It appears that handling of these call-progress signals in an SNA network would involve an expansion of the network services in the PU of the calling node. It might also involve an expansion of configuration services in the domain SSCPs for both the calling and the called nodes. However, the remainder of the architecture—for example, path control, half-sessions, LU services, and services in the SSCP—may not be affected at all.

Network features. In addition, the digital networks planning to use X.21 plan to offer a variety of valuable new optional services. In addition to auto-answer, auto-dial, and call-progress signals, optional features may include [17.1, 17.8] the following:

1. Direct Call: A facility that avoids the use of selection (dial) signals. The network interprets the call-request signal as an instruction to establish a connection with a single destination address that was previously designated by the user. This, in effect, can provide almost the same type of service offered by a nonswitched dedicated line.

2. Closed User Group: A facility that permits specified users to communicate with each other but precludes communication with others outside the group. (A user may belong to more than one group.)

3. Abbreviated Address Calling.

4. Outgoing Calls Barred.

5. Incoming Calls Barred.

6. Calling Line Identification: Enables a called terminal to be notified (by the network) of the address from which the call has originated.

7. Called Line Identification: Enables a calling terminal to be notified by the network of the address to which the call has been connected.

8. Multiple lines at the same address.

9. Charge Transfer (collect call).

Call Progress Signal	Brief Description of Circumstances
Selection signal procedure error	The selection signals received did not conform to the specified procedure.
Selection signal transmission error	A transmission error was detected in the selection signals by the first DSE.
Invalid call	Facility request invalid.
Access barred	The calling DTE is not permitted to obtain a connection to the called DTE. Incompatible closed user group or incoming calls barred are examples.
Not obtainable	The called number is not assigned, or is no longer assigned or there is an incompatible user class of service.
Number busy	The called number is engaged in another call.
Out of order	The called number is out of order (DTE "uncontrolled" not ready). Possible reasons include: 1. DTE not functioning; 2. Mains power off to DTE/DCE; 3. Line fault between DSE and DCE.
Changed number	The called number has recently been assigned a new number.
Call the information service	The called number is temporarily unobtainable, call the information service for details.
Network congestion	The establishment of the connection has been prevented due to: 1. Temporary congestion conditions; 2. Temporary fault conditions, e.g., expiry of a time-out.
Terminal Called	The incoming call was signalled to the DTE and call acceptance is awaited.
Controlled not ready	The called DTE is in the "Controlled Not Ready" state.

Fig. 17.8 Circumstances that give rise to call progress signals in circuit-switched data transmission services.

10. Connect When Free: Enables a call originator to request the network to establish the call when the busy terminal becomes free (sometimes known as "camp-on").

11. Redirection of Call: Permits a called user to request the network to transfer a call to another nominated address.

Features 1, 2, 3, 6, 7, and 8 above are from the X.2 definition by CCITT for international use. The others are expected to be popular in national usage.

Different products from different companies may support only a subset of these optional features. Again it appears that the effect of these features on an SNA network would probably be on

1. The data link control level (to route these messages appropriately).

2. The network services in the PU of both the calling node and the called node (to process these messages).

3. The configuration services in the SSCP (to assist the PUs when necessary).

It appears that the remainder of the architecture—for example, path control, the half-sessions, LU services, and session services in the SSCP—would probably not be affected.

X.21 BIS. Several communications carriers are also planning to provide, as an interim measure, the connection to public data networks of synchronous DTEs which are designed for interfacing to synchronous V-series (RS-232-C in USA) modems. This conversion interface facility is called X.21 BIS. It seems that there is no change required to existing products (that now use the V.24 or RS-232-C interface) to attach to an X.21 network when using X.21 BIS. The user may, however, pay extra for the X.21 BIS interface, and many new facilities offered by X.21 (for example, call-progress commands) are not then available to the user.

17.3   X.25 INTERFACE

17.3.1   Introduction

Some packet switching networks, such as Telenet in the United States, Datapac in Canada [17.12], and Transpac in France [17.11], use (or will use) an interface based on the X.25 recommendation. In packet switching (see Section 4.5.2) all messages (both user information and network call control information) are formed into discrete units called packets, which contain a header to specify packet control functions and packet network destination. *The packet network provides a virtual circuit, that is, one that appears to be a point-to-point connection for a pair of DTEs, but actually is a circuit that is shared (in part) by many DTEs through multiplexing (asynchronous time-division multiplexing) provided by the packet carrier.* These virtual circuits may be switched (in which case, a virtual-call set-up and clearing procedure is required of the DTE) or permanent (in which case a permanent association is maintained between the DTEs and no calling procedure is needed).

17.3.2   X.25 Structure

X.25 levels.   As stated in Section 17.1, the X.25 interface [17.10] builds further on both the X.21 interface and portions of the HDLC protocols. As such, it not only defines the conventions in which DTEs establish, maintain, and clear calls over a real access line to a DSE, and defines the protocols for the transmission of frames of information between the DTE and the DSE, but in a third level it also:

1. Defines formats for the packaging of data and control information into standardized packets, and
2. Manages the flow of data for many virtual calls over a single real circuit to and from the packet network.

The three levels of the X.25 interface, illustrated in Fig. 17.9, are:

1. The X.21 *physical level* (X.21 BIS may also be used).
2. The *Link Access Procedure* (LAP) or data link control level, which *uses the principle and terminology of HDLC.* The objective of studies by CCITT and the International Standards Organization (ISO) is to achieve general compatibility between LAP and HDLC.
3. The *packet level*, where packet headers are added and packet flow is controlled.

At the data link control level, the Link Access Procedure of the X.25 interface allows a point-to-point, duplex, asynchronous response mode whereby the DTE and the DSE each have both a primary and a secondary function. This may be thought of as two independent but complementary transmission paths superimposed on a single physical circuit. The use of these two paths rather than the newly defined HDLC Asynchronous Balanced Mode (ABM) (see Section 11.7.4) has been a subject of some debate. A compromise between ISO and CCITT has been reached and it appears that *both the LAP duplex asynchronous response mode and a version of the HDLC Asynchronous Balanced Mode* (sometimes called LAP-B) *will be allowed.* In the former, link commands flowing from the DSE to a DTE and their link level responses contain the address 1100000; link level commands flowing from a DTE to a DCE and their link level responses contain the address 10000000. (The ABM is described in Section 11.7.4.) Other HDLC modes for X.25 such as duplex normal response mode and half-duplex normal response mode (see Section 11.7.4) are also under study.

Logical channels.   One of the things desired in some data processing systems is to be able to multiplex many different sessions across a single interface when different messages have different destinations. This is

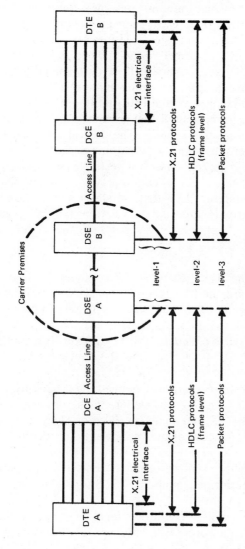

Fig. 17.9 Three levels in support of the DTE-DCE X.25 interface for packet switching networks.

roughly analogous to having different messages multiplexed on a multi-drop HDLC (or SDLC) link, each associated with a different station address [17.15]. The designers of the X.25 interface chose to achieve this multiplexing by creating a *logical channel ID to locally designate each virtual circuit.* For this, each virtual call or permanent virtual circuit is *locally* assigned a *logical channel group number* (≤ 15) and a *logical channel number* (≤ 255). For virtual calls, these are assigned during the call set-up phase. For permanent virtual circuits, these are assigned at the time of subscription to the service. The logical channel ID (logical channel group number plus logical channel number) then must be carried in every packet header (except those for restart packets where these ID fields are zero). Note that a virtual circuit may carry many different SNA sessions, concerning different LUs that are all located at the same logical channel. The TH (carried within the data field of the data packet) would identify each session. Alternatively, a separate virtual circuit (and logical channel) could be used for each session.

Packet headers. The Data Switching Exchanges (DSEs) of packet switching networks are built to recognize packets. Accordingly, in the current X.25 definition, *all of the data to be sent between DTEs are preceded by packet headers. In addition, all of the network control messages are also preceded by packet headers.* The key packet formats thus needed are shown in Fig. 17.10. Each packet is then enclosed in the data link control header and trailer as shown in Fig. 17.11.

Figure 17.10 shows the currently defined identifiers in the four high order bits of the first byte of each header. In the data packet the Q or data qualifier bit indicates that some special processing of that packet is needed (for example, for device control messages). Otherwise, Fig. 17.10 shows these four bits to be always the same. However, other identifier codes are used to identify similar formats when the sequence numbering of data packets is performed modulo 128. Still other codes are as yet unassigned.

Each packet header also includes the local *logical channel ID* for that virtual circuit and also a *packet type indicator.* The packet type indicator for the data packets is only a zero in the low order bit of the third byte, but is a full byte in the other packet types. (In the latter cases, there is a one in the low order bit.)

The Call Request packet includes space for the destination address (equivalent to selection or dial characters) plus an indication of its length (Ly). The Incoming Call packet may contain the address of the calling DTE. The facility field in the Call Request packet may optionally be used for things like reverse charging.

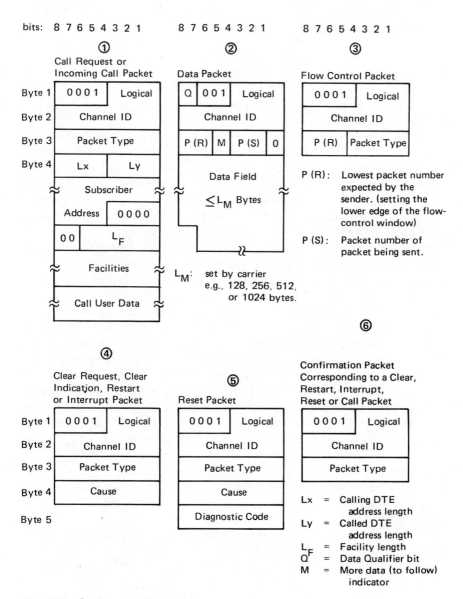

Fig. 17.10 Some packet formats.

F A C [Packet] FCS

F   = Flag
A   = Address
C   = Control
FCS = Frame Check Sequence

Fig. 17.11   Frame format (at level 2) using packets.

The third byte of the data packet header (see Fig. 17.10) is similar to the control byte of HDLC information frames except that the poll/final bit is replaced by the More Data bit (M). The M bit is used to indicate in a full data packet whether there is a logical continuation of data in the next data packet on a particular virtual circuit. The P(S) and P(R) numbers roughly correspond to the Ns and Nr of HDLC described in Section 11.5, but *the P(S) and P(R) are used primarily for controlling the data flow on each logical channel* to or from the packet switching network rather than for providing acknowledgments between stations. The objective is to have an ability to throttle the flow on each logical channel (to prevent overdriving the packet network). The P(S)/P(R) is defined to create a "window" that only allows a predetermined number of frames to be outstanding on a given logical channel at a given time. The actual maximum number of outstanding frames, called window size, W, is set for each virtual circuit either at subscription time or at call-establishment time, but it can never exceed a system parameter of 7 or 128.

Note also that (as in HDLC frames) some packets are not sequenced. One of these nonsequenced packets is the Interrupt packet, which will be transmitted by the network without waiting for all other previously sent packets to be delivered; moreover, it will be delivered to a DTE even when it is not accepting data packets. The Interrupt packet (see Fig. 17.10) can carry only one byte of user data (in the cause field).

Also (as in HDLC frames) there are Receive Ready (RR) packets and Receive Not Ready (RNR) flow control packets, which contain a receive count P(R) but not a send count.

When there is no data packet to carry the P(R), an RR packet is used by the DTE or the DSE to indicate that it is now ready to receive data packets *on a given logical channel* with the indicated P(R). (The number of packets to be sent without a response will be less than eight or less than 128 depending on the modulus used for sequence numbering.) An RNR packet, on the other hand, tells a DTE or a DSE of an inability to accept additional data packets on a given logical channel. The RNR can be cleared by an RR packet sent in the same direction.

X.25 also defines a series of reset and restart packets. Reset is used to reinitialize a virtual call or permanent virtual circuit when it is in the data transfer state. The reset packets are:

- Reset Request (sent by a DTE).
- DCE Reset Confirmation (DSE response to originating DTE).
- Reset Indication (sent by a DSE to a DTE).
- DTE Reset Confirmation (DTE confirms reset).

Either a DTE or a DSE can initiate a reset condition (via a Reset Request or a Reset Indication, respectively. In either case, the opposite party (DSE or DTE) responds with a confirmation packet. That would be a DCE Reset Confirmation or a DTE Reset Confirmation, respectively. The cause field in the reset packet (see Fig. 17.10) may be coded to indicate out of order, remote procedure error, local procedure error, or network congestion. The reset procedure removes all data packets that may be in a reset virtual circuit.

It has also been suggested [17.18] that the Reset and Clear packets be used to inform the using system of various other types of errors, including loss of packets, duplication of packets, mutilation of packets, and packets delivered out of sequence; this area, however, is still under study.

The restart procedure is used to simultaneously clear all the virtual calls and reset all the permanent virtual circuits at the DTE/DCE interface. The restart packets are

1. Restart by the DTE
   - Restart Request (sent by any DTE).
   - DCE Restart Confirmation (response from DSE).
2. Restart by the DSE
   - Restart Indication (from the DSE).
   - DTE Restart Confirmation (response from DTE).

How do packets relate to the SNA units of information? Within the data field of the data packet is the information to be sent from DTE to DTE. In the case of an SNA network, this could be one or more path information units (PIUs) being sent to a single destination address of the packet network. One possible arrangement of this is illustrated in Fig. 17.12.

Thus, the headers potentially involved, in an SNA network using X.25, are:

- FM headers (e.g., for presentation service selection, character string controls, format transforms, compaction, compression, and command-transformation) (see Sections 7.4–7.7);

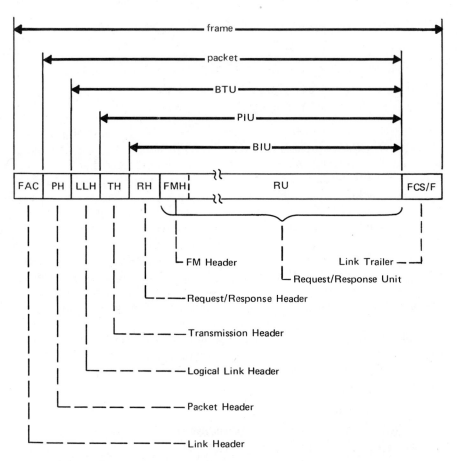

Fig. 17.12 One possible arrangement of an SNA path information unit (PIU), within a packet, in a frame.

- Request/Response header (e.g., for controlling the send/receive discipline, the request/response agreements, chaining, brackets, and end-to-end pacing) (see Section 9.2);
- Transmission header (e.g., to convey the session ID (OAF, DAF) and the end-to-end RU sequence number) (see Section 10.5);
- Logical link header (e.g., for DTE/DTE lost packet or out-of-sequence packet detection);
- Packet header (e.g., logical channel ID and DTE/DSE flow rate control);
- Link header (for DTE/DSE link control).

As emphasized throughout this text, a key to network design is the
selection of the appropriate function subsets in each of the layers of the
network; this selection then affects the headers in Fig. 17.12. (The link
header (FAC), the link trailer (FCS), and the packet header (PH) are
specified by the X.25 interface, but the others can often be subsetted to
meet the needs of the system or product designer.) As stated earlier, the
logical link header (LLH) may be necessary, but its content will depend
on experience with different packet carriers and the evolution of the X.25
interface. The content of the transmission header, request/response
header, and FM header correspond to the LU-types and PU-types chosen
and the function subsets thus allowed by a particular set of products. (See
Section 6.12 and Appendix B.)

Access circuits to a packet network.   The access line between the DCE
on customer premises and the data switching exchange (DSE) of the
carrier network is always a real (rather than virtual) circuit. The following
four cases have to be architected:

	Access circuit	Virtual circuit
1.	Nonswitched	Permanent
2.	Nonswitched	Switched
3.	Switched	Permanent
4.	Switched	Switched

Initially, at least, we can expect most of the access circuits to be
nonswitched analog circuits. A switched, real access circuit might be
either an analog circuit or a digital circuit. The call control for the
establishment/clearing of the real access circuit might be manual (for
example, by an operator in the case of analog circuits) or automatic. For
switched digital access circuits, the X.21 call controls are proposed
(whether the virtual circuit beyond the DSE is switched or permanent).

Call establishment and clearing.   The sequences in X.25 for virtual
circuit call-establishment phase, data transfer phase, and clearing phase
loosely resemble those of X.21, discussed in Section 17.2, *but use packets
for information exchange.* A simplified illustration of this is given in Fig.
17.13 (compare this with Fig. 17.7). Remember, however, that *the packets
for virtual circuit establishment and clearing are formed at level three and
flow at level two, whereas the signals for call establishment/clearing of a
real access circuit appear at level one (X.21).* Note also that the characters
of the virtual circuit call-progress signals are placed in the cause fields of
the Clear Request or Reset packets (see Fig. 17.10), whereas the characters of the real access circuit's call-progress signals appear at level one.

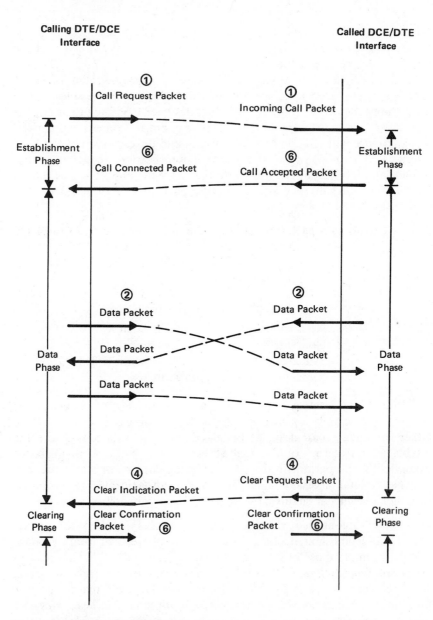

Fig. 17.13 Simplified illustration of call establishment, data transfer, and call clearing. (Circled numbers refer to packet formats in Fig. 17.10).

The sequence shown in Fig. 17.13 is as follows:

1. The calling DTE indicates virtual call request by transferring a Call Request packet across the DTE/DCE interface. This packet (see Fig. 17.10) includes the called DTE address.

2. The destination DSE indicates that there is an incoming call by sending to its DTE an Incoming Call packet, using the logical channel there that is in the ready state and has the lowest logical channel number.

3. The called DTE enters the virtual call data transfer state after it indicates its acceptance of the call by sending a Call Accepted packet. The latter specifies the same logical channel as that of the Incoming Call packet.

4. The calling DTE enters the data transfer state after it receives (from its DSE) a Call Connected packet that specifies the same logical channel as in the Call Request packet. (Note that the logical channel numbers at the two ends are usually different.)

5. In the data phase, traffic can flow in either direction at any time. Data, Interrupt, Flow Control, and Reset packets may be exchanged in the data transfer state.

6. A DTE may request that the virtual call be cleared by sending a Clear Request packet. However, the logical channel will not be returned to the ready state until the local DSE returns a DCE Clear Confirmation packet.

7. The remote DSE in turn can advise the other DTE by sending a Clear Indication packet. That DTE responds by sending a DTE Clear Confirmation packet and the DTE then returns to the ready state. The cause field (see Fig. 17.10) of the Clear Indication packet may be coded to indicate one of the following:

- Number busy
- Out of order
- Remote procedure error
- Number refuses reverse charging
- Invalid call
- Access barred
- Local procedure error
- Network congestion
- Not obtainable

(Note the similarity of these with the X.21 call-progress signals in Fig. 17.8.) State diagrams that define the X.25 sequences more precisely can be found in [17.10].

17.3.3   X.25 Evolution

There is still a great deal of study and discussion of various aspects of the X.25 interface, and an interface of this type can be expected to evolve gradually over many years. Although only a few of the many proposals will be noted in the following, these give a perspective of the alternatives in interface design.

Restructuring of X.25.   Pouzin [17.15] suggests that the X.25 packet level is redundant with other levels and that some of its functions could be performed by taking advantage of facilities already present in HDLC.

Another point Pouzin makes is that the vast majority of synchronous DTEs will be nodes that require only a single logical channel access, so a simplification of the interface for their benefit is in order. Since such a simple DTE need not multiplex virtual circuits, the X.21 or X.21 BIS call-establishment phase would appear to be all that is needed to reach the data transfer phase. Furthermore, it is claimed that flow control on a single logical channel between the DTE and DSE can be achieved as well with the HDLC RR and RNR commands. (Note that the HDLC Ns/Nr counts also provide an incidental flow control when the count of outstanding frames reaches the modulus minus one.)

Pouzin further observes that for more complex DTEs the multiplexing of virtual circuits can neatly be handled by the recently defined "balanced" HDLC procedure (see Section 11.7.4). Each physical circuit would support a number of independent logical data links, and each data link would be a point-to-point connection with a pair of balanced stations. Each data link then would have two station addresses, and by simply assigning consecutive numbers to address logical stations in the DTE and similarly in the DSE, *the frame address could be used as the data link identifier.* In that way, it appears that HDLC could also handle the multiplexing of independent logical channels for the DTE-DCE interface.

A consequence of the above might be that the data transfer phase could be pure HDLC, with no need for format identifier and with the logical channel group number and logical channel number taken care of by the address field of the HDLC frame.

Movements in this direction also would increase the possibility that the interface seen by a synchronous DTE would be essentially the same, whether the service used is a packet-switched service, a circuit-switched service, or a nonswitched service.

Another proposal, generated at the IBM Research Center in Zurich [17.20], uses the X.21 circuit-switched call set-up and clear protocol to establish and clear the packet-switched (virtual circuit) connection (whereas the X.25 recommendation uses a packet-oriented virtual call set-up and clear protocol which is functionally located above the X.21 level).

Still another proposal, following developments in Datapac, concerns priority of a virtual circuit over others that share the same facilities. That priority, it is proposed, would be indicated in a Call Request packet.

Other suggestions. A long list of less dramatic modifications or additions to X.25 is also under continuing consideration by the CCITT. In general, the objective is to reduce the cost of facilities in the DTE that are needed to

1. Permit attachment to the packet switching network.
2. Permit optional use of either circuit switching or packet switching networks.
3. Cope with new types of errors possible in packet switching networks.

Some of the suggestions along these lines, include the following [17.17, 17.21]:

1. An option for the simple (e.g., one virtual circuit) DTE (sometimes called a *frame DTE*) to utilize any of the HDLC "classes of procedure": For example, a low-cost means of attaching a DTE would be for it to operate in normal response mode and half-duplex send/receive mode as one of a number of secondary stations on a multipoint link. Following these HDLC procedures, according to the ISO standard, would not only reduce the DTE product cost but would also increase the feasibility of the user moving between different carrier services when desired.

2. *Segmenting by the carrier:* Redesigning simple DTEs so as to perform segmenting into packets for the convenience of the packet-switched network implies a cost that may not be easily justified. Therefore, it has been recommended that all packet-switched networks accept frame sizes of at least 1024 bytes and 4K bytes for networks with low error rates on local loops, and also consider frame sizes of up to 64K bytes for some applications like facsimile. The referenced suggestions [17.17] further ask that the carrier deliver the same frame size that it received so that the agreements on buffers remain between the two DTEs.

3. *Leased line simplicity:* When operating with a single permanent virtual circuit, no call/clear phases are needed and there seems to be no reason why the data transfer phase for a simple DTE could not then be

identical to that for a nonswitched line in a digital network using the X.21 interface. This flexibility for the user of the network would require that (in the data phase) the packet switching network (a) accept data from the simple DTE without packet headers and (b) strip off packet headers before delivery to the simple DTE.

4. *Call setup for virtual calls:* Even the simple DTE may have to add function to format packet headers for call establishment and clearing if that DTE is to set up a virtual circuit to more than one destination in a packet switching network. However, it still should not be necessary for the simple DTE to construct and handle packet headers during the DTE-DTE data transfer phase. In that phase, it should be no different from the data phase in the (above described) permanent virtual circuit; it could be just like a nonswitched network using X.21 interfaces.

If this is to be possible, however, the simple DTE must have an indication of when the DSE's messages concern call controls for DTE-DTE connection. (Remember that with packet switching networks, the X.21 call-establishment phase may be needed to set up a switched access line. Then, in the X.21 data transfer phase, we need to send another set of call-establishment signals for DTE-DTE connection via the packet switched network.)

The suggestion [17.17] is to *use a code in the HDLC control field* (the third byte of the link header) *to specify a nonsequenced frame and an HDLC information field that contains call-establishment and clearing information.* This simple use of HDLC would permit the DTE to route the call-control information field to call-control programs, without examining special headers in each information field as it comes. That way, packet headers would still not be needed in simple DTEs, except when call-control information is being exchanged.

5. *Simple versus multiplexing DTEs:* The above sounds attractive for simple DTEs, where the DTE is not concerned with multiple virtual circuits (even though the DTE may be only one of several stations on a multipoint line). However, there probably will also be some DTEs in the network that do wish to multiplex a number of virtual circuits over a single access line and use the full X.25 interface. We would want each DTE to use exactly the same protocol, regardless of whether the destination is a simple DTE or a multiplexing DTE.

If, however, the multiplexing DTEs use packet headers *for control purposes during the DTE-DTE data transfer phase,* then we would have some complications when a multiplexing DTE talks to a simple DTE. This is because the simple DTE should not need to handle packet headers *in the data transfer phase.*

The recommended solution [17.17] is that a small number of operational conventions also be defined, together with some mapping of control packets into HDLC commands and vice versa. For example, the occurrence of Command Reject (CMDR) at the data link control level of the DCE/simple-DTE interface would cause a Reset Indication packet to flow to the other DTE. This mapping would avoid requiring simple DTEs to handle such control packets during the data transfer phase.

The suggestions in [17.17] have been widely discussed, presented by a number of authors, supported in a submission to CCITT by IBM Europe, and assigned for study by a CCITT raporteur.

In addition to the above, other studies have resulted in a provisional recommendation (at the 1977 meeting of the CCITT committee VII) for an accommodation of devices using a start-stop data link control. This recommendation involves the use of a Packet Assembler Disassembler (PAD) to connect from synchronous, international alphabet #5, at speeds of 110, 200, and 300 bps, to the format and protocols of the X.25 interface.

Prognosis.   The acceptance of suggestions such as the five "other suggestions" above or comparable simplifications would seem to mean that simple (single virtual circuit) DTEs that use HDLC could then use *permanent virtual circuits* of packet switching networks with no change of the DTEs. The packet switching network, for them, would then be just another alternative carrier seen only at the data link control level. Other changes to X.25 possibly could also reduce or eliminate the changes needed to products using BSC (or other) line disciplines. However, it will take time to work out and obtain agreement on satisfactory solutions.

Those products that need to have call-establishment capabilities for virtual circuits would still need new supervisory functions. If the call establishment is not to be a manual operation, the additional capabilities would be needed to handle the call-establishment/clearing requests.

Those products that need the original full X.25 capability would, in addition, need other capabilities below the DTE/DTE DLC level. This would be needed to provide packet headers for each data transfer. Still other functions at this same level would be needed for those products that need to multiplex virtual circuits on a single access line or need to segment data so as to match the maximum allowable packet size.

In any event, the X.25 packet networks can appear as a more or less complex carrier below (or near) the data link control level. Because of the layered approach of SNA, the implementation of the additional capabilities needed to accommodate the X.25 interface can be either (a) integrated into an existing SNA node or (b) built into a stand-alone "network interface adapter," which would leave the SNA node unchanged. The cost of designing or adapting equipments to use the packet network will depend on the way in which the continuing development of the interface evolves.

17.4 CONCLUSION

As plans to use both X.21 and X.25 progress, the broader requirements of users become clearer. The above recommendations illustrate the process of interface evolution. As the needs become defined and solutions are set in place, the service can be expected to offer better configuration flexibility while still allowing the user complete freedom in the user's data field. Hopefully, the extensions will anticipate application growth, including those requiring terminal-to-terminal and facsimile-to-facsimile, as well as terminal-to-host, communication. Hopefully, too, the preservation of full transparency will keep open the potential for end-to-end services including the accommodation of unforeseen input-output mechanisms and newer system integrity techniques, such as end-to-end encryption on a message or message group basis (see Section 14.8.4).

17.5 REFERENCES AND BIBLIOGRAPHY

17.1 B. Allonen, L. Haglund, S. Hellman, and O. Olofsson, "Technical Description of the Nordic Public Data Network." TELE (January 1976): 13–23.

17.2 H. C. Folts, "X.21—The International Interface for New Synchronous Data Networks." *Proc. IEEE Control Conf. on Communications*, San Francisco (June 1975): 1/15–1/19.

17.3 *The Telenet Report.* Telenet Communications (August 1975).

17.4 U. C. Strahlendorf, "Access to Packet Switching Networks." *Nat. Electronics Conf.*, Chicago (October 1975).

17.5 L. Pouzin, "The Case for a Revision of X.25." *Computer Comm. Review* **6,** No. 3 (July 1976).

17.6 "Recommendation X.21 (Revised) General Purpose Interface Between Data Terminal Equipment and Data Circuit-Terminating Equipment for Synchronous Operation on Public Data Networks." CCITT Document APVI-No. 55-E, Geneva (1976).

17.7 "Recommendation X.96, Call Progress Signals in Public Data Networks." CCITT Document APVI-No. 55E (May 1976).

17.8 "Final Report on the Work of Study Group VII, Part IV: Proposals for New and Revised Definitions of Terms Concerning Public Data Networks." CCITT Document APVI-No. 56-E, Geneva (1976).

17.9 A. Rybczynski, B. Wessler, R. Depres, and J. Wedlake, "A New Communication Protocol for Accessing Data Networks—The International Packet Mode Interface." *AFIPS Conference Proc. National Computer Conference 1976* **45** (7–10 June 1976): 477–482.

17.10 "Draft Recommendations X.25, Interface Between Data Terminal Equipment (DTE) and Data Circuit-Terminating Equipment (DCE) for Terminals Operating in the Packet Mode on Public Data Networks." CCITT Document APVI-No. 55-E, Geneva (1976).

17.11 A. Danet, R. Despres, A. LeRest, G. Picko, and S. Ritzenthaler, "The French Public Packet Switching Service: The Transpac Network." *Proc. of the Third International Conference on Computer Communications*, Toronto (3–6 August 1976).

17.12 D. A. Twyver and A. M. Rybczynski, "Datapac Subscriber Interfaces." *Proc. of the Third International Conference on Computer Communications*, Toronto (3–6 August 1976).

17.13 G. F. Carleton, J. F. Pincosy, and R. M. Davies, "InfoSwitch and InfoDat." World Telecommunications Forum, Geneva Switz., 6–8 October 1975 (International Telecommunications Union 1975), pp. 2.3.8/1-8.

17.14 Y. Makino, "Perspectives on Data Communication in Japan." *Proc. of the Second International Conference on Computer Communications*, Stockholm (August 1974).

17.15 L. Pouzin, "A Restructuring of X.25 into HDLC." *Computer Communication Review*, ACM **7,** No. 1 (January 1977): 9–28.

17.16 L. Pouzin, "Virtual Circuits Vs. Datagrams—Technical and Political Problems." *AFIPS Conf. Proc. 1976 National Computer Conference* **45,** New York (7–10 June 1976).

17.17 "Possible Additions to Recommendation X.25 to Attach Frame Mode DTEs (FDTEs)." *CCITT Study Group VII Contribution No. 59-E* (January 1977).

17.18 "Further Study of Packet Mode Operation on Public Data Networks." *CCITT Study Group VII Contribution No. 60-E* (January 1977).

17.19 E. Port, K. Kummerle, H. Rudin, C. Jenny, and P. Zafiropulo, "A Network Architecture for the Integration of Circuit and Packet Switching." *Proc. of Third International Conference on Computer Communications*, Toronto (3–6 August 1976).

17.20 P. Zafiropulo, E. Port, and K. Kummerle, "Extension of a Circuit-Switched User/Network Interface to Packet Switching." *Proc. of Third International Conference on Computer Communications*, Toronto (3–6 August 1976).

17.21 IBM Europe Contribution to CCITT titled "Technical Comments Regarding CCITT Recommendation X.25." (November 1976).

Appendixes

Appendixes A through E contain certain details of the Systems Network Architecture for the purposes of illustration and to permit exercises in course work. These appendixes are not intended for use in product design, for which the up-to-date architectural or product publications must be consulted.

A
RH, TH, and Link Header Formats in SNA

A.1

The formats for the request/response header (RH) and the transmission header (TH) are given in Figs. A.1 and A.2, respectively.

A.2

The control fields in an SDLC (line control) frame are summarized in Fig. A.3.

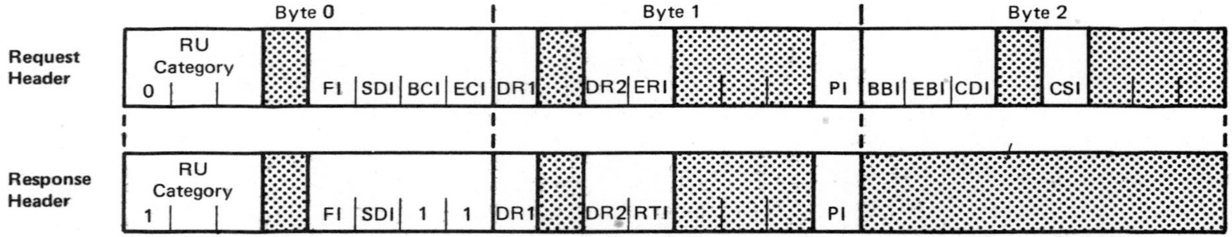

Request Header

| RU Category 0 | | FI | SDI | BCI | ECI | DR1 | DR2 | ERI | | PI | | BBI | EBI | CDI | | | CSI | |

Response Header

| RU Category 1 | | FI | SDI | 1 | 1 | DR1 | DR2 | RTI | | PI | |

Byte 0 — Byte 1 — Byte 2

Field	Description	Explanation/Usage
RU Category	Request-Response Unit Category	00 — Presentation Services (PS)
		01 — Network Control (NC)
		10 — Data Flow Control (DFC)
		11 — Session Control (SC)
FI	Format indicator	0 = no FM header (¬FMH), or character-coded (for network services);
		1 = FM header follows (FMH), or field-formatted (for network services)
SDI	Sense Data Included indicator	0 = not included (¬SDI); 1 = Included (SDI)
BCI	Begin Chain indicator	0 = not first in chain (¬BC); 1 = first in chain (BC)
ECI	End Chain Indicator	0 = not last in chain (¬EC); 1 = last in chain (EC)
DR1	Definite Response 1	(Note 1)
DR2	Definite Response 2	(Note 1)
ERI	Exception Response indicator	(Note 1)
PI	Pacing indicator	0 = ¬PAC; 1 = PAC (Note 2)
BBI	Begin Bracket indicator	0 = ¬BB; 1 = BB (Note 3)
EBI	End Bracket indicator	0 = ¬EB; 1 = EB (Note 3)
CDI	Change Direction indicator	0 = do not change direction (¬CD); 1 = change direction (CD)
CSI	Code Selection indicator	0 = code 0; 1 = code 1
RTI	Response Type indicator	0 = positive (+); 1 = negative (−)

Notes:
1. See Chapter 8
2. See Chapter 9
3. See Chapter 8

▨ Reserved

Fig. A.1 RH formats. (Reprinted by permission from SNA Format and Protocol Reference Manual, © 1976 by International Business Machines Corporation.)

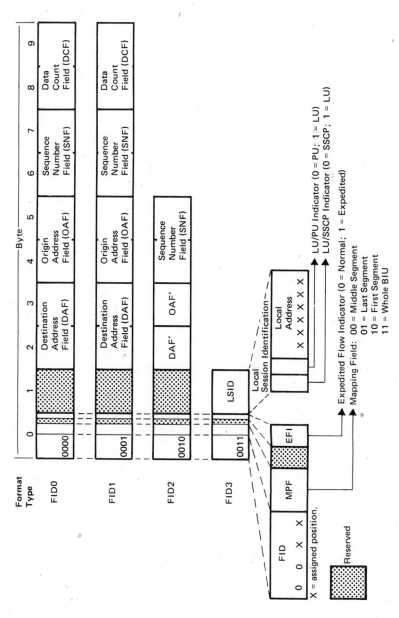

Fig. A.2 TH formats. (Reprinted by permission from SNA Format and Protocol Reference Manual, © 1976 by International Business Machines Corporation.)

Format (Note 1)	Binary Configuration (Sent First)	(Sent Last)	Acronym	Command	Response	I-Field Prohibited	Resets Nr and Ns	Confirms frames through Nr-1	Defining Characteristics
NS	1100 P/F	000	NSI	X	X				Command or response that requires nonsequenced information
	1110 F	000	RQI		X	X			Initialization needed; expect SIM
	1110 P	000	SIM	X		X			Set initialization mode; the using system prescribes the procedures
	1100 P	001	SNRM	X			X		Set normal response mode; transmit on command
	1111 F	000	DM		X	X	X		This station is offline.
	1100 P	010	DISC	X		X			Do not transmit or receive information.
	1100 F	110	NSA		X	X			Acknowledge NS commands
	1110 F	001	CMDR		X				Non-valid command received; Must receive SNRM, DISC, or SIM
	1111 P/F	101	XID	X	X	X			System identification in I field
	1100 0/1	100	NSP	X					Response optional if no P-bit.
	1110 P/F	111	TEST	X	X	X			Check pattern in I field.
S	1000 P/F	Nr	RR	X	X	X		X	Ready to receive
	1010 P/F	Nr	RNR	X	X	X		X	Not ready to receive
	1001 P/F	Nr	REJ	X	X	X		X	Transmit or retransmit, starting with frame Nr
I	0 Ns P/F	Nr	I	X	X			X	Sequenced I-frame

Note 1: NS = nonsequenced, S = supervisory, I = information

Fig. A.3 Summary of command or response control fields in an SDLC frame. (Reprinted by permission from IBM Synchronous Data Link Control, General Information, GA27-3093-1, © 1974, 1975 by International Business Machines Corporation.)

B
Profiles
and LU-Types
in SNA

An *Lu-type* supports only selected function subsets at one end of one or more sessions. As shown in Fig. B.1, an LU-type can be expressed in terms of three *function profiles*. These profiles identify selected function subsets in the SNA layers used by a half-session. Terminology is unclear, but sets of profiles have been referred to as:

1. Presentation Services (PS) profiles, dealing primarily with services in the FI.FMD elements.

2. Function Management (FM) profiles, dealing primarily with the data flow control layer.

3. Transmission Subsystem (TS) profiles, dealing primarily with the transmission control layer.

Figure B.2 illustrates how different LU-types may support different profiles. Some of the currently used FM and TS profiles are listed below in Appendixes B.1 and B.2. FM headers and character string controls that are included in some PS profiles are given in Appendix D.

B.1 FUNCTION MANAGEMENT (FM) PROFILES [13.3]

Currently defined FM profiles primarily concern data flow control, but also concern some presentation services. FM Profiles 0 and 2 through 5*

---

* Reprinted by permission from SNA Format and Protocol Reference Manual, © 1976 by International Business Machines Corporation.

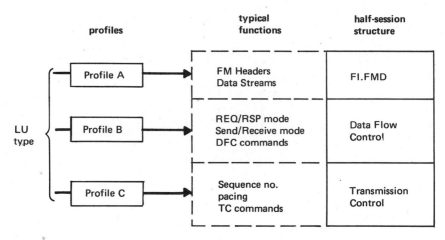

Fig. B.1 The logical unit type identifies function subsets of the SNA architecture.

(referred to in ACTPU, ACTLU, and BIND) are described here. All other profile numbers are reserved.

FM Profile 0

Profile 0 specifies the following session rules:

Primary and secondary half-sessions use immediate control mode and immediate response mode.
Only single-RU chains allowed.
No compression.
Primary half-session sends no DFC RUs.
Secondary half-session may send LUSTAT.
NS Headers are allowed.

LU-type	1	2

PS Profile
  Data Stream
  FM Headers
	SNA Character String
	A subset of FMH
	type 1, 2, 3
		3270 Character String
		none

FM Profile	3,4	3
TS Profile	3,4	3

Fig. B.2 Illustrative LU-types and their allowable profiles.

No FM headers.
No brackets.
No alternate code.
Normal-flow send/receive mode is half-duplex, contention (HDX-CONT).
Secondary half-session wins contention.
Primary half-session is responsible for recovery.

FM Profile 1

Profile 1 is reserved.

FM Profile 2

Profile 2 specifies the following session rules:

Primary half-session uses delayed control mode.
Secondary half-session uses delayed request mode.
Secondary half-session uses immediate response mode.
Only single-RU chains allowed.
Secondary half-session requests indicate no response.
No compression.
No DFC RUs.
No NS or FM headers.
Secondary half-session is first speaker if brackets are used.
Bracket termination rule 2 is used if brackets are used.
Primary half-session will send end-bracket (EB).
Secondary half-session will not send EB.
Normal-flow send/receive mode is duplex (FDX).
Primary half-session is responsible for recovery.

The FM usage fields defining the options for Profile 2 are:

Primary request mode selection
Primary chain response protocol (no-response may not be used)
Brackets
Alternate code

FM Profile 3

Profile 3 specifies the following session rules:

Primary half-session and secondary half-session use delayed control mode and immediate response mode.
No NS headers.

Primary half-session and secondary half-session support the following DFC functions:

    CANCEL
    SIGNAL
    LUSTAT (allowed secondary-to-primary only)
    CHASE
    SHUTDOWN (SHUTD)
    SHUTDOWN COMPLETE (SHUTC)
    REQUEST SHUTDOWN (RSHUTD)
    BID and RTR (allowed only if brackets are used)

The FM usage fields (e.g., in the BIND command) defining the options for Profile 3 are:

    Chaining use (primary and secondary)
    Request mode selection (primary and secondary)
    Chain response protocol (primary and secondary)
    Compression indicator (primary and secondary)
    Send end-bracket (EB) indicator (primary and secondary)
    FM header usage
    Brackets
    Bracket termination rule
    Alternate Code Set Allowed indicator
    Normal-flow send/receive mode
    Recovery responsibility
    First speaker (for bracket protocol)
    Contention resolution

FM Profile 4

Profile 4 specifies the following session rules:

    Primary half-session and secondary half-session use delayed control mode and immediate response mode.
    No NS headers.
    Primary half-session and secondary half-session support the following DFC functions:

    CANCEL
    SIGNAL
    LUSTAT
    QUIESCE AT END OF CHAIN (QEC)
    QUIESCE COMPLETE (QC)
    RELEASE QUIESCE (RELQ)

SHUTD
SHUTC
RSHUTD
CHASE
BID and RTR (allowed only if brackets are used)

The FM usage fields (e.g., in the BIND command) defining the options for Profile 4 are:

Chaining use (primary and secondary)
Request mode selection (primary and secondary)
Chain response protocol (primary and secondary)
Compression indicator (primary and secondary)
Send EB indicator (primary and secondary)
FM header usage
Brackets
Bracket termination rule
Alternate Code Set Allowed indicator
Normal-flow send/receive mode
Recovery responsibility
First speaker (for bracket protocol)
Contention resolution

FM Profile 5

Profile 5 specifies the following session rules:

Only single-RU chains allowed.
Primary half-session uses delayed request mode.
Secondary half-session uses delayed request mode and delayed response mode.
Primary half-session chains indicate definite response.
Secondary half-session chains indicate no-response.
No compression.
No DFC RUs.
NS headers are allowed.
No FM headers.
No brackets.
No alternate code.
Normal-flow send/receive mode is duplex (FDX.)
Primary half-session is responsible for recovery.

Note: If the FM usage field specifies a value for a parameter, that value is used unless it conflicts with a value specified by the FM profile. The FM profile overrides the FM usage field. The following table specifies which FM profiles currently may be used with certain kinds of session.

FM Profile	NAUs in session:		
	(SSCP, PU)	(SSCP, LU)	(LU, LU)
0	yes	yes	no
2	no	no	yes
3	no	no	yes
4	no	no	yes
5	yes	no	no

B.2 TRANSMISSION SUBSYSTEM (TS) PROFILES

TS profiles primarily concern facilities at the Transmission Control level. TS Profiles 1 through 5 (referred to in ACTPU, ACTLU, and BIND) are described here.

TS Profile 1

Profile 1 specifies the following session rules:

> No pacing.
> Identifiers rather than sequence numbers are used on the normal flows.
> START DATA TRAFFIC (SDT), CLEAR, REQUEST RECOVERY (RQR), and SET AND TEST SEQUENCE NUMBERS (STSN) are not supported.
> No maximum RU sizes for the normal flows are specified.

This profile does not require the use of the TS usage field.

TS Profile 2

Profile 2 specifies the following session rules:

> Primary-to-secondary and secondary-to-primary normal flows are paced.
> Sequence numbers are used on the normal flows.
> CLEAR is supported.
> SDT, RQR, and STSN are not supported.

The TS usage subfields defining the options for this profile are:

> Pacing counts
> Maximum RU sizes on the normal flows

TS Profile 3

Profile 3 specifies the following session rules:

> Primary-to-secondary and secondary-to-primary normal flows are paced.
> Sequence numbers are used on the normal flows.
> CLEAR and SDT are supported.
> RQR and STSN are not supported.

The TS usage subfields defining the options for this profile are:

> Pacing counts
> Maximum RU sizes on the normal flows

TS Profile 4

Profile 4 specifies the following session rules:

> Primary-to-secondary and secondary-to-primary normal flows are paced.
> Sequence numbers are used on the normal flows.
> SDT, CLEAR, RQR, and STSN are supported.

The TS usage subfields defining the options for this profile are:

> Pacing counts
> Maximum RU sizes on the normal flows

TS Profile 5

Profile 5 specifies the following session rules:

> No pacing.
> Sequence numbers are used on normal flows.
> SDT is supported.
> CLEAR, RQR, and STSN are not supported.
> No maximum RU sizes for the normal flows are specified.

This profile does not require the use of the TS usage field.

The following table specifies which TS profile currently may be used with each type of session.

TS Profile	NAUs in session		
	(SSCP, PU)	(SSCP, LU)	(LU, LU)
1	yes	yes	no
2	no	no	yes
3	no	no	yes
4	no	no	yes
5	yes	no	no

B.3   PHYSICAL UNIT (PU) TYPES

A PU-type supports only selected function subsets in the layers of the common transmission network. The following PU types are defined (all others are reserved).

PU Type 1 (PU.T1)

For all PIUs sent and received, the transmission header (TH) format is FID3.

PU Type 2 (PU.T2)

For all PIUs sent and received, the transmission header (TH) format is FID2.

PU Type 4 (PU.T4)

A PU.T4 is at a node that has intermediate and/or boundary function.

The TH format is either:

- FID0 or FID1 for all PIUs transmitted between the PU.T4 and adjacent PU.T4 | 5s.
- FID2 for all PIUs transmitted between the PU.T4 and adjacent PU.T2s.
- FID3 for all PIUs transmitted between the PU.T4 and adjacent PU.T1s.

PU Type 5 (PU.T5)

A PU.T5 is at a node that has intermediate and/or boundary function and also contains the SSCP.

The TH format is either:

- FID0 or FID1 for all PIUs transmitted between the PU.T5 and adjacent PU.T4s.
- FID2 for all PIUs transmitted between the PU.T5 and adjacent PU.T2s.

C
Request-Response Unit (RU) Formats in SNA

C.1 RU CATEGORIES

This appendix defines detailed RU formats. A categorized list of RU abbreviations is presented first, followed by an alphabetic list of request RU format descriptions, a summary of response RUs, and a list of response format descriptions for those positive response RUs that return data in addition to the request code.

The initial line for each RU in the two format description lists is in one of the following formats.

Requests

"RU ABBREVIATION; Origin NAU→ Destination NAU, Normal (Norm) or Expedited (Exp) Flow; RU Category (RU NAME)"

Responses

"RSP (RU ABBREVIATION); Origin NAU → Destination NAU; Norm or Exp Flow; RU Category"

Notes

1. The origin or destination service determines the *RU category* and is abbreviated as follows:

DFC Data flow control

SC Session control (in transmission control layer)

---

* Reprinted by permission from SNA Format and Protocol Reference Manual, © 1976 by International Business Machines Corporation.

NC   Network control (in transmission control layer)

NS(C)   Network services (configuration services)

NS(ma)   Network services (maintenance services)

NS(me)   Network services (measurement services)

NS(s)   Network services (session services)

2. The formats of character-coded NS RUs and LU → LU FMD-RUs (other than FM headers) are implementation-dependent.

3. All values for field-formatted RUs that are not defined in this section are reserved.

4.   ILU = Initiating LU   PPU = PU controlling primary link station

      TLU = Terminating LU   SPU = PU controlling secondary link station

   PLU = Primary LU (i.e., the LU supporting the primary half-session)

   SLU = Secondary LU (i.e., the LU supporting the secondary half-session)

   COMC = Communications controller

Summary of Request RUs by Category

NC

ANSC	LSA

SC

*ACTLU	CLEAR	RQR	UNBIND
*ACTPU	DACTLU	SDT	
BIND	DACTPU	*STSN	

DFC

BID	LUSTAT	RELQ	SHUTC
CANCEL	QC	RSHUTD	SHUTD
CHASE	QEC	RTR	SIG

NS(c)

ABCONN	CONNOUT	*DUMPINIT	IMLINIT
ABCONNOUT	CONTACT	*DUMPTEXT	IMLTEXT

* These request RUs require response RUs that, if positive, contain data in addition to the request code. See "Summary of Response RUs" and "Positive Response RUs with Extended Formats."

ACTCONNIN	CONTACTED	ESLOW	REQCONT
ACTLINK	DACTCONNIN	EXSLOW	REQDISCONT
ANA	DACTLINK	FNA	RPO
	DISCONTACT	INOP	SETCV
	DUMPFINAL	IMLFINAL	

NS(ma)

ACTTRACE	EXECTEST	RECTD
DACTTRACE	RECMS	RECTRD

NS(s)

BINDF	INIT-OTHER	SESSEND	TERM-SELF
CINIT	INIT-SELF	SST	UNBINDF
CTERM	NSPE	TERM-OTHER	

C.2   REQUEST RU FORMATS

Bytes   *Description*

ABCONN; SSCP → PPU, Norm; NS(c) (ABANDON CONNECTION)
0–2   X'01020F' NS header
3–4   Network address of link

ABCONNOUT; SSCP → PPU, Norm; NS(c) (ABANDON CONNECT
            OUT)
0–2   X'010218' NS header
3–4   Network address of link

ACTCONNIN; SSCP → PPU, Norm; NS(c) (ACTIVATE CONNECT
            IN)
0–2   X'010216' NS header
3–4   Network address of link
5   bit 0, type: 0 (only value defined)
           bits 1–7, reserved

ACTLINK; SSCP → PPU, Norm; NS(c) (ACTIVATE LINK)
0–2   X'01020A' NS header
3–4   Network address of link

ACTLU; SSCP → LU, Exp; SC (ACTIVATE LOGICAL UNIT)
0   X'0D' request code
1   Type activation requested: X'01' cold
2   bits 0–3, FM profile (see Appendix B)
           bits 4–7, TS profile (see Appendix B)

ACTPU; SSCP → PU, Exp; SC (ACTIVATE PHYSICAL UNIT)
0   X'11' request code
1   Type activation requested:
             X'01' cold
             X'02' error recovery procedure (ERP)

2	bits 0–3, FM profile (see Appendix B)
	bits 4–7, TS profile (see Appendix B)
3–8	A six-byte field that specifies the ID of the SSCP issuing ACTPU. The first four bits specify the format for the remaining bits.
	bits 0–3, 0000 format
	bits 4–7, PU type of the node containing the SSCP
	bits 18–47 implementation and installation dependent binary identification

ACTTRACE; SSCP → PU, Norm; NS(ma) (ACTIVATE TRACE)

0–2	X'010302' NS header
3–4	Network address of the resource to be traced
5	Selected trace: binary value specifying which trace is to be activated: X'01' link (only value defined)
6–n	Data to support trace

ANA; SSCP → PPU, Norm; NS(c) (ASSIGN NETWORK ADDRESSES)

0–2	X'010219' NS header
3–4	Network address of PU associated with the node to which LU network addresses are to be assigned
5	Number of network addresses to be assigned
6	Type: X'80' noncontiguous (only value defined)
7–8	First network address
9–n	Any additional network addresses (two-byte multiples)

ANSC; PU in COMC → SSCP, Exp; NC (AUTO NETWORK SHUT-DOWN COMPLETE)

0	X'07' request code
1	Reason code, indicating why the completed automatic network-shutdown procedure was initiated:
	X'01' operator-initiated
	X'02' unrecoverable timeout occurred on the link used for the session between the SSCP and the shutdown-initiating PU
	X'03' ACTPU (ERP) was received while (SSCP, PU) .SEC.SESS.RCV: ACTIVE
	X'04' DISC was received while (SSCP, PU).SEC.SESS.RCV: ACTIVE
	X'05' SNRM (SDLC command) was received while (SSCP, PU).SEC.SESS.RCV: ACTIVE
	X'06' unrecoverable link error occurred on the link used for the session between the SSCP and the shutdown-initiating PU

Note: ANSC is always sent with no-response indicated.

BID; LU → LU, Norm; DFC (BID)
0   X'C8' request code

BIND; PLU → SLU, Exp; SC (BIND SESSION)
0   X'31' request code
1   bits 0–3, Format: 0000 (only value defined)
             bits 4–7, Type: 0001 cold
2   FM profile (see Appendix B)
3   TS profile (see Appendix B)

             FM usage—primary half-session
4   bit 0, chaining use selection:
                        0   only single-RU chains allowed from primary
                            half-session
                        1   multiple-RU chains allowed from primary half-
                            session
             bit 1, request control mode selection:
                        0   immediate request mode
                        1   delayed request mode
             bits 2–3, chain response protocol used by primary half-
                        session for FMD-requests; chains from primary
                        will ask for:
                        00 no response
                        01 exception response
                        10 definite response
                        11 definite or exception response
             bits 4–5, reserved
             bit 6, compression indicator:
                        0   compression will not be used on requests from
                            primary
                        1   compresssion may be used
             bit 7, send end bracket indicator (reserved if brackets not
                        used, i.e., if byte 6, bit 2 = 0):
                        0   primary will not send EB
                        1   primary may send EB

             FM usage—secondary half-session
5   bit 0, chaining use selection:
                        0   only single-RU chains allowed from secondary
                            half-session
                        1   multiple-RU chains allowed from secondary
                            half-session

bit 1, request control mode selection:

    0   immediate request mode

    1   delayed request mode

bits 2–3, chain response protocol used by secondary half-session for FMD-requests; chains from secondary will ask for:

    00 no response

    01 exception response

    11 definite or exception response

bits 4–5, reserved

bit 6, compression indicator:

    0   compression will not be used on requests from secondary

    1   compression may be used

bit 7, send end bracket indicator (reserved if brackets not used; i.e., if byte 6, bit $2 = 0$):

    0   secondary will not send EB

    1   secondary may send EB

FM usage—common to both half-sessions

6   bit 0, reserved

bit 1, FM header usage:

    0   FM headers not allowed

    1   FM headers allowed

bit 2, brackets usage:

    0   brackets will not be used during this session

    1   brackets will be used

bit 3, bracket termination rule selection (reserved if brackets not used, i.e., if byte 6, bit $2 = 0$):

    0   Rule 2 will be used during this session

    1   Rule 1 will be used during this session

bit 4, alternate code set allowed indicator:

    0   alternate code set will not be used

    1   alternate code set may be used

bits 5–7, reserved

7   bits 0–1, normal-flow send/receive mode selection:

    00 duplex

    01 half-duplex contention

    10 half-duplex flip-flop

    11 reserved

bit 2, recovery responsibility:

    0   primary half-session responsible

    1   sender of request responsible

bit 3, brackets first speaker selection (reserved if brackets not used; i.e., if byte 6, bit 2 = 0):

    0   secondary is first speaker

    1   primary is first speaker

bits 4–6, reserved

bit 7, contention resolution (reserved if normal-flow send/receive mode is duplex or if brackets are being used; i.e., if byte 7, bits 0–1 = 00 or if byte 6, bit 2 = 1):

    0   secondary speaks first when data traffic (DT) FSMs are first activated if HDX-FF; secondary wins contention if HDX-contention

    1   primary speaks first when data traffic (DT) FSMs are first activated if HDX-FF: primary wins contention if HDX-contention

TS usage

8

bits 0–1 reserved

bits 2–7 secondary CPMGR's send pacing count (a value of zero means no pacing of requests flowing from the secondary)

9

bits 0–1 reserved

bits 2–7 secondary CPMGR's receive pacing count (a value of zero causes substitution of the value set by a system definition pacing parameter, if such exists; a value of zero received at the secondary is interpreted to mean no pacing of requests flowing to the secondary.)

10

Maximum RU size sent on the normal flow by the secondary half-session: if bit 0 is set to *zero*, then no maximum is specified and the remaining bits 1–7 are ignored; if bit 0 is set to *one*, then the byte is interpreted as $X'ab' = a*2**b$. (Notice that, by definition, $a \geq 8$ and therefore $X'ab'$ is a normalized floating-point representation.)

11

Maximum RU size sent on the normal flow by the primary half-session: identical encoding as described for byte 10

12

bits 0–1, reserved

bits 2–7, primary CPMGR's send pacing count: a value of *zero* causes the value set by a system definition pacing parameter (if the system definition includes such a parameter) to be assumed for the session; if this is also *zero*, it means no pacing of requests flowing from the primary

13	Reserved
14	*PS profile*
	bit 0, PS usage field format
	bits 1–7, LU-type
15–25	*PS usage*
	allowable subsets of FM headers and SNA character string
	controls.
26	bits 0–3 reserved
	bits 4–7 option field length
$27 - K$	reserved options
$K + 1$	Length of primary LU name
$(K + 2) - m$	Primary LU name
$m + 1$	Length of user data ($X'00'$ = no user data field present)
$(m + 2) - n$	User data

BINDF; PLU → SSCP, Norm; NS(s) (BIND FAILURE)

0–2	$X'010685'$ NS header
3–4	Network address of primary LU
5–6	Network address of secondary LU
7	Reason (multiple bits may be set to 1, indicating that the corresponding conditions have occurred).
	bit 0, BIND error at primary
	bit 1, BIND error at secondary
	bit 2, BIND reject at primary
	bit 3, BIND reject at secondary
	bits 4–7, reserved

CANCEL; LU → LU, Norm; DFC (CANCEL)

0	$X'83'$ request code

CHASE; LU → LU, Norm; DFC (CHASE)

0	$X'84'$ request code

CINIT; SSCP → PLU, Norm; NS(s) (CONTROL INITIATE)

0–2	$X'010601'$ NS header
3–4	Network address of secondary LU
5	CINIT format, specifies format for the remainder of RU: $X'00'$ (only value defined)
$6 - m$	BIND image: the BIND RU (see BIND description)
	Network name of secondary LU
$m + 1$	Type: $X'00'$ no length and name fields follow
	$X'F3'$ logical unit
$m + 2$	Length: binary number of bytes in symbolic name ($X'00'$ = no symbolic name present)

$(m+3)-n$ Symbolic name of secondary LU, in EBCDIC characters

Requester ID

$n+1$ Length: binary number of bytes in requester ID
                (X'00' = no requester ID present)

$(n+2)-p$ Requester ID, in EBCDIC characters, of the end user initiating the request. (May be used to verify end-user's authority to access a particular resource.)

Password

$p+1$ Length: binary number of bytes in password
                (X'00' = no password present)

$(p+2)-q$ Password, field used to verify the identity of an end user

User field

$q+1$ Length: binary number of bytes of user data
                (X'00' = no user data present)

$(q+2)-r$ User-specific data that is not processed by NS protocol machines but is passed to the primary LU (see the INIT-SELF and INIT-OTHER requests)

CLEAR; PLU → SLU, Exp; SC (CLEAR)

0   X'A1' request code

CONNOUT; SSCP → PPU, Norm; NS(c) (CONNECT OUT)

0–2   X'01020E' NS header
3–4   Network address of link
5   Address of link station
6   bit 0, type: 0 (only value defined)
                 bit 1, automatic manual:
                    0   automatic connect out
                    1   manual connect out
                 bits 2–7, reserved

                 Note: Bytes $7-n$ not permitted on manual-connect calls.
7   Retry limit: number of times the connect-out procedure is to be retried
8   Number of dial digits
$9-n$ Dial digits: decimal EBCDIC characters plus end-of-numbers (X'FC') and separator (X'FD') characters, where used

CONTACT; SSCP → PPU, Norm; NS(c) (CONTACT)

0–2   X'010201' NS header
3–4   Network address of PU in node to be contacted (the SPU)

CONTACTED; PPU → SSCP, Norm; NS(c) (CONTACTED)
0–2   X'010280' NS header
3–4   Network address of PU in node being contacted (the SPU)
5   Status of SPU:
     X'01' loaded
     X'02' load required
     X'03' error on CONTACT

CTERM; SSCP → PLU, Norm; NS(s) (CONTROL TERMINATE)
0–2   X'010602' NS header
3   Type UNBIND:
     bits 0–1, 00 terminate only active or pending active session;
          other values reserved
     bit 2, type termination:
         0   forced termination; session to be deactivated
            immediately and unconditionally
         1   orderly termination requested; primary LU to
            be given an opportunity to prepare for an or-
            derly shutdown before deactivation of the ses-
            sion
     bits 3–7, reserved
4–5   Network address of secondary LU

DACTCONNIN; SSCP → PPU, Norm; NS(c) (DEACTIVATE CON-
           NECT IN)
0–2   X'010217' NS header
3–4   Network address of link

DACTLINK; SSCP → PPU, Norm; NS(c) (DEACTIVATE LINK)
0–2   X'01020B' NS header
3–4   Network address of link

DACTLU; SSCP → LU, Exp; SC (DEACTIVATE LOGICAL UNIT)
0   X'0E' request code

DACTPU; SSCP → PU, Exp; SC (DEACTIVATE PHYSICAL UNIT)
0   X'12' request code
1   Type deactivation requested:
     X'01' final use, physical connection may be broken
     X'02' not final use, physical connection should not be broken

DACTTRACE; SSCP → PU, Norm; NS(ma) (DEACTIVATE TRACE)
0–2   X'010303' NS header
3–4   Network address of resource to be traced
5   Selected trace
6 – n Data to support trace deactivation

DISCONTACT; SSCP → PPU; Norm; NS(c) (DISCONTACT)
0–2   X'010202' NS header
3–4   Network address of PU in node to be discontacted (the SPU)

DUMPFINAL; SSCP → PPU, Norm; NS(c) (DUMP FINAL)
0–2   X'01208' NS header
3–4   Network address of PU in node being dumped (the SPU)

DUMPINIT; SSCP → PPU, Norm; NS(c) (DUMP INITIAL)
0–2   X'010206' NS header
3–4   Network address of PU in node to be dumped (the SPU)

DUMPTEXT; SSCP → PPU, Norm; NS(c) (DUMP TEXT)
0–2   X'010207' NS header
3–4   Network address of PU in node to be dumped (the SPU)
5–8   Starting address where dump data is to begin
9–10   Length of text: two-byte binary count of the number of bytes
           of dump data to be returned

ESLOW; PU → SSCP, Norm; NS(c) (ENTERING SLOWDOWN)
0–2   X'010214' NS header
3–4   Network address of PU

EXECTEST; SSCP → PU, Norm; NS(ma) (EXECUTE TEST)
0–2   X'010301' NS header
3–4   Network address of resource to be tested
5–8   Binary code selecting the test
9–n Data to support the selected test

EXSLOW; PU → SSCP, Norm; NS(c) (EXITING SLOWDOWN)
0–2   X'010215' NS header
3–4   Network address of PU

FNA; SSCP → PPU, Norm; NS(c) (FREE NETWORK ADDRESSES)
0–2   X'01021A' NS header
3–4   Network address of target link or SPU
5   Number of SPU or LU network addresses to be freed
           (X'00' = all: bytes 7–n not present
6   Type: X'80' noncontiguous
7–8   First network address to be freed
9–n Any additional network addresses (two-byte multiples)

IMLFINAL; SSCP → PPU, Norm; NS(c) (IML FINAL)
0–2   X'010205' NS header
3–4   Network address of PU in node being loaded (the SPU)
5–8   Entry point location with load module

IMLINIT: SSCP→PPU, Norm; NS(c) (IML INITIAL)

0–2	X'010203' NS header
3–4	Network address of PU in node to be loaded (the SPU)

IMLTEXT: SSCP→PPU, Norm; NS(c) (IML TEXT)

0–2	X'010204' NS header
3–4	Network address of PU in node to be loaded (the SPU)
5 – n	Text: a variable-length byte string in the form required by the node being loaded

INIT-OTHER; ILU → SSCP, Norm; NS(s) (INITIATE-OTHER)

0–2	X'010680' NS header
3	bits 0–3, format: X'0' (only value defined) bits 4–7, reserved
4–11	Mode: an eight-character symbolic name (implementation and installation-dependent) that identifies the set of rules and protocols to be used for the session; used by SSCP to build the CINIT request

Name of LU-1

12	Type: X'00' no length and name fields follow X'F3' logical unit
13	Length: binary number of bytes in symbolic name (X'00' = no symbolic name present)
14 – m	Symbolic name of LU, in EBCDIC characters

Name of LU-2

m + 1	Type: X'00' no length and name fields follow X'F3' logical unit
m + 2	Length: binary number of bytes in symbolic name (X'00' = no symbolic name present)
(m + 3) – n	Symbolic name of LU, in EBCDIC characters

Requester ID

n + 1	Length: binary number of bytes in requester ID (X'00' = no requester ID present)
(n + 2) – p	Requester ID, in EBCDIC characters, of the end user initiating the request (May be used to verify end-user's authority to access a particular resource.)

Password

p + 1	Length: binary number of bytes in password (X'00' = no password present)
(p + 2) – q	Password, field used to verify the identity of an end-user

User field

q + 1	Length: binary number of bytes of user data (X'00' = no user data present)

$(q+2)-r$ User-specific data that is not processed by NS protocol machines but is passed to the primary LU on the CINIT request

INIT-SELF; ILU → SSCP, Norm; NS(s) (INITIATE-SELF)
0–2   X'020681' NS header
3   bits 0–3, format: X'0' (only value defined)
             bits 4–7, reserved
4–11   Mode: an eight-character symbolic name (implementation and installation-dependent) that identifies the set of rules and protocols to be used for the session; used by SSCP to build the CINIT request

             Name of other LU
12   Type: X'00' no length and name fields follow
                  X'F3' logical unit
13   Length: binary number of bytes in symbolic name
                  (X'00' = no symbolic name present)
$14 - m$ Symbolic name of other LU, in EBCDIC characters

             Requester ID
$m + 1$ Length: binary number of bytes in requester ID
                  (X'00' = no requester ID present)
$(m+2)-n$ Requester ID, in EBCDIC characters, of the end user initiating the request (May be used to verify end-user's authority to access a particular resource.)

             Password
$n + 1$ Length: binary number of bytes in password
                  (X'00' = no password present)
$(n+2)-p$ Password, field used to verify the identity of an end-user

             User field
$p + 1$ Length: binary number of bytes of user data
                  (X'00' = no user data present)
$(p+2)-q$ User-specific data that is not processed by NS protocol machines but is passed to the primary LU on the CINIT request

INOP; PPU → SSCP, Norm; NS(c) (INOPERATIVE)
0–2   X'010281' request code
3–4   Network address of (1) an inoperative link or (2) an SPU (when the SPU or its secondary link station is inoperative)

5   Type: X'01' PU (loss of contact, unexpected loss
                           of connection, or connection
                           establishment failure)
                       X'02' link (link failure)

LUSTAT; LU → LU, Norm; DFC (LOGICAL UNIT STATUS)
0   X'04' request code
1–4   Status value + status extension field (two bytes each):
                   X'0000' + 'uuuu' no-op (no system-defined
                                     status) + user-defined field

                   X'0001' + 'cc00' component now available +
                                     component identification
                   X'0802 + 'cc00'   component failure (inter-
                                     vention required) + component
                                     identification
                                     (see Note)
                   X'081C' + 'cc00' component failure (permanent
                                     error) + component
                                     identification
                                     (see Note)
                   X'0824' + 'rrrr' function canceled +
                                     reserved field
                   X'400A' + 'ssss' "no-response mode" not
                                     allowed + sequence number
                                     of the request
                                     specifying no-response

       Note: Values for "cc" byte are:
       X'00' = LU itself rather than a specific LU component
       Otherwise,
       bit 0, set to 1
       bits 1–3, LU component medium class:
           000 console
           001 exchange (e.g., customer-removable diskette)
           010 card puch
           011 printer
       bits 4–7, LU component device address

NSPE; SSCP → ILU or TLU, Norm; NS(s) (NS PROCEDURE ERROR)
0–2   X'010604' NS header

3   Reason (multiple bits may be set to 1, indicating that the
                corresponding conditions have occurred):
                bit 0, BIND error at primary LU
                bit 1, BIND error at secondary LU
                bit 2, BIND reject at primary LU
                bit 3, BIND reject at secondary LU
                bit 4, UNBIND failure
                bits 5–7, reserved

                Network name of primary LU
4   Type: X'00' no length and name fields follow
                      X'F3' logical unit
5   Length: binary number of bytes in symbolic name
                      (X'00' = no symbolic name present)
$6 - m$ Symbolic name of primary LU, in EBCDIC characters

                Network name of secondary LU
$m + 1$ Type: X'00' no length and name fields follow
                      X'F3' logical unit
$m + 2$ Length: binary number of bytes in symbolic name
                      (X'00' = no symbolic name present)
$(m+3)-n$ Symbolic name of secondary LU, in EBCDIC characters

QC; LU → LU Norm; DFC (QUIESCE COMPLETE)
0   X'81' request code

QEC; LU → LU, Exp; DFC (QUIESCE AT END OF CHAIN)
0   X'80' request code

RECMS; PU → SSCP, Norm; NS(ma) (RECORD MAINTENANCE
STATISTICS)
0–2   X'010381' NS header
3–4   Network address of resource
$5 - n$ Maintenance statistics

RECTD; PU → SSCP, Norm; NS(ma) (RECORD TEST DATA)
0–2   X'010382' NS header
3–4   Network address of resource under test
5–8   Binary code selecting the test
$9 - n$ Test status and results

RECTRD; PU → SSCP Norm; NS(ma) (RECORD TRACE DATA)
0–2   X'010383' NS header
3–4   Network address of resource under trace
5   Selected trace
$6 - n$ Trace data

RELQ; LU → LU, Exp; DFC (RELEASE QUIESCE)
0   X'82' request code

REQCONT; PPU → SSCP, Norm; NS(c) (REQUEST CONTACT)
0–2   X'010284' NS header
3–4   Network address of link

Station ID
5   bits 0–3, reserved
           bits 4–7, PU type: a binary value corresponding to the PU
                type of the SPU with which the PPU has estab-
                lished a physical connection
6   Reserved
7–10   Block number (12 bits): see the individual product specifica-
           tions for the specific values used; ID number (20 bits): a
           binary value identifying a specific station uniquely within a
           customer network installation. The ID number can be as-
           signed in various ways, depending on the product. See indi-
           vidual product specifications for details.

REQDISCONT; SPU → SSCP Norm; NS(c) (REQUEST DISCON-
           TACT)
0–2   X'01021B' NS header
3   Type: X'00' normal
                X'80' immediate

RPO; SSCP → PPU, Norm; NS(c) (REMOTE POWER OFF)
0–2   X'010209' NS header
3–4   Network address of PU in node to be powered off (the SPU)

RQR; SLU → PLU, Exp; SC (REQUEST RECOVERY)
0   X'A3' request code

RSHUTD; SLU → PLU, Exp; DFC (REQUEST SHUTDOWN)
0   X'C2' request code

RTR; LU → LU, Norm; DFC (READY TO RECEIVE)
0   X'05' request code

SDT; PLU → SLU, Exp; SC (START DATA TRAFFIC)
0   X'A0' request code

SESSEND; PLU → SSCP, Norm; NS(s) (SESSION ENDED)
0–2   X'010688' NS header
3–4   Network address of primary LU
5–6   Network address of secondary LU

SETCV; SSCP → PU, Norm; NS(c) (SET CONTROL VECTOR)

0–2	X'010211' NS header
3–4	Network address of resource to which control vector applies, as described below.
5 – n	Control vector keys and related data, as described below.

Date-time control vector

3–4	Network address of PU
5	Key: X'01'
6–17	Date, in EBCDIC: MM/DD/YY.ddd (MM = month; DD = day of month; YY = year; ddd = Nth day of year, 1–366)
18–25	Time, in EBCDIC: HH.MM.SS (HH = hours; MM = minutes; SS = seconds)

Subarea routing control vector

3–4	Network address of link to be used for routing to the subarea specified in byte 6
5	Key: X'02'
6	Subarea address (left-justified)

SDLC secondary station control vector

3–4	Network address of SPU for secondary station
5	Key: X'03'
6	Reserved
7	PU type identifier for SPU
8	Type modifier (product-dependent)
9	SLDC BTU send limit
10	Maximum consecutive BTUs sent from the primary station to the specified secondary station without another secondary station on the link being polled or being sent BTUs
11	Error retry indicator
12–13	Link error recovery control information
14–15	Number of bytes in maximum segment length

NAU control vector

3–4	Network address of NAU
5	Key: X'04'
6	Local address form of NAU network address
7	n pacing
8	Reserved, set to a value of 1
9	Priority (0 or 1): denotes the DLC dequeuing priority to be used at the PPU node (receiving this SETCV) for all BTUs destined for the NAU specified in bytes 3–4

Channel control vector

3–4	Network address of the channel link
5	Key: X'05'
6–7	Channel delay: minimum interval between successive inbound transmissions (binary, in tenths of a second)

SHUTC; SLU → PLU, Exp; DFC (SHUTDOWN COMPLETE)

0	X'C1' request code

SHUTD; PLU → SLU, Exp; DFC (SHUTDOWN)

0	X'C0' request code

SIG; LU → LU, Exp; DFC

0	X'C9' request code
1–4	Signal code + signal extension field (2 bytes each), set by the sending end-user or NAU services manager; has meaning only to the NAU services level or above;

X'0000' + 'uuuu'   no-op (no system-defined code)
+ user-defined field
X'0001' + 'rrrr'   request to send + reserved field

SST; PLU → SSCP, Norm; NS(s) (SESSION STARTED)

0–2	X'010686' NS header
3–4	Network address of primary LU
5–6	Network address of secondary LU

STSN; PLU → SLU, Exp; SC (SET AND TEST SEQUENCE NUMBERS)

0	X'A2' request code
1	bits 0–1, action code for S → P flow (related data in bytes 2–3)
	bits 2–3, action code for P → S flow (related data in bytes 4–5)

Note: Each action code is set and processed independently. Values for either action code are:

00 ignore; this flow not affected by this STSN
01 set; CPMGR's value must be set to the value in bytes 2–3 or 4–5, as appropriate
10 sense, secondary end user (or NAU services manager) must return its sequence number for this flow in the response RU
11 set and test; CPMGR's value in appropriate bytes 2–3 or 4–5, and the secondary end-user (or NAU services manager) must compare that value against its own and respond accordingly

bits 4–7, reserved

2–3   Secondary-to-primary sequence number data to support
             S → P action code
4–5   Primary-to-secondary sequence number data to support
             P → S action code

Note: For action codes 01 and 11, the appropriate bytes 2–3
or 4–5 contain the value to which the CPMGR's value is set
and against which the secondary end-user (or NAU services
manager) tests its value for the respective flow. For action
codes 00 and 10, the appropriate bytes 2–3 or 4–5 are
reserved.

TERM-OTHER; TLU → SSCP, Norm; NS(s) (TERMINATE-OTHER)
0–2   X'010682' request code
3   bits 0–1, type UNBIND: 00 terminate only active or
                 pending-active sessions (only value defined); other
                 values reserved
             bit 2, type termination:
                 0   forced termination; session to be deactivated
                     immediately and unconditionally
                 1   orderly termination requested; primary LU to
                     be given an opportunity to prepare for an or-
                     derly shutdown before deactivation of the ses-
                     sion
             bits 3–7, reserved

             Name of primary LU
4   Type: X'00' no length and name fields follow
                 X'F3' logical unit
5   Length: binary number of bytes in symbolic name
                 (X'00' = no symbolic name present)
6 – m   Symbolic name of primary LU, in EBCDIC characters

             Name of secondary LU
m + 1   Type: X'00' no length and name fields follow
                 X'F3' logical unit
m + 2   Length: binary number of bytes in symbolic name
                 (X'00' = no symbolic name present)
(m + 3) – n Symbolic name of secondary LU, in EBCDIC characters

             Requester ID
n + 1   Length: binary number of bytes in requester ID
                 (X'00' = no requester ID present)

$(n+2)-p$ Requester ID, in EBCDIC characters, of the end-user initiating the request (may be used to verify end-user's authority to access a particular resource).

Password
$p+1$ Length: binary number of bytes in password
          (X'00' = no password present)
$(p+2)-q$ Password, field used to verify the identity of an end-user

TERM-SELF; TLU → SSCP, Norm; NS(s) (TERMINATE-SELF)
0–2   X'010683' NS header
3   bits 0–1, type UNBIND: 00 terminate only active or
          pending-active sessions; other values reserved
          bit 2, type termination:
               0 forced termination; session to be deactivated
                  immediately and unconditionally
               1 orderly termination requested; primary LU to
                  be given an opportunity to prepare for an orderly shutdown before deactivation of the session
          bit 3, last session indicator:
               0 not the last active session for sending LU
               1 last active (LU, LU) session for sending LU
          bits 4–7, reserved

          Name of other LU
4   Type: X'00' no length and name fields follow
               X'F3' logical unit
5   Length: binary number of bytes in symbolic name
               (X'00' = no symbolic name present)
$6-n$ Symbolic name of other LU, in EBCDIC characters

UNBIND; PLU → SLU, Exp; SC (UNBIND SESSION)
0   X'32' request code
1   Type UNBIND: X'01' normal end of session

UNBINDF; PLU → SSCP, Norm; NS(s) (UNBIND FAILURE)
0–2   X'010687' NS header
3–4   Network address of primary LU
5–6   Network address of secondary LU
7   Reason bits 0–3, reserved
          bit 4, 1 UNBIND failure (only value defined)
          bits 5–7, reserved

C.3 SUMMARY OF RESPONSE RUs

Apart from the exceptions cited below, response RUs return the number of bytes specified in the following table; only enough of the request RU is returned to include the field-formatted request code.

RU category of response	Number of bytes in RU
NC	1
SC	1
DFC	1
FMD-NS (FI = 1) (field-formatted)	3
FMD-NS (FI = 0) (character-coded)	0
FMD-(LU, LU)	0

Five positive response RUs (RSP(ACTLU), RSP(ACTPU), RSP (DUMP-INIT), RSP (DUMPTEXT), and RSP (STSN)) return additional data. See "Positive response RUs with extended formats."

All negative responses return four bytes of sense data in the RU, followed by the number of bytes specified in the table above. Negative-response RU length is four greater than the number of bytes in the table. See Appendix E for exception codes and their meanings.

C.4 POSITIVE RESPONSE RU WITH EXTENDED FORMATS

Bytes   Description

RSP (ACTLU); LU → SSCP, Exp; SC
0   X'0D' request code
1   Type activation selected: X'01' cold

RSP (ACTPU); PU → SSCP, Exp; SC
0   X'11' request code
1   Type activation selected: X'01' cold
                                       X'02' ERP
2–9   Contents ID: eight-character EBCDIC symbolic name of the load module currently operating in the node. Eight blanks is the default value.

RSP (DUMPINIT); PU → SSCP, Norm; NS(c)
0–2   X'010206' NS header
3 – n   Dump data

RSP (DUMPTEXT): PPU → SSCP, Norm; NS(c)
0–2   X'010207' NS header
3 – n   Dump data

RSP (STSN); SLU → PLU, Exp; SC
0   X'A2' request code

1	bits 0–1, result code for S→P action code in the request (related data in bytes 2–3)

bits 2–3, result code for P→S action code in the request (related data in bytes 4–5)

Note 1: Values for either result code are:

■ For set or ignore action code:

01 ignore (other values reserved); appropriate bytes 2–3 or 4–5 reserved

■ For sense action code:

00 reserved

01 reserved

10 secondary end-user (or NAU services manager) does not maintain user sequence numbers (appropriate bytes 2–3 or 4–5 reserved)

11 user sequence number, as known at the secondary, in bytes 2–3 or 4–5, as appropriate

■ For set and test action code:

00 reserved

01 value received in STSN request equals the user sequence number value as known at the secondary (appropriate bytes 2–3 or 4–5 return the secondary's value for the user sequence number)

10 secondary end-user (or NAU services manager) does not maintain user sequence numbers or cannot perform the requested test on the user sequence number (appropriate bytes 2–3 or 4–5 reserved)

11 value received in STSN request does not equal the user sequence number value as known at the secondary (appropriate bytes 2–3 or 4–5 return the secondary's value for the user sequence number)

bits 4–7, reserved

2–3	Secondary-to-primary normal-flow sequence number data to support S→P result code, or reserved (see Note 1 above)
4–5	Primary-to-secondary normal-flow sequence number data to support P→S result code or reserved (see Note 1 above)

Note 2: Where the STSN request specified as action codes two "sets," two "ignores," or a combination of "set" and "ignore," the positive response RU consists of one byte: X'A2' (the STSN request code).

D
FM Headers and Character String Controls in SNA

This appendix provides further description of some of the currently used FM headers and character string controls. Allowable subsets of both FM headers and character string controls, for a particular session, are specified in the PS usage fields (bytes 15–25) of the BIND command.

D.1 FM HEADERS

The formats for function management headers, type 1 and type 2, are shown in Figs. D.1 and 7.22, respectively. Both of these types pertain to a particular selected end-user component. The type-3 FM header carries information relative to all components involved in the session, unless qualified by parameters in the header.

For all of the following, byte 0 and byte 1 of the FM header contain the:

- FMH length
- FMH concatenated bit, and
- FMH type.

D.1.1 Device Selection (Type-2 FMH)

Peripheral Data Information Records (PDIR):

Byte 2	SRI and Code = X'01'
Byte 3	Identifier: X'00' = Standard PDIR
	X'01' = Job separator PDIR
	X'02' = System message

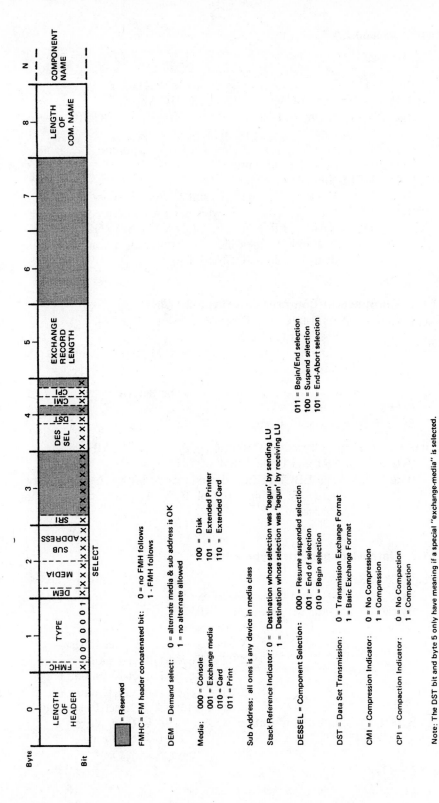

Fig. D.1 Type-1 FM header format.

Byte:

0	1	2	3	4	5	6	7	8	N
LENGTH OF HEADER	TYPE	MEDIA / SUB ADDRESS		DES SEL / DST / CMI / CPI	EXCHANGE RECORD LENGTH			LENGTH OF COM. NAME	COMPONENT NAME

Bit row: FMHC | x 0 0 0 0 0 1 (TYPE); DEM, x x x x x (MEDIA); SUB ADDRESS x x x x x; SRI x; x x x x x x x; DES SEL x x x x; DST x; CMI x; CPI x

SELECT

= Reserved

FMHC = FM header concatenated bit: 0 = no FMH follows
                                      1 - FMH follows

DEM = Demand select: 0 = alternate media & sub address is OK
                       1 = no alternate allowed

Media: 000 = Console   100 = Disk
         001 = Exchange media   101 = Extended Printer
         010 = Card   110 = Extended Card
         011 = Print

Sub Address: all ones is any device in media class

Stack Reference Indicator: 0 = Destination whose selection was 'begun' by sending LU
                           1 = Destination whose selection was 'begun' by receiving LU

DESSEL = Component Selection: 000 = Resume suspended selection   011 = Begin/End selection
                                001 = End of selection   100 = Suspend selection
                                010 = Begin selection   101 = End-Abort selection

DST = Data Set Transmission: 0 = Transmission Exchange Format
                                 1 = Basic Exchange Format

CMI = Compression Indicator: 0 = No Compression
                                 1 = Compression

CPI = Compaction Indicator: 0 = No Compaction
                                 1 = Compaction

Note: The DST bit and byte 5 only have meaning if a special "exchange-media" is selected.

Byte 4–11   Date of data set creation: MM/DD/YY

Byte 12–19   Time of data set creation: HH.MM.SS

Byet 20–27   Forms to be handled by operator, in EBCDIC characters

Byte 28–35   Forms Control Buffer name (for printers)

Byte 36–43   Printer train name

Byte 44–51   Number of copies

Byte 52–59   Volume: Number of print lines or number of cards

Byte 60–99   Data Set Name: 7 bytes each for JOBNAME, STEPNAME, PROCSTEP, DDNAME, SPINNO (SPINNO is a unique identifier to distinguish among data sets with the same JOBNAME).

D.1.2 Compaction/Compression (Type-2 FMH)

Compaction Table: (FMHC = 0, Type 2)

Byte 2   SRI and Code: X'02'

Byte 3–n   Number of master characters, M, and a Compact code table

Query for Compaction Table: (FMHC = 0; Type 3 FMH)

Byte 2   Code: X'03'

Bytes 3–n   Name of Compaction Table

Prime Compression Character Definition: (Type 2 or 3 FMH)

Byte 2   SRI and Code: X'04'

Byte 3   The EBCDIC hexadecimal value of the character to be used, by String Control Byte, as prime compression character.

D.1.3 Data Management (Type-2 FMH)

Create Data Set:

Byte 2   SRI and Code = X'20'

Byte 3   Data Set access method:

X'00' = Sequential

X'01' = Addressed Direct-Basic

X'02' = Keyed Direct-Unique

X'03' = Keyed Direct-Nonunique

X'04' = Keyed Indexed-Unique

X'81' = Addressed Direct-Restricted

Byte 4   Local Application Access: X'00' = Read/Write

X'01' = Read only

Byte 5   Fixed of Variable Length Records:
                 X'00' = Fixed Length
                 X'01' = Variable Length

Byte 6   Record Length (hexadecimal value)

Byte 8   Number of Records (hexadecimal value)

Byte 12−n Password for read access, for users of the data set being created.

Bytes $(n+1)-p$ Password for read/write access

Bytes $(p+1)-(p+6)$ For Keyed-direct data-sets only: Key length (1 byte), displacement to key (2 bytes), hash type (1 byte), and resolution space (2 bytes).

ERASE DATA SET: Byte 2 = X'22'

SCRATCH DATA SET: Byte 2 = X'21'

SCRATCH ALL DATA SETS: Byte 2 = X'2D'

QUERY FOR A DATA SET:

Byte 2   SRI and Code = X'28'

Byte 3   Query mode:
          X'00' = Immediate Reply; requested data must be sent on the next Type 1 BEGIN FMH.
          X'01' = Delayed Reply: requested data may be sent on any subsequent Type 1 BEGIN FMH.

ADD:

Byte 2   SRI and code = X'24'

Byte 3   Number of records to be added

ADD REPLICATE:

Byte 2   SRI and code = X'26'

Byte 3   Replication factor

REPLACE:

Byte 2   SRI and code = X'25'

Byte 3   Number of records to be replaced

REPLACE REPLICATE:

Byte 2   SRI and code = X'27'

Byte 3   Replication factor

ERASE RECORD:

Byte 2   SRI and code = X'2C'

Byte 3   Number of records to be erased

NOTE:
Byte $2 = X'29'$

NOTE REPLY: (FMHC = 0)
Byte 2   SRI and code = 10101010
Bytes 3-n Address of next available record (RECID)

D.1.4 Data Management Extensions (Type-2 Extension FMH)

RECORD ID:
Byte 2   SRI and code = $X'2B'$
Byte 3   Key indicator: $X'00'$ = Addressed direct key
              $X'01'$ = Keyed direct key 1
              $X'02'$ = Keyed direct key 2
              $X'03'$ = Application definition
              $X'04'$ = Control definition
Bytes 4 – n Key of record

PASSWORD: (concatenated to a type-1 or type-2 header)
Byte 2   SRI and code: $X'23'$
Bytes 3-n Password

VOLUME ID (VOLID): (concatenated to a type-1 or type-2 header)
Byte 2   SRI and code: $X'2E'$
Bytes 3-n Volume ID

D.2 CHARACTER SETS

Three characters sets are defined in the SNA character string (SCS).
These sets contain 48, 63, and 94 characters. Figure D.2 shows the codes
for these three character sets. On a serial line, bits of each character are
transmitted with the least significant bit first.

D.3 CHARACTER STRING CONTROLS*

The SNA character string (SCS) controls are shown in Fig. D.3. These
control codes are used primarily to format a visual presentation medium,
such as a printed page or an alphanumeric display screen. Other control
codes serve to set modes of device operation, to define data to be used in
a unique fashion, or to provide unique communication between a device
operator and an application program.

---

* Abstracted by permission from SNA Format and Protocol Reference Manual,
© 1976 by International Business Machines Corporation.

Hex Code		Graphic
EBCDIC	ASCII*	
48-character set:		
40	20	
4B	2E	.
4E	2B	+
50	26	&
5B	24	$
5C	2A	*
60	2D	—
61	2F	/
6B	2C	,
6C	25	%
7B	23	#
7C	40	@
7D	27	'
C1	41	A
C2	42	B
C3	43	C
C4	44	D
C5	45	E
C6	46	F
C7	47	G
C8	48	H
C9	49	I
D1	4A	J
D2	4B	K
D3	4C	L
D4	4D	M
D5	4E	N
D6	4F	O
D7	50	P
D8	51	Q
D9	52	R
E2	53	S
E3	54	T
E4	55	U
E5	56	V
E6	57	W
E7	58	X
E8	59	Y
E9	5A	Z
F0	30	0
F1	31	1
F2	32	2
F3	33	3
F4	34	4
F5	35	5
F6	36	6
F7	37	7
F8	38	8
F9	39	9

*ASCII hexadecimal codes do not
include VRC parity.

Hex Code		Graphic*
EBCDIC	ASCII*	
Additional for 63-character set:		
4A		¢
4A	5B	([ )
4C	3C	<
4D	28	(
4F		│
4F	21	(!)
5A		!
5A	5D	( ])
5D	29	)
5E	3B	;
5F		¬
5F	5E	(^)
6D	5F	_
6E	3E	>
6F	3F	?
7A	3A	:
7E	3D	=
7F	22	"
E0	5C	\
Additional for 94-character set:		
6A	7C	¦
79	60	`
81	61	a
82	62	b
83	63	c
84	64	d
85	65	e
86	66	f
87	67	g
88	68	h
89	69	i
91	6A	j
92	6B	k
93	6C	l
94	6D	m
95	6E	n
96	6F	o
97	70	p
98	71	q
99	72	r
A1	7E	~
A2	73	s
A3	74	t
A4	75	u
A5	76	v
A6	77	w
A7	78	x
A8	79	y
A9	7A	z
C0	7B	{
D0	7D	}

*ASCII Compatibles:
The four graphics in parenthesis are
ASCII characters that are not included
in the normal EBCDIC set. They are
included in the "ASCII compatible"
EBCDIC set, in place of the EBCDIC
characters listed immediately above
each parenthesis.

Fig. D.2   SCS character sets.

	0	1	2	3	4
0					
1					
2					
3					
4	SEL	ENP	INP	PP	
5	HT	NL	LF	TRN	
6		BS			
7		POC			
8					
9					
A					
B	VT		FMT		
C	FF	IFS			
D	CR	IGS			
E		IRS			
F		IUS			

SEL = Select
HT = Horizontal Tab
VT = Vertical Tab
FF = Form Feed
CR = Carriage Return
ENP = Enable Presentation
NL = New Line
BS = Back Space
POC = Program Operator
IFS = Interchange File Sep
IGS = Interchange Group Sep
IRS = Interchange Record Sep
IUS = Interchange Unit Sep
INP = Inhibit Presentation
LF = Line Feed
FMT = Format
PP = Presentation Position
TRN = Transparent

Fig. D.3 SNA character string (SCS) control code chart.

Functions such as media selection and data compression are performed via FM headers rather than by SCS control codes. Some of the more frequently used SCS control functions are described below.

BACK SPACE (BS, X'16')
BS moves the presentation position horizontally one position to the left.

CARRIAGE RETURN (CR, X'0D')
CR moves the presentation position horizontally to the left margin on the same line.

ENABLE PRESENTATION (ENP, X'14')
ENP is a device mode control that enables the presentation, at the entering device, of device-entered data. All data entered at the device after receipt of the ENP control function is presented in the normal fashion. The ENP control function is used in conjunction with the INP control function to provide a means for controlling presentation during the entry of sensitive data.

FORM FEED (FF, X'0C')
FF moves the presentation position to the top and left margins of the next presentation surface.

FORMAT (FMT, X'2B')

FMT is a data-defining control used with a one-byte parameter to define the start of a formatted data stream. Format types supported include Set Horizontal Format—SHF (X'2BC1'), and Set Vertical Format- -SVF (X'2BC2'). (SHF and SVF are defined below.)

HORIZONTAL TAB (HT, X'05')

HT moves the presentation position horizontally to the right to the next tab stop setting. Horizontal tab stop values may be set through the use of the Set Horizontal Format (SHF) function. (SHF is defined below.)

INHIBIT PRESENTATION (INP, X'24')

INP is a device mode control that inhibits the presentation of keyboard-entered data at the entering device, while allowing the entered data to be transmitted in the normal fashion. Presentation of all data entered at the device after receipt of the INP control function is inhibited. Data received by the device is presented, not inhibited.

INTERCHANGE SEPARATORS (IUS, X'1F'; IRS, X'1E'; IGS, X'1D'; IFS, X'1C')

The interchange separators consist of Interchange Unit Separator (IUS), Interchange Record Separator (IRS), Interchange Group Separator (IGS), and Interchange File Separator (IFS); they are used as logical separators. When used in hierarchical order, the ascending order is IUS, IRS, IGS, IFS. An information block must not be split by a higher order separator; for example, a record may contain a whole number of units, but may not contain a part of a unit.

Within SCS, the IRS character is used as follows:

- Terminates a secure data string headed by an SSR code.
- Indicates the end of a card in a data stream sent to a card punch or received from a card reader.

LINE FEED (LF, X'25')

LF moves the presentation position vertically down to the next line.

NEW LINE (NL, X'15')

NL moves the presentation position horizontally to the left margin and vertically down to the next line.

PRESENTATION POSITION (PP, X'34')

PP begins a three-byte format control sequence that moves the presentation position according to two parameter types: a function parameter and a value parameter. The PP code (X'34') is followed first by the function parameter (a single hexadecimal byte). The value parameter follows the function parameter; it consists of a one-byte binary number and denotes either an absolute or relative column or line number.

There are four basic operations defined by the function parameter:

1. Absolute move or relative move.
2. Horizontal or vertical.
3. Move and erase.
4. Erase to new position, then reset to old position.

When an absolute move is specified, the value parameter denotes a specific line or column number and the presentation position is moved to the line or column specified. For a printer, an absolute move to a line number less than the current line is a move to that new line on the following page. When a relative move is specified, the value parameter denotes a positive incremental value; the presentation position is moved the number of lines or column increments specified.

Function parameters for PP		Code
Absolute, Horizontal	Move to PP and do not erase	X'C0'
Absolute, Horizontal	Erase up to new PP, then reset to old PP	X'C1'
Absolute, Horizontal	Erase up to and move to new PP	X'C2'
Absolute, Vertical	Move to PP and do not erase	X'C4'
Absolute, Vertical	Erase column up to new PP, then reset to old PP	X'C5'
Absolute, Vertical,	Erase column up to new PP and move to new PP	X'C6'
Relative, Horizontal	Move PP and do not erase	X'C8'
Relative, Horizontal	Erase through new PP, then reset to old PP	X'C9'
Relative, Horizontal	Erase through and move to new PP	X'4A'
Relative, Vertical	Move PP and do not erase	X'4C'
Relative, Vertical	Erase column through new PP, then reset to old PP	X'4D'
Relative, Vertical	Erase column through new PP and move to new PP	X'4E'

PROGRAM OPERATOR COMMUNICATION (POC, X'17')

The POC function begins a three-byte sequence used to provide a communication mechanism between end-users, where at least one of the end-users is a terminal operator. The communication may be from a program end-user to an operator end-user, from an operator to a program, or from an operator to an operator.

Typically, the program *receives* a POC sequence identifying one of several program function keys that an operator has activated, or the program *sends* a POC sequence that lights an indicator light(s) visible to the operator. The meaning associated with POC character sequences is defined by the end-users.

There are two one-byte parameters following the POC code (X'17'). The first parameter defines a function and the second defines a value. Valid parameters are defined below.

Function parameters for POC

INDICATOR LIGHTS	FUNCTION KEYS	PARAMETER
No-op	No-op	X'C0'
Set Individual indicators on	Identify function key	X'C1'
Set indicators by mask		X'C2'
Set indicators by mask		X'C3'
Set all indicators off		X'C4'

Value parameters for POC

When the function parameter is X'C1' or X'C2', the value parameter is a binary number defining a unique indicator or function key. Valid values are from 1–255, depending on the number of indicators or function keys implemented. A zero value is a no-op. When the function parameter is X'C3', the value parameter is treated as an 8-bit mask, where each bit represents an indicator. A zero value in the mask causes the corresponding indicator to be set off, and a one value in the mask causes the corresponding indicator be set on.

SECURE STRING ID READER (SSR, X'0450')

The SSR code is used to distinguish between an operator identification number entered into the system from a magnetic stripe reader and an operator identification number entered from a keyboard. This is accomplished by delimiting a magnetic stripe card number with the SSR and IRS codes (See the Interchange Separator Characters Section, in this appendix, for the IRS code).

The device must apply the SSR code only to data from an operator identification card. These are distinguished by the use of an Operator ID (OID) code as the first data character on the card containing an operator ID. Before forwarding the data read from the card, the OID code is replaced by the SSR code and the "end of data" code from the card is replaced by the IRS code. Data designated as secure, through the use of the delimiting SSR and IRS codes, is not printed or displayed nor can it be edited in the buffer.

SELECT (SEL, X'04')
SEL is a device control with an associated one-byte function parameter used to control a function within a device.

SET HORIZONTAL FORMAT (SHF, X'2BC1')
The SHF function sets horizontal formatting controls, including maximum presentation column, left and right margins, and horizontal tab stops. A one-byte binary count follows the SHF code; it indicates the number of bytes to the end of the SHF string, including the count byte. The first three parameters following the count define the maximum presentation position, the left margin, and the right margin, respectively (defined below). Tab stop parameters in the SHF sequence start following the right-margin (RM) parameter position. Parameters of SHF are one byte each and contain binary numbers in the range 0–255.

The SHF sequence appears as:

$$(SHF)(count)(MPP)(LM)(RM)(T1) \ldots (Tn)$$

where

MPP = maximum presentation position; specifies the horizontal extent of the presentation surface (print-line length or display width, in number of characters). This value is used to define a line length less than or equal to the physical device line length. The MPP default value is the physical device line length.

LM = left margin value; specifies the column value of the leftmost presentation position. The LM also services as the first horizontal tab stop. Valid LM values are less than or equal to MPP. The LM default value is one.

RM = right margin; the RM is used to assist an operator in formatting keyboard-generated data streams. Its function is to warn the operator that the end of the line is approaching; the warning is issued only once, when the presentation position column number equals RM minus ten. Valid RM values are greater than or equal to LM and less than or equal to MPP. The default value for RM is MPP.

T1 . . . Tn = horizontal tab stop parameters; set column values for use with the Horizontal Tab (HT) function. The tab string does not have to be in order. Valid tab stop values are equal to or greater than LM and less than or equal to MPP. Note that the LM parameter is the first horizontal tab stop; repeating the LM value in the horizontal tab stop parameter sequence would be redundant. When no tab stop values are set to the right of the current presentation postion column value, the HT function acts as a Space function.

SET VERTICAL FORMAT (SVF, X'2BC2')
The SVF function sets vertical formatting controls, including maximum presentation line (i.e., page size), top margin, bottom margin, and vertical tab stops. A one-byte binary count follows the SVF code; it indicates the number of bytes to the end of the SVF string, including the count byte. The minimum sequence which can be sent is with a count of one, in which case all vertical format controls are set to their default values.

The first three values following the count define the maximum presentation line, top margin, and bottom margin, in that order. A zero value for any of these parameters is a no-op and results in the function assuming its default value. Vertical tab stop parameters in the SVF sequence start following the bottom-margin (BM) parameter position. Parameters of SVF are one byte each, and contain binary numbers in the range 0–255.

The SVF sequence appears as:

$$(SVF)(count)(MPL)(TM)(BM)(T1) \ldots (Tn)$$

where

MPL = maximum presentation line; defines the vertical extent of the presentation surface. This is the page depth for a printer, or the number of lines in a display. All values from 1 to 255 are valid. The default value is the device-fixed line capacity, for those devices that have a fixed line capacity, and is *one* for devices without a fixed line capacity.

TM = top margin; specifies the line value to be used as the top presentation line of the page. The default value for TM is one.

BM = bottom margin; specifies the line value that, if exceeded, causes an automatic skip to the top margin of the next presentation surface. The BM default value is the MPL value.

T1 ... Tn = vertical tab stop parameters; specify line values for use with the vertical tab (VT) function. Vertical tabs must be listed in increasing order. Vertical tab stops may be set at any line, except top margin, down to and including bottom margin.

TRANSPARENT (TRN, X'35')
TRN is a data-defining control used to denote the start of a transparent data stream. The data delimited by TRN is end-user defined and is not scanned for SCS control codes. A one-byte binary count follows the TRN

code; it indicates the number of bytes of transparent data (not including the count byte).

VERTICAL TAB (VT, X'0B')
VT moves the presentation position vertically down to the next tab stop setting. Vertical tab stop values may be set through the use of the Set Vertical Format (SVF) function.

E
Exception
Codes

The sense data included with an exception request (EXR) or a negative response is a four-byte field that includes a one-byte category value, a one-byte modifier value, and two bytes of implementation- or end-user-defined data (hereafter referred to as user-defined data).

Together, the category and modifier bytes hold the sense code (SNC) defined for the exception condition that has occurred.

The following categories are defined; all others are reserved:

Value	Category
X'80'	Path Error
X'40'	RH Usage Error
X'20'	State Error
X'10'	Request Error
X'08'	Request Reject
X'00'	User Sense Data Only

The category User Sense Data Only (X'00') allows the end-users to exchange sense data in bytes 2–3 for conditions not defined by SNA within the other categories (and perhaps unique to the end-users involved). The modifier value is also X'00'.

The sense codes for the other categories are discussed below. For

---

these categories, a modifier value of X'00' can be used (as an implementation option) when no definition of the exception condition beyond the major category is to be identified.

PATH ERROR (CATEGORY CODE = X'80')
This category indicates that the request could not be delivered to the intended receiver, due to a path outage or an invalid sequence of activation requests or one of the listed transmission header errors. (Some TH errors, i.e., SQN errors, are state errors, category X'20'.)

Modifier (in hexadecimal):

01 Intermediate Node Failure: Machine or program check in an intermediate PC; request discarded. A response may or may not be possible.
02 Link Failure: Data link failure.
03 LU Inoperative: The LU is unable to process requests.
04 Unrecognized DAF: An intermediate or boundary PC has no routing information for the DAF, or an end node PC has no LU with indicated DAF(FID1), DAF'(FID2), or local address (FID3).
05 No Session: No half-session is active in the receiving end node for the indicated OAF-DAF pair, or no BF.SESS.RCV is active for the OAF-DAF pair in a COMC node providing the boundary function. This exception does not apply to BIND, ACTPU or ACTLU. (Note 1)
06 FID: Invalid FID for the receiving node. (Note 2)
07 Segmenting Error: First BIU segment had less than 10 bytes; or mapping field sequencing error, such as first, last, middle; or segmenting not supported and MPF not set to 11. (Note 3)
08 PU Not Active: The (SSCP,PU).SEC half-session in the receiving node has not been activated and the request was not ACTPU for this half-session. (Note 1)
09 LU Not Active: A DAF addresses an LU for which the (SSCP,LU).SEC half-session has not been activated and the request was not ACTLU. (Note 1)
0A Reserved.
0B Incomplete TH: Transmission received was shorter than a TH. (Note 2)
0C DCF: Data Count Field inconsistent with transmission length.
0D Lost Contact: Contact with the link station for which the transmission was intended has been lost, but the link has not failed. If the difference between link failure and loss of contact is not detectable, link failure (X'8002') is sent.
0E Unrecognized OAF: The OAF (FID1) was not recognized.

0F Invalid Address Combination: The (DAF', OAF') (FID2) combination or the LSID (FID3) specified an invalid type of session, e.g., a
(PU,LU) combination.

Notes:

1. This error is listed as a path error since the request cannot be
delivered to the intended TC element.
2. It is generally not possible to send a response for this exception
condition, since information (FID, addresses) required to generate a
response is not available. It is logged as an error if this capability
exists in the receiver.
3. If segmenting is not supported, a negative response is returned for
the first segment only, since this contains the RH. Subsequent
segments are discarded.

RH USAGE ERROR (CATEGORY CODE = X'40')
This category indicates that the value of a field or combination of fields in
the RH violates architectural rules or BIND options previously selected.
These errors prevent delivery of the request to the intended half-session
protocol machine and are independent of the current states of the session.
They may result from the failure of the sender to enforce session rules.
Detection by the receiver of each of these errors is optional.

Modifier (in hexadecimal):

01 Invalid SC or NC RH: The RH of a SC or NC request was invalid.
02 Reserved.
03 BB Not Allowed: Begin bracket (BB) was indicated with middle of
chain (MOC) or end chain (EC)
04 EB Not allowed: End bracket (EB) was indicated with MOC or EC, or
by the primary when only the secondary may send EB, or by the
secondary when only the primary may send EB.
05 Incomplete RH: Transmission shorter than full TH-RH.
06 Exception Not Allowed: Exception response was requested when
not permitted.
07 Definite Response Not Allowed: Definite response was requested
when not permitted.
08 Pacing Not Supported: The pacing indicator was set on a request,
but the receiving CPMGR does not support pacing for this session.
09 CD Not Allowed: Change direction (CD) was indicated with begin
chain (BC) or MOC.
0A No-Response Not Allowed: No response was specified on a request
when not permitted. (Used only on EXR)

0B   Chaining Not Supported: Chaining bits indicated other than (BC, EC), but multiple-request chains are not supported for the session.

0C   Brackets Not Supported: A bracket indicator was set but brackets are not used for the session.

0D   CD Not Supported: The change-direction indicator was set, but is not supported.

0E   Reserved.

0F   Format Indicator Not Allowed: The format-indicator bit was set when not supported for the session, or when begin chain (BC) was not set.

10   Alternate Code Not Supported: The code-selection indicator was set when not supported for the session.

STATE ERROR (CATEGORY CODE = X'20')

This category indicates a sequence number error, or an RH or RU which is not allowed for the receiver's current session control or data flow control state. These errors prevent delivery of the request to the intended half-session protocol machine.

Modifier (in hexadecimal):

01   Sequence Number: Sequence number received on normal flow request was not one greater than the last.

02   Chaining: Error in the sequence of the chain indicator settings, such as first, middle, first.

03   Bracket: Error resulting from failure of sender to enforce bracket rules for session. (This error does not apply to contention or race conditions.)

04   Direction: Error resulting from a normal-flow request received while HDX-FF FSM was not in the receive state. (Contrast this sense code with X'081B', which signals a race condition.)

05   Data Traffic Reset: An FMD or DFC request received by a half-session whose SESS.(SEND/RCV) was active, but whose DT FSM was not in the ACTIVE state.

06   Data Traffic Quiesced: An FMD or DFC request received from a half-session which has sent QUIESCE COMPLETE or SHUT-DOWN COMPLETE and has not responded to RELEASE QUIESCE.

07   Data Traffic Not Reset: A session control request (e.g., STSN), allowed only while the DT FSM is in the RESET state, was received while the DT FSM state was not RESET.

REQUEST ERROR (CATEGORY CODE = X'10')

This category indicates that the RU was delivered to the intended half-session, but could not be interpreted or processed. This condition represents a mismatch in half-session capabilities.

Modifier (in hexadecimal):

01 RU Data Error: Data in the request RU is not acceptable to the receiving FI.FMD; for example, a character code not in the set supported, or a formatted data field not acceptable to presentation services.

02 RU Length Error: The request RU was too long or too short.

03 Function Not Supported: The function requested is not supported. The function may have been specified by a formatted request code, a field in an RU, or a control character.

04 Reserved.

05 Parameter Error: A parameter modifying a control function is invalid, or outside the range allowed by the receiver.

06 Reserved.

07 Category Not Supported: DFC, SC, or NC request received by a half-session not supporting any requests in that category; or an NS request with byte 0 not set to 01, or byte 1 not set to an NS category supported by the receiver.

08 Invalid FM Header: The FM header was not understood or translatable by the receiver, or an FM header was expected but not present.

REQUEST REJECT (CATEGORY CODE = X'08')

This category indicates that the request was delivered to intended half-session protocol machine and was understood and supported, but not executed.

Modifier (in hexadecimal):

01 Resource Not Available: The LU, PU, or link specified in an RU is not available.

02 Intervention Required: Forms or cards are required at an output device, or device is temporarily in local mode, or other conditions requiring intervention.

03 Missing Password: The required password was not supplied.

04 Invalid Password: Password was not valid.

05 Session Limit Reached: The requested session cannot be activated, as one of the NAUs is at its session limit. Applies to ACTCDRM, INIT, BIND, and CINIT commands.

06 Resource Unknown: The request contained a name or address not identifying a PU, LU, or link known to the receiver.

07 Reserved.

08 Reserved.

09 Mode Inconsistency: The requested function cannot be performed in the present state of the receiver.

0A Permission Rejected: The receiver has denied an implicit or explicit request of the sender.

0B Bracket Race Error: Loss of contention within the bracket protocol. Arises when bracket initiation/termination by both NAUs is allowed.

0C Procedure Not Supported: A named procedure (Test, Measurement, Trace) specified in an RU is not supported by the receiver.

0D Reserved.

0E NAU Not Authorized: The requesting NAU does not have access to the requested resource.

0F End User Not Authorized: The requesting end-user does not have access to the requested resource.

10 Missing Requester ID: The required requester-ID was missing.

11 Break: Asks the receiver of this sense code to terminate the present chain with CANCEL or with an FMD request carrying EC. The CHAIN.RCV FSM of the half-session sending the Break sense code enters PURGE state when Break is sent.

12 Insufficient Resource: Receiver cannot act on request because of a temporary lack of resources.

13 Bracket Bid Reject—No RTR Forthcoming: BID (or BB) was received while the state was IN-BRACKETS (INB), or while the state was BETWEEN-BRACKETS (BETB) and the first speaker denied permission. RTR will not be sent.

14 Bracket Bid Reject—RTR Forthcoming: BID (or BB) was received while the state was IN-BRACKETS, or while the state was BETWEEN-BRACKETS and the first speaker denied permission. RTR will be sent.

15 Function Active: A request to activate a network element or procedure was received, but the element or procedure was already active.

16 Function Inactive: A request to deactivate a network element or procedure was received, but the element or procedure was not active.

17 Link Inactive: A request requires the use of a link, but the link is not active.

18 Link Procedure in Process: CONTACT, DISCONTACT, IML or other link procedure in progress when a conflicting request was received.

19 RTR Not Required: Receiver of READY TO RECEIVE has nothing to send.

1A Request Sequence Error: Invalid sequence of requests.

1B Receiver in Transmit Mode: A race condition; normal-flow request received while the HDX-CONT FSM was not in the RECEIVE state. (Contrast this sense code with X'2004', which signals a protocol violation.)

1C Request Not Executable: The requested function cannot be executed, due to a permanent error condition in the receiver.

1D   Invalid Station/SSCP ID: The Station ID or SSCP ID in the request was found to be invalid.

1E   Session Reference Error: The request contained reference to a half-session that was neither active nor in the process of being activated (generally applies to network services commands).

1F   Reserved.

20   Control Vector Error: Invalid data for the control vector specified by the target network address and key. Applies to SET CONTROL VECTOR.

21   Invalid Session Parameters: Session parameters were not valid or not supported by the half-session whose activation was requested.

22   Link Procedure Failure: A link-level procedure has failed due to link equipment failure, loss of contact with a link station, or an invalid response to a link command. (This is not a path error, since the request being rejected was delivered to its destination.)

23   Unknown Control Vector: The control vector specified by a network address and key is not known to the receiver.

24   Component Aborted: The component (device indicated by an FM header) that was selected has been aborted, due to an error condition or resource depletion.

25   Component Not Available: The component (device indicated by an FM header) is not available.

26   FM Function Not Supported: A function requested in an FMD-RU is not supported by the receiver.

27   Intermittent Error—Retry Requested: An error at the receiver caused an RU to be lost. The error is not permanent and retry of the RU (or chain) is requested.

28   Reply Not Allowed: A request requires a normal-flow reply, but the outbound data flow for this half-session is quiesced or shut down, and there is no delayed reply capability.

29   Change Direction Required: A request requires a normal-flow reply, but the HDX-FF FSM state implies "not in the SEND state." Change-direction (CD) was not set on the request, and there is no delayed reply capability.

F
Answers
to Exercises

Chapter 6

6.1 Link Controls: a, c, j, 1
     Device Controls: b, e, h
     User Controls: d, f, i, k, m
     Path Controls: g
     Network Controls: n

6.2 c, d

6.3 a, b, d

6.4 Presentation services, data flow control, and transmission control

6.5 a) BIU = RH + RU
     b) PIU = TH + RH + RU
     c) BIU = RH + RU

6.6 a, c, d

Chapter 7

7.1 b

7.2 a, b, c

7.3 a, b

7.4 c, d

7.5 Byte 0:   0000 1100
     Byte 1:   1000 0001
     Byte 2:   1100 1111
     Byte 3:   0xxx xxxx

Byte 4:   0100 x00x
Byte 8:   0000 0011
Byte 9:   1110 0011
Byte 10: 1101 0110
Byte 11: 1101 0100

7.6 Byte 0: 0000 0100
Byte 1: 0000 0010
Byte 2: 0010 1000
Byte 3: 0000 0000

7.7 Bytes 0–2:   X'020681'
Byte 3:   X'00'
Bytes 4–11:   INTERACT
Byte 12:   X'F3'
Byte 13:   X'0B'
Bytes 14–24: BANKBALANCE
Byte 25:   X'0B'
Bytes 26–36: TELRAKJONES
Byte 37:   X'0D'
Bytes 38–50: DECEMBER41920
Byte 51:   X'06'
Bytes 52–57: NORMAL

Chapter 8

8.1 b, d
8.2 a, b, f
8.3 c, d
8.4 a, b

Chapter 9

9.1 d
9.2 c
9.3 c
9.4 b
9.5 a, b
9.6 a
9.7 a, c, d, e
9.8 b, d, f, g, h
9.9 a-4, b-1, c-8, d-2, e-3, f-6, g-5, h-7
9.10 000x 1011, 1x01 xxx1, 100x 0xxx
9.11 100x 0111, 1x01 xxx0, xxxx xxxx, 0100 0000, 0000 0011

9.12 02, 06, 81, 0X, 00, 00, 00, 00, 00, 00, C8, C9, F3, F2, D1, D6

9.13 Byte 0:   0011 0001
 Byte 1:   0000 0001
 Byte 2:   0000 0100
 Byte 3:   0000 0010
 Byte 4:   1111 xx11
 Byte 5:   1111 xx11
 Byte 6:   x111 0xxx
 Byte 7:   0010 xxxx
 Byte 8:   xx00 0001
 Byte 9:   xx00 0001
 Byte 10:   1000 0101
 Byte 11:   1000 0101
 Byte 12:   xx00 0001
 Bytes 13–26:   reserved
 Byte 27:   0000 0010
 Byte 28:   1101 0100
 Byte 29:   1101 0110

Chapter 10

10.1 a, c, d, e

10.2 a, b, e

10.3 a-2 & 4, b-1 & 4, c-3 & 4

10.4 1. FID-1
 2. TH = 1E003000100000070008
   RH = 0B8000
   RU = 01020A300A
 3. 0007
 4. normal (TH byte 0, bit 7 = 0)
 5. 1000
 6. Request (RH byte 0, bit 0 = 0)
 7. Presentation Services (RH byte 0, bits 1 and 2 = 00)
 8. X'0A' in byte 2

10.5 0011 01x1, 1110 0000

Chapter 11

11.1 011111011

11.2 c

11.3 Receive Not Ready

11.4 a, b, c, d, f

11.5 a

11.6 Nr = 2

11.7 The SIM command then initiates a local IPL/IML

11.8 Supervisory

11.9 REJECT

11.10 Frame Check errors are not specifically answered. Since that erroneous frame would not be accepted by the station, the Nr count would not be incremented. When the Nr count is returned to the other station, an error is indicated. If the link was duplex, the sequence error could be reported immediately via a REJECT command.

11.11 1–e
       2–c
       3–g
       4–a
       5–f
       6–h
       7–b
       8–d

11.12 b, g, a, c, f, d, e, h

11.13 01111110, 00010000, 10001011

Chapter 12

12.1 a, b, e, f, g, h

12.2 a, e

12.3 a, d

Chapter 13

13.1 Input, outputs, states

13.2 a, b, f, g

13.3 a, c, e, g, h

13.4 See Fig. F.1

13.5 See Fig. F.2

Chapter 15

15.1 c, d, e

15.2 b, c

15.3 a, b, d

15.4 b, c

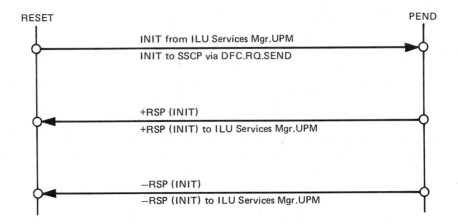

a) Part of FSM for: (SSCP, ILU).SEC.INIT (PLU, SLU).SEND

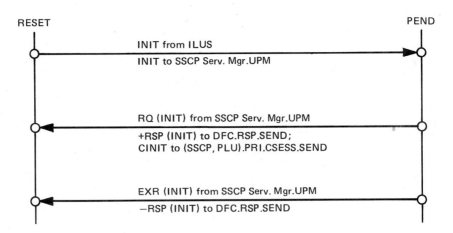

b) Part of FSM for: (SSCP, ILU).PRI.INIT (PLU, SLU).RCV

EXR = exception request
UPM = undefined protocol machine

Fig. F.1 Portions of FSMs for handling the INITIATE command.

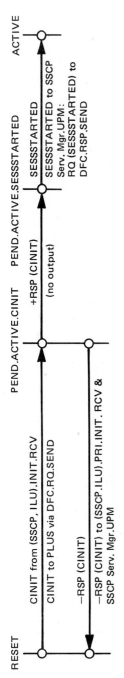

RESET   PEND.ACTIVE.CINIT   PEND.ACTIVE.SESSSTARTED   ACTIVE

CINIT from (SSCP, ILU).INIT.RCV

CINIT to PLUS via DFC.RQ.SEND

+RSP (CINIT)

(no output)

SESSSTARTED

SESSSTARTED to SSCP
Serv. Mgr. UPM:
RQ (SESSSTARTED) to
DFC.RSP.SEND

−RSP (CINIT)

−RSP (CINIT) to (SSCP,ILU).PRI.INIT. RCV &
SSCP Serv. Mgr. UPM

a) A Portion of the FSM: (SSCP, PLU).PRI.CSESS.SEND, in the SSCP.

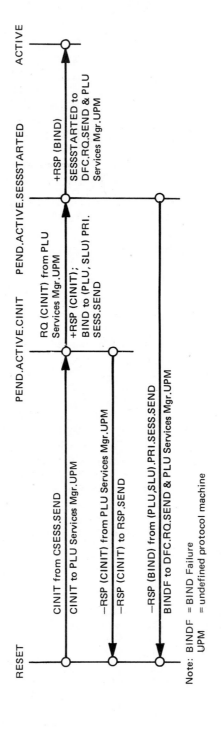

RESET   PEND.ACTIVE.CINIT   PEND.ACTIVE.SESSSTARTED   ACTIVE

CINIT from CSESS.SEND

CINIT to PLU Services Mgr. UPM

RQ (CINIT) from PLU
Services Mgr. UPM

+RSP (BIND)

SESSSTARTED to
DFC.RQ.SEND & PLU
Services Mgr. UPM

+RSP (CINIT);
BIND to (PLU, SLU) PRI.
SESS.SEND

−RSP (CINIT) from PLU Services Mgr. UPM

−RSP (CINIT) to RSP.SEND

−RSP (BIND) from (PLU,SLU).PRI.SESS.SEND

BINDF to DFC.RQ.SEND & PLU Services Mgr. UPM

Note: BINDF = BIND Failure
       UPM   = undefined protocol machine

b) A Portion of the FSM: (SSCP, PLU).SEC.CSESS.RCV, in the PLU.

Fig. F.2 Illustrative portions of the FSM called control sessions, used to handle the CINIT command.

G
Acronyms and Abbreviations

A	address (SDLC)
ABCONN	ABANDON CONNECTION
ABCONNOUT	ABANDON CONNECT OUT
ACF	Advanced Communication Function
ack	acknowledgment
ACTCDRM	ACTIVATE CROSS DOMAIN RESOURCE MANAGER
ACTCONNIN	ACTIVATE CONNECT IN
ACTLINK	ACTIVATE LINK
ACTLU	ACTIVATE LOGICAL UNIT
ACTPU	ACTIVATE PHYSICAL UNIT
ACTTRACE	ACTIVATE TRACE
ADCCP	Advanced Data Communication Control Procedure
ANA	ASSIGN NETWORK ADDRESSES
ANSC	AUTO NETWORK SHUTDOWN COMPLETE
Arpanet	Advanced Research Projects Agency Network
ASCII	American Standard Code for Information Interchange
ATDM	asynchronous time division multiplexing
BB	begin bracket
BBI	begin bracket indicator
BBIU	begin-BIU
BC	begin chain
BCI	begin chain indicator
BETB	between brackets
BETBIU	between BIUs
BETC	between chains
BF	boundary function

BIND	BIND SESSION
BINDF	BIND FAILURE
BIU	basic information unit
BLU	basic link unit
BS	backspace
BSC	binary synchronous communications
BTAM	Basic Telecommunications Access Method
BTU	basic transmission unit
CCITT	International Telegraph and Telephone Consultative Committee
CICS	Customer Information Control System
CD	cross domain
CD	change direction
CDI	change direction indicator
CDRM	cross domain resource manager
CINIT	CONTROL INITIATE
CLC	cluster controller
cmd	command
CMDR	Command Reject (SDLC)
CMI	compression indicator
CNTL	control
COAX	coaxial cable
COMC	communications controller
COMP	complete
CONFIG	configuration services
CONNIN	CONNECT IN
CONNOUT	CONNECT OUT
CONWIN	contention winner
CPMGR	Connection Point Manager
CPI	compaction indicator
CPU	central processing unit
CR	carriage return
CRC	cyclic redundancy check
CSC	common session control
CSESS	control session requests
CSI	code selection indicator
CTERM	CONTROL TERMINATE
C#	column number
d	device
d	decibel
DA	device address field
DACTCDRM	DEACTIVATE CROSS DOMAIN RESOURCE MANAGER
DACTCONNIN	DEACTIVATE CONNECT IN
DACTLINK	DEACTIVATE LINK

DACTLU	DEACTIVATE LOGICAL UNIT
DACTPU	DEACTIVATE PHYSICAL UNIT
DACTTRACE	DEACTIVATE TRACE
DAF	destination address field
DAF'	DAF prime
DASD	direct access storage device
DCE	data communications equipment
DCF	data count field
DDCMP	Digital Data Communications Message Protocol
DEM	demand select (FMH-1)
DEST	destination
DFC	data flow control
DISC	Disconnect (SDLC)
DLC	data link control
DM	Disconnected Mode (SDLC)
DOV	data over voice
DP/C	data processing/communications
DR1	definite response type 1
DR2	definite response type 2
DSE	data switching exchange
DT	data traffic
DTE	data terminal equipment
DUMPINIT	DUMP INITIAL
DUV	data under voice
EB	end bracket
EBCDIC	extended binary coded decimal interchange code
EBI	end bracket indicator
EBIU	end-BIU
EC	end chain
ECI	end chain indicator
EFI	expedited flow indicator
ENP	enable presentation
EOT	end of transmission (BSC)
ERCL	exchange record length field (FMH-type 1)
ERI	exception response indicator
ERP	error recovery procedure(s)
ESLOW	ENTERING SLOWDOWN
EXT	end of text (BSC)
EXECTEST	EXECUTE TEST
EXP	expedited
EXR	EXCEPTION REQUEST
EXRD	EXR indicating definite-response requested
EXRE	EXR indicating exception-response requested
EXRN	EXR indicating no-response requested
EXSLOW	EXITING SLOWDOWN

F	flag (SDLC) (see also P/F)
FCS	frame check sequence (SDLC)
FDX	full-duplex (duplex)
FF	form feed; flip-flop
FI	function interpreter
Fl	format indicator
FI.FMD	function interpreter for FM data
FID	format identification (field)
FM	function management
FMD	function management data
FMH	FM header
FMHC	concatenated FMH
FMT	format (control character)
FNA	FREE NETWORK ADDRESSES
FRMR	frame reject (= CMDR)
FSM	finite-state machine
FSP	first speaker
GEN	generator
HDLC	High-Level Data Link Control
HDX	half-duplex
HDX-CONT	HDX contention
HDX-FF	HDX flip-flop
HS	half-session
HSID	half-session identification
HT	horizontal tab
I	initiating
ID	identifier; identification
IFS	interchange file separator
IGS	interchange group separator
ILU	initiating logical unit (LU sending INIT)
ILUS	initiating LU services
IML	initial machine load
IMP	interface message processor
IMS	Information Management System
INB	in bracket (state)
INC	in chain (state)
INIT	INITIATE
INOP	INOPERATIVE
INP	inhibit presentation
I/O	input/output
IOS	input/output supervisor
IPL	initial program load
IPR	ISOLATED PACING RESPONSE

IRS	interchange record separator
ISO	International Standards Organization
IUS	interchange unit separator
JES	Job Entry System
Kb	kilobits
KB	kilobytes
LAP	link access procedure
LF	line feed
LH	link header
LM	Left Margin
LPS	logical presentation space
LRC	longitudinal redundancy check
LSA	Lost Subarea
LSB	least significant bit
LSID	local session identification field
LU	logical unit
LUS	LU services
LUSTAT	LOGICAL UNIT STATUS
L#	line number
LT	link trailer
Mb	megabits
MGR	manager
MOC	middle of chain
MPF	mapping field
MPL	maximum presentation line
MPP	maximum presentation position
Nr	frame number expected (SDLC)
Ns	frame sent (SDLC)
Na (or na)	network address
NAU	network addressable unit
NC	network control
NCP	network control program
NL	new line
NRC	network routing center
NRZI	non return to zero inverted (SDLC)
NS	network services
NSA	non sequenced acknowledgment (SDLC)
NSH	network services header
NSI	non sequenced information (SDLC)
NSP	non sequenced poll (SDLC)

NSPE	NETWORK SERVICES PROCEDURE ERROR
Network	network
OAF	origin address field
OAF'	OAF prime
P/F	Poll bit for primary station; final frame bit for secondary station
PAC	pacing request, pacing response (value of PI in RH)
parms	parameters
PC	path control
PCE	path control element
PCID	procedure correlation ID
PEND	pending (state)
PI	pacing indicator
PIU	path information unit
PLU	primary logical unit (i.e., the LU supporting the primary half-session)
PLUS	LU services in the primary logical unit
PP	presentation position
PPU	primary physical unit (PU at the node of a primary link station)
PRI	primary
PS	presentation services
PTT	Post, Telephone and Telegraph administration
PU	physical unit
PUS	PU services
QC	QUIESCE COMPLETE
QEC	QUIESCE AT END OF CHAIN
R	receive
RCV	receive
REC	recovery
RECMS	RECORD MAINTENANCE STATISTICS
recovery r	recovery for received request
recovery s	recovery for sent request
RECTD	RECORD TEST DATA
RECTRD	RECORD TRACE DATA
REJ	Reject (SDLC)
RELQ	RELEASE QUIESCE
REQCONT	REQUEST CONTACT
REQDISCONT	REQUEST DISCONTACT
RIM	Request Initialization Mode (HDLC) (= RQI)
RH	Request/Response header
RM	right margin
RNR	Not Ready to Receive (SDLC)
RPO	REMOTE POWER OFF

RQ	request
RQD	RQ indicating definite-response requested
RQE	RQ indicating exception-response requested
RQI	Request Initialization (SDLC)
RQN	RQ indicating no-response requested
RQR	REQUEST RECOVERY
RR	Ready to Receive (SDLC)
RRI	request/response indicator
RSET	Reset (HDLC)
RSHUTD	REQUEST SHUTDOWN
RSP	response
RT	response-type
RTAM	Remote Terminal Access Method
RTI	response type indicator
RTR	READY TO RECEIVE
RU	request/response unit
RUC	RU category
S	send
SABM	Set Asynchronous Balanced Mode (HDLC)
SABME	Set Asynchronous Balanced Mode Extended
SAF	switched network access facility
SARM	Set Asynchronous Response Mode (HDLC)
SARME	Set Asynchronous Response Mode Extended
SC	session control
SCB	string control byte
SCS	SNA character string
SDI	sense data included indicator
SDLC	Synchronous Data Link Control
SDT	start data traffic
SE	session ended
SEC	secondary
SEL	select (control character)
SERV	services
SESS	session
SESSEND	SESSION ENDED
SETCV	SET CONTROL VECTOR
SH	subhost
SHF	set horizontal format
SHUTC	SHUTDOWN COMPLETE
SHUTD	SHUTDOWN
SID	session identification
SIG	SIGNAL
SIM	Set Initialization Mode (SDLC)
SLU	secondary logical unit (i.e., the LU supporting the secondary half-session)

SLUS   LU services in the secondary logical unit
SNA   Systems Network Architecture
SNC   sense code
SNF   sequence number field
SNRM   Set Normal Response Mode (SDLC)
SNRME   Set Normal Response Mode Extended (HDLC)
SOH   start of heading (BSC)
SPU   secondary physical unit (PU at node of a secondary link station)
SQN   sequence number
SREJ   Selective Reject (HDLC)
SSCP   System Services Control Point
SSR   Secure string ID reader
SST   session started
STA   station
STSN   SET AND TEST SEQUENCE NUMBERS
SVC MGR   services manager
SVF   set vertical format

TAM   Teleprocessing Access Method
TC   transmission control
TCAM   Telecommunications Access Method
TCE   transmission control element
TERM   TERMINATE
TH   transmission header
TLU   terminating logical unit (LU sending TERM)
TM   top margin
TN   terminal node
TRN   transparent (SCS control characters)
TS   transmission subsystem
TSO   Time Sharing Option
TTY   teletype

U   Unnumbered (HDLC)
UA   Unnumbered Acknowledgment (= NSA)
UI   Unnumbered Information (= NSI)
UNBIND   UNBIND SESSION
UNBINDF   UNBIND FAILURE
UP   Unnumbered Poll (= NSP)
UPM   Undefined protocol machine

VCS   vertical channel select
VRC   vertical redundancy check
VT   vertical tab
VTAM   Virtual Telecommunications Access Method

WIN	contention winner
XID	Exchange Station Identification (SDLC)
¬	Not
|	or
−RSP	negative response
+RSP	positive response

ABOUT THE AUTHOR

Following several years of wind tunnel-control work at the Ames Aeronautical Research Laboratory of the National Advisory Committee on Aeronautics, Dr. Cypser was for six years on the research staff and faculty of MIT. As a member of the Servomechanisms Laboratory there, he worked on the numerical control of milling machines, and as an assistant professor he taught in the electrical engineering department.

After receiving his Doctor of Science degree from MIT in 1953, he joined IBM on the SAGE air defense project and was responsible for equipment to handle computer inputs from radar and keyboards and computer outputs to aircraft and to other computers.

His subsequent development responsibilities included advanced technology development, a computer prototype in the Army field data series and the technology for a large computing system at an Air Force control center.

After an assignment on the IBM corporate staff (Research and Engineering), he spent several years in Europe advising on technical programs in the six IBM laboratories there. Subsequent activities included product planning for tightly and loosely coupled multiprocessors, and for communications-oriented hardware and software in various products.

He has taught communications architecture for distributed systems at both the IBM Systems Research Institute and Syracuse University.

Index

Index

ABANDON CONNECT OUT
(ABCONNOUT), 438, 642
ABANDON CONNECTION
(ABCONN), 443, 642
Abbreviations and acronyms, 688
Abort, 375
Acknowledgment, 183, 327, 381
Access methods, 83, 91, 92
ACTIVATE CONNECT IN
(ACTCONNIN), 442, 642
ACTIVATE LINK (ACTLINK),
424, 642
ACTIVATE LOGICAL UNIT
(ACTLUO), 303, 430, 477,
642
ACTIVATE PHYSICAL UNIT
(ACTPU), 232, 303, 424, 642
ACTIVATE TRACE (ACTTRACE),
445, 643
Activation, session, 233, 548
Address, 335
    destination (DAF)/origin (OAF),
    341, 352
    element, 335
    extended, 376
    field (in SDLC), 375
    local (short form), 341

network, 153, 336
subarea, 335
Advanced data communications
    control procedure (ADCCP),
    360
Alternate host, 567
Alternate path, or route, 577
Application, classifications, 4, 38
    exits, 214, 498
    program, 156, 161
    subsystem, 94, 156
Arpanet, 201, 256, 325, 328, 570, 581,
    588
ASCII, 250, 667
Assembly (of segments), 343
ASSIGN NETWORK ADDRESSES
    (ANA), 440, 643
Asymmetric protocols, 192, 195
Asynchronous mode (HDLC), 397,
    608
Asynchronous signaling, 213
Authorization, 318, 512
AUTO NETWORK SHUTDOWN
    COMPLETE (ANSC), 643
Automatic calling unit (autocall),
    58
Availability, 111, 497

Bandwidth, 20
Basic information unit (BIU), 187
Basic link unit (BLU), 187
Basic mapping support (BMS), 252
Basic transmission unit (BTU), 187
Batch applications, 5
Begin-bracket indicator (BBI), 277,
    456
Begin-chain indicator (BCI), 270, 456
BID, 279, 284, 644
Bidder (bracket), 279
Bidirectional pacing, 302
Binary synchronous communication
    (BSC), 363
BIND FAILURE (BINDF), 647
BIND SEQUENCE, 483
BIND SESSION (BIND), 303, 311,
    312, 644
Bit rate, 20
Bit stuffing, 373
Block check (BC), *see* Frame check
    sequence
Blocking (of PIUs), 343, 347
Boundary function (BF), 100, 338,
    416, 447
  address transformation, 339
  pacing, 309
  path control (BF.PC), 339
  transmission control (BF.TC), 308
Bracket termination rules, 313
Brackets, 277
  bidder, 279
  first speaker, 279
  indicator, 277, 297, 456
Broadcast, 375, 398
Buffers, 133, 300, 344
Bulk store, 40
Bypassing host, 540

Call
  clearing, 597
  establishment, 596, 615
  progress signals, 602, 605
  virtual, 607
Camp-on, 606

CANCEL, 281, 647
Carriers, 19
CATV, 62
Centralization, 199
C-field, *see* Control field
Chains, 269, 296, 490
  begin, 470
  definite-response, 270, 272
  end, 270
  exception-response, 272
  middle-of, 270
  no-response, 272
Change-direction indicator (CDI), 297,
    456
Character sets, graphic, 251, 666
Character, separator, 669
Character string controls, 251, 666
Character-coded NS RUs, 228
CHASE, 283, 647
CICS, 288
CINIT sequence, 482
Classes of procedure (HDLC), 399
Cleanup, 556
CLEAR, 304, 648
Close destination, 325
Cluster controller, 104, 413
Code-selection indicator (CSI), 297
Code, sense, *see* Sense data code
Codes
  cyclic, 387
  detection, 386
  polynomial, 387
Command Reject (CDMR) (SDLC),
    380
Commands (link), 371, 378
Common carrier, 19, 60
Common network, 170, 195
Common session control (CSC), 308
Communications controller, 98, 111,
    416, 562
  twin-tailed, 532
Compaction, 246, 248, 664
Component, 187
Component selection, 243, 662
Compression, 246, 664

Compression indicator (CMI), 663
Configurations (link)
  duplex, 25, 268, 363
  half-duplex, 25, 363
  loop, 127
  multipoint, 123, 364
  point-to-point, 363
Concentration, 129
Conditioning, 24
Configuration services, 22
CONNECT OUT (CONNOUT), 438, 648
Connected services, 218
Connection point manager (CPMGR), 180, 292
CONTACT, 230, 425, 648
CONTACTED, 428, 648
Contention, 128
Control field (SDLC), 376, 627
  data flow, 170, 180, 265
  data link, 170, 180, 359
  delayed, 273
  domain, 198, 520
  functions, SCS, 251, 666
  host, 417
  network, 310
  path, 333
  resource, 521
  session, 292, 303
  transmission, 170, 180, 291
CONTROL INITIATE (CINIT), 319, 482, 647
Control mode
  request, 273
  response, 275
CONTROL TERMINATE (CTERM), 321, 649
Conversational applications, 4
Cost factors in DP/C systems, 30, 44, 47, 67
CROSS DOMAIN, 525
  CONTROL INITIATE (CD-CINIT), 550
  INITIATE (CD-INIT), 550
  SESSION ENDED (CD-SE), 556

SESSION STARTED (CD-SST), 550
Cross domain
  link, 558
  resource manager (CDRM), 541, 542
Cryptography (CRYPTO), 512
Customer Information Control System (CICS), 288
Cyclades, 327
Cyclic redundancy check (CRC), 387

Data circuit-terminating equipment (DCE), 594
Data count field (DCF), 354
Data entry, 5
Data flow control (FC), 170, 265
  control modes, 273
  request header (RH), 186, 294, 456, 627
  RUs, 185, 281
Data link control (DLC), 94, 170, 180, 359
Data management codes, 248, 664
DATAPAC, 66, 593
Dataphone digital service (DDS), 51, 593
Data rates, 42
Dataroute, 66, 593
Data switching equipment (DSE), 594
Data terminal equipment, 594
DB/DC, 94
DEACTIVATE CONNECT IN (DACTONNIN), 442, 649
DEACTIVATE LINK (DACTLINK), 425, 649
DEACTIVATE LOGICAL UNIT (DACTLU), 308, 649
DEACTIVATE PHYSICAL UNIT (DACTPU), 308, 649
DEACTIVATE TRACE (DACTTRACE), 649
DECNET, 354
  naming conventions, 257
  NSP, 203

Definite response
  chains, 270
  type 1 (DR1), 272
  type 2 (DR2), 272
Delayed control modes, 273
  delayed request, 273
  immediate request, 273
Delays, 26
Delta routing, 584
Demand select, 663
Design objectives, 141
Destination address field (DAF), 341,
    352
Devices, 162
  selection, 662
DFC-RUs, 185, 281
Dial, 430
Dial-in, 433, 442
Dial-out, 433, 435
Digital data communications message
    protocol (DDCMP), 360, 403
Digital transmission, 50, 138, 593
Direct call, 605
Disconnect (DISC) (SDLC), 379
Disconnect mode (DM) (SDLC),
    379
DISCONTACT, 428, 650
Distributed Communication Archi-
    tecture (DCA), 205, 258, 355
Distributed data, 77
Distributed function, 72
Distributed systems, 9
Domain, 198, 519
Domain resource manager (DRM),
    542
DUMP FINAL (DUMPFINAL), 443,
    650
DUMP INITIAL (DUMPINIT), 443,
    650
DUMP TEXT (DUMPTEXT), 443,
    650
Duplex, 25, 268, 363
Duplex multipoint, 124

EBCDIC, 250, 297
Element, 171, 336

Encryption, 63, 513
End-bracket indicator (EBI), 277, 456
End-chain indicator (ECI), 270, 456
End-to-end services, 166
End-user, 159, 213, 511
End-user components, 160
ENTERING SLOWDOWN
    (ESLOW), 445, 650
Equalization, 22
Error recovery, 498
Errors
  causes and reporting of, 501, 503
  detection, 385
  nonreporting, 504
  path errors, 676
  request rejection, 679
  RH usage errors, 677
  state errors, 678
  system-definition, 507
  transmission, 29
Exception codes, 504, 675
EXCEPTION REQUEST (EXR),
    296, 503
Exception-response chains, 272
Exception-response indicator (ERI),
    272, 456
Exchange Station Identification (XID)
    (SDLC), 380, 630
EXECUTE TEST (EXECTEST),
    445, 650
EXITING SLOWDOWN
    (EXSLOW), 445, 650
Exits, 214, 498
Expedited flow, 267
Expedited flow indicator (EFI), 352,
    456

F (final) (P/F bit), 378
Facsimile, 38
Failures, 498, 565, 568, 675
Fiber optics, 46
FID (format identification, TH), 349
Field-formatted data, 251
Field-formatted NS-RUs, 227, 642
FI.FMD, 169, 180, 212, 235
Finite-state machine, 465, 466, 471

First speaker (bracket), 279
Flag (SDLC), 373
Flows, normal/expedited, 267
FM (function-management) header,
    186, 241, 662
  concatenated bit, 242
  data, 169
  profiles, 197, 314, 453, 631
  type-1, 242, 663
  type-2, 243, 247, 662
  type-3, 662
  usage field, 315
FMD-RUs, 185
Format identifiers (FID), 349, 350
Format indicator, 295
Format transform, 255
Formatting function, 254
Forward error correction, 385
Frame, 370
Frame check sequence (FCS), 371,
    388
Frame DTE, 619
Frame reject (HDLC), 398
FREE NETWORK ADDRESSES
    (FNA), 650
Frequency division multiplexing, 130
Function codes, SCS, 251, 666
Function interpreter for FM data
    (FI.FMD), 169, 180, 212, 235
Function management, *see* FM
Function subsets, 196

Generator polynomial, 387
Go-ahead signal, 385
Graphic character set, 251, 666

Half-duplex, 25, 268, 363
  contention, 268
  flip-flop, 268, 490
Half-session, 164
  structure, 171
HDLC, 360
Headers, 185
  assembly, 456
  data link control (DLC), 371

FM (function management), 186,
    241
NS (network services), 227
request/response (RH), 186, 294,
    456, 627
transmission (TH), 186, 348, 627
Host, 86, 416
  failures, 565
Hub polling, 126

Identification, 166, 341, 380, 511, 512,
    630, 655
Idle (SDLC), 375
Image systems, 38
IML FINAL (IMLFINAL), 429,
    651
IML INITIAL (IMLINIT), 429, 651
IML TEXT (IMLTEXT), 429, 651
Immediate control mode, 273
Immediate request mode, 273
Immediate response mode, 275
Immediate services, 218
Infodat, 66, 593
Information Management System,
    94
Information spectrum, 37
INIT sequence, 481
Initialization (SDLC), 399
INITIATE-OTHER (INIT-OTHER),
    550, 651
INITIATE-SELF (INIT-SELF), 317,
    447, 481, 652
INOPERATIVE (INOP), 438, 445,
    653
INQUIRE, 317
Inquiry applications, 5
Interface message processor (IMP),
    328
Interfaces, 57, 593
Interlayer communication, 183
Intermediate function, 99, 416
International Standards Organization,
    360, 399
I/O Scheduler, 89
ISOLATED PACING RESPONSE
    (IPR), 300

Layers, 167
Length, RU, 300. *See also*
      Appendix C.
Line, 22, 83
Line switching, 135
Line turnaround, 26, 28
Link access procedure, 608
Link addresses, 339
Link commands, 371
Link header, 185, 370
Link responses, 371
Link trailer, 370
Load leveling, 579
Local address, 339
Local node, 338
Logging-off, 452
Logical channel, 608
   group number, 610
   ID, 610
   number, 610
Logical connection, 164
Logical link control, 600
Logical presentation space,
      253
Logical unit (LU), 158
   name, 537
   network services, 233
   services, 212, 215
   services managers, 217, 452
   type, 198, 631
LOGICAL UNIT STATUS
      (LUSTAT), 284, 653
Log-on
   exit, 323
   modes, 317
   sequences, 446
Long haul, 23
Longitudinal redundancy check
      (LRC), 386
Loop, 127, 385
Lost path, 498
Lost subarea, 446, 561, 562
LU-LU session, 310, 479

Maintenance services, 226

Manager
   connection point, 180, 292
   LU services, 217, 452
   NAU services, 155, 156, 168, 212
   PU services, 217
   SSCP services, 217
Mapping, 236, 350
Maximum RU size, 300
Measurement services, 226
Message, 7
   content validation, 501
   handlers, 214, 498
   sizes, 188
Message switching, 134
Migration, 145
Models, 256
Modem, 22
Modes
   control, 273
   request
      delayed request, 273
      immediate control, 273
      immediate request, 273
   response
      delayed response, 275
      immediate response, 275
Modes, normal-flow send/receive, 267
Modes (SDLC)
   asynchronous balanced, 397
   asynchronous disconnected, 397
   asynchronous response, 396, 397
   extended, 397
   normal disconnected, 397
   normal response, 396, 397
Multidomain networks, 113, 201, 519
Multidrop, 123
Multi-multipoint, 124
Multiplexing, 129
Multipoint, 123

Name
   alternate, 156, 535, 537
   network, 156, 535
   resolution, 316, 535
Narrowband, 21

NAU, 153, 155
NAU services, 156, 158
NAU services managers, 156, 168,
   212
Negative response, 185, 503, 675
Network, 109, 195, 520
   address(es), 155, 535
   addressable unit (NAU), 153, 155
   common, 170, 195
   control (NC), 292
   multidomain, 113
   operation support program, 201, 538
   operator, 222, 227, 538
   routing center, 582
Network services (NS), 211, 214, 222,
   227
   categories, 222
   character-coded RUs, 229
   field-formatted RUs, 228
   formats, 227
   header, 227
NETWORK SERVICES
      PROCEDURE ERROR
      (NSPE), 653
Networking
   forms of, 115
   transparent, 520
New data networks, 44, 593
Next node index, 586
Node, 162
   local, 338
   SNA, 411
   structural overview of, 413, 472
   transit, 541
Noncoded information (NCI), 39
Nonsequenced acknowledge (NSA),
   279
Nonsequenced commands (SDLC),
   378
Nonsequenced information (NSI)
   (SDLC), 378
Nonsequenced poll (NSP) (SDLC),
   380
Nonswitched network, 23
No-response chains, 272

Normal flow, 267
Normal response mode (SDLC), 396,
   397
Notify, 561
NRZI (SDLC), 374

Open destination, 323
Open session, 447
Operator intervention, 498
Optical fibers, 46
Origin address field (OAF), 341

Pacing, 101, 297, 299, 302
Packet headers, 610
Packet switching, 60, 134, 607
Parity check, 386
Password, 512
Path, 575
Path control (PC), 170, 180, 333
Path information unit (PIU), 187
Peer, 179
Peer processing, 17
Peer protocols, 180
Pending states, 471
Peripheral data information record
      (PDIR), 247
P/F (Poll/Final bit), 378
Physical unit (PU), 100, 158
Polling, 123, 384
Ports, 156
Positional significance, 369
Post, telephone, telegraph
      administration (PTT), 19, 60
Presentation services, 169, 211, 235
   data transfer, 242
   interactive environment, 251
   text processing, 250
Presentation space, 253
Pre-session routing, 308
Primary half-session, 194
Primary logical unit, 641
Primary station, 369, 397
Prime compression character, 248
Procedure correlation ID (PCID),
   542

Profiles, 197
   FM (function managements), 314, 631
   TS (transmission subsystem), 314, 636
   PS (presentation services), 314
Program maintenance, 71
Programming, 68
Propagation time, 28
Protocol, 82, 180, 192
   asymmetric, 192
   bracket, 277
   data link control, 371
   peer, 180
   per-NAU, 180
   session team, 181
PS profile, 197, 314
PU network services, 230
PU services, 212
PU services manager, 212, 214
PU types (in a node), 197

Qualified name convention, 475
Queues, queuing, 101, 553
QUIESCE AT END OF CHAIN (QEC), 281, 654
QUIESCE COMPLETE (QC), 282, 654

RAS, 497
READY TO RECEIVE (RTR), 279, 284, 655
RECORD MAINTENANCE STATISTICS (RECMS), 445, 654
RECORD TEST DATA (RECTD), 445, 654
RECORD TRACE DATA (RECTRD), 445, 654
Receive Not Ready (SDLC), 378, 395
Receive Ready (SDLC), 378, 391
Receive sequence count (Nr), 381
Reconfiguration, 222, 577
Recovery, 194, 500, 503
   aid, 501

in-session, 505
link-level, 381
multidomain network, 560
by network operation, 498
Reject (SDLC), 378, 395
RELEASE QUIESCE (RELQ), 282, 655
Reliability, 497
REMOTE POWER OFF (RPO), 655
Repair, 505
Request, 183, 579
REQUEST CONTACT (REQCONT), 439, 441, 655
Request Disconnect (RD) (SDLC), 381
REQUEST DISCONTACT (REQDISCONT), 655
Request Initialization (RQI) (SDLC), 379
Request Initialization Mode (RIM) (HDLC), 379
REQUEST RECOVERY (RQR), 304, 503, 655
Request/response header (RH), 186, 294, 456, 627
Request/response unit (RU), 184, 185, 640
REQUEST SHUTDOWN (RSHUTD), 283, 655
Request units (RUs)
   category (SC, NC, DFC, FI.FMD), 293
   data flow control (DFC), 281
   EXCEPTION REQUEST (EXR), 296, 503
   network services
      configuration services, 641
      maintenance services, 642
      session services, 642
   session control (SC), 303, 640
Resale, 63
Reset
   convention (state-transition graph), 476
   in HDLC balanced mode, 398

Response, 183, 297, 660
Response control modes, 273
Response indicator, 297
Response time, 26
Retransmission, 498
Route, 575, 576
  alternate, 577
  parallel, 577
  selection, 587
  switching, 586
Routing, 292, 334, 579. *See also* Path
    control.
  centralized, 580
  distributed, 580
  explicit, 580, 585
  stochastic, 580, 587
RU category, 640

Satellites, 47
Secondary half-session, 194
Secondary logical unit, 641
Secondary station, 369, 397
Secure string ID reader, 671
Security, 510, 514
Segment sequence, 354
Segments, segmenting, 188, 343, 344
Selective Reject (HDLC), 396
Send/receive modes, 267
Send sequence count (Ns), 381
Sense data, 185
Sense data code, 319, 504, 675
Sense-data-included indicator (SDI),
    296
Sensor base applications, 6
Separator characters, 669
Sequence counts
  SDLC, 381
  LAP, 612
Sequence number field (SNF), 353
Sequencing (of requests and
    responses), 298
Serializing, 26, 28
Services, 167
  configuration, 222
  connected, 218

  immediate, 218
  LU, 215, 233
  maintenance, 222
  network, 167, 214, 222, 227
  per-NAU, 167
  per-session, 167
  presentation, 169
  PU, 219, 230
  session, 222, 225, 318
  SSCP, 215, 228
  transmission, 166
Services managers
  LU, 127, 212, 452
  NAU, 155, 156, 168, 212
  PU, 212, 217
  SSCP, 212, 217
Session, 164
  activation sequence, 233, 548
  control (SC), 180, 292, 303
    boundary function, 309
    RUs, 303
  initiation, 320
  LU-LU, 310, 479
  recovery, 211
  services, 225
  team, 131
  termination, 321
SESSION ENDED (SESSEND), 655
Session identification, 166, 341
SESSION STARTED (SST), 324, 657
SET AND TEST SEQUENCE
    NUMBERS (STSN), 304, 305,
    657
Set Asynchronous Balanced Mode
    (SABM), 381, 397
Set Asynchronous Balanced Mode
    Extended (SABME), 397
Set Asynchronous Response Mode
    (SARM), 381, 396, 397
SET CONTROL VECTOR
    (SETCV), 439, 440, 656
Set Initialization Mode (SIM)
    (SDLC), 379, 429
Set Normal Response Mode (SNRM)
    (SDLC), 379, 396, 397, 425

Shared applications, 92
Shared communications controllers, 532
Shared lines, 92, 124
Shared terminals, 92
SHUTDOWN (SHUTD), 283, 657
SHUTDOWN COMPLETE (SHUTC), 283, 657
SIGNAL (SIG), 283, 657
Slowdown, 445
SNA character string (SCS), 251, 666
SNA network, 195
SNF (sequence number field), 353
Sperry Univac distributed communications architecture, 205, 258, 355
SSCP (system services control point), 158, 212, 215, 316, 501, 533, 541
START DATA TRAFFIC (SDT), 303, 320, 485, 655
Start-stop, 360
String control byte (SCB), 246
Subarea address, 336
Subhost, 109, 419
Subset, 196
Subsystem failure, 508
Supervisory commands (SDLC), 378
Switched access facility (SAF), 432
Switched backup, 509
Switched circuit, 23, 525
Switched network, 432
Synchronization, 362
Synchronous data link control (SDLC), 360
Synchronous transmission, 362

Takedown, 555
TCAM, 214
TC-RUs, 185
Technology trends, 35
TELNET, 571, 593
Terminal node, 105, 413
Terminals, 83, 162
TERMINATE-OTHER (TERM-OTHER), 658

TERMINATE-SELF (TERM-SELF), 321, 659
Termination rules, bracket, 131
Test (SDLC), 380
Time-division multiplexing, 60, 130
TP access method, 91, 92
Traces, line, 445
Transaction, 7
Transmission control (TC), 170, 180, 291
  boundary function (BF.TC), 308
  common session control (CS), 308
  connection point manager (CPMGR), 180, 292
  network control (NC), 310
  pacing, 300
  sequencing (of requests and responses), 298
  session control (SC), 303
Transmission facilities, 19, 44, 64,
  costs, 44, 47, 67
  performance, 67
Transmission header (TH), 186, 334, 348, 627
Transmission subsystem (TS), 176
  profile, 197, 314
Transpac, 593
Trends
  distributed function, 72
  programming, 68
  technology, 35
  transmission, 44
TS profile, 197, 314, 636
Turnaround, 26, 28
Two-way alternate, 369
Two-way simultaneous, 369
Tymnet, 581

UNBIND FAILURE (UNBINDF), 659
UNBIND SESSION (UNBIND), 303, 321, 659
Unformatted NS RUs, 228
Unit
  logical (LU), 158

network addressable (NAU), 153, 155
physical (PU), 100, 158
Units (message)
  basic information unit (BIU), 187
  basic link unit (BLU), 187
  basic transmission unit (BTU), 187
  path information (PIU), 187
  request/response unit, 184, 185
Universal data link control (UDLC), 360
Unnumbered acknowledgment, *see* Nonsegmented acknowledgment
Unnumbered information, *see* Nonsequenced information
Unnumbered poll, *see* Nonsequenced poll
Usage fields
  FM, 315

PS, 315
TS, 314
User record, 188

Value-added network (VAN), 60, 594
Virtual circuit, 60, 594, 607
  permanent, 607
  switched, 607
Virtual terminal, 256
Voiceband, 21
VTAM, 214, 225, 285, 321

Wideband, 21
Work stations, 162

X.21, 593, 595, 600, 607
X.25, 594, 595, 596, 607, 618

Zero insertion (SDLC), 374